The Critical Response
to Ann Petry

Recent Titles in
Critical Responses in Arts and Letters

The Critical Response to Mark Twain's
Huckleberry Finn
Laurie Champion, editor

The Critical Response to Nathaniel Hawthorne's
The Scarlet Letter
Gary Scharnhorst, editor

The Critical Response to Tom Wolfe
Doug Shomette, editor

The Critical Response to Ann Beattie
Jaye Berman Montresor, editor

The Critical Response to Eugene O'Neill
John H. Houchin, editor

The Critical Response to Bram Stoker
Carol A. Senf, editor

The Critical Response to John Cheever
Francis J. Bosha, editor

The Critical Response to Ann Radcliffe
Deborah D. Rogers, editor

The Critical Response to Joan Didion
Sharon Felton, editor

The Critical Response to Tillie Olsen
Kay Hoyle Neldon and Nancy Huse, editors

The Critical Response to George Eliot
Karen L. Pangallo, editor

The Critical Response to Eudora Welty's Fiction
Laurie Champion, editor

The Critical Response to Dashiell Hammett
Christopher Metress, editor

The Critical Response to H. G. Wells
William J. Scheick, editor

The Critical Response to Raymond Chandler
J. K. Van Dover, editor

The Critical Response to Herman Melville's
Moby Dick
Kevin J. Hayes, editor

The Critical Response to Kurt Vonnegut
Leonard Mustazza, editor

The Critical Response to Richard Wright
Robert J. Butler, editor

The Critical Response to Jack London
Susan N. Nuernberg, editor

The Critical Response to Saul Bellow
Gerhard Bach, editor

The Critical Response to William Styron
Daniel W. Ross, editor

The Critical Response to Katherine Mansfield
Jan Pilditch, editor

The Critical Response to Anais Nin
Philip K. Jason, editor

The Critical Response to Tennessee Williams
George W. Crandell, editor

The Critical Response to Andy Warhol
Alan R. Pratt, editor

The Critical Response to Thomas Carlyle's
Major Works
D. J. Trela and Rodger L. Tarr, editors

The Critical Response to John Milton's
Paradise Lost
Timothy C. Miller, editor

The Critical Response to Erskine Caldwell
Robert L. McDonald, editor

The Critical Response to Gloria Naylor
Sharon Felton and Michelle C. Loris, editors

The Critical Response to Samuel Beckett
Cathleen Culotta Andonian, editor

The Critical Response to Ishmael Reed
Bruce Allen Dick, editor
With the assistance of Pavel Zemliansky

The Critical Response to Truman Capote
Joseph J. Waldmeir and John C. Waldmeir, editors

The Critical Response to Robert Lowell
Steven Gould Axelrod, editor

The Critical Response to Chester Himes
Charles L.P. Silet, editor

The Critical Response to Gertrude Stein
Kirk Curnutt, editor

The Critical Response to Ralph Ellison
Robert J. Butler, editor

The Critical Response to John Steinbeck's *The
Grapes of Wrath*
Barbara A. Heavilin, editor

The Critical Response to D. H. Lawrence
Jan Pilditch, editor

The Critical Response to Marianne Moore
Elizabeth Gregory, editor

John Updike: The Critical Responses to the
"Rabbit" Saga
Jack De Bellis, editor

The Critical Response to John Irving
Todd F. Davis and Kenneth Womack

The Critical Response to Kamau Brathwaite
Emily Allen Williams

The Critical Response
to Ann Petry

Edited by Hazel Arnett Ervin

Critical Responses in Arts and Letters, Number 44

Westport, Connecticut
London

Library of Congress Cataloging-in-Publication Data

The critical response to Ann Petry / edited by Hazel Arnett Ervin.
   p. cm. — (Critical responses in arts and letters, ISSN 1057-0993 ; no. 44)
  Includes bibliographical references and index.
  ISBN 0-313-32282-1 (alk. paper)
  1. Petry, Ann Lane, 1911——Criticism and interpretation. 2. Women and
literature—United States—History—20th century. 3. African Americans in literature. 4. New
England—In literature. I. Ervin, Hazel Arnett. II. Series.
PS3531.E933Z64 2005
813′.54—dc22   2004043188

British Library Cataloguing in Publication Data is available.

Library of Congress Catalog Card Number: 2004043188
ISBN: 0-313-32282-1
ISSN: 1057-0993

First published in 2005

Praeger Publishers, 88 Post Road West, Westport, CT 06881
An imprint of Greenwood Publishing Group, Inc.
www.praeger.com

Printed in the United States of America

The paper used in this book complies with the
Permanent Paper Standard issued by the National
Information Standards Organization (Z39.48–1984).

10 9 8 7 6 5 4 3 2 1

Copyright Acknowledgments

The editor and publisher gratefully acknowledge permission for use of the following material.

Larry R. Andrews. "The Sensory Assault of the City in Ann Petry's *The Street*." In *The City in African-American Literature*. Edited by Yoshinobu Hakutani. Madison, NJ: Fairleigh Dickinson University Press, 1995. Reprinted with permission.

Author Unknown. "A Review of *Country Place*." *The New Yorker*. October 11, 1947.

Michael Barry. " 'Same Train Be Back Tomorrer': Ann Petry's *The Narrows* and the Repetition of History." MELUS, Spring, 1999. Reprinted with permission.

Bernard Bell. "Ann Petry's Demythologizing of American Culture and Afro-American Character." In *Conjuring: Black Women, Fiction, and Literary Tradition*. Edited by Marjorie Pryse and Hortense J. Spillers. Bloomington: Indiana Univerity Press, 1985. Reprinted with permission.

Arna Bontemps. "The Line." *Saturday Review*, August 22, 1953.

Arna Bontemps. "Tough, Carnal Harlem." *New York Herald Tribune Weekly Book Review*, February 10, 1946. By permission of New York Herald Tribune Morgue.

Ben Burns. "Off the Book Shelf." *Chicago Defender*, February 9, 1946.

Barbara Christian. "A Checkered Career—*The Street* by Ann Petry." *The Women's Review of Books*, July 1992.

Keith Clark. Excerpts from "A Distaff Deferred? Ann Petry and the Art of Subversion." *African American Review*, 1992. Reprinted with permission.

Arthur P. Davis, "Hard Boiled Fiction," *Journal of Negro Education*, vol. 15, no. 4, 648–649. Copyright © 1946.

Kimberly Drake. "Women on the Go: Blues, Conjure, and Other Alternatives to Domesticity in Ann Petry's *The Street* and *The Narrows*." *Arizona Quarterly*, Spring, 1998. Reprinted with permission.

Hazel Arnett Ervin. "The Hidden Hand of Feminist Revolt in Ann Petry's *The Street*." With the permission of the author. 2004.

Marjorie Pryse. " 'Patterns Against the Sky': Deism and Motherhood in Ann Petry's *The Street.*" In *Conjuring: Black Women, Fiction, and Literary Tradition.* Edited by Marjorie Pryse and Hortense J. Spillers. Bloomington: Indiana University Press, 1985.

Excerpts from "Race Trumps All Other Identity Markers: Reading Ann Petry's *The Narrows* as an Anti-Lynching Text" by Deidre Raynor. Reprinted with permission.

J. Saunders Redding. "A Review of *The Narrows.*" *Afro-American (Baltimore) Newspaper,* September 12, 1953.

Excerpts from "Women in the Novels of Ann Petry" by Thelma J. Shinn [Richard]. *Critique Studies in Modern Fiction* 16.1 (1974): 110-120. Reprinted with permission.

Barbara Smith. "A Familiar Street." *Belles Lettres.* January/February, 1987.

Excerpts from "A Review of *Country Place* by John Caswell Smith, Jr., published in *The Atlantic Monthly.* November, 1947.

Excerpts from "A Review of *The Street*" by John Caswell Smith, Jr., published in *The Atlantic Monthly.* April, 1946.

Richard Sullivan. "Injustice, Out of Focus." (a review of *Country Place* by Ann Petry). *New York Times Book Review,* November 29, 1970.

Ivan E. Taylor. "A Review of *The Narrows*" by Ann Petry. *Current Literature.* (Winter, 1954): 60–61.

Gloria Wade-Gayles. *No Crystal Stair: Visions of Race and Sex in Black Women's Fiction* (New York: The Pilgrim Press, 1984), 148–56. Copyright © 1984 by The Pilgrim Press. Used by permission.

Excerpts from " 'Beating Unavailing Palms Against the Stone': Spatiality, Sexual, Stereotyping, and the Myth of the American Dream in Ann Petry's *The Street,*" by Ama S. Wattley. Reprinted with permission.

Sybil Weir. "*The Narrows:* A Black New England Novel." *Studies in American Fiction* (Spring, 1987): 81–93. Reprinted by permission.

Sherley Anne Williams. "A Review of *The Street.*" *MS,* September, 1986.

Richard Yarborough. "The Quest for the American Dream in Three Afro-American Novels: *If He Hollers, Let Him Go, The Street,* and *Invisible Man, MELUS,* Winter, 1981. Reprinted with permission.

Every reasonable effort has been made to trace the owners of copyright materials in this book, but in some instances this has proven impossible. The author and publisher will be glad to receive information leading to more complete acknowledgments in subsequent printings of the book and in the meantime extend their apologies for any omissions.

To
Tony and Millicent Arnett
Vernon and Annette Gooden

and

Barbara Smith
of Albany, New York

Barbara Christian (1943-2000)
Professor of American Literature
The University of California at Berkeley

Mary Helen Washington
Professor of English
University of Maryland at College Park

Nellie Y. McKay
Professor of American and Afro-American Literature
University of Wisconsin at Madison

Deborah McDowell
Alice Griffin Professor of English
University of Virginia

Contents

Introduction

Once when asked to name the work or works for which she wanted to be remembered, Ann Petry answered unwaveringly, "I'd like to be remembered for everything I've written" (Ervin 101). Petry's *oeuvre* is comprised of three novels---*The Street* (1946), *Country Place* (1947), and *The Narrows* (1953); sixteen short stories, thirteen of which make up the collection *Miss Muriel and Other Stories* (1971); three juvenile works, *Harriet Tubman, Conductor on the Underground Railroad* (1955), *Tituba of Salem Village* (1964), and *Legends of the Saints* (1970); one children's book, *The Drugstore Cat* (1949); numerous articles and book reviews; and a weekly newspaper column "The Lighter Side," which appeared in *People's Voice* from 1942 to 1943. Petry is read often in the shadows of her male counterparts Richard Wright and Chester Himes, novelists, short story writers, essayists, and critics whose reputations are paramount. But, the female novelist, short story writer, author of books for juveniles and children, essayist, and columnist is a force to be reckoned with, both within and beyond African American literature. For example, when *The Street* and *The Narrows* were published, each soared in sales of more than one million copies, making Petry the first African American female author to hold such a distinction. Though fewer in sales, as a novel of manners, *Country Place* became a book of the month in London, England. Petry's short story collection *Miss Muriel* placed her on the short list of "first" for an African American female. Her short stories such as "Like a Winding Sheet" and "The Witness," and her novels *The Street* and *The Narrows* have appeared repeatedly in award-winning anthologies, including *The Negro Caravan, Invented Lives: Narratives of Black Women, 1860-1960, The Norton Anthology of African American Literature, Call and Response: The Riverside Anthology of the African American Literary Tradition*, and the *Heath Anthology of American*

Literature, and have been reprinted in anthologies abroad such as *Feminine Fiction from Across America* and *Daughters of Africa.* Finally, all three of her novels, several of her short stories, and the juvenile work *Harriet Tubman* have been translated into at least eleven different languages.

In this collection, the focus is not on "everything" that Petry has written. Instead, via a chronology, book reviews, articles, and a select bibliography, the focus is on Petry's novels and the critical responses to them from 1946 to the present. Comprised of book reviews and articles that are grouped chronologically and according to the order of Petry's published novels (*The Street, Country Place,* and *The Narrows*), this collection gauges the historical, cultural, aesthetic, and theoretical depths of Petry's novels, and it anticipates future receptions of them. Also, it fosters an understanding of and an appreciation for Petry's literary positions on the role of the novelist, the function of the novel, and the artistic responsibility of the audience to both.

Within the annals of African American literature, Ann Petry's novels were published during the Chicago Renaissance (1935-1953). In the lead article to a special issue of *Callaloo* (1986), dedicated to Richard Wright, the most influential writer of the renaissance, critic Robert Bone defines the movement as

> the flowering of Negro letters that took place in Chicago from approximately 1935 to 1950. . . . [Furthermore, it] was in all respects comparable to the more familiar Harlem Renaissance . . . .(448).. . . [A]s the writers of the Chicago school launched their careers[,] they wrote repeatedly of the Great Migration, and of the transformation that it wrought in the black community. They wrote of the pathology that was too often the price of adjustment to the urban scene . . . . Their basic outlook, reflecting the recent history of the black community, was integrationist. This orientation was reinforced by their contacts with the Chicago School of Sociology, which offered them a sophisticated theory of urbanization. (452)

While a renaissance took place in Chicago between the 1930s and 1950s, the major novelists of the movement were not all living in Chicago ---e.g., Chester Himes was living in Cleveland, Ohio, and, of course, Ann Petry was living in New York City. Nor were all of the major novels of the movement set in Chicago---e.g., William Attaway's *Blood on the Forge* (1941) is set in Pittsburgh; Chester Himes's *If He Hollers, Let Him Go* (1945), is set in Los

Angeles; and, of course, Ann Petry's *The Street* (1946), is set in Harlem. But, as stated, what identifies the Chicago Renaissance writer is his or her deterministic outlook for urban America.

Appearing in the 1950s are two book-length studies of major African American novelists (Robert Bone's *The Negro Novel in America* and Carl Milton Hughes's *The Negro Novelist: 1940-1950*). Of particular interest here is that in these works, critics set the patterns of critical approaches to the literary movement's female novelist, Ann Petry, and those were sociological. In addition, because of Hughes's and Bone's book-length critiques, which were quoted and excerpted well into the 1970s, critics often read Petry in the shadows of Wright---i.e., as his supposed disciple, writing in the urban school of naturalistic protest (Ervin xix). When studying Petry's works on their own, critics tended to limit their critiques to comparisons of Petry's *Country Place* and *The Narrows,* with her first novel, *The Street.* For instance, in a review of *Country Place*, Alain Locke dismisses the novel because it has "neither the surge nor the special significance of Petry's first novel" (7). Nick Aaron Ford analyzes *Country Place* as "greatly inferior to *The Street* due to its themes" (373). Petry's *The Narrows* received much more favorable criticism, but like *Country Place*, for all the wrong reasons. For example, in *Dark Symphony: Negro in Literature in America*, the editors James Emanuel and Theodore Gross conclude that *The Narrows* is a success due to its "modification of the basically sociological approach taken with the family's environment in *The Street*" (99). Noel Schraufnagel in *The Black American Novel* calls *The Narrows* an "accomplished novel" due to "its combination of Petry's earlier attempts [in *The Street*] to reflect the effects of racism and to analyze the human condition" (24).

Ann Petry never accepted critics' categorizations and labeling of her writings. Nowhere is she more adamantly opposed to, for instance, the categorization of herself as Wright's protege, or to the labeling of *The Street* as a "carbon copy" of *Native Son* than in her interviews and autobiographical essay "Ann Petry" (*Contemporary Authors*, 1988). For instance, in her interview with John O'Brien, she insists:

> Interviewer: Do you feel that you belong to a naturalistic school of writing?
>
> Petry: If I belong to a certain tradition, I don't want to belong, because my writing would be very boring if I always wrote in a particular style.
> (O'Brien qtd in Ervin 75)

In her autobiographical essay, "Ann Petry," she insists:

> My writing has . . . been influenced by the
> books I've read but it has been much more
> influenced by the *circumstances* of my birth
> and my growing up, by my family
> (*Contemporary   Authors   254-255*).
> (emphasis mine)

The second of two daughters to James Lane, a pharmacist, and Bertha James Lane, a licensed chiropodist and owner of an embroidery business, Ann Petry grew up in a "rich. . . [and] life-sustaining environment" in Old Saybrook, Connecticut, a quaint, and pervasively white, seaside town, located at the mouth of the Connecticut River *(Contemporary Authors* 257). Like her father, Ann became a pharmacist and practiced the profession in the family's drugstores in Old Saybrook and Old Lyme. Like both her parents and other relatives, she revered the family pastime of storytelling (*Contemporary Authors* 257). However, unlike parents and other relatives who created stories for entertainment, Petry, even at an early age, desired a larger audience. She desired a professional career as storyteller and writer.

In 1938, the would-be writer married George D. Petry (1907-2000) of New Iberia, Louisiana, and moved with him to Harlem. Following her relocation to Harlem, she decided to gamble on her future as a writer. She abandoned the family profession, and, for the next eight years, actively pursued a career as a writer of short stories and eventually of novels. If while living in Old Saybrook, past attempts to get published were indications of the difficult challenges ahead ("While I lived in Old Saybrook, I kept writing short stories and receiving rejection slips," *Contemporary Authors* 264), once in Harlem, Petry decided to chart a new course for success: "I [sought] and [found] jobs that were . . . related to writing" (*Contemporary Authors* 264).   The jobs included writing advertisements for *Amsterdam News* from 1938 to 1941; editing the women's page for *People's Voice* from 1941 to 1944; and during the same years at *People's*, covering general news stories and writing a weekly column. Also Petry enrolled in a highly recommended writing workshop and course at Columbia University, taught by Mabel Louise Robinson, took an art course at the Harlem Art Center, and joined the American Negro Theatre in Harlem. According to Petry, Robinson was an amazing creative writing instructor. In addition to having dedicated *The Narrows* to Robinson, on more than one occasion, Petry has recalled with gratitude her experiences in the Columbia educator's workshop and course:

> It was a great experience. She made me
> believe in myself. . . . [S]he taught me how
> to criticize my own work, and other people's
> work. Perhaps even more importantly, she
> made me believe in my own ability. (Ervin
> 101)

As a student in an introductory art course at the Harlem Art Center, Petry says she learned "to look at objects---people, landscapes, everything---with great care" (*Contemporary Authors* 267). The theatre, she says, allowed her "[to] experience firsthand the ways in which . . . dialogue . . . furthered the action" (*Contemporary Authors* 268). While growing up in Old Saybrook, Connecticut, Petry's relatives---those "spinners of yarn" (*Contemporary Authors* 257)--- were her sources of inspiration, but in Harlem while juggling careers as student, journalist, editor, and columnist, Petry's sources of inspiration were mainly her teachers and peers in the fine arts.

In a 1946 article "Harlem Portrait" that appeared in the *Pittsburgh Courier,* the interviewer, James E. Fuller, calls Ann Petry "Harlem's adopted daughter," primarily because she gave voice to the men, women, and children of Harlem who had touched her life. Indirectly, the people of Harlem inspired Petry's writing, as well. Petry says as much in the interview/article "Harlem Made Ann Petry Write Her Novel":

> Just go into some of [their] houses. You'll
> see rooms so small, and halls so narrow . . . .
> Just live in one of those houses for a week . .
> . . Life will become a dismal, hopeless thing,
> and you'll want to write a novel. (*PM* 4).

In the same interview, Petry also narrows her influences to other black women:

> Most books that have delineated Negro
> women have shown them as prostitutes or
> other disreputable characters. These women
> have had no particular moral code, and such
> writing has given the impression that this is
> the true Negro woman. That, of course,
> isn't so. You have all kinds of Negro
> women, just as you have all kinds of women
> in all groups. In *The Street*, I have tried to
> portray a [working-class] struggling woman,
> with aspirations, with decency. Negroes are
> not the comics they have been portrayed nor
> are they criminals. They are people, and I
> have tried to show "just people." (*PM* 4)

The overall suggestion is that Ann Petry was influenced by the Chicago School and its naturalistic writers (Wright, Himes, Attaway, William Gardner Smith, and others). In fact, in an interview in 1988, Petry admits to having "read them all" (Ervin 101). But, when one considers Petry's unorthodox education in creative writing, which was in her parents' home, on the job, and in her various classes, Petry's influences are too numerous to be limited to any one.

II.

In her 1946 interview with reporter Earl Conrad of the *Chicago Defender* ("The Woman's Place in Harlem"), Petry probes the question of woman's place in the mid 1940s. The interview adds yet another dimension to discussions of Petry's apprentice years, or, as Petry remarked earlier: "[to] my writing . . . influenced by . . . circumstances" (*Contemporary Authors* 254). In the mid 1940s, patriarchal ideology reinforced the notion of domesticated women as wives, mothers, and homemakers, and argued that the proper sphere for women was the home. To realize a role outside of tradition was to go against great odds. Ann Petry grew up in a "warm and life-sustaining environment," and the women in her middle-class family were "business-women, financially independent, and [ones] who refused to be traditional housewives" ("Artspectrum" qtd in Ervin 101). But, in the real world in the 1940s, where Petry attempted to establish herself as a writer, like some women in general, who may have worked outside the home, and like black women in particular, who worked inside and outside of the home, Petry felt the weight of sexual politics. As she explains to Conrad:

> [The success of the black woman writing in the 1940s] is understandable only when you realize the condition of the mass of [black] women. The fact that few [black] women have had the opportunity to write, to secure the leisure, study, and to do the reading necessary to write, itself shows where the [black] woman has been: She has been hard at work earning a livelihood, not only for herself but often for a whole family. (13)

In addition, Petry says:

> The [black] woman, with the responsible matriarchal role she has had to play, has been a principal bearer of the economic burden. No wonder, she could not enter into the field of the novelist. (13)

So how does Petry, a woman of social identity and one who has known security since childhood regard her "place" in the larger world (or in the man's world of publishing) in the 1940s? On more than one occasion, this has been her response:

> I regard myself as a survivor and a gambler,
> writing in a tradition that dates back to 1859
> when *Our Nig*, the first novel written by a
> black woman in this country, was published
> in Boston, Massachusetts . . . .I regard
> myself as a survivor because I have written
> books and had them published . . . . I regard
> myself a gambler because each one of these
> books was written against odds that it would
> ever be finished, odds that only a gambler
> would have accepted . . . . Like all writers . .
> . , I work against odds, real or imaginary,
> against   hostility,   against   indifference.
> *(Contemporary Authors* 253)

Tillie Olsen, writing in *Silences* (1965) has addressed the "indifference" experienced by women writers prior to the 1960s. Olsen's assessment mirrors Petry's assessment: "We [women] who write are survivors, [and are] 'only's' " (42). Olsen who looks primarily at white women writers but includes black women writers Ann Petry, Margaret Walker, and Pauli Murray assesses women in a profession occupied largely by men. According to the concerned Tillie Olsen, in the profession prior to the 1960s, men evaluated the women. In her assessment of male evaluators, Olsen alludes to the Bones, Hughes, Locks, Schraufnagels and Fords who helped to set the patterns of critical approaches to women like Petry in the early 1950s:

> [When] still in our century, women's books
> of great worth suffer the death of being
> unknown, or at best a peculiar eclipsing. . . ,
> [When] still, [there is] the injurious reacting
> to a book, not for its quality or content, but
> on the basis of its having been written by a
> woman---with   consequent   misreading,
> mistreatment; [When] women writers are
> still suspect as unnatural if they concern
> themselves with aspects of their experiences,
> interests, being beyond the traditionally
> defined women's sphere . . . . [These
> women] who are writers are [gamblers] and
> "survivors." (40-42)

In her seminal essay "Toward a Black Feminist Criticism" (1977), Barbara Smith adds to the discussion of women writers being silenced---to their "invisibility," "misreading," and " unnatural spheres." On behalf of black women who write, Smith adds for emphasis:

> Black women's existence, experience and
> culture and the brutally complex systems of
> oppression which shape these, *are* in the
> "real world". . . *beneath consideration,*
> *invisible,* [and] *unknown.* (Smith qtd in
> Ervin 162) (emphasis mine)

In the late 1970s, a new level of feminine consciousness emerges among women critics about women who write. The central effort by feminist critics such as Tillie Olsen, Barbara Smith, Barbara Christian, Mary Helen Washington, Nellie McKay, and so many others is to get men and women to discuss and to analyze in a truly scholarly way the works of women writers---i.e. to approach the works of women writers on their own merits. As Barbara Smith puts it in "Towards a Black Feminist Criticism" books by black women "must be examined in such a way that the basic intention[s] of the writer[s] are at least considered" (Smith qtd in Ervin 164).   Furthermore, Smith retorts "the realization [is] that the politics of sex as well as the politics of race and class are crucially interlocking factors in the works of black women writers." In short, the realizations here forego any set patterns of introduction and critical examination of Ann Petry (Smith qtd. in Ervin 164).

III.

Prior to 1939, when attempting to publish, Ann Petry "[was] just getting back rejection slips"*(Contemporary Authors* 264).   In 1939, one year after taking a job with *Amsterdam News*, using the pseudonym Arnold Petri, she published her first short story, "Marie of the Cabin Club," an amateurish action-filled romance. However, in 1943, following her apprentice years with *People's Voice* as editor, columnist, and reporter, and following her years of study in art and theatre with creative writer and teacher Mabel Robinson and others, using her real name, Petry published in the *Crisis,* the short story "On Saturday the Siren Sounds at Noon." A somewhat probing story about a father who loses his favorite child in a house fire, murders his wife because she neglected the child, and then takes his own life, "On Saturday" points toward Petry's later, more mature fiction. As Hilary Holladay, writing in *Ann Petry* (1996), reveals,

> ["On Saturday"] contains key elements
> familiar to readers of [Petry's] later works
> [e.g., an environment that not only reflects
> the characters' torment but contributes to it]
> (11).   .   .[Furthermore, according to
> Holladay] Betrayal, deep-seated anger, and

> murderous victims all recur in [Petry's]
> three novels. . . . (11)

Equally important, Holladay states,

> [in "On Saturday"] . . .[u]nderstated, exact
> description[,] and the use of indirect
> discourse to convey a character's thoughts
> are also hallmarks of Petry's [longer]
> fiction. (11)

"On Saturday the Siren Sounds at Noon" is the story that heralded the beginning of Petry's writing career. Appearing in the *Crisis*, the story caught the eye of an editor at Houghton Mifflin. The editor (whose name and gender are lost to literary history) encouraged Petry to enter Houghton's literary contest in fiction. As Petry once recalled

> In December 1944, I entered *The Street* in
> the Houghton Mifflin Fellowship contest. I
> submitted five chapters of the novel, a
> complete synopsis, and two letters of
> recommendation. (*Contemporary Authors*
> 265)

In 1945, to Petry's "absolute astonishment"*(Contemporary Authors* 265), she won the contest, receiving from Houghton $2400 in prize money, and the publication of her novel, *The Street*. By February of 1946, some eight years after her decision to abandon the family profession and to pursue a writing career, Ann Petry's gamble had paid off. As Nick Aaron Ford has written, she went from "test tube to typewriter"---i.e., from pharmacist to best-selling novelist and short story writer (3).

The Street, a story about a single mother who is defeated in her attempts to make a home for herself and her eight-year-old son in an urban environment, is Petry's most known and celebrated novel. In its advance sales, in 1946, the novel, sold more than 20,000 copies. Following its publication, the novel went on to sell over 1,500,000 copies in hardcover and paperback. At present, it has gone through numerous reprints (domestic and abroad) and a re-issuance by Houghton Mifflin. The debut of *The Street* in 1946 was celebrated with a prepublication party in New York City's Hotel Biltmore. Guests included Henry Laughlin, president of Houghton Mifflin, honored American novelists John Dos Passos and Bucklin Moon, and American playwright Cornelia Otis Skinner (Ford 3). To follow were countless interviews, teas, citations and awards, invitations to speak, and photo shoots ---all, however, to Petry's disapproval. "I began to feel as though I was public property" (*Contemporary Authors* 226). Or, might one infer that what followed were "silencers" of this woman writer? After all, had not the public begun to interfere with the one thing Petry desired most—to write? Beset by notoriety, in 1947, following the publication of her second novel, *Country Place*, with her husband (who by now had returned from the Army), Petry escaped the public. She returned to Old Saybrook, settling into a home on Old Boston Post Road.

Guarding her privacy, in Old Saybrook, Petry completed her third novel, *The Narrows*, a story that explores the themes of miscegenation, greed, classism, racism, and betrayal among blacks and whites in a small New England town. The latter themes of classism, racism, and betrayal exist also in *Country Place*, although the characters are mostly white. From Old Saybrook, Petry would go on to complete additional short stories and her juvenile literature. Leaving Old Saybrook in 1958 to work on a movie script in Hollywood; in 1972, to lecture at Miami University of Ohio; in 1974, to lecture as a Visiting Professor at the University of Hawaii; and in 1983, 1988 and 1989, to receive honorary degrees from Suffolk University, the University of Connecticut, and Mount Holyoke College respectively, Petry returned always to the quaint seaside town of Old Saybrook, where she remained until her death on April 28, 1997.

IV.

The Critical Response to Ann Petry is the "first" collection of criticism of the writer's novels.[1] It is also the first collection to bring analytical attention to this Chicago Renaissance writer who is female. As will be reflected in this collection, Petry's critics move beyond any set patterns of criticism to arrive at various conclusions about the writer and her novels. For instance, she is viewed as a naturalist; an "unblushing realist"; a neighborhood novelist; a New Englander; a "novelist with a conscience"; a womanist; a feminist ally; and a female writer who approaches her characters (female and male) with the "penetration of a psychiatrist" and the "delicate care of a mother." In this collection, there are 16 reviews and 26 articles. The organization of the reviews and articles focus on all three novels in somewhat chronological order. While the articles are arranged most often to address the novels in descending order, the articles can be grouped and read also under the following sub-categories: (1) narrative voice and structural space and time, (2) cultural and literary traditions, (3) genre-based study, (4) gender-based study, (5) culture-based study, and (6) interdisciplinary studies. For teachers, critics, students and others who wish to read criticism of a particular novel, listed respectively in the Index are the reviews and articles under *The Street, Country Place,* and *The Narrows.* As stated earlier, collectively the reviews and articles gauge the historical, cultural, aesthetic and theoretical depths of Petry's novels, and collectively narrow other readings of them, but there is more. While specific articles offer an overview of Petry's life and/or works (see Lattin, Joyce, McDowell, McKay, and Bell), others offer evaluations of her style and structure (see Wade-Gayles, Ervin, Clark, Hernton, Holladay, Wattley, Garvey, Perkins, Fitzsimmons, Barry,

Andrews and Raynor); name her British and American literary influences (see Yarborough, Joyce, Weir, Fitzsimmons, Perkins, Hicks and Holladay); identify her aesthetic positions on the role of the novelist and the functions of American and African American novels (see Yarborough, Weir, Raynor, and Japtok); and define her positions in larger discussions of the female in general and the African American female in particular (see Wade Gayles, Shinn, McKay, Pryse, Clark, Ervin, Drake, Hicks, Wattley, and Henderson), as well as the male hegemony (see Bell, Pryse, McDowell, Henderson, Hernton, Ervin, Wade Gayles, and Hicks). Finally, other reviews and articles proffer evidence of future receptions and criticism of Petry's novels (see McKay, Bell, Holladay, Wade-Gayles, Hernton, Clark, Ervin, Hicks, Henderson, Raynor and Lancaster). Whether *The Critical Response to Ann Petry* serves today's readers or readers of tomorrow, Ann Petry gets her wish, and that is to be remembered for what she has written.

A number of people have assisted me in completing this compilation and I wish to acknowledge them. I am grateful to all of the contributors in this collection (in the book reviews, articles, and bibliography)–scholars par excellence. My heartfelt gratitude goes to Elizabeth Potenza, my editor, and to George Butler who first acknowledged my query for such a collection. To both of them, but especially to George Butler, thanks a million for recognizing the benefits of such a collection (and other recent Petry collections) to teachers and students at the secondary and post-secondary levels and to critics and scholars worldwide. Last, thank you Tony Arnett, Harrison Miller Arnett, Jr., Emily Williams, the librarians in Reference (particularly interlibrary loans) at the R. W. Woodruff Library at the Atlanta University Center, and the following staff members in Government Documents and Bound Series at the F. D. Bluford Library at North Carolina A&T State University: Raymond Hawkins, Brenda Saddler, and Inez Lyons. To all, I appreciate your invaluable service to scholarship.

Works Cited

"An Interview with Ann Petry." *Artspectrum* (Windham-Regional Arts Council, Willimantic, CT), September 1988, 3-4. Reprint. Hazel Arnett Ervin, *Ann Petry: A Bio-Bibliography.* New York: G. K. Hall, 1993. 98-100.

Bone, Robert. "Richard Wright and the Chicago Renaissance." *Callaloo* 9.3 (Summer 1986): 446-68.

Busby, Margaret. *Daughters of Africa: An International Anthology of Words and Writings by Women of African Descent from the Ancient Egyptian to the Present.* New York: Ballantine Books, 1994.

Christian, Barbara. *Black Feminist Criticism: Perspectives on Black Women Writers.* New York: Pergamon, 1985.

Conrad, Earl. "A Woman's Place in Harlem." *Chicago Defender,* 2 February

1946: 13.

Davis, Arthur P., Sterling A. Brown, and Ullysses Lee, eds. *The Negro Caravan.* New York: Arno, 1941.

Emanual, James A. and Theodore L. Gross. *Dark Symphony Negro in Literature in America.* New York: Free Press, 1968.

Ervin, Hazel Arnett. *Ann Petry: A Bio-Bibliography.* New York: G. K. Hall, 1993.

_____. *African American Literary Criticism, 1773 to 1993.* New York: Twayne, 1999.

_____. "Interviews." *Ann Petry: A Bio-Bibliography.* New York: G. K. Hall, 1993. 69-103.

Ford, Nick Aaron. "From Test Tube to Typewriter." *Afro-American* (Baltimore), 11 December 1948. 3.

Fuller, James E. "Harlem Portrait." *Pittsburgh Courier*, 9 February 1946: [Special Collections, Boston University].

Gates, Henry Louis, Jr. and Nellie Y. McKay, eds. *The Norton Anthology of African American Literature.* New York: W. W. Norton, 1997.

"Harlem Made Ann Petry Write Her Novel" *PM* (3 March 1946): M4.

Hill, Patricia Liggin, Bernard W. Bell, Trudier Harris, R. Baxter Miller, Sondra A. O'Neale, and William J. Harris, eds. , with Horace C. Porter. *Call and Response: The Riverside Anthology of the African American Literary Tradition.* Boston: Houghton Mifflin, 1998.

Holladay, Hilary. *Ann Petry.* New York: Twayne, 1996.

Hughes, Carl Milton. "Common Denominator: Man." In *The Negro Novelist: 1940-1950, A Discussion of The Writings of American Negro Novelists 1940-1950.* New York: Citadel, 1953. 147-193.

_____. "Portrayals of Bitterness." In *The Negro Novelist: 1940-1950, A Discussion of The Writings of American Negro Novelists 1940-1950.* New York: Citadel, 1953. 41-113.

Lauter, Paul and Richard Yarborough, eds. *Heath Anthology of American Literature*, vol 2. Boston: Houghton Mifflin, 2000.

Locke, Alain. "A Critical Retrospect of the Literature of the Negro for 1947." *Phylon* 9.1 (First Quarter 1948): 7

O'Brien, John. ed. *Interviews with Black Writers.* New York: Liveright, 1973. 153-63. Reprint. Hazel Arnett Ervin. *Ann Petry: A Bio-Bibliography.* New York: G. K. Hall, 1993. 72-77.

Olsen, Tillie. "One Out of Twelve: Writers Who Are Women in Our Century." *Silences.* New York: Delacorte/Seymour Lawrence, 1965.

Petry, Ann. "Ann Petry." *Contemporary Authors: Autobiography Series*, vol 6. Detroit: Gale Research, 1988.

Schraufnagel, Noel. "The Protest Tradition in the Forties." In *The Black American Novel.* Deland, FL: Everett/Edwards, 1972.

Smith, Barbara. "Toward a Black Feminist Criticism." *Conditions: Two* 1.2 (October 1977): 25-42. Reprint. Hazel Arnett Ervin, ed. *African American Literary Criticism, 1773 to 2000.* New York: Twayne. 162-171

Tetsuo, Yamaguchi, Midori. *Feminine Fiction from Across America.* Tokyo:

Bunri Company, 1978.
Washington, Mary Helen. *Invented Lives: Narratives of Black Women 1860-1960*. Garden City: NY: Doubleday, 1987.

---

[1] For years, Henry Louis Gates, Jr. and K. A. Appiah have been cited for editing *Ann Petry: Critical Perspectives Past and Present* (New York: Amistad Literary Series), but my research suggests the collection does not exist.

Chronology

1943   Publishes in the *Crisis* under her own name "On Saturday the Siren
        Sounds at Noon" which attracts attention of editor at Houghton
        Mifflin; prepares newspaper releases and recruits volunteers for
        Harlem-Riverside Defense Council; prepares newspaper releases
        for National Association of Colored Graduate Nurses while serv-
        ing as its publicity director; serves as recreation specialist of
        Harlem's Play Schools Association Project at Public School No.
        10 at St. Nicholas Avenue and 116th Street

1944   Competes for Houghton Mifflin's Literary Fellowship in fiction (sub-
        mits application made up of an outline and several chapters of a
        manuscript)

1945   Wins Houghton Mifflin's Literary Fellowship Award in fiction and
        receives a stipend of $2400

1946   Publishes *The Street* and dedicates the novel to her mother, Bertha
        James Lane; publishes short story "Like a Winding Sheet" in *The
        Best American Short Stories, 1946*, edited by Martha Foley and
        receives recognition as short story writer from Foley who dedi-
        cates the collection to Petry; is honored by New York's Women's
        City Club for her "exceptional contributions to the life of New
        York City"; translated is *The Street* (*Gaden* in Copenhagen)

1947   Publishes *Country Place* and dedicates the novel to her father, Peter
        C. Lane and to her husband, George D. Petry; relocates with her
        husband to Old Saybrook, Connecticut; donates autographed cop-
        ies of *The Street* and *Country Place* to the Countee Cullen Memo-
        rial Collection in the Trevor Arnett Library, Atlanta University (now
        Atlanta University Center, Woodruff Library); turns over manu-
        script for *The Street* to Carl Van Vechten for inclusion in the James
        Weldon Johnson Memorial Collection of Negro Arts and Letters
        located in the Beinecke Rare Book and Manuscript Library, Yale
        University; translated is *The Street* (*A Rua*. Translated by Ligia
        Junqueira Smith; *En Kvinne I Harlem*. Translated by Oversatt Av
        Erik Farland; *Gatan*. Translated by Olof Hogstadius; *La Rehob*.
        Translated by Aaron Amir); reprinted is *The Street* in London

1948   Donates letters, autographed publications (in English and in numer-
        ous translations), reviews, photographs, and the manuscript for
        Country Place to the James Weldon Johnson Memorial Collection
        of Negro Arts and Letters located in the Beinecke Rare Book and
        Manuscript Library, Yale University; translated is *The Street* (*De
        Straat*. Translated by Vertaald Door and H. W. J. Schaap; *La Rue*.
        Translated by Martine Monod, Nicole Soupault, and Philippe
        Soupault); reprinted is *Country Place* in London

1949   Translated is *Country Place* (*Tempeste*. Translated by V. E. Bravetta);
        publishes children's work *The Drugstore Cat* and dedicates to
        Anna Houston Bush and Anna Louise James; birth of daughter,
        Elisabeth Ann Petry; death of father

1950   Translated is *The Street* by Ryo Namikawa

1953   Publishes *The Narrows* and dedicates the novel to Louise Robinson

1954   Reprinted is *The Narrows* in London

1955   Publishes juvenile work *Harriet Tubman, Conductor on The Underground Railroad* and dedicates to her daughter; is censored for *The* Narrows and the censorship is protested by The American Civil Liberties Union in its Censorship Bulletin and Statement on Censorship; death of mother; translated is *The Narrows* (*Link and Camilo* in Berlin)

1958   Works as a writer for Columbia Pictures in Hollywood on the screenplay for Kim Novak's film *That Hill Girl*

1960   Transposed into Braille under the auspices of the Library of Congress is *Harriet Tubman, Conductor* on the Underground Railroad

1964   Publishes juvenile work *Tituba of Salem Village* and dedicates to uncle Frank P.Chisholm; transposed into Braille under the auspices of the Library of Congress is *Tituba of Salem Village*

1965   Is reelected to the Board of Directors of the Author's Fund (the Author's League of America)

1968   Donates to the "Ann Petry Collection" in the Special Collections at Mugar Library, Boston University, the following: research notes, galleys, manuscripts, photographs, autographed publications (in English and numerous translations), letters, numerous newspaper clippings of articles and reviews, and other miscellaneous memorabilia

1970   Publishes juvenile work *Legends of the Saints* and dedicates to sister Helen L. Bush

1971   Publishes collection of short stories *Miss Muriel and Other Stories* and dedicates to brother-in-law Walter J. Petry

1972   Lectures at Miami University of Ohio

1974   Is Visiting Professor of English at the University of Hawaii; enters biography in *Who's Who of American Women*; interviews with John O'Brien for *Interviews* with Black Writers; Publishes poems "Noo York City 1," "Noo York City 2," and "Noo York City 3" in *Weid: The Sensibility Revue* (Bicentennial Issue II, American Women Poets)

1975   Enters biography in *Who's Who Among Black Americans*

1978   Is awarded creative writing grant by the National Endowment for the Arts

1981   Publishes the poems "A Purely Black Stone" and "A Real Boss Black Cat" in *A View from the Top of a Mountain*

1982   Delivers the Fourth Annual Richard Wright Lecture at Yale University

1983   Receives Doctor of Letters from Suffolk University

1984   Receives award for literature from Connecticut

1985   Historical Society (Black Women of Connecticut: Achievement Against the Odds)

1986   Receives a citation for her literary achievements from the City of
        Philadelphia on 9 April; reprinted is *The Street* by Beacon Press
        (the Black Women Writers' Series; Deborah McDowell is the Gen-
        eral Editor)

1987   Enters biography in *Great Women in Connecticut History* (The Per-
        manent Commission on the Status of Women, Hartford, CT); pub-
        lishes the contemporary short story "The Moses Project" in Harbor
        Review (English Department, University of Massachusetts)

1988   Interviews with Mark Wilson for MELUS; receives a citation from
        the United Nations Association of the United States of America
        States of America on 28 January; receives Doctor of Letters from
        University of Connecticut; reprinted are *The Narrows* and
        TheDrugstore Cat by Beacon Press (the Black Women Writers'
        Series; Deborah McDowell is the General Editor)

1989   Interviews with Hazel Arnett Ervin for *Ann Petry: A Bio-Bibliogra-
        phy*; receives Lifetime Achievement Award at the Fifth Annual
        Celebration of Black Writers' Conference (presented at a recep-
        tion held at the Friends of the Free Library in Philadelphia on 4
        February; receives Doctor of Humane Letters from Mount Holyoke
        College; enters biography in *Who's Who in Writers,Editors and
        Poets;* reprinted is *Miss Muriel and Other Stories* by Beacon Press
        (the Black Women Writers' Series)

1992   Reissued is *The Street* by Houghton Mifflin; receives the Connecticut
        Arts Award from the Connecticut Commission on the Arts (Stam-
        ford); reads from writings during broadcast of "Connecticut Voices"
        on National Public Radio (NPR) in Hartford; attends "Tribute to
        Ann Petry," organized by Farrah Jasmine Griffin at Trinity College
        where Gloria Naylor is guest speaker; is honorguest speaker, is
        honored by Mayor of Hartford with "Ann Petry Day" on 14 No-
        vember

1993   Assists to promote accuracy in biographical and bibliographical data
        in *Ann Petry: A Bio-Bibliography*, compiled by Hazel Arnett Ervin

1996   Celebrated is the fiftieth anniversary of *The Street* in New York City.
        Included is a reading from the novel by actress Alfrie Woodard;
        published is *Ann Petry* by Hilary Holladay

1997   Death of the writer on 28 April

Reviews

The Street (1946)

Four-Star Novel (1946)
Merle Nance

When beautiful Lutie Johnson moved into the grubby apartment on 116th Street, she stepped right into the middle of evil. Her desperate struggle to free herself and her son from the enveloping tentacles of that evil makes one of the most absorbing, most vivid and alive novels of recent months.

Miss Petry's craftsmanship is one of highest competence. She builds her plot, interweaves her characters, with an architectural solidity. The story moves, and the people breathe. Her style is honest and unpretentious, with no false overtones striving for effect.

In addition to these virtues, Miss Petry has accomplished one of the most difficult feats of novel-writing: she has made as her really central character, not the individual, but the sprawling, malevolent, teeming locale---"the street." Like Egdon Heath, in Hardy's "Return of the Native," "the street" is not merely background, not merely symbolic, but is the acting, influencing all its own, and the preservation of that identity is assured as it gulps into its great maw everyone who moves within its reach. In this sense one might say that Miss Petry's book is a novel of circumstance.

If one would quarrel with the desperation and hopelessness of "The Street," if one would insist on an affirmative rather than a negative view of life and its possibilities, one would have to do so on the basis, not that such circumstances are not true, but that such circumstances can be changed. If one feels that Miss Petry is defeatist, it is because she gives no indication that such circumstances need not necessarily and forever be master of the individual, that they cannot be conquered by concerted will, "the street" with its poverty, greed, violence, social maladjustment and depravity, is true of the moment---has been true for too long a time. But with the dreams and courage and determination of all the Lutie Johnsons of the world, it is more likely that 'the street" is doomed. Some feeling of this impending doom would have leavened the heavy tragedy of the book's ending, and cast it more in line with the growing resolution and efforts to destroy those social forces which have made such tragedy for so long inevitable.

It is cause for comment that Miss Petry's very able novel finds its publication during Negro History Week. To anyone who watches the publishers' list it is apparent that the Negro writer is beginning to swim with the stream; that slowly, but with the inevitability of historical process, he is forcing recognition to his rightful place in American culture. No one will deny that there isn't still a fight ahead; but the increasing number of Negro titles among the book lists is but one additional sign that "the sun do move."

And with its moving, the neglected one-tenth of the American people will also move---out of the shadows of the wasteland of violence and defeat, out of "the street." Miss Petry should know.

A Review of *The Street* (1946)
John Caswell Smith, Jr.

Few people ever see this version of Negro poverty, because it is a condition that is unspectacular. It is a story of quiet, obscure, fear-laden living, denying the conception of the stereotype, the happy-go-lucky Negro. In winning the Houghton Mifflin Literary Fellowship, Ann Petry has given us a better than good novel, written with great honesty and insight. There are thousands upon thousands of girls like Lutie Johnson in some isolated Harlem in every industrial city of the nation, but to those who know these unhappy sociological islands only by their night clubs and their violence, she may seem a strange, unreal character.

Lutie and her kind are the direct descendants of other black men and women who fled the hunger and oppression of the rural South in search of the bright but phantom opportunities of the urban North. These families accepted and absorbed the shock of frustration in these harsh, lusterless lands-without-promise in exchange for an assured forty weeks of school for their children. But the ensuing generations discovered that this idolized Education was neither the key to opportunity nor the solution *per se* to race prejudice.

The girls married men who could not get jobs. They went to work in domestic service, because that was the only occupation abundantly open to them, and left their men at home to rear the children. And, paradoxically, while they kept their employers' families running smoothly, their own families disintegrated and fell apart.

The instability of the Negro family, seen in its true light, is not a "racial characteristic" but a response to our culture wherein successful family life depends upon the man's going out to do a man's work, and upon the daily presence of both parents in the home. The American man does not flourish emotionally if his virility is shunted for long periods into ungainful employment. Eventually he escapes into some other way of life, good or bad, which holds some promise of restoring his self-esteem. The wives and children of such men go to live in some cruel, ghetto-like street, and gradually drift outside the pale of social services and away from social organization.

Our sociologists have described all of this before, but *The Street* makes it live through characters who are only partially fictional.

Current Literature (1946)
Arthur P. Davis

The Street tells the story of the pathetic but futile efforts of Lutie Johnson to
provide a decent home for her only son---an [eight]-year-old Harlem "key-child"
---on 116th Street. Neither the child nor Lutie has a possible chance in the fight
with 116th Street, the antagonist in the story; because the "street" represents all
of the evil inherent in the bad housing, the bad sanitation, the violence, and the
bestiality of a segregated, oppressed, and frustrated people. The depraved,
superintendent who tries to rape Lutie and who finally proves her undoing, the
sinister figures of Junto, the white man who desired Lutie, of Mrs. Hedges, the
brothel-keeper, and of Boots Smith, the slimy band-leader, are all parts of the
street and are all in league against the heroic efforts of Lutie to give her son a
home and security.

The street---116th in New York in this case---is symbolical of all the slums of
America. Miss Petry has seen the evil effects of such places on the lives of
essentially fine characters, and that is the thesis of her work. As a thesis it is
sound, but a thesis is one thing, a good novel another. There is almost too much
thesis lurking behind the characters in *The Street*. As a result, some of them
become puppets to motivate the plot and not flesh-and-blood human beings.
Junto, for instance, the mysterious behind-the-scenes controller of Harlem bands
and night spots, is more melodramatic than real. The same holds true for Mrs.
Hedges, although she is a fascinating figure.

All the way through the book, the reader keeps wondering why Lutie, who is
an intelligent person, doesn't take an intelligent course of action when some
emergency arises. This is particularly true at the end when she seeks a lawyer to
get her child out of a detention home. As a matter of fact, the whole ending
seems forced. The author evidently felt that she needed a strong climax and
proceeded to obtain one at the expense of reality. A sensational ending it
certainly is, but it is not convincing.

In spite of these obvious weaknesses---weaknesses often found in first
novels---*The Street* is a fascinating work. Its sensationalism makes for fast and
"easy" reading. Moreover, Miss Petry knows her street intimately; and her
theme, though she has made it Negro, is not essentially racial but human, and
therefore, has a universal appeal. . . .

With her profound knowledge of Negro slum life, her flair for the
sensational, and her ability to dramatize social ills, Ann Petry has the makings of
a great protest novelist.

In *The Street* her thesis was not wholly sublimated into art, but with her
intelligence and obvious ability she will surely profit from the experience of this
first effort. It looks as though the Hard Boiled School has another able scholar.

Off the Book Shelf (1946)
Ben Burns

Portrait of "The Street"

Richard Wright's Bigger Thomas will have to move over this week to make room for Lutie Johnson.

What *Native Son* did in profiling the life and times of a slum-shocked Negro youth on Chicago's Southside, Ann Petry's new novel, *The Street.* . . does with virtually the same devastating, appalling effects in her story of a Harlem tenement. Her Lutie Johnson is a grim, heart-rending portrait of a struggling Negro housewife in the toils of one of the most terrible villains ever described in a book—*The Street.*

The Street is the octopus-like monster that claws out with relentless tentacles to enmesh its innocent victims in the web of hunger and prostitution, superstition and crime, sickness and immorality. "The Street" is Ann Petry's vivid symbol of all that is wrong in race hate.

It is the frightful, harrowing story of the inexorable doom that clamps down on the dwellers of the ghetto. In the graphic, stirring story of how the slums close in inevitably on Lutie Johnson, there is all the mood and tempo of Edgar Allan Poe's never-to-be-forgotten "Pit And The Pendulum."

Story of a Harlem Housewife

Lutie Johnson is a divorced Harlem housewife who lives alone with her eight-year-old son, Bub, in a miserable hovel on Harlem's 116th [Street]. Her marriage shattered by the shadow of poverty, she becomes a working mother who is forever tormented by the worry that "the street" will make her son another one of the army of juvenile delinquents who rove Harlem. She is forced to rent an apartment over a brothel where over and over again she is bidden to accept the favors of white men who covet her beautiful body.

Then there comes a chance to escape---a pick-up by Boots Smith, a band leader, who offers her a chance to sing with his band. But the odds are against her. "The Street" beats her down, shoves her roughly back into "her place" when Boots' white sponsor tells the musician he wants Lutie for himself. Slowly but surely fate closes in on her, driving her back and back into the corner where she finally strikes out like a cornered animal and commits' a capital crime against the white man's laws. Miss Petry has given a terrific suspense to her story. She describes her villain best when she writes:

> Streets like the one she (Lutie) lived on were
> no accident. They were the North's lynch

> mobs, she thought bitterly; the method the
> big cities used to keep Negroes in their
> place. From the time she was born, she had
> been hemmed into an ever-narrowing space,
> until now she was very near walled in and
> the wall had been built up brick by brick by
> eager white hands. (323)

Memorable Reading

Ann Petry is no Richard Wright in writing technique but with a certain, steady hand she has made her first published book, which won her a Houghton-Mifflin literary fellowship, a memorable experience, which will haunt readers long after shutting the covers. She has searched and sifted the mind of a typical Negro girl confronted with the painful problem of bringing up a child decently in the hell that is Harlem. With the penetration of a psychiatrist and the delicate care of a mother, she has delved into the social pressures that push good, everyday, common people over the brink into the chasm of desperate crime.

The former Negro newspaperwoman has avoided one pitfall which marred Wright's "Native Son." She has always emphasized the social implications of her story and stayed away from the phony melodrama which sometimes detoured Wright from his main theme. And despite her essential interest in social background, her book never lags in interest once it gets past its slow start.

The Street is an alarming, disturbing book. It will dismay and terrify many white readers in the same manner that *Native Son* did. In some ways its negative aspects will have a disheartening, defeatist reaction that cannot but disarm many and cause them to turn to cynicism.

But others---like Lutie---will be incensed, will be moved to a vengeful anger and strike out desperately at the virus of racism that creates characters like Lutie. That is the asset of *The Street* for all its hopelessness. It is a book to move people to action, perhaps wiser, more organized action than Lutie's hysterical, crazed murder of Boots, the man who would sell her into white hands.

Tough, Carnal Harlem (1946)
Arna Bontemps

Harlem won a spot on the literary map of the United States in the 1920s. In the publication of novels like Carl Van Vechten's *Nigger Heaven* and Claude McKay's *Home to Harlem*, in poems like Countee Cullen's "Color" and Langston Hughes's "Weary Blues," in related work by short story, drama and non-fiction prose writers like James Weldon Johnson, Rudolph Fisher and Wallace Thurman the first phase of dark Harlem's consciousness was detailed in arresting colors and compelling rhythms [,] Harlem was an island of primitive pleasures and passions in those days. Imaginary palm trees lined the streets. The moon was a ripe fruit too sweet for mortal taste. Africa's burnished, "copper sun" was suspended over the dingy rooftops. Harlem was "a city of refuge," a "promised land," a jungle of song, a flood of wine, a "shining tree," [and] "a nude young dancer."

Of course, the depression took care of all that. But not even the hardships of the 1930s could completely check the stream of Harlem books. Neither did the sobering blight of the bad times quite finish off the rhythms and passions of that "great dark city." The simple fact is that whatever we may think of it, the Harlem story is a hard one to put down.

It is at once fascinating and disturbing. Two years ago Roi Ottley caught its spirit and brought the record up to date in "New World A-Coming," a factual report. Now Ann Petry, a fresh new talent, gives her view in a fictional account centering around a handful of simple folk who live between Seventh and Eighth Avenues on 116th Street. *The Street*, Miss Petry's first book, won the Houghton Mifflin Literary Fellowship Award for 1944. It deserves the prize.

The story itself is the struggle of Lutie Johnson to make a decent life for herself and Bub, her young son. Lutie is young and attractive, perhaps a shade too attractive for her own good under the circumstances, and Bub is a rugged and healthy eight-year-old who needs nothing so much as his mother's oversight in the afternoons when he comes home from school. Presently the street traps them both, and they find themselves up against an uneven fight.

The actual trouble goes back to Lutie's work in domestic service. This was necessary at the time to keep the home going, but the week and month-long absences wrecked her marriage. Perhaps the crack-up is explained by a certain loss of self-respect on the part of the young husband following his discovery that he was unable to support a wife and child. Perhaps it is explained better by the presence of another woman. In any case, Lutie suddenly found her place occupied. She and Bub were out. Naturally, she turned again to her own father. But this unhappy individual was himself hopelessly slum-shocked, and the environment he created was poisonous to a growing youngster like Bub. Lutie decided that she and Bub would be better off alone. They found a top-floor, three-room apartment and set out on the kind of existence that too many Harlem mothers know too well.

Lutie was not unaware of the specific hazards she faced. What she did not know was that the ghetto itself, the hedged in, restricted life of the street, was the villain. But this fact revealed itself in time, and Lutie learned that even Mrs. Hedges, the burned and disfigured old wretch who sat forever at the window of the apartment in which she carried on her shady business, was just another victim of the street. Jones, the super (to whom Mrs. Hedges observed, "You done lived in basements so long you ain't human no more. You got mould growin' on you, was a product of filthy underground passages and boiler rooms.

The young woman's fight against the corrupting influences of this crowded little world, her effort to safeguard her son and to keep herself unsoiled, is the challenging theme Miss Petry has chosen for her novel. She could scarcely have found a more important human problem in our urban life today. She has treated it with complete seriousness in a story that will bear a lot of thoughtful reading.

As a novelist Miss Petry is an unblushing realist. Her recreation of the street has left out none of its essential character. It is a part of her achievement, however, that the carnal life of the slum never seems to be hauled in for its own sake. Even the earthy language, like something overheard on a truck or in a doorway, fails to draw attention to itself; in every case it seems to blend into the situation. It will not be for such details that *The Street* will be read and discussed.

A Review of *The Street* (1986)
Sherley Anne Williams

This novel offers a penetrating and absorbing chronicle of a black woman's struggle to realize her dreams of upward mobility from the pre-civil rights ghetto of 40 years ago. Originally published in 1946 (and completed on a Houghton Mifflin Literary Prize fellowship), The *Street* earns Ann Petry an abiding place among American naturalist novelists. Petry, a registered pharmacist, was born in Old Saybrook, Connecticut, and worked in her family's drugstores before she married and moved to New York in the late 1930s. She acquired the intimate and disturbing knowledge of the inner city that informs her novel through experience as a journalist for two Harlem newspapers.

Lutie Johnson, the attractive, hardworking protagonist of Petry's novel, starts out believing that anyone can be rich in the "richest damn country in the world" if they work hard enough. Married right out of high school, and a mother soon after that, Lutie, when her husband is unable to find work, has little choice but to take a job as a live-in maid. Hurt and humiliated when her husband takes up with another woman, Lutie takes her son and moves in with her father. Working in a steam laundry by day and attending school by night, she manages to acquire the skills that eventually lead to a job as a file clerk. Her salary is not enough to live on, but, alarmed at the influence her father's drunken friends might have on her son and thinking of this as a stepping stone in her quest for independence and financial security, Lutie moves to a cheap apartment in a dirty and desolate side street in Harlem.

Petry has been praised for the effectiveness with which she renders external details: the congested, malevolent Harlem street environment that distorts and perverts the personalities of its residents. But the real power of the novel lies in her understanding the roles that gender and sexuality play in the exploitation of black women; this lifts *The Street* above the general run of proletarian novels. Mrs. Hedges, the grotesquely scarred madam of the discreet whorehouse in Lutie's apartment building, is one metaphor of that oppression. Obsessed with her own disfigurement, Hedges becomes a partner in exploitation with Junto, the white man who owns the brothel over which she presides. Min, the drab doormat of a woman who lives with the super in Lutie's building, is another. Jones, the building super, who is sexually obsessed with Lutie, is at once the brute Negro of stereotype and the symbol of Lutie's fears about her own sexuality. Petry's assessment of Lutie's predicament---that her options are determined not by her virtue or lack of it, but by the fact that everyone with whom she comes in contact sees her only in terms of her sexuality---still applies to the average low-income black woman today.

A Familiar Street (1987)
Barbara Smith

In the fall of 1973[,] I taught my first course on Black women writers. Ann Petry's *The Street* was an essential part of my syllabus, but the bookstore informed me that it had gone out of print. Determined to teach the novel, I called the publisher and found out that there were a few copies left in the warehouse, which they were willing to ship to their office in Manhattan. My sister, who lived in Brooklyn at the time, went and got the books and literally brought them to me in a shopping bag on one of her visits to Boston. Undertaking such a complicated odyssey to obtain a text was typical of the changes I routinely went through during the years that I was teaching Black women's literature regularly.

Like most titles by Black women authors, *The Street*'s availability has been quite unpredictable. Fortunately, Petry's first and most acclaimed novel, a pivotal work in the African American women's literary canon, has recently been reissued by Beacon Press as part of its series of Black women's reprints, edited by scholar and critic Deborah McDowell. This novel and many of her short stories reveal harsh but necessary truths about Black women that are especially useful to readers and feminists who are seeking more than a superficial understanding of the ways in which racism has undermined the lives of women of color.

Petry's novel, originally published in 1946, ranks as a classic if only because of its vivid descriptions, strong characterizations, and involving plot. What made it stand out, however, when I began studying Black women's literature at a time when no cohesive Black feminist analysis was available, was how clearly it demonstrated the connections among racial, sexual, and class oppression in the life of a particular Black woman. What happens to Lutie Johnson does not occur solely because she is Black, or a woman, or poor, but because she is all three.

Petry's account of a Black woman struggling to raise her child alone amid the destruction of the slums is an archetypal Black woman's tale. It is incredibly depressing how accurate this portrait of a ghetto street and family still is today when 41.5 percent of Black families are headed by women and 50.5 percent of these families live in poverty. Unlike the victim-blaming stance of a *Moynihan Report* or a *Bill Moyers' Journal*, the novel indicates how limited Black women's options are in a society that hates them. Petry writes:

> Streets like the one she lived on were no
> accident. They were the North's lynch
> mobs, she thought bitterly; the method the
> big cities used to keep Negroes in their
> place. And she began thinking of Pop

> unable to get a job; of Jim slowly
> disintegrating because he, too, couldn't get a
> job, and of the subsequent wreck of their
> marriage; of Bub left to his own devices
> after school. From the time she was born,
> she had been hemmed into an ever-
> narrowing space, until now she was very
> nearly walled in and the wall had been built
> up brick by brick by eager white hands.
> (323)

Petry makes Lutie's victimization by social forces seem both more inevitable and more tragic by portraying her as thoroughly heroic. She is bright, tenacious, and brave and possesses unswerving integrity, all qualities that would lead to success if she were not also Black and female in an era that permitted even fewer tokens than the present one. The novel repeatedly points to White people's role in implementing institutional racism, and White women are just as contemptuous of Lutie as are White men.

Although Petry defines racism as the primary factor in Lutie's oppression and often attributes her male characters' sexually oppressive behavior to racial causes, during the course of the novel it is overwhelmingly both Black and White men's sexual exploitation of Lutie that ultimately seals her fate. Except for Lutie's former husband, Jim, and her father, the significant men in the story are uniformly malevolent and view her as nothing but a sexual object. Because Lutie is physically beautiful, they assume she exists solely to gratify their sexual appetites. After Jones, the Black superintendent of Lutie's building, tries to rape Lutie, Petry writes:

> She climbed the stairs slowly, holding on to
> the railing. Once she stopped and leaned
> against the wall, filled with a sick loathing
> of herself, wondering if there was something
> about her that subtly suggested to the Super
> that she would welcome his love-making,
> wondering if the same thing had led Mrs.
> Hedges to believe that she would leap at the
> opportunity to make money sleeping with
> white men, remembering the women at the
> Chandlers' who had looked at her and
> assumed she wanted their husbands. It took
> her a long time to reach the top floor. (240)

The imperceptible thing that is "wrong" with Lutie is the fact that she has inherited the legacy of slavery that defines Black women as sexual chattel.

Lutie's refusal to go along with Junto, the supposedly unprejudiced White man who owns a casino, and with Boots Smith, his Black bandleader, has dire economic consequences. Her chances of improving her and her son's living situation are directly tied to her willingness to be sexually exploited by them. On the other hand, lack of physical beauty according to White European standards also affects the degree of access that Black women have to both economic survival and emotional companionship, as exemplified by Mrs. Hedges, of whom Petry writes:

> She began thinking about the period of her life when she had haunted employment agencies seeking work. When she walked in them, there was uncontrollable revulsion in the faces of the white people who looked at her. They stared at her enormous *size*, at the blackness of her skin. They glanced at each other, tried in vain to control their faces or didn't bother to try at all, simply let her see what a monstrosity they thought she was. (241)

Mrs. Hedges's only hope for marriage is to make enough money to "buy" a husband's love. Once again it is a White man who has the power to change her circumstances. Junto takes the unusual step of making Mrs. Hedges a partner in his financial ventures. Although she refuses his personal overtures, sexual exploitation is still a component of their relationship, since she keeps a house of prostitution in one of the buildings he owns.

Petry's major point is that Blackness and femaleness virtually ensure poverty and that poverty in turn undermines the stability of emotional and sexual relationships as well as family life. The impact of this circular sexual, racial, economic trap, embodied in the phrase "the street," is most painfully apparent in Lutie's efforts to better things for Bub. When compared to the luxury and greed she witnesses while working as a maid for the Chandlers, a rich White family in Connecticut, Lutie's American Dream is decidedly modest. Petry writes:

> Only a few hours had elapsed since she stood in this same doorway, completely unaware of the dim light, the faded, dreary paint, the filth on the floor. She had looked down the length of this hall and seen Bub growing up in some airy, sunny house and herself free from worry about money. She had been able to picture him coming home from school to snacks of cookies and milk and bringing other kids with him; and them

playing somewhere near-by, and all she had
to do was look out of the window and see
him because she was home every day when
he arrived. And time and Boots Smith and
Junto had pushed her right back in here,
deftly removing that obscuring cloud of
dreams, so that now tonight she could see
the wall in reality. (230)

The building that Lutie and her son inhabit is dark and squalid. Bub's bed is
the living room couch. Because she must work to support them, he comes home
every day to an empty apartment, and the only place he has to play after school
is the street. His White teacher views Bub and all of the Black children in his
segregated school as savages, incapable of learning, so she does not bother to
teach them. Lutie knows exactly what the street holds for her 8-year-old son,
but like so many Black mothers, she is ultimately powerless to counter its
effects.

Whenever I reread the novel, I am always struck by Lutie's isolation,
particularly from other Black women. Petry explains that Lutie lost track of all
her friends during the years when she was working in a laundry all day and
studying to be a clerical worker at night. At certain key points the advice or
support of a Black woman friend might have made a positive difference, but
Lutie's isolation is only a factor in her downfall, not the cause.

Proving that Lutie can win out over impossible odds was not the author's
purpose. It was instead to portray in wrenching detail the conditions that the
majority of Black women faced during the period when the novel was written.
Petry wanted to inspire her readers to question a system that spawned such
nightmares and to motivate them to do work that could bring about actual
political change. Despite the racial and sexual reforms that have been instituted
in the intervening years, the novel is still frighteningly descriptive of the
situation of most Black women. Obviously it takes longer than 40 years to
eradicate the massive injustices that destroy Lutie and her real-life counterparts.
If we take on the challenge to work for freedom that is inherent in *The Street* and
in the writing of most African American women, Lutie's tale will not be quite as
familiar 40 years from now.

A Checkered Career --- *The Street* by Ann Petry (1992)
Barbara Christian

Last February Houghton Mifflin reissued Ann Petry's first novel, *The Street*, which it was fortunate enough to publish to much acclaim in 1946. This work was the first novel by an African American women to focus on the struggles of a working-class black mother in an urban ghetto, and a reissue in a quality edition is long overdue.

In the 1920s and 30s, African Americans published novels centered on urban women. But these---Jessie Fauset's *Plum Bun* (1929), for example, or Nella Larsen's *Quicksand* (1923)---portrayed middle-class female protagonists, usually childless, whose lives, despite their class status, are gravely constrained by the sexism and racism of urban America. African American male writers--- Richard Wright in *Native Son* (1941), or William Attaway in *Blood on the Forge* (1941)---wrote protest novels to dramatize how the lower-class or working-class status of their black male characters determined their tragic fate. Zora Neale Hurston built *Their Eyes Were Watching God* (1937) on a black woman's search for fulfillment in a rural community. But few African American writers in the first half of this century attempted to gauge the effect of the urban ghetto on the sexism and racism that African American women had always confronted.

Ann Petry's graphic portrayal of the inevitable downfall of her character, Lutie Johnson, is remarkable for its intensity of focus. By constructing a proletarian protest novel from the point of view of a black woman, Petry both criticized and developed that genre. Given the fact that millions of African American women live in conditions like those of *The Street* and when one considers the emphasis on urban racial issues in the sixties and on women's issues in the seventies, one has to wonder why this novel is not better known, more accepted.

I first saw a copy of *The Street* in the early seventies. I'd been teaching supposedly "uneducable" (sic) Harlem blacks and Puerto Ricans at City College in New York, and had learned what might now seem obvious but was then considered radical---that if my students were presented with books that related to their lives, they "miraculously" became passionate about reading and writing. Because in those times only a few books by blacks were regularly available at "normal" bookstores, I periodically combed Harlem's thrift stores for discarded books.

It was in one of those unintellectual places that I found a dingy copy of *The Street*. I was drawn to its cover---a brash photograph of an attractive black woman in wintry urban clothing framed by bold print: "SHE WAS A SOUL ON ICE IN A BRUTAL GHETTO"---words which gave me the mistaken impression that the novel was influenced by that literary blockbuster of 1968, Eldridge Cleaver's *Soul on Ice*. Unconsciously registering the fact that a woman's book was being authenticated by a man's, I wondered how I could have missed such a rare event---a new novel by a black woman.

I would soon discover that the much-used paperback I'd bought for ten cents was the eighth printing of a 1961 reissue of a novel originally published in 1946. Ann Petry was not a new writer: my Pyramid reissue had been cleverly packaged to take advantage of the country's then intense interest in the black ghetto, particularly its raging male inhabitants, a result of the response to "race riots" that swept major US cities in the 1960s. That interest was too short-lived to keep many such books in print. The few that did survive were written by men: Richard Wright's *Native Son* (1940), James Baldwin's *The Fire Next Time* (1963), Ralph Ellison's *Invisible Man* (1953). Nor were even these books usually taught in literature classes, since African American literature apparently did not exist; they were more likely to turn up on sociology class lists, where blacks were seen as appropriate objects of inquiry.

No wonder then that *The Street* has had its ups and downs. In print and acclaimed in the late 1940s, it was ignored for much of the 50s. Reissued in the early 1960s, it was difficult to obtain for much of the 1970s and 80s. In 1985, it was reissued under Deborah McDowell's editorship in a series of black women's novels that had been long out of print but were brought to light through the efforts of African American women critics. Now Houghton Mifflin has not only reissued *The Street* but intends to add Petry's other works for adults: two novels---*The Narrows* (1953) and *Country Place* (1947)---and her collection of short stories, *Miss Muriel and Other Stories* (1971).

In tracing critical response or the absence thereof towards this novel from the fifties through the eighties, I mean not only to underline its significance but also to sound a cautionary note about our own biases when we read and study African American women's writing: it still seems difficult for readers and critics in this country to comprehend and appreciate that black women can have differing visions at one and the same time.

In the few literary analyses of African American fiction published in the 1950s, *The Street* was usually mentioned, but almost always as a foil to Richard Wright's *Native Son*, whose alienated, angry, male protagonist was seen as more emblematic of the black ghetto than Petry's industrious, upwardly mobile black woman. These novels do have much in common. Both Bigger Thomas and Lutie Johnson are trapped by the physical and social space which their race and poverty condemn them to move in. At a pivotal point in the novel, each is employed as a servant to a wealthy white family whose racial or sexual stereotypes influence their tragic fate. Both Thomas and Lutie Johnson kill in the course of each novel as a result of the racial or sexual myths imposed on them.

But there are also major differences between the two novels---in their respective authors' philosophical concerns and their delineation of their major characters. While Bigger Thomas does not care about his family or believe in the American Dream, Lutie Johnson, like many other poor mothers, believes---one is tempted to say, *must* believe---that if she works hard enough, is thrifty, follows Benjamin Franklin's example, she might be able to save her son from the degradation of those streets that attempt to destroy or at least entrap anyone who is black and poor. While Wright adopts major Western philosophical frameworks---Existentialism, Marxism---to articulate the psychology of Bigger Thomas, Lutie Johnson is worried not so much about her womanhood as she is about the mundane: about food (for example, the red dye in the meat she and other Harlem mothers are forced to buy); about housing---not only the rent she can barely afford but the claustrophobia of her three tiny rooms; about her son, and whether her attempts to protect him from the dangers of his own street are futile; about her own body as she maneuvers in the terrain of male desire where both black and white men see her as sexual prey.

Perhaps the most telling disparity between these two protest novels arises out of their parallel plots: both protagonists kill, but the conditions and the effects of their acts are very different. Bigger Thomas accidentally kills Mary Dalton, a white woman in whose bedroom he is trapped, because of his fear (a well-founded one) that he will be accused of having raped her. Lutie Johnson, defending herself against being raped, kills Boots, a black man. Bigger is psychologically liberated by breaking the Great American Taboo (that of a black man having sexual relations with a white woman); he is defended by a Marxist lawyer in a trial that is as much about the meaning of oppression as it is specifically about his crime; and he comes to some self-knowledge just before his execution by the State.

In contrast, Lutie Johnson flees to another ghetto after her act of self-defense, leaving her child behind to the white world of the juvenile hall because she is convinced that he is better off there than with her, his powerless and now criminal mother. Lutie does not draw the attention of Marxist lawyers. She does not become a *cause celebre*. After all, how could a black woman be raped? And even if she were, after all, all she did was to kill a black man. While Wright's novel employs the outlines of the crime story intact with a murderer on the run, Petry's novel is not about adventure so much as it is about cramped space, about doors of opportunity that shut one after another in Lutie Johnson's face.

No wonder then that Wright's novel overshadowed Petry's in the 1950s and 60s. The civil rights and Black Power movements emphasized the muscular path of black manhood. Since the U[nited] S[tates] was clearly a patriarchal society, how else could blacks achieve equality? One result of that assumption was the much-touted belief that black men had been castrated---not only by white society but by the overpowering black matriarch, the female head of household so domineering she prevented her sons from growing up to be responsible men. It was she who was to blame for the "breakdown" of the black family, for the epidemic of black juvenile delinquents who threatened the order of society.

That perspective was to culminate in the Moynihan Report of 1966. But as public policy it had been circulating among intellectuals and popular commentators since the 1940s. In writing *The Street*, Petry used the mass of detail gathered in the investigative reporting she'd done for the Harlem weekly *The People's Voice* on urban ghetto housing, on black male unemployment and its relationship to "broken" marriages, on education, childrearing and sexual violence in the ghetto to demonstrate that juvenile delinquency and the breakdown of black urban communities were due not to domineering black mothers but to rampant institutional racism. Petry underlined this point when at the end of the novel Lutie Johnson ironically asks whether there is really any difference between the Southern slave plantation and the urban ghetto.

In the fifties the prospect of integration raised hopes among many that U.S. racism might be eliminated once blacks finally "legally" gained access to the American Dream. But neither Benjamin Franklin's philosophy nor her own literacy, beauty, intelligence and morality [would]save Lutie Johnson. In its scathing critique of the benefits of access, *The Street* might have been seen as a throwback to a less enlightened decade. Too, protest as a literary form was becoming unpopular, not only because it dwelt so heavily on the "grim side of black life," but also because it reduced black characters to types, as James Baldwin would argue so eloquently in his essay "Everybody's Protest Novel."

But what about the sixties, the decade that dwelt so much on urban black American and fostered so much protest? Why didn't *The Street* receive more attention when it was reissued then, since it, perhaps more than any other African American novel I've read, details so completely the conditions that a person encounters every day in the ghetto: the crowded tenements, the smelly streets, the grimy food markets, the hostile police, the indifferent, tired educational system? Why didn't cultural nationalists celebrate this "realistic" novel as they did the philosophical *Native Son*?

Though they valued literature as protest, the Black Power movements of the 1960s portrayed women as adjuncts to men, a perspective that Alice Walter, June Jordan and Audre Lorde would later come to criticize. One has only to consider the killing of Boots---a black rapist, not a white one---to see the ideological difficulties that cultural nationalist might have with the novel. At a time when Black Unity meant that women should not protest their conditions as women, Petry's analyses of the ways in which black men vented their frustrations on black women must have seemed (at best) strategically incorrect.

When I taught *The Street* for the first time in 1971, many of my students who lived in Harlem were alert to that point---what they called Petry's fostering of disunity. However, as the women's movement gained momentum, students from the same background were intrigued by the fact that a novel written well before the explosion of African American women's literature in the 1970s had attacked sexism in the African American community. Now they objected instead to the way in which the black community was represented as a ghetto, an alienated place where there is no indication that community ties exist. Many of them pointed to Petry's own small-town New England background as a way to justify their sense that a different moral and social ethos was at work: Petry was an outsider who saw the ghetto only as a place of material deprivation, and not as a community with deep cultural vitality.

But why hadn't these same students raised this objection to *Native Son*? Didn't Wright also focus on the black urban environment as a deprived ghetto? Unlike Petry, he came from a devastatingly poor family and had suffered intense racism in his childhood, so what did background have to do with it? Might not Petry's as well as Wright's emphasis on the destructiveness of the ghetto have more to do with the intention of the protest novel---that its goal is to demonstrate the effects of oppression? Would these novels be as effective as protest if rich cultural vitality was their focus? June Jordan pointed out in an essay on *Native Son* and *Their Eyes Were Watching God* that novels of affirmation *and* novels of protest are necessary to African American intellectual and social expression: doesn't that also apply to *The Street*?

As my students examined their criticisms, it became increasingly clear that while they could accept, even applaud, Wright's representation of an urban black man as alienated and angry, they could not accept Petry's representation of an urban black woman as disconnected from the community and angry at the limitations of her environment. Black women, whatever their class or condition, had to be community-oriented, or how would the community survive? What they applauded was Janie in *Their Eyes Were Watching God*, a woman who desired community, was clearly sensual, and achieved her voice. Ironically, while Hurston's novel had been rejected for decades because it was *not* a protest novel, now *The Street* was being criticized because a woman's novel should be affirmative.

While my students' opinions are not exactly a definitive explanation of why *The Street* failed to attract more attention in the woman-centered seventies, I think their responses do indicate the discomfort this novel might have caused in the last two decades among readers who yearned (as we should have) for rebels like Morrison's Sula, or her wise Pilate in *Song of Solomon* (1977), or for political activists like Alice Walker's Meridian or Toni Cade Bambara's Velma in *The Salt Eaters* (1981). Although I do not share Hazel Carby's assessment of our idealization of *Their Eyes Were Watching God* as a return to a pastoral past, I do think we ought to reflect on why so few novels about working-class urban black women were published or celebrated during the 1970s---and why so many prominent African American women's novels of that period were set in small towns, villages of the past.

In the fiction of the 1980s the issue of class became more focal. Yet except for Gloria Naylor's *The Women of Brewster Place* (1980), most of these novels emphasized middle-class black women: Jadine in Morrison's *Tar Baby*(1981), Celie in Alice Walker's *The Color Purple* (1983), Sarah Phillips in Andrea Lee's 1984 novel of the same name. Whether or not that trend was due to a social climate in which working-class lives were less central to intellectual inquiry or to the perceptions of publishing companies, it is nonetheless true that African American women were then and are now a majority of the Black urban ghetto.

In the 1990s a new trend is beginning to emerge. Films like *Boyz N the Hood* and *New Jack City* indicate that the new black ghetto, the "hood," is causing the rest of American society much consternation. Perhaps *The Street* will receive more attention in this era, and find the place it deserves in the literary history of the US. For as Petry pointed out in a recent interview, the world it portrays is as real now as it was in 1946.

Country Place (1947)

Injustice, Out of Focus (1947)
Richard Sullivan

Gossip, malice, calculation, infidelity, adultery, attempted murder, sudden death, and a set of surprise bequests that more or less straighten things out---these are some of the dominant matters treated in *Country Place*. Yet this is, despite the violence of its events, a rather quiet book, carefully and economically phrased, and a good deal different from the author's best-selling *The Street*.

The novel deals, thematically, with justice and injustice clashing in a small New England town. Among the persons who serve to concretize this theme are (a) a young man just home from the war, (b) his fluttery and beautiful young wife, who has recently developed an unfortunate response to (c) the town rake, who has previously engaged in a brief affair with (d) the fluttery young wife's mother, who is married to (e) the middle-aged son of (f) a very solid, rich and integral old lady. The relationships of these persons are sadistically complicated by (g) the town taxi-driver, who seems to ferret out everything about everybody and then to pass it on where it will accomplish most damage; and the doings of all concerned are narrated by (h) the town druggist.

In his narration by the druggist there lies a technical defect which blurs the continuity of the book slightly, and does some harm to its general conviction. For what begins as a first-person narrative, presumably subject to the limitations of that approach, very quickly changes to an intimate and thorough rendering of experience in which the narrator has had no share, and which he therefore seems to lack authority to relate.

In occasional chapters, and at the end of the book, the straight first-person point of view is reestablished; but the considerable sections which lie between, though in themselves full of fresh, effective writing, are always darkened by the doubt arising from a switched point of view. Reading them, one is disturbed by a persistent, nagging uncertainty as to whether these pages are to be taken as the objective recreation of actual fact or as the subjective re-creation of what the alleged narrator imagines the fact to have been.

Yet despite this technical ambiguity *Country Place* is a novel which, on the whole, is decidedly better than average. Its style is bright and vigorous. Its feeling for place, for the small telling background detail, seems consistently right. Its characterizations are forceful. Its events, though weighted with melodrama, come together into a satisfying whole design. There are a few open and obvious touches of management at the end, so that right seems to triumph almost at the author's direction; and perhaps a few too many side-issues are forced into a final situation that doesn't quite seem to justify them all. But a passionate seriousness of intention, a good feeling of honesty and a general competence of execution make up adequately for the book's technical weaknesses.

A Review of *Country Place*
Author Unknown

A soldier returning to his hometown from the war suspects his wife's behavior in his absence. By the time he finds out that his fears are well grounded, the community has been shaken by the scandal, and Miss Petry has joined the company of the novelists who have described the American small town as a center of bigotry, marital infidelity, and astounding malice. Near the end, the story buckles somewhat under the weight of a couple of improbabilities, but on the whole the author has kept up to the form she displayed in *The Street*.

Tragedy on Two Levels (1947)
Rose Feld

Add *Country Place,* by Ann Petry, to the list of novels about returned soldiers who find their wives unfaithful. This comment is not intended either as disparagement of the theme or of Miss Petry's book. Simply, the tragedy of the returned soldier who has been betrayed is stuff, which, in the past few years, has enriched the mulch of human experience upon which novelists draw.

Miss Petry writes of Johnnie Roane, who, after four years of service overseas, returns to his home in Lennox, Connecticut. Here, with his parents, lives Glory, the girl he had married a year before he left. Wishing to surprise his mother and his wife, he takes a taxi at the station. It is driven by a sharp-faced little man who laughingly tells Johnnie that people call him the Weasel.

Mainly, it is the Weasel who gives substance and shape to the events of the story. He is a Dickensian creature, compounded of slyness, cruelty and viciousness. It is he who throws the first suspicion of Glory into Johnny's mind; he who later informs Mearns, son of Mrs. Gramby, diabetic dowager of Gramby House, that his wife has been unfaithful to him. The story, with the Weasel acting as self-appointed spy and informer, is told on two levels, that of Johnny's tragedy and its resolution and that of Mrs. Gramby's conflict with her daughter-in-law, Lil, who is also Glory's mother. A storm of hurricane proportions, excellently described, serves as a backdrop for the intensity of the human drama that is enacted under two roofs.

There is much that is exceedingly good in Miss Petry's book, the feel of a small town, the integrity of dialogue, the portrayal of Johnnie, of Glory, of Mrs. Gramby. But it is not quite as good as it gives promise of being at the start. For one thing, Miss Petry switches the identity of the narrator; for another, some of the high moments of her story err on the side of the obvious.

Review of *Country Place* (1947)
John Caswell Smith, Jr.

Ann Petry's writing in this second novel shows much of the improvement one was led to anticipate on reading her first. *Country Place* is a fast-moving, somewhat melodramatic tale of a small New England town as seen through the eyes of its druggist, Mr. Fraser.

Johnny Roane, a veteran of the recent war, returns home after a four-year absence, to find his home town a bit strange and his beautiful young wife, Glory, more than a little estranged from him; yearning, in fact, after the affections of the town's chief seducer. Glory's mother, having artfully achieved marriage with the not very manly son of one of the town's first families, broods over her failure to achieve status among the citizenry as well as over her complete frustration in attempting to become the recognized mistress of the Gramby estate, a post sternly and jealously presided over by her aged and ailing mother-in-law. Bits and pieces of unassembled gossip flit tentatively and covertly about the town, but The Weasel, a taxi-driver, is impatient with the normal speed of gossip and he frequently finds ways of helping it to take a jump or two ahead of schedule so that it will land in the places where it will do the most damage.

There is a hurricane, too, and the story is geared to its onset, climax, and departure. At the height of the storm, the smoldering hates, loves, and confusions of the main characters are whipped up into swift, decisive action; and in the wake of the big wind, the uncovered emotions of our main characters lead them into areas that might have, otherwise, taken years to reach.

Most of the characters are well done, but curiously enough, Johnny Roane, the hero, is not; for he is not filled out to real-life, believable proportions. It is hard to believe, for instance, that a young man, just home from four years of war, would not relate a great deal of that most recent experience to the events in his new existence as a civilian, especially when slogging about on a rainy night in a muddy forest; and a fight with a soft, middle aged civilian---a cardiac patient at that---would have been a much more businesslike piece of action than Johnny displays.

Taken as a whole, though, *Country Place* is a good story, worthy of the telling. It preaches no sermons, waves no flags. It tells a plausible narrative of, for the most part, some very human people in an earthy situation. It need not have been told through the eyes and perceptions of the druggist, and it might even be that this technique detracts from its readability; for you may find yourself wondering, on occasion, where in the world even so wise a person as Mr. Fraser could have found out so much about the thoughts and behavior of his fellow citizens.

The Narrows (1953)

A Review of *The Narrows* (1953)
J. Saunders Redding

The long wait for Ann Petry's new work is over. *The Narrows* was worth waiting for. It is a good novel. Its chief characters are fully realized and Miss Petry brings them fully to life.

It is natural to compare *The Narrows* with Miss Petry's other works, *The Street*, her first, and *Country Place*, her second. *The Narrows* shows a greater narrative skill than the first and a tighter, sounder thematic structure than the second. Miss Petry is still growing. Given her potentials, *The Narrows* is not the best work she will do.

Since *The Street*, Ann Petry has been working towards a creative philosophy and, I assume, an artistic creed that other novelists who happen to be colored--- William Attaway, Chester Himes, and Richard Wright for instance---have assumed disingenuously and affected impatiently.

One principal element in this philosophy and this creed is its realistic idealism, and this has expressed itself among these colored writers in a denial of any fundamental differences between the races.

An Assumed Pose

Now, whereas a philosophy is a thing of the intellect, a creed is a thing of the emotions, and Attaway, Himes, and especially Wright have not really had the emotional conviction that there are truly no fundamental differences between the races. They have affected the conviction.

It is only necessary to recall Wright's "How Bigger Was Born' to see the elaborate care he takes to say that he conceived Bigger Thomas as "a type of man everywhere."

One has only to remember Chester Himes' assertion that he writes "about people" and if they happen to be colored, then their color is only an incident, to see how affected the conviction is.

As philosophy they believe this; as experience they do not. They have been impatient for their souls' conviction, and forced their souls to accept that they cannot yet accept. The result is that they have writ large the differences and tried, always after the writing, to explain them away.

No Criticism Intended

It must be understood that this is no disparagement of them.

On the other hand, Ann Petry seems never to have believed in such differences. Lay it to her upbringing in New England, or whatever, the fact remains that she has never written the differences in, nor even implied them.

Whether she has consciously kept them out, one cannot say, but out they are, and her work gains strength and validity from the fact. Move Lutie Johnson of *The Street* out of Harlem to Greenwich Avenue, and you have the same story, the same problem, the same resolution.

Leave out the description of Abbie Crunch and Link Williams and the comparative description of *The Narrows*, and you have a story that could not have been in any basic way different from what it is.

Tale of Illicit Love

It it a love story---a story of illicit love. Link Williams and a married woman, Camile Sheffield, fall in love. Little by little the town finds it out; the husband learns it and his ego is hurt. The story couldn't have ended in any other way.

But as contrary as it may sound *The Narrows* is about race relations in a small New England town; and it is just here that one feels Miss Petry strained to make a point that she need not have made at all.

She makes the point that the tragedy that ensues was the fault of no one person definable as colored or white. It was the fault of people. Period.

As I have said, *The Narrows* is a good novel, but Ann Petry will write better.

The Complexity of Evil (1953)
Wright Morris

Literature is the place to cry havoc, as the havoc itself must be reduced, the disorder made orderly, if the cry is to be heard. The Negro in America has known this for some time. To his old cry of havoc something new, recently, has been added. The desire to give it permanence, to stake out a claim in the durable world of art. This ambition transforms the writer's conception of both his suffering and his raw material---he is made aware that his predicament is more than skin deep. Ralph Ellison's *Invisible Man* marked the transition to this higher ground. It set new standards by which the old material must be judged. *The Narrows* reflects these standards in its ambition and its theme of the complexity of evil, but the performance indicates that the goal is not easily attained.

The heart of Miss Petry's story is a love affair that various forces of evil bring to a tragic conclusion. The girl is Camilla Treadway, the beautiful daughter of a wealthy white family; the man is Link Williams, an educated Negro who has accepted the lowbrow life of The Narrows, a Negro community about two hours' drive from New York. Link is the adopted son of Abbie Crunch, who is a symbol of the old-fashioned virtues and discredited attitudes that Link has carefully examined and rejected. He chooses the more realistic world of Bill Hod and Creepy Williams at The Last Chance Saloon.

The girl meets Link Williams on the foggy night she drives into The Narrows to do a bit of slumming, and finds herself pursued by the Cat Jimmie, a human monster. Link rescues her---and, in the fog, she does not recognize him as a Negro until they enter a local night club.

Later they go for a drive in her red convertible. The high implausibility of this scene is symbolic of their subsequent love affair and the dilemma that Miss Petry is not able to resolve. The dramatic center of her story is never credible. The lovers meet many times, they have their troubles, quarrel. Finally, the girl, in a fit of temper, accuses Link of attacking her. This leads to his arrest, to scandal in the tabloids [,] and to murder.

The other half of the story, the past, as it is revealed in a series of flashbacks, is always credible, and sometimes extremely good. But the reader is caught between an unreal present and a convincing past. Mamie Powther, a café-au-lait Molly Bloom, is real enough, whenever the author gets around to her, and so, at times, is her husband, the Treadway butler. The canvas has depth and complexity, but the surface drama central to the tragedy is like a tissue of tabloid day-dreams, projected by the characters. The living past overwhelms the lifeless present, but the present is obliged to give the past its meaning.

It is hard to see why Miss Petry did not realize this herself. Her first novel, *The Street*, published several years ago, attracted well-deserved praise—and, though it dealt with the familiar elements of the Negro-problem novel, it seemed to point the way to a brilliant creative future. But *The Narrows* reads like the first draft of an ambitious conception that has not been labored into imaginative life. It indicates what the author might have done but did not do. The forces that have lowered the craft of fiction have made it more difficult, not less, to write the book that will cry havoc and be heard. Miss Petry can do it, but it will take more brooding labor---and less space.

Current Literature on Negro Education (1953)
Ivan Taylor

In a way, Miss Petry's latest novel, *The Narrows*, is a masterpiece. It is an exceedingly well-wrought book, and there is everything in it that should please the reader and even the critic. It is, nevertheless, a book that will displease many people, irritate others, and make still others angry. These effects will come about because of several reasons: the explosive theme of a white woman falling in love with a Negro and going to bed with him---that situation will offend many people; the fact that she brings about his undoing---his lynching--- will not sit well with some people; the polygot unassimilated Negroes in Dumble Street will irritate many who would rather forget them; and the author's brave effort to conceal a hard-to-define New England superciliousness is sure to displease many. Yet, this is a good book, good medicine, a good cathartic.

No ordinary review can quite do justice to *The Narrows*. It must be read to be appreciated, and it is going to be read by many people for a long time to come, and it deserves a second and perhaps a third reading. There is rich humor in it and a profound understanding of human nature, especially of women. Where else in all fiction, except perhaps in Dickens or Hardy, would one find more humorous names than Kelly and Shapiro Powther and tiny J. C. Powther, sons of Malcolm Powther, the Treadway butler; and Messrs. B. Hod, and Weak Knees of the Last Chance Café; and Mamaluke Hill (christened Mathew Mark Luke John Acts-of-the Apostles Son-of Zebedee Garden-of-Gethsemane Hill) son of the Reverend Ananias Hill; and One One, manager of the Moonbeam Café? These are not mere caricatures as the names may imply. Almost every one of them is a living vibrant character that one has met at some time or other on Dixwell Avenue in Hew Haven or 116 Street in New York or on the thousand and one Catfish Rows of Negro America. They come to life: the race-wise Mr. Weak Knees, the race-conscious prideful Abbie Crunch, the race-hardened female undertaker, F. K. Jackson, and B. Hod, the hoydenish Mrs. Mamie Powther, and many others. There is humor inherent not only in the characters' names but in their actions, but this is not a novel of humour. It is tragedy, stark tragedy.

Link Williams rescues blond Camilo Treadway who is running away from the incredible, Porgy-like Cat Jimmie. A torrid romance develops leading Link and Camilo down the half-ridden ways of cheap New York pads. Link is a proud lad though, and he balks at following the primrose path, perfumed and made plush by Camilo's millions. Link is a proud one, a Dartmouth Phi Beta Kappa, and well-bred in worldly-wisdom by those finest of teachers B. Hod, Weak Knees, and the Last Chance. When he tries to put an end to the adulterous romance, Nemesis, in the person of the dowager Treadway, overtakes him. With Captain Sheffield serving as Lord High Executioner, Jubine, the photographer-artist; Peter Bullock publisher-owner-editor of the Monmouth *Chronicle*; Mamie Powther, and Malcolm Powther are responsible for the tragic end. Indeed, they are all responsible in one way or another, and even Dumble Street shares in the blame. B. Hod would assume the role of avenging angel--- he who in his own hardened way has loved and nurtured Link. But this would never do; Abbie Crunch intervenes.

Miss Petry has many of the gifts of the good novelist, among them that of making the commonplace seem cosmic. This phenomenon occurs throughout the novel as in the instance when young Link discovers that the pillars of *The Emporium* movie house are not of marble but of wood, and in that wonderful piece of advice that rich old Jonathan Cooper gives to Mal Powther on how to choose a wife. Miss Petry, moreover, handles the flash-back technique with consummate skill, weaving into the narrative fabric by this method many of the essential threads of this story.

In a very real sense, *The Narrows* is a novel of propaganda, subtle at times, but at other times rather obvious. A single instance will suffice: Miss Petry makes a deft thrust at one of the most vicious situations in American life, namely, the malevolent way in which the daily newspapers, North and South, manipulate news pertaining to crimes and misdemeanors committed by Negroes. That theme deserves an entire well-documented book, and Miss Petry with her rich knowledge of persons, places, and things-in-general would be a good one to undertake the writing of it. Miss Petry knows many things about Connecticut and its people of all races. She is intimately familiar with New Haven, Bridgeport, Saybrook, of course, and New London, and with what goes on at the big plant, such as Winchester, and in the Big House. She also knows a thing or two about Negro business establishments---barber shops, funeral parlors, cafes, and drug stores. In addition to this knowledge, she is a discerning and sympathetic sociologist. You should read this novel and others by Miss Petry, and hope, as I do, that she will write more of what she knows into other novels.

The Line (1953)
Arna Bontemps

There is no longer any doubt about it. The author of *The Street, Country Place,*
and now *The Narrows* is a neighborhood novelist. Just as some storytellers train
their sights on a roomful of people, a nest of simple folk, a company of travelers,
a town, a family, or an individual, Ann Petry elects the neighborhood as her unit.
In *The Street* her community was a block in throbbing Harlem. She found a
setting for her *Country Place* in rural New England. *The Narrows*, whose
history and way of life she chronicles in her newest novel, is the Negro area
around Dumble Street and along a section of the river in a New England town.

The eye that sweeps this little world of brick houses, ancient but still in good
repair, of lawns and white fences in the back yards, of the Last Chance Saloon
across the street and the massive tree known as The Hangman, belongs to Abbie
Crunch, age threescore and ten. It is in the upstairs apartment of her house that
big blowzy, noisy Mamie lives with her monstrous youngsters and her neatly
dressed, soft-spoken, and mannerly husband, who happens to serve the
wealthiest family of the town as butler. Abbie's deadly enemy is the proprietor
of the Last Chance.

Years ago the saloonkeeper had brought the Major, Abbie's beloved
husband, out of his place in a very sick condition, and the Major had not
recovered. A decade later Abbie had lost the struggle for her adopted son's soul
to the same evil genius. The boy Link had gone to work as a bartender in the
Last Chance. As if this were not enough to bow the head of the frail brown lady
with mended white gloves and a grocery basket on her arm, it now developed
that this same saloonkeeper, pretending to be Mamie's cousin, was carrying on
with that woman right in Abbie's house. It was all terribly discouraging---but
nothing to what it was about to become. On page 57, Mrs. Petry's novel catches
fire.

It was on a Saturday night, and Link was standing on the Dock in the fog at
the end of Dumble Street when suddenly he heard running feet. They belonged
to a panting, sweet-smelling creature who ran right into his arms, and not a
minute too soon. Right behind her was a shrunken beast in human form,
crippled but propelling himself on a cart, bent on running the young woman
down---or worse. Link would have dismissed the frightened girl with a shrug,
after kicking the cripple and his cart over, but she was much too upset. She
couldn't even return to her parked car alone. He had to walk her back.

Since all cats are gray in the night, neither Link, the strange white girl, the
dark folk of The Narrows, nor the people of the town generally saw anything to
be concerned with. When it came to light that the two had fallen in love,
however, everybody suddenly had eyes. The strain on the neighborhood and on

the town became so great something had to give.   Yet, with a problem as electrifying as this, Ann Petry's story does not get out of hand.

Her town, which is not prepared for as much racial equality as it was asked to accept, is not very hospitable to the man who was spending his lifetime photographing the river either. It couldn't fully approve of a man whose "laughter made the plates, the cups, and the saucers on the table rattle." And these attitudes it can reflect as easily through Abbie Crunch, the brown-skinned foster mother of the unfortunate Link, as through the family of millionaires across town or the publisher of the town newspaper.

A novel about Negroes by a Negro novelist and concerned, in the last analysis, with racial conflict, *The Narrows* somehow resists classification as a "Negro novel," as contradictory as that may sound.   In this respect Ann Petry has achieved something as rare as it is commendable.   Her book reads like a New England novel, and an unusually gripping one.

Critical Essays

(1970-1980)
Ann Petry and The American Dream (1978)
Vernon E. Lattin

Ann Petry's fiction too often has been mutilated or dismissed by the use of critical labels, especially the Scylla and Charybdis of Bone's assimilationist and Negro national nomenclature.[1] Although a number of critics have pointed out that Bone unwisely makes literary judgments on the basis of these sociological terms[2] his approach continues to haunt Petry's writings, Bone, himself, speaks disparagingly of the "siren spell of assimilationism"; although he views *Country Place* as "the best of the assimilationist novels," [3] his praise is obviously tainted. More severe is Nick Aaron Ford's view that the novel is greatly inferior to *The Street* because Petry is "conjuring up vicarious experiences of a white society with which she was not minutely familiar."[4] Hugh M. Gloster, on the other side of the Straits of Messina, sees *Country Place* as evidence of Petry's tilling "of broader fields than the circumscribed areas of racial life."[5]

Luckily, Ann Petry, speaking of her own work, has rejected labels and arbitrary categorization. She says she wrote *Country Place* not as a part of the assimilationist current of 1945-1952, but because she "happened to have been in a small town in Connecticut during the hurricane" and "decided to write about that violent, devastating storm and its effect on the town and the people who lived there."[6] Petry's matter-of-fact attitude does much to deflate the critics who are more concerned with their theories than her novels. It also invited one to look at the novels freshly and to reevaluate her work. The beginning of this necessary reevaluation can be seen in Addison Gayle's recent book, *The Way of the New World.* He correctly sees Petry as a rebel and iconoclast, rebelling against the older fiction of assimilationism and romanticism.[7] He limits his appraisal, however, to her "protest" novel, *The Street.* I think Ann Petry's rebellion is more profound and more extensive than Gayle or others have realized; a thread of deep-seated revolt and criticism runs through her white "assimilationist" novel as well as her "race" fiction. She rebels against the falsifications of life, the dreams, rationalizations, and illusions that distort one's grasp of reality; she rebels especially against the American Dream and all of its attendant illusions, which blind one to the stark, sordid existence that is America. Like all true rebels, she seeks freedom, a new order beyond the cages, walls, and prisons---dominant images of America.

Ann Petry's first novel cannot be discussed merely in environmentalist terms, as does Bone, as showing "a declassed *bourgeoise* who is driven to murder by the corrupting influence of 'the street.' "[8] Lutie Johnson, the protagonist, is not just the victim of the street; a complex character, she is both a conscious and unconscious fighter and rebel, a rebel, ironically, in the American tradition. Yet, paradoxically, she turns out to be a rebel against this tradition, its illusions, dreams, and false promises. Refusing to accept her life, to resign herself to "Negro" or "female" roles, Lutie Johnson struggles to fulfill the rags-to-riches formula only to discover that this illusion has prevented her from seeing the reality of her trap, that the American Dream itself is the spring that operates the trap. Lutie's discovery, at the end of the novel, also becomes the reader's discovery and one of Petry's major themes. Tragically, it is too late for Lutie, but she can subconsciously strike out against the illusion that has misled her.

At the beginning of the novel, the "cold November wind blowing through 116th Street"[9] reveals not only the powerful environmental forces that buffet and tear human fortune; it also reveals Lutie Johnson out in the wind seeking change. She is following her belief that if she [works] hard she can find a *place* in the world for herself and her eight-year-old son. Lutie has always believed in the rags-to-riches story and the protestant ethic of hard work and success. Even before going to work at the Chandlers', Lutie was a model of thrift and hard work; she only hears the Chandlers expressing what she has felt before: "'Richest damn country in the world--- . . . Hell! Make it while you're young. Anyone can do it---' " (43).

After listening to this for a year, she has absorbed the essence of the American Dream and confirmed her natural inclination. She swallows the idea "that anybody could be rich if he wanted to and worked hard enough and worked it out carefully enough" (43). Thus, in spite of her husband's inability to find work and the resulting destruction of their marriage, in spite of her struggle working at a laundry and going to night school to get a low-ranking civil service job that barely allows her to rent a twenty-nine-dollar-a-month flat, she still fantasizes that she is the spiritual offspring of Ben Franklin, with success for hard work just around the corner. "She shifted the packages into a more comfortable position and feeling the hard roundness of the rolls through the paper bag, she thought immediately of Ben Franklin and his loaf of bread. And grinned thinking, You and Ben Franklin . . . . .she couldn't get rid of the feeling of self-confidence and she went on thinking that if Ben Franklin could live on a little bit of money and could prosper, then so could she" (63-64).

In a section on the "American Dream" in that graduate-school tome, *The Literary History of the United States*, Gilbert Chinard cites Ben Franklin as the "living demonstration of the fact that in a republican society, where class distinctions do not prevent recognition of talent and genius, a poor boy may seize opportunities and rise to positions reserved to privileged classes in the Old World."[10] Lutie Johnson, although black, female, and poor, swallows this fantasy and dangles throughout the novel like a poor, caught fish. Although she is personally aware of racism, sexism, and economic slavery, she does not understand the ironic reality of the American Dream as it applies to her.

At times reality breaks into Lutie's fantasy, usually in the form of images of traps, cages, and walls enclosing her. Immediately after thinking herself Ben Franklin's peer, she is downcast by the conditions of her tenement life: "All through Harlem there were apartments just like this one, she thought, and they're nothing but traps. Dirty, dark, filthy traps. Upstairs. Downstairs. In my lady's chamber. Click goes the trap when you pay the first month's rent. Walk right in. It's a free country" (73). Unfortunately, Lutie, still believing in the success story, does not know what to do next, so she sends Bub to a movie (illusion), and she, seeing the walls of her flat pushing in on her, goes to the Junto for a beer "so that she could for a moment capture the illusion of having some of the things that she lacked" (144). The owner of the tavern, Junto, has, with Mrs. Hedges, built his fortune by understanding the miseries of Harlem, feeding illusions with bars and houses of prostitution. Both Junto and Mrs. Hedges have climbed the success ladder from the bottom to the top, collecting garbage and junk along the way. They are part of the system. That night at the bar, Lutie is offered a chance to sing her way out of her cage, and that same night Junto decided to have her sexually. Both Lutie and Junto fail to see reality. Lutie cannot escape by believing in the system, and Junto does not realize that Lutie will never be his whore: she has too much self-worth and rebellion within her.

The depth of Lutie's illusion appears as she returns from her first night of singing at the club. Instead of seeing the reality around her, she dreams: "It made her stand inside the door for a moment, not seeing the dimly lit hallway, but instead seeing herself and Bub living together in a big roomy place and Bub growing up fine and strong" (230). Her dream bursts as Jones, the Super of the building, who has been sniffing after her like a dog since the first day he saw her, grabs her and tries to drag her down into the cellar. Significantly, she sees this reality as "worse than any nightmare" (236) as he struggles to pull her down from her singing perch. The rape is prevented by Mrs. Hedges, but only to save Lutie for her " 'nice white gentleman,' " Junto. Very soon after this Lutie learns that she will not get paid for singing, since Junto wants her poor and in his power. Black and white rapists, Petry knows, are part of the same American system.

Lutie accepts her lost career as a singer, even recognizing for a moment that "she had built up a fantastic structure made from the soft, nebulous, cloudy stuff of dreams" (307-308). So she returns to the first dream of hard work, saving, scrimping, studying for a higher civil service rating. Returning home after discovering that she will not get paid for singing, she thinks " . . . time and Boots Smith and Junto had pushed her right back in here, deftly removing that obscuring cloud of dreams, so that now tonight she could see this hall in reality" (311-12). Of course, she sees only the hall; the whole illusion of American democracy and of the American Dream is still beyond her vision. Symbolically, as she slowly tiredly climbs the steps to her flat, the walls seem to be closing in on her; she can hear the sounds on the other side of the walls as they offer alternative illusions: " 'Buy Shirley Soap and Keep Beautiful' " to the revival hope, " 'This is the way, sisters and brothers. This is the answer' " (312).

Lutie is not distracted from her dream that easily; rejecting easy answers, she refuses to resign herself to her existence. She has not yet learned, as the narrator of *Invisible Man* will later discover, that the American Dream is designed to " 'Keep This Nigger-Boy Running.' "[11] Inevitably, Lutie's final revolt against this system will be violent, for she has believed in it too long. Only when she ends up in Boots's apartment as he procures [her] for Junto does she catch a glimpse of the naked truth: " . . . Junto has a brick in his hand. Just one brick. The final one needed to complete the wall that had been building up around her for years, and when that one last brick was shoved in place, she would be completely walled in " (423).

When Boots tries to seduce her before he passes her on to Junto, she smashes his head into a bloody mass. Her rage is an accumulation of her life, more furious because it has been fed by the illusions given her to live by. And reality for a moment has overtaken illusion: the reality of the dirty street, of hostile white women and lecherous men, of a white world which has built a prison for Blacks. Her act is a partially unconscious act of revolution; it is reality destroying , smashing the mask that Boots wears as his face. Lutie kills Boots, a black man, not primarily because he is going to rape her, or because he serves a white man, but because his is the face of the system, black and white; he is part of the American way. Thus, Petry's novel is a powerful statement of criticism, demanding that the American Dream be seen for what it is and that the American way be destroyed because it is not what it falsely promises to be.

Not only do Petry's black characters suffer from the illusions created by the American Dream and the professed American ideals. Most of the white characters in Petry's "assimilationist" novel *Country Place* have also been trapped by their illusions; this is particularly true of the protagonist.

When Sgt. Johnnie Roane comes marching home to Glory, his wife, after fighting to make the world again safe for democracy, he expects to return to the same town he left and the dream he created during his youth. After four years of war he remains essentially an innocent, a romantic planning his return to the American homestead, "thinking, Glory, Glory, Glory."[12] Not only does he expect time to have stood still, but he expects his dreams of his America to be reality. Yet he has never really seen America: he has never seen Lennox, a typical anti-Negro, anti-Catholic, anti-Jewish American town. Johnnie has been fed part of the same dream Lutie was fed; he has gone to war to defend this fantasy. He can return now only to see the dissolution of his dreams.

Significantly, one of the first people Johnnie sees while riding home from the railroad station is Ed Barrell. Ed, "like a tomcat" (15), will destroy Johnnie's dream of Glory by sleeping with her; more importantly, Ed, who reminds Johnnie of pictures he has seen of Mussolini, will destroy the whole fabric of Johnnie's American Dream. " 'Good old Ed'" is that tyrannical element at the heart of this American town; not only does he take advantage of everyone's wife, including young Glory; he also represents a serious flaw in Old Glory herself.

Johnnie's initial taste of disillusionment occurs on the first night home when Glory says she cannot stand for him to touch her. Glory, symbolic of the American flag, of everything beloved and fought for, as well as modern America and all its gaudy values, has been trying to get Ed Barrell to sleep with her. While Johnnie has been dreaming of Glory, Glory has been dreaming of Ed. After the rejection, Johnnie lets his thought travel from Glory to a questioning of the entire war effort: "What was a victory worth, what did it cost, and whose was it, anyway? Certainly not his. Technical Sergeant Johnnie Roane. He came, he saw, he conquered" (31). This initial questioning of the war effort leads Johnnie to think that reality eats the heart out of one's dreams. However, he quickly forgets his doubts when, on the second night, he sleeps with Glory: he decides that America and Lennox "with Glory . . . and the small white house and the contracting business" (128-29) are enough.

Johnnie is not alone in living the life of illusion and compromise; all the people of Lennox seem caught up in their own fantasies. Glory recreates herself as the heroine of movie illusion, while her mother dreams of owning the Gramby house and firing the servants who insult her. Mrs. Roane lives through her son's dreams; Mrs. Gramby lives the illusions of past glories, stifling her son's sexual and personal lives. Ed Barrell, the Mussolini of Lennox, deals in sexual conquest, hoping that he can thereby maintain an illusion of his youth (he had a bad heart) and his ego.

Uprooting illusions this pervasive requires a storm of hurricane force. To cleanse himself of romanticized America, Johnnie must walk several days in the wind and rain, finally crawling over fallen trees like an animal, grasping in the dark for the door to Ed's cabin so that he may confront and kill Ed and Glory together. He must return to the primitive in order to advance beyond his romantic illusions about America; he must, like Lutie, be blind (rage and darkness) in order to see the valuelessness of the American way of life. At first, he wants not only to kill Ed and Glory but to have all of Lennox "in at the death of their dreams" (186). Finally Johnnie does not even kill Ed. As he fights with Ed, he sees Glory sitting on a bunk with the same expression he has seen on her at the movies, "lapping up the gaudiest kind of melodrama" (194). He does not kill Ed and Glory because they are living only make believe. As Johnnie leaves the cabin and returns to his car, he hears the church bells tolling; he thinks that the storm has revealed the "rotten heart of the seemingly sturdy maples" of America (200). It is the death of his American Dream of glory, the "soapbubble" illusion that Petry finds throughout the American landscape.

Less extensively, but just as intensely, Ann Petry's last and very underrated novel *The Narrows*, contains a sharp criticism of the American way of life. The novel presents a love story of a Black and a White, Link and Camilo, who are destroyed by the racism and materialism that eat the core out of the American Dream. This system has perpetuated itself, linking slavery and money, from the first slave sales, through the Civil War, up until the present time. Appropriately, the protagonist is Lincoln Williams, nicknamed Link, a connection between past and present.

Link has an affair with Camilo, the white daughter of the influential Mrs. Treadway. Having found out that Camilo is married, however, Link feels like a "hired" lover and rejects her. Seeking revenge for this rejection and appealing to the stereotyped image of black man and white women, Camilo later claims that Link has attacked her.

The history of the *Monmouth Chronicle* reflects the history of the distortion of American ideals. Founded by Bullock's grandfather as an abolitionist paper, it ends up in the modern money world controlled by Mrs. Treadway and her wealth; Mrs. Treadway's money came not incidentally, from the invention of a new type of gun and then the manufacture of weapons and ammunition for war.

Bullock the editor, threatened by Mrs. Treadway's warning that she will discontinue her advertisements, cancels the story of how Camilo has run over a child while intoxicated. Later, he agrees to Mrs. Treadway's suggestion that he run a series of front-page stories on crime in The Narrows, Monmouth's black section, to help substantiate Camilo's claim that Link has assaulted her. The *Monmouth Chronicle* has descended from anti-slavery newspaper to a paper willing to portray Blacks as animals in order to please a patron. An illusion of black terror is created because Mrs. Treadway's advertising controls America, advertising that is itself the illusion of the American ideal. Bullock realizes that "if Mrs. Treadway took that institutional advertising with the American flag at the top, advertising that consisted of editorials on democracy, hymns of praise to the United States, out of his paper, it would just about fold up."[13] Thus, the illusion of the American ideal supports the materialism that supports the racism.

As his name suggests, Bullock is the castrated American male. A white man who has sold his freedom to search for wealth, he is the typical twentieth-century American trapped in the system of ranch-style homes, three-car garages, and do-nothing wives. " . . . he was a peon, he was a poor peon trying to act like rich peon because he was in love with an expensive beautiful redheaded female peon, and somewhere in the twentieth century they'd both lost the use of their legs, and their minds, and their will power" (360).

No wonder Cesar the Writing Man chalks in front of the *Chronicle* offices, " 'Thirty pieces of silver'" (364). Bullock is the white Judas, just as Powther, who points out Link to his murderers, is the black Judas. Similar to Bullock, Powther is trapped by his love for his wife Mamie and by his obsession to be part of the middle-class existence. Bought by Mrs. Treadwell and the values she represents, they sell their souls for acceptance by the American system.

Although only mentioned once, it is significant that the entire United States is hunting "witches" at this time, the period of the Un-American Activities Committee. Bullock, who has deliberately created the image of black terror in Monmouth, who has convinced the town that white women are not safe from black rapists, justifies his actions to himself by comparing the hunt for Negroes to the hunt for Communists: "Even the State Department was acting like a harried housewife . . . . So what difference does it make . . . whether we hunt down Communists" (378). To Ann Petry, of course, there is no difference, since both result from a way of life which limits the reality of an individual's existence in the name of American values. To be different in America is to be hunted down: Petry's constant revolt is against this dehumanizing system which is supported by the illusion of patriotism and democracy.

Ultimately, the trap closes on Link Williams, and he is murdered. Black men and white women do not fall in love in the American system Petry sees. To admit this possibility would be to destroy the system of economic slavery and caste division supporting the American way. Since anything is preferable to such a destruction, love between the races is denied through creation of the myth of the white harlot and the black rapist. Mrs. Treadway and Bunny, the wronged husband, kidnap Link and try to force him to confess rape, even though both know this to be a lie, while Abbie, the woman who adopted Link, can see Camilo only as a harlot. Since Mrs. Treadway and Bunny cannot accept the truth that Link refuses to deny, the Treadway gun explodes. Death is America's legacy for those who speak the truth, and Link dies saying it: " ' . . . we were in love' " (407).

Although certainly Petry's novel can be classified as a "race" novel, it is also a novel deeply attacking the American way of life that denies one freedom to love and develop as a human being. Not only are Link and Camilo trapped: Camilo's husband Bunny is trapped by Mrs. Treadway's money and his idea of the American way. Likewise, Bullock is trapped by his red-haired wife and American middle-class existence; Abbie and Powther are trapped by the illusion of middle-class respectability and the ambition to be more "American" than anyone, "so that white people would like colored people" (138).

Jubine, the photographer-artist of the novel, who keeps trying to get Bullock to do something worthwhile and significant, serves as the conscience and critic of the American Dream. Why does he keep trying, asks Bullock. In Jubine's answer Ann Petry speaks to her readers: " 'Because, my dear Bullock, I am trying to save you . . . from ulcers and the fate of ulcer victims, from slavery and the fate of slaves, from whoredom and the fate of whores—' "(44). In recording the beautiful, the ugly, and the damned, Jubine the artist is also both the prophet (" 'Am I the hand of God . . ?' " [45]) and the revolutionary (Bullock calls him a Communist). He consistently voices Ann Petry's revolt against the American Dream and the American system. He refuses to turn away from the truth his camera reveals; he refuses to be bought and sold, to let illusion blur his lens. Like Petry, he is a rebel, and his truth, he hopes, will set us free.

Ann Petry's fiction reveals an author who can see through the illusions of the American way of life that distort and destroy individuals. As a rebel, she seeks to tear down the walls that trap people, white and black, into meaningless existence. She has exposed the American Dream as a nightmare which forces Lutie Johnson to murder, which creates romantic visions of glory that blind one and must be rejected, and which leads to the death of Link Williams because he refuses to accept his assigned role in the system. Ann Petry, as a significant critic of American values, can no longer be dismissed by misapplied critical labels. Her work must be reread and reevaluated.

[1] Robert A. Bone, *The Negro Novel in America*, rev. ed (New Haven: Yale University Press, 1965), 3-7 and throughout the text.

[2] See especially Darwin Turner, "The Negro Novel in America: In Rebuttal." *CLA Journal,* 10 (1966): 122-34.

[3] *The Negro Novel in America,* 169.

[4] "A Blueprint for Negro Authors" (1950), rpt. In *Black Expression* ed. Addison Gayle, Jr. (New York: Weybright and Talley, 1969), 277.

[5] "Race and the Negro Writer" (1950), rpt. In *Black Expression,* 257.

[6] Quoted in *Interviews with Black Writers,* ed. John O'Brien (New York: Liveright, 1973), 16].

[7] (Garden City: NY: Anchor Press, 1975), 191-97.

[8] *The Negro Novel in America,* 180.

[9] *The Street* (Boston: Houghton Mifflin, 1948), 1. All future references are to this edition and will be included in the body of the text.

[10] Robert E. Spiller, et. al., eds. *Literary History of the United States*, 3rd ed., rev. (New York: Macmillan, 1963), 201.

[11] Ralph W. Ellison, *Invisible Man* (New York: Random House, 1952), 26.

[12] Ann Petry, *Country Place* (Boston: Houghton Mifflin, 1947), 7. All future references are to this edition and will be included in the body of the text.

[13] Ann Petry, *The Narrows* (Boston: Houghton Mifflin, 1953), 371. All future references are to this edition and will be included in the body of the text.

Ann Petry (1982)
Joyce Ann Joyce

Robert Bone, the white literary critic whose work *The Negro Novel in America* (1958) remains one of the first full-length studies of the Black American novel and Addison Gayle, Jr., a well-known Black Nationalist literary critic and author [,] have much in common. Yet Gayle will perhaps shudder if faced with this assertion. The obsessive tendency to divide our literary history into those works written by whites who either denounce or oversimplify the Black man's humanity and into those written by Black authors who either fight to prove the Black man's humanity or shun association with the mainstream of the Black American literary history underlines the racial realities that characterize American history, a history grounded in chattel slavery and all its cultural ramifications. Bone's study and Gayle's *The Way of the New World: The Black Novel in America* trace the history of the Black American novel from 1853 to the mid-twentieth century, categorizing according to historical period and theme.

The business of dividing the Black American novel into broad and superficial categories is akin to the academic process of categorizing historical periods, works, literature, and even people in order to facilitate discussion. In the midst of this misleading literary jargon and American racial limitations, literary historians not only lose sight of particular Black authors, but entire decades of them as well. The 1940's serve as a good case in point. In his study *Fiction of the Forties*, (1939-1953), Chester E. Eisinger lists approximately sixty-one white writers and three Black authors---Richard Wright, Ann Petry, and Ralph Ellison. Wright, Petry, and Ellison were not the only Black writers who published fiction during this expansive period. Others include Zora Neale Hurston's *Seraph on the Suwanee* (1948), Dorothy West's *The Living is Easy* (1948), William Demby's *Bettlecreek* (1950), and Gwendolyn Brooks' *Maud Martha* (1953), all of which merit at least a notable mention in a text with such an expansive goal. Even more important is Eisinger's total neglect to include in his comment on Ann Petry any discussion of the last two of her three novels. He gives her first novel *The Street* three sentences, focusing more on Wright and Ellison than he does on Petry. Addison Gayle is also guilty of the sin of omission in his treatment of Ann Petry, who is not only a major Black American writer of the forties, but also a major Black American writer whose contribution to Black American and American literature defies the stereotypes of academic and racial categorization. Dismissing the complexity of Petry's development, Gayle makes no mention whatsoever of Petry's second novel *Country Place* (1947) which depicts the lives of a white community in a small, provincial town in Connecticut, Petry's home state. He praises both her first novel *The Street* and her last *The Narrows*, works with Black characters.

In our assessment of a literary work, it is time that we follow Henry James' advice (although James sometimes forgot his ideas himself): we must give the fiction writer his/her donne; the writer should be able to write about whatever he/she chooses. Our main jobs as readers and critics are first to judge the extent to which the writer creates a plausible representation of reality and the human character as it really is and second to respond to the writer's skill, to the beauty of his craft. It is time that we slough off the ideas that whites are incapable of depicting full-blooded Black characters and that Blacks should only write about racial realities. Although the Black man's black skin indicates that Black men in various Black communities identify with each other through shared experiences, the Black community remains a pluralistic, heterogeneous society which contains levels of Black consciousness. Analogously, the Black American novel from William Wells Brown's *Clotel* to Toni Morrison's *Tar Baby* is not only as variegated as the Black heterogeneous culture from which it comes, but it also represents the same kind of diversity as the history of the white American novel. Literary histories, as Eisinger's study proves and others like Alfred Kazin's notable *On Native Grounds*, have done more to unearth the works of minor white authors, who have been buried with time than they have to bring to the forefront the works of major Black American writers.   The Black literary community contributes to this injury through its failure to approach the works of the past with new knowledge of the present. A part of Ann Petry's obscurity rests in the traditional American perception of Black literature which castigates what is called the protest novel and stereotypes an author's canon on the basis of his first successful work.

Consequently, in the hands of the literary critics, *The Street* marks Ann Petry as a protest novelist. If we are to appreciate fully her versatility as a literary craftsman and her uncanny insight into human nature, we must move beyond the Baldwin-Ellison condemnation of the protest novel in order to perceive the breadth and depth that underlie the characters that make up the *The Street*. Before discussing *The Street*, perhaps I should briefly characterize what is meant by a protest novel. In short, the protest novel blatantly and unflinchingly condemns racism and all its ramifications. The novel of protestation is far from subtle in its representations of the economic, sociological, and psychological effects of racism on Black lives.   James Baldwin's monumental essay "Everybody's Protest Novel," published by the Partisan Review in 1949, cemented the already unfavorable white attitude toward protest literature. He asserts that this type of novel is more akin to sociology than to literature and that by its very nature it categorizes human beings and thus robs them of their humanity. The Black writer, he adds, should not have to prove that he is human:

> . . . our humanity is our burden, our life; we
> need not battle for it; we need only to do
> what is infinitely more difficult---that is
> accept it. The failure of the protest novel lies
> in its rejection of life, the human being, the
> denial of his beauty, dread, power, in its
> insistence that it is his categorization alone

> which is real and which cannot be transcended.[1]

While Baldwin here emphasizes the limitations of the subject matter of the protest novel, Ellison focuses on what he believes to be the banal craft of most protest fiction. He says,

> . . . protest is not the source of the inadequacy characteristic of most novels by Negroes, but the simple failure of craft, bad writing: the desire to have protest perform the difficult tasks of art: the belief that racial suffering, social injustice or ideologies of whatever mammy-made variety, is enough. I know, also, that when the work of Negro writers has been rejected they have too often protected their egos by blaming racial discrimination, while turning away from the fairly obvious fact that good art . . . commands attention of itself, whatever the writer's politics or point of view . . . skill is developed by hard work, study and a conscious assault upon one's own fear and provincialism.[2]

These passages from Ellison and Baldwin open a Pandora's box that I have no intention of closing. What is most important here is what these artists-critics have in common---they both desire to be respected on the merit of the breadth and skill of their craft and they assert that the protest novel lacks both range and precision.

Although Ellison and Baldwin are ambivalent in their attitude toward Richard Wright, his fiction is the primary rung on the ladder of Black American literature that led to their prominence. Ann Petry's *The Street*, published in 1946, commonly referred to as a novel of the "Wright School," rarely escapes the naturalistic criticism that characterizes the books written on Richard Wright's early fiction. Richard Wright used naturalism, popularized by Theodore Dreiser in the American novel of the thirties, as a vehicle for his ideas in his first published major works *Uncle Tom's Children* (1938) and *Native Son* (1940). Essentially, the naturalistic novelist transforms Darwinian determinism into literary thought. Man becomes a victim of his environment encaged by socio-economic forces he cannot control. Driven by his fundamental desires, the naturalistic character is often simple and prone to violent actions. Both Richard Wright and Ann Petry transcend the limitations of naturalism through their depiction of the psyches of their main characters. Whereas Bigger

Thomas's intelligence grows as Wright's novel *Native Son* progresses, Lutie Johnson, the protagonist of *The Street*, is always aware of the environmental forces that attempt to subdue her.

When the story opens, Lutie Johnson is about to rent a run-down shabby apartment on Harlem's 116th Street so that she can rescue her son from the influence of her father's drunken mistress.   The pivotal point in the plot surrounds the lascivious, even monstrous, superintendent Jones who attempts to rape Lutie.   She is no monster like Frank Norris' McTeague nor is she as one-dimensional as Stephen Crane's Maggie. We see her complex, human response to her husband, to her son and we experience her feelings of compassion as she watches a succession of events in which the people on the street evince their resignation to the socio-economic factors that enslave them. Although the main narrative line focuses on Lutie Johnson's life, Petry adroitly weaves into the fabric of the novel a part of the life stories of Jones, the superintendent; Min, his mistress.   Mrs. Hedges; Junto; and the Chandlers, giving the characters a psychological depth that move them beyond one dimensional stereotypes although their characterizations remain symbolic as does Lutie's. In a novel of this kind, the difficult task is to show that the characters' lives are shaped by environmental forces, and simultaneously give the characters that age-old human trait we call ambiguity. Throughout the novel, Lutie's main concern is the welfare of her son. Yet, in a moment of violent anger she kills a man. Ironically, he's the man whose aid she seeks to acquire a lawyer to bring her son home from the detention center. Her flaw is a human one: she momentarily forgets her son. Intense anger, humiliation, and entrapment overshadow the ratiocination that she had practiced in an earlier scene when Bub (her son) asked her if she were mad at him

> She framed her answer carefully, trying not to let the hard, cold anger in her color her reply.   She frowned, because her only explanation would have to be that they needed to save more than they were doing. "I've been worried about us," she said. "We seem to spend so much money. I'm not able to save very much. And we have to save, Bub," she said earnestly, "so that we won't always have to live here."
> During the next week she made a conscious effort to stop talking to Bub about money. Yet some reference to it inevitably crept into her conversation.
> When she was mending his socks, she caught herself delivering a lecture about being careful and watching out for nails and splinters that might snag them. "They have

to last a long time and new ones cost
money."

If he left a cake of soap soaking in the
bowl in the bathroom, she pointed out how it
wasted the soap and that little careless things
ate into their meager budget. When she
went to bed, she scolded herself roundly
because it wasn't right to be always harping
on the cost of living to Bub.[3]

Lutie's desire to protect her son and the murder she commits give her that
juxtaposition of opposites that embodies human nature. Although literary critics
espouse that Lutie's life like Bigger Thomas' naturally led to violence, there is
nothing in the novel before the final scene to indicate that Lutie has the
proclivity to kill.

While *The Street* shines best in its portrayal of character, *Country Place*,
Petry's second novel, works beautifully through an intermingling of skillful
characterization and ambiguity. The story is narrated by the town druggist, who
tells the reader from the outset that he has no love of women and that the reader
must remember that the personality of the teller shapes all stories. Thus in its
narrative technique *Country Place* is more like the early English nineteenth-
century novel in which the narrator addresses the reader than it is like the
twentieth-century novel, which is characterized by the narrator's objective
distance. The story proper begins with young Johnny Roane's return from the
war. The Weasel, the town gossip and the most interesting, yet grotesque
character in the novel, picks Johnny up in his taxi at the train station. Because
of the hints dropped by the Weasel, Johnny begins to suspect that his wife Glory
has been having an affair with Ed Barrell, the town Lothario.

The story is intriguing. The motive behind each of the characters' actions
gives the novel its depth. We learn more of their fears, desires, aspirations, and
shortcomings than we do of the characters in *The Street*. Although the story
begins with Johnny Roane, he is not the thread that ties all the parts together.
Instead, the Weasel, the grotesque little man who looks so much like a weasel
that he accepts the name and the actions of this repulsive creature, is the story's
unifying point. His malicious actions underlie the unfolding of the plot. In
Petry's treatment of the environment and its effect upon the human psyche,
Country Place is much *The Street*. The people in this small country town are
characterized by the fear, the provincialism of any small, isolated community.
The confines of Lennox, Connecticut, shape their lives in much the same way
that 116th Street circumscribes the desires, fears, and aspirations of its
inhabitants. *Country Place*, however, is not a naturalistic novel. No one
escapes the horror of the environment in a truly naturalistic work.

Country Place is psychological realism.   While Petry focuses on the characters' motives and on how interaction between characters illuminates each character's individual personality, her characters maintain a certain ambiguity and mystery much like the people we know in our lives.   We never fully understand the druggist, who narrates the story and who is also a character in the story.   We can and cannot trust his insight.   He begins:

> I have always believed that, when a man writes a record of a series of events, he should begin by giving certain information about himself: his age, where he was born, whether he be short or tall or fat or thin. This information offers a clue as to how much of what a man writes is to be discarded as being the result of personal bias. For fat men do not write the same kind of books that thin men write; the point of view of tall men is unlike that of short men .
> . .
>
>   It is only fitting and proper that I should openly admit to having a prejudice against women---perhaps I should say a prejudice against the female of any species, human or animal.[4]

The druggist's admittance of his dislike for women at the outset of the novel should make us question his reliability as narrator in a work in which all the action revolves around the selfish, insensitive, and malicious acts of two women. Petry, however, presents a beautiful conflict between how Glory and her mother present themselves and how the community sees them.   The druggist, of course, belongs to the community.   Although we find Glory's and her mother's actions as distasteful as the Weasel's, we do not leave the novel with the same kind of dislike for women as the druggist's.

    For through her explorations of the psyches of her characters, Petry gives them human depth and thus assures our understanding of their actions.   The druggist's attitude toward women compared to the motive behind Glory's and her mother's attitude toward life suggests that *Country Place* is a novel that explores the emotional life of women as it differs from traditional expectations. A look at Glory's thoughts as she watches other women board the bus makes this point clear:

> Glory eyed the women who got on, thinking, a few more years and that's the way Johnnie will have me looking. I'll have four or five children and never quite enough money to

go all the way around. I'll be riding buses to
get to the markets where the food is
cheapest; and wearing a house dress under a
winter coat; and I'll put on wrinkled cotton
stockings in order to save my best ones for
Sunday; and carry a cloth knitting bag
instead of a pocketbook. I'll start for home
at this hour of the day so's to have the
supper ready for Johnnie and he'll wolf it
down and grunt and reach for the
newspaper. Then he'll take his shoes off
and sit sprawled in a chair half-asleep until
time to go to bed.[5]

The druggist's moral condemnation of Glory and her mother represents the traditional perspective of the community or, in larger terms, of society. Glory seeks the freedom of movement and romance unsanctioned by the community.

Although the druggist tells the reader that he will narrate the story, the reader too often loses sight of him as in the above passage which reveals insights into Glory's intimate thoughts unknown to him. Consequently, we find an obvious inconsistency in Petry's use of narrative point of view in *Country Place*. This technicality, however, does not minimize the plausibility of the story nor does it make the characters less believable. *Country Place* embodies the complexities reflective of real life: we learn the full scope of a character's personality as the novel unfolds. A character is not ready-made or symbolic and thus set for the reader when the story begins as in a naturalistic novel like *The Street*. This difference in approach prepares the way for Petry's last very impressive novel, *The Narrows*, an amalgamation of the best craftsmanship that went into *The Street* and *Country Place*. As in *The Street*, Petry returns to the use of typed characters. However, this time, much like human beings who have both static and dynamic components to their personality, the major characters of *The Narrows* are not symbolic. And as in *Country Place*, she depicts the complex interaction between a host of characters whose lives reflect the subtle interrelationship of people living in a circumscribed area. The narrative point of view is omniscient, perhaps, because of the large number of characters that make up the community called the Narrows.

The Narrows is a more challenging novel than both of Petry's previous works. Set in Monmouth, Connecticut, a small New England town far more urban than Lennox in *Country Place*, this last novel returns to the perspective of the Black community. The central character is Link Williams, the adopted son of Major Crunch and his pious, prudish, snobbish wife Abbie Crunch. Published in 1953 one year after Ellison's *Invisible Man*, *The Narrows* illustrates either that Petry and Ellison are influenced by the same contemporary thought or that Ellison's novel significantly influences Petry's work. Ellison's

Invisible Man is the modern novel that traces the Black man's history from the South to the North and records the effect that this history has had on his protagonist's consciousness. *The Narrows* is a kind of *Bildungsroman*, which charts the experiences that make up Link Williams' growth from innocence to maturity, from childhood to adulthood. Like Ellison's Invisible Man, Link Williams also struggles from early adolescence to come to terms with his relationship to the white society.

Link and Ellison's Invisible Man are equally intelligent characters. Although Link has already graduated from high school with honors and from college Phi Beta Kappa when the novel begins, we do not learn of these aspects of Link's life until the last third of the novel. Petry is a careful craftsman. She wants the reader to perceive first the extent to which his being an orphan isolates him from the mainstream of the community and how Abbie Crunch's unconscious rejection of him after Major Crunch's death makes him even more of an outsider. Unlike the Invisible Man, the young Link Williams possesses a spontaneity, a rebellious drive, and an intuitive insight that cause him to seek some answers to his questions about the relationship between Blacks and whites early in life. He learns self-respect and pride in his blackness from Bill Hod--- who owns the Last Chance, a jook joint----and from Weak Knees, Bill Hod's wise cook.

While Ellison's Invisible Man is blind to the richness of his Black culture, Link intuitively embraces it. Early in life he chooses between Abbie Crunch's middle-class embarrassment and rejection of her blackness and the rich, warm, common life of Bill Hod, Weak Knees, and the Last Chance. A central theme in the novel is the contrast between the sterility and order of the type of life Abbie represents and the lack or order and sensuality embodied in Mamie Powther, the wife of Malcolm Powther. Powther and his family of three children rent an upstairs apartment from Abbie Crunch. He is the male counterpart to Abbie Crunch: for he too is imbued with a middle-class morality and accepts an inferior role in his relationship with whites. His unending lust for Mamie Powther, who carries on an affair with Bill Hod, is perhaps his deepest weakness. Mamie Powther represents the center of the life-giving force in the Narrows. Petry consistently contrasts the passionate rhythm of the blues songs Mamie sings of love and loneliness to the lifelessness of the extemporaneous rhymes Abbie Crunch obsessively composes. The Moonbeam Bar, The Last Chance, Mamie Powther, her blues songs, the grotesque Cat Jimmie, and the ghost that Weak Knees sees any time he is in the midst of trouble all make up a part of the folkloric tradition that Petry uses to inform her novel.

While Ellison's concern with communism gives *Invisible Man* its global quality, Petry focuses on the power of the rich whites whose money controls the media; and through the character of Jubine, the esoteric young Black photographer, she illustrates the malign effects of bourgeois society. Because Jubine lives in a loft, wears GI pants and shoes, and rides a motorcycle, Peter

Bullock, the editor of *The Monmouth Chronicle* asks him why he doesn't wear "decent" clothes. Jubine responds:

> "For what? My clothes keep me warm. My loft keeps the rain and the wind away from my person. And I am free. But you, dear Bullock, you are a slave, to custom, to a house, to a car. You have given yourself little raw places in your stomach, little sore burning places, so that you cannot eat what you want and you cannot sleep at night, because you have turned so many handsprings to pay for that long shiny car, and you've got to keep on turning them so that you can buy expensive tires for it, so that you can buy the expensive gas that goes in its belly. It's a slave ship. Think of it---a slave ship right here in this beautiful little New England city called Monmouth---"[6]

Jubine spouts Marxist ideology in which he divides society into the proletariat and the bourgeoisie as he mocks the white editor of the *Chronicle*, who is constantly burdened by the pressure of maintaining his middle-class income.

In order to protect his job, Bullock later yields to blackmail by the wealthy Mrs. Treadway when he highlights denigrating stories about Black men in an effort to move the white community to hysteria against Link Williams. When everyone in town learns of Link Williams' affair with Camilo Treadway, all the major themes merge to a close. Although Link loves Camilo, his being a Black man and the Black man's collective history prevent his giving his inner self up to a white woman. And Camilo's background has not taught her how to humble herself in such a way that she can communicate her love to anyone, especially a proud Black man. Consequently, they talk at cross purposes. Their problem has its roots in their race and class differences. All other characters embody this same conflict between race and class. The Treadways are the epitome of the destructive power of bourgeois sterility. Peter Bullock, who is closest to the Treadways in power, consistently strives to amass more money and thus security. Abbie Crunch and Malcolm Powther reflect the self-imposed alienation of Blacks who emulate bourgeois ideals. Mamie Powther, Weak Knees, and Bill Hod represent the stability of the Black community which understands its true relationship to white society and accepts itself without pretense and social hokum. Link Williams is an embodiment of both the beauty and confusion of the Black community. For he too accepts himself for what he is and he is the novel's hero. He is quite aware that the dynamics of his black heritage and his intelligence cannot stop his falling in love with a white woman. This heritage foretells the afflictions of miscegenation. Though Link has a sharper sense of himself, of his community, and of the white world outside his community than Ellison's Invisible Man his fate proves more destructive.

With the publication of *The Narrows*, Ann Petry joins Ellison in increasing the range of Black fiction. Like *Invisible Man, The Narrows* is a modern Black American novel which depicts the contemporary cultural and political forces that shape the Black community in the aftermath of World War II. And the differences in Petry's form and subject matter in *The Street, Country Place,* and *The Narrows* illuminate not only the versatility of her individual talent, but also highlight the diversity of approach and variegated ideas that distinguish one Black writer from another. The Black American novel is as varied as its individual creators. John O'Brien, in an interview with Ann Petry asks her to respond to the arbitrary grouping of Black American writing in most anthologies of Black literature. She responds:

> That's because we're all black. As I said, we do have a common theme. We write about relationships between whites and blacks because it's in the very air we breathe. We can't escape it. But we write about it in a thousand different ways and from a thousand different points of view.[7]

Ann Petry's works demand more reading and fresher insights than they have so far been given. Instead of entrapping her in the quagmire of the protest novel and ignoring *Country Place* altogether as Addison Gayle does, we could learn much about the human condition from Petry's insights. Admittedly, a large part of our response to the subject matter in a work is determined by the artist's skillful shaping of the novel's form. *Country Place* serves as an excellent example of how reality becomes art. In this same interview, O'Brien also asks Petry why she chooses to write about whites in *Country Place.* She explains:

> I don't know what impelled other black writers to stop writing novels about blacks. I wrote *Country Place* because I happened to have been in a small town in Connecticut during a hurricane---I decided to write about the violent, devastating storm and its effect on the town and the people who lived there.[8]

For someone who just "happened " to be in [a]small town during a hurricane, Petry knows its inhabitants well enough to create a world that has the mark of genius . . . . .

[1] James Baldwin, "Everybody's Protest Novel," in *Notes of a Native Son* (New York: Bantam Books, 1964), 17.

[2] Ralph Ellison, "The World and the Jug," in *Shadow and Act* (New York: Vintage Books, 1972), 137.

[3] Ann Petry, *The Street* (1946; rpt. Pyramid Books, 1961), 196-97.

[4] Ann Petry, *Country Place* (1947; rpt. Chatham, New Jersey: Chatham Bookseller, 1971), 1. All subsequent references appear in the text.

[5] Ibid.

[6] Ann Petry, *The Narrows* (1953; rpt. Chatham, New Jersey: Chatham Bookseller, 1973), 43.

[7] John O'Brien, ed. *Interviews with Black Writers* (New York: Liveright, 1973), 157.

[8] Ibid, 161.

The Quest for the American Dream in Three Afro-American Novels: *If He Hollers Let Him Go, The Street,* and *Invisible Man* (1981)
Richard Yarborough

America is a dream
The Poet says it was promises
                    ---Langston Hughes, "Freedom's Plow![1]

The experience of Afro-Americans in this country has been marked by two major ironies which would seem to preclude any widespread, longterm endorsement of that body of cultural ideals called the American Dream. The first is the disappointing fact that the society which claims to be founded upon the principles of freedom and equality nonetheless supported a brutal chattel slave system for over two hundred years. Abolitionists like Frederick Douglass and Martin R. Delany frequently alluded to this tragic inconsistency. With emancipation and the victory of the North in the Civil War, however, it seemed to blacks that America was finally beginning to fulfill the promise of its bright conception. Afro-Americans felt that they would only have to follow the rules which white society prescribed in order to attain the American Dream. It was at this point that blacks on a large scale began to confront the second, galling irony regarding their status in the United States. They discovered that essentially the same racist distortions which had been used to justify slavery now served to thwart the Afro-American's participation in the great national drive toward prosperity and apparent fulfillment.

Despite severe disappointments, however, Afro-Americans have generally been among the most fervent believers in the American Dream. The primary source of this stubborn faith lies, oddly enough, in the very racial prejudice which so sorely tests it. Most blacks perceive that it is because of their race that they have been refused entrance into the American *sanctum sanctorum*, that imaginary arena of freedom and fair play where an individual may prove his or her worth and, upon doing so, earn the security, peace, material comforts, and happiness identified with success in the United States. Accordingly, pre-1920s Afro-American novelists most frequently portray the failure of the American Dream for the black as yet another result of racism in this country. An important assumption underlying this particular treatment is that the American system does indeed work. In other words, while many white social critics have contended that the American game of success is meaningless, that there are no winners, most Afro-American writers have instead argued that the rules of the game have never been fairly applied to blacks.

As a result, Afro-American novelists have had to perform a peculiar kind of thematic gymnastics in order to reflect in their works both the realistic awareness that racist oppression has persisted after slavery and the idealistic faith in America as the land of opportunity for all. One striking example of this delicate balancing act is Frank J. Webb's portrayal of free blacks in mid-nineteenth century Philadelphia, *The Garies and Their Friends* (1857). This novel is thematically torn by two ultimately unreconcilable concerns. The first is Webb's endorsement of capitalist individualism as a sure means to rise in America. At one point, the affluent, heroic Mr. Walters observes to another member of the black bourgeois community:

> Do you ever find them [whites] sending
> their boys out as servants? No; they rather
> give them a stock of matches, blacking,
> newspapers, or apples, and start them out to
> sell them. What is the result? The boy that
> learns to sell matches soon learns to sell
> other things; he learns to make bargains; he
> becomes a small trader, then a merchant,
> then a millionaire.[2]

However, Webb also is committed to an accurate presentation of the brutal racism in the North; Thus, he describes a white riot in violent, horribly explicit detail.

The conclusion of the novel typifies his dilemma. On one hand, we have the apparent validation of the mainstream American belief that anyone can rise to prosperity. For instance, Kinch, a former street urchin, evolves into a well-heeled dandy through the inheritance of his father's property, which has dramatically escalated in value. Further, the once embattled black characters seem again secure in their middle-class status. Symbolically dominating the scene, however, is the invalid Mr. Ellis, whose spiritual and physical crippling as a result of the riot reminds us that the achievement of bourgeois success for the Afro-American means little in the face of racial prejudice.[3]

Afro-American fiction in the twentieth century reveals the increasing difficulty black writers have had in maintaining both an unflinching willingness to confront white America's treatment of blacks and faith in the American Dream. After four decades of innumerable promises upon which America has almost inevitably reneged, the dialectical tension in Afro-American thought between hope and despair begins to produce a new synthesis: the agonizing recognition that white racism may forever keep the American Dream out of the black's grasp.

The first modern Afro-American novel to embody this dispair, pain, and rage is Richard Wright's *Native Son* (1940).[4] It is no coincidence that three black writers deeply influenced by Wright---Chester Himes, Ann Petry, and Ralph Ellison---share an acute sensitivity to the frustrations of the black individual striving for the American ideal of success. Further, the resolutions of Himes's *If He Hollers Let Him Go* (1945), Petry's *The Street* (1946), and Ellison's *Invisible Man* (1952) define the predominant reactions evoked by the failure of the

Dream: the cynical acceptance of defeat; explosive rage and then despair; and finally, the desperate hope that something of the American Dream can be salvaged.

> Go West, young man.
> ---Horace Greeley
>
> Swing low, chariot, come down easy,
> Taxi to the Terminal Line;
> Cut your engines, and cool your wings,
> And let me make it to the telephone,
> Los Angeles, give me Norfolk, Virginia,
> Tidewater 4-10-0-0,
> Tell the folks back home this is the Promised Land
> callin' and the poor boy's on the line.
> ---Chuck Berry, "The Promised Land" [5]

Physical mobility has always been an important facet of the American Dream. Most Americans have seen the freedom to pick up and leave their homes in search of better conditions as an inalienable right, and the awesome geographical space of the North American continent has accommodated their restlessness. For most of this nation's history, there has been a frontier to serve as a safety valve for America's restive energy.[6] Even after the land resources have largely been exhausted, spiritual equivalents (for example, outer space as "the new frontier' in the 1960s) were found. Americans, the majority of whom are of immigrant stock, have never really settled down; they have become emigrants within their own country.

Afro-Americans have shared this national endorsement of flight as a means to solve their problems. In her study of the great black migration in the early twentieth century, Florette Henri notes that "American blacks had always been moving from one part of the country to another, and also out of the country, looking for freedom and opportunity."[7] In both the fugitive slave's escape from the South and the black emigrationist's search for a homeland, flight becomes an act of rebellion, a rejection of oppression. For Americans, in general and for Afro-Americans in particular, self-determined movement has been an important declaration of independence.

The most important geographical movement in Afro-American culture has been northward, but nonetheless, a large segment of black society has shared America's fixation upon the West as the land of promise, waiting to yield up its treasure---whether it be gold, oil, crops, stardom, political or economic power, adventure, or even merely relief from the settled society in the East.

One of the most vivid examples in Afro-American literature of the lure of the frontier is Oscar Micheaux's autobiographical novel, *The Quest* (1913). This work is especially relevant here, for in justifying his decision to homestead, the narrator continually alludes to the opinion shared by many Americans of the time that in the West the American Dream was still alive and well. The protagonist's faith in the American way has already been reinforced by his success in Chicago, where he has earned $2,340 in an appropriately up-by-one's bootstraps manner. Now, he strikes out for new challenges:

> The odd forty I drew out, and left the remainder on deposit, packed my trunk and bid farewell to Armour Avenue and Chicago's Black Belt with its beer cans, drunken men and women, and turned my face westward with the spirit of Horace Greely [sic] before and his words "Go west, young man, and grow up with the country" ringing in my ears. So westward I journeyed to the land of raw material, which my dreams had pictured to me as the land of real beginning.[8]

The crucial premise underlying the protagonist's sanguine expectations is that "if white people could possess such nice homes, wealth and luxuries, so in time, could the colored people."[9] This belief that race cannot prevent success is the key to any acceptance by blacks of the relevance of the American Dream for their own lives. Throughout much of modern Afro-American fiction, this assumption is called into question and frequently proven fallacious. Such optimism as that displayed by the narrator of *The Conquest* is actually an accurate indication of the protagonist's naivete.

Chester Himes's *If He Hollers Let Him Go* is the powerful examination of one black man's painful growth from naivete to cynicism as he searches for the American Dream in Southern California. Bob Jones, the protagonist, moves to Los Angeles from Cleveland in the early 1940s, not just for better employment opportunities but for something far more elusive and difficult to define---a secure sense of his own manhood. But he has become quite familiar with white American racism. Early in the novel, he describes his previous encounters with prejudice: "Cleveland wasn't the land of the free or the home of the brave either. That was one reason why I left there to come to Los Angeles; I knew if I kept on getting refused while white boys were hired from the line behind me I'd hang somebody as sure as hell."[10] Los Angeles, however, promises to be an open society which will allow him to start over. Arriving in California, he optimistically believes that he has left his troubles behind: "I felt fine about everything. Taller than the average man, six feet two, broadshouldered, and conceited, I hadn't a worry. I knew I'd get along" (IHH 6-7).

What makes Bob's experiences in Los Angeles particularly troubling is that his expectations are merely those shared by most of his fellow countrymen. While he acknowledges the restrictions imposed upon him because of his race, Bob cannot help but partake of the same values and goals as other Americans:

> I'd learned the same jive that the white folks had learned. All that stuff about liberty and justice and equality . . . . All men are created equal . . . . Any person born in the United States is a citizen . . . . Learned it out the same books, in the same schools . . . . I was a Charles Lindbergh fan when I was a little boy, and thought George Washington was the father of my country---as long as I thought I had a country. (IHH 141-142)

His inability to abandon the notions that "being born in America gave everybody a certain importance" (IHH 143), that he does indeed have "a country," and that he is fully an American predetermines his fate.

His first major disillusionment in California involves his search for work. He comments: "It was the look on the people's faces when you asked them about a job . . . . They just looked so goddamned startled that I'd even asked. As if some friendly dog had come in through the door and said, 'I can talk' "(IHH 7). If, in Cleveland, he found it difficult to be recognized as an American citizen, he finds his very humanity denied in Los Angeles.

His anger and frustration turn to fear and anxiety with the internment of the Japanese-Americans during the war. The sight of "little Riki Oyana singing 'God Bless America' and going to Santa Anita with his parents next day" epitomizes for Bob the awesome power white society holds over his own head and the frightening ease with which that power can be exercised. After Pearl Harbor, Bob becomes especially sensitive to the "tight, crazy feeling of race as thick in the street as gas fumes." He admits: "Every time I stepped outside I saw a challenge I had to accept or ignore. Every day I had to make one decision a thousand times: *Is it now? Is now the time?* (IHH 7). The sheer nervous tension of maintaining a state of constant mobilization frays Bob physically and emotionally.

After his initial disappointment, Bob strikes an uneasy truce with the hostile white society in which he finds himself. He still believes that some accommodation can be reached, that he can attain some degree of success, American style. This qualified optimism is grounded in Bob's sense of his own manhood, and his tough, desperate pride is tied directly to three possessions which have typically buttressed the confidence of American males throughout the twentieth century: his car, his job, and his relationship with a woman. Himes describes how, in each case, white America flaunts its power over Bob.

In wartime Los Angeles, Bob's '42 Buick Roadmaster is a sign of his superior status; he comments, "rich white folks out in Beverly couldn't even buy a new car now" (IHH 13). Further, in his daily confrontation with the whites who can flourish their ascendancy with a condescending glance, Bob's car is a tool of aggression and an outlet for his frustrations. The limitations of his Buick as a symbol of prestige and as a source of power are brought home, however, the night he and his girlfriend, Alice, are pulled over by two white motorcycle policemen. The officers' insults and the fact that it is Alice who, using the political clout of her father, finally gets the police off their backs, both remind Bob of his impotence. After he and Alice have been taken to the police station and fined, Alice exclaims angrily: "I wish I was a man." Bob's cynical retort---"If you were a man what would you do?"---is directed as much at himself as at Alice (IHH 62).

The second important evidence of his own worth is his job as a "leaderman" at the Atlas Shipyard. His feelings as he dresses for work in the morning suggest the degree to which his position as a "key man" in the war effort defines him as a valuable and potent man and assuages somewhat his sense of helplessness: "Something about my working clothes made me feel rugged, bigger than the average citizen, stronger than a white-collar worker---stronger even than an executive. Important too. It put me on my muscle" (IHH 12). Despite his title, however, Bob is confronted daily with the nominal nature of his authority. Not only must he put up with members of his own black crew who blame him for their mistakes, but he finds that he is the subordinate of every white worker. His union representative is ineffective; his superior insults him by telling a "darky" joke in his presence; and he must acknowledge that a less qualified white leaderman can get the black crew better jobs than he can. He learns his true status in the yard when he calls Madge, a white, Texas-bred tacker who insultingly refuses to work for him, a "cracker bitch" (IHH 29). As a result of this exchange, he is downgraded and threatened with the loss of his military deferment.

His most precious source of masculine pride and the situation that most convinces him that he has a foot up on the ladder to American middle-class prosperity is his relationship with Alice. While Bob is an inveterate flirt with most of the black women he encounters, he believes that Alice Harrison is something special: "It gave me a personal pride to have her for my girl. And then I was proud of her too. Proud of the way she looked, the appearance she made among white people; proud of what she demanded from white people, and the credit they gave her; and her position and prestige among her own people" (IHH 10). Yet Bob abhors the pompous superficiality of Alice's parents and her fatuous friends, and he is equally exasperated by the stiff social worker manner Alice cannot seem to leave at her office. Their relationship is further strained by a series of events, each of which seems designed to mortify him. The first involves the harassment they receive when they go to an elegant hotel for dinner. Then comes the confrontation with the police. The ultimate insult stems from the more direct intervention of white society in their relationship several days later. Incensed by the racist behavior of whites, Bob seeks refuge at Alice's house, where he must endure the glib comments of her white co-worker, Tom Leighton.   Bob is particularly aggravated by the white man's condescension, which makes him "look like a goddamned fool" in front of Alice (IHH 85).   When he later encounters Tom and Alice on their way to a date, he feels that he is in danger of losing everything which defines his masculinity.

In his desperate need to retaliate for his humiliation, Bob first decides to get revenge on a young white who struck him during a crap game. Determined to make the man "feel as scared and powerless and unprotected as I felt every goddamned morning I woke up," Bob finds that having "a peckerwood's life in the palm of my hand . . . made all the difference" (IHH 37, 45). Soon, however, merely threatening the white man no longer seems either satisfying or practical; confronting white America's ultimate racial taboo, Bob turns his attention to Madge.

While there is something of the appeal of the sexually forbidden underlying Bob's obsession with Madge, revenge is the strongest motive: "I was going to have to have her. I was going to have to make her as low as a white whore in a Negro slum---a scummy two-dollar whore . . . . I was going to have to so I could keep looking the white folks in the face" (IHH 116). Despite his resolution to get back at white society through Madge, Bob is denied even this satisfaction, however, when her aroused cry of surrender---"All right, rape me then, nigger!"---literally unmans him "I let her loose and bounded to my feet. *Rape*---just the sound of the word scared me, took everything out of me, my desire, my determination, my whole build-up" (IHH 138). Having been thwarted in his every attempt to assert his manhood, Bob surrenders: "I was through and I knew it; the white folks had won again and I wanted out" (IHH 139).

At the height of his pride, Bob has contended: "If I couldn't live in America as an equal in the minds, hearts, and souls of all the white people, if I couldn't know that I had a chance to do anything any other American could, to go as high as an American citizenship would carry anybody, there'd never be anything in this country for me anyway" (IHH 144). Now, however, his goals are much simpler: "All I want is peace" (IHH 150). Admitting defeat, Bob seems willing, at long last, to resign himself to his second-class status. Alice and her circle of bourgeois blacks exemplify how such an adjustment might be made: "They hadn't stopped trying, I gave them that much; . . . but they have recognized their limit---a nigger limit" (IHH 141). As agonizing as it is for him to accept this "nigger limit," Bob also acknowledges: "(A)s long as I was black I'd never be anything but half a man at best" (IHH 153). Determined to make the best of his unavoidale plight, Bob promises Alice that he will swallow his pride, and he accepts the patronizing advice of his white department supervisor, who tells him: "Take your punishment like a man, then make a comeback. That's the *American way*, my boy. Prove yourself" (IHH 164); emphasis added).

In Himes's pessimistic view, however, Bob's decision to resign himself to the crumbs white society offers does not prevent the ultimate destruction of his remaining ambitions.   Accidentally trapped with Madge in a locked cabin aboard a ship, Bob is victimized by her second cry of "Rape," an accusation used for years to justify the emasculation of black men. While, for a short time, he naively expects to be somehow vindicated, Bob finally admits that he has no chance: "The whole structure of American thought was against me; American tradition had convicted me a hundred years before" (IHH 175). The idealism which has carried Bob to California is dead. He ends up "pressed, cornered, black, as small and weak and helpless as any Negro sharecropper facing a white mob in Georgia" (IHH 182).

Mauled physically and spiritually, Bob is finally bereft of all idealism, hope, anger, and even hatred. In the closing scenes, when he is offered the choice of going to prison or taking part in a war about which he cares little, he must fight down hysterical laughter at the bitter irony of his fate. After traveling West in the attempt to attain his portion of the American Dream---"just to be a man" (IHH 190), he must enlist in the Jim Crow Army which has long advertised its ability to "make" men. His final words---"I'm still here" (IHH 191)---mark the nadir of his aspirations; he has survived: that is all he can claim.

> *Or does it explode?*
>   ---Langston
> Hughes, "Dream Deferred" [11]

> *(D)iligence is the mother of goodluck*, as
> Poor Richard says and *God gives all things*
> *to industry*.
>   ---Benjamin   Franklin,
> "The Way to Wealth" [12]

A crucial component of the American Dream is the conviction that the United States is the land of infinite economic opportunity. This myth is firmly based on the widespread belief in the inherent justice of the U. S. economic system---that is, that hard work and dedication not only can but will lead to success.

In her novel, *The Street*, Ann Petry demonstrated that for Lutie Johnson, an industrious, intelligent, sensitive, and idealistic young black woman, the American Dream is impossible. A staunch, real-life proponent of the Dream, J. D. Rockefeller, once remarked: "They have but to master the knack of economy, thrift, and perseverance and success is theirs."[13] In *The Street*, Lutie displays the necessary "economy, thrift, and perseverance"; however, her path leads not to prosperity but to murder, despair, and the abandonment of her every aspiration, including her dreams for her son.

Like Himes's Bob Jones, Lutie Johnson has been raised to accept mainstream American values. Lutie's goals are grounded in the traditional optimistic American view of economic achievement traceable inevitably back to Benjamin Franklin. Lutie's explicit allusion to a famous scene from Franklin's *Autobiography* reinforces the conventionality of her ambitions. Walking home one day with a bag of rolls,

> she thought immediately of Ben Franklin and his loaf of bread. And grinned thinking, You and Ben Franklin. You ought to take one out and start eating it as you walk along 116th Street. Only you ought to remember while you eat that you're in Harlem and he was in Philadelphia a pretty long number of years ago. Yet she couldn't get rid of the feeling of self-confidence and she went on thinking that if Ben Franklin could live on a little bit of money and could prosper, then so could she.[14]

The last sentence of this excerpt is crucial, for it is this confidence which best characterizes Lutie throughout most of the novel.

In addition to the philosophy Lutie imbibes through her reading and schooling, she also encounters first hand proof that the American Dream is attainable. One example is the Pizzinis, who run a small local store. When, to her surprise, Lutie discovers that this old Italian couple "had a fine house and they had sent their daughter to college," she wonders: "How had they managed to do that on the nickels and dimes they took in selling lettuce and grapefruit?" Lutie believes that "if she could fine out how the Pizzinis had managed, it might help her and [her husband] Jim." (TS 26)

Lutie's second and more important contact with American success occurs during her tenure as a live-in domestic with the wealthy Chandler family. The main street in the Connecticut where the Chandlers live, their house ("a miracle"), and even the clothes Mrs. Chandler wears impress Lutie with the distance between their life and hers. She feels as though she were "looking through a hole in a wall at some enchanted garden. She could see, she could hear, she spoke the language of the people in the garden, but she couldn't get past the wall" (TS 31). Exposure to "an entirely different set of values" forces Lutie to reexamine her entire conception of white American goals:

> When she was in high school, she had
> believed that white people wanted their
> children to be president of the United States;
> that most of them worked hard with that
> goal in mind . . . . Even the Pizzinis'
> daughter had got to be a school-teacher,
> showing that they, too, had wanted more
> learning and knowledge in the family.
> But these people were different . . . .
> They didn't want their children to be
> president or diplomats or anything like that.
> What they wanted was to be rich - - - -
> "filthy" rich, as Mr. Chandler called it. (TS
> 31, 32)

Lutie's stay with the Chandlers, however, involves far more than a pleasant education in the values and aspirations of the American upper class. She is shocked and angered to discover that whites "all had the idea that colored girls were whores" (TS 31). Further, the moral bankruptcy of the Chandler family becomes increasingly difficult to ignore. From Mrs. Chandler's lack of love for her child and Mr. Chandler's alcoholism to the marital infidelity and the horrible suicide of Mr. Chandler's brother on Christmas morning, Lutie is confronted with indications that their money is no panacea for the emptiness of their lives. Ironically, however, even her unpleasant experiences with the Chandlers serve to tantalize Lutie with the power of money. While she does see that the "mere possession of it wouldn't necessarily guarantee happiness," the ease with which the Chandlers turn an obviously deliberate shooting into an "accident" with a few phone calls convinces Lutie that "when one had money there were certain unpleasant things one could avoid" (TS 35). [15]

The key to Lutie's optimism about her own chances to become affluent is that she ultimately sees little difference between the Chandlers and her own family. She is firmly convinced that "anybody could be rich if he wanted to and worked hard enough and figured it out carefully enough" (TS 32). If Ben Franklin, the Pizzinis, and the Chandlers can rise in the world, then why can't she? To Lutie, the problem is not that of overcoming peculiarly racial obstacles; rather, she feels that she has only to discover the right formula, the right sequence of steps and prosperity will be hers. Where Bob Jones's innocence lies in his belief that an acceptable balance can be struck between his own proud need for self-determination and white society's control of him, Luties's lies in the deeply American presumption that what others have attained is accessible to her as well. Like the ideal self-reliant American hero, Lutie believes that through a sheer act of individual will, she will succeed: "As she had been able to get this far without help from anyone, why, all she had to do was plan each stop and she could get wherever she wanted to go" (TS 44). As Lutie's story unfolds, this idealistic faith in the American Dream is slowly and excruciatingly undermined as white society frustrates her every ambition.

Lutie's path from hope to despair is marked by three crushing defeats: the breakup of her marriage, her ill-fated attempt at a singing career, and her son's arrest for stealing mail. Each incident strips Lutie further of the energy and optimism which nourish her dreams.

The initial blow to her self-confidence is the disintegration of her relationship with her husband, Jim; and what makes this so painful to Lutie is that, given her choices, she has done what society deems necessary to succeed. First, when Jim cannot find employment, Lutie scrimps and sacrifices in order to support her family on what they receive for taking in "State children." Over Jim's objections, Lutie's alcoholic father moves in with them, and soon thereafter the police raid a raucous party the old man gives when Jim and Lutie are gone. As a result, the foster children are taken away and all of Lutie's ingenuity, hard work, and obsessive budgeting go for naught. Then, after she takes the only available job---the live-in position with the Chandlers, her tremendous drive to get ahead economically leads to further disaster. In an effort to save as much money as possible, she visits Jim only once every two months. Petry describes the outcome of his resultant humiliation and loneliness, "He got used to facing the fact that he couldn't support his wife and child . . . . Slowly, bit by bit, it undermined his belief in himself until he could no longer bear it. And he got himself a woman so that in those moments when he clutched her close to him in bed he could prove that he was still needed, wanted" (TS 108). Upon her discovery of Jim's infidelity, Lutie moves out, taking their young son, Bub, with her.

Lutie recognizes that white society often subverts the Afro-American's access to the American Dream by preventing the black man from gaining work, and thereby weakening the entire family structure; but she refuses to acknowledge that the breakup of her marriage is the first step in her own entrapment. Her appointment to a civil service job after four years of extreme hardship encourages her dreams of security for herself and her son. The extent of Lutie's self-confidence is clear in her reflections on the destructive power of the "street," where she and Bub share a tiny apartment: "As for the street," she tells herself, ". . . she wasn't afraid of its influence, for she would fight against it" (TS 40).

Lutie's second major disappointment occurs after she has received the "lucky break" which plays such a crucial role in traditional American tales of success. "The Alger hero," Russel Nye observes, "is honest, manly, cheerful, intelligent, self-reliant, ambitious, moral, frugal, and all else that he need be, but it is not by reason of any of these attributes, admirable as they are, that he becomes rich. The fact is that wealth in Alger comes by reason of the lucky break, by seizure of the chance opportunity."[16] Lutie Johnson possesses most of the requisite traits for getting ahead; according to the American formula, she needs only the chance to prove herself. When she is "discovered" in a neighborhood bar by a black bandleader named Boots Smith and offered a chance to sing professionally, she apparently gets this chance. After having nearly given up hope, Lutie now experiences a powerful resurgence of optimism and confidence which belies the disappointments she has endured. However, her cocky "intention of using Boots Smith' is naïve; and her determined boast---"she could do it and she would," but a tragic underestimation of the opposition. (TS 107).

When she learns that she will not get paid for singing, she is crushed by the realization that success has once again been snatched seemingly out of her grasp. Lutie apparently resigns herself to her situation:

> The trouble was with her. She had built up a
> fantastic structure made from the soft,
> nebulous, cloudy stuff of dreams. There
> hadn't been a solid, practical brick in it, not
> even a foundation . . . . It had never existed
> anywhere but in her own mind.
>   She might as well face that she would
> have to go on living on the same street. (TS
> 191)

Her despair proves short-lived, however, for she quickly reaffirms her determination to apply herself, to meet whatever unwritten demands America imposes on those bold enough to strive for the American Dream: "She thought of the Chandlers and their friends in Lyme. They were right about people being able to make money, but it took hard, grinding work to do it---hard work and self-sacrifice. She was capable of both, she concluded. Furthermore, she would never permit herself to become resigned to living there" (TS 195). Her idealism reborn, she renews her struggle to make a better life for herself and Bub.

The remarkable resilience of Lutie's optimism, rather than insuring her success, ultimately sets her up for the next stage in her defeat. Still harboring the dreams of singing for a living, she visits the Crosse School for Singers. After Mr. Crosse's vulgar suggest that she become his mistress in exchange for music lessons she cannot afford, Lutie despairs of ever improving her lot.

In Horatio Alger's *Ragged Dick*, a wealthy character advises the young hero, "[I]n this free country poverty in early life is not bar to a man's advancement . . . . Remember that your future position depends mainly upon yourself, and that it will be high or low as you choose to make it."[17] In the case of Lutie Johnson, however, if poverty is no obstacle, race and sex certainly are. Lutie's world is governed not by some vaguely benevolent embodiment of justice but by impersonal, amoral rules of power---physical, sexual, and economic. Lutie is unwilling to parlay her worth as a source of sexual pleasure---the only value society places upon her---into the financial security she desires for herself and Bub. Consequently, she must reconcile herself to her total lack of power in American society. And without power, the door to success will remain forever closed to her. In Petry's view the traditional formula of self-reliance plus hard work plus moral uprightness plus opportunism equals success is fallacious if one is poor and black and female.[18]

If, as she thinks, "now she was very nearly walled in and the wall had been built up brick by brick by eager white hands," then the last brick is cemented in place with Bub's arrest for theft (TS 200-201). Confronted with her inability to protect her son, Lutie is forced to acknowledge not only the inevitability of her failure but also her own culpability in driving Bub to crime:

> The men stood around and the women worked. The men left the women and the women went on working and the kids were left alone . . . . The women work and the kids go to reform school. . . . [T]he little Henry Chandlers go to YalePrincetonHarvard and the Bub Johnsons graduate from reform school into DannemoraSingSing.
> And you helped push him because you talked to him about money. All the time money. And you wanted it because you wanted to move from this street, but in the beginning it was because you heard the rich white Chandlers talk about it. "Filthy rich." "Richest country in the world." "Make it while you're young."
> Only you forgot. You forgot you were black and you underestimated the street. (TS 240-241).[19]

All that remains of Lutie's ambitious goals is the desire to free her son. However, when Boots refuses to give her the money she thinks she needs for Bub's release, even this last and dearest hope is blocked. Boots' insulting slap after she rebuffs his sexual advances triggers the release of a lifetime of suppressed rage and violence in Lutie. Her subsequent murder of Boots is the culmination of years of frustrated plans and aborted dreams.

One of the many sad ironies of Lutie's fate is that while Boots is the handiest embodiment of an oppression she can bear no longer, he too is a victim. Humiliated by white society throughout most of his adult life, Boots is, like Lutie's father and Jim and Himes's Bob Jones, a black man who must struggle to retain the scraps of his pride by any means necessary in order to live with

himself.   His impoverishment during the Depression, his experience as a
Pullman porter, and his catching his lover cheating with a white man all have
chipped away at Boots's self-esteem. In order to survive, much less live with
dignity, Boots---like others on the "street"---has accepted the terms of his own
oppression; tragically, he thereby becomes in turn an oppressive force in others,
including Lutie. [20]

In her quest for the American Dream, Lutie Johnson has followed all the
rules; yet she has failed miserably. Her defeat is all the more complete because
not only has her own life been ruined, but she has likely insured that her son has
lost before he fully enters the fray.   She perceptively recognizes the
deterministic lives of those around her, those who have accommodated
themselves to their degrading environment.   However, like Bob Jones, she
refuses to abdicate her right to aspire to any goal available to white Americans.
Indeed, her training and personality both militate against such a concession. She
observes, "Perhaps it was better to take things as they were and not try to change
them. But who wouldn't have wanted to live in a better house than this one and
who wouldn't have struggled to get out of it?---and the only way that presented
itself was to save money" (TS 252). In Petry's pessimistic view of America,
Lutie's admirable determination assures nothing; that, according to popular
American mythology, she is deserving of success has little bearing on her fate.

Lutie's pursuit of the American Dream frustrated, the novel concludes on a
note of unqualified despair. In an ending as bitterly ironic as that which marks
Bob Jones's futile search for manhood, Lutie abandons Bub and unconsciously
takes part in another aspect of American myth---the trip West. Here, however,
Lutie is not looking for the American Dream; she has given up on that. She
heads to Chicago hoping desperately that "it would swallow her up" (TS 268)
. . . .

---

[1] Langston Hughes, *Selected Poems* (1959; rpt. N.Y.: Random House, Vintage
Books, 1974), 295.
[2] Frank J. Webb, *The Garies and Their Friends* (1857; rpt. N.Y.: Arno Press,
1969), 62-63.
[3] A similar thematic problem arises in Charles W. Chesnutt's *The Marrow of
Tradition* (Boston: Houghton Mifflin, 1901).
[4] William Attaway's *Blood on the Forge* (1941) also deserves note as an
important, largely-ignored black critique of the American Dream.
[5] Chuck Berry, *Anthology* (N.Y.: Arc Music Corp., n.d.), 49.
[6] For a discussion of the "safety valve" theory, see Henry Nash Smith, *Virgin
Land* (1950; rpt. N.Y.: Random House, Vintage Books, 1970).
[7] Florette Henri, *Black Migration: Movement North, 1900-1920* (Garden City,
N.Y.: Anchor Press-Doubleday, Anchor Books, 1976), 49.

[8] Oscar Micheaux, *The Conquest* (1913, rpt. Miami, Fla: Mnemosyne Pub. Co., 1969), 47.

[9] Micheaux

[10] Chester Himes, *If He Hollers Let Him Go* (1945); rpt. N.Y.: New American Library, Signet Books, 1971), 7. All future references to this edition appear in parentheses in the text following the abbreviation IHH.

[11] Langston Hughes, *The Panther and the Lash* (1967); rpt. N.Y.: Alfred A. Knopf, Borzoi Books, 1971), 14.

[12] Benjamin Franklin, "The Way to Wealth," in *The Norton Anthology of American Literature*, ed. Ronald Gottesman, et al (N.Y.: W. W. Norton and Co., Inc., 1979), 1, 269.

[13] Cited by Carl N. Degler, *Out of Our Past*, 2nd rev. ed. (1959; rpt. N.Y.: Harper and Row, Harper Colophon Books, 1970), 257.

[14] Ann Petry, *The Street* (1946; rpt. N.Y.: Pyramid Books, 1961), 44. All future references to this edition appear in parentheses in the text following the abbreviation TS.

[15] Lutie's appreciation of the power of money in American society is reinforced by her contact with Boots Smith, a black musician who not only bribes a white policeman when caught speeding but also avoids military service through the intercession of his wealthy boss, Junto. See TS, 106.

[16] Russel Nye, *The Unembarrassed Muse* (N.Y.: Dial Press, 1970), 65.

[17] Horatio Alger, *Ragged Dick*, for example, the young hero starts out as a bootblack. Lutie realizes, however, that because Bub is black, "if he's shining shoes at eight, he will be washing windows at sixteen and running an elevator at twenty-one, and go on doing that for the rest of his life." (TS 47)

[18] At first glance, two minor characters, Junto and Mrs. Hedges would seem to exemplify the American bootstrap rise to prosperity. Junto, however, is a white male. Not only is Mrs. Hedges largely dependent upon Junto's good will but her main source of income is a prostitution operation, the exploitative nature of which mocks the American myth of success.

[19] Lutie once slaps Bub because he is trying to earn money by shining shoes. This is another ironic inversion of the Horatio Alger myth, which is under attack in *The Street*. In *Ragged Dick*, for example, the young hero starts out as a bootblack. Lutie realizes, however, that because Bub is black, "if he's shining shoes at eight, he will be washing windows at sixteen and running an elevator at twenty-one, and go on doing that for the rest of his life." (TS 47)

[20] Compare the importance of their cars to both Boots and Bob Jones. Further similarities between the two characters include their bitterness toward the American effort in World War II and their resentment when their women associate with white men.

Ann Petry's Demythologizing of American Culture and Afro-American
Character (1985)
Bernard W. Bell

The novels of Ann Petry have been overshadowed and her talent misrepresented
by their frequent comparison to the fiction and achievement of Richard Wright
and Chester Himes. Robert Bone, for example, claims that *The Street* (1946),
her first novel, suffers by comparison to Wright's *Native Son* [1940] because "it
is an attempt to interpret slum life in terms of *Negro* experience, when a larger
frame of reference is required."[1] In contrast, he considers *Country Place* (1947),
her second novel, "one of the finest . . . of the period" because it is "a
manifestation not so much of assimilation as of versatility."[2] He does not
mention *The Narrows* (1953), the best of her three novels, in either edition of his
The Negro Novel in America. Neither does critic Addison Gayle, Jr., who
discusses only *The Street* in his more recent book, *The Way of the New World*.[3]
For Gayle, Petry is similar to Himes in that she develops characters with some
status and education, and to Wright in that "both were interested in the effects of
environment upon the psychological makeup of characters."[4] Unlike Wright,
however, Gayle concludes, "Miss Petry is more interested in the effects of the
environment upon her characters than she is in the character themselves."[5]
Whether valid or not, these critical views do not adequately express the
complexity and distinctiveness of Ann Petry's aesthetic vision and achievement.

Ann Petry actually moves beyond the naturalistic vision of Wright and Himes
in her realistic delineation of cultural myths, especially those of the American
Dream, the city and small town, and black character. In exploring the black
community's place in time and space, its relationship to the American past and
future, she effectively debunks the myths of urban success and progress, or rural
innocence and virtue, and of pathological black women and men. Embodying
the values and beliefs of a community, *myths*, as we are using the term here, are
stories people in a particular society tell to organize, explain, and understand the
realities and metaphysics of their world. "Myths are not rational," writes James
O. Robertson in *American Myth, American Reality*, "at least in the sense that
they are not controlled by what we believe to be logic." They are sometimes
based on faith, on belief rather than reason, on ideals rather than realities."[6]
Thus myths are a kind of behavioral charter that leads to both negative and
positive responses.

Since the "truth" about America and Americans is found in both American
myths and American realities, Petry dispassionately explores both in her novels.
Like realist writers from Sinclair Lewis and Theodore Dreiser to Zora Hurston
and Richard Wright, she realizes, moreover, that not all Americans participate in
the same myths or use them in the same ways. Race, color, class, sex, and
region are the major realities that determine the degree and manner of
participation of individuals and communities in our national myths. While, for
example, myths of the Founding Fathers like Benjamin Franklin, who is the

colonial paradigm of the successful self-made man, are available to all Americans, black Americans rarely refer to them. "On the other hand," as Robertson states, "many black Americans use the stories and myths of Abraham Lincoln more frequently than other Americans."[7] Despite turn-of-the century attacks on small-town life such as Sinclair Lewis's *Main Street*, the rural vision of the city is characterized mainly by sin, crime, and violence. At the same time, however, younger Americans, especially blacks, dream of the city as a place of opportunity, wealth, and progress. The truth, as Petry reveals in her novels, is actually more complex and paradoxical. So, too, is the socialized ambivalence, the pride and shame of one's identity, and double-consciousness, the struggle to reconcile one's dual heritage, of black American character.

The setting and themes of Ann Petry's novels are a natural outgrowth of her intimacy with the black inner-city life of New York and the white small-town life of New England. . . .

The Street is a conventional novel of economic determinism in which the environment is the dominant force against which the characters must struggle to survive. The novel opens symbolically with the November wind and cold and dirt and filth of 116th Street overpowering the hurried Harlem pedestrians, including the apartment-hunting protagonist, Lutie Johnson; it closes with Lutie leaving the city by train after killing the man who assaults her, the snow falling symbolically, "gently obscuring the grime and garbage and the ugliness" of the street. As the plot progresses episodically, we apprehend the street in the same sociological manner as the protagonist:

> It was a bad street . . . . It wasn't just this street that she was afraid of or that was bad. It was any street where people were packed together like sardines in a can.
>
> And it wasn't like this city. It was any city where they set up a line and say black folks stay on this side and white folks on this side, so that the black folks were crammed on top of each other---jammed and packed and forced into the smallest possible space until they were completely cut off from light and air.
>
> It was any place where the women had to work to support their families because the men couldn't get jobs and the men got bored and pulled out and the kids were left without proper homes because there was nobody around to put a heart into it. Yes. It was any place where people were so damn poor they didn't have time to do anything but

> work, and their bodies were the only source
> of relief from the pressure under which they
> lived; and where the crowding together
> made the young girls wise beyond their
> years.[8]

Poverty and race are inextricably linked to the "Dirty, dark, filthy traps" in which the characters live and die. It was "Streets like 116th Street or being colored, or a combination of both with all it implied" that drove the protagonist's father to drink and the mother to her early grave. It was the same combination of circumstances that

> had evidently made the Mrs. Hedges who sat
> in the street-floor window turn to running a
> fairly well-kept whorehouse . . . and the
> superintendent of the building---well, the
> street had pushed him into basements away
> from light and air until he was being eaten
> up by some horrible obsession; and still
> other streets had turned Min, the woman
> who lived with him, into a drab drudge so
> spineless and so limp she was like a soggy
> dishrag. (40)

Lutie Johnson was determined that none of these things would happen to her "because she would fight back and never stop fighting back." But her will to succeed is ineffectual against the relentless economic and racist forces that Ann Petry saw as the direct cause of streets like the one on which the protagonist lived. Far from being an accident, we learn through the narrator's probing into Lutie's mind, "They were the North's mob. . . the method the big cities used to keep Negroes in their place" (200).

Unlike Wright's and Himes' protagonists, Lutie Johnson is neither psychologically tormented nor driven by a fear of white people. Raised by her tale-telling, Puritan-minded grandmother, she is a respectable married woman, driven by a hunger for the material trappings of middle-class success for herself and her family; she longs for a better life and a place to be somebody. She seeks to satisfy this hunger by naively subscribing to the Protestant ethic and the American Dream as expressed by the Chandlers, the wealthy white New England family for whom she worked for two years as a live-in maid, and as embodied in Benjamin Franklin, with whom she compares herself. Ignoring her own social reality---a working-class black woman with an eight-year-old son to support; separated from her unfaithful, unemployed husband; living in Harlem during World War II; struggling to maintain her moral principles and to share equally in the wealth of the nation---she fantasizes "that if Ben Franklin could live on a little bit of money and could prosper, then so could she" (44). After a year with the Chandlers she finds herself influenced by their material values and belief in the American Dream. They promoted the "belief that anybody could be rich if he wanted to and worked hard enough and figured it out carefully enough . . . . These people had wanted only one thing---more and more money---so they got it" (32).

The irony is that Lutie sees, yet fails to act on, the price that the Chandlers pay in spiritual and personal alienation for their material success. In blind pursuit of the American Dream, Lutie loses her family and her hope for happiness, but not her self-respect. When she fails to get the singing job she had counted on to move off 116th Street and up the ladder of success, social reality begins to displace her dream world. "The trouble was with her," she concludes. "She had built up a fantastic structure made from the soft, nebulous, cloudy stuff of dream. There hadn't been a solid, practical brick in it, not even a foundation. She had built it up of air and vapor and moved right in. So of course it had collapsed. It had never existed anywhere but in her mind." (191).

Although some critics see the sensationalism of the denouement as a weakness, it is inconsistent neither with the naturalism of Dreiser and Wright nor with Petry's use of symbols of confinement and contrasting images of the white world and black world to give structural and thematic coherence to the novel.[9] The wide, quiet, tree-lined, sunny main street of Lyme, Connecticut, where the Chandlers live in gracious luxury is contrasted with the drab, violent, overcrowded streets where Lutie's economic, racial and sexual circumstances trap her. "From the time she was born, she had been hemmed into an ever-narrowing space until now she was very nearly walled in and the wall had been built up brick by brick by eager white hands" (200-201). The white world had a different set of values from those her grandmother had taught her. It was a strange world in which money was more important than people and young, black women were considered potential whores. Her grandmother had warned her so often about the lust of white men for black women that she found them repulsive. Thus, when Boots Smith, a black musician, attempts to persuade her to exchange sexual favors with Junto, the Jewish owner of the major clubs and whorehouses in the black community, for the two hundred dollars she needed to help keep her boy out of reform school, all she can think is: "Junto has a brick in his hand. Just one brick. The final one needed to complete the wall that had been building up around her for years, and when that last brick was shoved in place, she would be completely walled in" (262). Angrily responding to Boot's actual and threatened violence, she beats his head into a bloody pulp with an iron candlestick, realizing afterwards that "a lifetime of pent-up resentment went into the blows" (266).

Although the story is told by a disembodied third-person, omniscient narrator, Petry allows Lutie's consciousness to dominate the narrative and scrupulously avoids moralizing. The action and setting are subordinated to Lutie's impression of their impact on black women and the black family, thus encouraging our sympathy for her and other black women, who incredulously have no contact with the black church. Except for the denouement, the author-narrator explores the social evils of segregated communities, white and black, with restraint and objectivity. But it is clear that neither Petry nor her protagonist simplistically blame black men for the broken homes, poverty, and hopelessness that characterize too many urban black communities. The cause of these social problems is not black men like her alcoholic father and adulterous husband, nor black women like Mrs. Hedges, the whorehouse madam, but white people like Junto and the Chandlers, whose prosperity is based on the economic exploitation of blacks. If it is impossible to escape the corruption and despair of the black inner city, it is equally impossible, as the Chandlers reveal, to escape the degeneration and despair of small white towns.

In *Country Place*, Petry moves beyond economic and racial determinism to explore the realities beneath the myths of rural, small-town communities. In contrast to traditional stories and images of the beneficence, continuity, integrity, and homogeneity of values in small, rural American communities, her narrative reveals the hypocrisy, violence, prejudice, and stagnation of a small, post-World War II, New England town. *Country Place* is the first-person, retrospective narrative with the town druggist, George Fraser, as the on-the-scene chronicler of events. In the opening five pages, the friendly, sixty-five-year-old narrator immediately establishes his reliability ("I am neither a pessimist not an optimist"), the setting "a quiet place, a country place, which sets at the mouth of the Connecticut River, at the exact spot where the river empties itself into Long Island Sound"), and the major theme: " . . . wheresoever man dwell there is always a vein of violence running under the surface quiet."[10] Confessing his own petty prejudice against women, he is nevertheless sympathetic toward the townspeople, especially his friend Mrs. Gramby, and intimately knowledgeable about them and the "untoward events" that occurred during and after a storm the previous year when Johnnie Roane, the protagonist, returned home from the war.

The predominantly white characters of Lennox, Connecticut, are trapped by time, prejudice, and their own illusions. Refusing to sell land on Main Street to the Catholic Church, ostracizing the Jewish lawyer Rosenthal, and impugning the moral character of the black maid Neola and her admirer, the Portuguese gardener Portulacca, who are only sketchily delineated, the townspeople belie the myth of the beneficient small town. Glory Roane, the protagonist's wife, and Lillian Mearns, her mother and daughter-in-law to the wealthy Mrs. Gramby, are shallow, covetous women, fighting futilely against time with diets and hair dye while cheating on their husbands and dreaming of inheriting the Gramby house and fortune. Mearns Gramby, the frustrated, middle-aged heir of the wealthiest family in town, is trapped by his mother's illusion of him as "the last of a long and honorable and distinguished family" (84) and by his addiction to vitamin pills and his marriage to a middle-aged, acquisitive bigot.

Only two major characters manage to transcend the moral and social stagnation of the town. The first is Johnnie Roane, who has outgrown the town while serving in the Army and who returns there from the war only because of the love and memory of his wife Glory. When, at the height of the storm that dramatizes the realities beneath the town's surface serenity, he discovers her infidelity to Lennox's middle-aged Lothario, Ed Barrel, Johnnie breaks free from his idealized past to pursue his dream of becoming a painter in New York. The second is Mrs. Gramby, who embodies the virtues of New England Puritanism. She moves beyond the narrow-minded bigotry of her townspeople and the nostalgia of her personal dreams for her son to become the instrument for social change in the town. In death she, herself, becomes that instrument, for she wills land on the main street of town to the Catholic Church; leaves her house, its contents, and money for its maintenance to her black maid, Portuguese gardener, and cook; and provides six thousand dollars to subsidize Johnnie's pursuit of his dream to become an artist. Marred by the melodramatic conclusion of the reading of the will following Mrs. Gramby's and Ed Barrell's fatal heart attacks, *Country Place* is nevertheless an artistically impressive, realistic treatment of small-town life in New England in which time and place are more important thematically than color and class.

In *The Narrows* Petry moves even further beyond economic determinism as she continues to explore the impart of time and place on the shaping of character. The setting is the black community in Monmouth, Connecticut, another small, typically provincial, white New England town, during the era of Senator Joseph McCarthy's witch hunt for Communists in the State Department. The red neon signs on Dumble Street tell the story of its change; we learn through septuagenarian Abigail Crunch's reverie that

> It was now, despite its spurious early-morning beauty, a street so famous, or so infamous, that the people who lived in Monmouth rarely ever referred to it, or the streets near it, by name; it had become an area, a section, known variously as The Narrows, Eye of the Needle, The Bottom, Little Harlem, Dark Town, Niggertown---because Negroes had replaced those other earliest immigrants, the Irish, the Italians and the Poles.[11]

Petry's fine craftsmanship is immediately apparent in the compelling manner that the structure, style and theme of the narrative fuse as Abbie reflects on what in addition to the hate in the world has brutalized her adopted son Lincoln (Link) Williams, the protagonist. "In Link's case---well, if they hadn't lived on Dumble Street, if the Major had lived longer, if Link had been their own child instead of an adopted child, if she hadn't forgotten about him when he was eight, simply forgotten his existence, if she hadn't had to figure so closely with the little money that she had . . . and eke it out with the small sums she earned by sewing, embroidering, making jelly. If" (13-14).

The theme, simply stated, is that our lives are shaped as much by chance as they are by time and place. "On how peculiar, and accidental, a foundation rests all of one's attitudes toward a people," Abbie thinks. "Frances hears the word Irish and thinks of a cathedral and the quiet of it, the flickering light of the votive candles, the magnificence of the altar, and I see Irishwomen, strong in their faith, holding a family together. Accident? Coincidence? It all depended on what happened in the past. We carry it around with us. We're never rid of it" (235-36). This theme is developed in the main plot---the love affair between Link, a black orphan and Dartmouth graduate, and Camilio Williams, the internationally known heiress to the wealth and power of Monmouth's most prominent white family, the Treadways---and the several tributary subplots. The movement of the main plot is more psychological than chronological, for its pace is frequently interrupted by digressions and flashbacks some eighteen years to Link's childhood. The meeting of the couple in *The Narrows*, their falling in love, the discovery that she is rich and married, his rejection of her for betraying his trust and using him as a black stud, her revenge by claiming he attempted to rape her and thus appealing to traditional color and class prejudice are all influenced by chance and the historical past. The weight of their personal histories and the history of American racism and New England hypocrisy are too heavy a burden for Link and Camilio's love to survive. For breaking the American tribal taboo, Link is murdered by Camilio's mother and husband.

Link, as his name suggests, is the major connection between the past and the present, the white world and the black, the rich and the poor; and it is his consciousness that dominates the third-person point of view that shifts from character to character. Adopted when he was eight by Abbie and Major Crunch and having grown up in Monmouth, Link, at twenty-six, has lost faith in himself and other people. Most of the plot unfolds in his and Abbie's minds. His interior monologues, reverie, and flashbacks and those of the other characters weave a gossamer, impressionistic pattern of events that suggest why he is content to be a bartender at the Last Chance although he was a star athlete and Phi Beta Kappa student at Dartmouth, where he majored in history. Abbie's urge to whiteness and New England respectability confused and frightened him when he was young, making him feel ashamed of his color and "as though he were carrying The Race around with him all the time." These feelings were reinforced in school, where he was cast as Sambo in a minstrel show. But Bill Hod, the influential black owner of the most popular bar and whorehouse in town, and Weak Knees, his cook, who became his surrogate parents when Abbie forgot he existed for three months, taught him the positive aspects of blackness and to fight back if he is attacked.

Because Abbie and Bill had betrayed his love and trust---Abbie by rejecting him during her depression over her husband's death and Bill by severely beating him after finding him in a whorehouse---his belief in his ability to control his life and his desire to conquer the world were destroyed. Although his love for Camilio revives his belief in himself and others, he again feels betrayed when he discovers that she has lied to him about who and what she is. Kidnapped at the end of the novel by Camilio's mother and husband, Link remembers the sensational front-page pictures of a drunk Camilio and an escaped black convict under headlines that inflamed historical color and class prejudice by emphasizing that The Narrows bred crime and criminals: "So it was Jubine Lautrec's Harlot and The Convict by Anonymous that got me in this black Packard. That is one-quarter of the explanation. The other three-quarters reaches back to that Dutch man of Warre that landed in Jamestown in 1619" (399).

The frequency, length and occasional remoteness to the events at hand of the digressions and flashbacks give complexity to the characters but annoyingly impede the progress of the plot and emotionally and psychologically distance the reader from the tragedy of the central character. This is most apparent in the denouement when Link is kidnapped and murdered. Equally passive but more strikingly individualized are Abbie and some of the minor characters. Abbie, a black New England Puritan, is an old widow who is driven by an ambivalence about black people and an obsession with aristocratic values; Major, her dead husband, was a robust, sensitive mountain of a man who used to tell stories about the legendary members of his family, whom he affectionately called "swamp niggers"; Jubine, the "recording angel' of Monmouth, is a man with a deep compassion for "the poor peons" like himself, a man "who spent a lifetime photographing a river, and thus recorded the life of a man in the twentieth century"; Malcolm Powther, a black Judas, is a pompous, worshipful servant to rich white people, whose values he embraces, and to his sensual, promiscuous wife, whom he fears will leave him for another man; and Peter Bullock, the unprincipled owner and publisher of the *Monmouth Chronicle*, which has been transformed over the years from an antislavery newspaper into an anti-black tool of the white ruling class, is a slave to custom, to a house, to a car, to ulcers, and to the major advertisers in his paper, especially the Treadwell family. Petry's use of symbolic characters like Cesar the Writing Man, the wandering poet who scribbles biblical verses on the sidewalk in Monmouth, is also dramatically effective. Early in the novel Cesar gives philosophical resonance to the characters, plot, and theme when he writes the following passage from Ecclesiastes 1:10 in front of the café where Camilio and Link rendezvous: "Is there anything whereof it may be said, See this is new? It hath been already of old time, which was before us" (91).

Petry, like Himes and Wright, is adept at character delineation, but her protagonists are cut from a different cloth than those of her major contemporaries. Rather than sharing the pathology of a Bigger Thomas or Bob

Jones or Lee Gordon, Lutie Johnson and Link Williams are intelligent, commonplace, middle-class aspiring blacks, who, despite the socialized ambivalence resulting from racism and economic exploitation, are not consumed by fear and hatred and rage. Petry's vision of black personality is not only different from that of Himes and Wright, but it is also more faithful to the complexities and varieties of black women, whether they are big-city characters like Mrs. Hedges in *The Street* or small-town characters like Abbie Crunch in *The Narrows*. Ann Petry thus moves beyond the naturalistic vision of Himes and Wright to a demythologizing of American culture and Afro-American character.

---

[1] *The Negro Novel in America*, rev. ed. (New Haven: Yale University Press, 1965), 180.

[2] Ibid.

[3] (Garden City: Anchor Press, 1975), 192-97.

[4] Ibid, 192.

[5] Ibid.

[6] (New York: Hill and Wang, 1980), xv.

[7] Ibid, 18.

[8] Ann Petry, *The Street* (rpt. New York: Pyramid Books, 1961), 130. Subsequently references to this novel will be included parenthetically in the text.

[9] See Noel Schraufnagel, *From Apology to Protest: The Black American Novel* (Deland: Everett/Edwards, Inc., 1973), 42; and Bone, *The Negro Novel*, 185.

[10] Ann Petry, *Country Place* (rpt. Chatham: The Chatham Bookseller, 1971), 1, 3, and 4. Subsequent references to this novel will be included parenthetically in the text.

[11] Ann Petry, *The Narrows* (Boston: Houghton Mifflin, 1953), 5. Subsequently references to this novel will be included parenthetically in the text.

Women in the Novels of Ann Petry (1974)
Thelma J. Shinn

Ann Petry is black; she is also a woman. Yet her novels are not limited
ethnically nor sexually. Her first novel, *The Street* (1946), tells the story of a
young black woman in Harlem; her second, *Country Place* (1947), tells of two
white females in a small Connecticut community; her third, *The Narrows*
(1953), tells of a black man and a white woman in Massachusetts. Petry has
penetrated the bias of black and white, even of male and female, to reveal a
world in which the individual with the most integrity is not only destroyed but is
often forced to become an expression of the very society against which he [she]
is rebelling. She shows that the weak, regardless of race, are misled by illusions
and stifled by poverty.

Particularly for Lutie Johnson in *The Street*, the struggle for survival alone is
so demanding that even her *attempt* to struggle also for some status as a human
being---despite poverty, racial and sexual stereotypes, and loneliness---gives her
more stature in her failure than most people earn in victory.

Lutie can scarcely be said to be attracted to the stereotypes which would
define her as a black woman. Her tension grows out of the seeming inevitability
of her conforming to the stereotypes despite all efforts she may make to break
free, because she is born into a life that gives her new goals but fails to give her
any way to achieve them. She has been born and raised in Harlem; her mother
is dead, and her father is a drunken bootlegger who is more a burden than a
protector.   What family values she has are inherited from her wise and
understanding grandmother. She is separated from her husband and trying to
support herself and her son, Bub. Loneliness, poverty, the apathy and violence
of ghetto life, and prejudice oppose every step she tries to take to improve
herself.

Lutie faces a very different set of problems than do most American heroines.
She never has the alternative of remaining dependent; even the desirable
dependency of marriage is closed to her: "The only way of getting out was to
find a man who had a good job and who wanted to marry her. The chances of
that were pretty slim, for once they found out she didn't have a divorce they lost
interest in marriage and offered to share their apartment with her."[1] She must
make her way in the world on her own. Since survival---preferably at a human
level------is her foremost problem, her "values" seem mainly materialistic; she
dreams of a better job, a cleaner apartment, a more decent neighborhood.

However, Lutie is "handicapped" by a sense of moral integrity which reveals
much of what a woman could be if social pressures did not destroy her first.
Lutie will not live with a man, for instance, without the sanction of marriage,
even though most of the women around her do so freely and thus escape the
necessity of supporting themselves. She maintains her moral stand---and it is

moral because she believes it to be---even in the face of New York divorce laws which at that time made re-marriage nearly impossible.

She is also held back because she refuses to prostitute herself. Every route off "the street," which symbolizes the poverty and its concomitant evils which she is trying to escape, seems to be through offering herself to some man for the alternative he can offer her. Again, such behavior is expected of her: "Sure, Lutie thought as she walked on, if you live on this damn street you're supposed to want to earn a little extra money sleeping around nights. With nice white gentlemen" (57). But she refuses to conform.

Nor are Lutie's strengths all negative. She is attractive and hard-working, has struggled through high school and business school to be eligible for a better-paying job---although the next civil service rating that she is currently struggling to earn will still not pay her enough to enable her to move. That she is warmly loving and sensitive to the feelings of children can be seen when she is working as a maid for the rich white Chandler family. When Mrs. Chandler's brother commits suicide on Christmas morning, the parents forget Little Henry, and Lutie turns to him:

> She picked him up and held him close to
> her, letting him get the feel of her arms
> around him; telling him through her arms
> that his world had not suddenly collapsed
> about him, that the strong arms holding him
> so close were a solid, safe place where he
> belonged, where he was safe. She made
> small, comforting noises under her breath
> until some of the whiteness left his face.
> Then she carried him into the kitchen and
> held him on her lap and rocked him back
> and forth in her arms until the fright went
> out of his eyes. (35)

She not only loves her own son but also tries to treat him with the respect due another human being:

> She wanted to put her arm around him and
> hug him, for he still had tears in his eyes, but
> he had obviously been screwing up his
> courage to the point where he could tell her
> whatever he had on his mind, even though
> he wasn't certain what her reaction would
> be. So she turned toward him and instead of
> hugging him listened to him gravely, trying
> to tell him by her manner that whatever he

had to say was important and she would give
it all her attention. (48)

Her compassion and understanding extend not only to those she loves but even
to those she hates or those who have hurt her. A critic has admired Petry's own
"genuine and generous and undiscriminating . . . creative sympathy" by which
she "*becomes* each character she mentions."[2] and Lutie shares with her creator
this emphatic insight: "As she changed her clothes, she thought, this is the same
thing that happened to Jim. He couldn't stand being shut up in the little house in
Jamaica just like I can't stand being shut up in the apartment" (56). Thus, she
understands the tensions that drove her strong, unemployed husband to another
woman while she worked at the only job she could get---as a maid in
Connecticut---and came home once a month.

Yet this strong, moral young woman---attractive and willing to work---finally
conforms to the worst stereotypes of the black woman. She lives in a dark,
garishly-painted apartment (she had asked for white walls) and, leaving her son
alone, goes to a bar:

> No matter what it cost them, people had to
> come to places like Junto, she thought.
> They had to replace the haunting silences of
> rented rooms and little apartments with the
> murmur of voices, the sound of laughter;
> they had to stay and empty two or three
> small glasses of liquid gold so they could
> believe in themselves again. (95)

As much as she tries to be a good mother, she strikes her son twice, once when
she sees him lighting a cigarette for her father's blowzy mistress, Lil: "And
what was far more terrifying giving Bub a drink on the sly; getting Bub to light
her cigarettes for her. Bub at eight with smoke curling out of his mouth" (12).
The second time she strikes him publicly, when she comes home to find him
shining shoes with a box he made himself: "It's also that you're afraid that if
he's shining shoes at eight, he will be washing windows at sixteen and running
an elevator at twenty-one, and go on doing that for the rest of his life" (470).
Finally, she even commits murder, when the man she has hoped to borrow
money from locks her in his apartment and intends to sleep with her and then to
pass her on to his white boss, Junto. Ironically, she is borrowing to pay a lawyer
to save her son from reform school, but even the lawyer knows that Bub would
be freed without his assistance. Lutie does not know, but she still refuses to
prostitute herself. When she rejects Junto and then Boots as well, Boots tells
her: "I don't take that kind of talk from dames, . . . not even good-looking ones
like you. Maybe after I beat the hell out of you a coupla times, you'll begin to
like the idea of sleeping with me and with Junto" (265). In angry defense, she
grabs a heavy iron candlestick and attacks him: "A lifetime of pent-up

resentment went into the blows . . . . First she was venting her rage against the dirty, crowded street. Finally, and the blows were heavier, faster, now, she was striking at the white world which thrust black people into a walled enclosure from which there was no escape" (265).

Lutie becomes exactly what her society has defined her to be through its stereotypes. In a similar though more gentle way. Betty Friedan has asserted that the society of the 50's created a mystique and real women filled its role: "When a mystique is strong, it makes its own fiction of fact. It feeds on the very facts which might contradict it, and seeps into every corner of the culture, bemusing even the social critics."[3] Lutie Johnson, the very woman who set out to contradict her stereotype, becomes a vehicle of her society. Would we have preferred that she slip quietly into being one of the "little lost girls" working for Mrs. Hedges and Junto as prostitutes? Or like the self-effacing Min who melts into the background because of a "shrinking withdrawal in her way of sitting as though she were trying to take up the least possible amount of space" (20) but who survives because she has learned that "a woman didn't stand much chance along; and because it was too lonely living by herself in a rented room. With a man attached to her she could have an apartment---a real home" (86)?

Lutie Johnson, alone now in Chicago, running from the law, has abandoned her child, the person she loved most in the world. Her problem is compound: she is black and a woman. But the integrity she shows; the strength, love, compassion, and understanding she demonstrates, despite her failure, show what can come from one woman. Her destruction by a society which prefers to foster the survival of the passive Mins argues strongly for a needed change in that society. "The protest," a critic has pointed out, "is that decent human beings are ruined by social forces they cannot come to terms with."[4]

To show that her arguments do not stop with blacks or with the ghetto, Petry follows *The Street* with *Country Place* (1947), which, we are reminded, takes place in a small Connecticut town and in which "the cast . . . is almost entirely white."[5] Although her narrator is a male, Petry announces through him that the topic of women will be discussed:

> It is only fitting and proper that I should
> openly admit to having a prejudice against
> the female of any species, human or animal;
> and yet, like most of the people who admit
> to being prejudiced, I am not consistent, for
> I own a female cat, named Banana. Though
> I am devoted to her, I am well aware that
> she is much closer to the primitive than a
> male cat.[6]

His cat reveals other characteristics well: "Like most females she makes no effort to control her emotions" (2). Of course, our narrator sees men in animal terms as well---especially when those men are involved with a woman: "Ed at that moment was like a tomcat walking stiff-legged toward a female---ready, waiting, hungry" (15).

The novel centers around a mother and a daughter, Lil and Glory, and their respective in-laws. Glory is married to Johnnie Roane, who is just coming home from the war, and she has been living with his mother while he was gone. Lil is married to Mearns Gramby, the richest man in town, who married her when he was forty-seven and took her to live with him and his mother. The story is really of the infidelities of Lil and Glory with the same man---Ed Barrell, the town rake---and of the mothers of their respective husbands. In *Barbary Shore,* Mailer did not write of the effects of the war on the women back home as he had planned; in *Country Place* Petry completes the task for him. She not only demonstrates the collapse of tradition but also showed what society has become; Lil and Glory are vehicles of their society as Lutie is of hers, without, however, her underlying integrity.

Johnnie Roane comes home from the war eager to see his young wife, Glory, and through her to forget what he had been through: "this gives you back some of what you lost---this makes you forget wars and rumors of wars" (30). Glory is wearing a flimsy "Victory" nightgown: "designed by someone who had never been to war, but who knew that wars were won and lost in the bedrooms" (31). Glory is not ready to accept him back: "Women aren't made the same as men," she tells him; "They don't enjoy sexual intercourse" (39).

The cliché, or course, is only an excuse. Glory is a product of the collapse of traditions, and Johnnie's absence has brought out the worst in her: "Instead of a sharp life of demarcation between right and wrong, Gloria and her generation had found only the vague blur made by erasures---it was all that remained of a moral code after the impact of two world wars" (86). Glory has the additional handicap of being beautiful---a handicap also for Lutie, who was "too good-looking to be decent." Glory lacks the moral foundations Lutie gained from her grandmother. Her mother, Lil (interestingly, the name Petry gave to the mistress of Lutie's father), has quickly dismissed her as soon as she marries Johnnie, saying: "I won't have to think about you any more. I can put my mind on myself" (72). Glory is left thinking: "What was it like? Oh, like expecting to find a strong hand which would help you down from a high and lonely place, and then, just as you reached for it, the hand was withdrawn---deliberately, coolly" (72).

Added to these weaknesses in her heritage is her boredom with housewifely tasks after being so popular in high school: "sometimes she quarreled with Johnnie just to break the monotony of their existence" (44). When Johnnie goes into the army and she gets a job at Perkins's store, she feels "free for the first time in her life" (44-45). She makes a decision: "But she knew what she wanted. She did not intend to return to a life of cooking and cleaning in that frame house of theirs . . . . She was the prettiest girl for miles around and all the men who came in the store paid homage to her" (46). The contrast between her beauty and popularity and the dowdiness of wives who shopped at the store was too much for her:

> A few more years and that's the way Johnnie will have me looking. I'll have four or five children and never quite enough money to go around. I'll be riding buses to get to the markets where the food is cheapest; and wearing a house dress under a winter coat; and I'll put on wrinkled cotton stockings in order to save my best ones for Sundays; and carry a cloth knitting bag instead of a pocketbook. I'll start for home at this hour of the day so's to have the supper ready for Johnnie and he'll wolf it down and grunt and reach for the newspaper. Then he'll take his shoes off and sit sprawled in a chair half-asleep until time to go to bed. (74)

The picture she draws, pessimistic though it is, seems hauntingly accurate. The male druggist narrator, although he "found it easy to think of Glory with contempt" once she starts seeing Ed Barrell, cannot improve on the picture much:

> Yet I could not help wondering if she would have remained faithful to Johnnie if there had been no war to interrupt the normal course of their life together. Under other circumstances, she might have remained one of those pretty, more or less useless girls who get married and cook unappetizing meals and keep a house middling clean, and then later on have children, not because they want them but by accident---born of a moment of careless lazy passion. (98-99)

When Glory is given the slightest hope of an alternative to her all-too-normal life, she cannot see that she is choosing an illusion. Rather, she has been brought up to believe in illusions; as Mrs. Roane says about the "fancy ladies" at a trial in town:

> I think that's why so few girls in Lennox used to get in trouble back in those days. They could see for themselves what could and did happen. Nowadays it's not so easy for a girl to see that. I blame the movies more than anything else. They make it easy for a girl to believe that somewhere there's a beautiful carefree life if they could just find it. (126)

Just so does Glory see the glamour of an affair, even up to the time she watches Johnnie fight with Ed after he finds them together in a cabin:

> The expression on her face held him [Johnnie] motionless. Her lips were parted, she was bending forward, her eyes fixed on him. He had seen that same expression on her face when they used to go to the movies. She would sit on the edge of the seat, not moving, lapping up the gaudiest kind of melodrama, so entranced that you knew that she had transformed herself into the glossy heroine on the screen. (194)

So has Glory followed the dictates of her society and made herself a heroine in her own life.

Glory lives in illusions today because she cannot face the realities of tomorrow; her mother, Lil, is living the future of the illusory choice. She had supported herself and her daughter as a seamstress: "And you needed sleep so badly you could cry because you had been sewing all day long and your back ached from bending over the machine; your eyes hurt from putting some special piece of handwork . . . on . . . for some rich bitch who wouldn't want to pay but a fraction of what it was worth" (166). Knowing that the only alternative for her lies in a good marriage, Lil manipulates and plots to win the rich Mearns Gramby---only to find her life "geared to Mrs. Gramby's. " 'Mother doesn't go out in the evening any more. We must stay home with her!' " (167).

Mearns has other ways to keep Lil in line: he never gives her any money unless she "humbly" requests it, and then he expects " a proper show of gratitude" (214). She has a mink coat but nowhere to wear it. She turns for comfort to Ed Barrell because "she needed the undivided attention of a lover; needed and wanted that attention to use as a bulwark against the indifference and the hostility she had found in this house" (162). Barrell, however, wants only "to get her undressed and in bed with him in the shortest possible time" (162). Lil, it seems, cannot win; but she is very good at losing. She even loses when Mrs. Gramby dies, because the will---which Mearns had a hand in as well---gives her anticipated inheritance to the servants.

The older generation of women---Mrs. Roane and Mrs. Gramby---are somewhat more favorably presented. Mainly however, they serve to show the collapse of values.   Mrs. Gramby does have the capacity to see her own mistakes---she recognizes that she has over-protected her son---and to admit that , if Lil were

> Someone else's daughter-in-law, I would
> say that I could see how she came to
> intimacy with the bowlegged man. For she
> must have been desperately disillusioned,
> too, what with the bedroom door kept open
> at night, the cats stalking in and out, the cats
> sleeping on her bed, no money of her own,
> no place of her own in another woman's
> house. (214)

Petry shows once again that the sordidness of reality, the inequities and false illusions of society, and the inadequacies of the possibilities for women rob strong and weak alike of a chance for personal development and a sense of security.

The picture does not brighten in Petry's last novel of this period. *The Narrows*, which brings together the whites and the blacks in another small New England town and shows that when individuals publicly oppose society---when a black man dates a white woman---the problems increase astronomically.

In Link Williams, the young black hero of the novel, Petry has succeeded in creating in depth a man of integrity and stature, no mean feat for a woman writer. But Link, too, is driven to violence and eventually destroyed despite---or because of---his integrity. His death seems to be the inevitable outcome of his love for Camilo, the daughter of a multi-millionaire gun manufacturer and wife to the "Captain." Camilo is white, rich and bored, a beautiful blond, who is used to having her way. Perhaps she is "trying to compensate for not becoming an English instructor at Barnard, a job she was tentatively offered before she married: "It was something that I did by myself with my own brain. Don't laugh at me. I would have been good at it. I would have been somebody in my own right and instead---instead."[7] Whatever the reason, she gives herself to Link with such "absolute and complete surrender, the abandonment to surrender," that he feels her very nature would have forced him to end the affair whatever the outside pressures might or might not be: "it would eventually have been a matter of survival, a refusal to be suffocated, owned, swallowed up" (317). When he does break with her, however, she is sure that the reason is another woman, and she forcefully fulfills the role of the woman scorned: she screams, tears her clothes, and accuses him of rape.

Camilo conforms to female stereotypes---some of the most negative, in fact---just as all of Petry's other women do eventually, whether or not they struggle against such conformity. A good example is Link's "aunt" Frances Jackson, whose first description is given by Link himself: "F. K. Jackson is right at least ninety-nine times out of a hundred. It's very difficult for us average humans to love a female with a batting average like that" (14). Frances then fills in the portrait herself:

> I see my father . . . and he's saying, "Frank, you know you're got a man's mind." Anywhere I go here in Monmouth, I can always see myself---too tall, too thin, too bony. Even at twelve. And too bright, able , and unable and unwilling to conceal the fact that I have brains. When I finished high school I went to college, to Wellesley, where I was a kind of Eighth Wonder of the World, because I was colored. I hadn't been there very long when the dean sent for me and asked me if I was happy there. I looked straight at her and I said, "My father didn't send me here to be happy, he sent me here to learn." . . . A college graduate. All hung over with honors and awards and prizes. And I knew I'd never get married, never have any children. So I was going to be a doctor . . . . My father was along here and I couldn't bear to leave him, and there was the business he had built up so slowly and so carefully. So I became an undertaker too. (234-5)

She knows that her future has been determined for her; despite her intelligence and talents, Frances is doomed to live her life as circumstances have shaped it.

Ann Petry does not ignore the particular problems [of] blacks; her portrayals, especially of Link Williams and L[utie] Johnson, in both their individual triumphs and their socially-caused failures, display potentially enough for admiration and oppression enough for anger to satisfy any black militant. Her first concern, however, is for acceptance and realization of individual possibilities---black and white, male and female. Her novels protest against the entire society which would contrive to make any individual less than human, or even less than he can be.

---

[1] Ann Petry, *The Street* (New York: Pyramid Books, 1961), 55. Subsequent references are to this edition.

[2] David Littlejohn, *Black on White* (New York: Viking Press, 1966), 155.

[3] Betty Friedan, *The Feminine Mystique* (New York: Dell, 1963), 53.

[4] Chester E. Eisinger, *Fiction of the Forties* (Chicago: University of Chicago Press, 1963), 70.

[5] Littlejohn, 154.

[6] Ann Petry, *Country Place* (Boston: Houghton Mifflin, 1947), 1. Subsequent references are to this edition.

[7] Ann Petry, *The Narrows* (Boston: Houghton Mifflin, 1953), 95. Subsequent references are to this edition.

(1980-1990)
Journeying from Can't to Can and Sometimes Back to Can't
from *No Crystal Stair* (1984)
Gloria Wade Gayles

Lutie Johnson was the first female protagonist in black American fiction to commit murder as an expression of her rage, and the novel in which she appears, *The Street*, was the first novel by a black woman in this country to receive significant literary attention beyond the decade in which it was published. It has not, however, received literary applause. Robert Bone considers it worthy of comment in *The Negro Novel in America* (1958), but he calls it a *"roman`a these . . .*which offers a superficial analysis of life in a northern ghetto."[4] Noel Schraufnagel, in *From Apology to Protest: The Black American Novel* (1973), praises *The Street*'s realistic illustration of "the effects of environment and oppression on an individual," but considers "the melodramatic conclusion" more appropriate for "popular pulp fiction [than for] a fine novel."[5] Addison Gayle, who rates many black proletariat novels highly for their theme and craft, writes that Petry's work, though "provocative and powerful," is weakened by her failure to develop a "denouement [and] to revarnish her work, add color to her painting." Common to all these critical assessments is a comparison of *The Street* with Richard Wright's *Native Son* [1940]. "Change the characters," Addison Gayles writes, and *The Street* becomes "little more than a carbon copy" of *Native Son*. "Both Wright and Petry wrote in the naturalistic idiom; both were interested in the effects of the environment upon psychological make-up of characters; both were aware of the images handed down from the past";[6] and both created antiheroes driven to murder by the exigencies of black life in white America.

In reciting the similarities between *Native Son* and *The Street*, critics ignore the significance of a major dissimilarity: the sexual identities of the protagonists of the two novels. Wright's protagonist, Bigger Thomas, is male. Petry's protagonist, Lutie Johnson, is female. By definition, then, their realities are different, just as Wright's vision as a male artist is, by definition, different from Petry's vision. Moreover, Bigger Thomas is a young male in his late teens who has not functioned in the sexual roles of husband and father. Lutie Johnson, on the other hand, is a mature woman in her early thirties who has functioned in the role of wife and is the mother of an eight-year-old son. Critics who see Petry's vision as but a "carbon copy" of Wright's ignore the extent to which a character's age, sexual identity, and sexual roles affect his or her reality. Critics do recognize that Petry's aim is to show that a black woman, like a black man, struggles against forces in the environment that would circumscribe her life. However, writing from a male perspective, they ignore the added burdens that being a woman places on her. They do not understand that Petry's decision to place a black woman in an environment that is a "carbon copy"of the environment in which Bigger Thomas is victimized suggests that Petry intended to document not only the impact of racial oppression on the psychological makeup of her character, but the impact of sexual oppression as well. They fail to understand the thesis that Beatrice Royster develops with skill and sensitivity in her work: "*The Street* is the ambience of tragedy for the black family of the twentieth century"[7] in that it documents the brutal attacks made upon her because she is black and because she is female.

When the novel begins, Lutie Johnson, estranged from her husband, is alone with her eight-year-old son in a world of violence and corruption. Lutie looks for a reasonable apartment on 116th Street, in the very heart of Harlem. This will be but a temporary residence because she intends to fight her way out of poverty and into prosperity. The opening scene of the novel, considered by some critics a masterpiece of symbolism and imagery, introduces Petry's "dismal view of human nature" and her belief that "tragic disharmony" characterizes both the universe and human nature. A cold November wind "announces . . . the discord between man and nature"[8] and foreshadows Lutie's struggles in the ghetto. Like a monster with a mind of its own and an indomitable will to destroy, the wind

> did everything it could to discourage the
> people walking along the street. It found all
> the dirt and dust and grime on the sidewalk
> and lifted it up so that the dirt got into their
> noses, making it difficult to breathe; the dust
> got into their eyes and blinded them; and the
> grit stung their skins. [9]

The people on "the street" quickly submit to the wind's onslaught, for they have learned the futility of struggle. Theirs is a conditioned response that sends them "stooping" or rushing for cover. Lutie has no such conditioned response, for she is a newcomer to this environment of poverty, violence, and helplessness. She has lived amid opulence and power as a maid for a "filthy rich" white family in suburban Connecticut and, from their matter-of-fact discussions of stocks and bonds, has come to believe in the American capitalist dream. Into her very soul she has absorbed the philosophy that "anybody could be rich if he wanted to and worked hard enough and figured it out carefully enough" (32).

Petry draws heavily on her experiences as a newspaper reporter in the bowels of Harlem and, enraged by what she saw firsthand, she attempts to "show why the Negro has a high crime rate, a high death rate, and little or no chance of keeping his family intact in northern cities." In fact, she succeeds, as Richard Wright does not, in giving us the concrete particulars of this reality. She explains that "there are no statistics in the book . . .not as columns of figures," but they are "present in the background," in the hardships of people "who live in overcrowded tenements."[10] "The street" is a wasteland of human suffering, "bordered by garbage cans" that symbolize how life here is discarded with impunity by a system that "sucked the humanity out of people---slowly, surely, inevitably" (144). On "the street" the women work as domestics, hand pressers, or prostitutes; the men work in menial, low-paying jobs, or not at all. The children, left unattended because of chronic family breakdown, begin in their preteens to prepare for a lifetime of taking drugs, pimping, or anything that short-circuits their sordid reality. All the people on "the street" are confined to narrow and suffocating roles prescribed by white America, and too many have "lost the ability to protest against anything" (125).

Lutie Johnson protests against everything that hinders her because she is black. In fact, in attitude and behavior she is a forerunner of the black militant of the sixties, refusing to "scrape and bow" to white people. Her pride will not let her wear the expensive clothes Mrs. Chandler gives her after a few wearings. Her pride will not permit her to laugh and jest with white butchers who, rumor has it, use embalming fluid on the meats sold in Harlem. And her pride will not let her accept change from the hands of a white grocer, "because he was white and forcing him to make the small extra effort of putting the change on the counter gave her a feeling of power" (44). The central point of Petry's racial portrait of Lutie is the character's desire for wider options than those synonymous with the black experience.

Petry foreshadows Lutie's tragedy at the very beginning of the novel with an image of walls that move gradually and persistently to narrow the already small space in which she is trapped: the walls in the apartment "were reaching out for her ---bending and swaying toward her in an effort to envelop her" (13). After each new wave of self-confidence---always without cause---Lutie pushes harder against the "bending and swaying" walls. Everytime she returns to the apartment after being on "the street," she finds that the "walls seemed to come in toward her, to push against her with more force and persistence" (58). On the night that she emerges from her self-imposed isolation to enjoy a evening of forgetfulness in Junto's Bar and Grill, the walls seem to "walk at" her (56). When she learns that she has no chance of making money singing at Junto's, when she senses intuitively that her relationship with her son is being threatened by their poverty and by her growing impatience, and when her funds are depleted and she can no longer believe in her lofty goals, she realizes that "from the time she was born, she had been hemmed into an ever-narrowing space, until now she was very clearly walled in" (201). The stage is set for Lutie's initiation into a world of violence.

From well-articulated plans for success that would be easy to carry out if she "worked hard enough," she moves to a sense of urgency about the need to fight against the doors that "have been slammed in her face" because she is "poor and black." She would "shove [them] open; she would beat and bang on [them] and push against [them] and use a chisel in order to get [them] open" (118). Lutie is "both a conscious and unconscious fighter and rebel," writes Vernon Lattin, "a rebel, ironically, in the American tradition."[11] The irony to which Lattin refers is present in every scene of the novel and saturates every effort Lutie makes to "fight her way out." She fights for lofty alternatives to the suffocating exigencies of black life, but she does not understand the omnipresent force of "the street" and its various "traps," so she fails to choose the proper weapons for her battle. She does not recognize that, in spite of all of her plans and hard work, she will always be the offspring of black people who are systematically programmed into powerlessness.

The story progresses swiftly to tragedy. Her son, Bub, atttemps to earn money decently to contribute to their living expenses, but he falls innocently into a trap the super set for him and ends up in juvenile detention. From this moment on, Lutie's blinding naivete is presented as a tragic flaw in her character. She goes, naively, to an attorney on "the street" for assistance with her son's case, not realizing that neither bond nor legal service is required to get her son out of detention. Naively, she seeks a loan from Boots Smith, a seasoned veteran of "the street," who cannot enter into a contract of dignity, for, as Lutie herself sees, he is a man who has "no softness, nothing to indicate that he would ever bother to lift a finger to help anyone but himself" (98). When he attempts to rape Lutie in exchange for the money, the walls close in on her. Consumed by rage, Lutie strikes Boots Smith again and again, venting her rage against all the forces that have relentlessly conspired to destroy her. In the end, a murderer, she has no dreams, no plans, and no future. She has learned in the most tragic way, writes Vernon Lattin, that the American Dream that shaped her ambitions was always "itself . . . the spring that operated the trap."[12]

In interviews Ann Petry has emphasized that race stands at the center of her artistic vision. I have already quoted her intention to demonstrate the crippling effects of racism and capitalism on the lives of the people who live in ghettoes across America---and this literary goal she achieves brilliantly. The fact that Petry does not speak of sexual oppression in interviews about her novel does not mean that she fails to include it in her artistic vision. It is no accident that she opens her novel with a scene juxtaposing racial oppression and sexual violence, suggesting the forces that will victimize Lutie Johnson. The scene introduces the reader to the filth and poverty of "the street," but its drama is the sexual violence of the superintendent. It is significant that Lutie can tolerate the filth of the apartment, but she is "drunk with fear" (12) of the superintendent's sexual desires. She sees him "eating her up with his eyes" and knows, even when her back is turned, that he was 'sniffing on my trail, slathering, slobbering after me like some dark hound of hell seeking out, tonguing along the back of me" (21).

Critics do not overlook the role the superintendent plays in Petry's protest against the environment, but they often see only half of that role. They understand that he symbolizes the ultimate in victimization, for he "has come to represent the underground forces symbolized by the street itself . . . and survives mainly on sexual fantasies," writes Addison Gayle.[13] But critics do not understand that the superintendent's perversity is but an exaggeration of the sexual exploitation that runs rampant in the ghetto, unchallenged and institutionally supported. Consequently, they fail to see that Lutie, as a *woman*, responds to the first appearance of the superintendent with *"instinctive, immediate fear"* (18).

This fear is obviously the result of the socialization that teaches black women about their physical vulnerability. Lutie remembers marrying at the young age of seventeen because her grandmother believed marriage would save her from men like the super. And she has always known that as a black woman she is hated by white women and sought after by white men. In the home of the white family in Connecticut, she is suspect not because she is black and therefore must be dishonest and lazy (purely racial stereotypes), but because she is presumed to be promiscuous and whorish (racial and sexual stereotypes). White women assume that "all colored girls [are] whores" (31), and white men "ain't never willing to let a black woman alone. Seems like they all got a itch and urge to sleep with 'em" (33).

The image of the black woman as whore is not confined to white people. It festers in the minds of black men and creates a code of sexual behavior that sometimes results in the abuse of black women. Wright alludes to the problems of black women in his moving portrait of Bessie, who drowns her despair in drink and expresses her self-denial in sex that is at best an abusive, pleasurable way for Bigger to assert his manhood. That Wright understands the plight of such women is demonstrated in Bessie's tragic plea for her life:

> All my life's been full of hard trouble. If I
> wasn't hungry, I was sick. And if I wasn't
> sick, I was in trouble. I ain't never bothered
> nobody. I just worked hard every day as
> long as I can remember, till I was tired
> enough to drop.[14]

But Wright's emphasis is on the forces that thwart Bigger's manhood, not on those that thwart Bessie's womanhood. Ann Petry, on the other hand, reaches into the souls of black women for their peculiar agony. *The Street* is an explosion of the sounds of racial and sexual agony. The sounds from the run-down apartment buildings are the sounds of men beating their wives or abusing their mistresses. They are heard in the super's treatment of Min. They are heard crashing through broken windows as nameless men scream their obscenities at nameless women: "you black bitch, I oughta' killed you long ago" (136). And they are heard in Boots Smith's announcement that he will teach Lutie a lesson. As a man, he does not "take that kind of talk from dames . . . . Not even good-looking ones like you. Maybe after I beat the hell out of you a couple times, you'll begin to like the idea of sleeping with me and with Junto" (265).

The central point of Petry's novel is that poor black women are beaten spiritually and economically by "the street," and because they are women, they are beaten physically by black men. All of the violence on "the street," writes Beatrice Royster, "grows out of or is precipitated by, sexual encounters between men and women."[15] This fact does not mean black men are "the enemy." They are not. They are the "other" victims of "the street." Like Brownfield in Alice Walker's *The Third Life of Grange Copeland,* they have been programmed into sexism and destroyed by racism, and the two experiences are inextricable in America. While they elicit Petry's rage, they are within reach of her sympathy.

Petry repeatedly describes women who work and men who do not work, painting a picture of inequality in the thirties and forties that is not far from Sojourner Truth's observation in the nineteenth century that "colored women go out washing, which is about as high as a colored woman gets, and their men go about idle, strutting up and down."[16] But she immediately explains that the men are idle because white people enslave black women in white homes and crush the manhood of black men by keeping them unemployed. This history explains why Lutie's rage is heavily commingled with a sense of guilt. Because she chose to work and function in a role society assigns to men, Lutie believes she was partly responsible for the failure of her marriage.

Lutie's attitude toward "woman's place" is shaped by her middle-class aspirations. Indeed, Petry suggests that Lutie is partly responsible for her own failures by calling into question her strivings for upward mobility. Lutie believes that she and her son, Bub, are better than other blacks in Harlem because she has seen inside the workings of white America and therefore knows how to dream the right dreams. The world of stocks and bonds, of luxury and waste, of things and treasures, is the world to which she aspires. She wants Bub to sleep in rooms that are decorated with carpets, curtains, and fine mahogany furniture. She wants him to wear knickerbockers and attend the best of prep schools, as the Chandler boy does. And for herself, in her hidden fantasies, she wants to be like the white middle-class women whose lives are glorified in subway ads, magazines, and movies.

She believes that women should stay in the home because that is what middle-class white women do. Class, then, causes Lutie to internalize cultural assumptions about both her race and her sex, and it prevents her from seeing the direction from which the light in the tunnel of her darkness might possibly come.

Making it possible for black women to stay in "their place," as women is one of the solutions Petry proposed to the problems of family disorganization and teenage crime she wrote about as a journalist. She believed that if women could stay home and tend the hearth, the family unit would be stronger; and if the family unit were stronger, black youths would be sheltered from the pervasive violence in Harlem. In the novel she implies that if all things were in place for blacks in white America, Lutie would be home and her husband, Jim, would be gainfully employed. Petry's response to "woman's place," then, like Lutie's is unquestionably tied to the problems of racism and poverty. However, by documenting the double jeopardy of women in white America, Petry was a harbinger of the sexual consciousness that broke through in the late sixties and seventies, allowing black women to question the assumption that race is the only deterrent to their self-actualization. No matter how deeply she felt about the victimization of black men, Petry did not conceal from the reader her observation that black men are yet another force with which black women must contend.

Implicit in every sympathetic portrait Petry draws of victimized men is her conviction that they in turn victimize black women. They use women as buffers against the cold wind of "the street," as givers of pleasure, as money-making objects if they are pimps, and as credentials of their masculinity. Lutie's father, "Pop," for example, brings "a procession of buxom lady friends" home, exposing Lutie at a young age to the sordid in life and going against "Granny's unconcealed disapproval," because "using women was a way of demonstrating his manhood" (55). The same point is made about Jim, who attempts to regain his lost manhood by bringing in another woman as cook, housekeeper, and lover. All the men in the novel partake of woman's emotional nourishment, woman's body, and sometimes woman's earnings to keep themselves on their feet.

Lutie Johnson's struggle to maintain her dignity as a woman is as difficult as her struggle to achieve the American Dream. In her life they are inseparable struggles, though failure in the one need not preclude success in the other for the black woman. The point critics often miss in their analysis of Lutie Johnson is that she never compromises her woman's pride for her black aspirations. When all the signs indicate that Lutie could, in fact, make her way out of the filth and violence of "the street," she holds fast to her image of herself as a woman of dignity and hopelessly confronts Boots Smith. Surely this fact alone makes the novel more than a "carbon copy" of *Native Son*. As Beatrice Roysters claims, *The Street* is one of the most powerful "mandate[s] for black women to dismantle the cloak of blind innocence, to recognize the falsity of the American Dream . . . [and most significantly] to resist exploitation of their bodies by men of all races." [17]

---

[4] Bone, *The Negro Novel in America*, 180.

[5] Schraufnagel, *From Apology to Protest*, 42.

[6] Gayle, *The Way of the World, 196.*

[7] Beatrice Royster, "The Ironic Vision of Four Black Women Novelists," Ph.D. diss. Emory University, 1975, 158.

[8] Ibid, 154.

---

[9] Petry, *The Street*, 7. Subsequent references to this work appear in the text.

[10] Ivy, "Ann Petry Talks About Her First Novel," 198.

[11] Vernon Lattin, "Ann Petry and the American Dream," 69. [See elsewhere in this text]

[12] Ibid, 70.

[13] Gayle, *The Way of the World,* 194.

[14] Richard Wright, *Native Son* (New York: Harper and Row, 1940; Perennial Classics, 1966), 215. For an interesting discussion of Wright's treatment of black women characters, see Sylvia Keady's study, "Richard Wright's Women Characters and Inequality," *Black American Literature Forum* 10 (1976): 123-126.

[15] Royster, "The Ironic Vision," 155.

[16] Truth, 566.

[17] Royster, "The Ironic Vision," 171.

The Significance of Ann Petry (1987)
Calvin C. Hernton

In 1946, with the publication of *The Street*, Ann Petry made a very special contribution to the tradition of black literature. Her novel includes all of the themes of protest historically associated with black writing. But the novel goes beyond these themes and is a milestone in the development of black writing because of its import for the specific tradition of black women writers. In one sweep, *The Street* captures the essence of the literature written by black women in the past while it brings to light the issues of the literature proliferated by today's black women. Moreover, in 1946, Petry made the boldest stroke that a black woman author has ever dared. *The Street* was the first writing in which a black man is killed by a black woman for being an unmitigated villain in the oppression of that woman.

It should be repeatedly emphasized that black women have always cried out against injustice. The first American-born woman to speak in public was black. In the early 1800s in Boston, Marie Stewart rallied in defense of her black sisters. "Oh, Ye Daughters of Africa!" she called to them. Although Stewart spoke and wrote for the uplifting of both women and men, she was jeered by the men because she was a female. Pleadingly she cried out to the men, "What If I Am a Woman!" Again, in 1827, in the first newspaper owned by black men (*Freedom's Journal*), Stewart sent in a letter under a pseudonym, "Matilda," pleading with the men to include specifically black women in the uplifting of the race. During the heyday of the anti-slavery and women's rights struggles, another voice, Sojourner Truth, cried out to the world, "Ain't I a Woman!" Then when the men were pursuing their newly won freedom, another black woman, Anna Julia Cooper, pleaded the question of "When and Where" would black women enter. All during the 1800s and well into the twentieth century black women writers, poets, and novelists, continued to plea for the humanity of black women. It should be noted also that Frank J. Webb, W. E. B. DuBois, Benjamin Brawley, Wallace Thurman, and especially Jean Toomer and Langston Hughes, along with other early black men writers, had also written of the hardships and virtues of black women. But no one until Petry, male or female, had so thoroughly portrayed black women as victims of Multiple Oppression, and no one had so boldly portrayed black men as the levelers of a significant measure of that oppression.

The Street marked the juncture between the restraining colorations of nineteenth-century Victorian "colored lady's" writings (as in Frances Harper's *Iola LeRoy*, 1892, and even later in Gwendolyn Brooks's *Maude Martha,* 1953) and the forging of a proletarian black woman's fiction. Since the first wave of black migration out of the South shortly after the demise of Reconstruction, black women had been coming to the northern cities. But there had simply been no serious treatment of black underclass women, neither in the narratives and early novels, nor in the "primitivist" and "tragic mulatto" portrayals of Harlem

Renaissance writers, such as Claude McKay and Nella Larsen or Jessie Fauset. Although Janie in Hurston's *Their Eyes Were Watching God* (1937) was a breakaway from the restraining Victorian portrayal of black women, and despite Dorothy West's Cleo Judson in *The Living Is Easy* (1946), until Petry there had been no such women as Lutie Johnson, Min, and Mrs. Hedges in the entire history of black fiction. No one had made a thesis of the debilitating mores of economic, racial and sexual violence let loose against black women in their new urban ghetto environment. In both texture and substance, *The Street* is the first work of social realism and naturalism written from an all but complete Womanist Perspective.

[2]

Similarly, what Petry achieved for the history and future of black women's literature, the 1940 publication of *Native Son* by Richard Wright achieved the same thing for black men's literature. Wright and Petry had been preceded by a whirlwind cultural movement in the 1920s which was dubbed the New Negro/Harlem Renaissance. The first movement of its kind, the Renaissance writers vigorously debated the age-old issue of how should Negroes be portrayed in works of art. As already mentioned, Dubois and Langston Hughes published manifesto articles---"Criteria for Negro Art" and "The Negro Artist and the Racial Mountain"---in which they respectively set forth their views of what amounted to a "Black Aesthetic" for the first time in the annals of black writing.[1] Again, a decade later, in 1937, a third black aesthetic manifesto--- "Blueprint for Negro Literature"---was published in *Challenge* magazine (later *New Challenge*) by Richard Wright. Black male writers during the 1930s, such as Langston Hughes, Roi Ottley, Walter White, and others, as well as those before and after them, were always concerned about, in the words of Langston Hughes, the "elevation and illumination of the Negro people." In his article, however, Wright incorporated the unprecedented assertion that a Marxist philosophy should be the ruling principle in the treatment of the Negro situation in America. Thus, in 1940, *Native Son* became the first black social realist-naturalist novel to depict consciously the sundry effects of racism and capitalism on black males in the American urban ghetto environment. Highlighting the black family, and connecting the political with the personal, the novel decisively emphasizes the plight of black male youth in a torrential masculine landscape in which the protagonist, Bigger Thomas, murders two women, one white and one black.

In addition to similarities in genre (social realism and naturalism), there are other apparent similarities between *Native Son* and *The Street*. The protagonists of both novels, Bigger Thomas and Lutie Johnson, are young American-born blacks living in ghetto areas of two sprawling urban cities, Bigger on the South Side of Chicago, and Lutie on 116th Street, Harlem, New York. Both are conscious of being hated and oppressed by white society. Both share a sense of fear and are haunted by feelings of guilt. Lutie is estranged from her family and loved ones; although Bigger lives with his family, a brother, sister, and mother, there is no understanding between them and their relations are strained by distance and coldness. Both Bigger and Lutie are ambitious. Though he knows not what, Bigger yearns to be "something." Although Lutie is sure of what she wants out of life, she, like Bigger, feels trapped, thwarted, is nagged by an underlying sense of impending doom. In all of this they seem to be kindred spirits.

Although the situations of Bigger and Lutie appear to be the same, and while the similarities may be real enough, a closer look reveals that the qualitative, substantive aspects of Lutie's and Bigger's conditions are miles apart. There is no familyness among members of Bigger's family, nevertheless Bigger is living in the house with his family, and he has never been married. Lutie, on the other hand, has been married and is now estranged from her husband as well as from her parents. She is a "single parent" living in a cramped room in a run-down building with her young son. While Bigger has his gang cronies and a girlfriend, Bessie, Lutie is completely alone, with no friends of either sex. Lutie murders one person, a black man who has persistently offended her and who attempts to rape her. She murders him in an explosion of rage without aforethought. Bigger, on the other hand, murders two women out of "instinctive" fear---one, a white woman, "accidentally"; the other, his girlfriend, he murders with calculated brutality after having raped her, because he perceived her as a liability to his safety.

For all of Wright's Marxist analysis, *Native Son* is at heart of a psychological novel. Wright was possessed by a driving pursuit of the effects of oppression on the psychology of its victims. Although the novel is written in the third-person narrative, and though the Chicago landscape blanketed with the whiteness of snow is very present, it is Bigger, and Bigger alone, who dominates the novel. Or, rather, it is Richard Wright himself who dominates every page of the gruesome tale.

It was this way with almost everything Wright wrote, the sheer power of his imposing narrative always makes you know it is Wright writing and talking to you. The much criticized Marxist analytical summation speech of Bigger's lawyer, Max, is nobody but Richard Wright expounding.

The Street, by contrast, is written in the third person in earnest. So earnest, in fact, that frequently the third-person narrative easily translates into the first person. Petry sets Lutie loose on her own: I see what Lutie sees, I feel her feelings, I experience her being, I get angry with her for her blindnesses and for having emotions and beliefs with which I disagree. The same applies to the other characters, both the major and minor ones as well. They exist independently of Ann Petry. Likewise, so does the world in which the characters grapple with the forces of existence; without any effort on our part, we experience the milieu of 116th Street and the surrounding white world as living organisms in themselves.

The Street, moreover, deals with not just one dominating character, but with lots of people. In addition to Lutie Johnson, Min, and Mrs. Hedges, there are in-depth portrayals of Boots Smith and William Jones (the "Super"), and the white man, Junto. There are a host of other "minor" characters both black and white, including Lutie's husband and family and, of course, her son, Bud (sic). There are the ever-present women, men, and children of 116th Street, the young girls, the older "bag ladies," and the eternal "domestics" of all work. We experience the changing of the seasons along with the moods and countenances of the *black masses* hanging out on corners, on stoops, and in the joints, hustling, fighting, laughing, drinking, trudging along, existing and being. *The Street*, the novel, becomes more than a work of art. It is a living, organic life, utterly real and altogether natural.

In *Native Son*, none of this is portrayed. There is only Bigger, only Wright, dominating the scene. Despite the singular power of Wright's heady prose, *Native Son* is far from being comparable to the richness of *The Street*.

Yet the publication of *Native Son* established Richard Wright as the patriarch of black writing. He, of course, had his detractors. But Wright's greatness as the first revolutionary black man writer is unquestionable. During his lifetime, he was accorded worldwide recognition and achieved immortal fame.

By comparison, Petry has received only a meager amount of acclaim, and that was short-lived. Lots of people thought *The Street* was a "carbon copy" of *Native Son* (which was also said of *Knock on Any Door*, by Willard Motley). The great white critic of black fiction, Robert Bone, wrote ---*incredibly!*---that Petry's novel offered a "superficial analysis of life in the ghetto." Petry was judged as just another one of those Negro women writers. Only recently has her contribution begun to receive adequate evaluation, and solely on the part of black women literary purveyors. In her Ph.D. thesis, *The Ironic Vision of Four Black Women Novelists*, Beatrice Royster included *The Street* as an example of an immortal, visionary piece of writing. Gloria Wade-Gayles devoted about fifteen cogent pages to *The Street* in her water-breaking literary work, *No Crystal Stair: Visions of Race and Sex in Black Women's Fiction.*

Let's face it. *Native Son* is an astounding Patriarchal achievement. In its pages Richard Wright is exclusively concerned with the denial of Manhood to black American youth and the resulting demise of psychological health of inner city black men. Nothing at all is said about the womenfolk. The fact of a singular dominance in *Native Son* is sufficiently indicative of the novel's overriding phallic perspective. In the room, as Bigger smothers to death the limp drunken white woman, and in the abandoned tenement building, as he actually rapes and slaughters his black girlfriend, he experiences a violent inner passion that is orgasmic.

In a revised version of his "Blueprint" manifesto, Wright acknowledged the Triple Oppression of black women.[2] He also depicted black male sexism in various later works, such as, for example, in the posthumously published novel *Lawd Today*. Wright, moreover, held in great esteem the writing of Gertrude Stein and formed a mentor-type friendship with her. Nevertheless, he never got around to treating or portraying black women in his work from a woman's perspective. Again, this is not to take away from Wright. Wright, along with John A. Williams and Chester Himes, is among the world's greatest socially committed male-oriented writers.

[3]

In *The Street*, however, Petry's concern richly varies over a wide range of people and sensibilities. Most of all, she treats black women as both black *and* female, and, in addition to racism and capitalism, Petry incorporates the third dimension in black women's lives---sexism. *The Street* is a pioneer Womanist Feminist novel, depicting the nature of Geometric Oppression that is imposed on black women from both without and within the black race. To refer to this oppression as simply "triple"---merely to add up in an arithmetic way the effects of capitalism, racism, and sexism---does not begin to calculate the Terribleness of *Geometric* Oppression. The diagram shown will help to illuminate the multiple machinations of geometric oppression in *The Street*. . . .

On all sides Lutie Johnson is trapped by the big three *isms* of American white and black societies. At the top is Capitalism, represented and personified in the novel by the Chandlers, for whom Lutie works as a "domestic." The Chandlers (both the men and the women) are also racist and sexist toward Lutie. Wealthy and decadent, they are in possession of the American Dream, they have all the "finer things" of the American way. Below the Chandlers is Junto, a misfit white man who owns property and joints in the black ghetto, along with other such enterprises elsewhere. He is a parasitic exploiter of the misery and poverty of the black community. He controls Mrs. Hedges, who lives in one of his run-down tenements, and who runs a whorehouse. On either side of the diagram are Racism and Sexism. To the left there is William Jones, the superintendent of the building in which both Lutie and Mrs. Hedges live. Beneath Jones is Min, the battered girl-woman he keeps and treats like he treats his dog. Still on the left are Jim, Lutie's husband, and Pop, Granny, and Lil, members of her family household. There is a lawyer on the right, a minor character who is nevertheless significant in Lutie's terribleness.

Down the center are Junto's Bar and the men, women, girls, and boys of 116th Street. On the right is Boots Smith, another one of Junto's ghetto puppets.

On the left is Bud's white school-teacher, Miss Rinner. Mr. Crosse is on the right, owner of a singer's school where Lutie seeks employment.

Lutie Johnson is in the center. She and her young son, Bud, are in the JACKPOT.

All of these people, in and through the machination of the big three *isms*, are gunning for Lutie Johnson, and keep her in an ever-mounting state of frustration and insecurity. The dimensions of Lutie's oppression are not one plus one plus one, but one time two times three times all the people and impersonal forces she encounters. The sheer weight of this oppression is indeed *terrible*.

[4]

Lutie's situation is that she has been married to Jim, and they have a son, Bud. Soon the family runs into trouble, Jim loses his job, cannot find another one, and Lutie has to work as a "domestic" requiring her to "live in," and can only visit her family once every two weeks. One day Lutie comes home unexpectedly and catches Jim with a woman. Jim is drunk, as he has taken to drinking since being unable to countenance his wife's working "outside the home." Lutie is hurt to the quick, a fight ensues, after which Lutie takes Bud and leaves the family. Short of money, she and Bud find a cubbyhole of a place in the heart of the ghetto on 116th Street. Alone, isolated, a "single parent," Lutie desperately seeks to find suitable employment and to raise her son in a decent manner. But everywhere she turns she runs head-on into people perceiving and behaving toward her as but a sex object. The superintendent of her building, William Jones, gets the "hots" for Lutie, constantly harasses her, and eventually attempts to rape her.

Mrs. Hedges' apartment is a whorehouse; she sits all day peering out of her window down on the street looking for prospective whores among the young girls newly arrived from down south. She perceives Lutie as a "prized catch" for her boss and friend, Junto, who owns the building and provides protection for Mrs. Hedges through his "connections" with the local cops.

Nobody perceives Lutie as she is, but merely as a potential whore; they *insist* on it. The rich white family, the Chandlers, for whom she is obliged to work as a "domestic," regard her as a workhorse and as a sexual threat to the female Chandlers, who believe all black women are promiscuous sluts ready to jump in bed with any and every white man. Lutie receives racist and sexist harassment from Mr. Crosse at his singer's school, where she answered an advertisement for prospective singers, and she is rebuffed by other white and black employment prospects all along the way. "A nice-looking girl like you . . . a nice-looking girl like you . . . should not have to worry about money . . . a nice-looking girl like you . . . ."

Growing grim, Lutie maintains her determination to "make it" in the world in a manner befitting a respectable colored woman with a young son, a son who by now is mystified by his mother's growing bitterness and her being away from home so much, and who fares poorly in school where his white teacher, Miss Rinner, hates the "smell" of her black pupils. Also, by now, Jones has become totally crazed over not having Lutie and begins to dog and batter Min, his live-in sex servicer, who in turn harbors feelings of resentment toward Lutie. "Everything was all right until *she* came," growls Min.

Tired and frustrated, one evening Lutie wanders into Junto's bar and grill on the corner of 116th Street. As when she walks along the street, in the bar she is instantly perceived as "ready meat." Boots Smith, the black henchman of Junto, spots Lutie and proceeds to "hit" on her. Boots "dates" her for an instant, rides her in his shiny pimp's car and, when rebuffed, offers her a singing job with a band he manages. Junto hears of this and persuades Boots to set a trap for Lutie. Junto wants her for himself.

Meanwhile, because of Jones, Bud has gotten arrested. Desperate, Lutie goes to a lawyer who does not inform her that she does not need a lawyer because Bud is under age and will no doubt be released on probation into Lutie's custody. Instead, the lawyer says his fee will be $200. Seeking to borrow the money from Boots (who is "rolling dough") Lutie is lured to Boots's apartment on "Sugar Hill" under pretense of being lent the money. Here, finally, and fatally, Lutie strikes back.

[5]

All of this is portrayed in painstaking, graphic, naturalistic detail. *The Street* is populated with frustrated, twisted, deformed, victimized, beaten-down, improverished people, a few of whom, such as Boots, Jones, and Mrs. Hedges, claw their way off the bottom of the heap and prey upon the rest. Mrs. Hedges is a "mountain" of a woman, and is utterly "unattractive." Down south, when she was young, she was trapped in a fire, suffering burns all over her body; her hair was burned away and she must wear a wig. Stubbornly embittered, she made her way north, to Harlem, where she roamed the streets pilfering garbage cans and living in doorways. One night she meets a white man in the same condition as she, an ugly, dumpy wretch, and they are drawn to each other. The man is Junto, who is also endowed with sheer stubbornness. Together they form a team, and start a junk business. The white man and the black woman are beyond racial prejudice and hate. But, observing the rules of society, Junto puts the money earned through his brains and Mrs. Hedges' labor to good use; he works his way up the ladder, acquires property and several bars and nightclubs in Harlem and other parts of Manhattan; he makes the necessary connections with the big boys downtown, and becomes a kingpin of a sort. He sets Mrs. Hedges up in the whoring business and provides protection. In turn, she is loyal to Junto and steers some of her "girls" his way.

Though she has money, an apartment, and "security" of a sort, all Mrs. Hedges ever really wanted in life is what she cannot have, "a man who will fall in love with her"! But she is "repulsive," with burn scars and no hair, Lord *no hair*! So she sits framed in her window, with a bandanna around her head, casting eyes of prey down on the street in search of "girls" for her business. She calls everybody "dearie."

As soon as Mrs. Hedges sights Lutie she greets her, "dearie," and is convinced that the young, well-dressed, dignified newcomer is fit for her trade, or better yet, for Junto who, she knows, wants to sleep with a nice, warm, colored girl. Though Mrs. Hedges shows some human kindness by stopping Jones from raping Lutie in the darkened hall and invites Lutie to tea, she is thinking all the while of "catching" Lutie for Junto. Mrs. Hedges is a vampire who puts the "girls" out of doors when they have earned no money. It requires much stamina of Lutie to keep from being sick in her presence.

Then there is Min, who fearfully believes in the decree which says, "A woman alone has no chance." The fear that she must have a man to protect her drives her from man to man. Thus, after the last man, Min "took up" with Jones. Though she is "protected" from other men, she is not protected from the incredible beastliness of the very man with whom she lives. Similar to nearly all underclass women, Min has been beaten down by facile forces of oppression on every side. In order to survive, she has succumbed and accommodated herself to nothing less than enslavement. She knows it is wrong, but she feels helpless against white people, women in particular, who work her like a mule of the world and slander her black sexuality, which makes her, we're told, more accepting and expecting of the battering she receives from the men in her life. More than one of the men she has lived with (for "protection") has pimped her, taken her money, used and abused her, stayed drunk, and then left her. In the dimly lit hovel of Jones's apartment, she exists as though she were a hostage. Silent, inarticulate, tipping about, she is forever trying to make herself invisible. She feels "ugly," she feels at fault, for what?---she does not know---for being a woman, surely. In her crampy room there is a caged canary and Min's table with crawfoot legs: these are Min's signs. She is utterly confined without friends, male or female. Jones treats her like he does his dog, whom he abuses whenever something irritates him.

But things were not as bad as they became after Lutie Johnson moved into the building and Jones became fixated with her. After his failure at raping Lutie, Jones becomes insanely cruel. He beats Min and hates her "ugliness," because he wants Lutie and cannot "get" her.

Similar to Albert in *The Color Purple*, who beats Celie because Celie is not Shug, the taking out of frustration on the woman in the house is standard traditional procedure. Men oppress, batter, and make women 'ugly." Then men turn around and beat them some more for being "ugly." This is precisely what happens in Alice Walker's novel *The Third Life of Grange Copeland*. Significantly, Petry points out that all the men in Min's life have treated her as have her white employers, even worse.

But Min is a survivor. She has heard of a "root doctor," Prophet somebody or other, who can cure "nocturnal disappearances" of husbands and lovers.

Although Jones comes to have a constant urge to "kick her ass," Min obtains from the Prophet some conjure potion and a golden cross which she hangs over her bed, along with candles that she burns constantly. Held at bay by Min's newly acquired "mojo," Jones kicks the dog's ass instead. By now, though, Min has come to fear for her life. Jones, a "sick crazy animal," might kill her at any time. The sheer instinctive reflex for self-preservation signals her that it is time to run. Through all the torture that has been inflicted on her, Min has somehow held on to the belief that "a person has a right to live." She sneaks out, and takes up with a familiar pushcart man of the neighborhood. We know, and fear, what is going to happen here too. But Min survives for another day, at least.

[6]

While Min's life is her life, it is at the same time a representation of the lives of all the women in *The Street*. As Lutie walks up and down 116th Street, back and forth to her apartment, there are constant references to the women who populate the neighborhood. Lutie sees them, smells them, she hears their talk, their laughter, their complaints and wails. The young females and teenagers, catering to the attention of boys and men; the older and aged women sitting, standing, leaning against lampposts and buildings, moving along, burdened down from their "domestic" jobs, long ago deserted by their husbands, or shouldering the responsibilities of providing for their families, since their men cannot or will not find employment.

As she witnesses, 116th Street, Lutie is fearfully haunted by the thought that she might end up like these women, broken, worn out before their time, and resigned bitterly to their fate. She rejects the feeling, determined to get away before it becomes too late. Lutie is aware of the buildings themselves: the hallways and rooms are like dungeons inside, the walls reach out for Lutie. The shops, stores, and groceries along the street are stuffed with expensive cheap clothing fit for one wearing only, and inferior food selling for the highest prices. "Burley Negro," headlines in the newspapers. Old black men "aimlessly staring." Gangs of boys. "Hey, fine momma! Hey, ugly bitch." The homeless girls. Lutie sees and does not see Mrs. Hedges leaning eternally out of her window, bandanna-covered head, vulture eyes ever-watchful for a nice young "catch." As she mounts and descends the dreaded stairs to and from her apartment, Lutie sees whores and johns, boys and girls in the hallways, plying their trades and shortening their lives.

Cold, cheerless nights; hot, crowded days. The cursing in other people's apartments, the fighting. "Black bitch, I oughta kill you long ago!" The loud music on radios, the advertisements for "beauty" products. The church music, the smell of alcohol. No hope, no life. The bitter resignation, the crowded hospital every Saturday night, the blood spilled, the jobless men, the broken families, the desolation, the sense of loss, the white cops, always the white cops, and the poverty. Oh yes, poverty! The lack of money, money, money.

Lutie is in any ghetto anywhere in America: Cleveland, Chicago, Detroit, Boston, Los Angeles, Washington, D.C. A quarter century will pass and Gwendolyn Brooks will pen the line "sick and influential," describing the stairs Lutie has to climb, and will again portray in great poetic language the draconian irony of the "Mecca" that Lutie is witnessing in 1946.

[7]

In 1965, two decades later, a renowned black social scientist, Kenneth Clark, would publish a book entitled *Dark Ghetto*, in which he would write:

> The dark ghetto's invisible walls have been erected by white society, by those who have power, both to confine those who have no power and to perpetuate their powerlessness. The dark ghettos are social, political, educational, and ---above all---economic colonies. Their inhabitants are subject peoples, victims of the greed, cruelty, insensitivity, guilt, and fear of their masters. (*Dark Ghetto* 11)

Dark Ghetto is an authoritative study of black America, the first of its kind by a black social scientist. But when it comes to black women in the ghetto, the book is a failure. On pages 67-74, it even adhered to the viewpoint of black males' being unable, "due to slavery and lack of wherewithal," to "act out their *normal* desires for dominance" (my emphasis). The book also propagates the myth of "matriarchy" among black women, while it says nothing of value about the oppression and violence imposed on black women by black men.

Twenty years before the publication of Clark's book, *The Street* anticipated all that *Dark Ghetto* encompasses, and went beyond it to include the lives of more than half of the black population whom Clark chose to leave out of his most acclaimed work. When it comes to the beliefs, feelings, and behavior that are maintained by black men toward black women, Petry's novel is worth more than all the man-sociology ever written on the subject.

The Street does not philosophize, preach, or theorize. It depicts and portrays. It shows that the black ghetto is not only a social, political, educational, and economic colony, but that the black ghetto is also, and foremost, a *sexual* colony. If black people are little more than colonized slaves, then black women are multiple slaves. They are slaves of the white racist society, which exploits their labor and services while holding them at bay in the apartheid-like "homeland" ghettos; they are a "marker," a reserve of slaves for white men who plunder and pillage them as sex objects in white homes and in "brothels" in side and outside of the ghettos; they are once more slaves of black men within the confines of the ghettos, in their homes and along the public streets. In this last instance, black women are slaves of slaves, they are "game" and "sport" for black men who harass them, hold them hostage, batter them, hate, demean, oppress them, repress them, pimp, exploit and kill them, and dare black women to regard this behavior as offensive, let along make it public.

[8]

In *The Street*, Jones the super, and Boots the henchman of Junto, are archetypical paradigms of all the woman-hating sexism that black men at large and black society in general harbor toward and level against the women in their midst. Because of the political, economic, and social racism of white society and culture, Jones and Boots have "righteous excuses" to be all the more dehumanized and all the more monstrous toward the "opposite" sex, and toward Lutie in particular. But they are sexists anyway. Their specific experiences with the white world merely exacerbate their already deeply ingrained sexist dispositions.

Jones, for example, is depicted as a beast. His apartment is like the hold of a cargo ship, darkened and crowded with his junky stuff. We learn that he drove all the women out of his life by his violent sex. On the street, lounging in front of the building, he undresses women with his eyes, molests them in his mind. His feelings toward the women are about performing sexual harm on them, to prove how powerful and dominating he is. He hates the images he conjures up in his mind of Lutie and her husband having sex. Then he hates Lutie and "desires" her even more. To Jones, Lutie is a "piece of meat," an assemblage of body parts, a "thing" on which he can take out his hatred against the female sex, in and through the violence of "fucking."

In the opening scenes of the novel, when Lutie encounters him as she comes to apply for the apartment, I was unbelieving of Petry's description of Lutie's perception of Jones. We have been conditioned to deny the ugliness that men impose on women, and blame the women. "Men may not be angels but they are not as bad as women depict them," is what we are conditioned to say. Lutie's impressions of him must be "paranoia." She has just met the man. How can she think so badly of him? She thinks Jones's eyes are "hungry." As he follows her up the stairs to show her the apartment, Lutie observes that he has "a long black flashlight . . . the rod of its length . . . as black as his head." She feels his presence as "menacing," and that Jones is lusting after her. I am thinking, as I read, that this middle-class-oriented woman thinks she is better than this old worn-down Negro man. She must be "color-prejudiced" against him because he is so black and she is a smooth brown. She must have some kind of Freudian complex as well.

But Lutie's impressions prove to be more than accurate. Obsessed and enraged, Jones enters her apartment when she is at work and ingratiates himself to Bud, who is there. While pretending to make repairs, he rambles through her personal things. When he is done, he can be heard gulping down beer and emitting orgasm sounds.

Jones is so certain that Lutie is nothing but a "whore," that when she wards off his repeated advances, he believes at first that she does not comprehend his intentions, he has not made himself clear enough. But after Lutie, along with Mrs. Hedges, fights off his rape attempt, Jones decides he knows the reason Lutie will have nothing to do with him. "She was in love with Junto, the white man. Black men weren't good enough for her. He had seen women like that before." He fantasizes about Lutie and "the white man" together in copulation; his anger almost kills him. He vows "revenge." He plots and succeeds at getting Bud into trouble.

[9]

Boots Smith is a younger version of Jones. He had been a down-and-out pianist during the Depression days, playing in low-class joints. He hated playing in those joints, with the drunken white people shouting "nigger" insults and giving "Hey, boy" commands. He finally landed a regular job as a Pullman porter, and it was more of the same, "Hey, boy! Come 'mere, boy!" But it was better than playing in those joints, and he vowed he would never play the piano again. He got married to Jubilee. Then, upon returning from being on a Pullman run, he got a glimpse of a white man descending the fire escape leading from their apartment window. He had noticed the curtain blowing in the breeze as he entered the apartment. He beat Jubilee and would have killed her, but she ducked under his arm, grabbed a kitchen knife and sliced his face, leaving him scarred for life.

There had been lots of women since, but Boots could not remember them, except that he had kicked most of them around, always remembering the curtain blowing in the breeze. He ended up frequenting Junto's bar, which he liked because there was no racism in there. Even though he had sworn off the piano, on one occasion he sat down and began playing. A white man, Junto, came over and complimented him, and offered him a job as manager of the bar's fledgling band. There had not been any white-black bigotry from Junto, who was impressed with Boots's successful building of the band and rewarded Boots accordingly, such that by the time Lutie comes to the neighborhood Boots is able to "buy anything in the world he wanted."

Boots saw Lutie and wanted her. He saw her the way he saw Jubilee, and saw all women. He regarded her the same way Lutie's husband, Jim, regarded her and the same way that Jones felt toward all women. His lust for her was a lust for power over her, a lust to dominate and "revenge" himself for what white men had done to him, for surely they had robbed him of his manhood. Boots had been made to feel, "less than a half man, because he didn't even have a woman of his own, because he not only had to say 'Yes, sir,' he had to stand by and take it while some white man grabbed off what belonged to him."

The curtain in the window began to blow in the breeze of Boots's mind. He offers to drive Lutie in his shiny pimp's car to her place of "domestic" employment. His attitude is blasé, pimpish, superior, mannish. Wheeling the car at accelerated speed through the city "made him feel he was a powerful being who could conquer the world . . . . It was like playing god."

On a single page Boots addresses Lutie as "baby" more than a half dozen times, he never calls Lutie by her name throughout the novel. When she replies that she is single, he guns the car forward and flippantly remarks, "Never saw a good-looking chick yet who didn't belong to somebody," as though it were against the law for a woman to belong to herself.

Boots is wearing suede gloves; Lutie observes him and knows that he considers her a "pick up." As he hurls the car through the night, she thinks that he is making up for a lot of the things that have happened to him to make him what he is, that he is "proving all kinds of things to himself." But she is so desperate for a better job, and he has offered to get her an audition with the band, that she decides to "play the game," thinking to pull out before the kill. She tells him the reason she broke up with her husband, and how Jim accused her of "other niggers" and beat her, "because the fact that he couldn't support his wife and child . . . undermined his belief in himself until he could no longer bear it. And he got himself a woman . . his self-respect was momentarily restored through the woman's desire for him." After Lutie tells him this, Boots say to her, "You don't have to be poor any more. Not after tonight. I'll see to that. All you got to do from now is just be nice to me, baby."

But, fighting off his repeated advances, Lutie refuses to be "nice" to him. Plus, by now, Junto wants her and orders Boots hands-off to string her along about the singing job with the band. He tells Boots to promise her but not to pay her; instead, he is to give her presents. "Women like to receive presents," says Junto, believing what men believe and foster on women to make them feel like grateful children rather than like grown women. To convince Boots that he means what he says, Junto issued him a warning, saying "Whoever makes a man can also break him!" Boots considers the alternatives, but Lutie did not weigh enough against a lifetime slaving for and "uncle tomming" to white men.

On Page 171, we find that Boots would sell out a hundred Lutie Johnsons, a hundred black women, to keep money in his pocket. Anyway, the urgency of his desire for Lutie was but an urgency that Petry portrays as being at the base of men's desire for women---to "conquer and subdue." Boots's attitude toward Lutie is every man's attitude toward every woman, only now in the extreme. He exploits Lutie's desperation for the $200 lawyer's fee that the lawyer has misled her to believe she needs to get her son, Bud, out of police custody. Boots arranges an appointment at his apartment. The "appointment" is a deliberate set-up for Junto, who is to be there. Lutie arrives, Junto is hiding in a back room and overhears Lutie refusing to become his concubine. She is indignant, hurt, outraged. Junto slips out of the apartment. Boots says to him, "Don't worry, Mack. She'll come around. Come back about ten o'clock." Then:

> He closed the door quietly behind Junto . . . .
> He thought of the thin curtain blowing in the
> wind . . . this time a white man can have a
> black man's leavings . . . . This would be his
> revenge. . . . He reached out and slapped her
> . . . he slapped her again. "Maybe after I
> beat the hell out of you a coupla times,
> you'll begin to like the idea of sleeping with
> me and with Junto." (262-263)

[10]

But Boots is mistaken. Lutie Johnson will not be compromised by him, or Junto, or by anybody or anything. From the very beginning, as the cold November wind violently assaults the world of the street, Lutie is presented with a certain dignity and strength of character. The wind mounts a ravishing attack but it fails to vanquish her. She braces her body against the wind and refuses to be blown about.

Throughout the novel, through all the debilitating things that happen to her, though shaken, Lutie is steadfast until the very end. Men, the street, and the world at large beat and batter her. But they do not conquer or subdue her.

On the other hand, Min accepts and expects the degradation that everyone imposes on her, and she has no aspiration, no vision of herself, except the bare instinct to survive. By contrast, Lutie knows who she is and what she wants. She has aspirations for herself and her family, she has a strong sense of independence and high self-esteem. She is a Negro lady seriously in pursuit of worthy ideals. Placed in the context of overwhelming adversity, Lutie is made of the stuff that all heroines are made of.

But the concrete circumstances of both Lutie and Min contain the same social realities. First and foremost, both of them are black women. Secondly, although Min more so than Lutie, both are victims. They are regarded by society and by the men of both races as nothing but sex objects. Both are poor and are denied better employment opportunities because of their sex and their color. Both are "domestic servants" working for white folks who view black women as nonpersons and promiscuous whores. They live in the same building and the same neighborhood. Altogether, because of their sex and race, they are subject to the same general oppression. But when it comes to their inner worlds, to their attitudes and their character, they are completely two different women---almost.

[11]

The origins of the differences in the psychology of Lutie and Min are complex and yet quite simple. There is the age difference in the years of their experiences. Min is forty or more. She has been demeaned and stepped on all of these years. From what has been ascertained about women who come to be like her, Min is almost certain to have been sexually abused and battered during her childhood. Her household was probably one in which battering and quite possibly incest and alcoholism occurred. She may not remember some of the incidents, since they were so horrible when experienced that they are unbearable, resulting in "blank spots" in order to deny and shut them out. Then, too, Min's complexion is black, her features are blatantly Negroid, and she has been treated as being "ugly" all of her life---and has been made to feel that it was all her fault. This is especially so since she is not only black but a female too. Therefore, all of her experiences have inflicted in her a "double negative" concept of herself. Plus, she is of obvious common, peasant background, of little education, and has been so persistently tortured that she has been rendered inept and left with only the barest instinct for survival. As mentioned, Min is any number of women in the pages of fiction written by black women. She is Pecola in Toni Morrison's *The Bluest Eye*, She is the young Celie all over again. She is Eva in Gayl Jones's *Eva's Man*. Min is herself, and at the same time she represents untold numbers of black women in real life whose stories are never made public.

It is significant that Lutie, *and* Min, are both protagonists of *The Street*, as it is significant that the two women, although victims of the same oppression, are completely divorced from each other. Lutie was married when she was seventeen, and when the novel opens she is barely in her twenties. Although her Pop drank a lot and regarded women like all men regard them, and though no mention is made of her *mother* (no mention was made of Bigger's *father*), there is no evidence that Lutie experienced any abuse as a child. She has a brown complexion, which meant that she could "stick around," whereas if she had been solid black, she would have had to "get back." Through the "luck" of being not exactly the "wrong hue," Lutie enjoyed some "good fortunes" which Min was denied. She therefore was permitted to acquire a sense of self-worth. At one point of extreme frustration, she cries out, "What possible good has it done to teach people like me to write!"

But the most glaring difference in the psychology of Min and Lutie is *class*. Not class in the material sense, because both women are in the same boat when it comes to the reality of their lot---they are poor. But class in the sense of orientation and identification. Min's inner world may be described as comprising a set of what Richard Wright called "dim negatives." She possesses a victim psychology, a consciousness that sums herself up as being nothing but a "common, nigger wench." Lutie Johnson identifies herself with the "better class" of colored people. She knows racism has rendered her people the way they are. But at the same time she disassociates herself from the "niggerhood" imposed on them and inflicted in them, and she harbors a middle-class bias toward them. When she discovers Bud, her son, with a shoe-shine box, she admonishes him and expresses her wish for him not be be "just like the rest of these niggers." Angry and hurt over her husband's being with another woman, she refers to the woman as "that black bitch!" She exemplifies not only a class bias but a color bias against darker-skin members of her race.

Lutie's class (and color) biases may be further described as being identified with capitalistic values of the white American middle class. Working for the rich Chandler Family, she experiences first-hand the decadence in white middle-class life, the racism, Christian hypocrisy, and general "soap-opera" degeneracy of their family relations, including infidelity, incest, and suicide. She is terribly aware that America is bent on denying black people the "better things" in life. Nevertheless, she staunchly believes in the "higher values" of white America, and that she can achieve these values.

Lutie is in pursuit of the American Dream. This is her *quest*. She believes in all the virtues of the Protestant Ethic: the virtue of middle-class respectability, the virtue of hard work leading to getting ahead, the virtue of moral restraint leading to clean living, the virtue of serious personal purpose, and the virtue of thinking, grooming, dressing, and behaving "respectable"---all leading to happiness. She identifies with Ben Franklin as a model. She is determined to better her situation for herself and for her young son. She wants and demands respect as a Negro *Lady*, and she is nobody's "nigger wench."

Again, while Lutie rejects the hypocrisy and degeneracy displayed in the Chandler Family, she nonetheless wants the things they possess. She is lured by the beautiful "miracle kitchen." She reads the magazines the Chandler women read, *Vogue, Harper's Bazaar, Town and Country, House Beautiful.* Down under, she judges herself as always looking up at the standards of the whites and gauges her aspirations accordingly.

The class bias and the racial self-loathing tendency, with their innumerable machinations, are not only at the roots of the alienation between Lutie and Min. But this class bias and this self-hating tendency are at the roots of the fragmentation and disunity among black women and black people in general. Though Lutie and Min, and all the women in *The Street*, suffer the same oppression because of their race and sex, they are completely divorced from one another, and suffer in separate, isolated, invisible enclosure.   Through the machinations of race and class, they are manipulated, divided, and rendered helpless against their common enemies.

But most of all, throughout the novel, over and over again, Lutie's consciousness and actions are totally dominated by the supreme value of capitalistic life---*money*, or, more correctly, the lack of money.   Boots was correct about one thing. The reason Lutie plays the game with him in the first place is because she needs money. The oppressors know money can lead to independence. This is why no one does anything to help Lutie find a well-salaried job. This is why Junto instructed Boots not to pay Lutie a salary for singing in the band, but to give her "presents" instead. Keep Lutie dependent, as Min and the rest of the women are kept dependent. Though the women work as hard at anybody, they are kept virtually slaves because of the low, inadequate wages paid to them, while the men, white men first and black men last, keep all the high-status, best-paying jobs as their own. Moreover, it is Lutie's lack of money and her all-consuming pursuit of it that leads to the alienation between herself and her son, Bud, and eventually leads to his delinquency and arrest, which, in turn, exacerbates Lutie's need for the all-mighty dollar. Since Lutie is away from home slaving at the Chandlers' far into the night and away in her spare time looking for better employment, Bud is left alone. He develops "fear" of the dark, he begins to feel bereft of love, and roams the streets. He dwells in the movies, fantasizing himself as a "cop or a detective." He observes his mother tired and moody all of the time, and he thinks it is because of him. She lets him know she is worried about money. It is significant that Bud's response, as a male child, is to buy his mother a "present," something he has doubtlessly learned from his sex group. Jones exploits the situation between Bud and Lutie. He tricks Bud into doing "detective work," stealing mail from the boxes in the halls of buildings along the street.   The "detective work" fits Bud's movie fantasies. Then Jones "fingers" him to the cops. Though Bud is under age, Lutie is led to believe she needs $200 to free her son, for the lawyer's fee.

[12]

In racist capitalistic America, the ever-binding necessity for money is a divisive, deadly trap for black people. Yet, it is altogether foolhardy to expect black people to renounce the only way of life that they know, that they are born into and is all around them and is constantly being glorified as the American Dream. In *Dark Ghetto*, Kenneth Clark wrote:

> It would be psychologically naïve and even cruel to ask the oppressed to transform the values of American culture. Before they can be motivated to try, they need to experience those values for themselves with all the satisfactions and all the frustrations and anxieties. (109)

In her unrelenting desire and quest for the American Dream and the equally unrelenting denial of that dream to her, Lutie becomes a classical tragic heroine, flawed by her virtues and fated for doom. Lutie Johnson is an Invisible Woman. No one will see and accept her for what she is and wants to be. Her travail is the saga of a Native Daughter in search of the American Dream. She is a black Womanchild in a white Promised Land.

But Lutie Johnson is not only a native of, and contradicted by, a racist capitalist world. She is also a native of, and contradicted by, a sexist world. The bind she is in is a triple bind, her oppression is geometric.

Throughout the novel, a plethora of evidence shows that Lutie is possessed by negative loyalties, just like Min and the other women. Herein lies the third tragic element in her character. In all oppressive situations, it is deemed a virtue for the oppressed to identify with the world-view of the oppressors. The oppressed are "praised" and "rewarded" for loathing themselves and for admiring their oppressors; they are derided, made to feel ashamed, and are punished for embracing any ways they themselves might develop, and are instructed and forced to manifest allegiance to the ways of those who oppress them.

The chief symptom of negative loyalty is self-blame. Though Lutie prides herself on being a lady and puts up a vigilant struggle as a human being, she constantly blames herself for the bad things that happen to her and her family. Like the rest of the women, black and white, she firmly believes that it is wrong for a woman to work; "it is not good for the man," she is told. She works simply because she is forced to. Jim, her husband, destroys their marriage, but Lutie blames herself. Jones set up her son, Bud, but Lutie blames herself for being a "single parent" away working instead of being at home. She gets angry at men, but in the end she always finds a way to excuse them and blame herself. She has completely identified not with any values that might be considered women's ways, but with the values and prejudices of the male world as pertaining to women's role and women's nature.

Lutie is by no means blind to the rippling effects of racism on black people, on the men in particular. Sitting in Junto's bar, she observes and laments the effects of this racism on her people, and vows that she will fight her way out of the hole that racial oppression has put her people in . Furthermore, toward the latter pages of the novel, she begins to see that racism had perhaps falsely divided the races, the women in particular, and that capitalism was the real common enemy. In the Children's Shelter where Bud was being held along with other boys of all races, Lutie observes that all the mothers, black and white, were as poor as she.

But when it comes to the role that both white and black sexism and patriarchy play in the oppression of women and specifically in her own oppression, Lutie Johnson is blind as a bat.

Just as black male culture socializes black men to be sexists, black women are socialized to internalize sexist assumptions and prejudices. Again, instead of the urge to kill her husband for sleeping with another woman, Lutie has the urge to kill the woman and calls the woman a "black bitch." Min does the same thing, she blames Lutie for the increase in Jones's barbarity. Lutie feels guilty for everything bad happening to her, especially for having to work and leave her children alone. Her granny schooled her on the fact of being "pretty." She had better hurry up and get married, which Lutie did. Like Min, Lutie too believes "a woman alone didn't stand a chance." But a woman with a man is repeatedly proved not to stand a chance either, and Lutie is forced to be along anyway, forced to work. Otherwise, she would rather be in a lady's proper place, in a nice middle-class home, servicing husband and children. Her desires, similar to the desires of most women, are simply to live the liberal life, free of the more brutal perpetrations of men. Writing in *No Crystal Stair*, Gloria Wade-Gayles made the following observation:

> . . . The artists write from a feminist perspective, but their characters are like most black women in real life. They are essentially traditional in their approach to life. They do not seek new definitions of sexual roles. Most of them . . . are willing to observe the old rules . . . . Their desires for wider options . . . are essentially . . . "alternatives to brutality" . . . . They want love, acceptance, respect, and, for several women, the freedom to express their creativity. Even when they realize that the "old rules" are by definition obstacles to these desires, most of the women would rather take their chances with the "old rules"; and struggle in small ways for a new

> reality. They live what most women live---
> lives of contradiction. . . . The contradiction
> is the result of their loyalty or conditioning
> (or both) . . . . (241)

Lutie and the other women in *The Street* seem to be utterly mystified as to what is happening to them. But we see it plain as day. In black and white, the reader sees it all.

[13]

The Street is a frontal presentation of the sexual politics in the relations between black males and black females, the politics of male power over female existence. Ultimately, when she is on the verge of being actually raped by this power, Lutie explodes.

> . . . everything that had served to frustrate
> her . . . the dirty, crowded street . . . the rows
> of dilapidated old houses . . . the small dark
> rooms . . .the long steep flights of stairs . . .
> narrow dingy hallways . . . the little lost girls
> in Mrs. Hedges' apartment . . . the smashed
> homes where the women did drudgery
> because their men had deserted them. She
> was all of these things and struck out at
> them. . . Jim and the slender girl she'd found
> him with . . . the insults in the moist-eye
> glances of white men . . . the unconcealed
> hostility in the eyes of white women . . . the
> greasy, lecherous men at the Crosse School
> for Singers . . . the gaunt Super pulling her
> down, down into the basement. . . she was
> striking at the white world. . . . (266)

Notice, however, that as she explodes she lays the ultimate blame on the white world, still not fully aware of, or not daring to declare, that black men have it within their own power to refrain from brutalizing black women. Even when she discovers Boots's wallet bulging with money and that he "could have given her two hundred dollars and never missed it," Lutie still seems incapable of condemning him as a black man. She is loyal even as she ironically bludgeons him to death with the phallic symbol of women's oppression, a sharp iron candlestick. Wade -Gayles comments on this "negative loyalty."

> . . . to challenge the sexual limitations raises
> fundamental questions that affect the
> women's personal lives, and the persons

> they challenge are often the men they love
> and whose children they have borne . . . .
> They often find themselves alone when they
> challenge sexual oppression. In fact, myths
> about women are so basic to our culture that
> women who attempt to reject them totally
> must reject a part of who they are. (147)

Clearly Lutie is "split in two" by what she is forced to do. This is why she "explodes" in the act of killing. All the love-hate, loyalty-resentment detonate out of her, for as Lutie kills Boots, she is also killing a part of herself. Wade-Gayles writes

> . . . the challenges to sexism and racism
> made by black women in the seventies were
> perhaps explosions of many years of
> suppressed resentment. . . public images are
> so fundamental a part of our reality that to
> repudiate them totally is tantamount to
> repudiating a part of ourselves. (147, 242)

Finally, Wade-Gayles writes that "we cannot cure an illness by denying that we suffer from its symptoms."

[14]

That *The Street* is a pioneer work of womanist/feminist protest is unmistakable. But it does not go beyond protest. What Alice Walker's novel *The Color Purple* does for rural blacks in the South, *The Street* achieves for black people in the urban North. However, unlike in *The Color Purpose*, Ann Petry's novel does not offer any positive process of affirmation and overcoming. Lutie revolts but she revolts alone; it is an emotional, unplanned revolt---she explodes.

In 1968, twenty years after Lutie Johnson explodes, two black psychiatrists, William Grier and Price Cobbs, published a best-selling study entitled *Black Rage*. They devoted fifteen pages to black women in a chapter entitled "Acquiring Womanhood," in which they made glaring Freudian endorsements about the value of "feminine beauty and narcissism" for black women, and discussed how hard it is for black women to feel beautiful and narcissistic in white racist America.

Nothing is mentioned in the entire book about the *rage* black women might feel from the political, economic, and sexist oppression that they suffer. The only concern black men have for black women is that the women feel beautiful, be good mothers, and provide and experience good sex.

The explosion of Lutie Johnson foreshadowed the necessities for the more positive processes of black women's liberation. The modern successors of Ann Petry are busy depicting and mapping out these processes: the coming together of all women in sisterhood; the organizing and raising of consciousness; acclaiming the value of womanist ways and women-identified women; the naming of women's oppression as *sexism*; the affirmation of nurturing women, blues women, such as Shug in *The Color Purple*, Mattie in *The Women of Brewster Place,* and the women in *The Salt Eaters*, to mention but a few. This is not to take away from Petry's novel. The issues are all there, precisely and painstakingly detailed. What is needed are the solutions and the tactics. One of the women in the beauty parlor sees Lute near the end of her rope, burdened and filled with the blues, and the woman remarks, "Somep't must have walked over your grave."

The explosion of Lutie Johnson marked her own death as a Negro Lady Heroine and initiated a new life as a Black Woman Hero. The explosion of Lutie Johnson, the murder she committed, is being transformed by today's women writers into a positive act of love and liberation. Bigger Thomas killed Mary Dalton and Bessie Mears with only thoughts of fear and trembling. Lutie Johnson killed Boots Smith in an explosion of pent-up rage against the oppression of herself, against the oppression of Min, against the oppression of all black women and all black people.

---

[1] For DuBois's article, see *Crisis*, Vol 32, No. 6 (October 1926). For Hughes's, see *Nation*, June 23, 1926.

[2] John A. Williams and Charles Harris, eds. *Amistad #1* (New York: Vintage Books, 1970).

From 'Patterns Against the Sky': Deism and Motherhood in Ann Petry's *The Street* (1985)
Marjorie Pryse

In an essay titled "Ann Petry: The Novelist as Social Critic," Theodore Gross points to Lutie Johnson's references to Benjamin Franklin in the novel *The Street* as being central to her characterization. Gross reminds us that "at the outset of the book, Lutie expresses an idealistic attitude that is in the traditional American manner." After she buys six hard rolls for herself and her son Bub, she thinks

> of Ben Franklin and his loaf of bread. And grinned thinking. You and Ben Franklin. You ought to take one out and start eating it as you walk along 116th Street. Only you ought to remember while you eat that you're in Harlem and he was in Philadelphia a pretty long number of years ago. Yet she couldn't get rid of the feeling of self-confidence and she went on thinking that if Ben Franklin could live on a little bit of money and could prosper, then so could she.[1]

Bernard Bell takes Gross's observation a step further by noting that although black Americans rarely refer to "myths of the Founding Fathers like Benjamin Franklin, who is the colonial paradigm of the successful self-made man," Lutie Johnson does so,

> Naively subscribing to the Protestant ethic and the American Dream as expressed by the Chandlers, the wealthy white New England family for whom she worked for two years as a live-in maid, and as embodied in Benjamin Franklin, with whom she compares herself.

In depicting the collapse of the American dream for Lutie Johnson, Bell accurately concludes, Petry "thus demythologizes both American culture and Afro-American character."[2]

The precise nature of the social criticism Petry offers in *The Street* relies on the reader's recognition of Lutie's references to Franklin and, even more, on our ability to place these references within the context of American idealism, expressed by Franklin---and others---whom we consider our "Founding Fathers." Once we have taken note of Lutie's specific references to Franklin, we find the early chapters of the novel larded with related allusions. For example, one of the members of the Chandler family, within Lutie's hearing, advises the others to " 'Outsmart the next guy. Think up something before anyone else does. Retire at forty' " (43)---as Franklin himself was able to do. And later, after Lutie leaves the Chandlers and moves in with her father (she learns that her husband Jim has moved in another woman in her absence), she forces herself to study shorthand and typing at night after working all day in a steam laundry to support herself and her son. "Every time it seemed as though she couldn't possibly summon the energy to go on with the course, she would remind herself of all the people who had got somewhere in spite of the odds against them. She would think of the Chandlers and their young friends---'It's the richest damn country in the world.' " (55).

Although Lutie Johnson may seem initially naïve in taking Franklin for her model---even when she learns at the Chandlers' house that white people view black women as whores (45), she fails to recognize the stigma of her race and sex and her consequent disqualifications for achieving her particular version of the American dream---by means of dramatic irony as a narrative technique Petry makes sure that the reader understands the limitations society places on Lutie even if she herself does not. The novel's strength lies in Petry's narrative control. For even though we know much more than Lutie does---the effect here is to place every reader, whether white or black, in the position of white society looking in on the world of the street---and even though we are not surprised when Lutie fails to raise herself and her son, we are still surprised, even shocked, at the extent of her fall by the novel's end. When Lutie murders the black band leader and pimp, Boots Smith, who has tried to seduce her, and abandons her son to reform school, we are disappointed and depressed---like some of Petry's early reviewers and critics[3]---even though we knew, both from our own knowledge of our society as well as by means of Petry's use of dramatic irony---that the model of the self-made man that Benjamin Franklin represents does not, was never intended to, include women or black men. Therefore the origins of Lutie Johnson's narrative fate as well as of her naïve faith lie with Franklin and everything he has come to represent about our colonial American origins.

Petry uses dramatic irony to hide from Lutie Johnson the truth that she reveals to the reader early in the novel: that the white bar owner Junto stands behind Lutie's failure to raise herself out of the street. It is Junto who wants Lutie Johnson for himself. Therefore Boots Smith cannot pay Lutie for singing in his band; therefore her son Bub falls under the influence of the atavistic super, Jones, and gets arrested for stealing mail out of post boxes; and therefore, when Lutie discovers that she is expected to pay with her body for a loan to keep her son out of reform school, she effectively strikes back at Junto as she kills Smith with a candlestick.

But the name *Junto* is also a direct allusion to the first significant men's club in American colonial history, the name Franklin gave his secret group of friends.[4] Formed ostensibly for moral and intellectual improvement, Franklin's Junto actually served its members as a central sphere of social and political influence. As Franklin himself implies in his *Autobiography*, and as his biographers reveal, the secret organization helped Franklin solicit trade at his printing shop, it enabled him to put together the capital he needed to dissolve his partnership and become sole proprietor of that shop, and it became, as one of his commentators described it, "an instrument to help him and his associates to rise in the community."[5] n Petry's novel as well, Junto's influence operates in secret, and there is a "club" which appears to be nameless forces of the street but which in reality includes Boots Smith and the apparently omniscient Mrs. Hedges in league with Junto. In naming her powerful white man Junto, Petry thereby places her references to Benjamin Franklin and Lutie's idealism within the context of the deism which formed the intellectual and philosophical foundations both of Franklin's club and of our country's founding, as *The Declaration of Independence* makes particularly clear.

In light of the novel's references both to Franklin and to his Junto, we can more clearly place Petry's portrait of Mrs. Hedges. Mrs. Hedges, whom Petry invests from the beginning with an omniscience that rivals only that of the narrator's, comes to possess the attributes of a deity. Resembling in particular the deist's god, Mrs. Hedges sets herself apart from events on the street---her "world" which she has even named (251)---even though she sits in her open window, whatever the weather, and watches them. Mrs. Hedges represents for Lutie the street's impersonal and indifferent omniscience. She thinks, "living here is like living in a tent with everything that goes on inside it open to the world because the flap won't close. And the flap couldn't close because Mrs. Hedges sat at her street-floor window firmly holding it open to see what went on inside" (68).

Mrs. Hedges's curiosity is impassive and arbitrary, like that of the watchmaker or the benign policemen whom eighteenth-century colonial and European thinkers envisaged as the First Cause who created the world, then stepped back to let it operate according to its own "laws."[6] Like that First Cause, Mrs. Hedges served as the inspiration and conceptual genius which helped Junto transform himself from gatherer of garbage and junk others have discarded to landlord and proprietor of Lutie's apartment house, various establishment of prostitution (the one Mrs. Hedges runs and the fancier brothel at Sugar Hill), the Junto Bar and Grill, and the Casino where Boots Smith's band plays. And like that impersonal deity, she chooses not to intervene in the lives of Petry's characters.

She becomes as well, for them, the source of knowledge. Lutie discovers that it is impossible to walk past Mrs. Hedges's window without being seen (84), and when Jones, the building super, walks past, "he was filled with a vast uneasiness, for he was certain that she could read his thoughts" (89). When Lutie wonders why all the women on the street are separated from their husbands, she thinks, "Certainly Mrs. Hedges should be able to explain it." (76). When Min, the aging woman who lives with Jones, decides to visit a hoodoo doctor, she goes to Mrs. Hedges for a recommendation. After Jones tries to get Mrs. Hedges arrested for running a house of prostitution, he discovers that she is locked into power with the white police. And Mrs. Hedges, appearing to read Jones's thoughts and thereby knowing that he is interested in Lutie, warns him away: " 'There ain't no point in you getting' het up over her. She's marked down for somebody else' " (90). The language of the warning---that Lutie has been "marked down"---suggests Mrs. Hedges's larger than human knowledge of her fate. All of these details contribute to Petry's portrait of Mrs. Hedges as godlike.

Even in her physical description Petry sets Mrs. Hedges apart from the other characters. From the first time Lutie Johnson turns toward the entrance of the apartment building on 116th Street she notices the "enormous bulk of a woman . . . silhouetted against the light," and the single feature about Mrs. Hedges which impresses itself on Lutie is her eyes. "They were as still and as malignant as the eyes of a snake" (5-6). Later, when Lutie enters Mrs. Hedges's apartment after the woman rescues her from Jones's attempted rape, Petry describes her, in Lutie's eyes, as "a mountain of a woman" who had "the appearance of a creature that had strayed from some other planet" (237). While she makes Lutie tea, Lutie thinks that "she should have been concocting some witch's brew" (239). Again it is the woman's eyes that strike Lutie: "her eyes were like stones that had been polished. There was no emotion, no feeling in them, nothing visible but shiny, smooth surface" (239). Petry describes the "uncontrollable revulsion in the faces of the white people" who once had looked at the young Mrs. Hedges. "They stared amazed at her enormous size, at the blackness of her skin" and viewed her as "a monstrosity" (241). Petry explains that the woman's coldness results in part from her physical appearance. For after the apartment-house fire which scarred her body and charred her scalp---her blackness further blackened---Mrs. Hedges (who never married) knew that she would never be able to buy, much less attract, a lover.

Yet for all of Mrs. Hedges's power, she is not finally omniscient, and although she reminds us of the deists' god, she is no deity. She fails to detect Jones's scheme to entrap Bub, and she does not see the white policeman when they take Bub away. She doesn't seem to know Boots Smith. And even after Bub's arrest, she limits her interest to what she can see from her window, "urging the contestant on" in the "desperate battle" which the young boys on the street seem to be perpetually enacting (416). Her presence in the novel, however, points to larger forces and gives those forces a tangible, physical agent.

The larger forces in the novel are white people---whom Petry embodies in the Chandlers, the Connecticut family who hire Lutie as live-in domestic; in Junto himself, who looms largely responsible for the street; and in other white representatives---the white reporter who turns a thin man who tries to steal a loaf of bread into a "burly Negro" (198); the white nightclub agent, Mr. Crosse, who promises Lutie a "scholarship" to singing school if she is "nice" to him (318-22); the white schoolteacher, Miss Rinner, who thinks teaching black kids is like "being in a jungle" (333); and the white lawyer who is willing to charge Lutie two hundred dollars instead of telling her she doesn't need him to keep her son out of reform school (392).

The attitude of hostility and indifference which pervades Petry's description of the landscape---both natural and urban---also connects the forces behind the street with white people. Early in the novel, when Lutie comes home from work to the street for the first time, she finds herself staring at---or being watched by---an advertisement on the subway. In the advertisement she sees a blond girl leaning against a white porcelain sink in a "miracle of a kitchen" accented by "red geraniums in yellow pots" (28). The advertisement leads her to recall the Chandlers' kitchen in Lyme---and the main street of that town. The contrast between that street and the one she now lives on is unmistakable. The Chandlers' street was wide and lined with elm trees whose branches met overhead. "In summer the sun could just filter through the leaves, so that by the time its rays reached the street, it made a pattern like the lace on expensive nightgowns . . . . In winter the bare branches of the trees made a pattern against the sky that was equally beautiful in snow or rain or cold, clear sunlight" (29). The pattern like lace which is beautiful no matter what the weather stands "against the sky"---as if there is a connection between the two. But the sky Lutie sees on her street is different. And the pattern is different.

The white people on the downtown streets stare at Lutie "with open hostility in their eyes" (70), and Lutie concludes that "it all added up to the same thing"---white people (206). It all adds up to white people in the novel because white people, following the lead of Benjamin Franklin, Thomas Jefferson, and John Adams---the committee which submitted the Declaration of Independence to the Continental Congress in 1776---gave the country its deistic foundation. We know, from the manuscript version of the Declaration, that the document Jefferson and his committee submitted was radically different from the one the Congress ratified in one significant respect. Jefferson, in drafting his document using the conventional antislavery political rhetoric of the eighteenth century, in which the colonists become the enslaved and George III the unredeemable tryant, built his list of colonists' grievances against the king to climax with a long statement condemning the Negro slave trade, blaming the king for refusing to put an end to it, and darkly warning against possible slave insurrections like the very revolution of the colonists themselves. We also know that a "political compromise" with congressional representatives from South Carolina and

Georgia led the Congress to delete the specific references to Negro slaves and to replace it with the vague. "He has excited domestic insurrections amongst us."[7]

The existence of the draft manuscript of the Declaration of Independence, with its consideration of Negro slavery as a separate issue from the statement that "all men are created equal," is not something about which school children in this country routinely learn. The discovery that had the founding fathers seen fit to address the question of slavery in 1776, American history might have taken a different course with respect to our treatment of black Americans, is currently reserved for scholars.

Yet in the process by which the Continental Congress saw fit to drop the condemnation of Negro slavery from the Declaration, we can see the process by which Negro slaves were not considered by other men as "created equal"---they became a case for special consideration; and in their exclusion from the document by means of political compromise, we see the indifference that the Declaration builds into our system. In all fairness, historians have observed that the founding fathers thought that slavery would die out on its own anyway---that they couldn't have foreseen Eli Whitney's invention of the cottin gin in 1792 that would make the slave trade economically practical for the South. Nevertheless, the deism of the document finally makes no provision for the humanitarian treatment of the slaves.

In a novel that points to Benjamin Franklin as its protagonist's model and which explains the failure of the American dream for black people in terms of colonial allegory, it seems no accident that when Petry describes her landscapes in *The Street* she uses language that evokes a deistic universe. Early in the novel Lutie agrees to go for a drive with Boots Smith, whom she has just met in the Junto. Petry gives us a "full moon---pale and remote," writes that the "streets had a cold, deserted look" and that "the sky . . . , too, had a faraway look. The buildings loomed darkly against it" (157). The cold distance of the sky, against which the buildings of Harlem loom "darkly," becomes associated with the invisible control white people have exerted over the black world. Behind the wheel of his car, Boots loses his identity as a black man and "plunged forward into the cold, white night," as if "he was a powerful being who could conquer the world." To Lutie, his driving seems "like playing God"; and his engine "roaring in the night" brought the people sleeping in the "white farmhouses . . . half-awake—disturbed, uneasy" (157). In this scene, the indifference of white people toward the plight of the black people on the street seems relegated to the landscape---but Petry makes it clear that Lutie and Boots are dealing with a more active deism, "a world that took pains to make them feel that they didn't belong, that they were inferior." Because of the "delicate balance" of the world white people moved in, "there was nothing left for them but that business of feeling superior to black people." If that was taken away, Petry writes, "even for the split second of one car going ahead of another, it left them with nothing" (158).

The apparently invisible and naturalistic forces behind the street, then, become closely linked with the political attitudes of the white people who founded, then proceeded to run, the country. When Lutie looks out from her apartment window early in the novel she sees not the laws of a street in league with Junto, but rather simply a world let run to chaos: "The rubbish had crept through the broken places in the fences until all of it mingled in a disorderly pattern that looked from their top-floor window like a huge junkpile instead of a series of small back yards" (73). But by the novel's end, Lutie has rejected Franklin's myth of the self-made man and "slowly she began to reach for some conclusion, some philosophy with which to rebuild her shattered hopes" (307). She realizes that "streets like the one she lived on were no accident. They were the North's lynch mobs . . . the method the big cities used to keep Negroes in their place . . . . From the time she was born, she had been hemmed into an ever-narrowing space, until now she was very nearly walled in and the wall had been built up brick by brick by eager white hands" (323-24). She comes to see a different "pattern against the sky."

The "laws" of the street, which white people have set in motion and allowed to run their course, hem Lutie and the others, particularly the women, into that "ever-narrowing space." The novel depicts, among such "laws," the following: if the women work, the children go to reform school; women become prostitutes when their men leave; women who move in with men must try not to be "put out"; men prey on women; and there in no justice. Unlike Bub Johnson's fantasy, in which, when he is working to steal from mailboxes for Jones, he is really trying to help the "cops catch the crooks" (350), the most powerful "law" on the street is that there is no justice for its inhabitants. Neither is there room for human love in such a world gone wrong, cast away from its mooring: therefore, Lutie's husband Jim learns a "pretended indifference" (34) when she decides to take the job as live-in maid for the Chandlers; and therefore Boots Smith weighs Lutie Johnson against all the indignities he has suffered in his life and decides she isn't worth the risk.

In Addison Gayle's view, The Street backs away from a denouement." Gayle praises the novel for delineating the nature of American racism, yet considers Lutie "lacking in power to substantially alter the course of her life."[8] Yet despite the despair of Lutie's life and the futility with which she at first tries to fight for her son, then flees, as Boots murderer, The Street does set up alternative forces which provide its thematic denouement. When we begin to recognize these forces, the novel itself becomes much less bleak---whatever the future holds for Lutie Johnson. Ironically, in light of the forces the novel proposes to counter the "laws" of the street in a world created by white gods, Petry presents Lutie as simply making the wrong choices, following the wrong models; but finally, the power she needs in order to counter the white world already exists, on the street itself.

The first of these alternative forces is represented by Granny. Granny never appears as a character in the novel but she exists as a memory in Lutie's mind: We learn that Lutie's mother died when she was seven and that her grandmother raised her (80). Perhaps if Ann Petry had been able to read recent novels by Paule Marshall, Alice Walker, Toni Morrison, and Toni Cade Bambara,[9] she might have been more aware of the fictional potential of Granny in her novel--- for Lutie's Granny (like her fictional predecessor, Janie's grandmother in Zora Neale Hurston's *Their Eyes Were Watching God*) seems to have given Lutie at least some of the right advice and knowledge she needs to counteract the street. Lutie remembers Granny's "tales about things that people sensed before they actually happened. Tales that had been handed down and down and down until, if you tried to trace them back, you'd end up God knows where---probably Africa" (15-16). Lutie tries to silence what Granny might have said by telling herself she doesn't believe in "instinctive, immediate fear"---even though she knows that Granny would have summed up the super, Jones, as " 'Nothin' but evil, child. Some folks so full of it you can feel it comin' at you---oozin' right out of their skins' " (20). And even though Lutie's grandmother taught her never to let " 'no white man put his hands on you' "(45), Lutie chooses as her model a white man, Benjamin Franklin.

The second alternative force is represented by Mrs. Hedges. Mrs. Hedges is capable of using her power to ward off the evil on the street: she intervenes when Bub is overpowered by the other boys, and she saves Lutie from being raped by Jones. She is also, in her relation to Mary and her other "girls," a mother of sorts. As the "madam" of a whorehouse, where she gives homeless young women a home in exchange for their prostitution, she is a false madonna. Yet she gives Min, Jones's live-in woman, just the right information when Min, oppressed by Jones, tries to do something, herself, to ward off the forces of the street. When Min comes to Mrs. Hedges with her version of Paradise---not being "put out" of Jones's apartment---and asks whether Mrs. Hedges knows of a good root doctor, Mrs. Hedges sends her to see Prophet David. The scene in which Min receives the information and leaves Mrs. Hedges's apartment is significant. Mrs. Hedges tells Min that she doesn't "hold with" root doctors herself, "because I always figured out that as far as my own business is concerned I was well able to do anything any root doctor could do' " (120). As we have seen, in terms of the power Mrs. Hedges possesses on the street, she certainly could work hoodoo---but chooses not to. And when Min leaves, she sees Mrs. Hedges "brooding over the street like she thought if she stopped looking at it for as much as a minute, the whole thing would collapse" (121). In this image, the deity becomes an inverted goddess, "brooding" over a world she hasn't made, but over which she has mysterious power.

The Prophet David, himself, represents the third and most promising alternative force in *The Street*. When Min is on her way to the Prophet's house, she thinks, "the preacher at the church she went to would certainly disapprove, because in his eyes her dealing with a root doctor was as good as saying that the powers of darkness were stronger than the powers of the church" (122). When Min sees him, Petry writes that "the whiteness of the turban accentuated the darkness of his skin" (129). In contrasting the powers of physical and metaphysical darkness with the "whiteness" of his turban, Min arrives at the first of several important moments of clarity. "It was like Mrs. Hedges and that bandanna she wore all the time . . . . And staring at the Prophet's turban she got the sudden jolting thought that perhaps Mrs. Hedges wore that bandanna all the time because she was bald" (132). In the presence of the Prophet, Min--- generally described as a passive, slow-witted creature---begins to see through even Mrs. Hedges herself. The "powers of darkness," however they might be viewed by the white world or the minister of Min's church who scorns root doctors, prove superior to all the doctors and ministers Min has seen in her life. For unlike them, the Prophet gives Min "all of his attention," listens to her in a "quiet way," and "when she came out from behind the white curtains the satisfaction from his attentive listening, the triumph of actually possessing the means of controlling Jones, made her face glow" (137).

The root doctor, representing the strongest evidence of a lingering cultural cohesion among the black community, acts as a potential force against the street's laws' and the white world. For although the men (and Lutie Johnson) go to the Junto to escape their fears and loneliness, Min sees only women at the Prophet's. The women she sees there want to solve human problems: they are there to keep their husbands in bed nights, or to ward off the specters of white people in their lives. And they all emerge from the Prophet's satisfied and confident. It is important that Mrs. Hedges, who doesn't "hold with" root doctors, is surprised at the renewed energy with which Min returns from the Prophet's. "There was such energy and firmness about the way she walked that Mrs. Hedges's eyebrows lifted as she craned her neck for a further look" (138). And as the novel progresses, Min serves as Lutie's foil for Petry. Lutie becomes more hopelessly lost, in her pursuit of the American Dream; but Min follows the Prophet's instructions and manages to protect herself long enough from Jones to make up her own mind about what she wants to do. The contrast between the two women has never been examined by critics---but Petry clearly offers Min's alternatives, if not Min herself, as models for Lutie. How might the novel, and Lutie's life, have been different, for example, had she gone to the Prophet David for help when Bub is arrested instead of the white lawyer who wants to charge her two hundred dollars? Might the Prophet have been able to tell her she didn't need a lawyer?

Min, then, despite her limitations, lives by the same instincts Lutie Johnson rejects when she refuses to listen to her Granny's voice. Min knows, when she goes to see the Prophet David, that she is "committing an open act of defiance for the first time in her life" (127). We never see Lutie Johnson defying anything or anybody in her world---until her rage becomes so uncontrollable that she commits murder. It is true that Min's situation is different from Lutie's; where Lutie wants a better life for herself and her son, Min, not a mother, wants only to survive. She excuses and explains why she moves from man to man "because a woman by herself didn't stand much chance; and because it was too lonely living by herself in a rented room" (133). Petry doesn't give us any alternatives to Min's situation---yet Min displays a certain heroic dignity in deciding to leave Jones. Unlike Lutie, who despairs of ever leaving the street, Min makes her decision and carries it out. Unlike Lutie, who cannot interpret the "pattern against the sky" which ought to help her follow her instincts instead of burying them, Min can read signs. As she packs to leave, "she took a final look at the sky" (355). She wants to get herself moved "before the snow started"---and in a novel where natural forces of wind and snow alternately reveal and obscure the reality of the street (and in which description of wind and snow frame the novel, in its opening and closing paragraphs), Min recognizes the timeliness of her decision. She glances at the street which she is about to leave and thinks, "It wasn't somehow a very good place to live, for the women had too much trouble, almost as though the street itself bred the trouble" (355).

In a closing scene with Jones, in which the super enters the apartment surprised to see Min at home instead of at work, Min explains her presence by saying that " 'My heart was botherin' me.' " As she speaks, she realizes that it is, indeed, her heart that is threatened, as she feels her heart, "making a sound like thunder inside her chest" (360). The scene recalls Bub's own feelings of vulnerability just a few pages earlier in the novel as he runs home from school, having bought his mother a present with money he has earned "working" for Jones, and finds himself pursued by Gray Cap and other boys: "his heart was thudding so hard, he thought it was just as though it had been running, too . . . . He could almost see it---red like a Valentine heart with short legs kicking up in back of it as it ran" (337). Jones's impotence and rage, when Mrs. Hedges tells him that Min has left, leads him to set up Bub once and for all---Min may have escaped him, he thinks, but Bub, and Lutie, will not.

Before Min leaves, she discovers the opened letters addressed to strangers and realizes that "Jones was doing something crooked. He was up to something that was bad" (365). Unfortunately, she leaves without even trying to find out what---and without being able to warn or save Bub. Still, the scene depicts Min as finally smarter than Lutie, more savvy. And Min will survive, away from this particular street. When she meets the pushcart man who arrives to move her belongings, she says softly to herself, " 'A body's got the right to live' " (368). And Min leaves the novel as well as the street with a "soft insinuation in her voice" for the pushcart man. She is clearly on her way to another small apartment with another man, this one whose strength is apparent in his black muscles which bulge as he pushes the cart.

Min is not the perfect foil for Lutie---who rightly aspires to a better life than Min will have with yet another live-in "husband"---but Lutie, with all of her own strengths, combined with some of Min's might have made more of her situation. Instead of idealistically looking to the American past, Lutie needed to see the founding as it really was: a deistic setting in motion, in which, for white people, there is no place for black people except on the street. Only Min escapes---because Lutie is even more alone than Min, cut off from the possibilities of both black and women's community by her aspirations to be Benjamin Franklin---or to be a mother deity in her own right, for Bub.

Deism and motherhood combine their forces, as the novel moves to its close, as remnants of American myth. In the depiction of Lutie's fall into despair as Boots's murderer, the novel reflects on the tragedy by which motherhood becomes Lutie's only alternative to the street, within the parameters of her attempts to make a decent life and to rise in society. The perversion of the mother in the portrait of the madam/madonna Mrs. Hedges finds its ultimate grotesqueness in Lutie---who believes that against all other odds she can protect her son. Therefore she refuses to allow him to shine shoes, to become the typical black boy in white society, yet contributes to her own fall by insisting on money as the ultimate value. After all, Bub does not initially agree to steal letters out of mailboxes---he only suppresses his own misgivings about working for Jones when Lutie, in her disappointment that Boots will not pay her for singing in his band, finds herself unable to control her own rage. " 'Damn being poor!" she shouts as she prepares Bub's dinner. " 'God damn it!" (325). And so Bub turns to Jones.

But for all of her efforts to protect him from the street, Lutie abandons her son at the novel's end. *The Street* depicts the world Bub will grow up in as worse than indifferent, worse than deistic: he is now motherless as well. Lutie's departure reinforces the indifferences of the landscapes in the street world white people have made; yet her departure, though cruel, seems fated. She was "marked down" to fail as a mother when she was "marked down" for Junto. The particular indifference of white society comes to seem much more planned and much less an accident of nature than the deist's conception of the eighteenth-century universe. The reader is left, above all, with Bub's isolation hovering in the background. His *own* "god"---his mother---departs, leaving him to his fate. And Petry doesn't need to dramatize Bub's reaction to his abandonment---she has already done so in the earlier scene in which, when Lutie leaves Bub alone to go out to sing, he finds himself "swallowed up in darkness," afraid to look and afraid not to look around him in the empty apartment, "here along, lost in the dark, lost in a strange place filled with terrifying things" (217-18). On second and subsequent readings of the novel, this scene, in which Bub lies terrified, yet in which he bravely tells his mother good-bye, becomes one of the most painful for the reader. For we know, when we read it, that when she leaves him for good, at the end, he won't have a chance to tell her goodbye.

Mrs. Hedges, whose apparent omniscience and indifferent curiosity lead the reader to perceive the connection between Lutie's references to Franklin and the novel's larger deism, also leads Lutie to the novel's denouement. As Lutie leaves the apartment building to go to Boots's for the last time, Mrs. Hedges reminds her of the " 'very nice white gentleman, dearie' " who wants to sleep with her. At first Lutie merely fumes; then she starts thinking more clearly, and at last she gives form to the forces of the street: "It was Junto" (418). In her final appearance in the novel, Mrs. Hedges reminds us of her role as madam. The deity/goddess who seems so much a part of the landscape of the street has failed to mother. And when Lutie, following her murder of Boots, abandons Bub and buys a one-way train ticket to Chicago, Petry's vision is complete. The feeling of the failure of the idea of America, its possibilities, its "dream," is conveyed in the feeling of the failure of the mothers/madams to help their children. The image of "homelessness" or "absence of mother" which Petry gives her reader when Lutie leaves Bub is more terrifying than the absence of God.

Yet in the failure of the mothers to listen to their grannies, or to turn to the black community and the women's community for wisdom, solace, and help, the novel portrays social desolation in fundamental human terms. If we focus not just on the novel's deism, on the withdrawal of human agency by which the street operates, but see it instead as systematically alienating children from their "mothers"---that is, from their roots (and root doctors)---and orphaning them culturally, then the betrayal of democracy for black people in Petry's novel becomes the destruction of human feeling in the world. Mrs. Hedges's eyes become every bit as powerful and empty as the eyes of Doctor T. J. Eckleburg, which emerge from the landscape of the "valley of ashes" in F. Scott Fitzgerald's *The Great Gatsby*. Despite her ultimate failure as a model for the women on the street, Min therefore points (minimally?) to the novel's meaning. In not wanting to be "put out" from Jones's apartment, she fights for human survival, and for the survival of women. She does not want to be "put out" from the human circle.

Ironically, then, the only "pattern against the sky" which the novel creates is, after all, motherhood---but a motherhood not of biology but of human connection, in which the Prophet David becomes the symbol of nurturing power in the black community, the force capable of countering the perverted indifference of feeling represented by Petry's portrait of Mrs. Hedges. Like the snow at the end of the novel, which "gently" obscures "the grime and the garbage and the ugliness," *The Street* does offer its readers an alternative in the vision of a black community which might embrace its grandmothers, its folklore, and the survival of human feeling, a street which might become, and thereby transform, "any street in the city"---even the street in Lyme, Connecticut, on which Petry shows us white people, like Mr. Chandler's brother, blowing their brains out.

In so doing, *The Street* stands as a connecting link in a fictional tradition that looks back to Zora Neale Hurston's portraits of black community and folkore and looks ahead to those contemporary novels by Marshall, Alice Walker, Morrison, and Bambara (and Ralph Ellison and James Baldwin and Al Young) which have taught readers to rediscover, reassess, and reclaim the human values signified by folk community in black fiction. Such fiction really proclaims our declaration of independence---our refusal to be any longer enslaved by human indifference in any form, in any culture.

---

[1] In A. Robert Lee, ed. *Black Fiction: New Studies in the Afro-American Novel Since 1945* (New York: Barnes & Noble, 1980), 43. Gross is quoting Ann Petry, *The Street* (New York: Houghton Mifflin, 1946), 63-64. In making references to this edition, I will cite further page numbers in parenthesis in the text.

[2] "Ann Petry's Demythologizing of American Culture and Afro-American Character." [See elsewhere in this text]

[3] Since its publication in 1946, *The Street* has been applauded by some critics and reviewers, damned by others. James W. Ivy, who first interviewed Petry from *The Crisis* (in February 1946; the interview is reprinted by Roseann P. Bell, Bettye J. Parker, and Beverly Guy-Sheftall, eds. *Sturdy Black Bridges: Visions of Black Women in Literature* (Garden City, NY: Anchor Press/Doubleday, 1979), 197-200), in a subsequent issue delivered a vicious attack on Petry in his review of *The Street* (*Crisis* 54 [May 1946], 154-55). In a contrasting review from *Phylon* in the same year (7:98-99), Lucy Lee Clemmons called the novel "good reading . . . Despite the sordidness, the squalor, the bitterness, there is a fundamental understanding of basic human qualities and realism concerning Negro life." And Alain Locke, in a review of Petry and other black writers who had published fiction during 1946, assesses both the novel and its controversy and concludes that *The Street* is "the artistic success" of 1946. Calling the novel "the cleverest kind of social indictment," he describes Petry's characters as symbolic of "the environment which made them," concluding that "in realism, that is the height of art." More recently, Petry's Lutie Johnson has frequently been termed "the female counterpart of Bigger Thomas" (see, for example, Alfred Maund, "The Negro Novelist and the Contemporary Scene" [Chicago *Jewish Forum* 12 (1954): 28-34]; or Robert Bone, *The Negro Novel in America* (New Haven: Yale University Press, 1958], who calls the novel a *roman a these* and an "eloquent successor to *Native Son*"). Other critics have moved beyond either attacking Petry's portrait of Harlem life or undercutting the value of her achievement by comparing her to Richard Wright. David Littlejohn, for example, advises the reader to skip the novel's "sordid plot" but praises its "female wisdom, the chewy style" with which Petry creates "people made out of love, with whole histories evoked in a page" (*Black on White* [New York: Grossman Bros. 1966], 155). Arthur P. Davis *(From the Dark Tower* [Washington, D.C.: Howard University Press, 1974]) calls the novel Petry's "most impressive," although he too characterizes it as "a depressing work" which implies "that the black poor in the ghetto do not have

much of a chance to live decent and meaningful lives, to say nothing of happy lives." (194).

The most incisive analysis emerges from Addison Gayle, Jr., who explores the novel's naturalism and suggests that Petry "has paved the way for future black writers" by portraying America as "an oppressive place for black people," thereby beginning "the exploration for realistic ways of combating the deterministic universe" (*The Way of the New World* [Garden City, NY: Anchor/Doubleday, 1975], 196).

[4] In his biography, *Benjamin Franklin: Philosopher and Man* (Philadelphia: J. B. Lippencott Co., 1965), Alfred Owen Aldridge notes that Franklin organized his Junto in the fall of 1727 (39), although he did not become a member of the Masons until February 1731 (44).

[5] Aldridge, 40.

[6] Set in motion by an Efficient Cause (54) and cites the deists' "central concept of God as a Passive Policeman" (56).

[7] See Edwin Gittleman, "Jefferson's 'Slave Narrative': The Declaration of Independence as a Literary Text," *Early American Literature* 8 (1974), 239-6, for a fuller discussion of the original draft of the Declaration, as well as for the text of the anti-slavery grievance, 252-53.

[8] Gayle, 196.

[9] I'm thinking especially of Marshall's *The Chosen Place, The Timeless People* (1969), Morrison's *Sula* (1973) and *Song of Solomon* (1977), Bambara's *The Salt Eaters* (1980), and Walker's *The Color Purple* (1982), all of which portray strong women who understand the power of black, female traditions.

The Narrows: A Fuller View of Ann Petry (1980)
Margaret B. McDowell

The Street (1946), which depicts a Black woman's struggles in a New York slum, established Ann Petry as a major figure in American naturalistic fiction, and critics immediately linked her work with Richard Wright's *Native Son* (1940). Petry's more intricate novel, *The Narrows* (1953), has sold over a million copies, but has not received full critical attention. Nor have critics been generally aware of her achievements with short stories or her two historical novels with female protagonists *(Harriet Tubman,* 1955 and *Tituba of Salem Village,* 1964).

Because of the social and literary impact of her first novel, *The Street* may be regarded as Petry's most important work. But the high quality and the variety of her fiction warrant further exploration into her contribution to American realistic and anti-realistic fiction to current preoccupation with racial themes and Black protagonists, and to the fiction produced by Black women.

A study of *The Narrows* provides a wider perspective for an assessment of Ann Petry's achievement than does a consideration of *The Street* alone.[1] In *The Narrows* Petry experiments with conveying the depths of psychic consciousness, with communicating emotional conflict thorough interior monologue, and with juxtaposing memory and present experience. She moves away from the qualities which characterize *The Street*: chronology, characters who remain relatively unchanged, dramatically compressed scenes, and tautness of plot. Expansiveness and flexibility mark her technique here as she shifts point of view and intonation, makes abundant use of flashbacks, and elaborates theme through the use of extended metaphor. Metaphorical and ironic implications lift the writing beyond realism to enlarged social and psychological significance. She often develops situations of emotional stress and complication with more subtlety in *The Narrows* than she does in *The Street*. Rather than presenting one or two individuals in relative isolation as she had done earlier, in *The Narrows* she frequently depicts more complex interactions among individuals and among these individuals and larger groups of people. She again mirrors indirectly a culture vitiated by racial intolerance through focusing upon the effects of intolerance in the lives of only a few characters. This intolerance destroys Link, the determined and dynamic hero. Abbie Crunch, his adoptive mother, possesses not only fortitude but also a protective evasiveness which permits her to survive her ordeals with a degree of satisfaction and self-respect.

By dramatizing a twenty-year period in which a mixed-ethnic neighborhood becomes a segregated Black locale, Petry emphasizes that Blacks must attain a historical perspective concerning race prejudice in America; and she also observes the growth of hostility against Blacks in a certain place during a specified time---one neighborhood in a New England mill town between the early 1930s and 1950s. She underscores the necessity for Blacks to keep a "racial memory" active by choosing a protagonist who aspires to write a history of slavery in the United States from the Black viewpoint. Throughout the book she demonstrates how the established and respected institutions---churches, schools, and news media---intensify the polarization between the races. Petry neither pretends to provide answers to the problems she presents nor evades any of the implications of these problems.

Petry focuses her story temporally on three months in Link's life, the period during which he abandons his studies of history to pursue an affair with a wealthy white woman, Camilla Treadway, who is unhappily married. When they meet for the first time in the dark on the Dumble Street dock in the Narrows, they do not immediately recognize that they are of different races. Later, Camilla, using a false name, hides from Link both her wealth and her marriage. By driving frequently to a Harlem hotel from their Connecticut town, they enjoy comparative anonymity. When Link finally learns everything about Camilla and recognizes that she had never intended to marry him in the spring, he breaks with her. On the same dock where they met, Camilla impulsively plays Potiphar's wife, hysterically accuses Link of rape and demands his prosecution. A few days later she is herself arrested for driving recklessly in the Narrows and severely injuring a Black child. Newspaper sensationalism, Link's race, and the wealth and power of Camilla's family all fan public prejudice---against Link but also to a degree against Camilla---before the rape trial opens. In a confused effort to keep the Treadway name out of a sensational trial, Camilla's mother arranges Link's kidnapping and murder. She attempts to dispose of his body, is fortuitously arrested for speeding, and is exposed as a conspirator in the murder.

Flashbacks insistently weave together the past and the present. Important in the flashbacks is the pastoral peace which once existed in the Narrows, particularly in the household where Link, before the age of eight, lived with Abbie Crunch and the Major. The child then felt great camaraderie with the Major, whose irrepressible humor pervaded the family. Their Irish, Polish, and Italian neighbors, moreover, respected Link's family in the integrated neighborhood. The family *chose* to attend a Black church, primarily to accelerate the Major's chances of becoming a deacon; Abbie was proud of being elected president of the white WCTU. Even so, Abbie self-consciously and continually sought to impress her white neighbors with the worth of her family, sometimes at the cost of holding herself from other Blacks. Such compulsion undoubtedly derived from the tenuousness of trust existing between Blacks and whites, a potentially unstable situation existing in spite of surface harmony. Petry leaves no doubt that antagonism based on race, if relatively quiescent, preceded the influx of a predominantly Black population into the neighborhood.

The idyllic life in the old brick house near the river on Dumble Street ceased when Link was eight. Bill Hod, owner of the Last Chance saloon, dragged the staggering and incoherent Major home one afternoon. Furious at his "drunkenness," Abbie ignored the Major---and allowed him to die of a stroke. For weeks her grief and guilt made her forget even the existence of Link, who found his own way to the Last Chance. Link moved restlessly for ten years between Hod's saloon and Abbie's house. His bitter memories remained a source of trauma for him in his adulthood---Abbie's sudden neglect, Hod's outbursts of physical cruelty toward him throughout his adolescent years, a teacher's discrimination, and a prostitute's betrayal of him at the age of sixteen.

The fullness and power of this novel contrast with its limited scope, or perhaps they derive from such concentration of Petry's creative energies. No single protagonist clearly dominates: the novel remains, in a sense, the saga of a community. Yet Link and his adoptive mother, Abbie Crunch, are vital characters because of the depths of their inner struggles. Both express their conflicts in fragmented interior monologues. Because of Abbie's centrality, the novel sustains intensity for a time following Link's funeral, and it ends with a fuller suggestion of hope and the significance of fortitude than Petry could attain in *The Street*, where her concentration on a youthful heroine and victim is not extended to a secondary figure of almost equal consequence.

In this book, Petry also created powerful lesser figures---notably Frances K. Jackson, a spinster who left medical school to return to serve the Narrows as an undertaker, and Malcolm and Mamie Powther, who live with their three children in Abbie's upstairs apartment. Frances K. Jackson's humanity helps Abbie survive spiritually after the Major's death; her practical, though brusquely delivered advice guides Abbie in bringing up Link. She is certainly the most stable and assured character in the book. Frances's sharp remarks as she copes with her two employees---an assertive cook and an unpredictable driver of the funeral car---establish a pervasive humor for the book despite its tragic overtones. And yet she is also a tragic figure as she presides over the griefs of the Black community year after year, allowing herself few feelings of her own. Frances's sensitivity in the presence of suffering, hysteria, and fear leads others to say that she always knows "when to retreat and when to advance."[2] Another minor character, the flamboyant Mamie Powther, dominates every scene in which she appears with her warmth and magnetism, her quick anger, her frank search for pleasure, and her unacknowledged isolation. Just as Mamie commands attention, Malcolm Powther arouses empathy, because Petry explores his mind with only less thoroughness than she does the minds of Abbie and Link. Malcolm provides a connection between the Narrows and the estate of the wealthy industrialists, the Treadways for whom he is butler; and he emerges not only as a man with an undue sense of decorum, but as a man given to passion and intense fantasies about his own life and situation. He is fascinated by Mamie's vulgarity and impulsiveness, which contrast with his own desire for stability and propriety. His fantasies of delicate blonde women and his preoccupation with the fairy tale of a golden princess, which he tells his little boys each night, conflict with the inexplicable pride with which he views his own intense marriage to a shabby and disorderly woman, despite the frustrations that it arouses in him.

As Petry shifts skillfully between past and present in the novel, she moves also with assurance between the mind of Abbie Crunch and that of Link Williams. Only a few scenes---mostly those centering on the Powther family--- move beyond the imaginative and emotional experience of Abbie or Link, and these the reader views through the eyes and memory of Malcolm Powther.

Three memorable eccentrics are peripheral to the plot but add mystery. They move above the streets day and night and at crucial moments provide a disturbing and grotesque dimension to the novel. First, there is Cesar the Writing Man, who writes prophetic Bible verses on sidewalks with chalk, as if to indicate that the Narrows is important to God, if only as a community that must be chastised. Second, there is Weak Knees, the cook at the Last Chance saloon, who, whenever he is agitated, flails his arms and mutters, "Get away, Eddie!" to the imagined presence of the man he killed years before in self-defense. In him, as in Abbie, guilt assails an individual who is basically good and highly conscientious. Third, there is Cat Jimmie, an inarticulate, legless and armless man, who terrorizes the women whom he pursues at high speed on his cart. He is a caricature, since one "deadly sin"---lust---motivates his every moment.

As in all her work, Petry excels in *The Narrows* in her use of concrete detail, her ability to dramatize a situation, and her ear for exact dialogue. She is a master at transcribing the details of a given milieu as she recreates, for example, the sound of the river lapping against the dock at night, the feeling that fog generates as it rolls up the street from the river, the smell of beer from the saloon across from Abbie's brick house, and the glare of sunlight on the River Wye. To help convey the sense of plenitude in the social scene that she recreates in her novel, she appeals to the auditory sense of her reader, as when Mamie Powther sings her plaintive blues throughout the novel.

Each place, object, and fragment of dialogue becomes important in creating the realistic milieu, but certain aspects of the Narrows generate abstract associations. The cemetery becomes segregated, as if the dead must not mingle across racial lines. A myriad of placards proclaiming rooms for rent and a growing number of drifters sleeping under Abbie's big tree suggest the increasingly transient nature of the population. The River Wye, though a beautiful stream, draws the desperate to suicide. In its growing pollution, the river symbolizes, to a degree, the economic exploitation of the area. The naming of the Last Chance saloon promises fellowship as well as food and drink for the survival of the down-and-outer, but the name also implies an impending finality to those who need more than food and drink. It offers no further opportunities for the repressed of society to attain for themselves security, love or justice. Its neon sign is ugly and cheap, its owner's temper flares in murderous violence, and it is linked with lucrative prostitution and gambling enterprises which exploit the poor while providing them with specious pleasure. The Treadway estate---remote from the Narrows---is also symbolic. It is the site for an annual festival for the workers in the munitions plant, but the celebration is an impersonal gesture which expresses no true concern of the employers for their workers. The laborers, in turn, gossip viciously about Camilla Treadway's presence on the dock at Dumble Street at midnight when she was allegedly threatened with rape.

The motor cars of the Treadways---the Rolls-Royce and their fleet of Cadillacs---are symbolic of power. Camilla's automobiles make possible the anonymity which she and Link achieve by driving to Harlem. Camilla's impulsive, reckless driving suggests her instability. Treadway automobiles, in a more sinister context, facilitate the kidnapping of Link and the hauling away of the body. Bill Hod's secondhand Cadillacs represent the rewards of his shady dealings, many of which exploit his Black brothers and sisters, while F. K. Jackson's funeral limousine (with its whiskey bottle for the weary and its case of long black gloves and lace veil, available for any bereaved woman to wear for a half hour of proper mourning) reflects how superficial and conventional the rites of grief are to the capitalist entrepreneur.

II.

The slow pace and intensive elaboration inherent both in the characters' reflections and in the numerous flashbacks allow Petry to develop fully three themes: the oppressiveness of guilt; the effects of historiography, tradition, and time on the attitudes of contemporary people toward race; and the limited veracity of sensory apprehension.

In her emphasis on the relationship of past and present and in her penetration into the depths of consciousness, Petry emphasizes the sense of inferiority which hangs over certain Blacks and makes them experience a general and irrational guilt for something that they cannot define. Because of the denigration that Blacks have suffered over the generations, both Abbie and Link are plagued at times by a feeling that Blacks perhaps deserve, in part, this denigration. Both characters occasionally seek to separate themselves from other Blacks, to avoid association that might be demeaning to them. This denial of their racial identity results in further guilt. The aging Abbie feels the strongest sense of oppression, having existed longest under the constraint which Martin Luther King, Jr. called "living at tiptoe stance." She tries anxiously to live without anyone reproaching her, to assert equality with her white neighbors by being always more virtuous and more socially correct than they are. Only the Major, and later Link, can laugh Abbie out of her compulsive concern for appearances, her attempts to build a façade of propriety that will gain her the immediate approbation of the respectable. Abbie not only mends the cotton gloves she wears to the grocery, but she also makes the stitches invisible. She not only keeps her house immaculate, but she also scrubs the wood trim around each tiny pane in her windows and daily polishes her brass door-knocker. As she walks down the street, she stretches her spine to attain an erectness that may make her seem tall, though she is short and plump. She appears always to be proud, but she is secretly vulnerable and fears that she may not fully be "measuring up." Abbie's primary concern is to be a credit to "the race." She insists, to the point of being oppressive, that Link also must worthily represent the Black world.

Other characters deal with excessive guilt feelings with violence. In an attempt to escape any sense of wrong-doing for either his violence or his illegal enterprises involving liquor, gambling, and prostitution, Bill Hod is preoccupied with certain properties, as evidenced by his perverse beatings of Link to keep the adolescent boy "innocent." Weak Knees, Hod's cook, is himself plagued by guilt for having murdered a friend in self-defense many years earlier, but he helps Link recognize that Blacks need not adopt an inordinate humility. He asserts that they must confront the injustice meted out by whites and the power which those in authority often use against them. Blacks must survive, he insists, by force and determination. Weak Knees, thus, contradicts Abbie's view that Link must, by incessant effort, attain worthiness in the eyes of whites. In reeducating the youth, Weak Knees systematically provides him with clippings about "smart white boys" who receive light sentences in court for embezzlement while Blacks are imprisoned for minor infractions of the law. The growing realization that society encourages conditions of inequity relieves Link's anxiety about his personal responsibility for "the race" and its progress, an emotional burden which Abbie had forced him to assume. From Weak Knees' clippings and from Hod's distrust of whites and his harsh punishment of him, Link learns that because he is Black, he simply cannot *afford* to disobey a law or convention. Following his kidnapping he expresses his full realization of this in his internal monologue while anticipating his death.

Near the close of the book Abbie gains a modicum of victory over the guilt that she has nurtured for eighteen years as a result of her neglect of the dying Major when she misperceived his stroke. Abbie returns from Link's funeral to find that little J.C. Powther has mischievously appropriated the Major's hat, which had hung in the hallway since his death as almost an object of veneration. Instead of shock and anger, she is amused with the child, whose impish face is largely covered by the hat. As she silently muses, she refers to the hat as "old clothes," a phrase of particular significance in her meditation, because the news stories of Link's murder had stated that the bag containing his body was at first described to police as containing "old clothes."

Abbie has finally realized that both husband and son are now dead. She knows that it will make little difference if one ever knows that exact cause of the deaths. In giving the hat to J.C., Abbie once more reaches out to a child, as she had in adopting Link. With renewed courage, she determines to remain independent, rather than to move to F. K. Jackson's home. She further determines to protect Camilla Treadway by alerting the police to Bill Hod's plan to kill the rich white woman in revenge for Link's death. In doing so, Abbie breaks the tyrannical cycle of impulsive action followed by excessive retribution or self-accusation which has dominated all the principle actions of the novel. On this one occasion, at least, Abbie does not maintain her own race and class consciousness but reaches out to protect a white heiress against the impending violence of a Black man who plans to avenge the death of Abbie's own son.

III.

Petry emphasizes the fallibility of human beings. Abbie, fortunately, recognizes by the closing scene that human behavior is too complex to be judged as expeditiously as a conventional society often attempts to do. Abbie's recognition of her false pride and narrowness is the first step to self-reliance and peace of mind. The recognition by society of its historical failure to treat all people as human beings can bring about its regeneration and peace; otherwise, only alienation and violence lie ahead.

Racial stress in *The Narrows* develops not only from the actions of a repressive society and the resentment of the oppressed but also from the uncertainties which the Black characters experience concerning their own place in history. Understanding the history of one's race is vital, in Petry's view, to the understanding of the self. Link attempts, therefore, to resolve his adolescent confusion about his Black identity by studying history in high school and college for what it may tell him about his origins; he hopes that a greater understanding of slavery in particular may provide Blacks with a key to their own history and identity. Full consciousness of past indignities may serve both symbolically to help Blacks understand the evil in human nature and spiritually to liberate Blacks in the present. Link sees such spiritual liberation, derived from identification with the oppressed, as parallel to the crucial insight into their culture which Jews gain from the celebration of Passover, with its ritual rehearsal of escape from slavery. But Link also is cynically aware that racial problems increase in complexity and that history will remain an enigma, even to the Black scholar seeking to understand his origins and his present identity.

Petry presents Abbie at her worst when she deflates Link's announcement of his ambition by taunting, "Whoever heard of a black historian!" Elsewhere, Abbie comments perceptively that history itself has enslaved Blacks by perpetuating the myth of racial inferiority. But she cannot honestly face her family's past. She finds too much that embarrasses her in the folk culture, as it is reflected in the Major's stories of his strong, eccentric, and vulgar relatives. Afraid of humiliation before whites, she allows false pride to confuse and annoy her and to separate her from her Black origins---and, to a degree, from even the Major and Link. Yet she forces Link to feel the burden of responsibility for an abstraction of which she would seem proud: "the race." Like Abbie, Link recognizes that history has become a storehouse of prejudice enslaving Blacks, but he also sees that it provides the resources to overthrow prejudice. Historical perspective provides the context for evaluating contemporary events.

Petry, in portraying the slow history of change in the Narrows over twenty years, does not imply that the culture moves away from racism as Blacks become the majority. For her, social history provides no evidence of moral evolution. As the area becomes mainly Black, not only does the polarization of Blacks from their neighbors increase but also the spirit of Black community and brotherhood fails to develop. Abbie is uncomfortable as she finds herself newly surrounded by Blacks. She has primly avoided her Polish neighbors because they yell and swear in domestic fights, and she has refrained abstemiously from the cooking of foods that might make her house smell like "colored folks' houses. She dresses with care to avoid looking "like an Aunt Mehalia." Attending a funeral of a Black, she looks askance at the conspicuous mourning of the widow, not only because of the hypocrisy involved in this particular case but because a Black is expressing herself with primitive abandonment and giving way to the irrational and demonstrative.

After the novel's publication Petry stated that she did not intend to imply that Link's tragedy developed from an interracial love affair.[3] In this novel the conflict and deception implicit in the relationship between Link and Camilla mirror the pervasive nature of prejudice even more effectively than does Link's historical research on slavery. Deception and distrust remain inevitable in all relationships in a society which makes assumptions primarily on the basis of the racial origins of its citizens.

If after twenty years of integration individuals in the Narrows remain imprisoned in prejudice, the long established institutions of society are not less free. In the school play, a teacher assigns Link a stereotypical Sambo role of sleeping in the sun, and fails to understand why Link feigns illness the day the play is to be performed. In the church, a Jewish child visits Abbie's Sunday School and goes home ashamed of his heritage because of the ridicule from Black children who fail to understand the rituals that he has been taught to revere. In the editorial offices of newspapers, a campaign exploiting hatred of Blacks occurs after Link's arrest and accusation by a member of a white family of wealth. Thus all the conflicts felt by the individual characters in this novel are intensified daily by patterns of racial intolerance which are deep-rooted in institutions and which change only sporadically and confusingly. Petry implies that if little hope for radical social change exists, the understanding of Black tradition and Black history may provide a liberating force which will ultimately have some positive and dynamic effects.

IV

Petry's third major theme concerns the nature and degree of truth which one can gain through observation and recognition of verifiable sight or sound.

Though a master of realistic detail, Petry demonstrates the fallacy of attempting to discover the "whole truth" and the need for recognizing the limits of individual recognition and interpretation of fact. Intellectual humility can lead to human tolerance. Much of her characterization and humor emerges from her ironic treatment of certain individuals who attempt to oversimplify human relationships---to name, define, and communicate with an objective exactness in realms which must retain complexity and mystery.

In grappling with racial confusion, divergence of interpretation rather than final and definitive answers must be sought. Petry develops this theme more fully through her presentation of the photographer, Jubine, and through the personality of Abbie than she does through the more pragmatic Link. Petry uses images connected with photography to delineate Abbie's mind, in the same manner as she employs sequences which involve Jubine, the photographer. If Jubine focuses his camera to present truth from his own viewpoint, Abbie adjusts her perspective so that she can acknowledge only those aspects of an event, a person, or a location which she can accommodate within her conservative and stable life. The camera both *lies* and presents truth. The objective recording of reality is subject to continual manipulation, that is sometimes conscious, sometimes not. By extension, Petry implies that in our society no one can envision the whole configuration of racial conflict in perspective. The individual, at best, confronts and shapes fragments of conflicting truths. In their concern for social propriety, Jubine and Abbie are at opposite poles. They share in common their understanding that basic moral truth lies in response to the question, "Am I my brother's keeper?"

Jubine pretends to be always an observer rather than a participant, but as the author's spokesman, he forces others out of complacent non-involvement. For example, early in the novel, he confronts the newspaper editor and insists that he buy and print in the Christmas issue a series of three photographs of the River Wye, rather than the single picture the editor wishes to buy. In the picture which the editor wants, the river lies snow-covered and tranquil beneath a steepled church and a single star, as if to suggest harmony in nature which seems also to exist in society during the Christmas season. Jubine's second picture, however, introduces a disturbing element. The river lies shadowed in the background, the steeple no longer dominates, and on the dock in the foreground a man sprawls, belly-down in dirty snow marred by black puddles. Harsh surroundings characterize the plot as the third photograph details in the broken snow the man's crawling , clawing, and staggering. Zigzag footprints lead to the edge of the dock; none return.

The editor's horror grows as he realizes that Jubine must have waited to record with apparent detachment the slow progress of a suicide. Jubine responds to the editor's shock with the rhetorical question: "Who *is* involved in what happens on the dock?" Basic in Petry's fiction is always her view that in any organic society we are our brother's keeper and that the sufferings of one individual should make their indelible mark on other individuals as well.

Later in the novel when prejudice against Blacks threatens Link's access to a fair trial, the same editor plays upon the prejudices of the community by featuring a sinister picture of an escaped Black convict. Jubine retaliates on Link's behalf by arranging for a New York tabloid to print an incriminating photograph which he has made of Camilla, Link's accuser, standing by her car with a frightened and guilty expression on her face just after she has run down a Black child. Beside this photograph is Jubine's portrait of Link standing handsome in the sunlight, his body, "possessing the solidity of fine sculpture." Jubine's photographs obviously serve a propagandistic aim in the novel's plot, in order to prejudice prospective jurors in Link's favor.

As with Jubine, Petry uses imagery associated with photography to analyze Abbie's mind. Just as she implies that Jubine's manipulation of fact is justified to awaken conscience, Petry also suggests that Abbie's evasive strategies--- which essentially limit her moral growth---are forgivable for the more timid individual in a hostile society. For the woman from a minority group, along and growing old, spiritual survival, rather than growth, may be the crucial objective. Abbie's ability to cope in the Narrows probably depends upon her facile limiting or shaping of that which she is willing to acknowledge as reality. The degree of disapproval of Abbie by other characters varies greatly in emphasis from Hod's hatred, Link's annoyance, and the Major's teasing, to Frances K. Jackson's straight-forward scolding. Always, however, these negative reactions to Abbie relate to her escapist patterning of her environment, her narrow vision, her dogmatic inflexibility, and her need to manipulate others in a manner that will leave her home, family, and familiar way of living relatively undisturbed.

Petry leaves little doubt that Jubine's shocking of society into awareness of injustice is laudable, but she is far more ambiguous in her judgment of Abbie's refusal to look straight at the world around her. If Jubine remains the same imperturbable character throughout, Abbie continually gives evidence of internalized conflict which eventually results in growth and acceptance of herself. She begins to come to terms with her weaknesses, her strengths, and her growing capacity to reach out in concern for others who differ greatly from herself. Abbie maintains just enough courage to see life steadily, but never achieves the imaginative and spiritual daring to see life wholistically. She is a heroine by virtue of her ability to survive and to grow to a limited degree in a hostile society. It is society's tragedy that she cannot confront it more fully. Abbie cautiously composes, balances, and frames her version of reality. Reflecting upon her mental "pictures," she ruthlessly crops those memories which might distract and mar her small and settled vision of herself, others, and her race. She never fantasizes wildly. She squints until she finds her necessary perspective.

In the opening pages of the novel Abbie stands in reverie on the dock, trying to see the river as a mountain pond, rather than as an industrialized waterway. A moment later, still focusing, cropping, and reframing, she tries to picture her own house apart from the ugliness of Dumble Street with its neon saloon sign and "For Rent" placards. In doing so, she closely centers on the maple in its autumn glory on her front lawn. But Abbie's mind flees always to the stasis of the quiet and unchanging picture: she decides to see her tree as one on a calendar for "September." She then can avoid seeing the drunks sleeping under it and she need not look ahead to the winter months when the beautiful leaves will be swept away by cold winds. Similarly, when she focuses upon her old house, her passive mind pictures the bricks not as red but as "rose-colored," a muted shade which to her suggests "an air of aristocracy." Continually, Abbie isolates and distorts to make her milieu acceptable.

Just as she mentally modifies her physical surroundings, she also deliberately examines, accepts or rejects people. Sitting at the breakfast table, for example, on the morning after the Powthers have moved into her upstairs apartment, she decides that Mamie Powther, hanging out her washing, does not fit appropriately into the picture which she expects to see each morning of her tidy back yard. With her big bosom, jingly earrings, high heels, and short red flowery dress that bares the backs of her thighs each time she dips into the basket of clothes, Mamie (and her blues song) disturb Abbie's orderly day and the perspective that she has been accustomed to view from her kitchen window:

> She simple did not belong in that neat
> backyard with its carefully tended lawn and
> its white fences. The brilliant red of the
> poppies on her dress made the red of the
> dogwood leaves look faded, washed out . . .
> She dominated the morning so that you saw
> nothing but Mamie. (24)

Abbie even extends this critical view to her portraits of herself, in which she must appear as the worthy image of the Black woman. She constantly checks that every strand of hair is kept in place as if an unseen camera will at any moment record her appearance and behavior before the whole world.

Besides framing selectively all that she sees, Abbie further simplifies and shapes her world by patterning that which she hears---news of change, a cutting phrase, a significant name, a demeaning epithet, a fearful rumor. In moments of stress she calms herself with a childish game in which she silently fits the unfamiliar word or phrase into a neatly-rhymed couplet. Once she closes the rigid verse---even nonsensically---she has imprisoned the disturbing element in a framework which she can control. She relaxes as if she has reached the end of a phrase in music or the resolution of an equation in mathematics.

Through such rhyming, and more particularly through the continual focus of her "camera eye," Abbie emerges as a woman who keeps her mind and heart in order by admitting into her life only that measure of experience which she feels ready to control. By classifying truth in terms of settled views and understandings and by condensing it to the simplistic statement or the undisturbing picture, she is, of course, following the patterns that have allowed the stereotypical attitudes which alienate the races to develop. Abbie certainly is not the spokeswoman for Petry. In the full portrayal of both Abbie's strengths and her weaknesses, however, Petry allows the reader to identify fully with the confusion and the insight, the fears and the courage, the false pride and the deep humility of one aging Black woman. She emerges as a woman who tries daily to make her "race" admirable in the sight of all who would judge it, but who also, paradoxically, separates herself from full fellowship with either Blacks or whites. A courageous heroine, she is also a victim of a history of prejudice. Though less dramatic than the tragedy of Lutie Johnson in *The Street*, Abbie's situation in which she is torn by the pressures of guilt, aloofness, and false pride also demonstrates the destructiveness of the society in which individual differences---in her case, largely racial in origin---promote hatred, intolerance, and alienation.

---

[1] *Country Place* (1947), Petry's second novel, is not discussed here because it seems to me of lower quality than the first and third novels. Like *The Narrows*, it is set in a Connecticut town; unlike *The Narrows*, it deals almost exclusively with white characters. Petry herself grew up as a member of the only Black family in the small Connecticut town where her father was the pharmacist. After receiving a degree in pharmacy at the University of Connecticut and writing in New York for a few years during World War II, Petry and her husband returned to her hometown, which provides the background for several of her stories.

[2] Ann Petry, *The Narrows* (Madison, NJ: Chatham Book Seller, 1953), 3. Future references will appear parenthetically in the text and refer to the 1953 edition.

[3] John O'Brien, *Interviews with Black Writers* (New York: Liveright, 1973), 162.

The Narrows: A Black New England Novel (1987)
Sybil Weir

When Ann Petry published *The Narrows* in 1953, the novel was reviewed in the leading newspapers and magazines. Since then, however, critics have neglected it, preferring to focus on Petry's achievement in *The Street* (1946) and in short fiction such as "In Darkness and Confusion." This neglect of *The Narrows* is undeserved because the novel reveals the maturing of Petry's literary vision beyond the limited sociological determinism of *The Street*. The rich and complex rendering of black and white relationships in a small Connecticut city continues to compel readers. Of particular interest is Petry's use of both Anglo-American and Afro-American literary motifs. As Arna Bontemps wrote in his review of *The Narrows* in *The Saturday Review of Literature*,

> a novel about Negroes by a Negro novelist and concerned, in the last analysis, with racial conflict, *The Narrows* somehow resists classification as a "Negro Novel," as contradictory as that may sound. In this respect Ann Petry has achieved something as rare as it is commendable. Her book reads like a New England novel, and an unusually gripping one.[1]

Arna Bontemps was right. To overlook the ways in which *The Narrows* is shaped by Petry's New England heritage is to miss part of its complexity, yet, aside from Bontemps, almost every critic who has analyzed Petry's work has done so solely in relation to other Afro-American fiction. This context has been necessary and valuable for recovering the contours of the Afro-American literary tradition. Nevertheless, it it time to take seriously Sherley Williams' proposal that the most fruitful approach to American literature is a comparative one.[2] Such an approach reveals that, in *The Narrows*, Petry is indebted to Nathaniel Hawthorne as well as to Richard Wright, that *The Narrows* belongs to the tradition of domestic feminism and realism created primarily by New England women writers as well as to the experience Petry had in Harlem in the 1940s.

The New England tradition is most clearly exemplified in Abbie Crunch, the seventy-year-old black matron in *The Narrows*. While it is important to note that Abbie Crunch is only one of the novel's three major characters from whose perspectives the novel is narrated, Petry's characterization of her is convincing, complex, and realistic.[3] Petry shows the emotional and psychic reality of a black mother who has embraced the values of New England culture at the expense of her own racial heritage. Petry's treatment of the theme of the psychic costs of racism, a theme central to much of Afro-American fiction before and since *The Narrows*, is particularly moving and convincing.

The Narrrows is set in Monmouth, Connecticut. The title refers to Monmouth's black ghetto, Dumble Street, variously known as "The Narrows, Eye of the Needle, The Bottom, Little Harlem, Dark Town, Niggertown--- because Negroes had replaced those other earlier immigrants, the Irish, the Italians, and the Poles."[4] To emphasize the universality of her vision, using a speech from *King Henry V* as her inscription:

> . . . I tell you, captain, if you look in the
> maps of the 'orld, I warrant you shall find,
> in the comparisons between Macedon and
> Monmouth, that the situations, look you, is
> both alike. There is a river in Macedon; and
> there is also moreover a river at Monmouth:
> it is called Wye at Monmouth; . . . but 'tis all
> one, 'tis alike as my fingers is to my fingers,
> and there is salmons in both (Act IV, vii).

In New England as in old Britian and Macedon, the river flows on, indifferent to the dramas of human aspirations and passions played out on its bank. The river is indifferent to human betrayal---Alexander killing his best friend in Macedon, Henry V shunning Falstaff, the black butler betraying the black bartender in Monmouth, Connecticut. And just as all the water in Wye cannot wash the Welsh blood out of Henry V's body,[5] so all the water of the Wye in Monmouth, Connecticut, cannot wash out black or white blood.

The plot traces the tragic consequences of a love affair between a black man, Link Williams, and a white woman, Camilo Treadway Sheffield. The two meet by chance on a foggy night in The Narrows, unaware at first of each other's race or class. The course of the love affair inevitably reflects America's pervasive racism: The white woman in a jealous rage gains her revenge by crying rape, the black man is callously murdered by her white family, who try to dispose of his body by disguising it as a bundle of old clothes for the Salvation Army. This is a predictable series of events given the sexual and racial politics of America, a series of events as predictable in Petry's Connecticut as in Wright's or Faulkner's South. Petry's rendering of the love affair between Link and Camilo is the weakest part of the novel, unconvincing because melodramatic. As Wright Morris noted in his review in the New York *Times*, the love story, the dramatic center of the novel, is never quite credible.[6]

In part, this weakness stems from the fact that Petry's concern in *The Narrows* is less with depicting an interracial love affair than with tracing its antecedents and charting the reactions to the affair of a variety of characters, black and white. The events in the present illuminate the major characters' attempts to puzzle out the significance of their past order to discover the meaning of their lives. Petry, therefore, uses multi-points of view to narrate the

events of the novel, making extensive use of interior monologues and flashbacks
to convey the mental life of her characters. Although one must agree with
Wright Morris' assessment that "the living past overwhelms the lifeless
present,"[7] the power of the past is precisely Petry's point, and the extensive
flashbacks reinforce this point.

Petry, like Nathaniel Hawthorne, believes in the chain of "dark necessity"
from which people can rarely, if ever, extricate themselves. As the character in
the novel most chained to "dark necessity" is seventy year-old Abbie Crunch.
Eighteen years before the novel opens, when her husband was brought home
comatose and Abbie was urged to call a doctor, Abbie assumed the Major was
drunk, not ill: "People would laugh at her. President of the local WCTU and
her husband so drunk couldn't stand up . . . . The colored president of the white
WCTU. Drunken husband. Well he's colored" (41). The deadly poison
America's racism leads Abbie to worry only about what whites will think
causing her to neglect her husband's stroke. Pathetically, her only concern is
with her living room carpet, her only ministration to put newspaper around the
couch where the Major lies snoring, dying. Guilt and suppressed grief over the
Major's death haunts Abbie throughout the novel causing Abbie to abandon her
adopted son, Link Williams, to forfeit love, and to give him over to the enemy,
Bill Hod, owner of the Last Chance Saloon, and the personification of evil for
Abbie.

Petry's characterization of Abbie is wonderfully compelling in psychological
realism. Indeed, that characterization represents the most telling indictment of
racism in *The Narrows* because it is Abbie Crunch whose psyche has been most
severely damaged by being black in a world in which the standards of conduct
are white. But Petry is not content, as she was in *The Street*, to demonstrate the
inevitable defeat of a black woman by white America. Rather, by the end of *The
Narrows*, Abbie Crunch transcends the moral bankruptcy of American society
and emerges as a spiritual victor.

At first glance, Abbie Crunch seems cast in the mold of the emasculating
black mother figure, a stereotype familiar to readers of Wright's work as well as
other fiction by black males. In a sensitive analysis of this stereotype, Daryl
Dance has concluded that

> these writers in their bitter attacks have been
> dealing in a symbolic way with only one
> aspect of the character of the Black mother
> and have been calling for the destruction,
> not of the Black mother, but rather of that
> aspect of her character that white racist
> society has forced her to develop---the
> repression of the spirit and vitality of her
> Black men, whether as a result of her blind

> acceptance of the dictates of white American
> society or her subservience to them.[8]

But Petry's characterizations are not the stereotypes they seem.[9] In Abbie, Petry reveals the anguished reality beneath the façade of the emasculating black mother. What the son feels as emasculation, the mother perceives as necessary for survival. Abbie Crunch adheres rigidly to genteel standards of ladylike conduct because she believes only those standards offer her a way to control her destiny in a chaotic, threatening world.

Petry's Abbie evokes the isolated women, the New England widows and spinsters, found in the fiction of such writers as Louisa May Alcott, Harriet Beecher Stowe, and Mary Wilkins Freeman. Nor is this surprising. Petry became a full-fledged reader, she writes, "when someone gave me *Little Women* and I discovered Jo March, the tomboy, the misfit, the impatient quick-tempered would-be writer. I felt as though she was a part of me and I was part of her despite the fact that she was white and I was black." Petry continues, "I wept over *Uncle Tom's Cabin* and *Black Beauty*." [10] In addition to Alcott and Stowe, the only other American writers Petry now remembers having read while growing up are Poe and Hawthorne. In view of the fact that Petry grew up in New England and read New England writers while young, it is not surprising that she would endow Abbie Crunch with a New England consciousness. The white code that Abbie chooses to embrace in order to control her destiny in Monmouth, Connecticut, is that code of conduct deemed "proper" to New England matrons, a code which has, in fact, seemed to confer gentility and respectability on many women, in and out of fiction, black and white.

Abbie Crunch is a descendant of the female characters found in the fiction written by New England women. For example, Abbie, like the two sisters in Mary Wilkins Freeman's " A Gala Dress," who are forced to alternate wearing their one proper Sunday dress, will not leave her house improperly attired. Her sense of self-worth necessitates a ritual Saturday morning shopping costume:

> She'd had this basket almost forty years . . . .
> It was a[s] much a part of her Saturday
> morning shopping costume as the polished
> oxfords on her feet, and the lisle stockings
> on her legs. The shoes had been resoled
> many times, but the uppers were as good as
> new. She glanced at her hands---the beige
> colored gloves were immaculate; true,
> they'd been darned, but she doubted that
> anyone would know it (14).

This passage reveals Petry's mastery of the tradition of domestic realism as she focuses attention on the commonplace, seemingly trivial detail, which reveals so much about the inner values of her character. [11]

Abbie's mind is also informed by domestic imagery:

> In this early morning light, the brick of the house was not red but rose colored---the soft pinkish red found on old Persian carpets. The wrought iron railing on each side of the front steps was so intricately and delicately worked that it resembled filet crochet, incredible that a heavy metal like iron could be twisted and turned and bent until it looked like lace. (13)

Not only does Abbie think in terms of images of the home, she also chooses work that can be done there. A schoolteacher before her marriage, Abbie does not return to the classroom after being widowed but supports herself by work associated with the respectable New England matron: she sews, embroiders, makes jellies. However, Petry, unlike Stowe, does not fashion Abbie as a life-giving, maternal figure whose home offers the spiritual and moral values missing in American society outside the family. Rather, Abbie's home has become a prison which she dares not escape; although it is a place of refuge from the terrors Abbie imagines to exist in the larger world, it is also a place that is sterile and deadly.

That Petry is consciously delineating Abbie's character within the confines of the New England tradition becomes even more evident when Abbie is contrasted with other female characters in *The Narrows* who also belong to this tradition. The spinster Frances K. Jackson, Abbie's close friend, not only works as an undertaker but once aspired to become a doctor. F. K., as she is known, describes herself as "too bright . . . and unable and unwilling to conceal that fact that I had brains" (281). After finishing Wellesley, "where I was a kind of Eighth Wonder of the world because I was colored" (281), F. K. is forced by the circumstances of her race, gender, and class to give up her aspirations in order to help her father in his undertaking business.

Frances resembles the spinster figures in later New England realistic writing, in particular, Olive Chancellor in Henry James' *The Bostonians*. As in James' portrayal of Olive, Petry suggests that Frances' friendship for Abbie is motivated both by a lesbian attraction and a wish to dominate her. In other words, the brainy, angular, bony, too tall woman is not quite a woman at all, at least if "woman' is defined as heterosexual and submissive.

Petry's characterization of Camilo Treadway Sheffield, the wealthy white lover of Link, is also informed by Petry's New England heritage. Petry's analysis of Camilo stresses that Camilo's unhappiness stems in part from the fact that her family did not permit her to do productive work as an English teacher.[12]   Instead, Camilo works as a fashion photographer, a parasite, who nevertheless fits in to an economy based on consumption rather than production, a white woman whose culture has forgotten the New England moral emphasis on useful work.   In Petry's formulation, women such as Frances and Camilo are prevented by their race, class, and gender from following the secular vocation to which they aspire.   In the novels of the pioneer New England women writers such as Alcott and Stowe, who inaugurated the tradition of domestic feminism and realism, the parlors and kitchens symbolize the warmth and security offered only by the home in American society.   In contrast, Abbie Crunch's parlor lacks warmth and joy, and her husband is chided for soaking his feet in a tub in the kitchen: " 'Dory, I told you not to do that here in the kitchen.   It's the kind of thing sharecroppers do'" (145).   Abbie Crunch has embraced a rigid New England code of genteel behavior in order to deny her blackness and in so doing has sacrificed love.

In *The Narrows*, Petry presents a "counterposed value" to the rigid repression symbolized by Abbie's joyless house.   The response to Abbie's sterile kitchen where neatness reigns is the kitchen belonging to Bill Hod, gangster and saloon owner, and his chef, Weak Knees.   Here is the vitality, warmth, and joy of black culture; it is a kitchen in which smells represent the Sunday morning cooking smells of The Narrows as a whole, the heart of the black community:

> Then they were in the kitchen, a kitchen
> almost as big as the barroom, and filled with
> such delicious smells of food that he [Link]
> was afraid for a moment he would cry,
> smells like on Franklin Avenue over near
> the bakery on Saturday morning when they
> were baking bread . . . . smells like on
> Sunday on Dumble Street, and he coming
> home from church with Abbie, . . . and his
> stomach sucking in on itself, and Dumble
> Street filled with the smell of fried chicken
> and baked yams, and kale cooked with ham
> fat. (140)

This passage represents Petry at her best.   The sensuous imagery, the evocative and realistic details, the use of the commonplace, all express the strength and love to be found in the black ghetto, although not by such as Abbie Crunch. Once again, Petry has used the New England tradition of domestic realism, here to evoke one Afro-American reality.

One of Petry's techniques in *The Narrows*, then, is to provide an Afro-American response to Abbie's New England way. For example, Abbie's need to control her fate in white America leads her, as it led many female characters in New England fiction, such as the protagonist in Freeman's "A New England Nun," to shrink from sexuality. The character of Mamie Powther enables Petry to posit a contrast to Abbie's inhibitions about sexuality. To Abbie, Mamie symbolizes the eruptive chaos of indiscriminate sexuality. Abbie recoils from Mamie's type, "young, but too much fat around the waist, a soft, fleshy, quite prominent bosom, too much lipstick, a pink beflowered hat, set on top of straightened hair" (25). Mamie, though married, is not known as Mrs. Powther because, according to Abbie, she is "not a man's wife, permanently attached, but an unattached unwifely female" (35); Mamie does not "belong in that [Abbie's] neat backyard with its carefully tended lawn and its white fences" (35). Worst of all, Mamie sings the blues, defined by Abbie as "the bleating that issued from all the gramophones and radios these days, all of it sounding alike, too loud, too harsh, no sweetness, no tune, simply a reiterated bleating about rent money and men who had gone off with other women, and numbers that didn't come out" (32-33). , Abbie concludes with contempt that "Mamie Powther was Dumble Street" (30).

For Petry, however, Mamie is an earth mother; what Abbie condemns as vulgar behavior, Petry presents as the embodiment of the spirit of the black ghetto. Mamie is the life-force figure found in the Afro-American blues tradition; according to Sherley Williams, "the ability to keep on pushing, to keep on keeping on, to go on about one's business, is the life-force, the assertion of self amidst collective and individual destruction that comes directly out of the blues tradition."[13] Abbie's outrage at what she conceives of as Mamie's vulgar behavior is a measure of her fear that the life-force will erupt and destroy her carefully controlled world, will lead to the emergence of the black heritage that she has so rigidly suppressed:

> Wind whipped the clothes back and forth,
> lifting the hem of Mamie Powther's shore
> cotton dress as though it peered underneath
> and liked what it saw and so returned again
> and again for another look. What a vulgar
> idea. I never think things like that I
> don't dance. I never could, Abbie thought.
> I haven't any sense of rhythm and yet she
> hangs clothes and I think about dancing.
> (33-34)

But Abbie does have a sense of rhythm, not permitted to emerge in music and dance, because that would be being black, emerging rather as a compulsion to make up jingles; Abbie has a witty mind and a rhyming gift. Abbie is pleased that she lives on Dumble Street, pleased because it offers so many opportunities to rhyme: "The people who lived near the waterfront fumbled and they mumbled and they stumbled and they tumbled, ah, yes, make up a word---dumbled" (31).

By endowing Abbie with a need to construct rhyming jingles, Petry is making a complex statement about her black matron. The jingles are more than an expression of Abbie's verbal intelligence. Abbie's gift has its roots in the rhythmic and linguistic inventiveness of black oral expression (Langston Hughes' poems are an example), yet for Abbie this oral heritage must also serve as a way to control her environment. Whereas Mamie Powther embraces her heritage and sings the blues, Abbie expresses her heritage through the structure of white nursery rhymes. For example, about Mamie Powther's cuckolded husband, Abbie thinks:

> Mister Powther Sat on a sowther
> Eating his curds and whey
> Along came a Mamie
> And said, You must pay me.
> And so he did pay, did pay. (30)

Abbie's rhymes, like Emily Dickinson's poems, tell the truth, but tell it slant.

On the surface, Abbie Crunch is indeed "upright as a darning needle" (the phrase Stowe uses to describe Miss Ophelia in *Uncle Tom's Cabin*), independent though poor, dismayed by vulgarity, emotionally repressed. Abbie is almost an elderly version of Stowe's Topsy, who incorporated the white contempt for blacks into her own self-concept. Underneath Abbie's pride and rigid stance pulse guilt, shame, and self-hatred. The pathological aspects of this syndrome, as well as its roots in the racism of American society, have been delineated in books such as *Black Rage* by William Grier and Price Cobbs. But Petry does not simply condemn Abbie; rather, she presents her "case" with compassion and understanding. It is not the pathological in Abbie that interests Petry but her representativeness. In her conception of Abbie, Petry is following the lead of another Afro-American, W. E. B. DuBois, who, like Petry, grew up in the only black family in a small New England town. It was DuBois who first articulated the dilemma facing Afro-Americans searching to establish an identity "in this American world---a world which yields him no true self-consciousness, but only lets him see himself through the revelation of the other world." [14]

Abbie's consciousness comes only from "the revelation" of New England culture. Petry, however, remains always aware of the other half of DuBois's double consciousness, the strength and vitality of black culture. Petry explicitly links Abbie's destructive human failings---symbolized by her "cold house," her "house of weeping," her "house of darkness"---to her rejection of black culture. Abbie's contempt for Mamie Powther signifies her rejection of the sensual heritage of African dance, religion, song, and music, a heritage that celebrates the union of body and mind.   Another example of Abbie's rejection of the strength to be found in black folk culture in her horror of her husband's relatives, "swamp niggers," from South Carolina, who are legendary conjurors, witches, gypsies. Abbie dismisses these folk as an "ungodly crew" whose tales are never "about goodness and mercy, always death and cruelty" (50), whose tales , in other words, do not reflect New England Christian tenets but vestiges of African folklore merged with the horror of slavery and post-reconstruction black lives.

Abbie, of course, shrinks from The Narrows, the black ghetto vividly evoked by Petry.   Unlike her treatment of Harlem in *The Street*, Petry presents The Narrows as a milieu of vitality, a source of strength, fellowship, and spiritual warmth as well as a potentially violent and criminal place.   In The Narrows are saloons with ironic names such as "The Moonbeam" and "The Last Chance"; Dickensian grotesques such as Cat Jimmie, who has raw, red stumps for arms and legs and whom one can see "lie flat on his homemade cart and moan like an animal" (77) when looking up a woman's skirt; Cesar the Writing Man, who prophesizes and writes small sermons on the sidewalk, looking neat and clean yet always wearing the same clothes; large signs promising to reveal the "Strange Secrets of the Unseen Forces of Life, Time and Nature, Divine Blessings---Healings of Mind and Body" (11); clangs of trolleys, whines and sirens, redorange neon signs, drunks, prostitutes, obscene jokes about red-winged blackbirds; the river front blanketed with fog or in bright sunlight, the river the "blue of bachelor buttons, of delphiniums" (10).   Petry's ghetto inhabitants display bitterness and despair but also manage to endure, to hope, and to love. In short, Petry's capsule descriptions of The Narrows emphasizes the existence of a vital black folk culture behind the mask reserved for white America.

But Abbie Crunch sees only through the eyes of white America. As her foster son, Link, remembers:

> She said colored people (sometimes she just
> said The Race) had to be cleaner, smarter,
> thriftier, more ambitious than white people,
> so that white people would like colored
> people . . . . You had to be polite; you had to
> be punctual; you couldn't wear bright-
> colored clothes, or loud-colored socks; and
> even certain food was forbidden. Abbie said
> that she loved watermelons, but she would
> just as soon cut off her right arm as to go in
> a store and buy one, because colored people
> loved watermelons. (168-69).

Thus Petry's version of an experience central to the memories of so many blacks, fictional and actual.

Abbie's hatred of poor blacks, rural and urban, is concentrated in her hatred for Bill Hod, pimp, procurer, gangster, owner of The Last Chance saloon. Hod, more symbol than character in *The Narrows*, is a descendant of the legendary black bad man, presented in Afro-American folklore with what Lawrence Levine has called "unadorned realism" because "they never really tried to change anything. They were pure force, pure vengeance; explosions of fury and futility. They were not given any socially redeeming characteristics simply because in them there was no hope of social redemption."[15] Bill Hod, however, does have one socially redeeming characteristic, his love for Link, who becomes as much his foster son as Abbie's. As Link remembers just before his murder, Hod and Weak Knees, "had balanced that other world, the world of starched curtains and the price of butter, the world of crocheted doilies and what will people think, the world of white bedspreads and pillow shams and behavior governed by what The Race did or did not do" (482).

Abbie's New England way is inadequate to the reality of black experience. It is the father figure, Bill Hod, who gives Link that pride in race necessary to Link's psychic survival, who teaches Link that "Black was best-looking," that "the best caviar was black. The rarest jewels were black; black opals, black pearls" (176). Ironically, it is only because he has learned from Hod not to be ashamed of the color of his skin that Link can retain his admiration for Abbie despite the hurt and confusion she causes him. And Link is right. Abbie is a heroine, despite her contempt for her own race and culture. She has earned admiration because she has learned to survive in the only way she knows how; she is "upright as a darning needle" and that rectitude compels admiration even in the context of her flaws.

For seventy years Abbie has been asking herself "what will people think?" For seventy years, Abbie has accepted unquestioningly the New England code of conduct. Petry, on the other hand, examines the culture of Monmouth's whites by applying the moral standards of an earlier New England, and by this measure Petry determines the New England of the 1950s to be morally bankrupt. Petry uses Camilo Sheffield, Link's mistress, to expose the corruption at the heart of the New England girl, the heroine who, in earlier New England novels, had symbolized the moral values of the New England way.[16] In *The Narrows* the underlying reality of the New England girl is uncovered: "The princess of the fairy tales, all gold, was not gold at all, was flesh, human flesh, all too human, all too weak, capable of jealousy, of vengeance, capable of being ruined, like any other woman" (412). In Camilo Treadway Sheffield's case, the gold is even further debased by the fact that her fortune depends on the manufacture of munitions. She is, in fact, "the Duchess of Moneyland, young Mrs. Moneybags, of the gun empire" (432). Link's love, the golden heroine, who in nineteenth century New England literature represented the redemptive promise of America, now represents another reality of American culture: materialism, moral corruption, violence.

In *The Narrows*, as in Petry's other novels, the hollowness of the white society is a persistent theme. Petry's indictment resembles the New England jeremiads that called on the younger generation to live up to the moral vision and stern rectitude of their forebears, that invoked as a standard the moral heritage of the past against which the moral emptiness of the present is revealed. Ultimately, however, what most links Petry's novel to the New England literary and cultural tradition is her belief in what Hawthorne called the chain of "dark necessity." Petry's insistence that the past, collective as well as individual, determines the present.

In a modern day version of Calvinism, Petry argues that there is one original sin that must continue to burden America, the sin of slavery with its attendant racism. Petry's thesis in *The Narrows* is like that articulated by LeRoi Jones in *Blues People*. "The poor Negro," Jones writes,

> always remembered himself as an ex-slave and used this as the basis of any dealing with the mainstream of American society. The middle class black man bases his whole existence on the hopeless hypothesis that no one is supposed to remember that for almost three centuries there was slavery in America, that the white man was the master and the black man the slave. This knowledge, however, is at the root of the legitimate black culture of this country. It is this knowledge, with its attendant muses of self-division, self-hatred, stoicism, and finally quixotic optimism, that informs the most meaningful of Afro-American music.[17]

This knowledge with its attendant muses also informs *The Narrows*. In the character of Link Williams, Abbie's adopted son, Petry provides a response to Abbie's denial of her race's history. Whereas Abbie "always avoided the mention of slavery" (171), Link aspires to write the definitive history of slavery in America and to master the authentic texts and documents belonging to the Afro-American heritage.[18] Link knows that the explanation for his impending murder "reaches back to the Dutch man of warre that landed in Jamestown in 1619." (475)[19]

Petry insists that both white and black Americans must acknowledge their collective history and its consequences if they are to avoid moral and spiritual confusion. But it is only Abbie Crunch among the many white and black characters in *The Narrows* who transcends moral and spiritual confusion. Abbie overcomes her fear of whites and her self-hatred and recognizes that it is not only she who is responsible for Link's death, that "it was all of us, in one way or another, we all had a hand in it, we all reacted violently to those two people, to Link and that girl, because he was colored and she was white." (498). Abbie transcends her own racism to save Camilo, the white woman, from certain death at the hands of Bill Hod, the black man.

The Narrows demonstrates that in the United States racial and sexual politics are inextricably intertwined: both whites and blacks react with murderous rage to the love affair between a black man and a white woman. It is only the black mother, the repressed and respectable New England matron, who transcends that murderous rage to reach charity and forgiveness. Among Ann Petry's many achievements in the novel, one of her finest is her realistic and complex characterization of Abbie Crunch. And, in *The Narrows* as a whole, Ann Petry has accomplished what she told an interviewer in 1943 was her goal, to show Afro-Americans "as people with the same capacity for love and hate, for tears and laughter, and the same instinct for survival possessed by all men." [20]

Note:
A different version of this paper was first given at a M.E.L.U.S. sponsored panel during the National Women's Studies Association annual meeting, Storrs, Connecticut, June 1981. I would like to thank Ann Petry, Fauneil Rinn, and John Galm for their assistance.

---

[1] Review of *The Narrows, Saturday Review*, 36 (August 22, 1953), 11.
[2] Cited in Robert Hemenway's "Are You a Flying Lark or a Setting Dove?" in *Afro-American Literature: The Reconstruction of Instruction*, ed. Dexter Fisher and Robert B. Stepto (New York: MLA, 1978), 129.
[3] For a useful general introduction to *The Narrows*, see Margaret B. McDowell, "*The Narrows*: A Fuller View of Ann Petry," BALF 14 (1980): 135-41. [See elsewhere in this text].
[4] Ann Petry, *The Narrows* (New York: Pyramid, 1971), 11. All further references to the novel will be cited in the text.
[5] William Shakespeare, *King Henry V, IV, VII, 105-106.*
[6] Wright Morris, *New York Times Book Review* (August 16, 1953), 4. Petry, in a letter to this writer (September 13, 1984) responds as follows to the criticism that the love story is never quite credible: "Not true. Racism, especially as it manifests itself in reactions to miscegenation, is 'so deeply imbedded in American society, in its laws, in its social structures' (Baldwin) that it is impossible for most readers, reviewers, critics to look at Link Williams squarely,

forthrightly, head on, and recognize him for the 3-dimensional, fully-realized, compelling figure that he is and to recognize the reality and the validity of his love affair with Camilo."

[7] Morris, 4.

[8] "Black Eve or Madonna: A Study of the Antithetical Views of the Mother in Black American Literatare," in *Sturdy Black Bridges: Visions of Black Women in Literature*, eds. Roseann P. Bell, Betty J. Parker, and Beverly Guy-Sheftall (Garden City: Anchor, 1979), 126-27.

[9] Barbara Christian in *Black Women Novelists* (Westport: Greenwood Press, 1980) makes this point about *The Street*.

[10] Statements in a letter and in an enclosure, both sent to this writer on February 9, 1984.

[11] About *The Street*, Barbara Christian writes that "Petry employed the tone of the commonplace. She is particularly effective in selecting the many details and seemingly trivial struggles that poor women can seldom avoid" (64).

[12] Berndt Ostendort, in *Black Literature in White America* (New York: Barnes & Noble, 1982), borrows this term from Melville Herskovits to describe the give and take between the black culture and the dominant culture in America. See particularly "Double Consciousness: The Marginal Perspective in Language, Oral Culture, Folklore, Religion," 19.

[13] Sherley Anne Williams, "The Blues Roots of Contemporary Afro-American Poetry" in Fisher and Stepto, 85.

[14] *The Souls of Black Folk* (Greenwich: Fawcett, 1961), 16.

[15] *Black Culture and Black Consciousness: Afro-American Folk Thought From Slavery to Freedom* (New York: Oxford, 1977), 419, 420.

[16] In *The New England Girl: Cultural Ideals in Hawthorne, Stowe, Howells and James* (Athens: University of Georgia Press, 1976), Paul John Eakin provides an extensive analysis of the cultural significance of the New England heroine.

[17] Quoted in Ostendorf, 56, note 19.

[18] Link's quest for freedom and literacy places him within the tradition of the articulate Afro-American hero, delineated by Robert Stepto in *From Behind the Veil: A Study of Afro-American Narrative* (Urbana: University of Illinois Press, 1979).

[19] When Petry was asked by an interviewer in 1973 about the cause of the evil in *The Narrows*, she answered that although there was not just one cause, "racism comes closer to being *the* cause." See John O'Brien, ed. *Interviews with Black Writers* (New York: Liveright, 1973), 162.

[20] James W. Ivy, "Ann Petry Talks about First Novel" in *Sturdy Black Bridges*, 200.

(1990 to 2000)
Ann Petry's *The Street* and *The Narrows*: A Study of the Influence of Class,
Race, and Gender on Afro-American Women's Lives (1990)
Nellie Y. McKay

Although Ann Petry's three adult novels (she has also written four books for
juveniles) were favorably noticed at publication (1946, 1947, and 1953), and
The Street (1946) made her the first black woman writer to record book sales of
more than a million copies, it is interesting to observe the evolutionary changes
in the critical appraisals her work has received over these past four decades. In
the late 1940s and through the early 1950s, when, as a black writer, Richard
Wright enjoyed "most favored standing " among white literary critics, there was
a very different perception of Petry's works than now exists. As literary studies
gradually came to recognize that alternative (to white Western male paradigms)
but equally complex aesthetics are embedded in the writings of women and
people of color, Petry's works gained wider acceptance. For instance, while
earlier critics saw *The Street* as a weaker, less well conceptualized imitation of
Wright's *Native Son,* new feminist reevaluations of *The Street* reveal a more
complex structure that expands the boundaries of the traditional naturalistic
novel. In fact, as a consequence of the interests of these critics, discoveries of
previously overlooked agendas in Petry's writings have been useful in
reinforcing our awareness of a much-neglected black female, cosmological
perspective in literature that has existed through several generations of writers.

Nineteen eighty-seven Pulitzer Prize winner Toni Morrison has spoken
eloquently to this verity of a unique literary worldview "as perceived by black
women." In a 1985 interview with Gloria Naylor, she observed that each black
woman writer is engaged in an adventure analogous to the polishing of "one
facet of a prism, . . . just one side . . . [of its] millions of sides," only to discover,
in reading some other book, that "somebody who is [also] a black woman . . .
[with] a . . . [similar] . . . sensibility and power and talent . . .[is] writing about
[another] side of this huge sort of diamond thing . . . and then [the writer] read[s]
another book and [again finds that] somebody [else] has written about another
side."[1] Pre-1960s black women writer like Ann Petry are therefore eminently
important in the current discourse on the longevity of a unique black female
literary tradition in America which addresses issues important to women's lives
but is consistently neglected by others.

Unlike most well-known black writers of the 1940s and 1950s, Ann Lane
Petry came of age outside of the cultural milieu both of the dominant black
communities in the South and of the large northern urban centers with their
populous and /or growing concentrations of black people. Born in Old
Saybrook, Connecticut, in [1908], she grew up in that small New England town,
where hers was the only Afro-American family to reside there for many years.
Unlike another famous black New Englander, W. E. B. DuBois, who preceded
her by almost half a century and who grew up in a proud but poor family in

Great Barrington, Massachusetts, the Lanes, who boasted three generations of professionals, enjoyed stability, privilege, and success in the eyes of their white neighbors. . . . .Thus, in her early years, Ann Lane was sheltered from the disabilities of a poor education, an unstable family life, and the low socioeconomic status that many blacks of her generation experienced. Nor was gender role oppression part of her childhood and young adulthood experiences. Such good fortune, however, did not keep her from realizing the existence of a different order, and later she developed a profound sensitivity to the politics of racial, sexual, and class discrimination on black people as a group in America....

While notices in such important journals and newspapers as the *New Yorker*, the *New York Times Book Review*, and the *New Republic* brought Ann Petry to the serious attention of readers and critics in the 1940s and 1950s, her reputation at that time was overshadowed by comparisons of her work with the writings of Wright and Chester Himes, whose novels more closely fit the conventional paradigms of the naturalist tradition. These early judgments are not difficult to understand, but more recent critics realize that basic philosophical differences between Petry and the black men of her generation separate the general intent of her work from theirs and that her perceptions of women's lives, separate from those of men, led her to different ways of understanding the meanings of women's experiences. Far from being inadequate in comparisons with black male writers, Petry's narratives are revolutionary in their expansion of the perimeters of naturalism as perceived by black and white male writers. Furthermore, in an age when black writers were expected to assume exclusive literary loyalties to the concerns of race, she foreshadowed a later generation of women like Toni Morrison, Alice Walker, and Gloria Naylor in sharing with them a complex vision of the place that gender roles and economics play in the lives of black people. As these more contemporary writers explicitly establish, there can be no adequate representation of black women's (or men's) experiences outside of a recognition of the ways in which these are shaped by the overall historical context in which this group has lived for close to three hundred years. In this, race is only one aspect of their oppression.

Adopting this premise, this paper presents two of Petry's novels, *The Street* and *The Narrows*, as illustrations of this aspect of her prescient artistic vision. Although different from each other in style and content, both have black women as central characters, and in each, race, class, and gender intersect to become dominant forces in their fates. Her second novel, *Country Place*, does not focus on the lives of black people, but instead explores the role of bigotry and prejudice toward a number of minority groups: blacks, Jews, Irish, and Portuguese in provincial New England. This is an issue with which Petry was well acquainted. And if her characters are different from those in her other books, she remains consistent in her vision of the complexity of the human condition.

The Street introduces Lutie Johnson, the *first* black female protagonist in American literature to battle a hostile environment in the way that men are accustomed to seeing themselves pitted against social and economic forces. The novel is set in a decaying Harlem ghetto, and although Lutie loses the fight to transcend the limitations of her environment, she is an interesting heroine. Unlike many protagonists in naturalistic novels, until the end of the novel she refuses to admit defeat, in spite of the tremendous odds against her. Without a supportive community (which is most unusual for black women in America) and as the result of her self-confidence in her ability single-handedly to change the course of her life, she naively and erroneously places her faith in industry, thrift, individuality, and personal ambition, considering them the only important factors in the struggle against poverty and social disability. Her tragic flaw is her inability to perceive that this social construction for success fails to take the central impediments to that success for people of color into consideration: the disadvantages of her race, class, and for women, sex.

Lutie's mother dies when she is very young, and she is raised by a loving, morally conservative, God-fearing grandmother, who also dies by the time her charge reaches young adulthood. The young woman's only family then is an unemployed alcoholic father, who spends most of his time with a series of much younger, raucous, cigarette-smoking, beer-drinking girlfriends. Lutie, who has a much higher sense of self-esteem than her father, partially separates herself from this low-life environment when she marries a man whose ambitions for the "good" life are much like her own.

For a short time, the young black family seems to mirror, if less luminously, its white counterparts in the world outside of their immediate environment. Lutie and her husband Jim secure a small house in a modestly priced locale outside of Manhattan, and to them a son is born. But Jim, through no fault of his own, soon loses his job, and before long, in the struggle to meet their financial obligations, they deplete a small inheritance he received from his mother. Attempting to hold on to their home, the husband and wife, for a very small remuneration, become foster caretakers for homeless children who are wards of the state. But they lose that source of income when the oversight agency discovers that Lutie's father, who lives with them temporarily, hosts drinking parties at their home on the occasions when, to relieve emotional stress, the couple seek respite in a movie, or similar inexpensive entertainment. When the children are removed from their care, the Johnsons are completely without an income. As financial pressures close in on them, Lutie's determination to keep them afloat leads her, against Jim's wishes, to accept sleep-in domestic employment in Connecticut.

In the beginning she visits her family weekly, then, as time goes on, in an effort to save as much money as possible (even the train fare drains their resources), she sees Jim and Bub only once each month. Oblivious to the toll that such an arrangement might have on her marriage, Lutie's dreams or social stability and financial independence increasingly take on the sterile materialistic ethic of her wealthy employers, the Chandlers, while Jim's self-esteem, battered on the anvil of unemployment and a fragmented domestic situation, sinks lower. Listening to the Chandlers' conversations of Wall Street activities and the making of fortunes, she comes to believe that the answer to the dilemma in the lives of her and Jim rests solely in their need to work harder and concentrate on ways to earn and save money. Ironically, she neglects to look analytically at the unhappiness that pervades this wealthy home. For instance, when a Christmas morning suicide is transformed into an accident by the legal authorities and the media in order to save the Chandlers social embarrassment, she sees only the power of money at work. Predictably, Lutie's marriage falls apart; she and Jim lose the house, and she returns to New York to assume full financial and emotional responsibilities for herself and her young son.

Four years later, leaving her employment as a hand presser in a steam laundry where the heat was almost unbearable and, simultaneously, in spite of the test to her physical endurance, attending night classes to study filing, shorthand, and typing, Lutie secures a low-level position in the civil service. Even this minimal change reassures her, and she interprets it as a small victory in her struggle to achieve a stable social and economic place in the world. Alone and under extremely strained financial circumstances, she finds for herself and Bub a dingy apartment that she can barely afford on a street where the buildings are old, with small slit-like windows that let in no sunlight; the halls are dark and narrow, with rooms "hot as hell in summer and cold in winter." Surveying the decrepit block, she observes that streets like this were no accident. They represent "the North's lynch mob," the way in which blacks are kept in their place. Bitterly, she muses that in all of her life some force had attempted to wall her into an ever-narrowing space, and she imagines herself nearly walled in, with each brick being put into place by "eager white hands." Still, she does not succumb to despair. Although she struggles heroically to improve her condition and to find an escape for herself and her son from the dehumanizing influences of the [s]treet, she fails. Lutie reaches the end of her emotional rope when, in frustration, she bludgeons to death the black male hustler who, enraged by his own social and economic impotence, attempts to use her in his struggle against white male domination.

Clearly, Petry made use of naturalistic techniques in this narrative. As Bernard Bell accurately states, this is "a conventional novel of economic determination in which the environment is the dominant force against which the characters must struggle to survive."[2] But Petry also alters a number of plot conventions and opens up the space for Lutie to be more than a conventional victim. Lutie Johnson does not believe that poverty and race are inextricably linked, spelling her doom regardless of her efforts to transcend them. Unlike black fictional characters like Wright's Bigger Thomas, who internalize their victim status, Lutie has self-confidence; is without fear of white people or racism; and believes that individual ambition and hard work will bring the rewards she seeks. She begins her adult life full of optimism for her future. Her grandmother had loved her and in making that love known, had given her assurances that she could make her own life. At an early age her grandmother had instilled in Lutie a Puritan sense of the values of hard work, thrift, and morality and had warned her against the lust of white men. At the same time, she had failed to impress on her the subtleties of gender oppression. In fact, Lutie has so assimilated and accepted the values her grandmother touted that they became thought barriers that prevented her from realizing the true nature of her situation as a black woman in a white patriarchal society. She did not recognize that the Ben Franklin individualistic model, taken on face value, is a dangerous ideology for black women.[3]

Inseparable from each other, race and class discrimination exclude the young black couple, Lutie and Jim Johnson, from the American dream of upward mobility through ambition and the willingness to work hard to achieve their goals. While this is true at all times, social scientists agree that during the Depression, blacks comprised the group that suffered most from its effects. The most unskilled and expendable, as last hired they were the first to be fired, and no new jobs were available to them. Thus, Jim, coming into manhood during the worst years of that national disaster, inevitably found himself on the outside of the employment rolls. With no jobs and an absent wife whose income was insufficient to compensate for the disruption in their lives, his morale crumbles, and he loses his will to continue what seems to him no more than meaningless struggle.

On the other hand, when Jim abdicates responsibility to the family, Lutie, young and beautiful, finds herself a black woman alone in the world, and her vulnerability increases considerably. Barbara Smith, who calls this an archetypal text, notes that left alone to raise her child amidst the destruction of the slums, Lutie's story tells the "harsh but necessary truths about [b]lack women that are especially useful [for those] seeking more than a superficial understanding" of the oppression of these women.[4] The racism that prevented Jim from finding work also keeps Lutie from other than the most menial jobs. Thus, race and poverty create and maintain a social underclass. For four years Lutie suffers the subhuman conditions of the steam laundry; throughout that time, with barely sufficient strength at the end of each awful day, she attends night school in hopes of eventually achieving a better position. When that comes, in the form of civil service employment, her position is so low that she enjoys no financial advantages. When she seeks the kind of work that would permit her to take advantage of her beautiful singing voice, the men in control of such businesses see her only as a sexual object. They will advance her ambitions only at the cost of her sexual integrity. Nor is this attitude on the part of white people (or men) new to her. As early as in the days when she worked for the wealthy Chandlers, she learned that the white women who visited with Mrs. Chandler for luncheons and bridge parties assumed, without knowing anything about her, that her presence threatened their marriage, since they believed that what she wanted most was to entrap their husbands in sexual liaisons. White women and all men saw her only as a sexual object. Again, Toni Morrison cogently encapsulates the essence of black women's designated place in a male society: " 'Well, you're a woman,' what does that mean? . . . usually . . . somebody's handmaiden . . .[but] when you think of . . . the women that you admire and what . . . you admire about them as women, it would never be what men would think."[5] Thus, as Smith further points out, to be black and female in a system of white patriarchy, "virtually ensures poverty, and poverty undermines the stability of emotional and sexual relationships as well as family life."[6]

In addition to its focus on a female protagonist, *The Street* is significantly different from its male counterparts in that while Petry lashes out uncompromisingly at racism, classism, and sexism, she undercuts the conventions of the naturalistic novel by refusing to make Lutie a mere victim of her social environment. Nor does this step on the part of the author lessen the impact of the oppression of that environment. Lutie may well have had greater success in achieving her goals had she been less innocent of the politics of race, class, and gender. Her uncritical acceptance of white middle-class values and the capitalist tenets of the American dream make her an easy prey for the greed and sexism of the black and white men who surround her. In addition, Lutie serves herself poorly by separating from any support she might have had from the black community and those values that have insured black survival in America since the first slaves arrived on its shores. Preoccupied with her ambitions for herself and her son to escape the poverty and disillusionment of black ghetto life and wholly uncritical of the white models to which she is exposed, she has no friends or relatives with whom she seeks association, attends no church, and in her attitudes, denies the possibilities of communal sources of strength. Consequently, she was vulnerable to the greed, anger, and sexism of those who were capable of destroying her.

In *The Narrows*, located in a different locale, Ann Petry continues to examine these crucial issues. This discussion focuses on Abigail (Abbie) Crunch and Frances Jackson, her friend of more than twenty years. These are the two black women who most influence the life of Abbie's adopted son, Lincoln (Link) Williams, the main figure in this novel. Minor players in the contemporaneous action of the plot, the women's character portraits fill in the background of the life of the protagonist and provide an image of black women's lives in this small area of the country. Although the central plot revolves around the historically forbidden relationship between a black man (Link) and a white woman (Camilo Treadway), Petry turns what might otherwise be no more than a sensational story of interracial love---a melodrama of clichés and stereotypes---into a novel that seriously explores issues of race, class, and gender roles. Earlier reviews of this book were mixed, from black writer Arna Bontemps's commendation that it was less a novel about black people than of New England, to those (mostly white) who condemned it as shocking, sordid, and scandalous for its handling of an American sexual taboo. None of these, however, gave attention to women's roles, except as Link's rich white girlfriend is a necessary ingredient in the making of the tragic ending. New readings, however, demonstrate that black and white women's experiences and actions are crucial to the development of this narrative, and their place in the complex of entangled relationships it embodies cannot be overlooked in any understanding of the novel.

The Narrows is set in Monmouth, Connecticut, a small New England town, where class, as much as race, had always defined the terms of black and white people's lives in this area. That had not changed in the 1950s. Unlike the Old Saybrook of Petry's youth, Monmouth has a sizable black community, and most of this population is poor and dependent for employment on the town's one rich family, the Treadways, owners of a munitions factory. Black people live along the River Wye---a beautiful river, "the blue of bachelor buttons, of delphinium [with] small frothy waves, edged with white."[7] Against this setting, the squalor of the black community---its proliferation of Rooms for Rent signs and the ugly neon light of the local bar—stands out in sharp contrast. This river area has many names, including the Narrows and Niggertown, in Petry's continuing exploration of white America forcing black people's lives into constricting spaces that, as Lutie Johnson visualizes, provide no room for escape. Unlike Lutie Johnson's one-dimensional "Street," however, Petry sees complex tensions at work in the Narrows. It is a vital place, both spiritually energizing and full of crime and violence.

Abbie, who owns her own home, is a seventy-year-old widow—a poor, genteel, and brown-skinned would-be aristocrat with rigid standards of religious morality. Frances, past middle age but younger than Abbie, is an unmarried Wellesley-educated woman, formidable and independent in word and deed. Much earlier in her life, realizing that in a world dominated by men, her education and ambitions were a deterrent to romantic love and marriage, to motherhood, and even to sexual love as an equal partner, Frances decides on a professional life to which she could devote her energies without compromise. She wants to become a doctor. However, loyalty to her widowed undertaker father, who needs her assistance, keeps her at home and out of medical school. Later, she takes over his business, assuming the role of the son he never had.

Abbie Crunch and Frances Jackson, unlike Lutie Johnson, are middle-class black women, but their lives are also affected by issues of gender, race, and economics. Also different from each other, they represent ways in which northern black women of their class perceived options for independent selves in the 1930s and 1940s. Class privilege is clearly a significant factor here, and the Monmouth black community, although oppressed by the white world that surrounds it, is not the Harlem ghetto.

Although the incomes of these women, especially Abbie's, are very small, both are self-employed and self-supporting, unlike Lutie, and thus they escape many of the daily humiliations that majority of black women cannot avoid. Geography plays a role in their race and class situations. Southern black women and black women in large urban centers have even fewer options for independence than those in smaller northern towns. Looking back over the years of her life, Abbie Crunch sees herself in a series of "jumps." Initially, she was a school teacher, one of the few respectable professions open to women of her class and color at the time. Her first "jump" was to become a coachman's wife---for white marriage is always preferable to remaining single, it is also accepted that it seldom improves the social status of professional black women, since the women are usually better educated and more socially refined than the men. Later, as a widow, facing pecuniary straits, Abbie is a needlewoman-landlady, occupying a financially precarious but respectable place on the social ladder.

At the same time Petry does not idealize the achievements of this woman, for Abbie has many qualities that are less admirable. Her meticulous preoccupation with her personal appearance, her consciously held upright posture, hurried short steps, simple unadorned clothes, and delicate handkerchiefs, for instance, indicate her acceptance of a class-based female socialization. In spite of her race and class, she considers herself a "lady." So that if race and economic means compel her to live with poor, uncouth black people (she does not identify with poor, uncouth people either) rather than with white royalty, she does not engage in the crudeness of speech or actions of the former. Her flaws, like Lutie Johnson's, come from her uncritical acceptance of certain white patriarchal values that demean black people and black culture and keep all women enslaved by oppressive ideas of the meaning of womanhood.

Still, Abbie has a core of moral toughness that is possessed only by those for whom the struggle for psychic survival is intrinsic. She exhibits that toughness both in her life as an independent, professional woman and as a wife fulfilling a male-defined woman's role. During her marriage it is Abbie who insists on buying the house they own, who is Link's "whole world" in his early years, even though it is her husband's need for a son that initiates the adoption. Unexpectedly widowed in middle life, with the emotional support of her friend Frances, she quickly, except for a momentary lapse, pulls her life together. She does needlework, the oldest black women's profession not requiring manual labor; she converts a part of her home into rental property; and she plans and manages her meager resources superbly, enabling her to live financially independent of others. Her son is correct when he thinks there is "something indestructible" in her. At the end of the novel, in spite of the tragedy of that son's lynch-style murder by the wealthy Treadways, Abbie, unlike Lutie Johnson, emerges a transcendent figure, having spiritually overcome the forces of American racism.

Frances, on the other hand, is different. She is neither haughty nor pretentious, and she never capitulates to the male-centered, female-oppressive standards the culture defined for women of her class. She lives with feeling less-than-female for most of her life, but does not allow that to deter her actions. At age twelve, her father called her Frank, not Fran, and noted that she had a "man's mind," not that she would become a brilliant woman. At Wellesley College, with its long tradition of brilliant women, her abilities were appreciated and rewarded, but her color separated her from the rest of the community. As an adult woman, her physical appearance, independence, and intelligence earn her labels like "unfeminine," "man-like," and the "old-maid" type. Petry, however, gives her stamina, uncompromising integrity, clarity of vision, compassion, and the ability to love unselfishly. Although her dreams for family happiness were thwarted, she is professionally successful, and her position permits her to make choices she otherwise would not have. In her private life, after the death of Abbie's husband, she adopts Abbie and Link as her own; caring for them becomes the fulcrum in all of their lives. If what she creates for herself falls short of her original goals, Frances belongs to that stalwart band of black women of all classes---feminists before the word was even known to their generations. These are the women who, in spite of external limitations, made a way for themselves and others where none previously existed. Their class does not alleviate the problems of race for them, although it affords them a wider range of options for independence. Nevertheless, they are trapped in the same gender roles as their less fortunate sisters. In spite of this, Abbie and Frances maintain dignity as black women in a world that values neither blacks nor women.

Petry's novels are unique for their time, and brilliant expositions in the intricacies of their literary, political, philosophical, and social implications. Written in a period when deliberate black feminist fiction and black feminist interpretations of fiction were ideas whose time had not yet come, they were revolutionary. There is no question that Petry had a unique black female vision. *The Street* and *The Narrows* are complex novels with entangled relationships that hold multiple implications for contemporary feminist criticism of blacks and whites, men and women. Petry's vision of the complicated dynamics of black women's lives is especially compelling. Her black women, even in a racist, sexist, classist society, seek individual autonomy as their human right. They do not always win, but they are heroic figures.

---

[1] Gloria Naylor and Toni Morrison, "A Conversation," *Southern Review* 21 (July 1985), 590.
[2] Bernard W. Bell, "Ann Petry Demythologizing of American Culture and Afro-American Character," in *Conjuring: Black Women, Fiction, and Literary Tradition*, eds. Marjorie Pryse and Hortense J. Spillers (Bloomington: Indiana University Press, 1985), 107. [See elsewhere in this text].

[3] Throughout the novel, Lutie's attitudes indicate her identification with Ben Franklin as a model for the individual search for success. At one point, as she walks home in the evening with packages from the grocery store, including hard rolls she bought for breakfast, she "thought immediately of Ben Franklin and his loaf of bread. And [she] grinned thinking, You and Ben Franklin. You ought to take one out and start eating it as you walk along" (Ann Petry, *The Street*, 63).

[4] Barbara Smith, "A Familiar Street," in *Belles Lettres: A Review of Books by Women* , 2 no. 3 (January/February 1987), 4. [See elsewhere in this text].

[5] Naylor and Morrison, "A Conversation," 571.

[6] Smith, "A Familiar Street," 4.

[7] Ann Petry, *The Narrows* (Boston: Beacon Press, 1988), 4.

A Distaff Dream Deferred? Ann Petry and the Art of Subversion (1992)
Keith Clark

The "American Dream" has been a prominent subject in American literature, especially during the first half of the twentieth century. Dreiser, Fitzgerald, Miller---all of these writers have depicted characters in search of the utopian dream, few of whom find it. Their African-American counterparts' variation on this mythic search has followed a similar pattern in that their characters have also sought psychological and material fulfillment—a fact making Ralph Ellison's declaration that "the values of my own people are neither 'white' nor 'black,' they are American" (*Shadow and Act* 270) particularly resonant. But unlike Jay Gatsby or Willy Loman, men whose demons are internal, most black protagonists prior to the 1960s have faced "flesh-and-blood" demons. *Black* Bigger Thomas differs substantially from *white* Jay Gatsby or Willy Loman, for the race and class of the black character preclude even marginal access to the Dream and its attendant creature comforts. At least prior to the Civil Rights [m]ovement, then, "Lift yourself up by your bootstraps" rang as a specious aphorism, since typical black protagonists in protest fiction neither owned the bootstraps nor had access to the means of acquiring them.

While something of an anachronism in the 1990s, the African-American protest novel of the 1940s and 1950s maintained a symbiotic relationship with the mythic American Dream: It decried a history of American racism which made achieving the Dream a chimera for blacks. While Richard Wright is considered the "father" of the genre, and *Native Son* (1940) its quintessential document, Ann Petry emerged as another strident voice---a progenitor or native daughter. While her novel *The Narrows* (1953) deviated somewhat, it nevertheless continued the Wrightian tradition. Link Williams, the protagonist, differs superficially from Bigger in that he has attained a Dartmouth education and enjoys relative freedom from economic hardships; it would *appear* that he has the means to acquire the bootstraps over which Bigger can only ruminate. However, Link's "success" cannot shield him in an America which insists upon his inhumanity. When he breaks the taboos of class and race by having an affair with a white New England heiress, his violent murder becomes ritual---an inexorable response to a black stepping out of his "place." While Petry's "New England" novel echoes *Native Son* thematically, more ostensibly it also foregrounds the black *male* as the victim of an America which denies African-Americans their very personhood. But in *The Street* (1946), Petry recasts the Herculean quest for the American Dream in an unequivocally female context. Indeed, the novel represents the "distaff" side of the African-American literary tradition, emerging as a groundbreaking work in its examination of the black woman's pursuit of happiness. Not only does Petry depict how women pursue the Dream in traditionally "American" terms, but, most deftly, she illustrates how black women subvert the quest for the American Dream and fulfill their own version of it.

II

Given the spurious nature of the American Dream, one would assume that the African-American writer would vigorously expose its shortcomings—for instance, the myopic measuring of "success" in monetary and materials terms. But the tendency has not been so much to attack the Dream as to *protest* whites' insistence on treating blacks as outsiders and interlopers. Indead, the hue and cry of the Biggers and the Walter Lee Youngers emanate from their staunch loyalty to the hallowed Constitution, which stipulates that "all men are created equal"; they cry only because they want *their* slice of the pie. As Richard Yarborough points out, "Despite severe disappointments, . . . Afro-Americans have generally been among the most fervent believers in the American Dream" (33).

Lutie Johnson, the protagonist in *The Street*, embodies the female version of the archetypal quest. Patterning her life after Benjamin Franklin's, Lutie embarks on an expedition she hopes will bestow the trappings of success upon herself and Bub her eight-year-old son. However, Lutie's odyssey from Jamaica, New York, to Lyme, Connecticut, to Harlem bestows upon her little more than disillusionment. Ultimately, what Calvin Hernton calls the "three isms' (65)—racism, capitalism, and sexism—launch an implacable assault on Lutie, precipitating the novel's tragic conclusion.

While it would be tempting to view the novel as a treatise on how men, black and white, collude to destroy the All-American black girl, Petry's text discourages this sort of naturalistic preoccupation with character as subject and object. Instead, one might view this seminal examination of the black woman's search for the Dream as a mosaic—much like Alice Walker's tropological quilt---that includes other women, other stories, and other voices. In addition to presenting Lutie and her blind adherence to American values, Petry depicts two black female characters who circumvent the quest: Mrs. Hedges, who operates a bordello in the apartment building where Lutie lives and who also oversees the day-to-day events on "the street," and Min, the downtrodden and subservient companion of William Jones, the building superintendent.

Far from being minor characters, Mrs. Hedges and Min embody what I see as a history of black women *subverting* the vacuous Dream myth through an almost innate ability to secure their own space despite the twin scouges of racism and sexism.[1] Existing in a milieu where the Dream's core assumptions belie their lived realities, these black women *undermine* the myth, altering it to ensure both economic survival and varying degrees of emotional stability. And because "traditional" principles have been the bane of black people since America's inception, questions involving the "morality" of how these women survive become ancillary ones given their predatory, hostile environment.

Superficially, Mrs. Hedges and Min adhere to the ideals of "hard work" and "ingenuity" in a country where "anything is possible." However, these women more accurately replicate techniques used by such archetypal African-American trickster figures as Charles Chesnutt's Uncle Julius or black folklore's Peetie Wheatstraw in (re)inventing lives independent of the white American Dream. While denied opulent lifestyles and material objects, Petry's "minor" women attain life's basic necessities, and, given their tenuous existences, they (re)construct their own "dream" by tapping into a tradition of what Peter Wheatstraw in *Invisible Man* calls " 'shit, grit and mother-wit' " (176). Thus, *The Street* transcends the boundaries of the *"roman-`a-these,"* the thesis presumably being that white racism extinguishes all black hope.[2] The denizens of Petry's Harlem face a world more Darwinian than Franklinian, and they act according to their individual circumstances.

Clearly, Lutie Johnson's plight serves as the novel's primary concern, for Petry privileges her in terms of narrative space and point of view. A literary relative of black maids such as William Faulkner's Dilsey Gibson and Toni Morrison's Pauline Breedlove, both of whom worship their white employers, Lutie epitomizes mimetic desire: She deifies her white employers, the Chandlers, as living proof that, with a lot of hard work, the Dream can become reality. One of Susan Willis's observations is apropos here:

> The situation for the black woman was somewhat different [from that of the black man].   Usually employed as a maid and therefore only marginally incorporated as a wage laborer, her alienation was the result of striving to achieve the white bourgeois social model (in which she worked but did not live) which is itself produced by the system of wage labor under capitalism. (265)[3]

The converted Lutie buys into the Chandlers' "new philosophy" about being "filthy" rich and about America's being the "richest damn country in the world" (32). In Lutie's new "religion" she will become a disciple of the father of such declarations, Benjamin Franklin. But after several harrowing experiences, Lutie ultimately realizes, albeit too late, what the "Emersonian" Invisible Man must also face: Hackneyed beliefs based on a prescription of "hard work" and "self-reliance" are not panaceas for black folks. However, by allowing Mrs. Hedges and Min into Lutie's narrative space, Petry deftly depicts how black women (re)configure the mythic American quest for economic and emotional security.

Perhaps more indicative of the type of "pioneering" spirit that fails Lutie is Mrs. Hedges, who runs a brothel in the apartment building. Indeed, her history resembles a Horatio Alger "rages-to-riches" fable. Having undertaken what has become the black character's archetypal movement, from the South to the North, Mrs. Hedges overcomes a hand-to-mouth existence of scavenging for food in garbage cans. Most assuredly, she has encountered economic hardships more caustic than Lutie's.

Petry portrays Mrs. Hedges as relying on 'ingenuity," a basic ingredient in the American Dream formula---or what blacks might call mother wit. Upon encountering the white man Junto (who will eventually wield immense control over the lives of band leader Boots Smith and Lutie), Mrs. Hedges brings to their relationship an acumen for business and entrepreneurship. First, she encourages him to expand his "business"; he is a "pushcart" man, collecting bottles and other refuse to exchange for money: "It was she who suggested that he branch out, get other pushcarts and other men to work for him" (152). Mrs. Hedges's association with Junto eventually pays further dividends, as he gives her "the job of janitor and collector of rents" (traditionally male occupations) when he acquires some tenements in Harlem. Their collaborative efforts culminate in a thriving prostitution business, the brainchild of a woman, who has mastered the rudiments of supply and demand.

On the surface, Petry's depiction of Mrs. Hedges might represent the author's disdain for a society that would reward "vice." If this were the case, Petry would be echoing sociologist Horace R. Cayton's excoriation of the Dream:

> We have embraced and are the victims of a configuration of shoddy values, the "get-rich-quick' compulsion, and our surrender to the bitch goddess of material success. Our emphasis is on sex for gratification rather than deep organic emotional expression, experience and communication . . . and [we are] unable to rid ourselves of an archaic economic system that defies all laws of logic, humanity and downright common sense. [Yet] this is the most bountiful country in the world; a country birthed in principles both noble and bold, familiarized to us all as the American Dream. (41)

In this context Mrs. Hedges would symbolize capitalism gone awry. However, that Mrs. Hedges immediately exploits her "chance" meeting with Junto demonstrates that she recognizes the locus of power---the white male. Because she has experienced racism and sexism and their attendant hardships firsthand, Mrs. Hedges's actions become laudable, a prime example of what Booker T. Washington would call casting down one's bucket. She understands the patriarchal system and thus *subverts* it by accepting her place as the "brains" behind Junto's conglomerate, performing her own updated form of "masking."

I believe Addison Gayle accurately assesses Mrs. Hedges's talents: "Given Mrs. Hedges's entrepreneurial skills, energy, ability, and a white skin, she might have created a capitalistic enterprise, might have become, like the Chandlers, a purveyor of stock market receipts and dividends" (194). However, it is precisely because Mrs. Hedges *cannot* become like the Chandlers that she resorts to procurement, a "black-market" activity.   She successfully parlays her "entrepreneurial" skills in the best tradition of the American Dream. Presented with a set of circumstances which do not merely limit but deny her access to wealth and power, she creates a viable alternative: She erects a "capitalistic enterprise." Her mother wit allows her to survive, her endeavors being logical and acceptable ones. Just as Chesnutt's Uncle Julius cunningly weaves a design to "fool ole massa" into guaranteeing economic security, so too does Petry's Mrs. Hedges subscribe to a higher "moral imperative"---self-preservation.

Having the acuity to align herself with the powerful white male hegemony, Mrs. Hedges effectively adopts a "masculine" persona to maintain the place she carves out for herself. The text buttresses the notion that the American Dream not only is the domain of white men, but it also involves the subordination and objectification of women. White Mrs. Chandler owes her opulent lifestyle to her good looks and her capitulation to white men; and in a billboard advertising kitchen sinks, Lutie notices the white woman's "incredible blond hair" (23).

Given the limitations placed on white women, one can surely surmise the black woman's cramped choices---to become either a whore or a mammy. While Petry painstakingly focuses the reader on Lutie's physical beauty and how it works detrimentally, she simultaneously alerts us to Mrs. Hedges's grotesqueness. She dons a "red bandanna tied in hard, ugly knots around her head" (173) because a fire in Junto's apartment building has left her bald. Petry also describes her as a "mountain of a woman" (148).   Her physical "deformities" have also prevented her from finding work:

> When she walked in [employment agencies],
> there was an uncontrollable revulsion in the
> faces of the white people who looked at her.
> They stared amazed at her enormous size, at
> the blackness of her skin. They glanced at
> each other, tried in vain to control their faces
> or didn't bother to try at all, simply let her
> see what a monstrosity they thought she
> was. (151)

The inability to support oneself through no intrinsic fault might have sealed the fate of most women, but Mrs. Hedges continues to display an acute understanding of America's "work ethic" and the value of perseverance.

By ardently resisting "feminization"---Mrs. Hedges's unwillingness to exploit her own body in the sex-money nexus---she retains her hard-fought place in the white-male power structure. Petry elucidates this idea further when Junto gives Mrs. Hedges a wig in an attempt to "beautify" her. By staunchly refusing his "gift," Mrs. Hedges maintains her leverage and power in the street's economic hierarchy. Indeed, not only is she an integral part of the omnipotent Junto-police axis, but she exerts a control over black men that women seldom have---the power to determine the availability and price of sex. Along with the economic benefits, Mrs. Hedges's defeminization brings positive results: She thwarts the Super's attempted rape of Lutie and keeps his parasitic sexuality in check; in her role as "procurer," she enables young hopeless black women to work *off* of a street that would probably devour them; and she acts as a guardian for other female tenants (in addition to Lutie). Certainly, Mrs. Hedges has at least a reciprocal relationship with the community, if not a purely *quid pro quo* one. In an environment which commodifies and objectifies *ad infinitum*, Mrs. Hedges operates deftly on the outskirts of the American Dream---a marginal domain where scores of black women and men have made a way out of no way.

The emphasis on sex as commodity and the concentration on physical beauty place the black woman in an untenable position. As Horace Cayton has observed, "American culture places high value on appearances, and beauty---by all means one must be beautiful---must conform to stereotyped norms of so-called Anglo-Saxon beauty and appearance" (41). While Petry portrays Mrs. Hedges almost paradoxically---her physical unattractiveness and her "success" being directly proportional---the incongruity emphasizes the importance of "tricksterism" and living by one's wits.

Another of Petry's female characters displays ingenuity, given her restricted possibilities. Min, Mrs. Hedges's neighbor and the Super's live-in companion, endures a particularly brutal life not unlike Celie's in *The Color Purple*. Petry portrays her as a ne'er-do-well whose initial objective is to save enough money to purchase some false teeth. Petry's Min fits a classic "abused-woman" paradigm: Conditioned by her society to see herself as worthless, she tolerates and rationalizes a life of violence---physical, sexual, and economic. Her possibilities slim, Min enters the economic arena as a maid and incurs hardships similar to Lutie's. Unlike Mrs. Hedges in that the most important men in her life are black, Min must still face an American society which privileges men--- even miscreants like Jones, who, as the Super, holds a limited amount of power. Jones treats Min slightly better than he does his dog, tormenting her physically and psychologically. The abuse escalates when Lutie moves into the building and evokes the Super's lascivious sexual desires. In terms of America's patriarchal system, Min's perpetual dependence on the "kindness" of men--- perhaps a basis for her name---mirrors the experiences of countless black women in America. Indeed, Min's plight recalls Janie Stark's grandmother's folk metaphor: " 'De nigger woman is de mule uh de world so fur as Ah can see' " (Hurston 29).

Petry's complex depiction of black women is a testimony to her years as a reporter, where she witnessed firsthand the harrowing circumstances many Harlemites faced. Against the backdrop of Lutie's monomaniacal pursuit of the American Dream, it would appear that Petry uses Min contrapuntally to illustrate what happens when the desire for "security" takes a pathological turn. But closer examination elucidates how she grants Min the same type of *improvisational* talents that sustain Mrs. Hedges---the ability to ensure survival in a crumbling, life-abnegating America. It is precisely because Lutie has become so enslaved to the American Dream and the "white" means of attaining it that she lacks the ability to modify and act accordingly.

Mrs. Hedges plays a crucial role in Min's life: She passes along the name of a "root doctor" (which Mrs. Hedges, in turn, has gotten from one of "her girls"), although she says she does not " 'hold with'em myself, because I always figured that as far as my own business is concerned I was well able to do anything any root doctor could do' " (79). Unlike Lutie, Min does not engage in the type of sententious "moralizing" that estranges Lutie from other black women in the community. By refusing to judge Mrs. Hedges by a white code of "ethics"---as "pimp" and therefore out-of-bounds---Min avails herself of one of the community's greatest sources of information and power. I would disagree with Barbara Christian's assertion that "*The Street* is different from most novels by Afro-American women in that its female characters are so cut off by everyone and everything" (64). Although not a flourishing one, a black female community---some sort of network that attempts to sustain its members---does exist. Mrs. Hedges (along with "her girls") thus becomes a crucial conduit in Min's search for economic stability.

Inexplicably, Lutie discounts similar sources of oral, "folk" wisdom which might have helped her. The memory of her grandmother ("Granny") haunts Lutie's life long after the old woman has passed on, and she thus represents a potential mentor. Whether it be through practical wisdom about how butchers in black neighborhoods adulterate tainted meat or how Lutie might deal with men like the lecherous Boots Smith, the sagacious Granny looms as a tangible presence throughout the novel---a veritable "mother" figure much like the perspicacious "ghost father" who guides Pilate Dead in Morrison's *Song of Solomon.*

Even in economic matters, Granny could teach Lutie some lessons. On the one hand Granny disapproves of the bootlegging business run by "Pops" (her son and Lutie's father). Granny reveals to Lutie that " 'men like him don't get nowhere . . . . Think folks owe'em a livin'. And mebbe they do, but not nowhere near the way he thinks' " (55). But despite her outward distaste for Pops's "business," Granny, perhaps internally, realizes that blacks have often had to engage in "immoral" activities given their financial exigencies; thus, she refrains from castigating her son.

Lutie, on the other hand, reacts violently when Bub attempts to aid his Dream-crazed mother by shining shoes in front of their apartment building. Upon learning of his venture, she slaps him "sharply across th face. His look of utter astonishment made her strike him again---this time more violently, and she hated herself for doing it, even as she lifted her hand for another blow" (46). Lutie's preoccupation with stereotypes about black boys shining shoes blinds her to the grim reality she and Bub face. Neither Granny's guidance nor the reasons behind Bub's ingenuity can penetrate the funk in which Franlkin's and the Chandlers' dogma has left Lutie.[4] Thus, Petry portrays Lutie as maniacally enslaved to a dysfunctional ideology, a woman who has swallowed whole the spurious rhetoric of the American Dream.

Juxtaposing Lutie and Min in terms of their ideological "role models" illuminates a fundamental difference between Euro-American and African-American cultures. In a lengthy essay, "Black Poetry, Blues, and Folklore," Berndt Ostendorf makes a perceptive distinction between "oral" and "literate" culture"

> Oral cultures are dramatic, literate cultures epistemic in their focus of attention, *the first develops the resources of spontaneity, style, affective performance, and catharsis, the second scrutiny, contemplation,* or what Romantic art called "recollection in tranquility." *Oral folklore openly reveals its social genesis and function, whereas the relative "autonomy" of literary texts has been postulated on the basis of the constitutional self-reflexiveness of literary products. Literacy engenders historical norms for the production and reception of culture; the resultant lag between past and present forms or habits of reception has to be made functional (i.e., usable for the present) through constant hermeneutical effort* . . . . Literacy also puts a brake on semantic freedom and development; semantic ratification and adoption into usage are slow and laborious processes. *Innovations, adaptations, and neologisms are treated as intruders, and subcultural improprieties run into a wall of purists.*
> (224; emphasis added)

Ostendorf's meticulous delineations illuminate the core differences between Lutie and the novel's other black characters. Mrs. Hedges, Granny, and Min (and, to some degree, Boots Smith) are grounded in an African-American ethos which has served blacks well historically; concomitantly, this more demonstrative and practical culture facilitates the development of improvisational techniques, such as the "subversive" acts of Mrs. Hedges, Pops, Boots, and Min. Antithetically, Lutie is mired in a fruitless "hermeneutic" process: She spends the entire novel trying to decipher Franklin's encoded, phallocentric text---a "white" book blacks were never meant to read in the first place.

In terms of white versus black role models, David the Prophet assumes an even greater significance in the text. Ostensibly, he "cures" Min of her economic ills, passing along the "roots" that will prevent Jones from banishing her. Crucially, David's "text" is neither indecipherable nor cryptic. Min does not have to "interpret" him, and he listens to *her* story attentively, witnessing and validating her life: "The satisfaction she felt was from the quiet way he had listened to her, giving her all of her attention. No one had ever done that before" (88). Thus, Petry affirms the power of orality for blacks in both tropological and practical contexts.

In aiding Min in her subversive actions, the Prophet David epitomizes the power of "conjure" in eradicating evil and effecting change in an unjust, amoral society. Just as Chesnutt demonstrated how the animistic folk "remedies" of the "Conjure Woman" served as a corrective force in the dehumanizing antebellum South, so too does Petry show how similar folk beliefs benefit blacks in the postbellum urban North. Ultimately, David's stimulation of Min and the resurgence that results mark the height of subversion (as well as paralleling the Hedges-Junto relationship)---she by rejecting a black "Christianity" that mimics the ineffectual white one; he by giving her a cross, a key piece of white Christian iconography, to place over her bed in warding off evil. Thus, they subvert a sacrosanct but hypocritical institution which most Americans profess to worship, exploiting it for their own ends. Vis-'a-vis Min's activism, Lutie's comment " 'What possible good has it done to teach people like me to write? ' " (27) becomes particularly resonant and ironic. Precisely because she based her life on a white, "literary model, she loses sight of the invaluable "black book of life"---a hallowed, Afrocentric text that instructs blacks to "read" what is not written, to draw from their own cultural guideposts.

III

What Petry's women attain is not emblematic of what the American Dream should produce in its most sanguine form. But Mrs. Hedges and Min do "get over," and their actions and choices appear free of the author's judgment. Given Petry's position in her relation to the text, I wish to spend the last section of this essay discussing the novelist's own act of subversion in constructing *The Street* and the assumptions that go into treating Petry as an American "naturalist"---a purveyor of social "protest" and Richard Wright's native daughter.

On the surface, the view that *The Street* fits snugly into the "social criticism" school of Dreiser---and even more cozily into the "protest" tradition of Wright---seems plausible enough. W. Lawrence Hogue examines why critics in the 1940s welcomed Petry and Wright into the bosom of the American literary "tradition," while responding tepidly to Zora Neale Hurston's *Their Eyes Were Watching God*, which appeared contemporaneously:

> During the first half of the twentieth century, the naturalist movement was one mode of writing that dominated the American literary scene. It became a kind of literature that was judged "fine." Naturalism's literary themes and motifs---determinism, survival, violence, and taboo---became the standards by which the worth of a literary text was assessed and judged. These themes were a part of the definitions of reality that belonged to the ruling ideological apparatus. (29)

Hogue concludes that, "in examining the favorable reception during the 1940s of Wright's *Native Son* and Petry's *The Street* and the unfavorable reception of Hurston's novel, the reader can see how normative criticism functions: as an active and ongoing part of literary tastes and theories of literature" (31). Clearly, one could read *The Street* as a commentary on why America fails the black woman (and man). Petry's discourse---that of "social criticism"---is one that the writer herself embraces.[5] Writing in the vein of the male "naturalists," she therefore assumed a place denied Hurston, whose bucolic "folk portraits" were simply not in vogue.[6]

But if we look at Petry's depiction of Lutie in terms of the options available to other women in the book, the pervasive critical stance that views Lutie as a perpetual victim becomes somewhat troublesome. I would not go so far as to say that she should not be perceived as acting heroically. I do question, however, the degree to which we can see Lutie as a "tragic heroine," notwithstanding the author's claims to the contrary.[7] To understand more fully what Petry achieves in portraying Lutie as she does, I think we must recall the black female characters' primary resource---the ability to subvert.

One explanation for seeing Lutie as an "anti-heroine" lies in her obtuseness and gullibility. In this respect, Petry's depiction of Lutie resembles Jonathan Swift's presentation of Gulliver. The satirist ridicules his protagonist for his own ideological and rhetorical purposes. Harlem becomes Lutie's Brobdingnag and, like her "dwarf" predecessor, she is almost parasite-like in a voracious world. Indeed, Lutie's "travels" intersperse the comic and the absurd: In one episode, "She pushed [Bub] away and unlocked the door and the can of peas slipped out from under her arm to roll clumsily along the hall in its brown-paper wrapping. While Bub scrambled after it, she opened the door" (48); and in another she is duped into believing that a lawyer can free Bub from the detention home. In this context, then, Gayle's suggestion that "*The Street* takes on the dimensions of a mock-heroic epic" (193) is quite salient. By having her protagonist refuse to read the black "book of life" in lieu of Franklin's unintelligible, quixotic *auto*biography, Petry forces the reader to take an incredulous stance. Lutie's choices strain our sense of acceptable behavior, given such implacable circumstances. Ostensibly, Lutie's plight differs little from that of a character like Stephen Crane's Maggie, whose sordid environment eventually drives her to suicide. But because Lutie is so naïve, so anesthetized by the nectar of the mythic American Dream, one cannot help but wonder whether Petry was---albeit obliquely---criticizing not only Lutie's choices but also naturalistic conventions, where an individual bears such immense suffering and squalor that his or her tragedy borders on the banal and the clichéd.

Lutie's superciliousness and naivete combine to render her less the apogee of the "tragic victim" who populates the naturalist's landscape and more the black-faced "gullible Gulliver," the object of the satirist's derision. Petry thus achieves something rather paradoxical: She pledges allegiance to the godhead of American naturalism while depicting a hopelessly naïve black American woman through whom the author appears to challenge the validity of such abstractions as "determinism" and "victimization."

Looked at from a different perspective, then, *The Street* transcends the limitations of "thesis literature" and naturalism, which concentrate microscopically on a single victim and the violence that society inflicts upon him or her. As I mentioned at the outset, Petry presents Lutie's story as the central one, but it also functions organically, spawning others' as well. By effectively shifting narrative focus away from Lutie in the novel, Petry's lens becomes more panoramic: other stories encroach upon Lutie's *mise-en-scene* and take on a tension and drama all their own.

Using multiple viewpoints as a structural device deviates from the naturalist's narrow eye, placing Petry closer to a tradition of African-American writers who view the black community in its totality, harboring several stories. Like Mrs. Hedges and Min, Petry has mastered the skill of "improvisation," which defined the democratic "free jazz" of iconoclasts such as Ornette Coleman and Albert Ayler in the 1950s. She gives each of the text's characters her own "solo." By deemphasizing character and instead accentuating community, Petry moves away from the exalted American naturalism which privileges men (Dreiser and Wright), and anticipates African-Americanists

James Baldwin, Toni Morrison, and Gloria Naylor---writers who see the blackness of blackness, a layered universe and not a single stratum.

Masking, signifying, disguise/concealment---black characters have exploited these techniques in order to survive in a country bent on their annihilation. Linda Brent, Uncle Julius, and Janie Crawford invent lives far different from those of Alger, Franklin, and Greeley. In her groundbreaking, gynocentric novel, Petry reaffirms the value of tactics that have enabled blacks to endure a lifetime of physical and psychological slavery. While her "main" protagonist, Lutie Johnson, murders and flees, other black women carve out existences, although somewhat meager and unglamorous. Min and Mrs. Hedges also prefigure women like Frances Jackson, the successful mortician in *The Narrows*. Subversion as a prominent skill---on the part of author and characters alike--- catapults black women from the confines of a patriarchal, dehumanizing America to another country, where they can operate businesses, keep a roof over their heads, and move beyond restrictive and male-dominated literary configurations.

---

[1] Hernton's reading of the novel might be termed "feminist" in that he isolates and examines the complicity of men, both black and white, (and to some degree Mrs. Hedges, whom he calls a "vampire" [70]) in Lutie's demise. However, I believe that privileging Lutie as the sole, almost infallible, victim becomes somewhat problematic: Albeit obliquely, it perpetuates myths about helpless, prostrate women who are incapable of acting on their own behalf. Marjorie Pryse offers an especially insightful exegesis of the text, primarily because she does not limit her examination to Lutie's "victimization." Pryse focuses on how American history informs the characterization and plot of the novel. Specifically, she links what she calls "deistic forces" in the novel to their historical antecedents: "The apparently invisible and naturalistic forces behind the street, then, become closely linked with the political attitudes of the white people who founded, then proceeded to run, the country' (122). Pryse goes on to adduce that Granny, Mrs. Hedges, and David the Prophet represent viable "alternative forces" to Lutie's white ones. However, while she sees them as women who adapt better than Lutie does, Pryse holds a rather pejorative view of Min and Mrs. Hedges, particularly the latter. While Min possesses traits which might have benefited Lutie, she is not the "perfect foil for Lutie" (127). Mrs. Hedges functions as a "false madonna" and an "inverted goddess" who is ultimately complicit in Lutie's demise: "The deity/goddess who seems so much a part of the landscape of the street has failed to mother" (128). I would counter that Mrs. Hedges functions much more affirmatively, as seen by her ability to "mother" Min. That Lutie fails as miserably as she does says less about Mrs.

Hedges and more about Lutie's own inability or unwillingness to subvert American institutions which have been the bane of blacks for centuries.

[2] See Bone and Davis, who both perform---to varying degrees---a "reduction" of Petry's novel. Bone labeling it a *roman-a-these* (180). He goes on to criticize Petry in terms of Wrightian protest for her insufficient political analysis: "Here the ideological limitations of Wright's disciples become evident: they attack the slum without understanding that social system which produced it. Their novels fall between the stools of racial and social protest, lacking the historical sweep with which Wright synthesized the two" (159).

[3] Historically, black women who entered the work force as maids have been particularly vulnerable to a sort of "white disease," perhaps the natural result of living in the "big house." Discussing Lutie specifically as a maid, Trudier Harris elaborates on how she has been "seduced" by the American Dream and her 'belief that dedication to getting money will solve all problems" (92).

[4] See Bell, who speaks to the futility of the Franklinian Dream which Lutie assiduously pursues: "While, for example, myths of the Founding Fathers like Benjamin Franklin, who is the colonial paradigm of the successful self-made man, are available to all Americans, black Americans rarely refer to them" (106).

[5] In "The Novel as Social Criticism," Petry elaborates on the symbiotic connection between "art" and "life": "*The novel, like all other forms of art, will always reflect the political, economic, and social structure of the period in which it was created* . . . . The moment the novelist begins to show how society affected the lives of his characters, how they were formed and shaped by the sprawling inchoate world in which they lived, *he is writing a novel of social criticism whether he calls it that or not*" (33; emphases added).

[6] Lamentably, if understandably, critical response to Wright's *Uncle Tom's Children*, which appeared a year after *Their Eyes Were Watching God*, reflects the tendentious nature of the "liberal" literary establishment. In its eyes the works of self-professed "angry young men" such as Wright, Baldwin, and Amiri Baraka are acceptable means of protest; the flagellation is welcomed, albeit in a patronizing way. Regrettably, critics ignored Hurston's work and lavishly praised Wright's ---despite some basic similarities between the two texts. Wright himself attacked Hurston's book in a now-infamous "review."

[7] See "Ann Petry Talks about First Novel" (*Crisis* 53 [Jan. 1946]: 48-49). This brief essay/interview is the source of Petry's often-quoted "paean" to naturalism: "In *The Street* my aim is to show how simply and easily the environment can change the course of a person's life. For this purpose I have made Lindy Johnson [sic] an intelligent, ambitious, attractive woman with a fair degree of education" (49).

The Hidden Hand of Feminist Revolt in Ann Petry's *The Street* (1993)[1]
Hazel Arnett Ervin

Ann Petry once stated, "The normal thing when you write it to write about those things which interested you."[2] What appears to have interested Petry in her novel *The Street* (1946) is the resurgence following World War II of traditional attitudes about the woman's place being in the home. In response to the re-imposition of patriarchal domesticity, Petry undermines prescribed gender roles in a subversive subtext. Writing in specific chapters in *The Street*, she creates recognizable portraits of domesticated women as wives, mothers, and homemakers, and, then, by pointing out contradictions and double standards of women's lives, or the ironic circumstances of their social realities, especially on behalf of working-class black women, she subverts traditional attitudes concerning the roles and behavior of women. Petry seems interested also in empowering women. After raising questions about patriarchal ideology, using, again, specific women in *The Street*, she offers a solution to the contradictions or ironies of prescribed female roles---a new level of social consciousness about what constitutes common womanhood.

Over the years, critics have recognized nineteenth-century women writers Harriet Jacobs in *Incident in the Life of a Slave Girl* and Francis Harper in *Iola Leroy* and twentieth-century women writers Nella Larsen in *Quicksand* and *Passing* and Zora Neale Hurston in *Their Eyes Were Watching God* (1937) as major black women writers who challenged traditional assumptions concerning women's roles and behavior. I wish to add Ann Petry to the list, for with the possible exception of Harriet Jacobs who consistently attacks male domination, none of the novelists mentioned here is as consistent as Petry in opposing patriarchal ideology, especially on behalf of working-class black women. Other concerns such as Harper's "uplifting the race," Larsen's ambivalent black middle class, and Hurston's oral folk tradition, preoccupy their respective texts. In addition, in contrast to the 1880s, when Jacobs and Harper were writing respectively *Incidents* and *Iola*, to the 1920s when Larsen was writing *Quicksand* and *Passing*, or to the 1930s when Hurston was writing *Their Eyes Were Watching God*, the 1940s was a time when men were waging a concerted campaign to get women out of the workplace and back into the home (Chafe 94).[3] It was a time that almost demanded a female novelist's unrelenting resistance to cultural ideology. Petry, I contend, is a novelist who questions and undermines the patriarchy and cultural assumptions of the 1940s, especially on behalf of working-class black women.

Writing in *No Crystal Stair* (1984), Gloria Wade-Gayles is the earliest of critics to recognize in *The Street* Ann Petry's interest in the re-enforcement of traditional roles of men and women. While Wade-Gayles does not offer a lengthy or detailed analysis of Petry's critique of patriarchal gender roles in *The Street*, she alerts readers of the writer's indirect and subtle intent, especially on behalf of working-class black women:

> What is [Ann] Petry's response to the
> prevailing notion of the forties that
> 'woman's place' is in the home? [Petry]
> seems to challenge . . . indirectly . .. [the]
> cultural assumption [that woman's place is
> in the home] . . . . We can speculate that the
> negative portraits of white women who
> remain in their 'place' are comments on the
> sterility of women's 'place.' There is no
> need to speculate on Petry's opinion of the
> impact the assumption [that women should
> remain subordinate] has on black women.
> She attacks the system for believing in that
> 'place' and denying it to poor black women.
> (124)

The rest of this article will be devoted to identifying the subversive text alluded to by Wade Gayles and to analyzing the presence of women characters in *The Street* who strive to achieve a new level of feminine consciousness.

It is within a patriarchal context in *The Street* that Petry reveals her subversive text which undermines prescribed gender roles. Like most women writers prior to the 1960s, Petry's contempt comes in her work "not in thunder, but in electric whispers"; her text of revolt is submerged in the conforming naturalistic/protest narrative of the times (Dobson, "The Hidden Hand: Subversion of Cultural Ideology in Three Mid-Nineteenth-Century Women's Novels, 223-241). On the surface, Petry appears to conform also to a patriarchal society. For example, all of the women in the novel either yearn to become or strive to maintain their roles as homemakers, wives, and mothers. Main character, Lutie Johnson does not go outside her home without wearing her white gloves---the symbolic trappings of an ideally chaste and pious woman. Mrs. Pizzini responds to Lutie's request to write a letter of recommendation for a job by reminding her that a high priority of the ideal woman is "domesticity." All of the men in the novel dominate aspects of life outside the home. They are lawyers, entrepreneurs, grocers, musicians, skilled laborers, and even heads of organized crime. While Petry appears to reinforce a patriarchal society, actually she undermines it. Close citings of how Petry interrupts narrative conventions (e.g., narrative sequencing or narrative order) and of when she slants textual language will alert readers to a hidden text of revolt and will reveal also the writer's contempt for a system that believes in 'that place' yet denys it to poor black women.

As early as Chapters One, Two, and Three of *The Street*, Petry disrupts traditional sequencing of the novel, and along with persistent contradictions, double standards, and ironic circumstances in these chapters, particularly

Chapter Two, she alerts the reader to a subversive text. Chapter One of *The Street* ends with Lutie having secured an apartment for herself and her eight-year-old son Bub. Because Lutie and Bub live with Lutie's father and his girlfriend Lil, and because Lil allows Bub to smoke and to bring her beer from the refrigerator, Lutie considers the arrangement as undesirable, especially for Bub. She decides to move. If Chapters One, Two, and Three in *The Street* were in expected sequences, Lutie's concerns about getting herself and Bub settled into their own apartment would continue in Chapter Two. Instead, it is Chapter Three that continues with Lutie's having "solved [the] problem" of her and Bub's "living alone" (59). Chapter Two unexpectedly breaks the sequential ordering of the novel; it is not really connected to either Chapter One or Three. On the surface, Chapter Two consists primarily of flashback to familial moments when Lutie and her husband Jim were married, to when Lutie took a job as a live-in domestic to bring money into the house for food and mortgage payments, and to Lutie's separation from Jim. Not so visible, however, in Chapter Two is Petry's slant on domesticity.

As part of her slant, Petry manipulates language to achieve her end. For instance, in Chapter Two, she repeats the phrase "that kitchen" and indirectly returns the reader to the postwar story of domesticity. Then, she undermines the ideology of male domination. Early in the chapter, Lutie Johnson enters a crowded subway and positions herself in the crowded aisle. Directly in front of Lutie is an advertisement in which a white woman leans closely to a white man wearing a navy uniform. The two are standing in front of a white porcelain kitchen sink. While Lutie gazes intently at the advertisement in front of her, through flashback, she "enter[s] a small private world" (20) which takes her back in time when she worked not in her own kitchen or home but as a live-in domestic for two years in a kitchen "almost exactly like the one" in front of her (28). Within the context of the 1940s postwar story, advertisements like the one before Lutie replaced advertisements that once encouraged women to work outside the home. Previous advertisements once presented "Rosie the Riveter"---a woman in bib overalls, standing in front of an airplane, which she had built, with a power drill in one hand. Like millions of women during the early 1940s, Rosie worked outside the home. By 1945, however, as the war neared an end, men returned home, expecting to get back their old jobs. Thus, advertisements with Rosie the Riveter that once encouraged women to work outside the home were being replaced with ones like the one before Lutie that encouraged women to return to their proper sphere---the kitchen.[4] Yet, with the repeated phrase "that kitchen" and the ironic circumstances surrounding Lutie's social reality "(live-in domestic, separation from husband and child, etc.), Petry suggests Lutie had a "completely different kitchen" (28), and she forces readers to question the contradictions in patriarchal ideology of the 1940s, particularly on behalf of working-class black women like Lutie Johnson who desires to be home with family but can not because the husband cannot find work.

Further evidence in Chapter Two of a critical slant against domesticity is by way of Petry's use of indirect discourse. She "bends" textual language and renders inappropriate responses to the social functions of the language---all to signal her "narrative commentary."5 For instance, early in Chapter Two, Petry writes several declarative sentences about the kitchen in the advertisement viewed by Lutie:

> That kitchen sink in the advertisement or one just like it was what had wrecked [Lutie] and Jim. The sink had belonged to someone else---she'd been washing someone else's dishes when she should have been home with Jim and Bub. Instead she'd cleaned another woman's house and looked after another woman's child while her own marriage went to pot; breaking up into so many little pieces . . . . (30).

The social function of these sentences is "stating." Because of the social function of these sentences, one would expect the subsequent paragraph to be declarative, as well. On the contrary, Petry changes the direction of the narrative by posing in the next paragraph the following question: "Yet what else could she have done?" (30). Petry's interrogative sentence is an inappropriate response to the social function of the language in the sentences that precede it. Readers that are expecting a follow-up statement or two about the kitchen are forced abruptly to focus on the role of the African American woman who is compelled to work in another woman's kitchen, and readers are urged to respond to the repeated question, "Yet what else could she have done"?

On another occasion, Petry writes, "That kitchen in Connecticut had changed [Lutie's] whole life" (56). Again, the social function of the sentence is "stating." As before, Petry's expected response to the social function of the declarative statement is inappropriate. As if she were intentionally changing the focus of her narrative, Petry follows: "[T]urning to take one last look at the advertisement [in disgust, one might add], she [Lutie] left the car" (56). Here and earlier, Petry's inconsonant responses to the declarative statements about "that kitchen" abruptly force readers to question patriarchal ideology and prescribed roles, particularly on behalf of working-class black women who are working in kitchens owned by other women.

In subsequent chapters devoted to the female characters Lutie, Min, and Mrs. Hedges, Petry returns the reader to a questionable ideology. Using free indirect discouse or what Henry Louis Gates calls bivocal utterance ["third-person narrator's discourse"which has "in its syntactic and semantic structures . . . the discourse of a character Petry and characters, to coin a phrase by Karla Holloway, "create, tell, and talk back" with regard to the postwar story and prescribed roles.   Petry removes any distinctions between the omniscient narrator who basically repeats speech and represents events and the characters who actually think and react. For instance, in the quotation on the symbolic kitchen [" . . . that sink in the advertisement or one just like it was what had wrecked Lutie and Jim"] and in the quotation concerning a particular kitchen ["that kitchen in Connectitut had changed her whole life"], Lutie and narrator appear to speak directly about how she [Lutie] had been taking care of someone else's home and looking after someone else's child while her own marriage, family and home became fragmented. There are no quotation marks to indicate that Lutie is actually speaking, but when one replaces third-person pronouns with first-person pronouns, there is an identifiable fusion of the narrator's direct speech and the character's indirect speech. Furthermore, there is an apparent mental state of consciousness of the character Lutie. As a bivocal utterance, the quotation on the symbolic kitchen would reveal

> [I] relaxed [my] hand and then tightened it.
> Because   that   kitchen   sink   in   the
> advertisement or one just like it was what
> had wrecked [me] and Jim. The sink had
> belonged to someone else---[I had] been
> washing someone else's dishes when [I]
> should have been home with Jim and Bub.
> Instead [I had] cleaned another woman's
> child while [my] own marriage [and home]
> went to pot . . . . (31-32)

As a bivocal utterance, the quotation referring to the particular kitchen, would reveal

> That kitchen in Connecticut had changed
> [my] whole life --- that kitchen all tricks and
> white   enamel   like   this   one   in   the
> advertisement. (56)

When presenting the present thoughts, memories, and reflections of her black female characters, especially on traditional attitudes of the patriarchy, Petry returns most often in *The Street* to bivocal utterances.   The following observations of Lutie, Min, and Mrs. Hedges are to serve as analytical evidence of the latter. Provided also is evidence of how Lutie, more so than Min and Mrs. Hedges, moves toward a new level of feminine consciousness about what constitutes womanhood.

Lutie

When the reader meets Lutie Johnson, she and her husband Jim are having difficulties with their living expenses, particularly the mortgage. The major reason for their deficit is that Lutie's husband cannot find a job. In the 1940s, unemployment among African American men is alarmingly high. Thus, is order to keep the Johnson's home somewhat intact and to maintain the cultural assumption that the man is the provider and the woman is the caretaker, Jim and Lutie agreeably decide to care for six state children and to use the income received for the children to support themselves. This use of the state children to provide an income is seen by Jim and Lutie as temporary. Jim sees himself one day having a job and being the sole provider for his wife and son. And Lutie sees "[herself] and Jim and Bub . . . together ---safe and secure and alone" in their own home (175). In other words, Lutie desires to realize the traditional roles of housewife and mother. Lutie's desire to remain in the home does not materialize, however, because according to Jim no one would hire a black man and allow him to support his family:

> God damn white people . . . . I don't want
> favors.   All I want is a job.   Just a job.
> Don't they know if I knew how I'd change
> the color of my skin? (30)

As pointed out already, in the 1940s, there is a cultural effort to return women to the home in order to give jobs to men and to maintain stability in the family. But, via contradictions and ironic circumstances, Petry deconstructs patriarchal ideology of the 1940s by showing that patriarchal ideals are less than universal or absolute in Western culture. Should not society's cultural ideology of the 1940s (i.e., men are the protectors and providers in the home and women are the homemakers and nurturers) apply to the African American male and female? Jim is unemployed because no one will hire him. Because of his inability to be the provider in his home, he feels worthless. Eventually, he deserts the family. Lutie is forced to support herself and her son in a nontraditional role. She is forced to work outside of the home.   Petry helps the reader to understand that African American men are not being hired and that African American women are being forced to work in other women's homes. And when the men allow themselves to feel useless, they leave the women alone to provide for themselves and the children.

In a patriarchal society, the woman is also expected to remain in the home as the nurturer of the child. But Petry undermines this cultural notion in order to prove that in the 1940s in Western society, the nurturer of the African American child is not always the African American mother. Lutie Johnson desires to fulfill her role as mother to her son Bub. She wants for Bub an "airy, bright home" (311). She wants to be home each day when Bub returns from school (305). Contrary to cultural expectations, such a role, however, is denied Lutie.

In Lutie's absence, the street becomes the surrogate mother: "The street . . . played nursemaid to [the African American mother's]kid . . . . It became mother . . . and train[er] . . . , and it was a vicious mother . . . ." (407).

Firmly rooted in patriarchal ideology are the notions that as a female and as an American citizen, the woman has a "biological destiny" (Clinton 21). She is to provide her husband with heirs; as an American citizen, she is to produce citizens (Clinton 21).[6] But Lutie Johnson becomes a struggling mother who works outside the home; she is unable to provide proper guidance for Jim's heir, Bub. Because Lutie must work long hours, Bub is "[a]lways alone" . . . [and] Bub [will not] stay in the house after school because [he is] afraid of the empty, silent, dark rooms" (231). Bub turns to "the street." And as Petry concludes, the street responds to African American children by "reach[ing] out and suck[ing] them up [Bub included]" (213). Put another way, in this mother's absence, "the street" does not help to mold Bub into an exemplary citizen. Rather, "the street" creates a citizen bound for reform school. The commentary here is that society charges mothers with the task of producing ethical citizens but then forces the African American mother to be out of the home during those important hours and years in children's lives. Here lies contradiction in the ideological expectations of the 1940s.

Petry is concerned also with the notion that ideal womanhood includes white women (implied by advertisements like the one witnessed by Lutie while riding the subway) and excludes African Amreican women. On different occasions in the novel, the reader observes how Lutie is told indirectly that she falls outside ideal womanhood---i.e., she is an unlikely respectable woman. First, there is Mrs. Pizzini, who firmly warns Lutie against working outside the home as if she [Mrs. Pizzini] believes the true woman's place is in the home. Then, there is the mother-in-law of Lutie's employer, Mrs. Henry Chandler, who never bothers in Lutie's presence (as if Lutie were invisible) to conceal her thoughts about the African American woman. According to Mrs. Chandler's mother-in-law: "That girl is unusually attractive and men are weak. Besides, she's colored and you know how they are---" (45). Accordingly, Mrs. Chandler's friends say:

> Sure, she's a wonderful cook. But I wouldn't have any good-looking colored wench in my house. Not with John. You know they're always making passes at men. Especially white men. (40-41)

In essence, by twentieth-century definition, this "wench" is a whore; she cannot control her sexual desires when it comes to men, especially white men. She is regarded as *persona non grata* in a society where the pious and chaste ideal woman is encouraged.

But Petry forces the reader to question if the very white women who attempt to exclude Lutie from ideal womanhood are not themselves questionable representatives of ideal womanhood. For example, it is acceptable for Mrs. Pizzini to work with her husand in their business, but according to Pizzini, it is not acceptable for Lutie to work and help out her husband, who cannot find a job. Mrs. Chandler's mother-in-law is a questionable ideal mother. Following the suicide of her own son on Christmas morning in front of the Christmas tree, she comments" "The nerve of him.   The nerve of him.   Deliberately embarrassing us. And on Christmas morning, too" (48). When the young Mrs. Chandler hires Lutie as a live-in domestic, she implies that she is seeking help with her role as homemaker—that is, she wants someone to help with the cooking and cleaning and to share being a companion to little Henry Chandler. But Mrs. Chandler, who frequently gives bridge parties and elaborate dinners and travels to New York City to shop, leads a life of leisure. Too, while Mrs. Chandler's friends are concerned about Lutie sleeping with Mr. Chandler, Mrs. Chandler, their best friend, is sleeping with their husbands. Or, as Lutie and the betrayed Mr. Chandler observe, Mrs. Chandler is at least always "leaning much too close" (44) to the husbands of her friends. Lutie never considers Mr. Chandler as a possible lover because she loves Jim and, after years of being taught by her grandmother that she was never to let a "white man put his hands on [her]" (45), she detests the idea of being involved with a white man. On the other hand, Lutie does pity Mr. Chandler. She sees him as the husband betrayed by his less -than-ideal wife.

In the final analysis, using double standards, ironic circumstances, and contradictions in Lutie's narrative, Petry undermines cultural standards and patriarchal notions of ideal roles and behavior of women---black or white—in Western society.

Min

When the reader meets Min, it has been years since her husband Big Boy deserted her. Like many working-class African American women in urban areas in the 1940s, Min cannot afford a divorce. Neither can she survive financially on her own. As a result, Min attaches herself to any available man willing to take her in as his common-law wife. Min becomes the common-law wife of Jones who is the super at an apartment building on 116th Street. In free indirect discourse, Min summarizes her arrival at Jones' apartment:

> [I] hadn't seen [my] husband in twenty-five
> years. [I] had stayed with the others [other
> men] because a woman by herself didn't
> stand much chance, and because it was too
> lonely living by [myself] in a rented room.
> With a man [Jones] attached---[I] have an
> apartment---a real home (133).

In these lines, there are patriarchal sensibilities, and it can be concluded that Min embraces prescribed gender roles (i.e., men are the providers of shelter; women are the caretakers). To realize her prescribed role as homemaker and caretaker, Min is willing to become Jones's live-in lover and to be responsible for cooking his meals and cleaning his apartment. Such an arrangement is unconventional, for Min is bartering sex and housekeeping skills in exchange for shelter. What Min has is an economic arrangement. Even the narrator suggests Min's co-habitation with Jones is an economic arrangement:

> [Jones] thought it was kind of cheerful to
> have [Min]˙ around . . . [because she] kept
> the place from getting so deadly guiet (98).
> Since [Jones] never asked [Min] for [rent]
> money when [Min came] home from work
> she cleaned the apartment and cooked for
> him and ironed his clothes. (416).

What Min also has are false illusions of security and happiness. More than anything, Min considers her arrangement with Jones advantageous because she is "free from the yoke of that one word: rent. . . . That word that meant [for struggling African American woman] padlocked doors with foul-mouthed landlords standing in front of them or sealed keyholes with marshals waving long white papers in their hands" (127). Min also considers her arrangement with Jones advantageous because, as she explains in emotive language, she is free to save her money and have things:

> I ain't never had nothing of my own before.
> No money to spend like I wanted to . And
> now, I'm living with [Jones] where they
> ain't no rent to pay. Why, I can get things
> that I see (119)

When Min's arrangement is threatened, which is after the young and attractive Lutie Johnson moves into the Super's building, she reaffirms that it is the loss of economic stability that worries her. To quote Min , she is fearful of "goin' back to having nothing. Just paying rent and fearing eviction" (119). Min is willing to fight to maintain her arrangement with Jones. For instance, she is willing to accept Jones's abuse if it means the proliferation of their arrangement. Speaking in free indirect discourse, Min shares with the reader to what extent she is willing to hold on to her arrangement:

> Only last night when [I] leaned over to take
> some beans out of the oven, he kicked [me]
> just like [I] was the dog. I had managed to
> hold on to the pan of beans . . . , swallowing

> the hurt cry that rose in [my] throat, because
> [I] knew what was the matter with him. He
> had been comparing the way [I] looked from
> behind with the way young Mrs. Johnson
> would look if she stooped over. (117-118)

Again, what Min has are false illusions of security and happiness.

In an attempt to find ways to prevent Jones from abusing her and from having him "[put] her out," Min , who concludes "prayer couldn't possibly help" (210), turns to the root doctor Prophet David. First, to prevent Jones from abusing her, the root doctor prescribes for Min a ritual. She receives a red liquid, one drop of which every morning she is to put into Jones's coffee; a cross that she is to hang over her and Jones's bed; a powder which she is to carry with her at all times; and candles that are to be burned for five minutes starting at ten o'clock every night. Then, to guarantee Min's continued stay in the apartment, the root doctor, while emphasizing the word "everyday," instructs Min that everyday she is "[to] clean the apartment until there isn't a speck of dirt any where. In the corners. On the cupboard shelves. The window sills" (135).

Critic Marjorie Pryse in "'Pattern against the Sky': Deism and Motherhood in Ann Petry's *The Street*"[see elsewhere in this text] praises Min's attempts to remain in Jones's apartment. Pryse suggests that Min's fight not to be "put out" is a fight for "human survival and for the survival of women." Pryse, in her feminist reading, is convinced that Min does not want to be "put out" from the "human circle"---that is from the African American community or the community of women which includes Mrs. Hedges and the other women in the apartment building (129). But Petry seems to suggest that when the African American woman must barter her very soul to maintain a home, in the manner that Min does, there is never stability. In other words, there is ironic instability in what Min thinks she has---i.e., "a real home" of security and comfort.

There is irony in the role of the root doctor within Min's community, as well. In the African American community, the conjurer or root doctor is considered attuned to the needs of the community. But is Prophet David merely another male enforcing patriarchal dictates? In " 'Pattern against the Sky'," Majorie Pryse calls Prophet David the "symbol of nurturing power in the African American community," especially when the betrayal of democracy for the African American in the novel is behind the destruction of human feeling (129). But how aware is the root doctor of the feminine perspective in the community? He seems oblivious to the predicaments of African American women who are trying to realize ideal womanhood but cannot because society has fragmented the real African American home. And he appears aligned to cultural ideology, especially when he directs Min to perform more vigorous work in her home when really she has never had "a real home" of security.

Convinced that Jones has become interested in Lutie Johnson, Min moves out of his apartment. She does not end up, however, living alone. While in the process of moving, Min meets another man with whom she decides to live. According to Min, "This man was a very strong man." As if sizing up cattle, Min reports that "[h]is black muscles bulged as he pushed the cart [in which he moved her belongings]" (321). According to Min, because this healthy-looking man worked and because she worked, in an arrangement with him, "if one got sick the other one could carry on . . . . [Too,] [t]here'd still be food and the rent would be paid" (371). In other words, Min is telling us, "It was [again] possible to have a home that way . . ." (371). As commentary, Petry's "that way" points to contradictions in the ideal home and to degrading compromises made by working-class women desiring a place in the home. Petry's "that way" also points to endless and degrading ways of life by which working-class women like Min must subject themselves in order to obtain food and shelter. In essence, Min is reduced to a survivor---a female survivor in *unconventional* terms.

Clearly, in the chapters devoted to Min, Western society is implicated for having created circumstances within the African American community that destabilize the home and forces arrangements between African American men and women like Jones and Min. Of course, Min does regard her living arrangement with Jones and the imagined co-habitation with the man with the pushcart as the closest she will come to having the ideal home as prescribed by society. But, the fact remains that for working-class African American families of the 1940s, the traditional home is always vulnerable to disorder.

Mrs. Hedges

Petry concludes her commentary on patriarchal ideology with Mrs. Hedges---a woman who goes from being obsessed with the idea of marriage to being indifferent. The reader is told that Mrs. Hedges moves from Georgia to New York City for one reason: She wants to find a man who will fall in love with her. In the 1940s, this means Mrs. Hedges wants to get married. In Georgia, Mrs. Hedges is made to feel that the prospects of a husband are nil because of her "enormous size . . . and the blackness of her skin" (241). In metropolitan New York City, however, she expects that her outside appearance will become insignificant and that she will find love and marriage. But, as Petry reveals, New York society is no kinder to Mrs. Hedges than Georgia society. In the 1940s, ideal images of African American beauty exclude the obese, the very tall, and the very dark-complexioned female. What is somewhat acceptable is the petite and fair-complexioned female with an abundance of hair.

Of course, once Mrs. Hedges arrives in New York City, there are specific incidents that persuade her that in the North her femininity is unacceptable. In free-indirect discourse, she summarizes:

> [I] had haunted employment agencies
> seeking work. When [I] walked in them,
> there was an uncontrollable revulsion in the
> faces of the white people who looked at
> [me]. They stared amazed at [my]
> enormouse size, at the blackness of [my]
> skin. They glanced at each other, tried in
> vain to control their faces or didn't bother to
> try at all, simply let [me] see what a
> monstrocity they thought [I] was. (241)

Another incident is even more revealing to Mrs. Hedges. She is involved in a house fire. She is the only survivor because she literally squeezes herself out of a very narrow window. Public reaction to her appearance after the fire, however, is not sympathic:

> They couldn't conceal the expressions on
> their faces. Sometimes it was only a flicker
> of dismay, and then again it was sheer
> horror, plain   for   anyone   to   see---
> undisguished, uncontrollable. (247)

In the end, society undermines Mrs. Hedges's psychology and it teaches her how to define her femininity and her feminine beauty: "monstrosity" and "sheer horror." As a result of her rejection by society, and as a result of her permanent scars caused by the fire, the woman adopts the title of "Mrs." And withdraws to an apartment on 116th Street, vowing "never to expose herself to the prying, curious eyes of the world" (247). Mrs. Hedges says she is withdrawing from society because of her appearance after the fire. But is she not withdrawing because, through its "prying and curious eyes," society has made her feel less than the ideal woman?

There is never a direct word from Mrs. Hedges to suggest that because of her size and permanent scars (which contrast with the cultural definitions of ideal feminine beauty), she has been psychologically scarred. But circumstances following Mrs. Hedges's release from the hospital point to a psychologically marred woman. For instance, Mrs. Hedges starts a prostitution business with girls who reflect culture's definition of ideal beauty---the very standards used by society to exclude her and to force her to retreat permanently to her apartment on 116th Street. Her girls are petite. They have long thick hair that can be "piled high above their small pointed faces" (254). Mrs. Hedges declares that her motive for managing the prostitution enterprise is that people need to "make love in order to forget their troubles" (251). But when one considers that all of Mrs. Hedges's girls are petite when she is obese, fair-complexioned when she is dark-complexioned, and possessing bountiful heads of hair when she is bald, one must ask, is there a self-hatred for her obesity, blackness, and baldness?

Although Mrs. Hedges does not articulate how her experiences as an obese, dark-complexioned and bald woman have affected her self-identity, the reader is aware by now that in the forties women of her appearance are not the ones most men desire to marry.

Before Mrs. Hedges's scars and before her prostitution enterprise, she is obsessed with falling in love and getting married. After the scars and after her internalization of society's rejection, she takes the title "Mrs." and creates "for herself a comfortable home." In fact, a significant room in the home is an impeccable kitchen which Petry takes time to describe:

> [A]nd there was bright linoleum on the
> floor, the kitchen curtains were freshly done
> up, and the pots and pans hanging over the
> sink had been scrubbed until they were
> shiny. There were potted plants growing in
> a stand under the window. (118)

With yet another kitchen (Mrs. Hedges's kitchen), Petry renders her whisper of contempt against the patriarchy (against "that kitchen') and with Mrs. Hedges who allows society to define [or undefined] for her ideal femininity, Petry brings her slant in *The Street* full circle. But Petry's critique of the patriarchy does not end until she has offered some solution to the contradictions and ambiguities raised by patriarchal ideology.

A New Level of Social Consciousness:

In particular, Lutie Johnson gains insight into the conditions of men and women around her when she comes to look objectively at the breakup of African American marriages and families. Lutie blames the racist society in which she lives:

> Why do the women work? . . . .The women
> work because the white folk give them [not
> their men] jobs---washing dishes and clothes
> and floors and windows. . . .(388). . . .The
> men get out of the habit of working and the
> houses are old and gloomy and the walls
> press in . And the men go off, move on, slip
> away, find new women. . . . (389)

From daily observations and personal experiences, Lutie also arrives at her own answers as to how women like herself, who wanted nothing but to live happily ever after, end up living alone. Again, she blames a racist society:

> [O]n this street, the women trudged along
> overburdened, overworked, their own homes
> neglected while . . . the men on the street
> swung along empty-handed, well dressed,
> and carefree. Or, they lounged against the
> sides of the buildings, their hands in their
> pockets while they stared at the women who
> walked past, probably deciding which
> woman they should select to replace the
> wife who was out working all day. (64)

Lutie also arrives at her own answers as to how women like herself who
wanted nothing but to be good mothers, ended up losing their children to "the
street." This time, it is because she is poor:

> Was it because the mothers of white
> children had safe places for them to play in,
> because the mothers of white children didn't
> have to work? . . . . Maybe [losing your
> child to the street] doesn't have anything to
> do with color . . . . Perhaps. . .[it is] because
> [you are] poor. (409)

Lutie's realizations about African American marriages and families in general
and about the debilitating influences of poverty and racism are left to the reader
for consideration.

When it comes to ideal womanhood, Lutie realizes that African American
women must not define womanhood through the eyes of white society. When
Lutie considers "the patterns her life [has] followed" (428)---that is "going to
grammar school, going to high school, getting married, having a baby" (400)---
she concludes that such a step-by-step socialization meets white cultural
expectations for the female. But through the eyes of African American women,
reality was "growing up [getting married] working [losing your husband],
saving, and finally getting an apartment on a street that nobody could have
beaten" (399). At the start of *The Street*, Lutie Johnson is extremely naïve about
the ways of life for poor African Americans in urban America, but by the end of
the novel, she is an informed individual. She comes to realize and to accept the
fact that she had believed in cultural ideals that had no particular basis for black
life:

> Slowly she began to reach for some
> conclusion, some philosophy with which to
> rebuild her shattered hopes . . . .[of being a
> good wife and mother]. The trouble was
> with her. She had built up a fantastic

> structure made from the soft, nebulous,
> cloudy stuff of dreams. There hadn't been a
> solid, practical brick in it, not even a
> foundation. . . . So of course it had
> collapsed. It had never existed anywhere
> but in her own mind. (307-308)

In essence, what Lutie is saying is that for the working-class African American, society's ideal ways of life are impractical.

Perhaps Lutie's greatest insight comes from her efforts to escape poverty via education. When Lutie's various attempts to escape 116th Street fail, particularly her prospective job as a jazz singer, she decides to use the system to beat the complex cycle of hardship. She decides to advance her education. She studies for a civil service examination in order to obtain a higher rating and to earn more income (309). Of course, when Bub is lured into crime by the revengeful Jones and ends up in a juvenile detention center, Lutie's plan for social and financial advancement is aborted. But, still Lutie realizes what millions of African Americn women in the years to come would realize: education is the one means of escaping poverty and total male dependency. Unfortunately, Lutie's self-realization as an African American woman and her knowledge of what she must do in ordr to grow spiritually as well as financially will come too late. Soon after her awakening, Lutie is in the apartment of Boots Smith because he has promised to lend her money to pay Bub's lawyer. Boots, however, attempts to rape Lutie. While defending herself, Lutie accidentally bludgeons Boots to death. Out of fear, she flees to Chicago. Prior to Lutie's departure, however, she communicates (and so does Petry) an understanding of the socialization of women, and, in return, she encourages women in urban America to seek understanding of the cultural ideology that prescribes their roles and behavior by examining their own experiences and the experiences of other women.

---

[1] This essay is a revised portion of my dissertation, "The Subversion of Cultural Ideology in Ann Petry's *The Street* and *Country Place*," copyright 1993.

[2] "From Pestle to Pen," *Headline and Pictures*, March 1946, 42-43.

[3] William Chafe, *The American Woman: Her Changing Social, Economic, and Political Roles, 1920-1970* (New York: Oxford, 1972), 94.

[4] June Sochen, *Herstory, A Woman's View of American History* (New York: Alfred Knopf, 1974), 347.

[5] Henry Louis Gates, Jr., *The Signifying Monkey: A Theory of Afro-American Literary Criticism* (New York: Oxford University Press, 1988), xxv-xxvi.
[6] Catherine Clinton, *The Plantation Mistress: Women's World in the Old South* (New York: Pantheon, 1982), 21.

The Sensory Assault of the City in Ann Petry's *The Street* (1995)
Larry R. Andrews

Ann Petry's first novel, *The Street* (1946), reflects black disillusionment with the northern city after the 1920s. Lutie Johnson, its protagonist, sees her street, and by extension the city, as her monstrous antagonist. Like Petry's novella "In Darkness and Confusion" (1947), the work is set in Harlem, here largely on 116th Street. Her third novel, *The Narrows* (1953), with its appropriately claustrophobic title, is also set in a ghetto, but in a New England town. *The Street* has remained one of the most vivid and compelling evocations of city life in African-American literature, and it anticipates the superb urban landscapes of Paule Marshall and Gloria Naylor.

As a novel of the city, *The Street* touches on all of the major themes in modern urban literature. In a few passages, Petry suggests that the city can be aglow with life and that it can offer occasional experiences of community:

> The glow from the sunset was making the
> street radiant. The street is nice in this light,
> she [Lutie] thought. It was swarming with
> children who were playing ball and darting
> back and forth across the sidewalk in
> complicated games of tag. (64)

But the picture is largely negative. Barbara Christian speaks of the work's "relentless presentation of the dreary despair of the inner cities" (*Black Feminist Criticism* 11). Overcrowding deprives the inhabitants of needed personal space---on the subway, in the street, in the apartment houses, "so that the black folks were crammed on top of each other---jammed and packed and forced into the smallest possible space until they were completely cut off from light and air" (206). The dominant images of the novel are claustral and suffocating---walls, cages, cellars, even those people's stares. Alienation and isolation are a corollary of this spatial deprivation. Self-interest in the name of survival squeezes out compassion, and Lutie, on her own, working and raising a small boy, has no one to turn to whom she can trust. The street dehumanizes its inhabitants, destroying their spirit, as in the case of the aimlessly staring man in the hospital (201-2) or the resigned young girls. An endless cycle of poverty is especially destructive. "The most memorable quality of *The Street*," as Theodore Gross notes, "is its direct, unsentimental, ruthless, bitter description of poverty: the black characters are caught in a suffering that fills them with meanness and hatred, that diminishes their humanity" (45). Prostitution, crime, and sudden death complete this typically modern picture of the artificial urban environment bereft of nature's softer influences. In her growing awareness near the end, Lutie sums it up with understatement: "Perhaps living in a city the size of New York wasn't good for people . . . . Certainly it wasn't a good place for children" (Petry 396).

Many commentators on the novel have assigned this portrayal of the city to the naturalism of the Richard Wright "school." Petry herself laid the groundwork for this emphasis in an interview with James Ivy in *The Crisis* in February 1946:

> "In *The Street* my aim is to show how simply and easily the environment can change the course of a person's life . . . .
> "I try to show why the Negro has a high crime rate, a high death rate, and little or no chance of keeping his family unit intact in large northern cities." (49)

Class oppression is part of this picture, as the vastly unequal distribution of wealth creates extremes of rich and poor neighborhoods, the latter effectively trapping the inhabitants for life. Vernon Lattin and Marjorie Pryse have shown how the novel ironically explodes the American economic dream of the founding fathers. Robert Bone classifies the work as an "environmentalist" novel of the Wright school in its treatment of slum neighborhoods (157). Noel Schraufnagel says that it "indicates how a ghetto shapes the lives of its inhabitants into a rigid framework of poverty and hopelessness . . . . The environment is the controlling factor of the novel" (40-42). Addison Gayle especially emphasizes the forces of the environment: "Miss Petry is more interested in the effects of the environment upon her characters than she is in the characters themselves. The characters are products of the street; their lives are dominated by forces beyond their control" (192). More recently Barbara Christian has concurred that "Petry's major concern in the novel was most emphatically the hostile environment of Harlem and its effects on the people who must endure it" *(Black Women Novelists* 63). Bernard Bell calls the work "a conventional novel of economic determinism in which the environment is the dominant force against which the characters must struggle to survive" (107). Arthur Davis, on the other hand, denies the total domination of the environment (193-94). Lattin also has urged that the novel "cannot be discussed merely in environmentalist terms" (69), and he stresses Lutie's revolt and discovery. Mary Helen Washington agrees that the novel is naturalistic but complains that it tends to marginalize women and thus ignore "many of the deeply felt realities of women's lives" (298), whereas Gloria Wade-Gayles argues that the work treats gender issues as part of its naturalism (152). But again in her excellent recent essay Pryse points out positive alternatives to the supposedly determined choices Lutie makes, alternatives suggested by her grandmother's values, the conjuring tradition of Prophet David, and the successful revolt of her foil Min.

Beyond this larger naturalist tradition that portrays the city in general as a hostile environment impossible to overcome, critics have amply demonstrated that racism is the determining factor more than the city per se. The system of socioeconomic oppression that the white power structure has created is responsible for the heightened suffering of the Harlem ghetto. Lutie comes to realize that "streets like the one she lived on were no accident. They were the North's lynch mobs, she thought bitterly; the method the big cities used to keep Negroes in their place" (323). The lesson of her experiences is that white people have caged blacks in the ghetto, tossed them their refuse, and systematically destroyed the black family: "Streets like 116th Street or being colored, or a combination of both with all it implied, had turned Pop into a sly old man who drank too much; had killed Mom off when she was in her prime" (56). White people refused to hire black men and overwork black women, leaving the street to educate the children. White butchers, lawyers, detectives, landlords, bar owners, schoolteachers, and affluent women with hostile stares are merely the front for white capitalists like the Chandlers who live at a distance and pull the strings: "It wasn't just this city. It was any city where they set up a line and say black folks stay on this side and white folks on this side . . . . It all added up to the same thing, she decided---white people. She hated them. She would always hate them" (206). As Gross points out, Petry "does not permit the reader to forget that the white world had drawn the limitations and consequently caused the bitter despair of black people" (44). And Christian finds that "Petry clearly indicts the white society for the failure of many black marriages and implies that it consciously is seeking the fragmentation of the black family" (*Black Women Novelists* 66).

In addition to racism, sexism is a dominant force against which Lutie Johnson must struggle, for all of the white characters and many of the black characters, including Mrs. Hedges, see her primarily as a sexual object. Wade-Gayles and Beatrice Royster have been instrumental in analyzing the impact of sexual oppression on Lutie and other black women portrayed in the novel. Wade-Gayles finds that male critics who draw parallels between Lutie and Wright's Bigger Thomas "ignore the added burdens that being a woman places on her" (149). She says that Petry "reaches into the souls of black women for their peculiar agony. *The Street* is an explosion of sounds of racial and sexual agony" (154). Royster says that all of the violence of the street "grows out of, or is precipitated by, sexual encounters between men and women" (qtd. Petry 154).

Thus the interpretation of the role of the city in the novel has been well developed in terms of naturalism, class oppression, racism, and sexism. The ideology of this protest novel is manifest in the text itself, which contains thematic generalizations and numerous symbolic and metaphorical references to the street that represent this whole array of forces. But the work is far more than a *roman `a these* of the Wright school. It strikes the reader above all as an act of imagination and literary art. What I would like to focus on in this respect is the powerful physical way in which the city assaults the characters' senses through concrete detail. Some critics have noted this aspect of style in passing. Lattin gives some examples of the images of traps, cages, and walls (70), and Gross notes Petry's compelling portrayal of details of setting (42). Christian stresses her "voluminous use of external detail" in contrast to Wright's approach in *Native Son*, but focuses on the "tone of the commonplace" in these details (64).

What strikes me, however, is the extraordinary, nightmarish character of most of the sensory detail. Characters in the novel typically feel pressed upon or actually invaded physically, often to the point where their perceptions are distorted and they feel terror or hysteria. In this often surreal vision of the modern city the novel is thus akin not only to the naturalism of Zola, Crane, Dreiser, and Wright but also to the urban evocations of Poe and Dickens, and to the great modern portrayals of the city---St. Petersburg of Gogol, Dostoevsky, and Bely, the Paris of Baudelaire and Rilke's *Die Aufzeichnungen des Malte Laurids Brigge*, the Berlin of Doblin's *Berlin Alexanderplatz*, the Prague of Kafka's *Der Prozess*, and the Harlem of Ellison's *Invisible Man*. In these works, as in *The Street*, the psychological stress the characters undergo as a result of urban socioeconomic structures combines with the sensory assult of the urban physical environment to produce a dislocation rendered in an intense and nightmarish style.

In *The Street* this sensory assault occurs on several levels. To a small extent it is a general urban condition that creates crowded subways and streets and bombardments of noise and smells that affect more or less all inhabitants, black and white people alike. But clearly the city can be benign to the white and well off. The sensory assault is heightened, then, for inhabitants of the black ghetto, where poverty and racism are suffocating and "people were packed together like sardines in a can" (206). Yet even here people can occasionally expand compared to their sense of encroachment and violation in the downtown white world. Lutie reflects that

> once they are freed from the contempt in the eyes of the downtown world, they instantly become individuals. Up here they are no longer creatures labeled simply 'colored' and therefore all alike. She noticed that once the crowd walked the length of the platform and started up the stairs toward the street it expanded in size. The same people who had made themselves small on the train, even on the platform, suddenly grew so large they could hardly get up the stairs to the street together. She . . . stood watching them as they scattered in all directions, laughing and talking to each other. (57-58)

In most physical ways Harlem is claustrophobic and evokes a protective, survivalist response, or it is openly violent and breeds violence within characters. Most central to the novel, however, is the sensory assault related to sexual exploitation.   As an attractive black woman on her own, Lutie is subjected to the lustful looks of white men, the hostile stares of white women, the sexual propositions of Junto and Mrs. Hedges, and the attempted rapes of Boots and the Super Jones.   What is particularly effective stylistically is Petry's use of all the other detailed assaults of the setting on Lutie's senses as an indirect way of expanding and intensifying this vulnerability of black women. The walls that press in on her and the silence that threatens to get inside her constitute a kind of rape against which she must constantly protect herself. Such details, often repeated, thus express Lutie's gender situation as distinct from, though related to, her racial and urban situation.

Stylistically the city is palpable in a negative way to every character through powerfully described detail touching every sense, including the sense of movement and perception of space. Characters experience even inert objects as threatening and other people as invasive. Even natural elements such as the wind are often perverted by the city so that they participate in its punishing effects. Characters under stress from other causes are especially susceptible, and if they have lively imaginations and intuitive powers, their sense perceptions may become distorted and exaggerated to the point of disorientation. To some extent the ability of characters like Lutie to experience heightened sensation is a result of instincts that can be a powerful source of protection. Her grandmother had tried to tell her that evil was palpable: "'Some folks so full of it you can feel it comin' at you--oozin' right out of their skins' " (20). What counts is what other resources one has with which to act on these perceptions---folk wisdom, flight, conjuring, communal support.   Tragically, Lutie relies instead on rationalism, individualism, and the American myth of success until at the end violence explodes from her uncontrollably. Thus the sensitivity to the city's sensory bombardment is not in itself a weakness but may be a strength if it is supported by other qualities.   The numbling of Harlem's inhabitants ("sleepwalkers") into insensibility is a death-in-life, a fate worse than the fears with which Lutie has to live.

The physical assault on Lutie is established vividly in Petry's brilliant open chapter, when she first arrives on the street and takes an apartment. The initial description of the wind on the street is filled with vigorous verbs:

> It rattled the tops of garbage cans, sucked
> window shades out through the top of
> opened windows and set them flapping back
> against the windows; and it drove most of
> the people off the street . . . except for a few
> hurried pedestrians who bent double in an
> effort to offer the least possible exposed
> surface to its violent assault. (1)

The refuse the wind picks up from the street becomes a "barrage" that "swirled into the faces of the people" (2). The natural element is corrupted by the wind-tunnel effect of the narrow street and the dirt mingled with the wind as it hits the pedestrians:

> It found all the dirt and dust and grime on the sidewalk and lifted it up so that the dirt got into their noses, making it difficult to breathe; the dust got into their eyes and blinded them; and the grit stung their skins. It wrapped newspaper around their feet entangling them until the people cursed deep in their throats, stamped their feet, kicked at the paper . . . . And then the wind grabbed their hats, pried their scarves from around their necks, stuck its fingers inside their coat collars, blew their coats away from their bodies.
>
> The wind lifted Lutie Johnson's hair away from the back of her neck so that she felt suddenly naked and bald, for her hair had been resting softly and warmly against her skin. She shivered as the cold finders of the wind touched the back of her neck, explored the sides of her head. It even blew her eyelashes away from her eyes so that her eyeballs were bathed in a rush of coldness and she had to blink in order to read the words on the sign swaying back and forth over her head.
>
> Each time she thought she had the sign in focus, the wind pushed it away from her so that she wasn't certain whether it said three rooms or two rooms. (2)

This small opening passage encompasses the invasive, multisensory assault of the city, the sexual overtones of Lutie's vulnerability ("naked," "fingers . . . explored"), and the clouding of perception. Minutes later the angry wind again blows dust, ashes, and paper into her face, eyes, nose, and ears (4).

Lutie's first encounter with Mrs. Hedges as she enters the apartment building begins a series of "staring" assaults on Lutie by people who represent the hostile influences of the city:

> It wasn't that the woman had been sitting there all along staring at her, reading her

> thoughts, pushing her way into her very
> mind, for that was merely annoying . . . .It
> was the woman's eyes. They were as still
> and as malignant as the eyes of a snake . . .
> flat eyes that stared at her---wandering over
> her body, inspecting and appraising her from
> head to foot. (5-6)

Minutes later she encounters the Super Jones' lustful stare: "after his first quick furtive glance, his eyes had filled with a hunger so urgent that she was instantly afraid of him" (10). As she mounts the stairs ahead of him she feels that "he was staring at her back, her legs, her thighs. She could feel his eyes traveling over her---estimating her, summing her up, wondering about her" (13). Back downstairs, she feels him "eating her up with his eyes" (25). Later on she refers to the "moist" looks of white men and the hostile stares of white women. The entrepreneur Junto, her ultimate nemesis, watches her, studies her in the mirror of the bar (146-49), and Boots Smith, with his hard, expressionless, predatory eyes, watches her react to his job offer (150-52). In all of these cases her personal space is invaded physically and she is the object of sexual appraisal.

When Lutie first sees her house's interior, she is disturbed by its claustrophobic atmosphere. The dim light in the entrance hall deceives her into thinking she sees a piano there. The hall is narrow, the stairs steep and dark, and the upstairs halls very narrow and smelly. As she ascends to the fifth floor the temperature gets colder and colder, and she imagines that it must get hotter and hotter in summer until "your breath would be cut off completely" (12). When she recalls the fourth floor, "instead of her reaching out for the walls, the walls were reaching out for her---bending and swaying toward her in an effort to envelop her' (12). The rooms in her apartment are small and dark and face the back---a rubbishy backyard and a blind air shaft. Petry carefully describes the size and feeling of each nook of the apartment, and later repeats the same claustral adjectives whenever she refers to Lutie's apartment. In recognizing her limited choice in apartments, Lutie creates a metaphor from the corridors: "You've got a choice a yard wide and ten miles long" (19).

All of her perceptions of the physical setting are colored by the threat of Super Jones, who shows her the apartment. Her sense of this threat begins when she rings his doorbell. Petry gives astonishing emphasis to the assaultive force of the doorbell and Jones' dog:

> It made a shrill sound that echoed and re-
> echoed inside the apartment and came back
> out into the hall. Immediately a dog started
> a furious barking that came closer and closer
> as he ran toward the door of the apartment.
> Then the weight of his body landed against

> the door and she drew back as he threw
> himself against the door. Again and again
> until the door began to shiver from the
> impact of his weight. There was the horrid
> sound of his nose snuffing up air, trying to
> get her scent. And then his weight hurled
> against the door again. She retreated toward
> the street door. (8-9)

It continues with the "hot fetid air" and hissing steam that come at her out of his rooms. She feels stalked by Jones up the dark stairs, with his physical presence behind and beneath her.

In the apartment, with his flashlight pointed down, he becomes "a figure of never-ending tallness. And his silent waiting and his appearance of incredible height appalled her. . . he looked as though his head must end somewhere in the ceiling. He simply went up and up into darkness" (14-15). The repetition emphasized Lutie's sensory disorientation. At this moment she feels Jones' monstrous desire: "the hot, choking awfulness of his desire for her pinioned her there so that she couldn't move. It was an aching yearning that filled the apartment, pushed against the walls, plucked at her arms" (15). She thinks that he reaches out for her but is uncertain in the dimness. When she hears the choking sound of his repressed desire she imagines his turning out the light and attacking her in the dark. She senses the force of his will against her: "When he finally started down the hall, it seemed to her that he had stood there beside her for days, weeks, months, willing her to go down the stairs first" (18). And even though she gets him to go first on the descent, he still controls the pace. His effect on her is completed by the denizens of his apartment---Min, whom she mistakes for furniture in a Kafkaesque touch, the cowed dog, and the canary--- all "huddled" and "shrinking."

What does Lutie offer in resistance to this initial onslaught? She tries humor, imagining the landlord renting out cots in the entrance hall and thinking that the bathroom wasn't big enough for Methuselah's beard and that the only source of fresh air was the toilet vent pipe. She also tries rational common sense, reassuring herself that she is imagining things and that there is no cause for fear. She offers "determination," a fighter's will to overcome adversity. She also recalls her grandmother's storytelling wisdom and hums her grandmother's song about "no restin' place" (17). She falls back on a naïve faith in urban order:

> If he [Jones] tries to include making love to
> the female tenants, why this is New York
> City in the year 1944, and as yet there's no
> grass growing in the streets and the police
> force still functions. Certainly you can
> holler loud enough so that if the gentleman

> has some kind of dark designs on you and
> tarries to carry them out, a cop will
> eventually rescue you. That's that. (19)

Yet she is compelled to accept in herself "the instinctive, immediate fear she had felt when she first saw the Super" (20). She throws a final menacing look at him

> just in case some dark left-over instinct
> warned me of what was on your mind---just
> in case it made me know you were snuffing
> on my trail, slathering, slobbering after me
> like some dark hound of hell seeking me
> out, tonguing along in back of me. (25)

Although she can click her heels and click her purse shut with an air of angry determination, her defiant departure is undercut by the dog's yelps, Mrs. Hedges' flat stare, and the biting wind.

In the course of the novel Lutie's senses continue to be assailed by the apartment house and street. It is impossible to walk around in her rooms without bumping into something. As she washes dishes with the radio on, a "stillness that crept through all the rooms" becomes so palpable that "she found she kept looking over her shoulder, half-expecting to find someone had stolen up in back of her *under cover of the quiet*" (78, my emphasis). The halls are dank with the smell of urine, and every time she enters the apartment "the walls seemed to come in toward her, to push against her" (79). These two images of silence and of the pushing walls are constantly reiterated as Lultie struggles harder and harder to get out of the street. In Chapter 6 she sees Junto's bar as an escape from small dark rooms and the silence, and like the other patrons, she responds to "the sound of laughter, the hum of talk, the sight of people and brilliant lights, the sparkle of the big mirror, the rhythmic music from the juke-box" (145). But the big mirror behind the bar distorts everything in the bar. Underneath the illusory "gaiety and charm" reflected there is the reality of Junto (also magnified by the mirror), whose "squat figure managed to dominate the whole room" (146). The mirror lies to her when she feels "free here where there was so much space," where the mirror "pushed the walls back and back into space" (146). For this is the beginning of her ultimate entrapment by Junto, who first sees and desire her here. Her disoriented perceptions seem benign but are just as dangerous as her earlier fearful ones. When she returns home after the ride with Boots, she is depressed again by the "silence and the dimly lit hallway and the smell of stale air . . . . It was like a dead weight landing on her chest" (186).

In Chapter 8 Lutie has a remarkable nightmare of pursuit. When she finds out that Super Jones has been in her apartment she feels invaded and remembers the first day there. She now connects Jones with a life of "basements and cellars" and sees him as an embodiment of the street that threatens to destroy her. In her terrifying nightmare she sees him whining and crawling down the street after her with a building chained to his shoulders. Although she feels sympathy for him as an emasculated black man also imprisoned by the street, she must protect herself from his assault; he has merged with his dog and become the slavering hell-hound from Chapter 1:

> She reaches out her hand toward the padlock and the long white fangs closed on her hand. Her hand and part of her arm were swallowed up inside his wolfish mouth. She watched in horror as more and more of her arm disappeared until there was only the shoulder left and then his jaws closed and she felt the sharp teeth sink in and in through her shoulder. The arm was gone and blood poured out. (192-93)

Along with this image of Jones in the dream, the goadings of Mrs. Hedges and the transformation of the street's inhabitants into rats with houses chained to their backs bring to a climax Lutie's response to the city's assault. She awakens to a new "dread" of her room. "In the darkness it seemed to close in on her until it became the sum total of all the things she was afraid of and she drew back nearer the wall because the room grew smaller and the pieces of furniture larger until she felt as though she were suffocating" (194). It is then that she remembers the shoes of the murdered man in the street, the stabbed girl's "gaudy mask" of a face, and the psychopath's stare in the hospital. She vows to fight against becoming inured to the violence of the city and to escape the street with the added money from her hoped-for singing job.

For two days her new dream blinds her to the wind and the dim hallway (230), but this respite is short-lived. When Jones attempts to rape her, she is jolted back to reality and beyond it into surreality. Under the horror "not to be borne" of Jones's contorted face and sweating body and the stench of the dog on her back,

> She screamed until she could hear her own voice insanely shrieking up the stairs, pausing on the landings, turning the corners, going down the halls, gaining in volume as it started again to climb the stairs. And then her screams rushed back down the stair well until the whole building echoed and re-echoed with the frantic, desperate sound. (236)

Saving her, Mrs. Hedges appears balloon-like to Lutie's disordered perception, with her white nightgown against her intensely black and scarred skin, so that she looked like "a creature that had strayed from some other planet" (237). Henceforth Lutie will continually picture the trap of the street as Jones's "pulling her down, down, into the cellar."

After her disillusionment with the no-pay singing job, which has been a ploy of Junto's to make her his mistress, she again succumbs to the assault of her building---its pushing walls, its noises of flights that prevent privacy, its stairs "like a high, ever-ascending mountain" (313). On her visit to the Crosse School for Singers, the repulsive appearance of Mr. Crosse that assails her senses---his fat body, his soggy, shredded cigar, his rank smell, the skin of his hand "the color of the underside of a fish---a grayish white" (321)---is but the extended expression of yet one more attempt to exploit her sexually. In her righteous rage(throwing the inkwell at him) she finds herself increasingly violent and savage in her "cage," like the zoo tigers she remembers in vivid detail.

When Lutie discovers that Bub has been caught and detained by the police for the postal theft for which Jones has framed him, she begins to realize how the system has worked to destroy black families, a white system embodied in the "crisp, crackling white paper' of the court notice. Her sobs pervade the house and are echoed by the inhabitants' own pain, as if these cries are already within them (390). Without Bub in the apartment "the furniture had diminished in size, shrinking against the wall" (401), and the living room becomes "a vast expanse of space---unknown and therefore dangerous" (405). Under this new stress Lutie's perceptions are increasingly distorted.

In the last part of the novel (the last day) leading to Lutie's killing of Boots, the most vivid sensor stimulus is, remarkably, *silence*. Lutie's earlier sense of an invasive silence now becomes overwhelming as she desperately attempts to get money from Boots to keep Bub out of reform school. She is first "assailed by the stillness" at the Children's Shelter emanating from the "shrinking, huddled" women there (408-9). She begins "to believe the silence and the troubled waiting that permeated the room had a smell---a distinct odor that filled her nose until it was difficult for her to breathe" (409-10). The silence then successively drives her out of the apartment, where her throat is "constricting"; the movie house, where it "crouched along the aisles, dragged itself across the rows of empty seats . . . coming at her . . . coming nearer and nearer"; and the beauty shop, where it "crouched down in the next booth" and might leave with her and "somehow seep into the apartment before she got there, so that when she opened the door it would be there. Formless. Shapeless. Waiting. Waiting" (412-13). She begins to realize that she is "smelling out evil as Granny said." Finally, back in her apartment and again "assailed by the deep, uncanny silence that filled it," she is able to give the disembodied silence she could only "sense" before a clear shape in a terrifying but enlightening hallucination:

> It was Junto. Gray hair, gray skin, short
> body, thick shoulders. He was sitting on the
> studio couch . . . .
> If she wasn't careful she would scream.
> She would start screaming and never be able
> to stop, because there wasn't anyone there.
> Yet she could see him and when she didn't
> see him she could feel his presence. (418)

She hopes soon to "be free of this mounting, steadily increasing anger and this hysterical fear that made her see things that didn't exist" (419). But when she arrives at Boots, hallucination becomes real as the squat white Junto sitting on the couch whom she sees literally as "a piece of that dirty street itself" (422). At the moment she strikes Boots with the candlestick, motivated by a desire to kill Junto, her sense perception is seriously disoriented. She no longer "sees" Boots but instead sees the street and the small rooms, stairs, and halls. Ironically, the silence she would have destroyed, the evil represented by Junto, remains---it makes her feel as if she is "wading through water, wading waist-deep toward the couch, and the water swallowed up all sound. It tugged against her, tried to pull her back" (432). It nearly prevents her from getting to the door:

> The four corners of the room were alive with
> silence---deepening pools of an ominous
> silence. She kept turning her head in an
> effort to see all of the room at once; kept
> fighting against a desire to scream. Hysteria
> mounted in her because she began to believe
> that at any moment the figure on the sofa
> might disappear into one of these pools of
> silence and then emerge from almost any
> part of the room, to bar her exist. (433)

When all of the sensory assaults on her being coalesce into a clear white male enemy, Lutie finds that in succumbing to uncontrollable violence and striking out against him and his environment she has succumbed to the very mechanisms of control of that environment. She feels that she can only abandon her child and flee to yet another big city---Chicago---that could "swallow her up" (434).

Although Lutie is the central character who registers the sensory bombardment of the city, most of the other characters also react strongly to the physical environment and experience some of the same nightmarish disorientation. Super Jones has come to be defined and deformed by loneliness and lust. Mrs. Hedges labels him "cellar crazy"---a creature of cellars and basements (and ships' holds), as if the physical environment of his work has made him an imbalanced lecher seeking to express emasculated power through possession of women. On his first visit to Bub, the duress of his desire causes him to overreact to the sensory stimulation of Lutie's lipstick, the smell of her talcum, and the clothes in her wardrobe that "bent toward him as he looked inside" (108). When Min conjures him with a cross, he becomes so obsessed with its shape that he sees it everywhere. After she has left him he is uncertain whether her making the sign of the cross was real or hallucinatory. His misperception of Lutie's facial expression incites him to rape: "She seemed to fill the whole hall with light. There was a faint smile playing around her mouth and he thought she was smiling at the sight of him and bending and swaying toward him" (234). He is extremely vulnerable to Mrs. Hedges' invasive gaze not just because she mocks him and prevents his enjoying the street scene but because he thinks she can read his thoughts, can get inside him. The claustral ghetto environment has made Jones both victim and predator. His psychic imbalance makes him susceptible to heightened and distorted sense perceptions which in turn make him vulnerable to sexual desire, fear, and his own violence.

Bub's fear of being alone in the apartment at night may seem to be a normal child's anxiety, but it too is linked to the city's menace and it reinforces the reactions of other characters. His sensory orientation is dislocated: "The furniture changed in the dark---each piece assumed a strange and menacing shape that transformed the whole room" (211-12). He, too, feels invaded: "The floor would creak and the wind would rattle the windows like something outside trying to get in at him" (212). The corners are "wiped out in the dark," the chair becomes a "bulge of darkness," as though "quick, darting hands had substituted something else" (213). Sounds are magnified---heavy footsteps, a violent fight next door, the woman's sobbing so that "the room quivered with it until he seemed almost to *see the sound running through the dark*" (218, my emphasis). He was "lost in a strange place filled with terrifying things" (218).

Min, the Super's drudge, had retreated from the kind of lively engagement of the senses Lutie experiences, but as she begins to reassert control over her life by getting help from the Prophet David and later by deciding to leave Jones and the street, her responses are reawakened. From her point of view Jones's gloomy, silent anger "filled the small rooms until they were like the inside of an oven---a small completely enclosed space where no light ever penetrated" (352). At the same time her bed without Jones increases in size night after night until it seems to "stretch vast and empty around all sides of her." She has won protection from Jones, but now she no longer wants to stay:

> Having room to breathe in meant much
> more. Lately she couldn't get any air here . .
> . . It was because of the evilness in Jones.
> She could feel the weight of it like some
> monstrous growth crowding against her. He
> had made the whole apartment grow smaller
> and darker; living room, bedroom, kitchen---

> all of them shrinking, their walls tightening
> about her. (362)

Jones himself has become a monster in her distorted perception: "Every sound he made was magnified. His muttering to himself was like thunder, and his restless walking up and down, up and down, in the living room seemed to go on inside her in a regular rhythm that set her eyes to blinking so that she couldn't stop them" (363). She knows that she will die if she stays. With a final look at the street she thinks, "It wasn't somehow a very good place to live, for the women had too much trouble, almost as though the street itself bred the trouble" (355).

To a lesser extent other characters also suffer distortion of perception from the assault of the city. Mrs. Hedges' vision has been partly defined and distorted by being trapped in a burning house, stuck in a basement window, and being terribly burned. Her pain over her loss of any attractiveness centers on her burned-off hair, and her obsession with other women's hair occurs eight times in the space of four pages. She is capable of a kind of nurturing, as Pryse points out (124), but primarily she uses people's suffering and serves Junto's ends with schemes derived "from looking at the street all day" (251).

Boots's perceptions have been molded by the sounds of the bells and the racist commands of passengers on the Pullman cars where he formerly worked, and by the "curtains blowing in the breeze" in his apartment that have imprinted his girl's affair with a white lover on his brain.

Even Miss Rinner, Bub's neurotic white teacher, suffers from heightened and distorted sense perceptions. Educated in racist stereotypes by a segregated society, she is suffocated by the odors of the school, of the black children, and of "Harlem itself---bold, strong, lusty, frightening" (328). When she opens her classroom door on Monday morning "the smell had gained in strength as though it were a living thing that had spawned over the week-end and in reproducing itself had now grown so powerful it could be seen as well as smelt" (328). She is hysterically afraid of the black people she passes on the street "as though she had run a gantlet" (331). As a result of her obsessively exaggerated perceptions, she retreats from teaching the children anything and contributes to the oppression of the system.

The city, then, and particularly the ghetto streets and buildings, can create a disoriented perception that combines disastrously with the psychic imbalance created by other more abstract forms of oppression through class, race, and gender. Is the country any better? Lutie learns about "Country Living" from Chandlers' sleek magazines and their life in Lyme, Connecticut. Despite her memories of the wide, beautiful main street with its overarching elms, she senses the injustice it implies for her and the hollowness of its beauty, given the disintegration of the Chandler family. Her life on the Chandler's country estate is largely spent indoors, where she is subjected to guests' stereotyping her as a black wench. Later, on the drive with Boots, she finds that the hills along the Hudson River outside the city close in on her too much. Although two or three references point to the desirability of sun, sky, space, and farm work, the novel contains no clear opposition between city and country, as does, for example, Gloria Naylor's *Mama Day*.

And after all, the general descriptions of the street are not exclusively negative. Yet, in the sleet the "blobs of light" from windows make "no impression on the ever-lengthening shadows" (414), the buildings "loom darkly" against the distant sky, and the snow gets dirty quickly. But Lutie delights in the rope-jumping girls, Jones enjoys the activity on the street and yearns to join the circles of joking men, and the snow can momentarily transform the street, "gently obscuring the grime and the garbage and the ugliness" (436). Implied in the novel, however, faintly, is the hope that one's senses may also be receptive to beauty, that one may gather resources to accept realistically as well as resist, the menacing and the ugly, and that human community may transcend the inhuman environment.

Works Cited

Bell, Bernard W. "Ann Petry's Demythologizing of American Culture and Afro-American Character." In *Conjuring: Black Women, Fiction, and Literary Tradition*, edited by Marjorie Pryse and Hortense J. Spillers, 105-15. Bloomington; Indiana University Press, 1985. [See elsewhere in this text]

Bone, Robert A. *The Negro Novel in America*. New Haven: Yale University Press, 1958.

Christian, Barbara. *Black Feminist Criticism: Perspectives on Black Women Writers*. New York: Pergamon Press, 1985.

_____. *Black Women Novelists: The Development of a Tradition, 1892-1976*. Westport, CT: Greenwood Press, 1980.

Davis, Arthur P. *From the Dark Tower: Afro-American Writers 1900 to 1960*. Washington, DC: Howard University Press, 1974.

Gayle, Addison. *The Way of the New World: The Black Novel in America*. Garden City, NY: Doubleday, 1973.

Gross, Theodore. "Ann Petry: The Novelist as Social Critic." In *Black Fiction: New Studies in the Afro-American Novel Since 1945*, edited by A. Robert Lee, 41-53. New York: Barnes and Nobles, 1980.

Ivy, James. "Ann Petry Talks about Her First Novel." *The Crisis* 53 (February 1946): 48-49.

Lattin, Vernon. "Ann Petry and the American Dream." *Black American Literature Forum* 12 (Summer 1978): 69-72. [See elsewhere in this text]

Petry, Ann. *The Street*. Boston: Beacon Press, 1985.

Pryse, Marjorie. " 'Patterns against the Sky': Deism and Motherhood in Ann Petry's *The Street*." In *Conjuring: Black Women, Fiction, and Literary Tradition*, edited by Marjorie Pryse and Hortense J. Spillers, 116-31.

Bloomington: Indiana University Press, 1985. [See elsewhere in this text]
Schraufnagel, Noel. *From Apology to Protest: The Black American Novel.*
   Deland: Everett Edwards, 1973.
Wade-Gayles, Gloria. *No Crystal Stair: Visions of Race and Sex in Black*
   Women's Fiction. New York: Pilgrim Press, 1984. [See elsewhere in this
   text]
Washington, Mary Helen. " 'Infidelity Becomes Her': The Ambivalent Woman
   in the Fiction of Ann Petry and Dorothy West." In *Invented Lives:*
   Narratives of Black Women 1860-1960, edited by Mary Helen Washington,
   197-306. New York: Doubleday, 1987.

The Socially 'Forsaken Race': Dantean Turns in Ann Petry's *The Street* (2000)
Lorna Fitzsimmons

Beginning with the description of the "violent assault" launched by the "cold November wind blowing through 116th Street" (1), which attacks and scourges like the punitive winds tormenting the damned, Ann Petry's critique of racism in her first novel, *The Street* (Boston: Houghton Mifflin, 1946), deploys Dantean tropes to suggest that discrimination and prejudice in U. S. society reduce African Americans to the "forsaken race" of the doomed in the *Inferno* (tr. Mark Musa; NY: Penguin, 1984). The protagonist, Lutie Johnson, a working-class woman trying to raise her son, Bub, on her own, steps onto the street in Harlem buoyed by Franklinian optimism that she can succeed through hard work, planning, and frugality. The thought of Franklin's success repeatedly inspires her to hope for upward mobility, as Virgil guides the Pilgrim in his ascent. Instead, her life becomes a descent into hell spiraling into murder and sacrifice, through which Petry gives a searing deconstruction of the white patriarchal bias within Franklinian ideology.

Like many African American women during the 1930s, Lutie Johnson becomes a domestic servant when no one will hire her husband. Denigrating her within a sexually offensive hostile work environment, her employers, the Chandlers, lead her to believe that "anybody could be rich if he wanted to and worked hard enough" (Petry 43), making her feel guilty that her social status is due solely to lack of diligence by her husband, Jim, and her. When Jim is unfaithful, she leaves him, determined to work hard to make a home for Bub. Their new apartment in Harlem is supervised, however, by the demonic Williams Jones, whom she immediately senses is "evil" without realizing the depth of his depravity, foreshadowed by the violence of the Cerberus-like dog that repeatedly "threw himself against the door" (Petry 9) of Jones' apartment when she first approaches it. Boasting "respectable" inhabitants under the serpentine gaze of the madam Mrs. Hedges, the sign advertising the apartments, stained with blood-like rust and blowing in the wind at a sinisterly "impossible angle" (Petry 3), serves as an ironically proleptic *mise en abyme* inverting *The Inferno*'s claim that "JUSTICE IT WAS THAT MOVED MY GREAT CREATOR," inscribed upon the gate of Hell (Dante 89); for Lutie will be flayed by racist and sexist biases in media, educational, employment, police, and legal practices symptomatic of systemic weaknesses in U.S. society.

Just as Dante's text reflects upon the Bovaryesque effects of naïve reception in the tale of Francesca and Paolo, lovers whose passion is inflamed by reading of Lancelot (113), which dooms them to the Second Circle of the lustful, Petry lays bare Lutie's misguided over-identification with popular periodicals that Mrs. Chandler gives her, showing that the "college education free of charge" (50) she assumes they provide is, in fact, capitalist propaganda encouraging her to raise Bub to believe "how important it was that people make money and save money" (70). Developing a greater critical consciousness of media bias, she is upset when a "thin, starved" African American man is stereotyped as a "burly Negro" by the Caucasian press after he is killed while t[r]ying to rob a bakery (Petry 198-199); but her naïve tendency to consume patriarchal advertisements uncritically (28) makes her subject to sexual harassment when she answers an advertisement for singers that the "grayish white" Mr. Crosse runs in a "Negro newspaper" (318-321). Furious, she rejects his proposition and sinks into despair, reflecting upon her lot in terms smacking of the damned, "running around a small circle, around and around like a squirrel in a cage" (Petry 323).

Meanwhile, Lutie remains unaware that Bub is being undereducated by his prejudiced white teacher and corrupted by the resentful Jones, who pays him to rob mailboxes under the pretext of helping the police. Petry anticipates the racism of one of the detectives who comes to arrest Bub and assumes that Lutie is a "drunken bitch" (387) in her critique of the police's defense of segregated housing, when Lutie's father's drunken party incites an officer to sneer, "No wonder they won't let you all live near decent people" (178). Failing to inform her that the case doesn't require an attorney, the lawyer whom she consults exploits her like the usurers of the Seventh Circle whose greed interferes with human toil and thus "offends God's goodness" (Dante 171). Lutie takes time off work to visit Bub in custody at the Children's Shelter while worrying how to get the funds she believes necessary to pay the lawyer. Again she sees her life as socially condemned to circularity: "So it was a circle, and she could keep on going around it forever and keep on ending up in the same place, because if you were black and you lived in New York and you could only pay so much rent, why, you had to live in a house like this one" (Petry 407).

Prey of Jones' perverse machinations, Lutie turns to Boots Smith for cash and finds herself in the Cocytus-like depths of treachery, anticipated by the uncanny chilliness that grows colder the first time she goes up the stairs toward the apartment (Petry 12). The powerful white Junto for whom Boots works owns the Junto bar, a parody of the Junto through which Franklin promoted himself. Patronized by African Americans, the Junto is controlled by white males, laying bare the white patriarchal bias within Franklinian ideology. Resentful of Junto's power, wealth, and competition for Lutie, Boots seeks to take his revenge against Junto by possessing Lutie before him (Petry 428), like Count Ugolino biting the neck of his former associate Archbishop Ruggieri in the frozen hole of Cocytus (Dante 366). Boots plots to retaliate against Junto's dominance yet vents his rage against one of his own people, Lutie, as Ugolino's "hunger proved more powerful than grief," and he cannibalized his children (Dante 372). While snow falls on the street from which Lutie must flee after murdering Boots, the Franklinian hope for mobility to which she had clung deconstructs as a whitewashing of systemic injustice.

That Old Black Magic? Gender and Music in Ann Petry's Fiction (2000)
Johanna X. K. Garvey

Poised on the threshold between two centuries, W. E. B. DuBois looked both back into U. S. history and ahead into the nation's future as he made his prophetic statements about the twentieth century: its problem would be the "color line" separating black and white. In the concluding chapter of *The Souls of Black Folk* (1990), DuBois offered equally significant comments about African American culture, focused specifically on music:

> [B]y fateful chance the Negro folk-song---
> the rhythmic cry of the slave---stands today
> not simply as the sole American music, but
> as the most beautiful expression of human
> experience born this side the seas. It has
> been neglected, it has been, and is, half
> despised, and above all it has been
> persistently mistaken and misunderstood;
> but notwithstanding, it still remains as the
> singular spiritual heritage of the nation and
> the greatest gift of the Negro people. (180-
> 81)

A century later, both the opening and closing sections of *Souls* have proven accurate in a myriad of ways, some discouraging but others more inspiring; in particular, the continuing evolution of black music has sparked aesthetic endeavors that reach beyond song and instrumentation to numerous other fields, including literature. Rooted in Africa, marked by the horrors of the Middle Passage, and intertwined with the manifold experiences of enslavement, black music originates with a people denied the written word, kept illiterate by slave masters and thus forced to rely on oral expression throughout the antebellum years. As Franklin Rosemont notes, "Black music developed out of, and later side by side with, this vigorous oral poetry [field hollers, work songs] combined with dancing, both nourished in the tropical tempest of black magic and the overwhelming desire for "freedom."[1] Repression ironically---and felicitously--- led to amazing creativity. And from the early decades of the twentieth century to its closing years, African American writers have testified to the power of the music---gospel, blues, jazz, bebop, rap, and beyond.

"[The] capacity for love and [the] capacity to deal with loss and death through the expressive power of art": such attributes clearly apply to African American music, but the description comes from a discussion of the myth of Orpheus (Segal 193). To what extent can an ancient Greek figure---part historical, amplified by myth over many centuries---offer ways to think about contemporary African American literature? As Charles Segal states, "In Orpheus music, poetry, and rhetoric are composite, virtually indistinguishable parts of the power of art" (2). Several commentators point to the significance of orphic song as part of an *oral* culture, and to its power "as a magical drug (*pharmakon*) against death" (18).[2] The myth originated from shamans who "cross between the living and the dead, have magical power over nature and animals, and are closely associated with music and the ecstatic, trancelike effects of music, possess healing and prophetic powers, and can lead the dead forth from the lower world" (159).[3] Orality, magic, song, and dance: these are components of black culture in the United States, throughout the diaspora, and with connections to an African past.[4]

Playing his lyre and singing, Orpheus tames wild beasts and casts a spell over his audience---one primary element of the orphic involves *transformation*.[5] Orpheus does not rebel; he refuses to accept the world as it is; he does not lead the people, he charms them. Prometheanism aims for an outer transformation of society; it proposes to ameliorate man's lot by external action. Orphism proposes to transmute the inner man by a confrontation with himself and to alter society only indirectly, through the changes that man can effect within himself" (Strauss 10-11). Such a description evokes ambivalence in one looking to black Orpheus not only to express realities of African American experience but to chart a path for change. Yet this very ambivalence attests to the place of music in American culture, and specifically to the role of both music and literature in the struggles for freedom that have marked African American life since DuBois penned *Souls*.

Her life spanning these decades, the author Ann Petry (1908-1997) has written fiction that shows the multiple facets of music---in the collection *Miss Muriel and Other Stories* (1971), as well as in the novels *The Street* (1946) and *The Narrows* (1953). Throughout Petry's work, music figures centrally in plot, characterization, and thematic concerns, to illuminate African American experience, both urban and suburban. While sometimes indicating that black culture with roots in Africa can contest and subvert the patterns of the dominant systems, Petry also demonstrates how gender and class complicate the picture, especially when capitalism intrudes upon ritual and myth. Though the orphic powers of black music may challenge the status quo, they may also prove inefficacious in contending with political and social forces that reflect the values of the white middle and upper classes. In particular, through two contrasting female blues singers, Ann Petry delineates the dangers of subordinating black culture to racist and sexist designs, and highlights the importance of what Audre Lorde terms "the erotic" (53-59).

Dance, Drum, Song

"Traditional Africans came to God in particular circumstances with sacrifices and offerings---through the divinities, spirits, the living dead, and human intermediaries---and they came in Dance, Drum, and Song" (Floyd 19). Though set mostly in New York City and suburban towns in Connecticut and New York, during the middle decades of the twentieth century, several of the stories in *Miss Muriel* (1971) illustrate how music permeates diasporan experience and reveals African traces, roots both expressive and subversive.[6] We see what Samuel Floyd refers to as "African cultural memory" (5) and also how those survivals have been transformed by African American encounters with not only enslavement but other forms of capitalism and commodity culture. "Olaf and His Girlfriend," for instance, reveals foundations in Africa, the Middle Passage, and the resultant diaspora; ultimately it suggests that black magic is more powerful than the forces of the dominant societies in the Americas. This story is unique in the collection in that it begins not in the United States but in Barbados---the easternmost site in the West Indies, one might note, closest to Africa.[7] The Bajan dockworker Olaf, whose fear of the sea suggests deep memories of the Middle Passage, initially loses his girlfriend Belle Rose due to class differences: her guardian aunt considers him too "low" to marry her niece, whom she then whisks away to New York City. Seeking the disappeared lover, Olaf engages in a subversive underground communication system in which West Indian drummers form the key link. The opening paragraph of the story performs its own vanishing act, as the first-person narrator claims to be the only one to know why a young dancer and singer disappeared from a New York nightclub. We enter a narrative that will send us on a "queer, crazy voyage" anchored in the African past. The message telling Olaf news of Belle Rose traverses a route that replicates the Atlantic slave trade in reverse, with added tangents, as the boat travels from New York, to Liverpool, Africa, India, Barbados, "carrying guns and men and God knows what" (187). Olaf himself then embarks on a similar odyssey, aiming to find Belle Rose in New York. Though each voyage appears routeless, guided only by chance, the repeated reference to *messages* underscores the importance of communication---a network made possible by Olaf's love and the cooperation of Black musicians. These several-layered travels form the first stage in subverting the status quo, to blur the class divisions arising from values of the colonizers.

Belle Rose herself performs the second, most dramatic step, at the Conga club, itself a space that colonizes as it exoticizes and eroticizes black culture.[8] Backed by drums that "talked as plainly as though they were alive," Belle Rose becomes the obeah woman: "[Her singing] was an incantation to some far-off evil gods" (194), and her dancing "was the devil dance---a dance that's used to exorcise an evil spirit" (195). Music and religion combine to cast a spell that combats all the fear and pain evoked by Olaf's long sea journey, a bridge across the diaspora and the slave trade that created it. As Belle Rose dances in front of Olaf, "she reached back into that ancient, complicated African past that belongs to all of us and invoked all the gods she knew or that she'd ever heard of," and her singing casts a spell like that of the conjure and obeah women (196). She becomes a shaman of sorts, taming not only Olaf's anger and erasing his remembered fears, but also rejecting both the colonizer and the colonized.[9] Her aunt, after all, has intended that Belle Rose marry a schoolteacher like her father---a product of British influence via education---but the dancer's grandmother was an obeah woman and that heritage proves more powerful, an old black magic that cures pain and restores what has been lost. In this story, black Orpheus is a woman who uses song and dance to reclaim her lost love, to cast a spell on her audience, and to displace acceptable or "mainstream" artistic forms. Her singing, according to the narrator familiar to the city, "didn't belong in New York. It didn't belong in any nightclub that has ever existed anywhere under the sun" (194). At story's end, she and Olaf have indeed disappeared from the city.

In two other stories in the collection, we also see versions of orphic themes that connect black music to African roots and offer vitality and power, disrupting and challenging middle-class mores assimilated to the dominant culture. Both also introduce the blues as theme and aesthetic, which will emerge more fully in Petry's novels. "Solo on the Drums" performs a jazzy blues, as the drummer Kid Jones employs his music to recall and "talk" his own (mostly woman) troubles, expressing the story of his love, the story of his hate (24). His lover has told him she's leaving him for the piano player. This performance begins with the collective when instruments speak to each other, a conversation and symbolic knife fight: "When he hit the drums again it was with the thought that he was fighting with the piano player . . . . He was putting a knife in clean between his ribs" (239). Gradually, the individual takes over: the narrative repeats how drummer melds with drums, conveying his message viscerally, and how his act resembles African practices. "The drums . . . took him back, and back, and back, in time and space," sending news of chiefs, foreigners, forests (239), while also telling his own story of love and loss. The connection back to African culture preserved in drumming proves the most available and effective means of self-expression---just as drums during slave times allowed the enslaved to communicate and thus were outlawed by those in power to prevent insurrection.[10] On one hand, then, the story implies that black music is most potent when rooted in an African past.

Yet the conclusion to "Solo on the Drums" carries the ambivalence raised by the orphic myth as applied to African American literature. For the drummer performs an urban blues, a form removed from country origins and (some would argue) tainted by the contact with capitalist systems that made the blues a popular commodity.[11] When Kid Jones stops playing, he is *not* part of the drums, and realizes instead that he has been "[s]elling himself a little piece at a time," and this time, "he had sold all of himself" (241). As he bows to the audience, he thinks he looks "like one of those things you pull the string and it jerks, goes through the motion of dancing" (241). Similar to the Sambo doll in Ellison's *Invisible Man*, this image of black performer as marionette in others' hands collides with the earlier, more positive images of the drum solo.[12] The musician receives applause, but the acclaim comes at a cost---he has used his pain, communicated it to strangers, not only to fight the piano player but to entertain and make money. Black Orpheus *has* transformed loss into art, performed magic in crossing time and space, but the effects are temporary, the situation ultimately unchanged.

While the drummer's evocative and potentially restorative solo thus concludes on a troubling note, another male musician more closely resembles the magical and subversive figure of myth. In the title story, "Miss Muriel," differences of race and class cause collisions that confuse and unsettle the young female narrator.[13] The primary catalyst for these challenges to a middle-class environment of propriety is a musician who suddenly appears in the quiet town of Wheeling, New York. Music is not foreign to the narrator, but she has known it in safe familial circles, music lessons, a piano at home, a father who sings in the "Italian fashion": a fairly Eurocentric version of this performing art. Chink Johnson, the stranger of mysterious origins, is "a very dark-colored man," with a shaggy, goatlike beard and shaggier hair. A piano player and singer, he talks to the music: a "very peculiar kind of musical performance . . . what he does with those songs is known as the 'talkin' blues' "(29). Proclaiming that " 'All us black folks is lost' " (18), he becomes the guide, a driving force in the narrative as he pursues the narrator's Aunt Sophronia, subverts middle-class black mores, and challenges the culture that subordinates black to white, specifically that allows white men easy access to black women.

Unlike the drummer Kid Jones, Chink Johnson plays a music closer to Southern rural origins, more country blues than urban. His "fast, discordant sounding music" (28) and his seemingly constant body rhythm and movement arise from an oral culture. Instinctively, the narrator recognizes these qualities of Chink's blues, as she tries to play the piano *his* way: "I pretend that I am blind and keep my eyes closed all the time while I feel for chords. He must have a special gift for this because it is an extremely difficult thing he is doing and I don't know whether I will ever be able to do it. He has a much better ear for music than I have" (29).[14] His music also disturbs the sensibilities of the narrator's father, who sings in the church choir, causing him to tap our new rhythms, but mostly enraging him; calling Chink all sorts of names but his real one, the father compares him to a stallion running after a mare and wants to banish him from the house. The narrator herself thinks of Chink "violating" both the piano and her aunt---clearly, the energy he brings via the music is sexually charged and dangerous in the eyes of the bourgeois blacks. He also becomes protean, not only in the names the pharmacist father calls him, but in the roles he plays: "Just in that one short summer, he seemed to take on all kinds of guises---fisherman, dancer, singer, churchgoer, even delivery boy" (41). He does not conform to the behavior dictated by middle-class convention, especially when interacting with women; on a rather tame level, he transforms Aunt Sophronia, teaching the staid, quiet woman to dance. His powers of seduction do not stop there, however, as his "rough, atonal voice," "singing a ribald song," accompanies his appearance with a wagon full of women, driving off into the forest---"a kind of panting excitement in that wagon" (42, 43). He might be Orpheus with the Maenads, about to be attacked and beheaded, but this orphic figure not only survives but subverts the narrative embedded in the story's title.[15]

Angered when the young narrator repeats the tale of black men told by whites to say "Miss Muriel" when asking for a box of cigars with the picture of a white woman's face on the lid, Chink says: "'It ought to be the other way around. A black man should be tellin' a white man, 'White man, you see this picture of this beautiful black woman? *White* man, you say *Miss* Muriel!' " (37). These words prefigure the ending, when Chink leads the way in chasing out of town the white cobbler Mr. Bemish, who has been tirelessly pursuing Aunt Sophronia. Seeking to reverse relations built on racial and gender inequities, Chink the piano player certainly performs as black Orpheus---not only in his seductive music making and in his nonconformity with middle-class mores, but in his efforts to contradict racist and sexist attitudes, and to protect black womanhood. Yet, like "Solo on the Drums," this story, too, ends with ambivalence, for the narrator has sympathy for Mr. Bemish and is still trying to grasp the ways that "race" works to label and categorize people. Earlier in the story, she talks of having been "trained," to be a Christian, to think in racial terms (30). Watching Mr. Bemish threatened by Chink and forced to pack up his belongings and leave town in the middle of the night, she is surprised, angry, and hurt. The story ends with her cursing the *black* man, saying, "You and your goddam Miss Muriel---"(57). Of course, the narrator is still young, leading a fairly protected life, and thus not yet exposed to behavior and attitudes reflecting deep-seated prejudice; nor has her family's lifestyle suffered markedly from the racist and sexist systems that Petry explores in her first novel, set not in a lovely suburban town but in an impoverished neighborhood in Harlem.

Humming an Old Tune

Petry also uses music to evoke a Southern past and elements of black culture gradually displaced, muted, forgotten as a result of the Great Migration. By the time that *The Street* (1946) takes place (1944) in Harlem, waves of African American migrants had arrived in Northern cities, often with expectations of a better life. The novel's protagonist, Lutie Johnson, is of a generation knowing little of the South and of her family's past, which exist primarily in the character of her grandmother, no longer alive. Granny, a shadowy presence, embodies orphic qualities of wisdom and intuition, but is more memory or trace in Lutie's mind than active presence. Still, she does represent the "ancestor," and as Farah Jasmine Griffin (1995) argues, Granny offers a "safe space" to Lutie as she struggles against oppressive systems that stand as formidable barriers to success for a black woman attempting to escape poverty.[16] As Griffin notes, in the "urban North, the South---the ancestor---must live in the psyche because sophisticated, fragmented Northern power most effectively oppresses the urban dweller on this plane" (115). Unfortunately, though Granny *is* an internal voice speaking to Lutie at moments of peril, the younger woman seems unable to allow herself to listen to that voice, as her ears are filled instead with false promises of the "American Dream."[17]

The early pages of *The Street* establish not only the physical surroundings but also Lutie's ability to read urban signs and decipher their meaning, as she fights the wind and trash on a Harlem street, seeking an apartment for herself and her young son. She knows what a for-rent sign literally says, behind its deceptive phrasing, just as she recognizes the ills besetting this urban neighborhood. For example, "[p]arquet floors here meant that the wood was so old and discolored . . . . Steam heat meant a rattling, clanging noice in radiators . . ." (3). Similarly, she instinctively understands that the superintendent showing her the apartment lusts after her, his desire palpable as they climb narrow stairs and examine the dismal rooms. Even as she graphs his barely repressed feelings, however, she rejects this way of knowing, linking such intuition---negatively---to Granny.

> She was as bad as Granny, which just went on to prove that you couldn't be brought up like Granny without absorbing a lot of nonsense that would spring at you out of nowhere, so to speak, and when you least expected it. All those tales about things that people sensed before they actually happened. Tales that had been handed down and down and down until, if you tried to trace them back, you'd end up God knows where---probably Africa. And Granny had them all at the tip of her tongue. (15-16)

Lutie has been acculturated, accepting messages from the dominant culture and concomitantly dismissing the remnants of ancestral memory embodied in Granny. While Lutie has the skills to read accurately---whether to know the sort of rooms she can afford or to comprehend a man's physical desire for her---and while she also has a potential protector in Granny's voice, she cannot accept the validity of the ancient wisdom. Significantly, the ancestral connection often expresses itself through music.

Though taking place in New York City during World War II, and thus depicting experiences far removed from the South and slavery, *The Street* presents black women's struggles and insights as clearly rooted in systems and attitudes that took form in the antebellum period. As an attractive black woman separated from her husband and supporting a young son, Lutie battles on several fronts, the nexus of race, class, and gender continually putting her at risk---first and foremost as the target of male sexual desire, both white and black. What Granny offers, especially in *song*, could prove a link to community and a means of solidarity and salvation. As Lawrence Levine (1977) states, the orality of black culture provided a strong foundation for those enslaved: "In their songs, as in their tales, aphorisms, proverbs, anecdotes, and jokes, Afro-American slaves, following the practices of the African cultures they had been forced to leave behind them, assigned a central role to the spoken arts, encouraged and rewarded verbal improvisation, maintained the participatory nature of their expressive culture, and utilized the spoken arts to voice criticism as well as to uphold traditional values and group cohesion" (6). This rich tradition of oral expression persists in the spirit of Granny, whose tales and songs Lutie does remember, but so tragically wills herself not to hear. As the super Jones continues to scare her and the small apartment closes in around her, Lutie "started humming under her breath, not realizing she was doing it. It was an old song that Granny used to sing" (17). The lines she recalls come from one of the spirituals, those songs invoked by Du Bois as the quintessential heritage of the whole nation. In the spirituals, "slaves found a medium which resembled in many crucial ways the cosmology they had brought with them from Africa and afforded them the possibility of both adapting to and transcending their situation" (Levine19). Thus, in Granny we see vestiges of a worldview not only of earlier African Americans but traceable even further back, indeed to the Africa that Lutie scornfully pushes out of her mind.

Certainly, Petry does not condemn Lutie for her situation, as we see from the start the powerful forces arrayed against the protagonist. Compelled a few years earlier to take a job as a live-in servant for a White family in Connecticut, Lutie not only experienced the detrimental effects on her family life caused by poverty but also was exposed to the belief that money held the key to power and success. Combined with her commitment to hard work as a means to rise in society, these faiths have erased much of the "ancestor" from her consciousness. Though not middle class, Lutie has internalized the mindset imposed on and accepted by that general group, as described by LeRoi Jones (Amira Baraka). In the process of acculturation, Jones (1963) argues, the "African gods were thrown into disrepute first, and that was easy since they were banned by whites anyway." Discussing how some African Americans moved into U. S. society, he states that it was "the black middle class who believed that the best way to survive in America would be to *disappear* completely, leaving no trace at all that there had even been an Africa, or a slavery, or even, finally a black man" (124). While Lutie does not pursue her American Dream to this extreme, she does repeatedly deny the traces of Granny, the old song that rises to consciousness at moments of particular danger.[18] As a link to black women's wisdom as well as to community more generally, Granny potentially could serve as shaman or oracle, the one to turn to for strength, protection, guidance.[19]

In her pursuit of a more individual success and her reliance on Ben Franklin as mentor,[20] however, Lutie does not allow Granny's qualities enough recognition or respect. These powers ultimately do not possess the subversiveness necessary to combat the hegemonic systems that govern the city. While Lutie may recall phrases of folk songs and spirituals and invoke them as talismans to ward off racism and sexism in the urban environment, these ancestral fragments are insufficient weapons in the battle she wages. The evil that Granny helps Lutie to sense in Jones manifests itself more and more as the narrative progresses, his lust turning to anger, resentment, and jealousy as Lutie rejects him and he imagines (erroneously) that she is sleeping with the powerful white man Junto. Concocting an elaborate scheme to entrap Lutie's son Bub in mail theft, Jones succeeds in "bringing her down"---attacking her through the one person to whom she demonstrates any attachment. After Bub's arrest, alone in the dark, silent apartment, Lutie remembers Granny as a constant presence when she was a child: "Granny had always been there, her rocking chair part of the shadow, part of the darkness, making it known and familiar. She was always humming. It was a faint sound, part and parcel of the darkness. Going to sleep with that warm sound clinging to your ears made fear impossible" (404). Bub has not had such a reassuring presence in his life, but instead has gone alone to the movies or been kept company by the radio while Lutie goes out. Granny's song was missing from his childhood, and now Lutie perceives the enormous cost of living so isolated from family, from roots, from the values located in her grandmother's tales and songs. As the musician Sidney Bechet observes, there "was something happening all the time to my people, a thing the music had to know for sure. There had to be a memory of it behind the music."[21] Bechet specifically remembers his grandfather Omar, who held inside him a communal memory, one that can be heard when any good musician plays, Bechet says: "No matter what he's playing, it's the long song that started back there in the South. It's the remembering song. There's so much to remember" (Floyd 9). As Petry illustrates, a musician needs an audience willing and able to listen to that song if he is to perform his---or her---Black magic. Ears must be receptive, if the music is to perform its magical powers.

Black Man's Blues

The migration to Northern cities is intertwined with black music, and in themes, characters, and events associated with the blues Petry incisively engages issues of gender and sexuality, as well as class and race. In *The Street* we see yet another potential black Orpheus in "Boots" Smith, a rail-riding piano player and bandleader with enormous talent and an equally strong desire to "make it" in the fast lanes of New York City. Though evincing traces of a creative and nurturing blues aesthetic tied to earlier years,[22] Boots compromises himself in order to survive and succeed in the city's world of entertainment and capital. He has capitulated to the white man Junto who presides not only over the bar where Harlemites like Lutie gather and the nightclub where Boots plays, but also over the legal system, as well as the real estate and sex industries---essentially the whole power complex of the city. By the 1940s, the Great Migration and the era of the blues lie in the past; the music has become commercialized, and at the same time has combined with jazz and evolved in new directions such as swing.[23] In Boots, Petry has created a character who personifies a history of the blues, at least in its urban forms. Though we do not learn his origins or complete life story, Boots is not one of the first-generation bluesmen, but he embodies some of their spirit: "The pioneering rural blues artists . . . were the makers and carriers of a music that resisted cultural domination in both form and content. They used traditional African musical practices to spread the rebellion and to reinforce the powerful hold that African traditions had on African Americans living in the South" (Barlow 5). These musicians also represented freedom, movement---often traveling literally or figuratively by rail.[24] William Barlow further notes that the blues "were part of a widespread cultural response to renewed white oppression" (7) in the early decades of the twentieth century, and he as well as others connect the musicians to the West African griots.[25] The transition from South to North, from rural life to urban experience, is reflected in the music in complex ways. The blues might contribute to what Jones (1963) calls the "acclimatization" of migrants to the city (106), and blues performances might offer stability or fill a void in newcomers' lives (Griffin 54). Furthermore, as Lipsitz (1994) comments, under "industrial conditions, an oral tradition serves as a collective memory of better times, as well as a means of making the present more bearable" (327). Yet, despite such positive, even healing, powers, another important development arose: "transplanted to an urban setting, [the blues] were significantly influenced by two disparate cultural forms---the music industry and the redlight districts. These forces transformed blues culture by reorganizing its sphere of production to make it into a profitable commercial enterprise, which in turn tended to separate it from its folk roots. And, in the process, the music became more susceptible to white economic control" (Barlow 113). As Houston Baker (1984) points out, the blues manifest duality, as creative expression and as entertainment, raising questions of integrity and fidelity, versus masks and minstrelsy (194).[26] All of these tensions surrounding urban blues can be traced in Petry's character Boots Smith.

Like the super, Jones, the piano player also looks at Lutie in sexual terms, though his approach is more sophisticated, his methods matching his higher economic status. His career has followed an upward trajectory, largely due to his connections with Junto; from improverished musician during the Depression, to Pullman porter saving his meager earnings, to bandleader at the Casino, with an expensive car and a luxurious apartment on Edgecombe Avenue, he has climbed the proverbial ladder, with Junto's assistance. The white man controls him, having made him and able to break him: "There weren't many places a colored band could play and Junto could fix it so he couldn't find a spot from her to the coast. He had other bands sewed up, and all he had to do was refuse to send an outfit to places stupid enough to hire Boots' band. Junto could put a squeeze on a place so easy it wasn't funny" (264). These thoughts occur to Boots as he realizes that Junto wants Lutie, too, and can prevent anyone else from "owning" her. Despite his attraction, Boots weighs Lutie against where he has come from, and sexual desire is not worth a return to the servitude as nameless porter or the even more desperate life of an out-of-work musician. He recalls, sleeping in parks and playing for a meal, to audiences who "never heard the music that came from his piano, for they were past caring about anything or listening to anything" (266). His memories include scenes resembling minstrelsy, white folks drunkenly urging him to dance and sing, and in all these recollections, whites possess power, while he performs with a mask covering his hunger and hate.

Throughout the chapter that follows Boots's thoughts, the musician's identity is marked by race, gender, and class in such a way that despite his obvious talents, he repeatedly hits a wall---the color line that denies him true access to power, just as it dictates limits to his masculinity. His piano playing has won him a job with Junto and a decent salary, but it cannot perform the magic of transcending racism or transforming a deeply flawed social order. "The blues is an attitude of transcendence through acceptance, but not submission. We can accept reality without submitting to it. In fact, we sing Blues songs to transform that which we accept---namely our reality" (Kalamu ya Salaam 356). Boots's transformative powers are limited because he does not have a vision beyond his determination to avoid military service, seduce women, and maintain his lucrative career.[27] In him, we see a potential but ultimately failed black Orpheus who, with the white man, will attempt to control the black woman. Ironically, in their final encounter, Boots does play a version of Orpheus, with Lutie enacting the role of the Maenads. In that final act, they perform for no audience within the narrative, a fact that may point to why both Boots and Lutie (as we will see in the next section) fail as orphic figures. Performance involves *ritual*, as Levine (1977) notes, with sacred overtones, "elements of charisma, catharsis, and solidarity." He continues, "[C]ommon problems are enunciated, understood, shared, and frequently the seeds of a solution to them are suggested. Similarly, John Szwed has argued that the bluesman is something of a shaman:" 'He presents difficult experiences for the group, and the effectiveness of his performance depends upon a mutual sharing of experience' " (234). Boots may draw an audience, but as his thoughts show, he performs most often for whites and is indebted to Junto, rather than acting as shaman for his own group or expressing communal experience and concerns. When Boots tries to use musical performance as a lure to seduce Lutie---offering her a job singing with his band---he inadvertently places himself at a dangerous intersection: not the crossroads as empowering site of translation envisioned by Houston Baker,[28] but the place where lines are drawn based on race and gender, where tensions explode and lives are destroyed.

Woman's Trouble Blues

"When Black women sing the blues, we sing our own personalized, individualistic blues while simultaneously expressing the collective blues of African-American women" (Collins 100). This combination of individual and group expression, already noted as important to Black music in general, stands out as a critical factor for Petry's female singers. Lutie from *The Street* and Mamie from *The Narrows* (1953), both women of a lower socioeconomic class, both singers viewed largely in terms of their sexuality by the other characters in their respective narratives, illustrate two very different paths taken by female versions of black Orpheus. In commenting on the classic blues, Patricia Hill Collins says that these songs "can be seen as poetry, as expressions of ordinary black women rearticulated through the Afrocentric tradition." Not only does this music connect back through that past, but the "lyrics sung by many of the black women blues singers challenge the externally defined controlling images used to justify black women's objectification as the Other" (100). Stereotypes of Mammy and Jezebel, for instance, became powerful myths embedded nineteenth-century U.S. ideologies concerning "womanhood," as well as "race," and such images created a lasting impression stretching into the twentieth century.[29]   Black women's sexuality became a particularly fraught topic, not least for black women writers, singers, dancers, and other creative artists. While authors such as Jessie Fauset and Nella Larsen might be seen as muting or even denying black female sexuality to avoid the negative stereotypes, blues singers like Bessie Smith and Gertrude "Ma" Rainey certainly included among their songs many that directly addressed the concerns and needs of sexually active black women.[30]   Taken together, Petry's Lutie and Mamie illustrate the pressures placed on black women and the pitfalls awaiting them, even if they follow radically different trajectories.   Their singing, in particular, both embodies their struggles and signals reasons for failure---or success—or orphic figures.

Alone with her eight-year-old son in Harlem, determined to work hard, save money, and move into a better apartment, Lutie Johnson seeks community at the Junto Bar and Grill, a neighborhood site where "the music from [the] jukebox created an oasis of warmth" (141). She wants to hear voices, see people, enjoy the music: find an escape from the daily struggles to survive. As she hums along, "she felt free here where there was so much space" (146). Though the lights and rhythms have drawn her, she also sees the large mirror that creates the (false) impression of spaciousness, and reflected in it Junto himself dominating the room, his ear tuned to the cash register as his eyes observe everything. Listening to the record "Darlin'," Lutie begins to sing, using the power of song to express what spoken language cannot:

> The men and women crowded at the bar
> stopped drinking to look at her. Her voice
> had a thin thread of sadness running through
> it that made the song important, that made it
> tell a story that wasn't in the words---a story
> of despair, of loneliness, of frustration. It
> was a story that all of them knew by heart
> and had always known because they had
> learned it soon after they were born and
> would go on adding to it until the day they
> died. (148)

At this moment, Lutie would appear to have found that merging of personal and communal, to tap into traditional expression, connect it to her own troubles, and give voice to the feelings and experiences of the larger group---the informal audience at the Junto. Almost immediately, however, Boots intrudes into this scene, offering to pay for her beers and asking whether she sings for a living. He sees her as a marketable commodity (as a singer), while Junto has quickly assessed her as a sexual object: two powerful, interconnected systems with which Lutie will then repeatedly engage battle.

Focused on a success she defines primarily in terms of money, Lutie begins to fantasize a musical career while refusing to acknowledge her sexuality; the blues is a communal production, involving call and response, but Lutie also refuses this and most other forms of community.[31] As Audre Lorde (1984) astutely observes, "To refuse to be conscious of what we are feeling at any time, however comfortable that might seem, is to deny a large part of the experience, and to allow ourselves to be reduced to the pornographic, the abused, and the absurd" (59). In her blind drive for financial security, Lutie mistakenly models her identity on individuality that shades into isolation, and is repeatedly the target of male exploitation; unfortunately, she perceives her singing as means to wealth rather than as artistic expression and connection to community. Just as in the opening scene Lutie knows yet tries to deny the super's intentions toward her, with Boots she also easily recognizes the game, sees the offer of a singing job as "bait" set to lure and trap her. But she represses her insights, pushing them out of her consciousness in the way that Lorde describes, and convinces herself that she is making the right choice: "[S]he hadn't known where she was going. As a matter of fact, she had probably never known. But if she could sing---work, hard at it, study, really get somewhere, it would give direction to her life---she would know where she was going" (160). She knows she is playing a "dangerous, daring game" (163), and takes her chances---significantly, Granny's voice does *not* echo in her mind in the middle sections of the book, as Lutie attempts to re-create herself as singer: "And she started building a picture of herself standing before a microphone. . . . of a room full of dancers who paused in their dancing to listen as she sang. Their faces were expectant, worshiping, as they looked up at her" (207). She imagines her coming appearance at the Casino---an audition---as the key to her transformation, allowing her to leave "the street," and compares this step to the shedding of a worn-out dress. Certainly, in Lutie's visions we see her attempts at self-definition, just as she will resist others' defining of her purely in terms of her sexuality. Her vision is lacking, however, most obviously in her exclusive focus on money and her separation from any form of community, aside from her young son Bub. In fact, her main thought as she sings for the band is of *leaving* the street and the people surrounding her, of "getting out and away." She congratulates herself (too early) for having done it alone, with help from nobody.[32] This individualism, based on Lutie's white male model Ben Franklin, will lead to an isolation both extreme and self-destructive, far from the potent black magic of a Belle Rose or the ancestral wisdom of a Granny.

Lutie's fantasy of singing to a "worshiping" audience raises again the link between secular and sacred facets of black experience. Levine (1977) comments that "blues was threatening because its spokesmen [sic] and its ritual too frequently provided the expressive communal channels of relief that had been largely the province of religion in the past. Blues successfully blended the sacred and the secular. . . . Like the spirituals of the nineteenth century the blues was a cry for release . . ." (237). For such ritual to be effective, especially as a means of cultural resistance, *audience* stands with *vision* as crucial elements in the performance. A concept that helps to clarify these links is *Nommo*: "The process of naming is a fundamental aspect of African philosophy and religion. The Dogon's concept of *Nommo*, the word, is fundamental to an understanding of the development of the universe" (Saakana 33). [33] As Barlow (1989) explains in terms of the music, "[I]t was in singing the blues lyrics that [blues performers] evoked the spoken word, the 'nommo' of traditional African philosophy, in order to unleash its magical powers to heal and transform. They used the word as a catalyst for claiming and shaping their own culture. Performance was the true test of the blues artist" (326). Lutie Johnson may dream of herself singing to a secular congregation, but in fact she performs for appraising men: Boots, who looks her up and down; the men in his band, who assume she is Boots's "new chick" fallen for the "old come-on" (221); and Junto himself, who decides he wants Lutie and thus assumes he can determine her fate. Such is the group listening to her sing---a hierarchy of men, all seeing her only as female (black) body, arranged in ascending order of power from orchestra members to Boots to the white man who controls the "show" and whose attitude mirrors that of plantation owners who perceived black women in sexual terms, as objects at their disposal. Junto's command that Lutie not be paid for her singing replicates the power relations in existence for several hundred years, transplanted to the North. Without a different vision, her own *nommo* and the voice to express it, as well as a strong sense of community, Lutie will perform in vain.

Lutie's experiences illustrate how black music has been commodified, its power diminished, some would argue, in its merging with the dominant culture. It ceases to be subversive, and thus loses its orphic qualities. Looking at how black musicians performed for entertainment in the 1920s, Toni Morrison has discussed the commercialization of black music. Madhu Dubey (1998) explains: "The cultural and financial 'ownership' of jazz in this period disturbs Morrison because the global dissemination and commercialization of jazz occurred in a market characterized by unequal, racially determined access to cultural capital and economic profit" (295). A few short paragraphs juxtapose the commercial and the religious, showing how music has "evolved" in the 1940s. Lutie climbs the stairs to her apartment and hears a series of fragments from radio shows: a commercial jingle for Shirley soap, the beginning of the swing record "Rock, Raleigh, Rock," then a revival church's broadcast service.[34] These sounds overlap in a confusion of sound, which then is drowned out by a loud fight, its "angry violence . . . mingling with the voices on the radio" (313). Through Lutie we can clearly see the intersection of this process of commodification and the "commercialization of black female sexuality in the new urban music" (Dubey 300) that also began in the 1920s.

Lutie, too, one must acknowledge, participates in the belief that music makes money---the Casino where she sings with Boots's band has a fitting name, given that she has gambled, even knowing the odds, on a chance to escape. In the background, as Boots now tells her that the singing is not a job but "just experience," Lutie remembers not his voice but only "the thin, ghostly, haunting music," which will echo as a reminder of her fantasies. Boots reminds her, too, that Junto has the final word, for he "owns the joint" (304). In the fact of that power of possession: "She had built up a fantastic structure made from the soft, nebulous, cloudy stuff of dreams. There hadn't been a solid, practical brick in it, not even a foundation. She had built it up of air and vapor and moved right in. So of course it had collapsed. It had never existed anywhere but in her own mind" (307-308). Despite Lutie's harsh self-assessment in these lines, the cultural context would indicate that the systems of capital in which she is enmeshed have tainted or co-opted what might have been strong orphic powers, leaving Lutie vulnerable both to the promise of success through entertainment and to the obscene presumptions of men both black and white.

These interlocking forces manifest themselves in two later scenes, first as Lutie invests her faith once more in the power of music, then as she underestimates the lengths to which men will go to "possess" her physically. In both cases, rage drives her to violent acts, of increasing intensity. Unable to relinquish her vision of success, Lutie is lured by a newspaper ad promising to train singers for Broadway and nightclubs---"High-Paying Jobs"---and goes to audition at the Crosse School. In an office littered with paper,[35] the owner says he can tell "just from looking at [Lutie]" that she can sing and he almost guarantees her a job, then waives the fee for voice lessons " 'if you and me can get together a coupla nights a week in Harlem' " (321). Before she hurls an inkwell at him, enraged, Lutie draws a telling parallel: "It was a pity he hadn't lived back in the days of slavery, so he could have raided the slave quarters for a likely wench at any hour of the day or night. This is the superior race, she said to herself, take a good long look at him" (322). Once, again, sexism and racist stereotypes block her path, and the costs are too high for Lutie. She will not compromise her values, that is, sell herself, even though she might achieve her dream of a musical career by doing so. Perhaps this is the trade-off or result of her having looked to singing as a means to an end: financial gain, material comfort, individual achievement. As in her other fiction, however, Petry leaves this question open, ambiguous, as she presents the many complicated factors leading Lutie to this desperate state.

Lutie's altercation with Mr. Crosse foreshadows the final scenes of *The Street*, when she turns to Boots for money to hire a lawyer in order to get Bub out of juvenile detention. As she considers how she has arrived at such an impasse, "her thoughts were like a chorus chanting inside her head" (388), and the reasons boil down to insidious patterns constructed by racism. As she sobs in despair, neighbors tune up their music to drown out her voice---an ironic note, given Lutie's desire to sing for a worshiping audience. In Boot's apartment, Junto waits, too: both men continue to pursue her as sex object, still assuming she will prostitute herself for the needed money. As she begins to contemplate killing Junto, a tune from the Casino floats through her head, "a thin thread of music that kept getting lost . . .so that she wasn't' certain the music was real" (421). Throughout these scenes building to her actual killing of Boots, music weaves in and out of Lutie's consciousness, a counterpoint to her anger and despair.[36] Ultimately, she performs as the Maenads when she strikes Boots repeatedly with a heavy candlestick. Two potential embodiments of Orpheus have thus failed: Boots in his lack of conviction even becoming an enemy of the Orphic. Neither one has held a vision capable of true transformation---black magic---but instead both have been drawn into a system (embodied in Junto) that commodifies the music just as it subordinates black men and sees black women as objects to possess and discard. Tragically, no black Orpheus emerges at the end of this narrative.

While Lutie's experiences illustrate the difficulties for a black woman to play Orpheus in urban spaces run by men who perceive her purely in sexual terms, *The Narrows* offers a counterexample in the blues-singing Mamie Powther. Petry's third major novel is set not in Harlem but in the New England town of Monmouth, Connecticut; most of its scenes take place in the black section, called "The Narrows" or other, more derogatory names, and focus on the interracial relationship of a black man (Link) and a white woman (Camilla). Mamie might seem a minor character,[37] yet she is a constant presence throughout the narrative, her voice echoing in the neighborhood, her songs listened to and carried in memory by other characters, and the words themselves offering a running commentary on the main action of the book. Her singing also threads together the spaces and landmarks of The Narrows, from the Hangman tree to the foghorn, to the bar where Link takes Camilla on their first "date," just as Mamie affords a link between the South of spirituals and blues, and the North of Radio City Music Hall with its neo-minstrelsy. Parallel to Chink Johnson in "Miss Muriel," Mamie is a figure who makes middle class blacks uneasy. Nevertheless, in this character Petry presents an extended, effective rendering of black Orpheus---as a woman.

"There was music in the woman's voice, a careless, easy kind music" (18): this is the first impression readers receive of Mamie Powther, followed by a scene of her singing as she hangs clothes to dry, listened to by Link and his adoptive mother, Abbie:

> A big warm voice with a lilt in it, and
> something else, some extra, indefinable

> quality which made Abbie listen, made her
> want to hear more, and more; as though the
> singer leaned over, close, to say, I'm talking
> to you, listen to me. I made up this song for
> you and I've got wonderful things to tell you
> and to show you, listen to me. (22)

The effect on Abbie is "hypnotic," while Link asks whether he is hearing a record. That reference in turn leads to Abbie's thoughts on contemporary (1950s) music, "all of it sounding alike, too loud, too harsh, no sweetness, no tune, simply a reiterated bleating about rent money and men who had gone off with other women, and numbers that didn't come out" (23). Despite the way that Mamie's singing draws Abbie in, Mamie and her music repel the older woman, because she attempts to distance herself from black culture, to emulate whites. As Sybil Weir (1987) argues, "Petry [in Abbie] shows the emotional and psychic reality of a black mother who has embraced the values of New England culture at the expense of her own racial heritage" (82)[38] Mamie embodies elements of that heritage, especially as she sings the blues.

Significantly, when hearing her sing, Link wonders if he's listening to a *record*. When the narrative traces Mamie's life story, in the memories of her husband Malcolm, we find that his employer in Baltimore sent him to find a nursemaid for his baby grandson: "Go get a big fat colored woman to look after this brat, a big fat colored woman that can sing" (180), he commanded Powther. In the process of locating a suitable person, Powther met a Mamie *Smith*, whose "voice was music" and whom he eventually married. Her name repeated more than a dozen times in a few pages, Petry's Mamie Smith is unmistakably connected to a real-life blues singer from the 1920s: "A full-featured, curly haired colored woman from Cincinnati, Ohio, in her thirtieth year stood before the horn of the recording machine in the New York Studios of the Okeh Record Company." Five musicians began to play, and Mamie Smith sang, on February 14, 1920---the first record to be made by a black singer (Oliver 1).[39] On August 10, 1920, she recorded "Crazy Blues," which "set off a recording boom that was previously unheard of . The target of the publicity campaigns soon became known as the 'race market' " (Harrison 46). Smith herself received rave reviews from the black press: "She was pointed to with pride as the first artist of the race to record popular songs. Her entry into the market was a boom to music publishing companies as well as to music stores in every town and city" (47). One of the early "blues queens," Mamie Smith could be seen as an icon of black music---her success sent record companies scrambling to find black women singers, and in a reciprocal manner, the "recording industry was beginning to have a dynamic effect on the development of performers' careers and on the transmission of black popular music" (48). Petry's naming of her character pays tribute to this moment in music history.

To trace the history of blues records and black women singers is to demonstrate the complexity of the transformation of black music in the twentieth century. Zora Neale Hurston may have decried the appearance of "race records"as "a commercialization of traditional forms of music,"[40] but many other commentators emphasize positive assessments of the recordings, especially women's blues. Collins (1990), for instance, describes these songs as the "early written record" of major elements of Black culture. In part because these "race records" were made for an African American audience in which large numbers of women were not yet literate, "these recordings represented the first permanent documents expressing a black woman's standpoint accessible to black women in diverse communities. The songs can be seen as poetry, as expressions of ordinary black women rearticulated through the Afrocentric oral tradition" (100). In her book *Blues Legacies and Black Feminism* (1998) Angela Y. Davis discusses the significance of sexual politics, socio-economic realities, and the role of art when looking at the achievements of the classic blues women. "Considering the stringent taboos on representations of sexuality that characterized most dominant discourses of the time, the blues constitute a privileged site" (xvii), where individual problems could be conceived and articulated in communal terms and women could establish a position of strength. As Davis argues, the "blues woman challenges in her own way the imposition of gender-based inferiority. When she paints blues portraits of tough women, she offers psychic defenses and interrupts and discredits the routine internalization of male dominance" (36).

In feminist analyses of the blues, both Angela Davis and Hazel Carby focus on the mobility expressed in the lyrics. Carby, in "It Jus Be's Dat Way Sometimes" (1990), sees women blues singers appropriating motifs of trains and travel for their own purposes, to articulate movement and embrace the desire to migrate, as well as to "voice the nostalgic desires of urban women for home which was both a recognition and a warning that the city was not, in fact, the "promised land' " (242-43). Davis sheds an even more positive light on the theme of travel in women's blues: "Notions of independent, traveling women enter into black cultural consciousness in ways that reflect women's evolving role in the quest for liberation. At the same time, dominant gender politics within black consciousness are troubled and destabilized" (67). In these several evaluations, women blues singers appear as strong, mobile, expressive, and *subversive* versions of black Orpheus. It is worth noting that Lutie, two decades or so later, may aspire to a singing career, but her notion of mobility is to ascend the socioeconomic ladder and her train travel is limited to trips to and from employment, whether in Connecticut or in midtown New York City.

The fictional Mamie (Smith) Powther stands as a direct descendant of the women discussed by Collins, Davis, Carby, and others. In conjunction with--- and opposition to---Lutie, this character also raises issues of class, as well as race and gender. Recent analyses of black women's history and culture show the complicated nexus of these identities, helping to dispel assumptions based on dichotomies that oversimplify. Ann duCille (1993) coins the term *bourgeois blues* to consider Jessie Fauset's novels in contrast to Bessie Smith's songs, in order to displace notions of the latter as "the privileged signifier of the genuine, authentic, pure black experience" (72), and also notes the influence of vaudeville and (white) minstrelsy on the classic blues. She further questions Carby's stress on self-invention for blueswomen, wondering how much of their liberated sexuality was constructed by ideologies that eroticize the black female body (74). Such comments are cautionary in reading Petry'a Mamie, especially in a novel set in the 1950s: to what extent is she, too, a construct based in stereotype, the blueswoman as icon of sexuality? Madhu Dubey (1998) comments on this issue:

> Without diminishing the power of the classic women blues singers, it is nevertheless instructive to remember that these singers' projection of black women as sexual subjects was conditioned by their participation in the entertainment market. Record companies standardized and commodified the sexual content of classic women's blues songs for financial profit. Neither helpless victims of commercialization nor fully self-directed agents, urban women blues singers gained immense popularity because of their own opportunistic manipulation of the new cultural possibilities that migration opened. (300)[41]

If Mamie does seem to threaten the propriety that Abbie strives to maintain, her eroticism illustrated in her physical appearance, her singing, and her extramarital affairs, I would still argue that she does possess an awareness and honesty that contrast markedly to Lutie's refusal to acknowledge her own sexuality and her deafness to the cultural wisdom stored in song.

Where Lutie seems willfully blind to the realities of her situation, Mamie is perspicacious and wise; where Lutie denies her sexuality, Mamie accepts and acts upon her desires; where Lutie dismisses her granny's voice and warnings, Mamie not only sees the truth of situations but in her singing she voices what is occurring and prophesies the outcome. And where *The Street* is filled with paper, written words that dictate Lutie's life and documents that she herself takes seriously, Mamie represents orality: "Writing didn't come easy to her and even if it had, she would have preferred the direct contact offered by speech, not the impersonal business of using a pen or pencil to inscribe an explanation or an apology . . ." (164). Mamie performs as a communal voice throughout *The*

Narrows, singing spontaneously and *not* connecting herself to the commodification of the music.

Moreover, she always has an audience among the novel's black characters. As Mamie sings about a train, Link listens entranced to her voice, "listening, straining to hear as though something important depended on his not losing the sound" (124). The passage continues:

> He supposed that it was a song about death,
> and it might have been a spiritual originally
> though he'd never heard it before, but that
> smooth
> warm voice singing it now turned it into a
> song about life, about man and his first fall,
> about Eve and all the wonders of her flesh,
> about all the Eves for generations back and
> generations yet to come. She may have
> been singing about a female who rode on a
> train . . . . (125)

The three main narrative consciousnesses---Abbie, Link, and Mr. Powther---all follow Mamie's singing voice and respond to it, if in different ways. Her words and music serve as a chorus, commenting on the central plot of the text, the affair between Link and the wealthy White Camilla. This transgressive alliance raises issues of taboo still present in the national psyche, but within *The Narrows* it pales in importance, except as it serves to explore the interconnections and differences among the black population of Monmouth.[42] Eventually, jealous of Mamie and what she mistakenly assumes is Link's attraction to the black woman, Camilla will take revenge by staging an attempted rape, sending Link to prison, and ultimately to his tragic death at the hands of Camilla's mother and husband. The eroticism Mamie represents in the minds of the other characters is dangerous, on one level, not so much in its power over both men and women as in its potential misinterpretation by them. Petry shows how even one black woman can blame another, based on misconception and stereotype. Abbie, so anxious to be judged approvingly by the dominant culture, has always looked down on Mamie, as sexy, bluesy, loose; not surprisingly, she wants to make Mamie responsible for Link's murder: "It was that woman. That Mamie Powther. I should never have allowed her to stay under my roof.   A woman like that starts an evil action, just by her mere presence" (414). Abbie remembers Link leaving the house whistling one of Mamie's songs---drawn as if by Orpheus, one might say---but her attempt to fault Mamie fails, as Abbie arrives at a crucial recognition: "It was all of us, in one way or another, we all had a hand in it, we all reacted violently to those two people, to Link and that girl, because he was colored and she was white" (419). Abbie undergoes a transformation in this final scene, as she first admits that

Mamie is *not* the problem, that it is a communal one, then decides to warn
Camilla of a plot to kill her in revenge.

This ending has less to do with race relations, its significance lying more in
the role of song within the black community. Throughout the book, Mamie has
voiced themes of loneliness, of love and sex, and of racial identity, pointing
directly to what has been occurring between Link and Camila. The others have
not really listened, another willed deafness, until it is too late and Link has been
shot to death. Mamie emerges as a sort of shaman, perhaps, an Orpheus to hear
and learn from. I would connect her singing to a larger power that resembles
what Audre Lorde (1984) terms "the erotic," without which, she says, "our lives
are limited by external and alien forms, and we conform to the needs of a
structure that is not based on human need, let along an individual's "(58). Lutie
illustrates this mode of living according to outside forces, ones that ultimately
close in around her and offer no way out. On the other hand, according to
Lorde,

> when we begin to live from within outward,
> in touch with the power of the erotic within
> ourselves, and allowing that power to inform
> and illuminate our actions upon the world
> around us, then we begin to be responsible
> to ourselves in the deepest sense . . . . Our
> acts against oppression become integral with
> self, motivated and empowered from within.
> (58)

Such feelings must be *shared*, she asserts. In the context of my discussion,
music offers an optimal means of such mutual recognition, power, and creative
agency. One wishes, in fact, that Lutie might listen to Mamie singing, and begin
to form community with black women, along the lines of what Carby (1992)
describes in historical terms: "The blues women did not passively reflect the
vast social changes of their time; they provided new ways of thinking about
these changes, alternative conceptions of the physical and social world for their
audience of migrating and urban women and men, and social models for women
who aspired to escape from and improve their conditions of existence" (754-55).

In this discussion of music in Petry's fiction, I have emphasized particular
elements of orphic myths as most useful for thinking of a black Orpheus. I have
focused on characters within the narratives---from Belle Rose to Chink Johnson,
Granny to Boots, finally Lutie and Mamie. The existence of a vision and the
possibility of transformation, via subversion of oppressive forces and ideologies,
have lent themselves most readily to assessing the power of the music. Of
course, one must not place unlimited expectations on aesthetic enterprise or
creative endeavors as catalysts for change, as Davis (1998) reminds us:

> Art may encourage a critical attitude and
> urge its audience to challenge social
> conditions, but it cannot establish the terrain
> of protest by itself. In the absence of a
> popular mass movement, it can only
> encourage a critical attitude. When the
> blues 'name" the problems the community
> wants to overcome, they help create the
> emotional conditions for protest, but do not
> and could not, of themselves, constitute
> social protest. (113)

Certainly, the structures and stereotypes, the systems and ideologies, causing oppression have been formidable opponents, difficult to overturn or radically transform. Nevertheless, the positive power of Black music remains undeniable. "Black secular song, along with other forms of the oral tradition, allowed [African Americans] to express themselves communally and individually, to derive great aesthetic pleasure, to perpetuate traditions, to keep values from eroding, and to begin to create new expressive modes" (Levine   297). Ultimately, perhaps we should look beyond the fictional characters to the author who created them, to view Petry herself as a powerful version of black Orpheus---as woman writer.

---

[1] See Rosemont, Afterword in Paul Garon, *Blues and the Poetic Spirit*. (San Francisco: City Lights, 1996, 218). See also George Lipsitz, *Rainbow at Midnight: Labor and Culture in the 1940s.* (Urbana: University of Illinois Press, 1994, 306), and Lawrence Levine, *Black Culture and Black Consciousness.* (New York: Oxford University Press, 1977), Chapters 1 and 4.

[2] See also W. K. C. Guthrie, *(Orpheus and Greek Religion: A Study of the Orphic Movement*. London: Methuen, 1952) on tracing the evolution of the figure of Orpheus and Walter Burkert (*Green Religion.* Translated by John Raffen. Cambridge, MA: Harvard University Press, 1985) on the "problem of orphism" in classical studies. The difficulties point to the origins in oral culture and the complexities of tracing the figure through the written record of later centuries.

[3] See also Guthrie on various elements of the orphic myths, including magic: "[F]or some the name of Orpheus was associated with charms, spells and incantations" (3). See also Fritz Graf ("Orpheus: A Poet Among Men." In *Interpretations of Greek Mythology*, edited by Jan Bremmer, 80-106. Totowa, NJ: Barnes & Noble Books, 1986) for a detailed description of the story of Orpheus and orphic themes.

[4] On the connections of Africa, see Portia K. Maultsby, "Africanisms in African-American Music." In *Africanisms in American Culture*, edited by Joseph E. Holloway, 185-210. (Bloomington: Indiana University Press, 1990). See also Amon Saba Saakana, "Culture, Concept, Aesthetics: The Phenomenon of the African Musical Universe in Western Musical Culture." *African American*

Review 29.2 (Summer 1995): 329-40; and Samuel A. Floyd, *The Power of Black Music.* (New York: Oxford University Press, 1995), especially Chapter 1.

[5] See Walter A. Strauss (*Descent and Return: The Orphic: Theme in Modern Literature.* Cambridge: Harvard University Press, 1971, 3) who points to the influence of Ovid's version of the Orpheus story. See also Charles Segal, *Orpheus: The Myth of the Poet.* (Baltimore: John Hopkins University Press, 1989), especially Chapter 1; John Warden, ed. *Orpheus: The Metamorphoses of a Myth.* (Toronto: University of Toronto Press, 1982), especially the Introduction; and Emmet Robbins, "Famous Orpheus." In *Orpheus: The Metamorphoses of a Myth*, edited by John Warden, 3-23. (Toronto: University of Toronto Press, 1982).

[6] In her overview of themes in stories, Gladys Washington ("A World Made Cunningly: A Closer Look at Ann Petry's Short Fiction." *CLA Journal* 30.1 (September 1986): 14-29) includes entertainers and states: "Two most important aspects of that tradition, music and dance, have exerted a tremendous influence upon the lives of black people---from the tribal music and dances of Africa to the slave songs and minstrel shows to the blues and jazz rhythms of contemporary America" (27).

[7] In her novel *The Chosen Place, The Timeless People* (New York: Harcourt, Brace & World, 1967), Paule Marshall (herself of Barbadian heritage) uses this feature to help characterize the fictional Bourne Island.

[8] Petry appears to be in part responding to and rewriting the story of Rose in Claude McKay's *Home to Harlem.* For an insightful discussion of McKays' treatment of women in this novel, see Hazel Carby, "Policing the Black Woman's Body in an Urban Context." *Critical Inquiry* 18.4 (Summer 1992): 749-50).

[9] Bell Rose's song and dance demonstrate elements of African ritual, as described by Floyd: "The Yoruba believed that *ashe*---a dynamic, malleable energy, a life force that can be put to good or evil use---was "the true nature of things"…and here is the source of the spirit possession common to African ritual" (19-20), power tapped from the *orisha* or *vodun*.

[10] Of these aspects of drums, see royal hartigan, "The Heritage of the Drumbeat." *African American Review* 29.2 (Summer 1995): 234-36; Burton W. Peretti, *The Creation of Jazz: Music, Race, and Culture in Urban America.* (Urbana: Univeristy of Illinois Press, 1992); and Samuel A. Floyd, *The Power of Black Music.* (New York: Oxford University Press, 1995), especially Chapter 2.

[11] On this commodification, see especially Daniel Lieberfeld, "Million-Dollar Juke Joint: Commodifying Blues Culture." *African American Review* 29.2 *(*Summer 1995*): 217*-21. See William Barlow (*'Looking Up at Down": The Emergence of Blues Culture.* Philadelphia: Temple University Press, 1989, 114-115) on this process of incorporating Black folk music into the marketplace. See also Paul Oliver, *Blues Fell This Morning: Meaning in the Blues.* (New York: Cambridge University Press, 1990); Daphne Duval Harrison, *Black Pearls: Blues Queens of the 1920s.* (New Brunswick, NJ: Rutgers University Press, 1988); Richard Powell, *The Blues Aesthetic.* (Washington, CD:

Washington Project for the Arts, 1989; George Lipsitz, *Rainbow at Midnight: Labor and Culture in the 1940s*. (Urbana: University of Illinois Press, 1994); and LeRoi Jones, *Blues People*. (Westport, CT: Greenwood Press, 1963).

[12] In Ellison's novel (*Invisible Man*. New York: Vintage, 1990), the narrator comes upon Clifton, who had seemed as emerging Black hero, selling "Sambo" toys: "A grinning doll of orange-and-black tissue paper with thin flat cardboard disks forming its head and feet and which some mysterious mechanism was causing to move up and down in a loose-jointed, shoulder-shaking, infuriatingly sensuous motion, a dance that was completely detached from the black, mask-life face" (31). Petry's story was first published in 1947, five years before *Invisible Man*.

[13] Critics have noted the parallels between the narrator and the author, both growing up in suburban Connecticut, daughters of pharmacists and members of the only Black family in town. For a biography of Petry, see Hazel Arnett Ervin, *Ann Petry: A Bio-Bibliography*. (New York: G. K. Hall, 1993). See also Hilary Holladay, *Ann Petry*. (New York: Twayne, 1996).

[14] Lipsitz (308) notes the role of blind singers, closer to the oral tradition. In the myth, Orpheus loses his beloved when he *looks* back, trusting his eye instead of his ear.

[15] On Orpheus and the Maenads, Guthrie (32-36, 49). See also Graf (85-86) and Charles Segal, *Orpheus: The Myth of the Poet*. (Baltimore: John Hopkins University Press, 1989, 22).

[16] Griffin (*'Who Set You Flowin'?: The African-American Migration Narrative*. New York: Oxford University Press, 1995) sees three safe spaces available to Lutie---community, family, and her grandmother's voice: she focuses on the last of these in her discussion, and states: "Not unlike the blues singers discussed earlier, Lutie's grandmother gives her a map for her own survival" (116). Keith Clark ("A Distaff Dream Deferred? Ann Petry and the Art of Subversion." *African American Review* 26.3 (1992): 500) also points to Granny as potential mentor. See also Marjorie Pryse, " 'Patterns against the Sky': Deism and Motherhood in Ann Petry's The Street." In *Conjuring: Black Women, Fiction, and Literary Tradition*, edited by Marjorie Pryse and Hortense J. Spillers. Bloomington: Indiana University Press, 1985.

[17] On the American Dream as false myth, see Bernard W. Bell, "Ann Petry's Demythologizing of American Culture and Afro-American Character." In *Conjuring: Black Women, Fiction, and Literary Tradition*, edited by Marjorie Pryse and Hortense J. Spillers, 105-15. See also Clark. Nellie Mckay ("Ann Petry's The Street and The Narrows: A Study of the Influence of Class, Race, and Gender on Afro-American Women Lives." In *Women and War: The Changing Status of American Women from the 1930s to the 1950s*, 133, edited by Maria Diedrich and Dorothea Fischer-Horning. New York: Berg, 1990) blames Granny for this attitude of Lutie's, but the text offers evidence to the contrary.

[18] See Griffin (115). As noted, Clark also points to the potential protection afforded by Granny, which Lutie rejects, but he does not mention music/song per se as part of Granny's wisdom.

[19] "These 'oracles' constitute still another site of autonomous power within the slave community. To them the slaves could bring their dilemmas and uncertainties, in their knowledge slaves could try to find remedies and solutions to their numerous problems, from their aura of mystical authority slaves could attempt to draw assurance and strength" (Levine 70). See also Levine (33) on community and spirituals.

[20] On Petry's use of historical references to Franklin, see Pryse. See also Clark.

[21] Quoted in Floyd (8), from Sidney Bechet, *Treat It Gentle* (New York: Hill & Wang, 1960), 103.

[22] On these aspects of the blues, see Houston A. Baker, Jr., *Blues, Ideology, and Afro-American Literature: A Vernacular Theory* (Chicago: University of Chicago Press, 1984).

[23] On this evolution, see Leroy Ostransky, *Jazz City: The Impact of Our Cities on the Development of Jazz* (Englewood Cliffs, NJ: Prentice-Hall, 1978); Peretti; and Kathy J. Ogren, *The Jazz Revolution: Twenties America and the Meaning of Jazz* (New York: Oxford University Press, 1989).

[24] On this motif, see Baker ("Introduction") and Oliver (especially Chapter 2). See also Levine (262-63), Jones (Chapter 7), Barlow, and Garon (84-91). I will discuss the importance of travel to women blues singers in the final section.

[25] "Griots were both admired and feared by their fellow tribe members since they were thought to consort with trickster gods and even evil spirits" (Barlow 8). See also Floyd (33). Peretti (36) also notes a connection to voodoo.

[26] Baker cites Samuel Charters, as follows: "The blues has always had a duality to it. One of its sides is its personal creativity---the consciousness of a creative individual using it as a form of expression. The other side is the blues as entertainment" (194).

[27] On the further commercialization and effects on the blues, see Daniel Lieberfeld, "Million-Dollar Juke Joint: Commodifying Blues Culture." *African American Review 29.2 (Summer 1995): 217-21.*

[28] See Baker: "Fixity is a function of power. Those who maintain power, who decide what takes place and dictate what has taken place, are power brokers of the traditional. The 'placeless,' by contrast, are translators of the non-traditional . . . .[T]heir lineage is fluid, nomadic, transitional. Their appropriate mark is a crossing sign at the junction" (202), Barlow discusses the crossroads as domain of the Yoruban trickster god Legba: "In Yoruban folklore, a crossroads symbolizes the junction between the physical and the spiritual world, the human and the divine, where mortals sought out the god Legba in order to learn their fate" (49).

[29] See, for instance, Patricia Hill Collins. *Black Feminist Thought: Knowledge, Consciousness, and the Politics of Empowerment.* (New York: Routledge, 1990), Chapter 4 ,and Carby.

[30] In recent years, this charged issue has drawn stimulating discussions by a number of prominent critics, including Carby, Collins, Angela Y. Davis, *Blues Legacies and Black Feminism* (New York: Pantheon, 1998), Ann duCille, *The Coupling Convention: Sex, Text, and Tradition in Black Women's Fiction* (New York: Oxford University Press, 1993), and Harrison. I address some of the complexities below, especially in analyzing Mamie from *The Narrows*.

[31] Most discussions of Black music include the importance of call-and-response patterns. On the connection to community, see for instance Maultsby: "The fundamental concept that governs music performance in African and African-derived cultures is that music-making is a participatory group activity that serves to unite black people into a cohesive group for a common purpose" (187). She also cites Nketia on the public performance of Black music serving "a multiple role in relation to the community: it provides at once an opportunity for sharing in creative experience, for participating in music as a form of community experience, and for using music as an avenue for the expression of group sentiments" (188). See also McKay on Lutie: "Without a supportive community (which is most unusual for black women in America) and as the result of her self-confidence in her ability single-handedly to change the course of her life, she naively and erroneously places her faith in industry, thrift, individuality, and personal ambition, considering them the only important factors in the struggle against poverty and social disability" (130).

[32] While Lutie's singing seems a mixture of blues, jazz, and later forms of Black music, a comment from Harrison seems pertinent here: [T]he blues transcend conditions created by social injustice; and their attraction is that they express simultaneously the agony of life and the possibility of conquering it through the sheer toughness of spirit. That is, the blues are not intended as a means of escape, but embody what Richard Wright calls " 'a lusty, lyrical realism, charged with taut sensibility'" (65); "Neither the intent nor the result is escape, but, instead, the artistic expression of reality" (66)

[33] On Nommo, see also Davis: "The blues preserve and transform the West African philosophical centrality of the naming process . . . .[T]he process of nommo---naming things, force, and modes---is a means of establishing magical (or, in the case of the blues, aesthetic) control over the object of the naming process. Through the blues, menacing problems are ferreted out from the isolated individual experience and restructured as problems shared by the community. (33)

[34] One wonders if the ad for Shirley soap is a reference to Shirley Temple, a major icon of (White) femininity in the 1940s. Toni Morrison shows the destructive power of such models of beauty in *The Bluest Eye*. In "The Shirley Temple of My Familiar" [*Transition* 73 (1998): 10-32], Ann duCille offers an indepth analysis of the effects of Temple's film role on both Black and White audiences.

[35] Throughout *The Street*, Lutie exists in an environment strewn with paper and rules by written documents---a social system far from the oral culture that informs African American traditions and art forms such as music and song. It

seems significant in this context that she throws an inkwell at Mr. Crosse, symbolically turning the instruments of the dominant culture against it.

[36] On violence and blueswomen, see Harrison: "[J]ail and serving time are recurring themes in women's blues not only because of the bias in the legal system but because women in cities witnessed, were victims of, or sometimes resorted to violence to avenge mistreatment or infidelity. Women, at least in song, used violence, or the threat of violence, as one means of retaliation" (70).

[37] The few critical studies of this text ignore or touch only briefly on this character (Thelma J. Shinn, "Women in the Novels of Ann Petry," *Critique* 16.1 (1974): 110-20; McKay; and Margaret B. McDowell, "The Narrows: A Fuller View of Ann Petry." *Black American Literature Forum* 14.4 (1980):135-41). See, however, Sybil Weir, " The Narrows: A Black New England Novel." *Studies in American Fiction* 15.1 (Spring 1987): 81-93), who discusses Mamie as blues singer in opposition to Abbie Crunch, the "matron" who emulates New England (White) culture.

[38] Weir also comments: "Abbie's contempt for Mamie Powther signifies her rejection of the sensual heritage of African dance, religion, song, and music, a heritage that celebrates the union of body and mind" (88).

[39] On the historical Mamie Smith, see also Ogren (91) and Harrison (Chapter 2).

[40] See Carby ("The Politics of Fiction," 75), citing Robert Hemenway's biography of Hurston. But also see Carol Batker, " 'Love Me Like I Like to Be': The Sexual Politics of Hurston's *Their Eyes Were Watching God*, the Classic Blues, and the Black Women's Club Movement." *African American Review* 32.3 (Summer 1998): 199-213, especially 199-200, who points out Hurston's positive responses to the music, friendship with performers such as Ethel Waters and Bessie Smith, and familiarity with various venues for the classic blues singers.

[41] See also Batker, who summarizes some of the opposing assessments of whether the blues continued derogatory stereotypes, concluding, "Far from uniform in their treatment of sexual legitimacy, then, the classic blues reinforce, invert, and deconstruct the opposition between middle- and working-class sexualities, respectability and desire" (204-205).

[42] On responses to the interracial affair in this novel, see Ervin for summaries of early reviews of the book; see also the interviews included in Ervin (especially 76-77, 99, 101).

Women on the Go: Blues, Conjure, and Other Alternatives to Domesticity in
Ann Petry's *The Street* and *The Narrows* (1998)
Kimberly Drake

> When a woman get the blues, she goes to
> her room and hides.
> When a woman get the blues, she goes to
> her room and hides.
> When a man gets the blues, he catches a
> freight train and rides.
>
> Clara Smith, "Freight Train Blues" (1924)
>
> Sitting in the house with everything on my
> mind.
> Sitting in the house with everything on my
> mind.
> Looking at the clock and can't even tell the
> time.
> . . . Oh, the blues has got me on the go
> They've got me on the go.
> They roll around my house, in and out of my
> front door.
>
> Bessie Smith, "In House Blues" (1931)

Throughout the first half of the twentieth century, literary depictions of African-
American female sexuality continue to be extremely rare. With the exception of
Nella Larsen's Helga Crane and Zora Neale Hurston's Janie Starks, female
protagonists are largely asexual , the result of authors' attempt to fight the
Jezebel stereotype and to prove that black women could and did adhere to
middle-class values even if they were, by virtue of their color, excluded from the
"cult of true womanhood." These protagonists, specimens of the black
bourgeoisie who consider themselves a "credit to the race," construct their
identities against the Jezebel image; their behavior and values are well within
the bounds of middle-class respectability, but more importantly, their "female
desire" is expressed as a "desire to uplift the race" (Carby, " 'It Jus Be's' "
(240).[1] The black heroine's participation in community politics, however, often
occurs only after her marriage and enclosure in domestic life; women like
Pauline Hopkins's Sappho Clark or Frances E. W. Harper's *Iola LeRoy* do not
engage in public work until after their marriage (to politically involved
husbands). An asexual middle-class domesticity, then, is the literary "safe
space" for black female characters, a place which protects them from sexual
objectification so that they can work to transform and protect the reputation of
other black women.[2] While single, the black heroine is at risk from the sexual
dangers of the "outdoors," the culture of white supremacy; once sheltered in the

institution of marriage, her reputation secure, she can venture into the political realm knowing that she is protected in her "safe space" of marriage and domesticity.[3]

Yet not all women writers celebrate domesticity as the solution to the problems faced by black women: Nella Larsen's *Quicksand* depicts domesticity as another kind of slavery. Forced to choose between her "desire for sexual fulfillment" and her "longing for social respectability," Larsen's Helga Crane attempts to sanction her sexuality in marriage (McDowell xvii). This choice results not in safety but in suffocation; domesticity is a death sentence for Helga, in which she is slowly destroyed by consecutive pregnancies and the exhaustions of childrearing and housekeeping. Larsen's critique of marriage and domesticity is one of the first in the African –American literary tradition, adding a racial dimension to similar critiques made by white authors such as Emily Dickinson, Kate Chopin, Charlotte Perkins Gilman, and Edith Wharton. Twenty years later, Ann Petry inflects Larsen's critique further by adding the element of class as a central focus.[4] With the publication of *The Street* (1946) and *The Narrows* (1953), Petry portrays the working-class black woman's experience of domestic ideology while simultaneously acknowledging the limitations of previous black women writers' rigid moral standards. She does so not by breaking with the tradition of the asexual heroine, but by including sexualized minor female characters who act as foils to female protagonists with bourgeois values. Significantly, Petry does not portray her minor characters as fallen or degenerate, thereby highlighting the purity and goodness of the protagonists; rather, the minor characters survive and even flourish during the course of the novel, while the protagonists suffer. Through her narrative support of characters with working-class morals and lifestyles, Petry challenges the white-identified bourgeois standards of the female protagonists; in doing so, she is the first black woman writer to create a literary space for the "legitimate" expression of black female sexuality. [5]

In other words, Petry allows her minor characters to become powerful, sexually active working-class black women, almost a contradiction in terms in literature up to 1946. At this time, the only cultural precedent for such a woman was the female blues singer. Blues singers in urban areas performed in redlight districts, "The hub of a local underworld economy, the site of a night-life subculture, and a haven for American have-nots" (Barlow 115). Considered by the black church to be the "Devil's music," the blues quickly became associated in the public mind with the other elements of this underworld culture: gambling, prostitution, the numbers racket, voodoo and conjure, and, most importantly, the working classes (Oakley 116; Oliver 155).[6] And the effect was mutual: "nurtured by an underworld ethos," blues discourse "remained in opposition to the prevailing white culture," but it came to "illuminate the day-to-day realities of African-American life in the tenderloin enclaves" instead of those of Southern agricultural life in which it originated. (Barlow 117)

Blues singers consciously played with these "underworld " themes, developing them into a "blues praxis": "as cultural rebels, the blues artists adopted any number of personas." For female singers, these personas included "hoodoo queens, matriarchs, wild women [and] lesbians," and they "achieved mythical stature in the black community, constituting a black pantheon separate from ---and in many ways antithetical to ---the white heroes and heroines of middle-class America" (Barlow 327). Bessie Smith, for example, was an "unabashed rebel, openly defiant of bourgeois conventions and the oppressive social relations between the races, between the sexes, and between the classes in American society" (Barlow 165). As a "cultural rebel," then, a blues woman would consider the Jezebel persona a necessary part of both her performance and her lifestyle; that persona was accepted by those (artists and most of the working classes) sharing her values.[7] Middle-class blacks or working-class blacks who retained a bourgeois Christian morality could not condone blues music or its attendant culture.[8] The blues singer was considered by the bourgeois-identified black woman to be "fallen," promiscuous, disgraceful---the worst example of black womanhood.

Perhaps because of the risk to the image of black women, female blues singers would not appear as literary protagonists until three decades later, beginning with Gayl Jones' *Corregidora* (1975). In general, however, women blues singers depicted in literature typically do not appear on center stage but rather as "liminal figures that play out and explore the various possibilities of a sexual existence" (Carby " 'It Just Be's ' " 241). While an openly sexual female character might be intended to subvert the dominant culture's attitudes toward black female sexuality, the fact is that a reader titillated by that character's performance is continuing to objectify that performer both racially and sexually. Similarly, a prominent figure such as Bessie Smith, whose performance and music helped to transform the image of black women by making them "sexual subjects," was still making herself into a sexual spectacle in her shows. Blues singers dressed elaborately and ostentatiously, emphasizing "all the desirable aspects of their body," and Smith was no exception.[9] Michele Russell acknowledges that in this display, "blues singers like Bessie reduced black women's collective shame at being rape victims . . . by emphasizing the value of [their] allure" (131). On one hand, Russell celebrates Smith's display of "allure" as subversive, seeing her as a black woman assuming control of her own sexual image. On the other hand, she avoids discussing Smith's performance as a titillation of her (white and black) audiences, as what bourgeois blacks might consider a self-objectification that degrades all black women.[10]

A version of this double bind in the display of black female sexuality directs Petry's portrayal of her minor female characters, Min and Mamie; Petry seems to want to challenge the literary repression of black female sexuality, yet she cannot explicitly celebrate their transgressive sexuality without offending bourgeois black readers and confirming stereotypes in the minds of white readers. She skirts these risks by creating minor characters who fulfill the function of the "liminal" blues woman Carby describes, in that they resist allowing their sexual identity, and thus their female identity, to be determined by a class to which they do not belong. Petry does not mark these women as heroines, only gradually introducing the reader to an understanding of their points of view and circumstances. Initially, Min (of *The Street*) and Mamie Powther (of *The Narrows*) are dismissed and detected by their respective protagonists, Lutie Johnson and Abbie Crunch, and thus by the reader (who is aligned with the protagonist's point of view). Seen through a narrative filter, Min and Mamie are judged by the standards of the central characters; when they are eventually given their own point of view, the judgments grow more sympathetic.[11] The reader's corresponding judgment of the protagonists' morals thus undergoes a change; the protagonists now seem somewhat repressed, snobbish, and white-identified (although still heroic in their struggle against oppression), which is precisely Petry's point. Moreover, the main character's dismissal or avoidance of the "blues woman," eventually leads to her downfall: because Min and Mamie are familiar with sexuality and violence, they know a way out of the oppressive prison in which Lutie and Abbie are trapped, but they do not end up sharing their knowledge. By setting her minor characters against her protagonists in this way, Petry avoids controversy in her challenge to bourgeois sexual values.

A central part of the middle-class value system to which Lutie and Abbie adhere is white domestic ideology; they use its standards to judge (and reject) their neighbors Min and Mamie. A "crucial institution of civilization" to "middle-class women and men," the home "preserved those social virtues endangered by the public world," or the world of the street; along with the woman who "keeps" it, it is meant to be "enclosed, protected, and privatized" (Stansell 93). Working poor women such as Min and Mamie (before her marriage) find it difficult to practice this ideology in their own homes. Their long hours at low-paying jobs (most often, ironically, as domestics in the homes of white women) deprive them of the resources to make their rooms or apartment feel like the middle-class version of "home." Failing to become the middle-class housewife, the working-class woman has another available model: the persona of the female blues singer, who rejects domestic ideology and makes herself comfortable in the "uncivilized" world of the street. She has "broken out of the boundaries of the home" and taken her "sensuality and sexuality out of the private into the public sphere," into the dangerous "outdoors" (Carby " 'It Jus Be's' " 247). Petry's minor characters reside somewhere between these two fantasies of female identity. Min and Mamie wish to avoid the dangers of the streets, but the practice of domesticity is extremely difficult and ultimately harmful to them. Petry certainly doesn't romanticize street life for a single woman; ultimately, though, she maintains in these two novels that the attempt to perform white domestic ideology destroys the African American family.

Acknowledging the necessity of shelter while critiquing the type of shelter that constitutes the middle-class norm for women, Petry defines home apart from domestic ideology. In their positions at the margins of domesticity, in the space between the home and the street, her minor characters challenge the dichotomies which define society, separating the classes and genders: public vs. private, mobility vs. stasis, single vs. married, Jezebel vs. housewife. Women whose "blues" are caused by a deadly combination of racism, sexism, and poverty cannot act like a man and "catch a freight train," but neither should they "go to their rooms and hide." Rather, they must learn to move between the home (the pure, private domestic space) and the street (the "dirty," communal public arena). Neither space provides them with a home, but the culture and community they find in the street can help them transform domestic ideology to suit their needs, which in turn fortifies them to brave the dangers of the street. Both finally develop their liminal position into a personal security which does not depend on domestic space (and which thus challenges ideas of respectability); in doing so, they achieve a measure of freedom normally accorded only to men.

In mainstream society, the two spheres, home and street, are mutually exclusive to some degree; if a woman has a public, sexual identity, she is by definition not "pure' and private. Min, in fact, initially (and unsuccessfully) attempts to combine these two spheres, as she tries to use her sexuality to keep herself housed and domesticated. Yet Petry's novel indicates that sexual freedom, and thus personal satisfaction, for black women will be achieved only when they are freed from these dualities. Bessie Smith flaunts this freedom in her song, "Tain't Nobody's Business If I Do":

> If I go to church on Sunday,
> Then just shimmy down on Monday,
> Tain't nobody's business if I do do do do.
> (1923)

Her celebration of the seeming incongruity of her behavior reveals that she has managed to create a new version of female identity in which the spiritual comfort of religious practice does not conflict with the sexual delight of "shimmying down" in public clubs. Petry's Mamie also refuses to participate in these dualities, making use of the blues to secure for herself just such an identity; similarly, after seeing a root doctor, Min begins to question domestic ideology and to develop an inner security, an internal "home."

As part of her challenge to bourgeois convention, then, Petry questions the topological basis for the "ideal" home and thus for the "ideal' female identity; if a secured space is prerequisite for both, then how can working-class women achieve either? Analysis of the concept of "home" and house agree that, as Elaine Scarry notes, the walls of the house prevent "undifferentiated contact with the world" and secure "for the individual a stable internal space" in which to develop an identity (38-39). Gaston Bachelard has analyzed the image of the house as "the non-I that protects the I," a protected space (one with great depth and significance in the human imagination) which shelters "daydreaming" and integrates our "thoughts, memories and dreams" (5-6). Using the term "homeplace," bell hooks describes the ideal African-American home as a protected yet communal space where people can be "subjects, not objects" where "black people could affirm one another and by so doing heal many of the wounds inflicted by racist domination" (42, 47). These images of shelter stress the fundamental need for a secure and protected space which can allow the inhabitant to rest, heal, and then to daydream---a space that is typically unavailable to working-class black women for both financial and gender-based reasons (a woman of any class dependent on a man, with or without children, is not guaranteed with safety or privacy). Neither Min nor Mamie owns her home; both live in the homes of others, Min living rent-free in her abusive lover's apartment, and Mamie first living along in a run-down rooming house and then renting rooms (with her family) in Abbie Crunch's house. Without a private space, neither woman can be considered an ideal housewife. Both, however, finally realize that space is not necessary for home.

To construct alternative forms of home that would nurture the kind of "daydreaming" (Bachelard 6) or "affirmation" (hooks 42) they require, Min and Mamie turn to two forms of "low culture," conjure and blues, respectively. Each of these forms was labeled "primitive" by the dominant culture of the time, denoting that those who participate in it are equally primitive, uneducated, and "slavish," characteristics considered inappropriate to the modern era in which Min and Mamie reside.[12] Yet these cultural practices allow Min and Mamie to develop the capacity for reflection and analysis, both of which enable an inner peace and security. Sherley Anne Williams argues that blues songs are themselves "the creation of reflection," that the "blues singer strives to create an atmosphere in which analysis can take place" (125). The typical blues song acts as a reflection on and interpretation of a common social problem, allowing members of the audience to discover themselves mirrored by the singer; they then contemplate the singer's interpretation and develop their own. Root doctors, too, provide a mirror for the problems their clients face by accepting and understanding these problems and drawing on their clients' personal narrative and interpretation in order to develop solutions. They "aid the sufferer in mobilizing his psychological, spiritual, and bodily resources to return to a state of well-being" (Watson 15).[13] Both cultural forms allow poor black women, often kept running after the elusive dream of survival for themselves and their children while fending off pressure and oppression by black and white men, to meditate on themselves and their lives. Blues and conjure are not greatly affected by dominant ideologies such as domesticity or individualism (another ideology Petry critiques in *The Street*), which tend to tear down the confidence of poor women unable to fulfill their tenets and, in fact, tend to interfere with poor women's ability to create adequate homes. Rather, blues, and conjure provide these women with the tools to create alternative versions of home.

While both characters challenge middle-class domestic standards, Min and Mamie are not identical, but rather depict progressively more radical points along a continuum of unconventional female behavior. I argue that this continuum mirrors Petry's own increasing interests in challenging the bourgeois morality of both her protagonists and her readers, and in creating a new space for working-class black women's identity, sexuality, and culture. As Petry's first sexualized female character, Min is initially less interested in breaking rules than in preserving the status quo (her precarious position as working "housewife"). Min is a character in flux; it is only at the end of the novel that she can begin to discard the value system she's absorbed from her white employers and her surroundings, one which finds power in consumerism, domestic improvement, and traditional gender roles. Petry's second novel, *Country Place*, depicts the sexual transgressions of a middle-class white woman, Glory, whose husband Johnnie (also white) has been away fighting the war. The narrator of this novel, a white male druggist, is admittedly "prejudiced against women," considering them to be "closer to the primitive,' so that Glory's extramarital affair marks her as degraded from the narrator's viewpoint. Yet Petry's portrayal of Johnnie's marital rape complicates this judgment; Glory is a victim of domestic ideology even as she breaks its rules.[14] She is more transgressive than Min, but less so than Mamie of *The Narrows*, who has adopted "blues praxis" as her personal philosophy and completely transforms her own household so as to provide herself with maximum pleasure and power. Mamie Smith Powther is a true blues woman, named by Petry after the first recorded blues singer, Mamie Smith.[15] Mamie plays at the role of housewife and mother, but does not absorb domestic values in the process; rather, she adheres to the values of the "street," of the blues singer: in full control of her sexuality, using it to recreate her home. Mamie is an extremely appealing character. This, and the fact that she is able to create a change in the rigid attitudes of her foil, Abbie Crunch, is a mark of the development of Petry's critique of bourgeois values and her support for black working-class cultural products such as blues and conjure.

The blues woman makes use of her voice and her body, aspects of her person traditionally controlled by men, to give herself agency in the public realm; she transforms qualities which have traditionally made her a sexual object into aspects of immense female power. Men in the home train black women to talk what bell hooks calls "the right speech of womanhood" (6). While white women are often overtly silenced, hooks claims, black women are encouraged to speak, but their speech, "is itself a silence" because it is "talking that is simply not listened to," a kind of chattering or nagging ignored by husbands and even children (6-7). The blues woman, in contrast, is paid to sing---her every word is absorbed, repeated, and discussed by her audience. But blues singers put on a physical show as well; the classic blues women of the 1920s were "gorgeous," and their physical presence was both "a crucial aspect of their power" and a "representation of female desire" (Carby, " 'It Jus Be's ' " 247). Flashy and voluptuous, Mamie Powther too is "gorgeous"; according to protagonist Abbie Crunch, she is "young," but has "too much fat around the waist, a soft fleshy, quiet prominent bosom, too much lipstick, a pink beflowered hat, set on top of straightened hair . . . good teeth, even strong" (*The Narrows* 17). Abbie disapproves of Mamie's appearance, which is intended to emphasize her "allure," but she feels drawn to Mamie—perhaps *because* Mamie represents her "female desire" so strongly. Mamie's voice, too, draws attention: "there was music in the woman's voice, a careless, easy kind of music," Abbie notes with irritation (18). As a blues woman, Mamie confronts Abbie's bourgeois sense of decency, but her hypnotic voice and her buxom figure capture Abbie's attention, just as they capture the admiration and desire of everyone else in Monmouth.

Perhaps to minimize the impact of her first sexualized female character, Petry initially portrays Min as insignificant, practically invisible to the other characters and to the reader. Min's strategy for survival has been the opposite of Mamie's; where Mamie commands attention, Min camouflages herself, the better to keep out of range of male violence. Thus in her first appearance in *The Street*, Min (who is not initially given a name) is described by Lutie as "shapeless,' "small," "toothless," and "dark." Lutie is charismatic and strikingly beautiful, thus the description makes Min forgettable as a character (although the word "dark" is a subtle comment on Lutie's colorism). A "shrinking withdrawal in her way of sitting, as though she were trying to take up the least possible amount of space," erases Min from Lutie's consciousness; after a few minutes, Lutie "completely forgot the woman was in the room" (24). The only other time Lutie thinks of Min, she describes her as a "drab drudge so spineless and limp she was like a soggy dishrag" (57). This overdetermined description turns out to be incorrect, as Min's backbone becomes gradually more visible to the reader (if not to Lutie). But apart from her appearance, what signifies Min's class status and value system, and thus allows Lutie to categorize and dismiss her, is her prized possession, her table:

> It was a very large table . . . looking at it
> [Lutie] thought. That's the kind of big ugly
> furniture white women love to give to their
> maids. She turned to look at the shapeless
> little woman because she was almost certain
> the table was hers. (24) [16]

Like Min, Lutie has worked as a domestic, but she has refused to accept unappealing castoffs from her own employer, seeing them as degrading, a sign of "lower-class" culture. Because middle-class readers are accustomed to admire those who share their value systems (even those in the working class, like Lutie) and to ignore "shapeless" and seemingly degraded characters, they too "forget" about Min easily enough. Particularly in novels of social realism,

readers are encouraged to view characters like Min as part of the cultural waste
which the Algeresque hero must transcend.

But Petry does not allow the reader to erase Min so easily, and in giving her a
voice partway through the novel, she forces readers to correct their
preconceptions and acknowledge Lutie's class snobbery, if not their own. What
Lutie doesn't know about Min's table is that its value inheres not in its
appearance, but in its function as a survival mechanism: the "best place to keep
money[Min] had ever found." "Min "loved" the way it looks, "but the
important thing about it was that secret drawer it contained. Until she got the
table she had never been able to save any money . . . the table would protect her
money" from her abusive "husbands" (116). As Bachelard notes, in the poetic
imagination, objects like wardrobes and desks with drawers are "veritable
organs of the secret psychological life" (78). Min's ugly table misleads Lutie
into overlooking Min's "secret psychological life,' one which mirrors Lutie's in
many significant respects. Min's secret drawer shelters her dreams; saving
money is part of her plan to make herself more appealing to men and middle-
class society (she plans to buy false teeth) so that she can achieve a secure
middle-class home---which is what Lutie wants, too. However, Lutie refuses to
see herself reflected in Min, thus losing the chance to develop a friendship that
could have saved Lutie's life from destruction; Min is aware that the Super is
planning to harm Lutie and her son, and although she contemplates exposing
him, she never does so, primarily because of the distance Lutie has placed
between them (114). In this way, Petry forces the reader to see that it is
precisely Lutie's middle-class ambitions which cost her a valuable ally and, as a
result, her own happiness. [17]

Min also comes up short in Lutie's estimation for her apparent lack of
interest in domesticity; Lutie's sense of self-worth depends on having a clean,
comfortable home, and she judges the worth of others on these criteria. Lutie
claims with distaste that nothing has been done to "make [Jones's apartment]
like homelike," a job that clearly falls to Min, the woman of the house (24). Yet
Min is quite interested in the appearance of her home, in part because she wants
"to show how grateful she was" to Jones for letting her live with him rent-free.
She buys "a canary bird and a large ornate cage . . . because she felt she ought to
pretty the place up a little bit." She also cooks and cleans, adhering to
traditional domestic values including being fulfilled simply by Jones' need for
her: "she didn't know when she had ever been so happy" (117). For the greater
part of the novel, Min longs for the resources to fulfill more adequately her
domestic duties, but she succeeds in making the apartment more "homelike"
even without them. Jones admits that when Min had come to live with him two
years previously, "it was kind of cheerful to have her around, she kept the place
from getting so deadly quiet" with her "talking, talking, talking" (98). Min's
attempts to communicate and her cheerful attitude are the makings of a home,
but neither Lutie nor Min can see this because they view themselves and others
through the lens of middle-class domestic ideology.

Having dismissed Min, the reader might be taken aback when Petry gives her a narrative point of view, particularly when it reveals her strength, common sense, and ambition. The first indication of Min's intelligence is, paradoxically, her own awareness that Jones thinks she's stupid: "he don't know me. He thinks I don't know what's the matter with him" (113). And while Min's transgressive sexuality is what most clearly marks her as "degraded," she is relatively unashamed of her sexual unions, calling the men in her life her "husbands" although she knows they are not.[18] While she regrets the way she is forced to live, she doesn't condemn herself as "fallen"; Min is not ignorant of middle-class moral standards, which she certainly respects, but rather she is aware that her own moral standards are derived from a different culture and class. Min's ability to resist some of the aspects of bourgeois ideology that could interfere with her physical and emotional survival eventually prepares her to criticize and even reject that ideology.

At first, however, Min directs her strength and her skills of manipulation and secrecy (derived from her experience of invisibility) toward her goal of entering the middle-class by purchasing its trappings. When Jones develops an obsession with Lutie and decides to get rid of Min, the taste for consumer power Min has developed during two rent-free years drives her to seek help from Mrs. Hedges, the intimidating madam who lives in the building. "I ain't never had nothing of my own before," she says to Mrs. Hedges. "No money to spend like I wanted to." And now that "that Mis Johnson come here to live," Min knows that Jones will "be putting [her] out pretty soon." She vows, " I ain't goin' back to having nothing . . . And I ain't goin' to be put out" (119-20). Min's goal is to prevent Jones from evicting her, not to create a better relationship with him. Her extra money has allowed her to outfit herself and her domestic space with a few middle-class accessories; having created what she sees as a bourgeois-style "nest" for herself in Jones' apartment, she vows to fortify its walls by securing her position there.

Yet Min steps outside the bounds of middle-class moral codes when she takes Mrs. Hedges' suggestion to seek the services of a root doctor, a practitioner of voodoo who combines herbs, roots, and human and animal parts with ceremonies to effect "curses" or "cures" for various ills.[19] Min's solution is thus in tension with her dilemma---how to retain her "bourgeois" domestic space. Petry doesn't comment on or attempt to resolve this contradiction, nor does she use it to portray Min as confused. Min realizes that her preacher would disapprove of her actions, yet she considers conjure to be far more powerful than the church: "even the preacher must know there were some things the church couldn't handle, had no resources for handling. And this was one of them---a situation where prayer couldn't possibly help" (122-23). In acknowledging the church's limitations as a practical source of aid, Min reveals her perhaps unconscious belief that it is a trapping, at least in her life. Nowhere in the novel does she explain the benefits she received in attending church, easily abandoning it for folk remedies in her time of crisis. Petry's narrative silence serves, in my view, as a subtle acceptance of folk belief as a supplement or even an alternative to mainstream Christianity.

Unsurprisingly, dominant society has considered the belief in conjure to be a sign of working-class values, of a lack of education and sophistication. The common "educated" attitude toward practitioners has been that, "overt and natural means of obtaining justice being forbidden," to them, it is natural that, "brought up in ignorance, and trained in superstition, [they] should invoke secret and supernatural powers to redress [their] wrongs" (Bacon and Herron 360). Viewed from a more sympathetic standpoint, however, practitioners of folk medicine are not irrational, but logical in their worldview; they assume "a total coherence in the operation of the world" so that "whatever happened was *caused*," not accidental or random (Jackson 261, his emphasis). The appeal of conjure was the idea that what had been caused could be altered---that circumstances could be controlled by those who were otherwise powerless: "there was no justice in the courts for [poor blacks] and no regular source of financially reasonable medical aid from the white doctors in town" (Jackson 267). Unable to trust any aspect of white-dominated society, believers like Min placed "the most implicit faith in the conjure doctor's power," a faith which frequently allowed conjuration to succeed (Bacon and Herron 361). Because this faith in the power of conjure was shared by those it was used by and against, a good part of its efficacy was psychological; one who knew he had been conjured would manifest the symptoms expected of him. This faith in conjure gave it the power to elude attempts by the dominant belief system to destroy it; belief in conjure because only stronger as it went "underground."

While the use of conjure is not necessarily subversive simply because it is unsanctioned by the dominant culture, Min's use of it constitutes an act of protest. According to John Dollard, magical practices are reformist, not revolutionary: magic "accepts the *status quo*; it takes the place of political activity, agitation, organization, solidarity, or any real moves to change status . . . . Magic, in brief, is a control gesture, a comfort to the individual, an accommodation attitude to helplessness" (qtd. Jackson 267). While Min's use of conjure is initially intended to preserve the status quo, it ultimately alters her view of herself and her society. As she sits in the root-doctor's office, Min realizes that her act of seeking community-based aid for her problem is the "first defiant gesture she had ever made." Going to the root doctor has given her the opportunity to reflect on herself, itself a radical change in her behavior. "Up to now," she realizes, "she had always accepted whatever happened to her without making any effort to avoid as a situation or to change one" (126). "Never once had she protested" the terrible working conditions she experiences as a domestic, or the abuse by her "various husbands" (127). Nor does Min plan to lapse into passivity upon meeting the Prophet David," as the root doctor is known; she analyzes the women around her and the Prophet himself, wondering if he is just "stringing along" the other customers. Min vows that she won't be taken in : she'll "look up another root doctor that was honest" if this one isn't (131). Not only in the process of taking action, but also in the very act of reflection and analysis, Min evolves from a passive person to an active one, from object to subject. Just as she becomes a speaking subject in the narrative when the story shifts to her point of view, we see her develop her subjectivity through the act of reflecting on herself. Min's willingness to use conjure can thus be considered personally "revolutionary."

The root doctor's power lies not only in the manipulation of occult forces, but in the manipulation of the psyches of both customer and "patient" (typically the customer's husband, lover, or relative). For women customers, receiving empowerment from the conjure doctor has an immediate effect that only adds to the "prescription's" effectiveness; Min decides while in the waiting room that the Prophet David at the very least "deserves some credit for making that fidgety woman look so happy" (131). The Prophet effects this transformation by creating a dialogue, what bell hooks defines as "the sharing of speech and recognition," with his customers (6). The Prophet listens to Min's words with attention and respect: his eyes "didn't contain the derisive look [Min] was accustomed to seeing in people's eyes" (133). Min is used to being ignored by men when she speaks "the right speech of womanhood," as are, no doubt, most of the Prophet's other female clients.[20] But talking to the Prophet David is "the most satisfying experience she had ever known . . . the satisfaction she felt was from the quiet way he had listened to her, giving her all of his attention. No one had ever done that before" (136). In creating a dialogue with Min, the Prophet gives her a fuller recognition of her value as a person and reinforces her desire to survive, to outwit Jones.

The powders and potions the Prophet sells to Min aren't simply meant to build her confidence in herself; the Prophet uses the objects to influence the "patient" as well, often to instill a fear of and respect for the customer. The Prophet tells Min that he can't "promise results" on "taking Jones' minds off the young lady" (Lutie), but he can "fix things so [Min] won't be put out" (134). He gives her a glass vial filled with a red liquid that he instructs her to put into Jones' coffee each morning---"just one drop. No more; he also gives her candles to burn, a crucifix to hang over her bed ("to keep [her] safe at night"), and a "very powerful" green powder which will stop Jones "if he gets violent" or if he tries to put her out (135). Finally, he instructs her to "clean the apartment every day . . . until there isn't a speck of dirt anywhere." The Prophet does not explain to Min how any of this functions on either a psychological or a magical level, nor is the magical aspect of the conjure ever made clear in the text, perhaps reflecting Petry's view that conjure's effectiveness is purely psychological. In any case, the conjure works. While Jones is unimpressed by the newfound "energy and firmness about the way" Min walks after her visit to the root doctor, he immediately restrains his violence when he sees the cross she's hung over the bed: "to him a cross was an alarming and unpleasant object, for it was a symbol of power . . . mixed up in his mind with ...the power of darkness it could invoke against those who outraged the laws of the church" (140). When she hangs the cross in the bedroom, Min claims that room, for Jones will no longer enter it. Jones soon begins to hallucinate crosses all over the apartment; combined with Min's cleaning frenzy, these undermine his control of their communal space. Min had "changed lately," Jones realizes: "she dominated the apartment. She cleaned it tirelessly, filled with some unknown source of strength that surged through her" (293). Cleaning gives Min the (obviously limited) power of "homemaker" she craves; instead of being a "shrinking" presence, Min uses conjure to claim a territory for herself---a domestic territory.

Mamie Powther also "dominates" any space she is in "so that you saw nothing but Mamie," but her power to do so comes from her revolutionary attitude toward domesticity and toward the street itself (*The Narrows* 25). After observing Mamie hanging laundry outside the kitchen window, Abbie Crunch, Mamie's very proper landlady, concludes that Mamie is neither maternal nor domestic. Exuding a powerful sexuality, she "simply doesn't belong in that neat backyard with its carefully tended yard and its white fences," that backyard which is the essence of home ownership (25). Abbie feels that it's "somehow natural to eliminate Mrs." from Mamie Powther's name because she doesn't act or appear like "a man's wife, permanently attached," but like "an unattached unwifely female" (25). Here Abbie reproduces the common distinction between "wife" (whose sexuality is contained) and "unwifely female" (whose sexuality is dangerously uncontained). In the final analysis, Mamie represents the street Abbie lives on, which has become a redlight area since she bought the house: "Mamie Powther was Dumble Street" (21).[21] Abbie has dedicated her life to maintaining a strict boundary between her home and the street; with Mamie inhabiting her upstairs apartment, the boundary breaks down and the street takes up residence. "Unwifely" and clearly sexual, Mamie embodies the qualities of the street, yet she appears to be somewhat "domestic," as she tends to the usual activities of a wife and mother (in this instance, doing the laundry). She is no sloven; nor is she a "lady." She is somehow both, and neither.

Through her blues praxis, Mamie breaks boundaries between home and street, between "housewife" and "streetwalker"; she also breaks down the moral and ideological boundaries in other people, luring them into her world of sensuality and pleasure. Mamie's movements and singing are a siren call to Abbie, who tries her best to resist Mamie's influence. Watching Mamie hanging her clothes on the line and listening to her sing, Abbie realizes that "there was an almost hypnotic rhythm about her movements," and that she "couldn't look away" (23).[22] Mamie's voice "seemed to be right there in the kitchen"; it has an "indefinable quality" in it as if the "singer leaned over, close, to say, I'm talking to you, listen to me, I made up this song for you and I've got wonderful things to tell you and to show you, listen to me" (22). Houston Baker notes that a blues singer's song is "an invitation to energizing intersubjectivity," one which draws the audience into a communal sense of identity (5). Mamie's voice penetrates the walls of the kitchen from the outside, breaking through Abbie's reservations to compel her attention. The subject of Mamie's song is itself an invitation---the refrain is "I'm lonesome." Abbie's moral standards and adherence to domestic ideology have made her 'lonesome" by isolating her from most of the neighborhood community. Whether her attraction to Mamie is unconsciously sexual isn't made clear, but she certainly experiences an urge to accept Mamie's invitation, despite the fact that she shares the dominant moral attitude that blues music is not only sinful but of inferior quality: "too loud, too harsh, no sweetness, no tune, simply a reiterated bleating about rent money and men who had gone off with other women, and numbers that didn't come out" (23). Abbie is dismayed to discover that Mamie's presence has begun to change her thought pattern. She observes that the wind lifts the hem of Mamie's dress "as though it peered underneath and liked what it saw and so returned again and again for another look," and then scolds herself for her personification: "what a vulgar idea. I never think things like that" (23). Yet Abbie actually enjoys creating rhymes and images about people she knows; her strong moral feelings about "vulgarity" have prompted her to avoid entire areas of thought which might have expanded her verbal arts and increased her pleasure in them. The reader experiences the influence of Mamie's blues, however subtle, on Abbie as welcome and necessary.

Of course, Mamie's songs invite her listeners not simply to partake in vulgar metaphor, but to partake in sexual relations; yet Petry allows Mamie to transcend the Jezebel stereotype, giving her a female-identified subjectivity rather than a male-identified one. Link Williams, Abbie's adopted son, sees "invitation to Mrs. M. Powther's eyes, in the curve of her mouth, invitation cordially, consciously, graciously extended" (125). Comparing her to both Eve and Venus, "goddess" of love, he decides that while the lyrics of Mamie's song concern "a female who rode on a train, a train that would come back again tomorrow," the "texture of the voice, the ripeness of it told you that there must have been a male aboard that train" (125, 100-1). Link enacts the typical male response to Mamie, viewing her body as oozing invitation and her song as sexual even while she performs household chores like hanging the laundry. However, while Mamie clearly delights in and plays with her ability to attract men of all ages and races, this ability is not her dominant characteristic. More striking to the reader are Mamie's fearlessness, confidence, and healthy appreciation of her own body. Her songs do not mention men, but focus on trains and roads and the women who make use of them, highlighting the singer's freedom to move on at any moment. In giving Mamie mobility, agency, and confidence, Petry insists that Mamie's "allure" is indeed a representation of her own sexual desire and not a self-objectification.[23] She thus breaks with one of the primary conventions of literary representations of women; she gives Mamie sexual and emotional independence and working-class values without punishing her for them.

Ultimately, Mamie disrupts all traditional notions of female identity and "women's place,' combining a decidedly "feminine" personality and appearance with a "masculine" attitude toward relationships, family, and security. When Mamie's husband Powther tells her that he doesn't like Bill Hod, Mamie's "cousin" (read:lover), coming by their apartment so much, Mamie replies calmly, "I'm right fond of him. If you don't like his comin' here, Powther, I can always go live somewhere else" (212). The ease with which she offers to leave her home and family astonishes both Powther and the reader. Mamie has been married to Powther for over nine years and they have three children, yet apparently she would abandon them rather than lose her sexual freedom. Mamie's choice of word reveals her lack of attachment not just to the Powther household, but to domestic space in general. The apartment is just a place where Mamie lives for the time being, and going to live "somewhere else" is always an option---one nearly unthinkable to female readers of the fifties. When Powther panics at the thought of losing her and retracts his comment, Mamie accentuates her threat, singing "same train carry my mother, same train be back tomorrer" (212). Powther dislikes this song, a not-so-subtle insistence on Mamie's freedom, on the train that is always around to take her away. [24] By singing it, Mamie insists that she is elsewhere, unreceptive to Powther's demands: not only is her song her threat to leave, but while she's singing, "he couldn't discuss anything with her that she didn't want to discuss" because "you had to listen" when Mamie sings (209). When she sings the blues, Mamie simultaneously draws her listeners to her and holds them at bay; she breaks down boundaries in others, but preserves a 'home" within herself---a "mobile home." Powther realizes that "if he hadn't packed" the "expensive clothes" he bought Mamie when he was courting her, "she would have left them there in that rooming house in Baltimore" when she married him, "left everything behind her, and never regretted the leaving" (212). Mamie does not seem to put down roots, or to require them; nor does she need possessions or a house. She is adept at creating a home for herself that does not rely on four permanent walls, and she is not afraid of the street.

Possessing a good deal less strength and power than Mamie, Min initially draws on working-class cultural materials in order to preserve her domestic space, but her developing "conjure psychology" allows her first to save her own life and then to rethink her conception of home. When Min unintentionally witnesses Jones committing a crime, Jones becomes enraged and comes after her. As Min prepared herself for "the feel of his heavy hands around her neck," an image of "the big, golden cross" comes to her mind (*The Street* 358). She realizes that "just looking at it never failed to remind her of the Prophet and the quiet way he has listened to her talk" (358). Half-consciously, Min internalizes the Prophet's respect for her, transforming the feeling of recognition she gained from talking to the prophet into an act of self-preservation. She makes "the sign of the cross over her body---a long gesture downward and then a wide, sweeping crosswise movement." The gesture stops Jones in his tracks; he screams "You god damn conjurin' whore!" and leaves the apartment (358-89). With this act of protection, Min holds Jones at bay just long enough to realize that living with him has begun to threaten not just her physical health but her state of mind.

"Lately she couldn't get any air here," she concludes, because Jones' "evilness" and violence have kept her "running, running, running" (362). The constant threat of male violence Min feels from Jones and her previous "husbands" has created a velocity in Min's life which has 'blotted out" her inner vision, her ability to reflect on her own actions and feelings (363). The Prophet restores that ability by giving her the means by which to protect herself from Jones' wrath, forcing him to keep his distance so that she can turn her attention away from her physical safety and toward her emotional state.

In helping Min to establish (if only for a short time) a "protected space" within which she can "affirm" herself and "integrate her thoughts," the Prophet has provided her with the "home" she longed for. With room to reflect on her situation, however, Min concludes that Jones' "constant anger, his sullen silence," has turned her "protected space" into a prison, "like the inside of an oven—a small completely enclosed place where no light ever penetrated" (352). Here Min finds her conception of "home," a "completely enclosed place" safe from the contaminating street, to be a threat rather than a safe haven. Jones is not a welcome inhabitant of her "nest" but rather resembles "some monstrous growth crowding against her" (362). Min realizes that household space can be a dangerous trap for women, and that access to the street---mobility---is of crucial importance.

Min leaves Jones' apartment and the street accompanied by a well-built pushcart man, according to some critics of *The Street* a sign that she is "clearly on her way to another small apartment with another man," that she has learned nothing (Pryse 127). Yet Min's use of conjure and her resulting development of an internal space for reflection, I argue, have given her the tools to create a better home for herself---albeit a home sharing some resemblance with the apartment she has just vacated. Min's financial circumstances and hostile environment have not changed; she is still poor and threatened by homelessness, and the street still isn't "somehow a very good place to live, for the women had too much trouble, almost as though the street itself bred the trouble" (355). Min's analysis perfectly describes the plight of the poor single woman; random male violence, disease, and harsh weather make the street unsafe for her, and because "a woman living along didn't stand much chance" of affording a decent (private and safe) apartment, she is forced to enter equally unsafe domestic arrangements---a fact which goes largely unacknowledged by middle-class society even today. Thus, Min's decision to find another man to live with is not a blind repetition of previous mistakes but an informed determination of her best option; two incomes provide a safety net ("if one got sick the other one could carry on and there'd still be food and the rent would be paid") as well as much – needed sexual and emotional companionship ("it wasn't right for a woman to be sleeping by herself night after night) and make it "possible to have a home . . . an apartment instead of just one hall room and with the table her money would always be safe" (370, 353). Nor does Min's desire for an apartment reflect a continuing attachment to middle-class definitions of home, for in leaving Jones' apartment, she abandons her bourgeois aspirations: "Funny how she got to believe that not having to pay rent was so important, and it really wasn't . . . . Having room to breathe in meant much more" (362). By placing primary importance on "breathing room," on her own peace of mind, she both repudiates materialism and middle-class gender ideology and establishes an inner strength and security that will see her through her next domestic arrangement. She has learned, like Mamie, that if her man threatens her, she can "always go live someplace else."

In *The Street*, Petry doesn't depict a revised version of domestic ideology, only suggesting it as a potential part of Min's future, but in *The Narrows*, she creates an attractive alternative to domesticity which provides a formidable challenge to the domestic ideology practiced by Powther and Abbie Crunch. As a butler, Powther works to create and maintain an immaculate, silent, tastefully furnished home for his wealthy white employers. Yet his own home is the opposite of this---Mamie, he realizes, enjoys "the heat, the light, the confusion, the noise, the boys scuffling on the floor . . . fragrance issuing from the oven . . . over it all the smell of her perfume, too strong" in her kitchen (*The Narrows* 166). As a result, Powther feels "like an alien, a stranger" in his own home. When he arrives after work at the doorway to the "hot, brilliantly lighted, filled-with-food-smell, noisy kitchen," he is startled to notice that the look in his children's "eyes questioned him, challenged his right to enter this place that was the heartbeat of the house, heartbeat pulsing with heat, sound, life" (166). Powther unconsciously senses that Mamie's home is vitally alive whereas his "home," the Treadway mansion, is a model of domestic perfection but lacking in life of any kind. Mamie's home has a "heartbeat" because she performs her domestic tasks with an eye to her own pleasure and fulfillment. When she's happy, the house is a haven of delicious food and playful affection, but when Mamie diets, she's 'so cross, so irritable, that nobody could stay in the house with her" and her sons often have to fend for themselves (167). Mamie creates a home not by giving up her individuality and selfhood (required by common models of marriage and maternity), but by insisting on her right to express her feelings and moods, by being selfish.

Much is made in the novel of Mamie's selfishness. Her openly sexual manner, her not-so-secret affair, and her messy house and seemingly gruff treatment of her children provoke the disapproval of her husband Powther, Abbie, Link, and no doubt even the reader. Yet Powther's attitude toward his wife is not unproblematic, but objectifying; she reminds him of "one of those big women in the paintings" owned by his employer, and he decides at their first meeting that he has "to have her if it . . . cost [him his] job and all [his] savings" (182). Given 1950s gender ideology, one might believe that Petry doesn't intend Powther's attitude about his wife to seem offensive; however, Petry certainly punishes Powther for that attitude by turning the power relations in his marriage upside down. Moreover, Powther derives all of his pleasure in life from his contact with Mamie, and is willing to put up with her unconventional (and hurtful) behavior in order to preserve their marriage:

> I, I, I cuckolded as I am , worried as I often
> am, after a night with you, you, you, soft
> warm flesh, smell of perfume, toosweet,
> toosweet, toostrong deep-soft-cushion feel
> of you, feel of the arms, the legs, the thighs,
> me incased in your thighs, all joy, all
> ecstasy, all pleasure, not caring, forgetting , .
> . . defying Bill Hod, conquering Bill Hod
> and you and the world . . . . (194).

The sexual and sensual ecstasy Powther experiences while "incased" in Mamie's thighs (a female-centered description of sex) return to him the masculine pride he loses whenever Mamie has sex with Bill Hod. To be "feminized" by Mamie, then, is not to be made weak but rather to be "energized" by intersubjectivity" with her (Baker 5). Mamie's refusal to conform to standard feminine modes of behavior may harm her husband's masculine pride, but it also exposes him to a powerful pleasure. This pleasure is visible in his very language, which is reminiscent of the "feminine" style of writing described by Luce Irigaray, in which the writing "privilege[s] . . . things *tactile*, " "*simultaneity,*" the "*fluid,*" and "resists and explodes every firmly established form, figure, idea, or concept," of masculine language (Irigaray 79). Helene Cixous describes feminine writing obliquely as "flying in language," as "jumbling the order of space, . . . disorienting it, . . .changing [it] around . . . dislocating things and values, breaking them all up, emptying structures, and turning propriety upside down" (291). Because this description applies both to Powther's interior dialogue and to Mamie's behavior, I argue that Mamie has achieved Cixous' version of "flying" not in "language" but in action, and that in her sexual contact with Powther, she passes this experience of "femininity" onto him, however briefly. Powther's emasculation by Mamie is matters of home and family upsets him (and no doubt many readers as well), but his experiences of "femininity" during sex with Mamie gives him a life-sustaining pleasure than tends to affirm Mamie's disruption and revision of domestic ideology and gender identity.

Perhaps the most significant sign that Mamie's unconventional views and practices challenge, not reaffirm (through a negative contrast), the status quo is Mamie's "rescue" of Abbie from a life of self-recrimination and loneliness. Having lost her husband because of her obsession with appearances and propriety, and having lost her son in part because she is unable to accept his interracial sexual relationship, Abbie realizes at the novel's end that her carefully maintained house and her adherence to bourgeois values are not only destructive but actually prevent her from creating a true home.[25] She comes to this conclusion because Mamie has broken through her barriers and lured her into her world of "heat, light, confusion, and noise." Abbie enters this messy world unwillingly, telling herself that "it was a mistake to let that woman [Mamie] stay in my house" because "a woman like that always changes things, her mere presence is like water working on stone, slow attrition, finally a groove, stone worn down" (217). But if the "stone" here is Abbie's heart, then Mamie's tradition of sending her son JC down to "Crunch's" kitchen for some "leftovers" has provided a welcome transformation, for it is Abbie's grudging affection for the noisy and dirty JC which eventually gives her a second chance of happiness. Mamie's "sharing" of her son with Abbie might seem purely thoughtless and self-centered, but she actually intends it to change Abbie; she speculates to Powther that Abbie's attempts to educate and reform JC will "work out the other way." By the "time she listens to that jaybird jabber of his, especially walkin' right along the street with him for a half-hour," Abbie will "be talking the same way he does," Mamie predicts (348). And Mamie is right--Abbie is changed by JC. At the novel's end, Abbie is poised to abandon JC, tell him to "run along now," but then, recalling that she abandoned her son Link with the same words, she changes her mind (428). In placing JC's needs before her own sense of propriety, Abbie relinquishes her tight hold on middle-class standards of decency and accepts JC as a part of her "family," an action which transforms her empty house into a home. [26]

John Lukacs argues that the notion of domestic privacy is itself a bourgeois invention, a claim which underlines the bourgeois-centered nature not only of the family and the home but of psychoanalytic theory, which is largely constructed on an image of the psyche as a private "home-like" space.[27] The idea that humans require a secure physical space in which to develop an individual sense of identity is commonplace, but the fact that poor people without access to secure shelter do manage to develop identities reveals that this idea is not "universal" but derived from middle-class ideals of individualism, domestic, ideology, and "home ownership." Social power has everything to do with the control of space, as Houston Baker notes, describing dominant society as "those who maintain place" and tradition, and the "placeless" (the homeless, the "street people") as "fluid, nomadic, transitional" (202). In requiring a secure personal space as the precondition to fully developed humanity, and in choosing women as the custodians of that space, dominant culture controls both working-class and female identity. Part of Petry's accomplishment in *The Street* and *The Narrows* is to portray the identities of poor women, who lack access to secure personal space, *not* as flawed or insufficiently developed (except when they attempt to conform to bourgeois ideals), but as powerful and vital (particularly when they can be sustained by their working-class culture and community). Petry's Min may be the only female character in American literature up to 1946 to disregard both bourgeois sexual codes and Christian religious beliefs and be rewarded for her behavior with the promise of a better life. In Mamie, Petry creates a wife and mother who is immune to the lure of consumerism and to domestic ideology because home is not as important to her as personal freedom and mobility.[28] She transcends the "home/street" (place/placeless) duality altogether by constructing her identity around her own sensual and emotional pleasure and moving freely between home and street, fully self-possessed in either world. With these characters, Petry has engaged in a labor of cultural reformulation, challenging traditional models of gender and class by drawing on working-class cultural practices to create a new model of female identity.

---

[1] While I claim that most black female writers of the late nineteenth and early twentieth centuries were reticent on the subject of sexuality, I realize both that there are exceptions to this rule, and that white women writers too were reluctant to allow their female protagonists any kind of active sexuality (and were attacked if they did so, as was Kate Chopin in reviews of *The Awakening).* For further discussion of the topic of black women writers' portrayals of black female sexuality, see Hazel Carby, *Reconstructing Womanhood* (New York: Oxford University Press, 1987); Pamela E. Barnett, " 'My Picture of You Is, After All, the True Helga Crane': Portraiture and Identity in Nella Larsen's Quicksand." *Signs: Journal of Women in Culture and Society* 20 (1995): 575-600); and Deborah McDowell, "Introduction." *Quicksand and Passing* by Nella Larsen. (New Brunswick, NJ: Rutgers University Press, 1986, ix-xxxv).

[2] Very few politically active black female characters are unmarried in novels of this time period, and none of those is presented as sexual (even Candace, the Ethiopian queen of Pauline Hopkins' *Of One Blood: The Magazine Novels of Pauline Hopkins* (New York: Oxford Univerity Press, 1988), is a virgin awaiting her king), revealing an author's adherence to the conventional belief that marriage protects women from sexual danger. Witness Janie Crawford's grandmother's belief in the iron-clad reputation that a "good marriage" provides to a black woman: Nanny claims that, once married, Janie will no longer be in danger of rape by a white man.

[3] The term "outdoors" is borrowed from Toni Morrison's *The Bluest Eye.*

[4] While Larsen's novel does include an attention to class (Helga's marriage to a rural preacher effectively places her in the working class, which only increases her domestic burdens), I would argue that the economic oppression is not a central issue in this novel.

[5] As Barnett has argued in her study of Nella Larsen's *Quicksand,* "there is no mode of representation of any legitimate space within society in which black women's sexuality can be expressed" because the only available representations at that time were "racist depictions of primitive sexuality and reactionary portraits of desexualized bourgeois black women" (580). My point is not only that Petry challenged both of these representations but that she did so in such a way that her readers have not commented on it. Critics such as Mary Helen Washington, *Invented Lives: Narratives of Black Women 1860-1960* (New York: Doubleday, 1987), Beatrice Horn Royster, "The Ironic Vision of Four Black Women Novelists: A Study of the Novels of Jessie Fauset, Nella Larsen, Zora Neale Hurston, and Ann Petry," Ph.D. diss. Emory University, 1975, and Thelma J. Shinn, "Women in the Novels of Ann Petry," *Critique* 16 (1974): 110-20, have not recognized Petry's support for female sexual expression, almost replicating traditional views of black female sexual identity in their

comments on Petry's characters Min and Mamie: "sexually liberated and aggressive" and therefore "vicious," "degenerate," and "debase[d]" (Royster 186-87); "powerless as well as amoral" (Washington 391); and even "passive victims of the feminine mystique (Shinn 114).

[6] As Giles Oakley, (*The Devil's Music: A History of the Blues.* New York: Taplinger Publishing, 1977), explains "for those who tried to maintain an ordered goodness, a recognized accepted shape of action in life that would bring freedom at least in death [the blues] was *the devil's music*" (is his emphasis).

[7] While there were dangers to this sexually free blues persona and the "blue" lyrics of their songs, which could combine to "become a burlesque of African-American sexuality," this kind of exploitation typically resulted from the white music industry's manipulation of the singers and the recordings (William Barlow, *"Looking Up at Down": The Emergence of Blues Culture.* Philadelphia: Temple University Press, 1989, 142.)

[8] Although blues music was popular to some extent with whites in its early years, this was due primarily to the white-controlled record industry, which "liked to record white performers' 'cover' versions of popular blues to entice that white public to buy the records and to 'upgrade' the music." The industry was thus able to "bring African-American music more into line with European musical conventions, while superimposing on it a veneer of middle-class Angle-American respectability" (Barlow 124).

[9] MaRainey considered her physical appearance as important as her voice: her "stage appearance was legendary," and she was "a flamboyant dresser" who wore "outrageous costumes and expensive jewelry to shows" (Barlow 157).

[10] While it is true that self-objectification is inherent in the entertainment business and is thus not necessarily peculiar to one race or gender, I would argue that the historical context here makes the blues singer's performance of allure more risky than for a white male, for example.

[11] Washington's account of Petry's women characters reveals the effects of this narrative circumscription; Washington (like Petry's protagonist Lutie) omits any consideration of Min; she also claims that Mamie is "powerless as well as amoral" because she is only seen by the reader "as framed in her husband's gaze" (300-1), This assessment isn't accurate, since readers are introduced to Mamie's point of view in the last quarter of the novel; more importantly, though, it reveals that Washington's reading is controlled by the viewpoints of the protagonists.

[12] The blues have "always tended to be associated with roughness and a lack of 'class' "by middle-class and educated blacks, a reminder of the slave and rural folk culture from whch the music emerged and of the underworld culture in which it trived (Giles Oakley, *The Devil's Music: A History of the Blues,* New York: Taplinger Publishing, 1977, 110). Similarly, people who frequented root doctors were looked on as "primitive and uneducated" and their beliefs to be "a matter for some shame and a throwback to the days of servitude" (Paul Oliver, *The Meaning of the Blues,* Toronto: Collier, 1960, 176, 156); for example, in each of his autobiographies (specifically, in his discussion of the root Sandy

gives him), Frederick Douglass marks conjure as part of a primitive, heathen African culture inferior to Western culture.

[13] For another essay which treats the use of conjure in African-American literature, see Helen Jaskoski, "Power Unequal to Man: The Significance of Conjure in Works by Five Afro-American Authors." *Southern Folklore Quarterly* 38.2 (1974):91-108.

[14] Johnnie repents his rape of his wife, which complicates the reader's tendency to feel that Glory "deserves" to be raped. Because her characters in this novel are white, Petry can explore Glory's sexual behavior and subsequent victimization without worrying that she will damage the public image of black women. However, *Country Place* has long been excluded from the "black canon" precisely because it is about whites. DuCille has developed these ideas further in "Canon Fodder: Rape and Resistance in 'Non-Traditional' Texts of the 1940s" (a paper given at MLA Convention, Toronto, 27 December 1993).

[15] According to Oliver, "the first vocal recording to employ a blues form" was "Crazy Blues" sung by Mamie Smith, recorded 10 August 1920 (21).

[16] Min's and Mamie's status as working women is signified immediately to Lutie and Abbie by their bunions, physical evidence of long hours on their feet and ill-fitting shoes. Not surprisingly, Lutie doesn't have bunions, which reveals the depth of her refusal to accept a working-class identity.

[17] Further complicating the reader's identification strategies, Petry depicts Lutie as having natural talent as a blues singer; this makes it less easy for the reader to blame Lutie's problems on her disdain for working-class culture. In a decidedly Algeresque moment, Lutie is "discovered" singing to herself at the neighborhood bar by a blues musician, Boots Smith, who offers her first an audition, and after the audition, a job. Boots plans to extort sex from Lutie as payment for the job, but Lutie is "certain" she can "put him off deftly, neatly, and continue to do it until she sign[s] a contract" (227). She believes, in other words, that she can engage with the working-class world but escape its power dynamics and immorality. However, her hopes are crushed by Junto, the white owner of the bar and the blues club as well as Boots' boss. After spotting Lutie singing in the bar, Junto decides that Lutie will become his mistress in exchange for being paid to sing. When Lutie rejects this offer, and goes to an agent for another audition, she gets the same line. In response, she throws an inkwell at the white agent, thinking, "this is the superior race" (322). It is not only Lutie's middle-class morality that determines her actions here, but also the economic power of white men; in an inversion of the Alger myth, Lutie's talent and beauty do not enable her to transcend her conditions, but rather lead to the destruction of her already meager life.

[18] A study of Kathy Peiss (" 'Charity Girls' and City Pleasures: Historical Notes on Working-Class Sexuality," 163, edited by Ellen Carol DuBois and Vicki L. Ruiz. *Unequal Sisters: A Multi-Cultural Reader in U.S. Women's History* (New York and London: Routledge, 1990), indicates that this lack of shame was not uncommon among working class women, many of whom believed that "respectability was not predicated on chastity."

[19] Conjure or voodoo is practiced in the United States today, although its specific techniques vary from place to place. As Hurston (*Mules and Men.* 1935. New York: Harper and Row, 1970) notes, "nobody knows for sure how many thousands in America are warmed by the fire of hoodoo, because the worship is bound in secrecy. It is not the accepted theology of the Nation and so believers conceal their faith . . . . Nobody can say where it begins or ends. Mouths don't empty themselves unless the ears are sympathetic and knowing" (185). For information on conjure or voodoo, see Hurston; Wilbur H. Watson (*Black Folk Medicine: The Therapeutic Significance of Faith and Trust.* New Brunswick and London: Transaction Books, 1988); Harry Middleton Hyatt, *Hoodoo-Conjuration-Witchcraft-Rootwork.* Hannibal, MO: Western Publishing, 1970; and Newbell Niles Puckett, *Folk Beliefs of the Southern Negro,* 1928. New York: Negro Universities Press, 1968).

[20] Jones compares Min's conversation to a "tortuously winding path that continually turned back on itself, disappeared in impenetrable thickets, to emerge farther on at a sharp angle having no apparent relation to its original starting point" (295). As readers, we never experience this kind of conversation first-hand, which might lead us to assume that Jones *causes* Min to speak this way by not listening.

[21] Earlier in the novel, the nighttime version of Dumble Street is described as "all light and shadow, all murmur of voices and ripple of laughter" (126). This description gives Dumble Street a beauty exemplified by its communal nature, by the interactions of the people who live on it. Similarly, Mamie could be said to practice intersubjectivity, seen in her blues signing and in her strong connections with her culture and community.

[22] Bessie Smith, too, broke down boundaries through combining elements of apparently competing cultural practices. Although "many churchgoers condemned the blues as sinful," the blues and gospel are similar styles, and Bessie drew on this similarly in her performances: she "did the same thing on stage" as "people like similarity in her performances: she "did the same thing on stage" as "people like Billy Graham" and could "bring about mass hypnotism" at her performances (Oakley 1).

[23] Petry insists on Mamie's subjectivity even as she is being objectified; Al, the Treadway chauffeur, sees "a curvy colored wench" (Mamie) on Dumble Street,and calls to her to come over. She turns and smiles "straight at him" but shakes her head, leaving Al to think "I'da paid good money for a piece of that" (215). Instead of ending the scene here, from Al's perspective, Petry shifts to "Mrs. Mamie Powther," who says to herself, "wonder where that big one came from," a smile playing around her mouth and in her eyes. Petry highlights both Mamie's status as wife and her freedom to be interested in another man's attentions.

[24] Powther thinks this song is "a spiritual," but Mamie "made it sound like the kind of song they banned on the radio" (209). While gospel and blues are musically related, I contend that Mamie's reinterpretation of a religious song

about the journey to heaven as a blues song about a woman's (sexual) freedom is natural given her refusal to suppress the sexual aspect of her identity.

[25] Perhaps because of Abbie's insistence on maintaining a distance between herself and Mamie, Mamie doesn't feel the kind of connection to Abbie and to her son Link which might have led her to intervene in a misunderstanding between Link and Camilo, Link's white girlfriend, a misunderstanding which leads directly to Link's murder.

[26] What makes Abbie's acceptance of JC even more subversive to Abbie's standards of decency are the hints Petry plants in the text indicating that JC is not Powther's son, but Bill Hod's. When Abbie first meets JC, she is "certain she'd seen the little boy somewhere" (13). Later, Mamie thinks to herself that "Crunch is . . . awful good to JC. I hope she never finds out Bill comes over here so much" (294). I suggest that Mamie links her affair with Bill to JC's relationship with Abbie because if Abbie finds out that Mamie is having an affair with Bill, she might realize why JC looks so familiar.

[27] John Lukacs ("The Bourgeois Interior." *The American Scholar* 39 (1970):616-30) defines the word "bourgeois" as pertaining to a philosophy of "freedom," "permanent residence," and "security" (620). The "Bourgeois Age" (1450-1950), he claims, is marked by the "internal deepening of human consciousness" and thus by an increasing concern with "interiority," comfort, contemplation, and privacy (622). One example of Freud's spatalized description of the psyche is his description of trauma as "a breach in an otherwise efficacious barrier against stimuli," as "excitations from outside" which "are powerful enough to break through the protective shield" (*Beyond the Pleasure Principle*. Ed. James Strachey. New York: Norton, 1961); another is his description of the "uncanny," which in German translates as "unhomelike" (*unheimlich*), as an alien presence which reintrudes into and disturbs the mind after having been repressed or expelled from it ("The Uncanny." *The Complete Psychological Works of Sigmund Freud*. Ed. James Strachey. Vol 17. London: Hogarth Press, 1962, 241).

[28] Mamie's privileging of mobility is visible both in her behavior and in her songs, which are about roads and trains ("same train carry my mother, same train back tomorrer" and "tell me what color an' I'll tell you what road she took"), images normally associated with men but reclaimed by female blues singers "as a sign that women too were on the move" (194, 109; Hazel Carby, " 'It Jus Be's Dat Way Sometime' In DuBois and Ruiz, 243).

The "Walking Wounded": Rethinking Black Women's Identity in Ann Petry's
. *The Street*
Carol E. Henderson

> It is a peculiar sensation, this double
> consciousness, this sense of always looking
> at one's self through the eyes of others, of
> measuring one's soul by the tape of a world
> that looks on in amused contempt and pity.
>
> W. E. B. DuBois, *The Souls of Black Folk*
>
> We wear the mask that grins and lies,
> It hides our cheeks and shades our eyes, ---
> This debt we pay to human guile;
> with torn and bleeding hearts we smile,
> And mouth with myriad subtleties.
>
> Paul Laurence Dunbar, "We Wear The
> Mask"

"Face," writes Gloria Anzaldua, "is the surface of the body that is the most noticeably inscribed by social structures, marked with instructions on how to be *mujer, macho*, working class, Chicana.   As mestizas---biologically and/or culturally mixed---we have different surfaces for each aspect of identity, each inscribed by a particular subculture.   We are 'written' all over, or should I say, carved and tattooed with the sharp needles of experience" (xv).   Here, Anzaldua speaks of the body as a patchwork of integral parts, a maze of topographical signifiers that represent the intimate aspects of our identity.   This is the landscape through which we view our human experience.

In this essay, I will probe the social landscape of the body in Ann Petry's *The Street*, paying particular attention to the ways in which the body---as material substance---interacts with other social structures.   "The more we understand about the body," writes Paula Cooey, "the more we understand about the role it plays as object of and vehicle for the social construction of reality [. . .]" (5).   To this end, Cooey proposes that we think of the body as "a battleground for mapping human values as these are informed by relations of and struggles for power" (9).   Encompassing conceptions of the body posited by Anzaldua and Cooey, Melvin Dixon reminds us in *Ride Out The Wilderness* that "images of physical and spiritual landscapes [. . .] reveal over time a changing topography in black American quests for selfhood [. . .].   Images of land and the conquest of identity serve as both a cultural matrix among various texts and a distinguishing feature of Afro-American literary history" (xi).   A close examination of Petry's novel reveals how these notions of selfhood, identity and landscape shape our understanding of the body as these same properties also frame a context for understanding African American female subjectivity in the urban setting. Considered by some to be a poor imitation of Richard Wright's *Native Son*, Petry's novel has been critically eclipsed by what Bernard Bell calls the misrepresentation of her talent. "Whether valid or not," Bell concludes, "these critical views do not adequately express the complexity and distinctiveness of Ann Petry's aesthetic vision and achievement" (105). This "aesthetic vision" includes, in my estimation, a substantive focus on the body as text. Petry presents an array of women who have, by some degree or another, been traumatized or "tattooed" by their experience in the city. Petry herself is quoted as saying her characters are the "walking wounded" ("Ann Petry" 253); they are marked, I argue, by the prejudices of race, class, and gender, and bruised by the many systems of oppression that relegate them to poverty, obscurity, and even death. I will explore the figurative and literal boundaries of these wounds, suggesting alternative ways to view the subtle and not so subtle ways women are examined or perceived through the veil of bodily (im)perfection. In finding those places of refuge and regeneration Dixon so clearly articulates in his study, I too hope that my explorations of place and space will lead to "the discovery and the performance of identity" (xi) as seen in Petry's novel.

The Street

> A crowd of people surged in to the Eighth Avenue express at 59th Street. By elbowing other passengers in the back, by pushing and heaving, they forced their bodies into the coaches, making room for themselves where no room had existed before. As the train gathered speed for the long run to 125th Street, the passengers settled down into small private worlds, thus creating the illusion of space between them and their fellow passengers. The worlds were built up behind newspapers and magazines, behind closed eyes or while staring at the varicolored show cards that bordered the coaches.
> ---Ann Petry, *The Street*

The title of Petry's novel is as important a dynamic in the study proposed here as it is in the structure of the narrative itself. Petry's personification of the street as a shrewd and willing ally to the wind, who "lift[s] Lutie Johnson's hair away from the back of her neck so that she fe[els] suddenly naked and bald" (2), details the street's ability to literally and figuratively change the dynamic of the body. As an institution, the street functions outside of mainstream society, creating its own microcosm within the infrastructures of larger social systems; it is often depicted as a university of higher learning, lawless and brutal in the punishment it yields to those who fail to learn from its "hands-on" training. Literary examinations of this cultural phenomenon vary depending on the writer's interest or perspective. Author James Alan McPherson, for example, characterizes the street as a site that seeks to silence women. In his brief narrative, "A Story of A Scar," women remain nameless, and their scars become the mnemonic devices that tell their stories.[1] In *sassafrass, cypress & indigo,* author Ntozake Shange depicts the street as a place where girls must protect their budding femininity from men who 'want to know what [they feel] like" (29). Here, Shange underscores the precarious position of young women who not only battle racial, economic, and sexual oppression in this space, but who also negotiate sexual landmines that would have them compromise their physical as well as their emotional and spiritual integrity. In Petry's novel, the street is portrayed as a prominent force, one that

> turned Pop into a sly old man who drank too much; had killed Mom off when she was in her prime [. . .] made the Mrs. Hedges who sat in the street-floor window turn to running a fairly well-kept whorehouse; and the superintendent of the building---well, the street had pushed him into basements away from light and air until he was being eaten up by some horrible obsession; and other streets had turned Min, the woman who lived with him, into a drab drudge so spineless and so limp she was like a soggy dishrag. (56-57)

These illustrations suggest that in the street, individual existence is predetermined by mitigating factors that affect not only how people live but also how their identities are constructed in the public and private spheres.

It hardly needs stating that the street---as national and cultural symbol---evokes strong sentiment from writers and critics alike. African American writers in particular have used this powerful image as a literary trope to ground their discussions of race, class, and gender. As Shange, McPherson, and others demonstrate, these instances provide the most stimulating view of cultural recreation, as the quest for dignity and selfhood become the impetus for a restructuring of African American subjectivity grounded in a concern for economic, social, and political equality. Moreover, this persistence in acquiring a (political) voice through the assertion of writing creates an emancipatory spirit that fuses feeling into action, and helps the disempowered see their circumstances differently and act to change them. As Henry L. Gates reiterates,

"The will to power for black Americans [is] the will to write; and the predominant mode that this writing [. . .] assumes[s] [is] the shaping of a black self in words" (3). This impulse to testify, to fashion a public self in language that protests dehumanizing conditions, undergirds the potency of African American writing and its ability to transform delimiting systems of critical interpretation through creativity and innovative ways of thinking.

In a provocative and underutilized study, Gaston Bachelard suggests that "the essence of life is but a feeling of participation in a flowing onward necessarily expressed in terms of time and secondarily expressed in terms of space" (201). One can extend this to argue that the life Bachelard speaks of is the life of the literary text---the living, breathing words of expression inherent in the text. Enclosed in the perimeters of this sphere are space and its extension, imagination, which operate as tools of implementation to express the inexpressible. Bachelard goes on to say that "poetic space, because it is expressed, assumes values of expansion" (201). That is, poetic space allows characters the opportunity to uniquely define themselves within the space of the novel. Broadening Bachelard's theory of textual expansion, Houston Baker argues that "where Afro-American women's expressivity is concerned, the particular construction and accountability of the critic must allow him or her to negotiate metalevels of space, place, and time in order to figure forth a new expressive world [. . .]" (50).

Thus Baker deems the critic responsible for proposing alternative ways to view African American female expression in the literary imaginary. I further suggest that this "new expressive world" Baker speaks of allows the observer to view phenomenologically the ways in which female characters express themselves through their interaction with their environment. "After all," Baker continues, "phenomenology seeks to move transcendentally beyond indicative signs that govern 'ordinary communication' [. . .]" (53). Thus one can presuppose that "the condition of possibility of movement" affords the voiceless individual the opportunity to gain a voice, "affirmed by sight or vision or touch" (72). In Petry's novel, these sensory mechanisms provide an arena for her characters to move from voicelessness to voice, and from invisibility to visibility, as they contend with the dehumanizing and often stifling conditions of the street.

Shapeless Forms

> Next to the sofa there was an overstuffed chair and she drew her breath in sharply as she looked at it, for there was a woman sitting in it, and she had thought that she and the dog and the Super were the only occupants of the room. How could anyone sit in a chair and melt into it like that? As

> she looked, the shapeless small dark women
> in the chair got up and bowed to her without
> speaking.   Lutie nodded her head in
> acknowledgment of the bow, thinking, That
> must be the woman I heard whispering. The
> woman sat down in the chair again. Melting
> into it. Because the dark brown dress she
> wore was almost the exact shade of the dark
> brown of the upholstery and because the
> overstuffed chair swallowed her up until she
> was scarcely distinguishable from the chair
> itself.   Because, too, of a shrinking
> withdrawal in her way of sitting as though
> she were trying to take up the least possible
> amount of space. So that after bowing to her
> Lutie completely forgot the woman was in
> the room, while she went on studying its
> furnishings.
> ---Ann Petry, *The Street*

At first glance, the character of Min---the woman in the chair---appears to be
of little importance.   Arguably, *The Street* revolves around the life of Lutie
Johnson, a single African American mother, whose futile attempts to escape the
poverty of New York's inner city provides the most startling example of the
corrosive effects of racism and poverty on the human psyche.   Much of the
criticism of this novel focuses on these aspects of the narrative.[2] Additionally,
when critics consider the personal struggles of other characters in this novel,[3]
Min gets little or no attention as a character of any theoretical significance. She
is overlooked, her presence veiled by the fact that she does not wish to pursue
the "American Dream."[4] Min instead dreams of finding a place---a safe space---
to exist free of pain or danger.   These attributes make Min an unattractive
character for some to analyze because on the surface she seems to embody the
typical characteristics of the submissive woman.   Yet, in my effort to
demonstrate that, on many levels, the body is voice, and *this* voice determines
whether one is seen or heard within the context of the competing forces of the
city, these were the very properties that drew me to take a closer look at her as a
character.[5]

As the above epigraph illustrates, when Min is first noticed she is neither
seen nor heard. Her body is void of any noticeable expression or form. She has,
in essence, become part of the environment.   Yet as Lutie continues to survey
the Super's apartment, one item---the table---"speaks" to her and causes her to
return her attention to Min: "opposite the sofa an overornate table shone with
varnish. It was a very large table with intricately carved, claw feet and looking
at it she thought that's the kind of big ugly furniture white women love to give
their maids. She turned to look at the shapeless little woman because she was

almost certain it was hers [. . .] (24). Min takes on ghostlike features as she is constantly referred to in these passages as "shapeless." And although she wishes to remain invisible, Min's desire is circumvented by the relationship she shares with the table.

Min's connection to her table becomes more intriguing when one takes Baker's theory of the (inter)relation of material or medium in space and examines how communication occurs between an object and a corresponding literary character. Bachelard, whose works inform Baker's ideas in *Working of the Spirit*, theorizes that "to give an object poetic space is to give it more space than it has objectivity; or better still, it is following the expansion of its intimate space" (202). Therefore, as the object retains its aesthetic boundaries, it transcends this space to become an extension or expansion of its owner's space. If "medium" is "an agency, such as a person, object, or quality, by means of which something is conveyed, accomplished, or transferred" (Baker 77), Min's table transfers the power of space and voice to her, accomplishing visibility for a woman who seeks invisibility. Min and the table seem, to reverse their roles in this instance as Min becomes the object, and the table the speaking subject. This relationship foreshadows the interaction of person and medium throughout the remainder of the novel, for in moments that would suggest a confrontation with individuals hostile and invasive of Min's personal space, Min's table speaks for her and challenges the individual for her, eliminating any chance of recourse.

Min's life, as described in the novel, is one of dependency on others who are often abusive. Jones, her current live-in companion, detests the sight of Min after Lutie Johnson moves into the building. In one instance, Jones brutally slaps and kicks Min "just like she was the dog" because, in her view, 'he had been comparing the way she looked from behind with the way the young Mrs. Johnson would look if she should stoop over" (117-18).[6] Min endured similar atrocities at the hands of her former husband, Big Boy, who would use her hard-earned money to fuel his drinking habit. It was at this time in Min's life that the table became her salvation, her protector. "She loved its smooth shiny surface and the way the curves of the claw feet gleamed when light struck them." But more importantly, the table contains a secret drawer that allows her to hide her money from her abusive partners. "Until she got the table she had never been able to save money." For Min, this table represents the site where she achieves independence within her dependent, co-addictive relationships. Min confronted Big Boy "with this table" because it frustrated him. "That was really why he had left her" (116). With Jones, who does not ask for money but, instead, encourages Min to move in with him, the table epitomizes presence, for it creates its own space and identity within the small apartment he and Min share on 116th street.

In assessing the intimate relationship she shares with her table, one can see how it encourages Min's development as a woman and as an individual. In protecting her money from her abusive partners, Min possesses the power to reverse her cycle of economic dependency.[7] This relationship also facilitates Min's movement from silence to voice, and from submission to self-confidence. With the money she saves in the secret drawer, Min acquires the economic freedom to "buy" her voice. This metamorphosis begins when Min purchases conjuring materials from the prophet David, the first man who allows her the opportunity to speak: "Tell me about it, 'the prophet said again [. . .] his manner was so calm and so patient that without further thinking about it she started talking" (133).

The confidence Min gains from this encounter is twofold. Her discussion with the prophet frames a cultural dialogue between two aspects of spirituality found in the African American community: that of conjure (rooted in African culture), and that of Christian theology (rooted in Euro-American culture). This dialogue does not necessarily imply that these religious practices are mutually exclusive. Nor does it suggest that one form of spirituality is uninfluenced by the other. Rather, this conversation makes clear that in some cases, Christian theology is not only privileged over other forms of religious expressions rooted in African culture, but it may even conflict with the spiritual needs of the individual seeking assistance from the community. Min's struggle to reconcile herself to these two forms of religious expression underscores her internal conflict over whom she should go to for help. "The preacher at the church she went to would certainly disapprove" of her going to see a root doctor, for her choice implies that "the powers of darkness [are] stronger than the powers of the church" (122). Although Min seldom goes to church, she feels "a little guilty" seeking the aid of the prophet. Yet, as Min concludes, "even the preacher must know there were some things the church couldn't handle, had no resources for handling. And this was one of them---a situation where prayer couldn't possibly help [. . .]" (22-23).

Embedded in this remark is Min's sense that her live-in relationship with Jones (a "sin" in the Christian theological sense) places her outside the reach of God's love, and outside the church's ark of safety. Prophet David does not judge her, and consequently Min's relationship with him differs greatly from the ones she has had with preachers in the past. "The few times she had a chance to talk to the preacher at the church, he interrupted her with, "We all got our troubles, Sister. We all got our troubles.' And he, too, turned away" (317). Min's ability to speak to someone who would listen to her recite her innermost fears empowers her to think about her own well being for the first time in many years. It is this encounter that forces Min to consciously rethink the way she sees herself within her immediate environment. Her initial attempt to refigure this space and claim the right to be develops when she returns from her visit with the prophet:

> Normally Min's key was inserted in the lock
> timidly, with a vague groping movement,
> and when the lock finally clicked back, she

> stood there for a second as though
> overwhelmed by the sound it made. This
> key was being thrust in with assurance, and
> the door was pushed open immediately
> afterward. [Jones] frowned as he listened
> because on top of that she slammed the
> door. Let it go out of her hand with a bang
> that echoed through the apartment and in the
> hall outside, could even be heard going
> faintly up the stairs [. . .]. (138-39)

The pivotal scene marks the end of Min's desire to be invisible, voiceless, and submissive. Her actions transcend all spaces, those in the apartment and those in the hallway. Min is heard. Subsequently, Min's newly acquired voice and identity forces her to leave Jones, for her presence in his apartment disrupts its previous order. Min realizes that staying with Jones would only create a desire in him to suppress and violently extinguish her new found voice: "He would probably kill her, she thought, and she waited for the feel of his heavy hands around her neck, for the violence of his foot [. . .] she knew how it would go, for her other husbands had taught her: first, the grip around the neck that pressed the windpipe out of position, so that screams were choked off and no sound could emerge from her throat" (357). Thus Min escapes to the street that gave her voice, keeping her table because "with the table her money would always be safe" (371).

Min's absence has a profound affect on Jones. Obviously, he no longer has a person upon whom he can vent his anger. But more specifically, in reflecting upon the arguments proposed in this essay, Min's table is emblematic of her absence or presence in Jones's personal space. In a passage where he feels threatened that Min will leave him, Jones concludes, "[S]he hadn't walked out. She'd be coming back. For the big shiny table with the claw feet was still there against the living-room wall" (112). Conversely, when Min does leave, Jones has difficulty filling the void that she and her table leave in his apartment: "[He pushes] the easy-chair over against the wall [. . .] where the table used to stand, dissatisfied. It couldn't begin to take the place of the table; instead it emphasized the absence of the gleam and shine of the table's length [. . .]" (375). Even in her absence, Min "speaks" to Jones, altering his physical as well as his mental "space." This encounter reinforces Jones's own feelings of inadequacy within the larger social structure of the street as the emphasis is placed, in this instance, on the value of space, and the importance of material possessions---two things Jones lacks in his own life. Disempowered and emasculated, Jones is left wandering the hallways of an apartment building he will never own, working towards a goal he will never achieve.

Min's table is intricately connected to her intimate space because it helps her create a voice and identity in *The Street*. With the action of hiding her money,

Min not only gains economic independence, but in a small sense, she acquires a self-assuredness that enables her to transform her abusive situation.   Her movement from invisibility to visibility, submission to self-confidence, and finally voicelessness to voice, provides an unsettling story of triumph and determination as a counter to Lutie's failure.[8] Min creates her own identity and is seen and heard.   Her narrative illustrates the contradictory impulse of the street as both a delimiting and immeasurable space.   In determining the varying dimensions of this site, it becomes evident that in order to be recognized as an individual, one must create a space where one can develop a self---vocalized and uniquely identified---within the context of one's immediate milieu.

Seared Bodies

> Lutie's mouth closed.   She had never seen Mrs. Hedges outside of her apartment and looked at closely she was awe-inspiring. She was almost as tall as the Super, but where he was thin, gaunt, she was all hard, firm flesh---a mountain of a woman.   She was wearing a long-sleeved, high-necked flannelette nightgown.   It was so snowy white that her skin showed up intensely black by contrast.   She was barefooted.   Her hands, her feet, and what could be seen of her legs were a mass of scars---terrible scars. The flesh was drawn and shiny where it had apparently tightened in the process of healing [. . .].   And watching the wide, full nightgown as it moved gently from the draft in the hall, Lutie thought Mrs. Hedges had the appearance of a creature that had strayed from some other planet.
> ---Ann Petry, *The Street*

Like Min, place and space are what define the life of Mrs. Hedges.   Her narrative offers the most vivid illustration of obtaining voice and visibility through the social landscape of the body.   Similarly, it is her rise to "overlord" of the street that presents the most compelling example where scarring of the body is directly attributed to class mobility and economic development and gain. For Mrs. Hedges, these developments materialize because her body, as scar, speaks to her indomitable spirit, and she, in turn, is able to use her body as a site for self-evaluation and self-redefinition.

The body, as sign or language, functions under the auspices of the visual, and it is in determining how the body is viewed that the process of self-creation occurs.   Mrs. Hedges understands the power of sight and how it relates to the concepts of invisibility and visibility. Doubly marked by her blackness and her disfigurement, Mrs. Hedges embodies two states of being---she is both seen (as a thing/object) and not seen (as a human being/subject). As the narrator relates, "[W]hen she had haunted employment agencies seeking work [. . .] there was an uncontrollable revulsion in the faces of the white people who looked at her. They stared amazed at her enormous size, at the blackness of her skin. They glanced at each other, tried in vain to control their faces or didn't bother to try at all, simply let her see what a monstrosity they thought she was" (241).

This reactionary reading of Mrs. Hedges is no different than the one she receives "in the small town of Georgia where she was born." There, "she was so huge that the people there never really got used to the sight of her." For these reasons, she goes to the city, where she feels "she would be inconspicuous' (241). Although Mrs. Hedges distinguishes the intent of the reading of her body by the townspeople from that of the employment agencies (this is supported by the tone of the language used to describe each incident), the adverse effects of these experiences, coupled with her inability to fit into the normative model of womanhood, create for her a void that sends "her big body [. . .] filled with a gnawing, insatiable hunger [. . .] prowling the streets at night, lifting the heavy metal covers of garbage cans, foraging through them for food" (241). In the street Mrs. Hedges can be inconspicuous, and can redefine the boundaries of place, space, and the creation of identity.

In an effort to rend the veils that confine the meaning of her body to ambiguity and non-productivity, Mrs. Hedges circumscribes what Bachelard terms "felicitous space," a space of human value that "may be grasped, that may be defended against adverse forces, the space we love" (xxxi). Because Mrs. Hedge's potential for developing a viable "economic" identity has been "shortchanged" by the social languages and discourses that govern the spaces of ethnicity and gender, Mrs. Hedges goes to the street, whose economy is based on the fluidity of its boundaries. As "janitor and collector of rents," Mrs. Hedges moves from the space of homelessness to a place of economic assuredness, where she is "careful to spend very little" so that she can attain the one thing her heart desires---"a man for herself [. . .] who would fall in love with her"(242). Although not the owner of the building, she creates for herself an interesting relationship with Junto, who is able to buy two buildings based on the advice and encouragement he gets from her.

Mrs. Hedges's transformation to the voice that we hear over the sound of the wind on the street, a voice "so distinct---that it [comes] to [the] ears quite clearly under the sound of the wind rattling the garbage cans and slapping at the curtains" (5), stems from her economic prowess, which moves her into a space traditionally associated with men. What is ironic about this "association" is that her subsequent disfigurement in the basement of the apartment building---the location of the business she helped "create" ---allows her the ability to reform what it means to be a woman economically, and this interrelationship grants her the power to design her own space on the street: "[T]he fire had started late at night. She was asleep in the basement and she woke to hear a fierce crackling---a licking, running, sound that increased in volume as she listened[. . .]." From the basement window she seeks an avenue of escape:

> It was a narrow aperture not really big
> enough for the bulk of her body. She felt
> her flesh tear and actually give way as she
> struggled to get out, forcing and squeezing
> her body through the small space [. . .] she
> could smell her hair burning, smell her flesh
> burning, and still she struggled, determined
> that she would force her body through the
> narrow window, that she would make the
> very stones of the foundation give until the
> window opening would in turn give way.
> (244)

In this illustration, Mrs. Hedges's body is representative of voice in action---the formation of creation. The burning and tearing of her flesh allows her to physically turn herself inside out, creating a new being. These actions are similar to the ones she exhibits as a homeless person, turning "bottles and pieces of metal" into a profitable business. As Junto states when he sees Mrs. Hedges in the hospital three weeks after the fire, "Getting out of that window was wonderful. Simply wonderful [. . .]you and me are the same kind of folks" (245). At this juncture in her recovery she realizes that her scars have banished her to a life different from the one she imagined for herself: "[S]carred like this, hair burned off her head like this, she would never have any man's love. She never would have had it, anyway, she thought realistically. But she could have bought it. This way she couldn't even buy it." (246). Realizing that the fire has marked her body to the extent that she will never obtain her ultimate desire, Mrs. Hedges, again, seeks to redefine how her bodily text is read as she moves into her position as overlord of 116th Street.

Mrs. Hedges's knowledge of the power she now possesses as the scarred partner of Junto unfolds in some interesting ways. She is well aware that Junto "would probably be the only man who would ever admire her" (245). She is also aware that the actions she took during the fire caused him to have "the kind of forthright admiration for her that he would have for another man---a man he regarded as his equal" (246). Armed with this ammunition, Mrs. Hedges develops another source of income, built on the bodies of others---a brothel house that took its customers from a space she knew well, the street. As she states, "the street would provide plenty of customers [. . .] men who were disillusioned with their lives, "men who had to find escape from their hopes and fears [. . .] she would provide them with a means of escape in exchange for a few dollar bills" (250). Although her economic goals appear to undermine Mrs.

Hedges's motivation for the start of this business, another desire also fuels her drive to establish this business---other women's bodies. Mrs. Hedges is able to re-vision her own scarred body through her association with young, disenchanted women who blossom under the auspices of her care. Moreover, just as Mrs. Hedges thought she could buy love, she foolishly believes that her scars and pain will be lessened by her association with the unscarred bodies of other young women.

In comparing Mrs. Hedges's role in the novel with other characters like Min and Lutie, whose subject and object positions cause them to operate within certain socially inscribed spaces, Mrs. Hedges's "lack" of femininity allows her to command spaces and places that the other two cannot. When Lutie is almost raped by the Super, for example, Min will not come into the hallway; instead, she opens the door and lets the dog out in an effort to rescue Lutie from the Super's vile attempts. It is at this moment that we see Mrs. Hedges in action. Because she is viewed as "an enormous bulk of a woman," she is able to command the hallway space with power as she prevents Lutie's rape: "[. . .] a pair of powerful hands gripped [Lutie] by the shoulders, wrenched her violently out of the Super's arms, flung her back against the wall. The same powerful hands shot out and thrust the Super's head against the cellar door" (236).

Curiously enough, Mrs. Hedge's vocal and bodily re-possession of this hall differs greatly from that of the hallway she was relegated to during her years of poverty, when "she slept on a cot in the hall of the apartment belonging to some friends of hers from Georgia" (241). Although the hall and hallway may be viewed differently in their geographical designation as sites of expression for Mrs. Hedges, her inability to find a job (which put her in the hall in the first place), and her ability to save Lutie (an economic investment in Mrs. Hedges's view) from the grasp of Jones in the hallway, function relationally, in that one action reverses the stigma of the other. In other words, Mrs. Hedges's ability to produce economic value in a space she has re-created serves to minimize the impact of her history as a homeless woman. Moreover, the scarring of her body amplifies what power Mrs. Hedges has, and her voice occupies the space of the hallway with force, to the extent that "her rich, pleasant voice filled the hallway, and at the sound of it the dog slunk away, his tail between his legs" (237). The Super's failed rape attempt, metaphorically referred to in this passage through his association with his dog, contributes to the frustration he feels at being unable to contain the mystical reach Mrs. Hedges appears to have over the street, and in particular, over those who occupy his apartment building. As he states, "[Mrs. Hedges] ain't never been able to mind her own business. If he could he would have had her locked up long ago. She oughta be in jail, anyway, running the kind of place she did" (90). But as the Super finds out, Mrs. Hedges's body exists outside the reaches of the law. Junto, "the white agent who collected the rents from him" (93) had seen to that. I would also argue that through her association with Junto, Mrs. Hedges is able to manipulate what

Baker terms the "placeless place of law," [9]creating for herself a distinct site for renewed bodily expression.

Thus, Mrs. Hedges's "felicitous space" becomes the street, and the window becomes the phenomenological venue through which she seizes this space. It is in this window that faces the street that Mrs. Hedges becomes deified, heard, recognized. She appears to possess godlike qualities: she warns Lutie of the arrest of her son before Lutie has knowledge of it; she reads Min's mind as she plans to move out of Jones's apartment; she tells Jones, before he sees his apartment, of Min's departure. In this respect, Mrs. Hedges's creation of place--a place *earned* through her ability to force her bulky body through the small aperture in the basement of this building---allows her to occupy and transcend traditional mediums of expression. Her actions change the very foundation of that building, and alter the notion of what it means to move beyond one's immediate spatial confinements. In her space in the window, Mrs. Hedges is on display for all to see---her body bares the marks and tells her story.

This return to the site of the visual is an important thematic current in Mrs. Hedges's narrative. Because she has often been read by other characters in the novel as an Other in the extreme, I don't find it coincidental that her eyes become the focus of much discussion in the novel. Mrs. Hedges knows the power of sight. She has seen in the eyes of others exclusion, disgust, and hatred. For this reason, she shields her innermost self with the construction of the malignancy of her eyes. This helps her hide the pain she feels at being seen as a freak, a nuisance, a monstrosity. The immensity of the street aids her in developing this armor; thus, as Mrs. Hedges watches the street, she feels that "if she stopped looking at it for a minute, the whole thing would collapse" (121). The street has given Mrs. Hedges the only source of comfort she has known---it is her spouse, her existence, her very being.

Barbara Christian concludes that "The Street marks a change in setting and tone in the literature of the black woman. After the publication of this novel, the black city woman could not be forgotten" (47). Indeed, *The Street* makes for compelling reading. Lutie, Min, and Mrs. Hedges offer startling portrayals of creation and re-creation, as each woman is allowed to utilize the qualities she possesses to refigure her space and to define new ways through which her self-expression may be viewed. The juxtaposition of these similar yet diverse encounters direct attention to the embodied experiences of African American women, and the uncanny ways their identities are formed, indeed shaped, by their personal interrelationships with their environments. In writing about the multiple systems of oppression that bind these women to the street, to their space and place in society, Petry moves the black woman's narrative to the forefront of urban literary studies, and in the process, reorders the very ways in which we view the very notions of material possession within the urban space.

[1] McPherson's short story presents a wonderful example of the narratological uses of the woman's body in fiction. Staged in a doctor's office, the plot of this story revolves around two patients---one male and one female. The male patient inquires about a scar on the nameless protagonist's face; McPherson proceeds to take the reader on a wonderful journey that investigates the concepts of power and control and who has the right to tell the story about "the scar."

[2] See Lindon Barrett, "(Further) Figures of Violence: The Street in the American Landscape." *Cultural Critique* 25 (Fall 1993): 205-237 and You-me Park and Gayle Wald, "Native Daughters in the Promised Land: Race, Gender, and the Question of Separate Spheres." *American Literature* 70.3 (1998): 607-33.

[3] I refer here to Mrs. Hedges and Lutie Johnson. There are other female characters in the novel, such as the women who service Mrs. Hedges' brothel, and the society lady Lutie works for---Mrs. Chandler---but their positions appear to revolve around their interaction with Lutie or Mrs. Hedges.

[4] Many of the studies on Petry's novel allude to the fact that Lutie embodies the contradictions of the American dream; see, for example, Bernard Bell's "Ann Petry's Demythologizing of American Culture and Afro-American Culture"; Farah Grifin's *Who Set You Flowin'? (*Oxford, 1995*)*, and Lindon Barrett's "Further Figures of Violence...." From the vantage point of class definitions, Lutie is a working-class woman, bound by her gender and her race, yet she aspires to the idealisms of the upper middle class through her insistent need to adopt the idealistic attitudes of Ben Franklin. As the novel bears out, these contradictions have tragic results for Lutie.

[5] I am not the first to notice Min's quiet power in the novel. Lindon Barrett notes in an analysis of Min by Marjorie Pryse, "[Pryse] consider[s] the character of Min and concludes that in some ways the timid Min is able to manage her own fate more successfully than Lutie Johnson" (qtd. in Pryse, "Patterns" 116). [See also elsewhere in this text].

[6] Jones' obsession with Lutie Johnson dominates his narrative in the space of the novel, and it is this obsession and his feelings of inadequacies that cause him to abuse Min after Lutie rejects his advances.

[7] This idea is illusive since all of us participate, to one degree or another, in the economic system of the United States, and for some of us, our role in this cycle becomes predicated on other factors, namely ethnicity and gender. I would also add that factors such as one's educational background and class standing influence one's participation in this cycle.

[8] See Christian (*Black Feminist Criticism*) and Griffin *(Who Set You Flowin'?)* for further discussions of Lutie's peculiar dilemma in the street.

[9] Baker defines the "placeless place of law" as the displacement and denial of African-Americans' viability within the Western economic community. Historically, people of African decent were denied their ability to claim commercial possession of their labor. Slavery provided the genesis of this way of thinking within North American society, but I argue that within certain urban centers, this same displacement holds true today. If one were to consider, for example, Mrs. Hedges's role in *The Street*, it becomes evident that she has

reinvented this space/place for her benefit, and has likewise co-opted the legal system in ways that tie economic viability to legal power. See Houston Baker's *Working of the Spirit* for further discussion of this concept.

Narrative Space in Ann Petry's *Country Place* (1996)
Hilary Holladay

Although William Faulkner is the author frequently credited with fully rendering the life of an American community, the same may be said of the African-American fiction writer Ann Petry. Petry's detailed portraits of communities are central to *The Street* (1946), *Country Place* (1947), *The Narrows* (1953), and *Miss Muriel and Other Stories* (1971). Like Faulkner, Petry examines a wide range of individuals and their relationships with each other, and she takes pain to place her examination of race relations in the context of an American community. But while Faulkner returns repeatedly to the intricacies of life in Yoknapatawpha County, Petry moves back and forth between urban, fragmented communities and small, insular ones. Her focus on relationships within the community, moreover, anticipates the work of younger African-American women authors such as Toni Morrison, Gloria Naylor, and Alice Walker.

Born in 1908 in Old Saybrook, Connecticut, a picturesque town on the Connecticut River, Ann Lane Petry is intimately acquainted with small-town New England. Except for the nine years she spent in Harlem after her marriage to George Petry in 1938 and a year teaching at the University of Hawaii in the mid-seventies, she . . . lived in Old Saybrook for her entire life. In her fictional portrayals of small towns in Connecticut and New York, she draws on her family background as the daughter of the town pharmacist, her first-hand knowledge of the region's terrain and climate, and her observations of the way people in small towns interact. She goes far beyond her own viewpoint as a native daughter of Old Saybrook, however, by exploring Northern communities from various perspectives of race, gender, social class, and age, and by refusing to flinch away from graphic depictions of racial prejudice and violence. The overall result is a multi-faceted portrait of small-town New England, where the pretty surface barely conceals a morass of social prejudices---some racial, others related to gender, sexual orientation, and age.

In *Country Place*, Petry explores the ways in which people's relationships determine the quality of their communal life, just as she does in her other fictional works. But while her second novel details the conflicts dividing classes, races, and genders, and makes use of the naturalistic techniques displayed In *The Street*, it is primarily concerned with relationships between creators and creations, real places and narrative spaces. The novel focuses on the implicitly contentious relationship between the first-person narrator, a pharmacist called Doc Fraser, and an unnamed, omniscient narrator; and the explicitly contentious relationship between Doc and his nemesis, a gossipy taxi driver known as the "Weasel." The novel's preoccupation with narrative control provides an intriguing analog to its complicated plot. *Country Place* reveals that storytelling and truth-telling go hand-in-hand, even when they seem to be at war.

Like Edith Wharton and Willa Cather before her, Ann Petry invokes a male narrator as a means of establishing credibility while simultaneously confusing her tale with irony. Since her father was a pharmacist, she is intimately acquainted with Doc's milieu. But since Petry is black and her white male characters are generally obtuse if not always racist and sexist, her choice of Doc Fraser as *Country Place*'s narrator is especially ironic. Educated as a pharmacist herself and employed by the family business for nearly a decade, Petry deliberately conceals in *Country Place* the autobiographical perspective informing her short stories set in and around a New England drugstore. By subjugating her black female pharmacist's identity to the persona of a white male pharmacist, Petry enacts the novel's first, and most blatant, assumption. As a novelist, she assumes the privileges---and concomitant biases---of a race and gender not her own. Doing so is an essential privilege of storytelling. Through Doc, Petry illustrates both the limits and possibilities embodied in any narrator, real of fictive.

Doc Fraser's portrayal of himself as a fair-minded storyteller ironically exposes the very blind spots he claims not to have. In the first chapter, he asserts, "I am the only druggist in the town of Lennox, and for that reason I believe I am in a better position to write the record of what took place here than almost anyone else" (4). He goes on to provide what he considers his vital statistics, because, as he says, such information "offers a clue as to how much of what a man writes is to be accepted as truth, and how much should be discarded as being the result of personal bias" (1). His repeated assurances that he is a "medium kind of man" (1) suggest that he considers himself fair and impartial--- that is, the ideal medium for presenting "a true account" of the town's history (4). Yet his idea of "medium" embraces extremes: He describes himself as "medium tall, medium fat, medium old (I am sixty-five), and medium bald" (1), And, as a bachelor, he admits to "a prejudice against women-perhaps I should say a prejudice against the female of any species, human or animal" (1). He then reveals, comically, that he considers his beloved female cat to be "much closer to the primitive than a male cat" (1).

Perhaps distracted by thoughts of his skittish pet, Doc neglects to mention his race. We can surmise that he is white, however, from the complete absence of racism directed his way and his conviction that he would have married Mrs. Gramby, a wealthy white widow, had they been closer in age. By overlooking race in his self-portrait, Doc implies that his whiteness is a given. He assumes that his readers would naturally expect a white narrator. The obvious irony here is that readers for generations have expected black authors to write exclusively about black characters. By creating a white male persona, Petry challenges our own assumptions about the limits authors must impose on their creative vision.

There is much more about Doc, besides his race, that he declines to specify. Although he presents himself as honest and forthcoming, he actually tells us very little about himself. We don't learn anything about his family history or his young adulthood in Lennox. We don't hear a rationale for his prejudice against women. And we never find out whether he has a specific audience in mind for his book: Is he writing solely for himself? For posterity? For a readership including or excluding his fellow townspeople?

Such questions lead us to an even more puzzling matter: What is Doc's relationship to the novel's omniscient narrator? Although Doc claims "an intimate, detailed knowledge" of his townspeople (4), an unnamed, omniscient narrator controls seventeen of the book's twenty-five chapters. This narrator knows a great deal that the pharmacist, grounded all day in his shop, could not possibly know. To give just a couple of examples, Doc could not know the intimate details of Johnnie Roane's bedroom conversations with his wife, Glory, nor could he know either Mrs. Gramby's or Ed Barrell's last thoughts as they fall down the courthouse steps to their deaths. The chapter describing Johnnie' attack on his sexually unresponsive wife would be pure imaginative speculation on Doc's part; likewise, Mrs. Gramby's senile hallucinations and Ed Barrell's final reminiscences about sex would be beyond Doc's ken.

Even if we accept Doc's aspirations to omniscience at face-value—if we believe that he knows everybody well enough to script their thoughts and private conversations---the more mundane issues of plotting still create problems. For instance, Doc would probably not have access to the note that the Weasel takes from Ed Barrell's wallet, nor would he know that the Weasel later presents the note (exposing a long-past assignation between Ed and Lil, Mearns Gramby's wife) to Mearns, who in turn presented it to his ailing mother. Suffice it to say that Doc would require a surveillance system far beyond a 1940s pharmacist's technological means in order to know all that the novel's omniscient narrator knows.

The presence of the unnamed omniscient narrator thus subverts Doc's claims to narrative control.[1]   Once we acknowledge this other narrator, whose supernatural leaps put Doc's mortal limits to shame, new questions arise: Is Doc the "real" narrator who creates an omniscient voice? Or is the omniscient narrator "real" and Doc the imagined one? How does Petry fit into this schema? Is the omniscient narrator her means of discrediting a spokesman who is white, male, and admittedly sexist? Is the omniscient voice a graphic warning, moreover, that every written account, no matter what its claims to "truth," contains a dose of fiction?

The fact that *Country Place* raises these knotty issues without resolving them suggests the book's difficult, often convoluted, nature. But its difficulties are at the crux of its meaning: In *Country Place,* narrators and characters repeatedly encircle and encroach on each other's territory. Truth seems to emerge as a byproduct of the concentric circles of what is real and what is imagined. As Wallace Stevens writes in "The Noble Rider and the Sound of Words," "It is not only that the imagination adheres to reality, but, also that reality adheres to the imagination and that the interdependence is essential" (Stevens 33). Petry probes this interdependence in *Country Place*, just as Stevens probes it in some of his finest poems.

Within the novel, Doc's stormy relationship with the Weasel embodies many of Petry's questions about narrative control. On the surface, the two characters appear quite different: Doc is a self-confident native with professional status; the Weasel is an outsider with a blue-collar job. Doc's language reflects his education; the Weasel's reflect his lack thereof. But the two men do share some traits. Both are bachelors, with time to scrutinize other people's lives. Conveniently, both have access to privileged information: The ever-attentive Weasel monitors his neighbors' comings and goings around town, while Doc keeps track of everyone's health problems and pharmaceutical needs. With their keen interest in other people, both men emerge as natural storytellers intent on squeezing a tale out of Lennox, no matter how small and seemingly bucolic a town it is.

Sneaky and malicious, the Weasel not only enjoys sniffing out trouble around town; he thrives on reporting it to Doc. Despite Doc's frequent censuring of the Weasel, we can surmise that these two have a symbiotic relationship: The scandal-hungry Weasel needs Doc to listen to his latest exposes, and Doc needs the Weasel to supply him with information he could not otherwise obtain. Because they must depend on each other for information, the upstanding Doc and the low-bred Weasel serve as each other's foils. They are competing narrators paradoxically engaged in a collaboration.

Given his crucial, yet disturbingly ambiguous, role in the narration, perhaps it is no surprise that the Weasel is the novel's most interesting character. His liabilities make him a perversely engaging figure. His real name is Tom Walker (14), but his appearance and behavior preclude anyone from addressing him by that name. He has a "sharp ferret's face" and "close-set eyes" (7). His "small hands" and "humped-over shoulders" set off his notably furtive visage (7, 16). For business attire, he wears a sweat-stained cap and keeps a cigarette tucked behind his ear (7-8). In short, the Weasel is a truly repugnant fellow who demands vigilant attention.

Doc, for his part, appears fascinated by the Weasel, though he never admits as much. Because he rarely leaves his shop, Doc requires a confidant of the Weasel's mobility in order to move the story along. Without the Weasel, in fact, Doc would not have much of a story to tell. But the Weasel boldly exceeds the bounds of the confidant or Jamesian *ficelle*, who provides information necessary to a story's plot. The Weasel does not merely report scandal to Doc; he actively courts and creates it from the raw materials at hand. Threatening to appropriate Doc's authority, he appears much closer in spirit to the novel's omniscient narrator than Doc does.

In the course of the book, the Weasel functions as an author setting up a series of crucial scenes: (1) He drives Mrs. Gramby and Mrs. Roane to Obit's Heights, where they spy Ed Barrell and Glory kissing; (2) he steals the incriminating note that Lil Gramby (Glory's mother) wrote during her own affair with Ed; (3) he gives the note to Lil's husband, Mearns, who in turn gives it to his mother, shocking her nearly to death; (4) he selects Ed Barrell to help Mrs. Gramby climb the courthouse steps; and (5) he steps nimbly aside as Mrs. Gramby angrily pushes Ed away, causing both of them to tumble to their deaths. Much more than a passive witness, the Weasel orchestrates the encounters central to the novel's progression.

Setting up conflict is not the Weasel's sole intent, however. The scandals that he provokes provide him with wonderful fodder for his own record of Lennox. His tale-telling prowess both maddens and impresses Doc, who recognizes a rival narrator when he sees (and hears) one. Although Doc must depend on the Weasel for information, he refuses to acknowledge the extent of his dependence. When the Weasel arrives fresh from his investigative visit to Obit's Heights, Doc feigns disinterest:

> In doing this, I was deliberately ruining The
> Weasel's performance. He prefers to have
> your undivided attention when he talks, so
> that he can observe the expression on your
> face and thus determine whether his words
> are pricking the bubble of some cherished
> illusion of yours. (91-92)

But, for all of his antipathy, Doc appears intent on memorizing the Weasel's storytelling technique.

Readers of *Country Place* will recognize Doc's description of the Weasel's narrative style as an accurate summary of his own methods: "He is something of a showman. He sets the stage before he tells a story, carefully identifying the characters, in order to sharpen the appetite of his listener" (92). Here we begin to see just how much Doc depends on the Weasel; it seems that he looks to the other man for style as well as content. Even in his attempt to wrest the story away from the Weasel, Doc leans heavily on the Weasel's presentation:

> The harsh rasp of his laughter filled
> the store. It seemed to point up the phrases
> he had used as he talked: gone to the bank
> to count her pearls, home from the war
> yesterday, falling all over herself to get in
> his car; couldn't get a straw between them;
> thought their eyes would fall out on the floor
> of the taxi.

> I could fairly see Mrs. Gramby in the
> bank at Clinton with her safe-deposit box
> open in front of her. I could hear the rustle
> of paper as she fingered through the stocks
> and bonds and the old letters; could see her
> face light up as she gazed at a pin or a ring,
> reliving the past as she examined it. (94)

Rehearsing and embellishing the events in his mind, Doc tries to make the story his own. Since the Weasel has already shaped the facts into a fully formed tale, Doc can only describe the way the story comes to him: "The Weasel's words had evoked a picture of raw hurt and pain and secret, furtive love. Now he was putting a frame around it---a frame of laughter" (94-95). Significantly, the Weasel's version of the tale is not our first encounter with the events on Obit's Heights; the omniscient narrator has beaten both Doc and the Weasel to the telling of this tale. By the time Doc rehashes the Weasel's account, we are reading about the episode for the third time. The telling and retelling of the story illustrate the expanding circles of narrative that any event can generate; these circles also suggest the control that a narrator wields via the framing of events.

Doc objects more to the Weasel's "frame of laughter" than any other element of the story. In an attempt to silence his adversary, he explodes: " 'For the love of God,' I said, 'can't you stop making that noise?' "(95). Although Doc dissociates himself from the Weasel's malicious reconstruction of events, he nevertheless lets us know that his version exists. His own self-righteous anger is just one more frame around the Weasel's frame. His subsequent censoring of the tale (" 'Don't tell anyone else what you told me' "[95]) indicates his desire to control all future framings. Although he warns the Weasel that rumor-mongering " 'will only make trouble all the way around' " (95), Doc does not have any tangible stake in protecting the town from gossip. He has much more of a stake in acquiring the story for his own use.

Doc's furious desire to control the story is illustrated again when he realizes that he has become the Weasel's *ficelle*. Once the Weasel obtains a valuable clue from Doc's prescription record book, Doc attempts to coerce the Weasel into silence. In an ironic reference to his dual occupation as pharmacist and author, Doc declares, " 'I don't know what you found out in this book, but whatever it was it's none of your business' " (136).

The Weasel's invasion of his narrative space so enrages Doc that he conjures up the worst punishment he can imagine: He says he will run his rival out of town. Expulsion from Lennox would be a kind of death for both of these storytellers, since Lennox provides them with the drama and intrigue that their competing, yet ultimately complementary, narratives require. But for all of his territorial bluster, Doc cannot afford to lose his main source of information about Lennox. Although he claims to be "too old now to turn informer" (137), he nevertheless includes the Weasel's sordid secret in his book, "partly as a means of relieving my conscience, and partly because it lends a further insight into The Weasel" (137). In effect, Doc settles for the best of both worlds: He enjoys the satisfactions of tattling, while protecting his informer from expulsion.

In another ironic twist, Doc's two-year-old story about the Weasel showcases the Weasel's narrative dexterity even as it exposes his immorality. Doc reveals that the Weasel courted Rosie, a mentally retarded girl who worked at a local inn. After the girl became pregnant, the Weasel "convinced her that he was Superman and that she was pregnant because of all the ice-cream sodas she had eaten" at Doc's pharmacy (142). Although Doc entreated the Weasel to marry the girl, he did not give away the Weasel's secret at the time. Hence, he considers himself "an accessory after the fact" (137), because he had erroneously assumed that Rosie would identify her baby's father.

Even though Doc is telling the story, the Weasel retains control of its outcome. The fiction that he spun for Rosie enabled him to escape community censure, and Rosie's pathetic insistence that "Superman" fathered the child ironically accords him mythic power (142). No matter that he is neither a comic-book hero nor a Nietzschean *Ubermensch,* the Weasel is an ace spinner of yarns. Doc can only conclude lamely that his nemesis lacks a conscience" (142). Such a belated, and futile, attempt to put the crafty Weasel in his place does little to secure Doc's control of the text.

Determined to force every moment to its crisis, the Weasel literally drives his townspeople to despair. He is so knowing, and nosy, that he appears all-knowing. His passengers even suspect the Weasel of the omniscience that Doc spuriously claims as his own. But the Weasel does not appear to be a truly omniscient, supernatural being, since he, too, is subject to the unnamed omniscient narrator's scrutiny. In the tenth chapter, we glimpse the Weasel's private thoughts. We discover just how much the Weasel resents the class distinctions separating him from his taxi passengers:

> He wished he could see Lil's face when she heard about Glory carrying on with Ed Barrell. She would be good and mad. First chance he got he'd needle her about it. After Lil got herself married to Mearns Gramby, she began acting like she'd never known anyone as common as a taxi-driver.

> But he never intended to let her forget that they were born in the same town. (105)

Even though the townspeople consider the Weasel synonymous with Lennox, he feels like a perennial outsider. But in this respect, the Weasel is more like the rest of the town than he knows. All of the other main characters, with the exception of Doc, voice feelings of disaffection and alienation from the community. A cloud of ambivalence, building toward open animosity, hangs over Lennox. The Weasel forces the other characters to confront their own hostilities even as he struggles with his own.

As an emblem of the town, the Weasel is frequently associated with mirrors. This association heightens the Weasel's intimidating aura of omniscience. During Johnnie Roanne's ride home from the station, for instance, he catches the Weasel giving him "sly, sharp looks in the mirror" (16). Like Lutie Johnson recoiling from Mrs. Hedges' stare in *The Street*, Johnnie cannot "stand having [the Weasel] pry into my mind' (14). He chafes against the Weasel's "sly way of looking at you so that you weren't quite aware of it at first, but before you knew it his glance was inside you, feeling its way around" (14). It is as though Johnnie realizes he is a character in a fictive world, and he has suddenly become cognizant of his loathsome creator, a dirty-minded deity who until now has always lurked just beyond his peripheral vision. The use of the second-person extends the omniscient narrator's reach to us. The phrasing suggests that we, too, should worry about authors scripting our lives, "feeling" their way around our minds.

The Weasel's persistent staring and suggestive conversation also have sexual overtones. Recalling the scene in *The Street* where Jones rummages through Lutie's closet just so he can touch her clothes, Johnnie thinks that "Listening to The Weasel was like having a dirty hand paw through your personal belongings, leaving them in confusion" (18). The Weasel's scrutiny is so intense that Johnnie silently declares, " I want to think. I don't want him sticking his mouth into my mind" (19). Johnnie's thoughts ironically enact the very process that he finds so objectionable, since the novel's omniscient narrator is giving voice to his unspoken concerns, that is, "sticking his mouth" into Johnnie's mind.

Although one would normally look for one's own face in a mirror, the Weasel provides an alternative reflection. When Johnnie catches the Weasel furtive glance in the mirror, he sees something of the Weasel, something of himself, something of the whole community. A brief conversation convinces Johnnie that "this little man represented [the town] and what came out of his mouth was the thinking of the town" (11). The mirror implicates Johnnie in the whole sordid enterprise. Grimly convinced that "The Weasel speaks for Lennox" (19), Johnnie admits by the chapter's end that the "rat-faced little man had managed to make him see that nothing ever was the same; nothing ever could be the same---either on the surface or deep underneath" (20). He feels just as uncomfortable about what he sees through the Weasel's eyes as he does about the Weasel's seeming ability to look inside his mind.

Glory and Mrs. Gramby likewise perceive the Weasel's alarming capacity for anticipating and shaping their lives. After the infamous events on Obit's Heights, Glory worries, legitimately, that the Weasel's actions will determine her fate: "It would be The Weasel who would pass the word around. He would tell all of his passengers, out of the side of his mouth, and his eyes would watch their reaction in the mirror" (78). Glory recognizes both the Weasel's power as a storyteller and the danger that such power poses to her. She knows that much of the real damage of her indiscretion will be done in the public revelation of it. Because the Weasel serves as a conduit to the town, Glory's story will soon become many different stories in many different minds. Glory is in no position to tell her own story, so she has no authority over the form that it takes.

It is only after she decides to resurrect Johnnie's attacks on her that Glory can seize control of her own narrative. In the process, she also re-scripts Johnnie's story. By painting bruises on her neck, she elicits her employer's sympathy and begins the process of rehabilitating her reputation:

> She smiled at Perkins---a small smile, piteous, helpless. She could tell from the expression in his eyes exactly how right the smile was; and also from the way he blinked and swallowed. He would tell his wife that Glory was a brave little girl and that skunk Johnnie Roanne has tried to kill her in a fit of rage; given to them like so many of these veterans who think they're still driving B-29's over Tokyo or something. The story would cling to Johnnie; it would crop up wherever he went: queer, not safe, not all there, Glory left him, tried to kill her, dirty skunk. (208)

Here Glory assumes the narrator's powerful role, building a new, useful story around the formerly humiliating one of Johnnie's assault on her. Perhaps Glory, like Doc, has learned from the Weasel's technique. In any event, she harnesses the strength that comes not just from speaking up, but from re-framing events to suit her own needs.

As usual, however, the Weasel arrives in time to re-script events according to his preferences. Glory expects the worst: "I don't want him staring at these bruises I painted on my neck. He's the kind would reach over and rub them to see if they would come off" (209). The Weasel actually goes Glory one better, revealing that he saw her leaving Ed's home that afternoon. The Weasel's revelation effectively ruins Glory's sympathy-inspiring account of herself; he remains the narrator supreme. Having succeeded in trumping Glory's amateurish attempt, the Weasel heads toward Perkins, an audience already in place: "He crossed the store, heading for the counter where Perkins was. He looked back at Glory over his shoulder; his glance, sly, knowing. Then he winked" (209). The Weasel's signature gesture reveals his confidence in his ability to control any scene, any story.

Mrs. Gramby never recognizes the Weasel's adversarial qualities, but like Johnnie Roanne, she marvels over the taxi driver's ability to read her thoughts. While ruminating over the town's prejudice against Jews, she is understandably startled when the Weasel brings up that very subject: "She glanced at the back of his head, and then looked out of the car window, Mr. Weasel had an uncanny and disconcerting way of following one's train of thoughts. She had often wondered how he managed it" (87). The personification of all the town's prejudices against minority groups, the Weasel speaks for Lennox whenever he gets on the subject of Catholics or Jews. Prejudice is on everybody's mind, it seems; the Weasel, who appears capable of entering people's minds, merely brings the topic out in the open. His snickering recollections of long-standing local prejudices reflect poorly on the town. But they also reflect the Weasel's ability to keep his finger on the community's pulse, as Mrs. Gramby's thoughts acknowledge. Nobody can accuse the Weasel of not knowing his subject matter; he is a consummate storyteller with a sharp eye for the damning detail.

Moments before her death, Mrs. Gramby finally tells the Weasel what she has been thinking for a long time: " 'I find you everywhere,' she said. 'Even in my thoughts. You reach them before I do.' " (254). Although Mrs. Gramby has no reason to dwell on the Weasel, who functions as her lackey at large, her comments imply that he is *literally* on her mind, reading her thoughts. Echoing Johnnie Roane's thoughts about the Weasel, Mrs. Gramby anticipates post-modernist concerns with authors and their texts. Her remark suggests a character's unnervingly direct appeal to the author.

As an emblem of omniscience, the Weasel appears to be a "Superman" who knows too much for anybody's good. He sets up scenes, anticipates his townspeople's thoughts, and then shapes everything into narrative form. But as the chapter from his perspective reveals, every narrator is subject to another narrator's "framing," and every mirrored image holds the potential for a new kind of truth. Even the Weasel occasionally sees himself in the town's mirror, as the following scene indicates:

> [The Weasel] lowered the car window
> and spit. Wind blew the saliva back against
> his hand. He wiped it off on the side of his
> coat."It's my own spit, ain't it?" he said
> defensively and glared at the mirror. (107)

Framed by the mirror, the Weasel addresses an image of himself as if it were a higher authority. For once, he has suffered the humiliating effects of his own crippling vision. His own spit is still spit, after all. Like Johnnie Roanne, Mrs. Gramby, Glory, and Lil, he engages in a destructively self-reflexive relationship with the town. Glaring at the town's mirror ensures only that the mirror will glare back at him.

After Mrs. Gramby's death, the novel ends swiftly, even abruptly. The narrative's tension is released, not by Johnnie Roane's departure of the deaths of Mrs. Gramby and Ed Barrell, but by Doc's open alliance with the Weasel. The two narrators within the novel finally have the opportunity to witness important events together. Doc does not need the Weasel as a source of information, and the Weasel cannot justify telling Doc a story that the drama-hungry pharmacist is witnessing for himself.

In the concluding chapter, Doc and the Weasel metamorphose into co-conspirators. They attend the reading of Mrs. Gramby's will together and leave together. They are even accorded similar recognition: Mrs. Gramby has bequeathed the Weasel five hundred dollars for "his careful driving" and "chivalrous assistance," while Doc, "her devoted admirer," receives a diamond ring (261). Mrs. Gramby makes no significant distinction between the two men: Both are relegated to the status of supplicants. But she views them in a much more flattering light than either man deserves. The Weasel's meddling has indirectly brought on her death, and Doc, having inadvertently aided and abetted the Weasel's plotting, is as much of an accomplice after the fact" in Mrs. Gramby's death as he is in the far-from-immaculate conception of Rosie's child.

Throughout the reading of the will, Doc keeps a close eye on his adversary. His story has been filtered through the Weasel for so long that he seems incapable of seeing events without the other man's guidance. After the lawyer Rosenberg announces that Mrs. Gramby left her house to the servants, for instance, Doc immediately turns to the Weasel: " I looked at him and he was nibbling at his thumbnail, putting it in his mouth and taking it out. In his excitement, his jaws were moving just as if he were chewing food, and pausing in between to swallow" (262). The Weasel appears to be processing raw spectacle, chewing it up and converting it into narrative. Later, when the two men leave together, "The Weasel did not speak as he drove through Whippoorwill Lane, though his lips kept moving, as though he were talking to himself" (265). The town's ever-changing history serves as the Weasel's sustenance, and the events he has just witnessed have been a royal feast. The events, moreover, have presented themselves to him like a gift. Lil's explosion and Mearns' confrontation with her have exceeded his own expectations of scandal. He can hardly believe his good fortune. Witnessing his townspeople in an ugly confrontation appears to be the Weasel's version of the American Dream. He does not mind saying as much: "He nudged me and whispered behind his hand, 'Hey Doc! I wouldn't a missed this for a million dollars' " (264). We can assume that nothing would have kept Doc away, either. The reading of the will (Mrs. Gramby's attempt to re-script Lennox's history) provides him with an unusual opportunity to watch the Weasel in action.

Doc and the Weasel continue to spar lightly, even after they have joined forces as fellow witnesses and narrators. When Doc explains the meaning of "chivalrous" to the Weasel, his definitions seems both ironic and indirectly self-laudatory: " 'Gallant. A gentleman in the old fashioned sense of the word. Polite to old women and babies and children. Even generous to, and considerate of, other men' " (266). His concluding remark—" 'Though I must say I fail to see how Mrs. Gramby came to that conclusion about you' " (266)---would have undercut the Weasel's moment of undeserved honor, had the Weasel heard him. But the Weasel appears lost in self -satisfaction.

Gazing at his reflection in a mirror on the book's last page, the Weasel emerges finally as the ugly, and accurate, mirror into which the whole town must look. While he, too, holds illusions about himself (he is clearly not so chivalrous as Mrs. Gramby's will has momentarily convinced him that he is), he spends most of his energies destroying other people's illusions about themselves. Yet for all the trouble that he causes, the Weasel helps hold the town together at the same time that he tries to break it apart. As taxi driver, he may drive people to ruin, but he also keeps them in contact with each other and thus keeps this depressed---and depressing---community alive. Thanks to his meddling, we see that

> Johnnie is not alone in living the life of illusion and compromise; all the people of Lennox seem caught up in their own fantasies. Glory recreates herself as the heroine of movie illusion, while her mother dreams of owning the Gramby house and firing the servants who insult her. Mrs. Roane lives through her son's dreams; Mrs. Gramby lives the illusions of past glories, stifling her son's sexual and personal lives. Ed Barrell, the Mussolini of Lennox, deals in sexual conquest, hoping that he can thereby maintain an illusion of his youth (he has a bad heart) and his ego. (Lattin 71)

Unified only by their selfishness and their penchant for illusion, these characters do not appear better off, however, after their illusions have been exposed. Along with the town's victims of racial and religious prejudice, they are still trapped by the community's limited mindset. Only Johnnie, on his way to New York, allows himself to believe that the world is "so vast and so complex that if a man were to seek out his role in it he would not have time to brood over a lost illusion" (247).

Doc's preoccupation with the Weasel suggests that he is finally more interested in his fellow-storyteller than in the startling events at hand. The Weasel has become the center of Doc's story as well as its main source. Once the Weasel bids him farewell after they return to the pharmacy, Doc literally has nothing left to say. The book ends with the Weasel's familiar adieu: "'Don't take no wooden nickels, Doc'" (266). Coming as it does at the novel's end, the directive resonates for Doc, and for us. In his inimical way, the Weasel suggests the importance of scrutinizing everything closely looking for fictive elements in objects that appear "real," and refusing to settle for other people's fabricated versions of truth.

Thanks to their rivalry, Doc and the Weasel have the town's most creative partnership. When the pharmacist and the taxi driver collide, Lennox becomes a shifting, dynamic presence---a story in the making. The two men are creating the town even as they hammer out its history. By the end of the novel, we see that for all the trouble that the Weasel has caused, his taxi nevertheless provides a nexus for the town at least as much as Doc's pharmacy does. He may drive his townspeople to ruin, but he also keeps them in contact with each other and thus helps keep the community alive. It is his meddling that enables us to conclude, as Vernon Lattin writes, that "Johnnie is not alone in living the life of illusion and compromise; all the people of Lennox seem caught up in their own fantasies" (Lattin 71). Only Neola and the Portegee, the black housekeeper and Portuguese gardener who inherit Mrs. Gramby's house, appear united by genuine love for each other rather than mutual self-delusion.

Country Place reveals in the paradoxes linking tellers, tales and interpreters. The book's title reinforces Petry's emphasis on the illusory of fictional qualities of reality. As readers, we inhabit *Country Place* the novel just as Doc and his cohorts inhabit Lennox, the so-called "country place." By reading and interpreting the book, we create the town of Lennox in our minds just as its citizens create it in theirs. Creating reality thus becomes the ultimate communal activity, joining people across time, both within and beyond any given place.

                              Works Cited
Petry, Ann. *Country Place*. Chatham, NJ: The Chatham
      Bookseller, 1971.
Stevens, Wallace. *The Necessary Angel. Essays on Reality and
      Imagination.* New York: Vintage Books, 1951.

[1] See also Hazel Arnett Ervin's reading of a feminist narrator's subversion of Doc's claim to narrative control in her dissertation "The Subversion of Cultural Ideology in Ann Petry's The Street and Country Place." (1993).

'Same Train Be Back Tomorrer': Ann Petry's *The Narrows*
and the Repetition of History (1999)
Michael Barry

In interviews and writings from the 1970s and 1980s, Ann Petry frequently
laments the decline in the current state of life in urban ghettos, remarking that it
is worse than it was when she wrote *The Street*, a 1946 bestseller. "The sad
truth about *The Street* is that now forty-one years later I could write that same
book about Harlem or any other ghetto," she writes in a 1988 autobiographical
essay (*Contemporary Authors* 265). In 1992, she told the *Washington Post*
something similar: where ghetto life and race relations in the United States are
concerned, "everything is worse-than it has ever been" (Streitfeld E2). Petry's
writing, especially *Country Place* (1947) and *The Narrows* (1953), is
preoccupied with this question---is the world getting any better?

Surely this is a universal human concern, especially as she asks this question
not only of ghetto life, but also of American society and of civilization in
general. But the question carries with it some obvious variations and
corollaries: "For whom is the world getting better?" and "In whose terms shall
we define 'better'?" The inquiry into the possibility of moral progress in society
maps out, roughly, as a variation on the momentous and familiar question that
African American writers have long been asked to address: whether or not to
take a stand on matters of politics and sociology. The "yes" side---commitment
to politically contentious fiction---implies the possibility of progress,
remediation, and transition, while the "no" side---an apolitical aesthetic---
implies in its resistance to historicism a belief in fallen human nature, mired in
repetition. So the very question of history's progress or stasis occupies the
shifting middle ground between what has been labeled sociology and what has
been labeled art.

In the years shortly following their publication, critics commended *Country
Place* and *The Narrows* because these novels transcended racial themes. In the
past two decades, critics often ignore them for what I suspect is the same reason-
--there is no clear message about group affiliations, either race or gender. While
some critics continue to think political messages preclude artistry, there has
come to be considerable disagreement on aesthetic matters. Cheryl Wall charts
the slightly more preponderant viewpoint of today when she points out that
African American writers, in contrast to writers in the white mainstream of
American fiction, are supposed to be political in their intentions (286).[1] Petry's
concern in her later novels with historical progress or its lack is perhaps
evidence of the alleged non-group---specificity of her themes. In *The Narrows*,
the novel to which I will devote most of my discussion, suffering is often
inescapable, an equal opportunity assailant. But the hope of easing racial
oppression by decrying it competes with this sense of inevitability, and one
significant sign of the world's improvement would be the improvement in the
status of oppressed groups.

Even allowing for early praise accorded to *The Narrows* for its universal themes, most of the scholarly work done on Petry has been devoted to her first novel, *The Street*, an attempt at realistic depiction of Harlem life during the depression. For advocates of a Black Aesthetic that collapses the distinction between politics and art, *The Street* offers a focused, unrelenting downward spiral that communicates an important sociological message about the hollowness of the American Dream; meanwhile, black feminist criticism is attracted to it for its image of multiple oppression, among the most successful early attempts at such images in black American women's fiction, particularly as its protagonist is a dark-skinned black (see, for example, Gloria Wade-Gayles and Barbara Christian). *The Street* goes beyond interrogating the categories of race, class, and gender, and in fact shows that when one is a member of several oppressed groups, the condition cannot be accounted for simply by adding or multiplying. This insight has been important in recent literary criticism. "[I]f women," says Hazel Carby, "as an undifferentiated group, are compared to blacks, or slaves, as an undifferentiated group, then it becomes impossible to see the articulations of racism within ideologies of gender and of gender within ideologies of racism" (25).[2] Perhaps because *The Narrows* locates the targets of oppression in different characters, it is studied less than *The Street*. When it has received attention---in essays by Nellie McKay, and Sybil Weir, and Mary Helen Washington, for example---the focus has usually been on the images of women.[3]

And so the more overt the social commentary is, the more widely praised has Petry's work been, and indeed, in her 1950 essay "The Novelist as Social Critic," she makes a case for art's social involvement and historical situation. Still, Petry as a rule avoids placing herself in a debate between "sociology" and "art": in most of her interviews, she uses a more universalizing rhetoric. She says, for example, that "We're all mixtures of good and evil" (O'Brien 76), and that "Men have fallen in love with pretty faces" (presumably always and everywhere) (*Artspectrum*, in Ervin 99) . . . . .

We can best appreciate Petry's view of history by sifting through the ironies of her texts; her view is ultimately progressive, but qualified by hints of determinism and even of a liberating ahistoricism---an affirmation of cyclicalness that offers an escape from a linear narrative that is not, after all, experienced universally as progress.

This ahistoricism deserves more treatment here, since, according to many scholars, its resistance to Western conceptions of progress typifies non-Western views of the world. In short, not every refusal of progress is deterministic. Folklore and oral culture's vision of history usually includes cycles of repetition, but these repetitions are not necessarily best understood as the forces of fate. Instead, they offer a resistance to any "progress" foisted upon an unwilling populace. While this worldview of repetition, founded upon or reinforced by folklore, is profoundly conservative in its suspicions of action in a modern world, its hope lies in open-endedness. Many critics have celebrated the redemptive and resistant qualities of folk elements in black fiction, particularly in black women's fiction.[4] Admittedly, they do not address the nagging self-reference problem of refutations of progress: how one might measure the growing acceptance of the arguments advanced in their writings. But we can at least see the potential for a new definition of progress that competes with a simple, technological and utilitarian one-progress as resistance to progress. The most prominent of these potentially resistant elements is the blues, an African American complement to the holism of a precapitalist African worldview. The blues and its political implications are defined in a variety of ways: as ritual and technique containing tragic and comic elements, by which "Negroes have survived and kept their courage" (Ellison 256-57); as the –changing same," where racial memory and spirit worship are transformed in new media (Jones 113, 115, and D. McDowell 182n); and as many-directional motion, with the train journey as the most vivid image (Baker 7).

It is noteworthy that few of the adherents to the resistant power of history's cyclicalness include Petry in their traditions or anti-traditions, of black women writers. Her absence from these accounts is not attributable to the lack of folkloric and blues elements in her fiction.[5] In fact, these elements figure prominently, as does the teleology of the Bible, which also undercuts Western progress narratives. What's more, Petry's fiction contains implications that improvement schemes are futile and that those who bear witness are not in the business of doing anything but bearing witness. But through all this, she does maintain a hope for action in a world already-historical, and thus for progress in moral terms. More justice and more peace may result from the revisioning of dominant ideology-revisioning that happens when new perspectives are sought. Consolation for suffering may come from the extraction of some of the affirmative aspects of tragedy: the assertion of free will in the face of destiny, and the continuity of meaning, if not peace, across enduring generations.

2

When Jubine, the self-assured maverick documentary photographer in *The Narrows*, takes the pictures that he later submits to the Monmouth Chronicle, he plays out the dilemma of the artist. A man has fallen in the snow at the end of a frozen dock on the Wye River. Some time later, in another shot, the setting is the same, but the man is gone. There are no returning footprints. In his typical dogmatic fashion, Jubine explains that he records events, but "never, never interferes" (45). For him, the artist bears witness, and this is enough. Anything else would be playing God. Though he is often insightful in his analysis of society, he does not seem, here, to have a supple enough theory to account for his own role in God's work. Petry knows what Jubine does not---that refraining from intervention is impossible. As a novelist, she too bears witness, and weighs the possibility that one can do little else. But still she insists on the ameliorative gesture.

A portrait of the black section of Monmouth, Connecticut, *The Narrows* initially seems to depict its people's finely conditioned character traits slowly growing into conflict. And things do in fact explode in the end. But we have to attend closely to the ironies of the text to decide whether the explosion could have been headed off, or whether it might simply be a consequence of the beast in humanity, unable to be suppressed. The outcome seems both contingent and determined, both as unforeseeable conclusion and a slight variation on an always repeating story.

We might be tempted to decide that history is open to individuals' free choice but still not susceptible to long term renovation. But can we be personally free and historically confined? It seems to me (most of the time) that wild contingency and predictability cannot ultimately go together. And what does a historical equilibrium imply? A determinism where the statistics come out the same at some imagined end point? This compromise would render an alteration of history's grand progress impossible, but since humans do not live long enough to appreciate a historical equilibrium---the forging of the equilibrium itself sometimes kills them---their actions might be better conceived of on individual levels, where their efforts are not always futile. The philosopher of history thus cedes ground to the novelist. A novelist sensitive to historical law still writes of contingencies, but they affect only people, not history.

Near the outset of *The Narrows*, Camilla Treadway Sheffield, heiress to the Treadway munitions fortune, meets Link Williams, and the ensuing romance alters the chemistry of the town. At age twenty-six, Link tends bar at The Last Chance, a bar presided over by Bill Hod, a father-figure for Link and a king of the local underground. Link is the adopted son of Abigail Crunch, a fussy, punctilious, old[-]fashioned woman who cannot abide the arrogance of Bill Hod. Abbie has been married, but when Link was eight, her husband died from not receiving attention for a stroke---he was not treated in time because Abbie attributed his condition to drunkenness. When her husband died, she grieved so much that she forgot Link for three months. He was thus forced to go across Dumble Street to live with Bill Hod and Bill's nurturing cook, Weak Knees.[6] Through his adolescence, Link either lives (he moves in temporarily again when he is ten) or works (when he is fourteen) with Bill Hod and Weak Knees and gets an education from them; this means not only learning more positive attitudes toward his color---but also being thrown down the stairs by Bill Hod for being caught visiting China's Place, the Dumble Street whorehouse.

Links hard-won independence and pride are tested when, one night, he meets this rich white woman in the fog, on the dock, in *The Narrows*. Link rescues her, without realizing she is white, from the perverted harassment of Cat Jimmie, a legless man on a wheeled cart, and she is grateful. She calls herself Camilo Williams. Link's and Camilo's ensuing meetings and romance are marked by the clash of strong wills. Meanwhile, Abbie Crunch welcomes

Malcolm Powther---a well-mannered, diminutive butler who happens to work at the Treadway mansion---when he asks to rent the upstairs apartment at her house. He is everything a black person should be in Abbie's view. He brings to Dumble Street his wife Mamie and three children, one of whom J.C., attaches himself to Abbie.[7]

We see most of the events of the novel through the eyes of Link Williams, Abbie Crunch, and Malcolm Powther, and a few episodes through the eyes of Mamie Powther. But some are also from the perspective of Peter Bullock, the editor of the Monmouth Chronicle, and Jubine, the freelance photographer. Bullock and Jubine have an important impact on the community's welfare after Link's and Camilo's fortunes become news: after, that is, Link tries a second time to end their relationship and Camilo cries out into the night and has Link arrested for rape.[8]

Ultimately, Link is shot and killed by Captain Bunny Sheffield for sleeping with Camilo. Powther fingers him before Sheffield abducts him. The damage to Camilo's and Link's reputation has moved irresistibly toward this climax after the Monmouth Chronicle reports Camilo's presence on the dock in the Narrows at midnight.

Or perhaps not so irresistibly. Link's destruction and Powther's treachery, which we can look upon with equal horror, seem to be highly contingent upon many peculiar events that precede them; this contingency is what prompts Bernard Bell to note the importance of chance in the novel.[9] These contingent events give the story its pathos. For example, even though Abbie is quite right when she intuits that Camilo finally gave up on her love for Link because she suspected that he had another woman, Camilo has made a mistake. She has heard Weak Knees's question to Mamie, "You wanta ham sandwich like the kind I made for you and Link?" (302) and taken it to signal a connection between Mamie and Link. What if Weak Knees had not asked? Or, to pursue another chain of events, what if J.C., indoctrinated in his fascination with golden princesses and bright jewelry by the stories Powther tells him, had not stolen Link's cigarette case? Powther later assumes Link left that cigarette case behind after an assignation with Mamie. He might not have made that assumption, and might not have subsequently pointed Link out for his employers, enabling them to execute him. If we trace events back further still, we may ask what would have happened if the Major, Abbie's husband, had not had liquor on his breath when he had his stroke? He would have lived, and Link would not have felt the abandonment that he felt for three months when he was eight. What if Mr. Copper had never commissioned Powther to get a fat black woman to nurse his grandson? Powther would never have ventured into Mamie's neighborhood in Baltimore, and later, never have committed his collaborationist crime. History, it seems, is wide open.

The Narrows, like *Country Place* before it, often considers what might have been. This radical contingency is no more fertile ground for social change than is radical determinism, for we cannot plan our most trivial act to yield more felicitous outcomes. Contingencies matter so much and so often that they do not matter after all. History is too wide open.

But if we seek a site of agency, *The Narrows* may offer some. Alongside the apparent contingency of its world, patterns of oppression can be identified over time: thus there is some historical law, some predictability of events. Emphasis on contingency overlooks, in its attempt to discover the uniquely requisite events in the procession of history; the character of the people whom the events force themselves upon. The narrative technique of frequently flashing back to formative moments in characters' lives highlights the motives of the principal characters: everyone walks around reliving important pieces of their history.

According to Abbie Crunch's theory, one's attitudes in life are always conditioned by "what had happened to you in the past" (236). Link remembers being forgotten when Abbie grieved for her mistake and for her husband; he remembers his betrayal by China, whose call to Bill Hod to report Link's visit to the whorehouse was unabashed treachery; he remembers that Bill Hod tried to kill him. Powther remembers that covetous look that his old boss cast on his wife Mamie. Weak Knees remembers his old friend Eddie, whose ghost still follows him around during stressful times. Camilo always remembers what it used to feel like to be laughed at.

Petry's characters seem sometimes to be too pat, but that is part of the point. They are overdetermined. Just as the major events are contingent upon earlier events, so are the personalities conditioned by formative events. But in the case of personalities, the prerequisites are not necessarily trivial or random. They are in fact systematic: *The Narrows* contains some of the same kind of social commentary as *The Street*. Characters struggle because of their group identity, and may use that identity to struggle out of the world they occupy.

The Narrows, for example, attacks racism. Because of insecurities largely effected by racism, Link resents an independent woman. He has learned to carry the burden of his race around with him from Abbie and her friend Frances. They taught him that everything he did he did as a representative of his race, so he had better be an ambitious, prompt, reliable young man who does not go in for bright clothing or watermelons. Link's elementary school teacher, Miss Dwight, contributes to his insecurities. She regularly emphasizes to her other students the fact that Link is different, she gives him the part of Sambo, the comic darky, in the class play, and she always calls the class attention to instances in which he fulfills her expectations of unreliable or uncooperative black kids. Bill Hod and Weak Knees lift some of the weight from Link's shoulders of always having to represent The Race, but the insecurity does not disappear. When he is twenty-six, he still remembers that at sixteen, he had read some histories of slavery and suggested to Abbie that he would become a historian; Abbie treated the aspiration with contempt: "Who ever heard of a colored historian?" she said (328).

Link has bound up this degradation and now passes it on, sometimes unwittingly, to Camilo. He laughs to himself about her being "a rather high-handed little female" (132). He calls her "little one," and, to himself, "this little exquisite." He is not used to a woman with her own ideas, a woman who can pay her own way---he does not like to be told not to interrupt (87), and he has "never been took to the movies before" (132). And when she mentions her own academic dreams, her prospects of teaching at Columbia, Link scorns her: "Professor Williams. That I can't picture" (95). He cannot picture this any more than he could ever picture a beautiful woman wanting to be an engineer or a dentist. Link's disrespect for Camilo has been present right from the outset. His domination is ultimately dependent on the threat of rape, which he thinks of several times, partly because he is reminded of the dominant culture's story about black men and white women. In their confrontations, one might think that Link's advantages in physical strength would be offset by Camilo's much higher position in the society.

But at key moments, it isn't. For sexism is also a powerful force. Camilo has no recourse when she is thrown out of Abbie's house, for if she is sleeping with Link, she must be a harlot. And when she gets the police to arrest Link for rape, her credentials are questioned, for she should not have been where she was at that time of night. Even if Camilo can be more free and confident in certain situations than Link could ever dream of being, she must conform to the expectations of the community to assure her good reputation. That required conformity is her reason for not telling Link her last name. She fears his knee-jerk response, and we have every reason to believe her judgment has been correct. She has always wanted to be "somebody in [her] own right" (95), but the opportunity has rarely presented itself.

Society's distortion of the personalities of Abbie and Powther is no less powerful than its effect on Link and Camilo, but it is not manifested in the same fierce independence. Powther feels he has to regularly prove himself to new employers and new colleagues, those who have learned to distrust blacks, just as Abbie believes that colored people "have to be cleaner, smarter, thriftier, more ambitious than white people, so that white people would like colored people" (138). Abbie worries about the smell of food in the house, for colored people's houses always smell of food (124), and Powther thinks the streets of Baltimore where he first met Mamie have "too many smells" (187). Their reasons for internalizing the dominant ideology are obvious enough.[10] Powther feels as if he has to go out of his way to earn the trust of distrustful white coworkers and employers because he does have to go out of his way. Otherwise he will be deemed untrustworthy.

Peter Bullock, to use Jubine's characterization of him, is a "poor peon" who "want[s] to be a middle peon" (362). He does not want his newspaper to fold up because of withheld advertising, but he blames his wife Lola for most of his mercenary cooperation with Mrs. Treadway. It is Lola who will have to "give up the green Buick, the maid, the laundress, the cleaning woman, and the new fall clothes" (371), so it is for her sake that he goes along with Mrs. Treadway's wishes---even though Lola has explicitly told him not to. To maintain the place in the community he requires, he must conspicuously provide for his wife.

Thus, some of the insecurities and fears that occasion hostility and violence are perpetuated by an ideology or racism, sexism, and classism. Indeed, we could blame everything on the forces of society and the opinions of the community, but these forces are managed—aren't they?---by the likes of Mrs. Treadway, Bullock, Camilo, and teachers like Miss Dwight. As in the case of *The Street*, we have in *The Narrows* a novel that traces social ills back to ideology---the largely unconscious belief system of society. It then offers a revision of ideology as about the only hope, and attempts that revision. Link, had he not been taught by Abbie and Miss Dwight to be ashamed of the color of his skin, might not have the chip on his shoulder about race that he in fact has. If China's Place did not present itself to his curiosity right on his own street, he might not have incurred his whipping at the hands of Bill Hod, and he might not have bottled up his anger and hatred for later use. Camilo, had she not felt pressured by family and newspapers to behave like an heiress, might not have treated everything as if she owned it. Powther and Abbie teach their charges to always be on the defensive with regard to their color, but if whites did not entertain inordinate suspicions and ignorant stereotypes of blacks, these two self-hating blacks would never have grown into who they are. If material possessions and a house in the neighborhood where millionaires live were not the only qualities he sees admired, Peter Bullock might have different ideas about what constitutes reputation, and might not have abandoned his ethics so readily.

Of these social blights, racism is the one most under attack.[11] Racism has separated economically interconnected people into their own worlds. The distinction between the rich white world and the poorer black world of Dumble Street and the Narrows is stark, and the segregation is not an accident. More houses are going up in the carefully groomed area at the edge of town where the Treadways live because that is where the millionaires live. Malcolm Powther comes to live on Dumble Street because the building he has lived in before has been condemned. Powther tries to keep the worlds of work and home separate, though he should know enough to doubt his ultimate success. In contrast, Link is the link between the two. There is "something wrong" with Link, as Camilo suggests (323), simply because he expects to integrate the two worlds. This course is even more prone to failure than Powther's. Inasmuch as Link has difficulty getting a share of respect in the white world consonant with what is just, he is poorly adjusted.

Link is inconsistent with white people's expectations, a black man with pride, too beautiful to live, able to look with pity on a cuckolded husband. He is sacrificed by those in power in order that they might suit their own convenience. The self-hating characters survive.

But let us retreat once more from outrage and activist zeal. We may feel an impetus for social change based on a revision of ideology, but we should realize that this novel does not enable us to affix the blame easily. All humans in Petry's world are prone to imperfection, and while the discovery of patterns of oppression offers structure to our interpretations, it also, on some occasions, excuses individuals from any part of the blame, and, on others, expresses simple prejudice. In some of his last moments, as he is being kidnapped, Link blames two newspapers for his predicament. Jubine's photograph of Camilo after she has hit a black boy with her car and a Chronicle photograph that exploits the ugliness of a black convict are "one quarter of the explanation" of why he (Link) is captive, in a black Packard. But quite naturally, he is tempted to trace events further back. "How far back shall I go?" he asks Camilo's mother and her husband as they are interrogating him (402). He goes as far as he can. The other three-quarters of the explanation, he decides, "reaches back to that Dutch man of warre that landed in Jamestown in 1619" (399), the beginnings of the slave trade in North America. Link's captors do not figure into his calculations at all. Admittedly, his attribution of causality is a fair account of consistent racial oppression. But it also shows that responsibility dissipates as we try to figure out who first "set the wheel in motion," and blame recedes to more remote times and stories. Link, when he has had his final falling-out with Camilo, decides to "blame it on China" (330). Abbie, after Link's death, apparently looks around for a dark face to blame, for she comes up with Mamie Powther (414). These are the less nimble readings of causality. In order for the analyses to be more accurate, they must be more complicated. Doris, the housekeeping of Abbie's friend Frances Jackson, does better: "It were everybody's fault . . . . It were purely like a snowball and everybody gave it a push, that twocent newspaper gave it the last big push" (415).

In one other way as well the novel suggests difficulty in assigning blame. The same ineluctable stories play themselves out again and again in the short history that we are privy to. The repetition obviously has great ramifications for the social protest content of the novel. For the social horrors resulting from twentieth century racism and corruption and cruelty appear to be eternal dilemmas. The same stories occur, for example, regardless of the race of the cast of characters. As Link likes to say, "When the candles be out, all cats be gray."

We find this repetition dyed in the fabric of the novel. Link knows what it feels like for Captain Bunny Sheffield to be shaking too much to fire a gun properly, for Sheffield is just reenacting a story that Link has already lived.

Years earlier, when he tried to kill Bill Hod after being whipped, he, too, was shaking. Malcolm Powther identifies with Sheffield too. Sheffield is living the anguish that Powther lived through several years earlier, when he first knew that his strongwilled wife was having an affair with another man, and when he struggled to keep her anyway. Camilo would understand the early period of Powther's relationship to Mamie, if she knew of it, for she is trying to buy Link---certainly Link thinks so---just as Powther bought Mamie, purchased her affection and her hand in marriage. The black convict whose picture Peter Bullock ran in his newspaper was finally brought in by the police after he broke into a woman's house for food, and that story, too, should sound familiar to us; Rutledge, Monmouth's current Chief of Police, had been beaten by police earlier in life when he was stealing food.

In Link's personal life, the recurrent story is of love and treachery, inextricable. The characters change: they are Abbie, Bill Hod, and China, acting as Bill's agent. And in the present time of the novel, Camilo Williams Treadway Sheffield fulfills the scripture. Cesar the Writing Man has prophesied on the sidewalk of Franklin Avenue: "It hath been already of old time, which was before us. Ecclesiastes 1:10" (91). Link sees immediately the applicability of this sentiment to his own life, a circle that started in The Last Chance when he, Camilo and Abbie are twinned as the two women whom Link has loved; when he was a child, he thought he would marry Abbie, and at twenty-six, he proposes to Camilo. Both deserve the appellation "lady" (308, 380). Camilo's hair shimmers like Abbie's (70). She sits up straight in her chair, as if she presides over the room, just as Abbie does (95). And, according to Link, she attempts his destruction just as Abbie has: "Don't all of them when it comes to the end decide to scorch the earth, if I go you will, too, if I go down I will take everything with me [?]" (319). Abbie's grief at the death of her husband gave her the –"subconscious" urge to destroy everything, and Camilo, by screaming into the night, is trying to do the same. The people whom Link loves all have ways of posting what he thinks of as eviction notices. "Abbie: Get out of my house. Mr. B. Hod: Get the hell out of my face. Camilo: Get out of my car" (257).

The same stories recur, and we continually meet similar characters as well, both across the boundaries of race, and within the black population of the Narrows, sometimes from one generation to the next. Mamie Powther's song captures this continuity:

> Same train carry my mother;

> Same train be back tomorrer;

According to Mamie, Link is like Bill Hod---they are the best built men she knows. Malcolm Powther thinks that they both belong to the same breed as his old boss, Copper, for they cannot be trusted around women (170). J.C. looks like Bill Hod when Hod is "being pure nigger" (292). And J.C. is like Link---he is neglected by his mother; his story threatens to be Link's all over again. (There is even a suggestion that Link and J.C. are brothers, fathered by Bill Hod). There are still other similarities as well. Link talks the same language as Jubine. Camilo sleeps like Bill Hod (264). And Mamie, because of her irresistible female charms, is linked in Link's mind with Camilo and China (126).

The most recurrent of stories is simply a battle of the sexes, and the requirements of that battle are responsible for some of the similarities between characters. Hence Powther's sense of the similarity between Link, Hod, and Copper; hence Link's sense of the similarity between Mamie, Camilo, and China. This all started long ago, according to Abbie. "It started when the first married woman whoever she was took a lover and went on living with her husband" (414). It all comes down to sex."[12] If we trace the plot back to what first set the wheel in motion, one of the originary moments we might come to is Cat Jimmie's sex drive, unable to be sated, responsible for his chasing Camilo down the dock in the fog.

The sexual motive is only slightly more preponderant than greed. In this tale, nearly everyone can be bought. Link feels most like a kept man, a stud, a plantation buck, when he and Camilo are at the hotel in Harlem, where Camilo has "bought bellboys, desk clerks, elevator men, doormen. Bought 'em up fast. Had bought him too" (283). Link tires the same tactic to get a look at the registration book; he gives the girl at the hotel desk five dollars to break the rules: "The girl smiled at him and located the Williams account in the record book for him, and he smiled right back at her thinking, You can buy any of 'em, they're a dime a dozen" (290). In a similar fashion, Mrs. Treadway finds Peter Bullock and Malcolm Powther to be easily purchasable. Bullock sells out the town's trust, and Powther sells out his race.

Link believes that he is no different, and he has discovered that he is no different in another respect---he can be an executioner, even of those he loves. And this is still another universal quality---everyone has the potential.

Abbie: Out of my house. Camilo: Black bastard. Bill Hod: I'll cripple you for life. And Mamie Powther? Sure. She hung little Mr. Powther from the sour apple tree, a long time ago, and keeps him there, not only refusing to cut him down, but rehanging him, there or four times a week, so that he will dangle, in perpetuity. China? Sure. Stand in a doorway and pull a curtain aside, watching and licking her lips while Mr. Hod tried to break my spine. Executioners, all (260). Link's manifestation of this instinct comes after Abbie ejects Camilo from her house and Camilo calls him a black bastard. He beats Camilo, thinking he would kill her if they were not out on the dock. Then he contemplates throwing Jubine, the snoop, in the river (260).

On top of the unmistakable suggestion of random contingency, then, and the futility of action in the face of it, *The Narrows* attests to systematic oppression, and on top of this, it features repetition and resemblance between events and characters across the lines of race, gender, class, and generation. This repetition and resemblance complicates any protest and constitutes an equilibrium of jealousy, greed, and violence. While at first glance, an equilibrium seems more attractive than a universe completely open to possibility (where individual trivial acts break open the future and cause history to unfold in a way unimaginable until they happen), it is premised on an evolutionary schema that rule out any renovation or reduction of suffering. Consistent with the Social Darwinism from which the American naturalist novel grows, an equilibrium implies that the society or the historical situation that we have arrived at has come before for good reason: it is best adapted, the one most consistent with our natural characteristics. Since this is likely to be the state which is least exalted spiritually, the model is a devolution as well as an evolution.

Petry's view of repetition, to my mind, is grim. It is not the affirmative open-endedness I described earlier, the theory that holds out a hope of repealing white supremacist Western progress. In Petry's fiction, the repetitions only hearken to earlier events in already----modern history. The archaic is not really in the equation. The social commentary does not aspire to great change. Petry says in "The Novel as Social Criticism" that her fiction is informed by a conviction that we are all our brothers' keepers,"[13] but respecting our brothers does not fully explain why so many prejudices in society are rewarded by its structural features: her call to respect urges an individual to transcend history, but it does not envision historical improvement or change.

This is true if the equilibrium is truly an equilibrium. The separation of the two perspectives (free individuals and historical law) is difficult to sustain, however. The effects on people of historically unimportant events start to extend a long reach, and ensuing events diverge from the ways they otherwise might have been. When we see that this causes some disasters to be founded upon, it is not surprising that we would be lured into trying to improve the world. Besides, human social structures, compared to the rest of nature, are still, in evolutionary terms, quite young. Humans do not know yet whether that which seems to be an essential feature of humanity is or is not subject to social construction, and do not know yet whether a society that nurtures a healthier human can survive. At any rate, treating the future as possibility rather than certainty is part of our patrimony, and we may as well fulfill it by attempting to create our own evolution. Because our determined course is undiscoverable ahead of time, the illusion of free will is the way that necessity comes into being."[14] Which leads Petry to settle for the modest reform potential of responsibility for one's brother, and perhaps to hope for more.

It is difficult to imagine Abbie Crunch's being for sale. It is difficult to imagine Weak Knees being an executioner. It is possible to believe that some people will attempt to change the ever-repeating stories. Even though Abbie decides we are never rid of the past, she does not ascribe necessity to the process of the selection of the stories. "The big things that happened to you were finally reduced to stories that you told, and the stories become fewer and fewer" (237). As one critic says, "Abbie emerges as a woman who keeps her mind and heart in order by admitting into her life only that measure of experience which she feels ready to control" (M. McDowell 140). This control is freedom, not the open-ended freedom of the refusal of progress, but the freedom of an individual in history to newly interpret determining conditions.

For our hopes to rest with a liberalism based on the symptomatic cures of a "lady" seems rather a false hope. But it is what *The Narrows* offers: the humanist solution that we are used to in novels: the world is a chaos, and does not reward our good behavior, but we must invent a moral code that pretends it does.

For Abbie Crunch, new stories are still possible. They do not grow out of very promising soil: she is living in hell again at the end of the story. She has lost her adopted son, seemingly by her own doing. If she had not thrown Camilo out on the street that night, none of this would have happened. So she now relives her husband's death, for which she saw herself as responsible. She decides, however, not to repeat her mistakes. Earlier, she has not alluded to her former hostilities with Link because, as Link says, "She's one of the last of a species known as lady" (308). She will go to the police station to tell the police of her suspicions that Camilo might be killed, and thus she might halt a cycle of revenge. She will take J.C. along; she does not want to neglect him in her moment of torment as she neglected Link. At seventy, she can still say, "I've never been inside a police station before" (428), and still be intent on trying something new.

---

[1] According to Carl Milton Hughes in *The Negro Novelist* and Hugh Gloster in "Race and the Negro Writer," *Country Place* and *The Narrows* are novels about humans, some of whose characters, it should be said, happen to be black. These critics are prone to regard as a work of immaturity any novel which has a sociological axe to grind. Of course it is hard to imagine how this dispute about an African American novelist's high points might translate to a discussion of a white male: he shows his maturity because instead of writing only about white males, he now writes about people?

[2] Valerie Smith's assessment is similar to that of Carby: "Black feminist theorists argue that the meaning of blackness in this country shapes profoundly the experience of gender, just as the conditions of womanhood affect ineluctably the experience of race" ("Split Affinities: The Case of Interracial Rape." *Conflicts in Feminism*. Eds. Marianne Hirsch and Evelyn Fox Keller. New York: Routledge, 1990, 47).

[3] Nellie McKay focuses on Abbie Crunch and Frances Jackson, who "represent ways in which northern black women of their class perceived options for independent selves in the 1930s and 1940s" (136-37). Sybil Weir, in her comparison of *The Narrows* to nineteenth century New England novels, also studies Abbie Crunch primarily, noting that Petry "consciously delineat[es] Abbie's character within the confines of the New England tradition" and that Petry reveals in Abbie "the anguished reality beneath the façade of the emasculating black mother" (84-85). Mary Helen Washington (*Invented Lives*) is distrustful of the environmental determinism of conventional social protest because it ignores the "realities of women's lives" (298). Washington shows the narrow possibility of Mamie Powther's role in *The Narrows* when it is seen in terms of Petry's conscious intention, but says it has nonetheless, lingering potential, aligned with the blues, for disruption and independence. Washington maintains that "[t]he attitude toward women in *The Narrows* would probably have gone unremarked in the 1950s since this view of women [with its emphasis on physicality] was the same as the one depicted in most of the popular culture of the day" (301). Washington's reading is itself a sociological reading, but a different sociology from one that emphasizes men entrapped by circumstance.

[4] The attraction of folklore and of traditional narrative is described by several critics I have read as a resistance to capitalist efficiency, to the fragmentation required for scientific method and instrumentalism, and to "progress." These critics' reasoning roughly follows the reasoning of Mircea Eliade, who, in *Cosmos and History: The Myth of Eternal Return*. Trans. Willard Trask. (New York: Harper, 1954), argues that archaic spirituality treats human existence in terms of repetition of archetypal gestures and eternal return. For Eliade, primitive cultures experience progress as the "terror of history": only a minority of moder men make history, over the heads of, and with the labor of, those who have to bear its consequences. Keith Byerman, in *Fingering the Jagged Grain: Tradition and Form in Recent Black Fiction*. (Athens: University of Georgia Press, 1985), is perhaps most explicit in his rejection of "progress" as it is conventionally defined. He is suspicioius of control schemes, of arguments for the "general good." His suspicion, I gather, is founded on the impossibility of a sufficiently broad definition of "general," or of a sufficiently flexible definition of "good." According to Byerman, folklore, like the trickster figure who sometimes embodies it, "resist[s] any system that demands sacrifice and suffering for its perpetuation," and undermines the pleas of the "apologists for oppression." Susan Willis, in *Specifying*, shares many of Byerman's theoretical commitments. She, too, appreciates the open-endedness of folk elements, and sees them as resistant to capitalist efficiency. Though the performers change, the content of the folklore outlasts any ideological purpose. Karla Holloway, Bonnie Barthoid (*Black Time: Fiction of Africa, the Caribbean, and the United States*. New Haven: Yale University Press, 1981), and James A. Snead ("Repetition as a Figure of Black Culture." In *Black Literature and Literary Theory*. Ed Henry Louis Gates, Jr. New York: Methuen, 1984, 59-79), without directly attacking instrumentalism and efficiency, address even more directly the

attractions of a cyclical view of history. In *Moorings and Metaphors*, Holloway argues for getting beyond the schism between myth and literature. Literature by black men, concerned with the present, with the act, and with "behavior," is surpassed by literature by black women, whose "voice" transcends time in a "synchronous realm." By finding cultural mooring places in women's shared ways of saying, Holloway hopes to avoid recapitulating the biases that have been contained hitherto in the disciplines of history and sociology. "It is hard [for the women characters in novels by black women] to believe in time, because the records of time are not reliable for what has happened to them, and prayer is not a responsible reaction . . . . Instead, just talking (telling) seems to be the way for memory and time to work out some sort of textu (r)al truce. History is reconstructed within such a frame and the author is able to write out of a matrix of memory that is both sensual and visceral, as well as to reconstruct a logic of repetitive circular complexity rather than a binary and linear polarity" (108). Barthold, in *Black Time: Fiction of Africa, the Caribbean, and the United States*. New Haven: Yale University Press, 1981), studies African and African American texts to show their resistance to linear notions of time and to whites' proprietary attitude toward time. Snead, in "Repetition as a Figure in Black Culture," sees repetition in literature as part of a broad tendency to modulate a view of history that includes only progression, and moveover sees black traditions, in their emphasis on rhythm and on the cycles of nature, as the forefront of this tendency. Snead does not say whether changes in individual fortunes reveal a pattern--an accumulation or an equilibrium---when they are studied as collective fortunes.

[5] Joyce Ann Joyce, in "Ann Petry," attributes certain elements in *The Narrows*, such as Mamie Powther's blues singing and the ghost that Weak Knees sees, to the "folkloric tradition that Petry uses to inform her novel" (19).

[6] At the risk of attributing too much credit to gender roles as they are traditionally defined, I'll say that Link has a mother figure and a father figure on each side of the street---on one side both mother and father are men, on the other side both are women.

[7] Like several other J.C.s in American literature, this J.C. is sometimes represented as Christ-like---Abbie reaches out of a dream to find him in the dark, for example. Since his relative abandonment echoes Link's plight, the suggestion of Christ in connection with J.C. links Christ in turn with Link, who is sacrificed. There is a Judas character here too (Powther), as there is in *The Street*.

[8] *The Narrows* reinscribes the belief that a woman's cry of rape is often the result of some quarrel and fabrication. This fact may undermine any feminist message it conveys. In her essay celled "Split Affinities: the Case of Interracial Rape," Valerie Smith shows the way such cases can highlight the problems of group analysis of society, and explains why black women might identify with a black male who stands accused of rape.

[9] Bell in "Ann Petry's Demythologizing of American Culture and Afro-American Character," says that Petry's theme is "that our lives are shaped as much by chance as they are by time and place" (112).

[10] In *The Afro-American Novel and Its Tradition,* Bell uses socialized ambivalence as a key term in his analysis of much of the fiction that he takes up.

[11] In an interview with John Murphy in *Black Authors,* Petry confirms that "racism comes closer to being the cause" of evil in *The Narrows*---closer, that is, than individual mistakes or other historical forces (162).

[12] It is worth noting that in *The Street,* Petry clearly identifies racism and poverty as socially constructed hierarchies, but sexism and violence against women are constants---virtually every man is a potential rapist----and thus might be construed as unsolvable problems.

[13] Margaret McDowell (1980) connects the importance of being our brothers' keepers with the social message of *The Narrows* as well (139).

[14] In his Discourse on Metaphysics, Leibniz defends his determinism from the charge that it forecloses on possibilities and thus prescribes apathy. He says: "But, you object, perhaps it is ordained from all eternity that I will in. Find your own answer. Perhaps it has not been" (50).

(2003 to the Present)
'This Strange Communion': Surveillance and Spectatorship in Ann Petry's *The Street* (2003)
Heather J. Hicks

From the time of its publication in 1946, Ann Petry's *The Street* has inspired comparisons to the work of prominent black male writers, including Richard Wright, Chester Himes, and Ralph Ellison.[1] In the first decades after its publication, especially, *The Street* was routinely classified as a naturalist novel of the "Richard Wright school." Later waves of critics have resisted thinking of Petry's novel in these terms, however, instead identifying "a more complex structure that expands the boundaries of the traditional naturalistic novel" (McKay 127). These more recent critical accounts have focused on Petry's feminist concerns, as well as specific thematic elements of the text, such as its recurrent allusions to Benjamin Franklin, conjuring, and the blues.[2]

This critical work has been vital to producing an understanding of how Petry's work stands apart from that of the black male writers by whom she was so long overshadowed. Yet, now that Petry's distinctive gifts have been acknowledged and her originality of thought and expression has been appropriately credited, I want to suggest that there is good to be gained by once more placing Petry's first novel in relationship to the work of Wright and Ellison.[3] Indeed, I believe that even briefly turning to their fiction illuminates a central concern within *The Street* that has never been addressed: namely, the dynamics of spectatorship and surveillance that animate the racist social formation of Harlem. Placing Petry in relation to her male literary forebears in these terms will serve to underscore further the degree to which she was an innovator, breaking new ground for the black feminist writers who have come after her.

In Wright's *Native Son*, of course, vision and failures of vision serve as a central trope for the racial animosity that has spawned Bigger Thomas's homicidal consciousness. In particular, Mrs. Dalton, the blind mother of Bigger's first victim, serves as a figure for the blindness of both blacks and whites to the complexities of racism. Bigger spells out Mrs. Dalton's symbolic function explicitly, reflecting that "a lot of people were like Mrs. Dalton, blind . . ." (107). At a critical moment of epiphany, Bigger suddenly understands the ideological apparatus that has shackled him in similar terms: "He felt that [his family] wanted and yearned to see life in a certain way; they needed a certain picture of the world; there was one way of living they preferred above all others; and they were blind to what did not fit. They did not want to see what others were doing if that doing did not fit their own desires" (106). Again, and again Wright returns to the idea that the blacks and whites in this text blunder forward, unseeing, toward fates that have been predetermined by power dynamics that render their environment as invisibly lethal as a minefield.[4] Twelve years after the publication of Wright's novel, Ralph Ellison would produce a brilliant meditation on racism in *Invisible Man*, and once again the experience of not being seen served as a central metaphor for the effects of American racism. While it is clear that a metaphorics of vision is central to the projects of both Wright and Ellison, virtually no notice has been given to the similar centrality of the ocular to Petry's own highly influential depiction of twentieth-century race relations. Wright and Ellison figured the power dynamics of race as matters of blindness and invisibility, respectively; Petry, on the other hand, depicts the dynamics of 1940s' Harlem in terms of visibility and, more particularly, in terms of looking and watching. At a number of key moments in *The Street*, which is set in Harlem in the 1940s, her characters attempt to articulate their experience of what E. Ann Kaplan calls the "imperial gaze."[5] In a crucial early scene Lutie, *The Street's* protagonist, for instance, struggles to explain to her eight-year-old son Bub " 'why . . . white people want colored people shining shoes' " (71). Lutie's reply suggests the centrality of the act of looking to the racism against which Petry's characters must incessantly struggle:

> She turned toward him, completely at a loss as to what to say, for she had never been able to figure it out for herself. She looked down at her hands. They were brown and strong, the fingers were long and well-shaped. Perhaps because she was born with skin that color, she couldn't see anything wrong with it. She was used to it. Perhaps it was a shock just to look at skins that were dark if you were born with a skin that was white. Yet dark skins were smooth to the touch; they were warm from the blood that ran through the veins under the skin; they covered bodies that were just as well put together as the bodies that were covered with white skins. Even if it were a shock to look at people whose skins were dark, she had never been able to figure out why people with white skins hated people who had dark skins. It must be hate that made them wrap all Negroes up in a neat package labeled "colored"; a package that called for certain kinds of jobs and a special kind of treatment. But she really didn't know what it was.
> "I don't know, Bub," she said finally. "But it's for the same reason we can't live anywhere else but in places like this"---she indicated the cracked ceiling, the worn top of the set tub, and the narrow window, with

a wave of the paring knife in her hand. (71-
72)

Petry establishes here the degree to which race must be regarded as a
specular matter.   At the heart of race is the "shock" of looking and the
complexities of embodiment that the superficiality of racial thinking resists.
Yet, as it is presented in this early scene, the connection between race and the
gaze is also a mystery, a riddle. Lutie cannot formulate the precise relation
between vision and race in response to Bub's question. Petry's larger project
can be understood in part as an attempt to capture the intricate mesh of vision,
race, and hate that the answer to a child's simple question could never
encompass[6]

As many critics have pointed out, however, race is only one part of the
puzzle in *The Street*. Racial dynamics co-mingle with economic imperatives
and sexual impulses in the text, creating a chaotic struggle in which the power
vested in acts of looking and watching seems the only constant. Indeed, in this
essay I want to explore Petry's distinctive variation on what bell hooks has
termed "black looks," and what E. Ann Kaplan terms "looking relations."[7] I
maintain that, in the acts of looking Petry foregrounds within the narrative, she
produces a distinctive view of the relationship between a mode of watching
driven by sexual desire and that propelled by a pervasive will to power---
between, that is, spectatorship and surveillance---within the context of American
constructions of racial identity.   In portraying both the tension and complicity
between these modes of watching, Petry presents a complex knot of oppression
and resistance between whites and blacks, men and women in 1940s' Harlem.

Most urgently, as I will demonstrate below, the dynamics Petry conjures
between these modes of watching emphasize the continuity between sexual and
racial oppression.   The Super begins as Lutie's sexual oppressor, yet by the
conclusion of the text, as a consequence of his sexual obsession with her, he has
learned to marshal the powers of a white government against his victim,
becoming complicit with its racist ideology.   Likewise, while Mrs. Hedges
initially functions as the primary figure of surveillance in the text, we are
ultimately made to understand that her complicity with the powerful white man
Junto springs from a history of sexual marginalization.   Meanwhile, Lutie is
chronically watched by Junto himself, who despite this ostensible racial
equanimity, comes to gaze upon her as a whore because of a racist ideology that
defines all black women that way.   The way her characters look at one another,
that is, serves as Petry's chief means of dramatizing the degree to which sexist
ideology inspires racist practice, and vice versa.   Petry's preoccupation with
spectatorship and surveillance becomes her primary means of expressing not
merely the burden a black woman faces as the object of both racism and sexism,
but also the degree to which these forms of hatred can treacherously morph into
one another.   Finally, however, ocular acts are not presented exclusively as
expressions of these deeply imbricated forms of hatred.   Instead, near the

conclusion of the text, she imagines a moment in which both racial and sexual hatred are shed through the act of looking itself and, in so doing, identifies potential in both modes of seeing to create solidarity and mutual understanding between the embattled blacks she portrays.

To better understand Petry's meditation on the "scopic regime" of 1940s' Harlem, I believe it is useful to turn to British art historian Griselda Pollock's remarkable essay "Feminism/Foucault---Surveillance/Sexualty."[8] I choose Pollock's work because, unlike a number of scholars who have addressed the interface between psychoanalytic theories of the gaze and Foucault's discussions of surveillance as a modern practice, Pollock insists on not only a profound interconnection between the two, but also important differences that prove crucial in Petry's work.[9] Specifically, Pollock interrogates "the conditions under which working[-]class women became the object of fascinated looking and of a disciplinary investigation in the nineteenth century" by investigating the ways female coal miners were regarded by the middle-class men who debated the decency of their choice to wear trousers in their mining work. In the course of her discussion, Pollock establishes a key distinction between "fascinated looking' and "disciplinary investigation." Connecting the former with "the mechanism and processes associated with the unconscious," she claims that these unconscious drives, in their "unpredictable and destabilizing plays of fascination, curiosity, dread, desire, and horror," complicate---or, to use her term, "furrow"---"the will to know and the resultant relations of power." (9)

Having posited this distinction between "sexuality and surveillance," Pollock proceeds to demonstrate the ways that these modes of perception "mutually constructed each other in the interests of bourgeois men" (10). Within the historical context she studies, sexualized "fascinated looking" occurs simultaneously with the disciplinary gaze while being distinct from it: "Sexual difference is a constant problem. Its deviations and instabilities must be monitored, explored, and tracked down by those with the competence to examine, assess, investigate, that is to subject these other populations to a surveying and disciplining gaze" (32). In short, the fascinated desire to watch sexualized bodies both impels and is impelled by the "exploitation [of the body] as an object of knowledge and an element in relations of power" (33). Ultimately, she claims, "sexuality both collaborates with and disrupts the technologies and discourses of disciplinary surveillance." (38)

While Pollock's discussion focuses on inter-class looking among whites, her formulations serve as a useful lens through which to understand the complex relations between blacks---and between whites and blacks---in Petry's vision of Harlem. Specifically, I want to demonstrate that Petry's novel constructs a picture of social relations in Harlem in which two distinct, but interdependent, modes of looking are in operation. As in the case of Pollock's discussion, they may be understood as spectatorship and surveillance, and they likewise exist in a relation of both tension and reciprocity.

There are two characters who most completely embody the looking relations that concern Petry---"The Super," the superintendent of the building into which Lutie reluctantly moves at the beginning of the novel, and Mrs. Hedges, the whorehouse madame who throughout the narrative remains stationed at a prominent window watching the eponymous 116th Street. Near the outset of the text, Lutie distinguishes between their specular modes, attempting to gauge which is more menacing: "Somehow the man's eyes," she muses, "were worse than the eyes of the woman sitting in the window" (9). As I will discuss below, it is far from clear that the text depicts one of their modes of looking as more dangerous than the other. Yet I believe that it is appropriate to take the cue Petry provides here and examine how she constructs their respective modes of watching as distinct from one another.

In his ceaseless ogling of women, the Super seems an exemplary case of the sort of "fascinated looking" Pollack associates with sexual desire and that psychoanalytic theory broadly treats as the "male gaze." In scene after scene in the novel, the Super stands on the street, "looking at the women who went past, estimating them, wanting them" (87). His gaze reduces them to objectified parts; they disintegrate, in his eyes, into "well-shaped hips" (85) or "well-shaped legs that quivered where the flesh curved to form the calf" (288).

Yet it is the Super's dogged pursuit of Lutie that becomes truly emblematic of a voyeuristic gaze. In their opening encounter, Lutie immediately experiences the Super's regard as an affront: "For after his first quick furtive glance, his eyes had filled with a hunger so urgent that she was instantly afraid of him and afraid to show her fear" (10). The degree to which the Super's aggressive watching of Lutie in this scene is a controlling, patriarchal act is symbolically conveyed by his possession of a "long black flashlight" (11). Overtly represented as the phallus ("The flashlight was as shiny black---smooth and gleaming faintly as the light lay along its length. Whereas the hand that held it was flesh---dull, scarred, worn flesh---no smoothness there" [12]), the flashlight symbolically equates the Super's ability to see with an ability to rape.[10] The power he commands is underscored in the scene, when, as he points the flashlight downward, it "turn[s] him into a figure of never-ending tallness" (14). In a scene that does justice to Petry's naturalist forebears, Petry telegraphs the degree to which sexual coercion and the act of looking will be conflated in the figure of the Super.[11]

Importantly, however, in this initial confrontation, Lutie is also armed with a flashlight, and although she is desperately afraid that she will drop the light ("she gripped the flashlight so tightly that the long beam of light from it started wavering and dancing over the walls so that the shadows moved ...shifting, moving back and forth" [17]), she manages to retain her own command of the light and, hence, the gaze. Indeed, at the conclusion of the scene, Lutie makes a final bid to resist the objectified position the Super's relentless staring imposes on her: ". . . she forced herself to look directly at the Super. A long hard look, malignant, steady, continued. Thinking, That'll fix you, Mister William Jones . . . . this look, my fine feathered friend, should give you much food for thought" (25). Lutie's choice to retaliate against the Super's oppressive attention by beaming at him a look of her own foregrounds the level at which Petry is methodically interrogating the stakes of looking in her narrative.

Yet Lutie is only momentarily successful---if at all---in resisting the Super's oppressive gaze. Eventually, the Super's obsession compels him to enter Lutie's apartment when only her son is home. Once again, Petry stages the scene in terms that foreground the Super's compulsive need to look and see. "He would see how the place looked," she writes. "He would see her bedroom" (101). Once again the scene culminates with an extraordinary presentation of phallic imagery. After investigating all of the rooms, the Super fixes on a lipstick that Lutie has left on her table:

> Jones was staring at a lipstick that was on the table-top. It had been lying close to the bowl of flowers so that he hadn't noticed it. The case was ivorycolored and there was a thin line of scarlet that went all the way around the bottom of it. He kept staring at the lipstick and almost involuntarily he reached out without moving his chair and picked it up. He pulled the top off and looked at the red stick inside. It was rounded from use and the smoothness of the red had a grainy look from being rubbed over her mouth. He wanted to put it against his lips. That's the way her mouth would smell and it would feel like this stuff, only warm.

Laura Mulvey has famously posited that, when gazing at women on the screen, male spectators escape their fear of lack of the phallus---their fear of castration---by either voyeurism or "the substitution of a fetish object" (438).[12] Here the Super clearly disavows castration by associating Lutie with the "red stick," and this projection becomes even more apparent when Bub, sensing the impropriety of the Super's apparent fixation on the object, snatches it from him "in a swift, instinctive, protective gesture" (105). The Super laments his loss:

> There ought to be some way of getting that lipstick away from him. It would be good to hold it in his hands at night before he went to sleep so that the sweet smell would saturate his nostrils. He could carry it in his

> pocket where he could touch it during the
> day and take it out and fondle it down in the
> furnace room.
> When he stood outside on the street, he
> wouldn't have to touch it, but he would
> know it was there lying deep in his pocket.
> He could almost feel it there now---warm
> against him. (106)

Possessing the lipstick would allow the Super to conquer his sense of lack: The proof of the phallus would be there, "lying deep in his pocket" (106).

This passage, like the flashlight episode, makes Petry's debt to the work of Freud unmistakable.[13] What is more striking, however, is the degree to which Petry's work anticipates that of Laura Mulvey and other feminist film theories. The moment in which Bub intercepts the lipstick becomes one of a series in which Petry depicts Bub and the Super as characters who understand one another ---who are, in fact, versions of the same man at different stages of experience. For my reading, Bub's function in these terms is crucial because Bub is also relentlessly constructed as a spectator---especially on film.

Bub's own---still latent---potential to become the sort of compulsive scopophiliac that we must understand the Super to be is framed in the broadest sense by the loneliness that he shares with the Super. We are told in our first extended glimpse of the Super's conduct as an ogler of women that his behavior is motivated by "the deadly loneliness that ate into him day and night. It was a loneliness born of years of living in basements and sleeping on mattresses in boiler rooms" (85). This loneliness, which figures as lack, likewise informs the actions of Bub. Lutie discovers early in the text that Bub, to endure the tedious hours when she is at work, had developed a game:

> He walked over to the window and stood
> there looking out, his chin resting on his
> hands . . . ,
> "What are you looking at?" she asked.
> "The dogs down there," he said, pointing. "I
> call one of 'em Mother Dog and the other
> Father Dog. There are some children dogs
> over yonder." She looked down in the
> direction in which he was pointing.
> Shattered fences divided the space in back
> of the houses into what had once been back
> yards. But as she looked, she thought it had
> become one yard, for the rusted tin cans, the
> piles of ashes, the pieces of metal from
> discarded automobiles, had disregarded the

> fences. The rubbish had crept through the
> broken places in the fences until all of it
> mingled in a disorderly pattern that looked
> from their top-floor window like a hugh
> junkpile instead of a series of small back
> yards. She leaned farther out the window to
> see the dogs Bub had mentioned. They were
> sleeping in curled-up positions, and it was
> only by the occasional twitching of an ear or
> the infrequent moving of a tail that she could
> tell they were alive.
> Bub was explaining the details of the game
> he played with them. It had something to do
> with which one moved first. (72-73)

Here Bub views the spectacle of Harlem itself, but his gaze in this scene eventually shifts to the face of his mother. In her construction of this scene, Petry deftly merges the spectatorial gaze that Bub is cultivating in his private game with the full-blown scopophilia of the man who functions increasingly as his mentor:

> She was holding him so tightly that he
> turned away from his game with the dogs to
> look up in her face.
> "You're pretty," he said, pressing his face
> close to hers. "The Super says you're pretty.
> And he's right." (74)

Bub's need not only to watch but to conceive of his environment as a spectacle, Petry implies, is an embryonic form of the compulsion that drives the Super.

More often, however, Bub's spectatorship involves going to the movies. In a number of scenes throughout the novel, Bub effusively narrates his response to films he has seen. Yet the significance of his spectatorship becomes clearer during the stalking scene I have quoted from above. At the opening of the scene, when the Super has first entered Lutie's apartment in her absence, Bub exclaims, " 'I been to the movies . . . . You shoulda seen it' "(102). Throughout the remainder of the passage, the Super's compulsive examination of Lutie's apartment is accompanied by Bub's endless telling of the movie" (104). By so closely connecting the gaze of the Super and Bub, Petry both presciently links Freud with masculine film spectatorship and points to the larger cultural forces that perpetuate what Mary Ann Doane terms the "masculinization of the spectatorial position" (188).[14]

The Super's fixation on Lutie as an object of the gaze culminates predictably in a scene in which he attempts to rape her. At this point, however, the Super's own status as the object of a policing gaze comes into dramatic relief. For throughout the Super's scopophilic gambit, he is consistently represented as suffering under a complex scopic regime that emanates from a network of power beyond his understanding. It is Mrs. Hedges who interrupts the Super's bid to assault Lutie, exclaiming, " 'Ever you even look at that girl again, I'll have you locked up' " (238). In her compelling reading of *The Street*, Marjorie Pryse argues that Mrs. Hedges figures in a larger discourse of design that Petry invokes throughout the text. What Pryse and others have seemingly discounted, however, is the degree to which Mrs. Hedges embodies a mode of controlling surveillance that exists in a dynamic tension with the fascinated looking the Super exemplifies.

Mrs. Hedges is introduced into the action of the text almost immediately, and from the first instant she appears she possesses a surreal and enigmatic scale that is the text's most consistent and marked gesture toward naturalism. As Lutie examines the sign advertising the apartment she will soon rent, she becomes aware of a woman sitting in a first-floor window. Unsettled to realize that "the woman had been sitting there all along staring at her, reading her thoughts, pushing her way into her mind" (5), Lutie immediately focuses on the sinister intensity of Mrs. Hedges's eyes: "They were as still and as malignant as the eyes of a snake. She could see them quite plainly---flat eyes that stared at her--- wandering over her body, inspecting and appraising her from head to foot" (6). Lutie's immediate sense of violation---of her mind invaded, her body scrutinized---is clearly akin in this initial scene to the impact of the Super's obsessive gaze. Hedges, that is, might be understood to be looking at Lutie with the same sort of sexual interest that the Super addresses to her. And we do, in fact, soon learn that Hedges assesses Lutie's body here and elsewhere as a sexual object.

Yet Hedges's treatment of Lutie in these terms is mediated by her work as the madame of a "fairly well-kept whorehouse" (57), and while I will return later to the place of "fascinated looking" in the dynamics of Mrs. Hedges and Lutie, Hedges's role as madame functions as an entry point into her more important "looking" function in the text. For though Hedges's first imposing gaze upon Lutie can be read as a sexual act, Hedges's gaze here and later is generally characterized in terms that are more systematic than libidinal. While the Super, that is, in his exercise of what Doane calls the "masculine axis of vision," perceives Lutie primarily in terms of sexual difference, Hedges scans the content of the world around her with a wider band spectrum, "reading thoughts"---apparently to control them---even as she takes in Lutie's body as a saleable object (Doane 188).

This more comprehensive and systematic mode of looking is reflected by Hedges's vast knowledge of the street before her. Early in the novel, Min, a woman who has shared the Super's bed as a hedge against loneliness and impoverishment, turns to Mrs. Hedges for counsel on how to neutralize the

Super's obsession with the younger, more beautiful Lutie. Mrs. Hedges, she reasons, is the perfect source of advice because she "knew everything that went on in this house and most of the other houses on the street. . . .she knew this block between Eighth Avenue and Seventh Avenue better than most people know their own homes" (75-77). The Super perceives the scope of Mrs. Hedges's knowledge as even wider, feeling simply that she "know[s]. . . everything" (290).

As Pryse has suggested, this omniscience can be understood as "godlike" (119). Min, for example, sees in Hedges's brooding vigil the possibility that, "if she stopped looking at [the street] for as much as a minute, the whole thing would collapse" (14). While Pryse locates in this and other passages an essential gesture toward deism, I believe the more important power that Hedges represents is a worldly one. Ultimately, Mrs. Hedges's acquisition of knowledge of the street through her tireless surveillance is revealed to be an exercise of power on behalf of Junto, the white racketeer who controls the local economy. It is Junto who controls the larger prostitution ring into which Hedges channels the women she recruits to her own bordello. It is to him that she relates many of her observations regarding the activities on the street. Mrs. Hedges reflects,

> Yes. She and Mr. Junto had gone a long way. A long, long way. Sometimes she had surprised him and surprised herself at the things she had suggested to him. It came from looking at the street all day. There were so many people passing by, so many people with burdens too heavy for them, young ones who were lost, old ones who had given up all hope, middle-aged ones broken and lost like the young ones, and she learned a lot just from looking at them. (251)

Junto himself is repeatedly characterized as a chronic watcher; as Lutie enters his bar early in the text, she reflects that, "whenever she had been in here, he had been sitting at the same table, his hand cupped behind his ear as though he were listening to the sound of the cash register; sitting there alone watching everything---the customers, the bartenders, the waiters" (146). Pervasive and unobtrusive, Junto's own surveillance is a regulative one; he watches in order better to control the flow of capital through Harlem:

> . . .Junto's squat-bodied figure was all gray---gray suit, gray hair, gray skin, so that he melted into the room. He could sit forever at that table and nobody would look at him twice. All those people quzzling drinks at

> the bar never glanced in his direction. The
> ones standing outside on the street and the
> ones walking back and forth were dumb,
> blind, deaf, to Junto's existence. Yet he had
> them coming and going. If they wanted to
> sleep, they paid him; if they wanted to drink,
> they paid him; if they wanted to dance, they
> paid him, and never even knew it. (275)

There is much to say about the figure of Junto that the space constraints of
this article do not permit; yet for my purposes, the most striking element of
Junto's character is his very diffuseness---he is, as Wurst puts it, "invisible,
invincible, and omnipotent" (21). His very grayness in the black-and-white
optics of a segregated America suggests his strange non-presence.

And in many senses, Junto is less of a subject than any other character in the
text. As Pryse has suggested, the name Junto seems a calculated invocation of
the sort of cabal of powerful men that propelled Ben Franklin---a figure who
haunts Petry's novel---on his road to success.[15] In this sense, Junto is not one
man but a figure for a power that feeds on the color line but is not reducible to it.
Importantly, Junto is the one major character in the text from whose eyes we
never see events. We are denied the possibility of understanding him as a
single, coherent consciousness. His increasingly abstract, disembodied quality
seems an exemplary expression of what Reginald Twigg characterizes as the
"feeling of alienation and weightlessness in the observer" that is produced by
"the conceptual distance necessary for the operation of surveillance . . . because
the fiction of a transcendent gaze is accomplished only by the rigorous denial of
the body" (320). Indeed, by the conclusion of the text Lutie perceives Junto as a
sinister, shapeless figure of evil---a profound stillness that isolates her and drives
her toward her own destruction:

> Before it had been formless, shapeless, a
> fluid moving mass---something disembodied
> that she couldn't see, could only sense.
> Now, as she stared at the couch, the thing
> took on form, substance. She could see
> what it was. It was Junto. Gray hair, gray
> skin, short body, thick shoulders. He was
> sitting on the studio couch. The blue-glass
> coffee table was right in front of him. His
> feet were resting, squarely, firmly, on the
> congoleum rug.
> If she wasn't careful she would scream. She
> would start screaming and never be able to
> stop, because there wasn't anyone there.
> Yet she could see him and when she didn't

see him she could feel his presence. She
looked away and then looked back again.
Sometimes he was there when she looked
and sometimes he wasn't.
She stared at the studio couch until she
convinced herself there had never been
anyone there. Her eyes were playing tricks
on her because she was upset, nervous.
(418)

Omnipresent and insidious, Junto finally seems to exemplify the Foucauldian axiom that modern surveillance is internalized by contemporary subjects, producing in them a mode of self-regulation that serves power. In the case of the subjects with whom Petry is concerned, moreover, this self-regulation has everything to do with race and segregation. The very existence of black ghettoes like Harlem was enforced by the fear among blacks that the white U.S. government was constantly watching each of them. Junto himself profits from the segregation enabled by this culture of surveillance by economically manipulating Harlem's captive consumer base. It should be noted, however, that Petry complicates Junto's relationship to this nexus of surveillance and racism by repeatedly emphasizing Junto's own indifference to race---an indifference exemplified by his alliance with and deep affection for Mrs. Hedges. Again and again throughout the text, Junto is depicted as never "stop[ping] to think whether folks are white or black." (251)

There are several possible ways of understanding Petry's depiction of Junto in these terms. On the most basic level, because Junto himself is represented as having had to struggle up from desperate poverty, it is possible to read his apparent fair-mindedness as an understanding of blacks arrived at through a similar class experience. Or perhaps Petry wished to document what she perceived to be a tendency among the white businessmen of Harlem to treat the blacks with at least superficial respect. On a more abstract level, it is also possible to see Petry's depiction of Junto as a means of speculating that a thoroughly systematic structure of power, driven primarily in this case by economic forces, might generate a culture that so dismantles human subjectivity itself that racial categories become inconsequential: In this reading, Junto dwells in a gray zone of economic imperative, where race is neutralized by an optics of dollars and cents. Yet no matter which interpretation one brings to Junto's ostensible color-blindness, it is crucial to understand that his actions remain contextualized by the rigid hierarchy that the system of white power holds in place. Junto can afford to bypass the usual discourses of race, that is, as long as the racial hierarchy remains so naturalized that his power is unquestionable. And it is surveillance itself that maintains this complex hierarachy.[16] It is in these terms that I link surveillance with racism in Petry's text.

The Super and Mrs. Hedges (as the "eyes" of Junto), then, seem to represent a sexualized, fascinated looking and surveillance, respectively. Yet, as in the cultural history that Pollock traces in her essay, the two modes of looking collapse into one another in striking ways in *The Street*. As I will now show, while the Super's ceaseless gazing is framed in a language of objectifying sexual desire, his mode of looking ultimately shifts toward a paradigm of surveillance that is underwritten by racist white power. Likewise, while Mrs. Hedges and Junto clearly figure within a system of surveillance in the text, both are also implicated within the sexual dynamics that propel fascinated looking.

The Super's aggression toward Lutie does not in fact end with his foiled rape attempt; rather, his aim shifts from raping her to destroying her by destroying her son. The Super misinterprets Lutie's rejection of his sexual advance, finding in it evidence that she believes that "black men weren't good enough for her" (282). This misinterpretation is in a sense the culmination of a pattern of mistaken visions and hallucinations that constitute the other form of seeing that Petry associates with this figure. From the very outset of the text, the Super is represented as a man who "got notions in his head about things" (114). In his sexual drive to possess Lutie, for example, he indulges in extended fantasies in which he sees her welcoming---even initiating---a sexual liaison.

Yet the more striking instances of the Super's tendency to see falsely the world around him are the consequence of Min's efforts to quell his pursuit of Lutie. Desperate to ensure that the Super does not ask her to move out of his apartment, Min secures the services of a root doctor. The doctor's "prescription" includes the placing of a large cross over the bed the two share. The prescription proves effective, for the Super is nearly overcome by panic each time he sees the cross. When he first spies it over the bed, "he started backing away from the sight of it, retreating toward the living room where he wouldn't be able to see it" (140). Throughout the remainder of the text, the Super is plagued by visions of it:

> Finally it seemed to him that he met it at every turn. Wherever he looked, he saw a suggestion of its outline. His eyes added a horizontal line to the long cord that hung from the ceiling light and instantly the cross was dangling in front of him. He sought and found the shape of a cross in the window panes, in chairs, in the bars on the canary's cage. When he looked at Min, he could see its outline as sharply as though it had been superimposed on her shapeless, flabby body. (231)

The Super's hallucinatory dread of the cross, we quickly learn, is produced by the association he makes between it and "the retribution which . . . awaited men who lusted after women---men like himself":

> Hence to him a cross was an alarming and
> unpleasant object, for it was a symbol of
> power. It was mixed up in his mind with the
> evil spirits and the powers of darkness it
> could invoke against those who outraged the
> laws of the church. (140)

What is striking about this passage is the degree to which the power of the Church has produced a mode of self-regulation in the Super that in turn transforms his vision. Noel Peacock has described the ways in which "hallucination . . . signifies a psychological internalization of the scopic regimes's gaze" (118). The Super's hallucinatory response to the cross, then, must be understood in part as a by-product of the power that the modern church---with its apparent capacity to monitor and record every indiscretion---exerts upon his imagination. [17]

Yet I would argue that the Super's tormented visions also derive from the constant surveillance to which Mrs. Hedges subjects him. For while the Super projects his sense of sexual guilt and corruption onto the cross, it is actually Mrs. Hedges who more overtly polices the Super's sexual desire. Indeed, while, as I have established above, Mrs. Hedges's gaze captures every movement on the street. The Super accurately perceives that he is the particular object of a "constant, malicious surveillance" on her part (379). The Super's compulsion to watch women on the street is relentlessly subverted by Mrs. Hedges's watching presence:

> In a sense, Mrs. Hedges even spoiled his
> daily airings on the street, for he became
> convinced that she could read his mind. His
> eyes no sooner fastened on some likely
> looking girl than he became aware of Mrs.
> Hedges looming larger than life itself in the
> window---looking at him, saying nothing,
> just looking, and he was certain, reading his
> mind. (93)

This controlling of the Super's sexual desire becomes even more pronounced once he begins to stalk Lutie. At her first opportunity, Mrs. Hedges obliterates the pleasure he takes in gazing at the young woman:

> Now standing here on the street watching
> Lutie walk toward the corner, he was aware

> that Mrs. Hedges was looking at him from
> her window.   He was filled with a vast
> uneasiness, for he was certain that she could
> read his thoughts . . . .
> "Ain't no point in you lickin' your chops,
> dearie," she said, "There's others who are
> interested."
> He frowned up at her. "What you talkin'
> about ?"
> "Mis' Johnson, of course. Who you think
> I'm talking about? . . . There ain't no point
> in you getting' het up over her. She's
> marked down for somebody else." (89-90)

The ultimate instance of this regulation of the Super's sexual desire, of course, comes when Mrs. Hedges physically arrests the Super's attempt to rape Lutie.

The stakes of this intersection of surveillance and spectatorship can be understood in several ways. Both the quelling function of the cross and the aggressive conduct of Mrs. Hedges can be understood as instances in which black women use surveillance to control the masculine gaze. It is Min, after all, who installs the cross in their apartment.   Her decision to do so is the consequence of her own observations of the Super:

> She had seen him look at that young Mrs.
> Johnson the night she paid the deposit on the
> top-floor apartment. He had almost eaten
> her up looking at her, overwhelmed by her
> being so tall, by the way her body fairly
> brimmed over with being young and
> healthy. Three different times since then she
> had opened the hall door just a crack and
> seen him standing out there watching young
> Mrs. Johnson as she went up the stairs. (113-
> 14)

Both Min and Mrs. Hedges, then, watch the Super watch Lutie, and both exercise a regulatory control over his objectifying gaze. This use of surveillance to check male spectatorship and attendant sexual aggression could be understood to affirm Lutie's early assessment that "the man's eyes were worse than the eyes of the woman sitting in the window" (9). That is, the capacity of the surveying gaze of Min and Mrs. Hedges to protect Lutie from the immediate threat of rape that the Super poses could be understood to signal that black women are less damaged by surveillance than by spectatorship---that indeed surveillance empowers them. And since Mrs. Hedges and Min are enabled in their acts of surveillance by an underlying matrix of white power, represented by Junto and the Church, respectively, we must reflect on whether Petry's text also implies that black women must ally themselves with whiteness to free themselves from victimization at the hands of black men---that they must either be surveying watchers coopted into a white system of power or objects of a controlling black male gaze. In this sense, the surveillance of the Super figures in a too-familiar dynamic of white policing of black male sexuality.[18] Such an interpretation would suggest the inverse of Pollock's reasoning that "sexuality both collaborates with and disrupts . . . disciplinary surveillance," implying instead that surveillance disrupts sexuality. (38)

Yet, understanding Petry's novel to assert a connection between white surveillance and black female sexual empowerment would be too reductive, I think, given the text's climax, where Junto's systemic power and his male gaze fully fuse to set in motion Lutie's devastation. Certainly, it is Junto's black henchman, Boots Smith, who attempts to rape Lutie, a narrative turn which continues to place the emphasis on the threat of black male sexual desire. Yet Junto's systematic manipulation of Lutie's financial life, through his control of her nascent singing career, is what renders her vulnerable to that attack and its consequences, suggesting that ultimately Lutie, as a black woman, is at the mercy of both the dynamics of surveillance and spectatorship that the text depicts.

Finally, perhaps the most interesting outcome of these complex looking relations is the Super's own gradual movement from a spectatorial to surveying mode of looking. Once Mrs. Hedges bars his access to Lutie---not merely stopping the rape attempt, but clarifying that it is the powerful Junto who has claimed Lutie---the Super is cast fully into an awareness of the complex field of power in which he is suspended. Recalling his earlier attempts to battle Mrs. Hedges, he sees connections that were previously invisible:

> His thoughts jumped back to Mrs. Hedges.
> So that was why he couldn't have her locked
> up that time he went to the police station.
> He remembered the police lieutenant,
> "What's her name?" and his eyes staring at
> the paper where it was already written down.
> Junto was the reason he couldn't have her
> arrested that time. Sometimes during the
> summer he had gone to the Bar and Grill for
> a glass of beer and he had seen him sitting in
> the back---a squat, short-bodied white man
> whose eyes never apparently left the crowd
> drinking at the bar. The thought of him set
> Jones to trembling. (279)

Certainly, even after his insight, the Super remains somewhat delusional, thinking with complete conviction that Lutie "was in love with the white man, Junto, and she couldn't bear to have a black man touch her" (281). Yet, the revelation of the power network seems to transform the Super's consciousness:

> Well, he'd fix her. He'd fix her good. He
> searched his mind for a way to do it and was
> surprised to find that his thinking had grown
> cool, quite, orderly . . . .
> He strained his eyes in the dark of the room
> as though by looking hard enough in front of
> him he would be able to see the means by
> which he would destroy her. He walked up
> and down thinking, thinking, thinking. . . .
> (283)

As he strains into the dark, the Super begins to see in a new way. The next day he engineers a plan in which he will himself manipulate the field of power to destroy Lutie:

> He stood transfixed by the wonder of what
> he was thinking. Because he had found
> what he wanted. This was the way to get the
> kid. Not even Junto with all his money
> could get the kid out of it. The more he
> thought about it, the more excited he
> became. If the kid should steal letters out of
> mail boxes, nobody, not even Junto, could
> get him loose from a rap like that. Because
> it was the Government. (291)

The scheme in which he persuades Bub to steal mail for him, then turns him into postal investigators, becomes another remarkable moment in the text where fascinated looking and surveillance become implicated in one another.[19] It is through Bub's love of movies that the Super entices Bub to commit the crime, speaking to him in an idiom of "crooks" and "detectives" that the movies Bub views romanticize. And, indeed, once Bub begins the work, the boy frames it in these terms:

> It was a pleasant tingling similar to the
> feeling he got at gangster movies. These
> men behind him, these people passing by,
> didn't know who he was or what he was
> doing. It could be they were the very men
> he was trying to catch; it could be the
> evidence to trap them was at that very

> moment reposing in the pockets of his
> jacket.
> This was more wonderful, more thrilling,
> than anything he had ever done, any
> experience he had ever known. It wasn't
> make-believe like the movies. It was real,
> and he was playing the most important part.
> (342)

In a sort of infinite regress of fascinated looking and surveillance, Bub is lured into the Super's trap by watching films that in turn fetishize the surveillance activities of detectives. The pleasure for Bub here is the invisibility that attends surveillance---or as Seltzer puts it, the "seeing without being seen [that] becomes the measure of power" (41); even as the Super shifts from a spectator to a surveyor, so does his protégé.[20]

Finally, the Super's inclinations to be a spectator resurface, as he revels in his opportunity to "stay and watch [Lutie] and laugh at her efforts to get Bub out of it" (384). Yet his activation of the incriminating authority of the government to effect Lutie's undoing suggests Petry's awareness of the complex relays between the masculine gaze and a mode of surveillance that marshals the more diffuse and systematic regulatory powers that emerge from and support the racist ideology that has created Harlem.[21] Bub's fate in the aftermath of the Super's trap, moreover, only intensifies the Super's apparent complicity with racist disciplinary power: Bub is consigned to reform school at the end of the text---an institution that represents the very essence of the disciplinary structures associated with modern surveillance.

Likewise, one can understand Mrs. Hedges not simply as a figure for surveillance in the text, but also as an emblem of how the powers and pleasures of looking are entwined. The narrative of how Mrs. Hedges has come to occupy a permanent, surveying post at her window comes late in the text and surfaces as a memory triggered by gazing upon Lutie. Mrs. Hedges recalls a life of brutal traumas produced by her physical appearance:

> She began thinking about the period in her
> life when she had haunted employment
> agencies seeking work. When she walked in
> them, there was an uncontrollable revulsion
> in the faces of the white people who looked
> at her. They stared amazed at her enormous
> size, at the blackness of her skin. They
> glanced at each other, tried in vain to control
> their faces or didn't bother to try at all,
> simply let her see what a monstrosity they
> thought she was. (241)

Driven by misery from a small town in Georgia where, because of her giant size, "people . . . never really got used to the sight of her," Mrs. Hedges had hoped to find love and acceptance in New York. Specifically, she "hoped that she would find a man who would fall in love with her" (242). Yet, instead, Mrs. Hedges becomes ever more conscious that she will never be the object of a desiring male gaze.

This reality becomes indelible when after making Junto's acquaintance and moving into a tenement he owns, she is horribly burned. "Scarred like this, hair burned off her head like this," she reflects "she would never have any man's love" (246). Instead, she must endure an even more uncomfortable visibility in her disfigurement:

> When the nurses and doctors bent over her to change the dressings, she watched them with hard, baleful eyes, waiting for the moment when they would expose all the ugliness of her burnt, bruised body. They couldn't conceal the expressions on their faces. Sometimes it was only a flicker of dismay, and then again, it was sheer horror, plain for anyone to see---undisguised, uncontrollable. (246-47)

The affront of existing as a horrific spectacle drives Mrs. Hedges into seclusion: "She stayed in the hospital for weeks during which the determination never to expose herself to the prying, curious eyes of the world grew and crystallized" (247). At the end of her hospital stay, she moves to her new post at the window on the street, where she can watch while controlling her own visibility.

In Mrs. Hedges, then, we find another complex variation on the relay between surveillance and fascinated looking. While Lutie is victimized by the excess of the Super's objectifying gaze, Mrs. Hedges experiences the absence of such a gaze as a punitive denial of sexual difference. Though she perceives that Junto has strong feelings for her, she understands them as fundamentally platonic: " . . . even he would never want her as a woman. He had the kind of forthright admiration for her that he would have for another man---a man he regarded as his equal" (246). Her alliance with Junto, which is cemented by her disfigurement in the fire, moves her into an abstract realm of surveillance where, though she seeks an escape from watching eyes, she still experiences the absence of the gaze as a form of deprivation. That deprivation of the gaze, and her attendant perceived masculination, propels her both to become an agent of Junto's scopic regime and to gaze upon women like Lutie as sexual objects. [22]

As I hope I have now established, Petry's novel is a subtle meditation on the relays and intersections between fascinated, sexualized looking and a regulatory gaze of surveillance that serves a racist system of power. As Petry orchestrates one encounter after another among Lutie, the Super, Mrs. Hedges, Bub, and Junto she foregrounds the gaze in its myriad forms as the central preoccupation of her text. It is crucial to note, however, that in a single, late passage Petry allows for the possibility of a form of looking that is free from hegemonic associations altogether. In this single scene, Petry's novel replaces the dynamics of what Kaplan calls "subject-object" looking, with an interaction in which two black characters gaze at one another without any assertion of dominance. In this passage Mrs. Hedges intervenes after a gang of young neighborhood boys surround Bub and begin to beat him. At the point where the boys begin to taunt Mrs. Hedges as well as Bub, she commands the boys to leave, and in the aftermath of the exchange, Bub and Mrs. Hedges regard each other from their relative positions:

> Mrs. Hedges remained at the window, her arms folded on the sill. She and Bub looked at each other for a long moment. They appeared to be holding a silent conversation--acknowledging their pain, commiserating with each other, and then agreeing to dismiss the incident from their minds, to forget it as though it had never occurred. The boy looked very small in contrast to the woman's enormous bulk. His nose was dripping blood---scarlet against the dark brown of his skin. He was shivering as though he was cold.
> Finally their eyes shifted as though some common impulse prompted them to call a halt to this strange communion. (348)

What is truly distinctive about this moment is that it proves to be the single instance in the text when two characters regard one another as equals, using their capacity to see as a means of solidarity and understanding. This "strange communion" is the coalescence of Bub's male gaze and Hedge's surveying one, but rather than initiating a power struggle, the meeting of eyes becomes a means of mutually resisting the forms of cruelty and oppression that the attacking boys represent.

Certainly, the commiseration between Bub and Hedges might seem more politically significant if they united their gazes against a white oppressor, rather than a cohort of young, black boys. This instance of sharing pain, however, remains a signal episode of what Kaplain calls " a looking relation," which she characterizes as "mutual gazing, mutual subject-to-subject recognition" (79). As such, the episode contrasts sharply with the many instances in which *The Street* portrays the visual dynamics of Harlem an unilateral and hegemonic.

Finally, then, Petry represents acts of looking in Harlem both as a primary vehicle of racial and gender oppression and as a potential means of solidarity and resistance. In offering a complex map of the intersections between the operations of surveillance and spectatorship, Petry exposes the insidious degree to which the sexist objectification of women can mutate into complicity with racist systems of power, and vice versa. By illuminating these relays between the two forms of oppression Petry reminds the reader that, to battle either racism or sexism, one must battle both. And, interestingly, the very acts of looking which so often serve as the merciless conduits of these interlocked forms of hatred are ultimately pinpointed as one means of conquering them. In portraying a moment of communion between a mature black woman and a young black boy in which these once destructive forms of looking build a bridge of understanding, Petry suggests that the racial optics of hate may still be revised with time and across generations.

To battle either racism or sexism, one must battle both.

---

[1] See, for instance, Robert Bone's (*The Negro Novel*) unfavorable comparison of Petry to Himes and Wright, and Eisinger's (*Fiction of the Forties*) identification of Petry along with Wright and Ellison as the only three notable black writers of the period between 1939 and 1953.

[2] See, for instance, McKay's reading of Lutie at the nexus of "race, class, and gender" (130); Park and Wald's analysis of Petry's negotiation of notions of the public and private; Wurst's and Pryse's respective readings of the centrality of the mythology of Benjamin Franklin to Petry's narrative; and Drake's contextualization of Lutie within the social practices of the blues and conjuring.

[3] My intention in this essay is to suggest only in the broadest terms how the work of writers such as Wright and Ellison can help to illuminate central concerns in Petry's fiction. Much more detailed comparative scholarship remains to be done.

[4] Two of the most compelling discussions of Wright's depiction of ocular matters in *Native Son* are those by Jonathan Elmer ("Spectacle and Event in Native Son." *American Literature* 70 (1998): 767-98 and Katherine Fishburn ("The Delinquent's Sabbath; Or, The Return of the Repressed: The Matter of Bodies in Native Son." *Studies in the Novel* 32 (1999): 202-21.

[5] According to Ann E. Kaplan (*Looking for the Other: Feminism, Film and the Imperial Gaze*, New York: Routledge, 1997), "The imperial gaze reflects the assumption that the white western subject is central, much as the male gaze assumes the centrality of the male subject" (78). While Kaplan is specifically concerned with (post)colonial relations in her text, I use her term here because it represents an important effort to assess the role of looking in the construction of racial identity. Kaplan states, "The gaze of the colonialist . . . refuses to acknowledge its own power and privilege: it unconsciously represses knowledge of power hierarchies and its need to dominate, to control. Like the

male gaze, it's an objectifying gaze, one that refuses mutual gazing, mutual subject-to-subject recognition" (79).

[6] The only critic to give extended attention to the focus on visuality in Petry's text is Larry R. Andrews, whose discussions of acts of looking are framed in terms of his very general argument regarding "the powerful physical way in which the city assaults the characters' senses through concrete detail" (199). Petry's fascination with vision and looking continued to be evident in her two other novels, *Country Place* and *The Narrows*. In the former, this preoccupation is most apparent in the character of the "Weasel," a voyeuristic cab driver who manipulates the residents of the small town in which the narrative is set by wielding the knowledge he acquires through his relentless surveillance. *The Narrows*, however, is a more comprehensive meditation on the gazes, and one that merits further critical attention. While McDowell has briefly discussed the ways issues of visuality, knowledge, and perspective are explored in Petry's last novel, much more remains to be said about her discussion there of photography, the male gaze, and the relationship between race and acts of looking. I concur with McDowell's assessment that the primary focus of such an analysis should be the photographer Jubine. Characterized by "eyes . . .[that] held you, embarrassed you, bold bulging eyes that made no pretense of not looking, that couldn't get enough of looking," Jubine becomes a new and complicated means by which Petry continues to explore issues of surveillance, male gazing, and the complicity of acts of representation in the expansion of modern forms of power.

[7] Both hooks (*Black Looks)* and Kaplan have produced important scholarship on the ways whites and blacks look at one another; while this reading is, in part, an extension of these discussions, it also considers how Petry comments on how blacks look at one another and how this is shaped by the interracial looking of which they are the object.

[8] While the term scopic regime is most closely associated with the work of Jay Martin (*Downcast Eyes: The Denegration of Vision in Twentieth-Century French Thought*. Berkeley: University of California Press, 1994), here I am interested in the particular definition Noel Peacock attaches to it in relation to Conrad's *Under Western Eye* ("The Russian Eye: Surveillance and the Scopic Regime in Under Western Eyes." ed. Alex S. Kurczaba. Vol 5 of *Conrad: Eastern and Western Perspectives*. Lublin: Maria Curie-Sklodowska University Press, 1996, 113-33). In that text, according to Peacock, the scopic regime is a "political mode of perception that is monstrous both in its functioning and in its relationship to the perceiving eye of the narrator" (115). This is an apt definition of the scopic regime of Harlem in Petry's text, as well.

[9] In his focus on the "nexus of policing and entertainment" Seltzer locates in acts of looking in realist texts, for example, he tends to discount any distinction between the drives that propel surveillance and spectatorship (33). Likewise, Reginald Twigg ("The Performative Dimension of Surveillance: Jacob Riis' How the Other Half Lives." *Text and Performance Quarterly* 12 (1992): 305-28) elides the differences between these forms of looking when he writes that " . . . surveillance imbues the act of looking at Others with sexual power.

Objectification is simultaneously a sexual and political act whereby the Other is rendered naked and vulnerable in the performance of the gaze. As passive objects offered up to the transcendent gaze, a gaze that invades the most private and vulnerable moments, Others are put on display and visually consumed" (321). And in her suggestion that "the 'male' gaze and the 'imperial' gaze cannot be separated within Western patriarchal cultures," Kaplan also tends to conflate acts of spectatorship and surveillance (xi). While I agree with these critics' suggestion that on some levels the two modes of watching can be understood as inextricably implicated in one another, I believe that distinguishing the origins of these modes of looking can yield important insights about the relationship between desire and power. Griselda Pollock ("Feminism/Foucault—Surveillance/Sexuality." *Visual Culture: Images and* Interpretations. Ed. Norman Bryson, Michael Ann Holly, and Keith Moxey. Middleton: Wesleyan University Press, 1994, 6) effectively articulates these distinct origins when she writes that "the will to know and the resultant relations of power are furrowed by the move unpredictable and destabilizing plays of fascination, curiosity, dread, desire, and horror."

[10] This use of the flashlight as a symbol of the phallus is also reminiscent of the scene in *Native Son* in which Bigger refers to his act of masturbation as "polishing [his] nightstick" (30). According to Elmer, this scene suggests that "Wright evidently wishes us to follow the lateral associations and overdeterminations of the terms 'nightstick' and 'beating' until we recognize that the need for stimulation to which Bigger has just attested is here enacted as a kind of 'self-flagellation' (778). Elmer also reads Bigger's choice to masturbate within a movie theatre as part of a larger, complex meditation on "spectacle and event" in Wright's novel. Petry's choice meanwhile to render the phallus in terms of an implement of light reinforces the degree to which she is preoccupied with issues of vision in her own novel.

[11] While my interests in this scene focus on the dynamics of the gaze in this battle of flashlights, this is one of a number of important passages in which Petry generates a complex interplay between light and darkness. Light, of course, as Peacock points out, is the "precondition" of vision (114). Yet I believe that Petry's applications of light and darkness throughout the text could also be profitably read in relation to the sort of symbolic register of whiteness and blackness that Morrison identifies as a routine means by which American writers have commented on the sweeping ideological impact of racial thinking.

[12] According to Tania Modleski ("Cinema and the Dark Continent: Race and Gender in Popular Film." Eds. Katie Conboy, Nadia Medina, and Sarah Stanbury. *Writing on the Body: Female Embodiment and Feminist Theory*. New York: Columbia University Press, 1997), the use of any fetish is an attempt "to restore the wholeness and unity threatened by the sight of difference" (212).

[13] Marilyn Mobley (*African American Writers*. Ed. Valerie Lee. New York: Scribner's, 1991) points out that Petry was "widely" read in "psychology, psychiatry, and sociology" (350).

[14] See Doane (Conboy, Medina, and Stanbury), 188. This is not to say, of course, that issues of the gaze had not been discussed much earlier than the 1940s when Petry was writing. As Gertrude Koch ("Ex-Changing the Gaze: Re-Visioning Feminist Theory." *New German Critique* 334, Winter 1993) points out, by 1913 social commentators were attempting to grasp the nature of the gaze that new film technologies were both bringing into being and, in turn, being shaped by (140). The connection between male desire and film-watching that Petry implies in these scenes also marks one of her important debts to Wright's *Native Son*, where film-going precipitates more direct acts of sexual violence.

[15] While Pryse provides more information about Franklin's relationship to his Junto, Wurst provides the most comprehensive discussion of the ways Petry incorporates the mythology surrounding Ben Franklin into her novel.

[16] For an interesting discussion of Petry's complex and ambiguous depiction of Junto, see Wurst 18-19.

[17] The references to the cross, of course, are also evocative of the passages in *Native Son* where, after seeing a burning cross elevated by the Ku Klux Klan, Bigger continues to see its image before his eyes.

[18] As bell hooks observes, "The black male gaze was always subject to control and/or punishment by the powerful white Other" (118).

[19] Interestingly, it was an account in the newspaper of a young boy arrested after a superintendent had taught him to steal mail that was the initial seed for Petry's entire novel (Condon 5). At the very origins of the novel, then, was a fascination with power and surveillance.

[20] For a brief discussion of the ways surveillance in particular figures in Bub's entrapment, see Lindon Barrett "(Further) Figures of Violence...," 228.

[21] The Super's actual function as the building "superintendent" of course should not be overlooked when considering his (belated?) shift toward this more regulatory, less libidinal persona.

[22] For other accounts of the role sexuality and fascinated looking plays in Petry's depiction of Mrs. Hedges, see Lee Greene *(Blacks in Eden)*, 192; Rosemarie Garland Thompson (Ann Petry's Mrs. Hedges and the Evil, One-eyed Girl),"611; Keith Clark ("A Distaff Dream Deferred?), 498.

The Effects of Evil in Ann Petry's *The Street*: Invoking Biblical and Literary
Tradition (2004)
Annie S. Perkins

Ann Petry's first novel, *The Street*, ends in murder and abandonment.[1] Critics
have attributed this disastrous conclusion to the blind materialism of protagonist
Lutie Johnson or to the insuperable obstacle of racism and its attendant ills. No
one has examined the extent to which individual acts of evil contribute to
Lutie's failure to gain economic self-sufficiency, yet these acts are central to the
progress of the narrative and to the development of Petry's theme, the
deleterious effects of evil upon human effort and aspiration. Lutie, in her
willful, unthinking desperation, places her family in grave jeopardy among a
community of predators who aim to exploit and even destroy her. Petry
underscores this evil intent by accumulating around these predatory antagonists
damning biblical and literary associations. The novel rushes headlong toward
one inescapable conclusion: Lutie's plans are thwarted because she is no match
for the evil she confronts.

St. Thomas Aquinas defines evil as "an activity that is not only out of right
order but injurious to another as well" (166). *The Oxford English Dictionary*
lists the denotation of *evil* as "anything that causes harm or mischief" and the
meaning of its root as "overstepping proper limits." All of these meanings posit
a concept of community in which the positive values of human interaction---
nurture, protection, and support---flourish unimpeded: any deviation from these
values, that is, any assault on another's personhood, becomes "an activity . . .
out of right order," an "overstepping[of] proper limits"---in other words, an evil.
This evil unleashes (and is) malevolence, exploitation, and manipulation---all of
which cause physical, emotional, or psychic harm. In such a perverse
community where evil is the norm and the potential for harm remains constant,
one must have the moral fortitude and insight to withstand its inevitable assaults.
As Petry charts the heartless machinations, the syrupy temptations, and the
calculating covetousness of Lutie's antagonists, she reveals Lutie's lack of these
defenses and her consequent vulnerability to evil influences.

Early ascetics and theologians formulated evil as sins they believed led to
"damnation and the death of the soul" (Bloomfield 44). Their formulation,
rooted in Gnosticism, Neo-Platonism, and the monastic tradition, evolved into
the Seven Deadly Sins (Bloomfield 56). An understanding of five of these sins--
-lechery, wrath, envy, avarice, and pride---affords insight into the evil embodied
in Lutie's human antagonists (Jones, Boots, and Junto), and into the nature of
the danger they pose for her and her son, Bub. With these sins, or evils, as
backdrop, Petry weaves in conventional animal imagery and elements from the
biblical and literary tradition of Satan to create an atmosphere of palpable evil
that engulfs, infects, and ultimately destroys Lutie's family.

One of the engines of this destruction is the lechery of Jones, the building superintendent. The last in the list of the Seven Deadly Sins, lechery occupies a primary position in the novel. Indeed, Jones's lustful obsession with Lutie precipitates the disastrous climax of Bub's arrest and Boots Smith's death. To reveal Jones's lechery, Petry surrounds him with negative images: a goat, a dog/wolf, and a snake. First, as Jones shows Lutie the apartment she is considering renting, Petry writes that Lutie "half-expected to see horns sprouting from behind his ears . . .and a cloven hoof that twitched and jumped as he walked down the stairs" (20). With this image, Jones becomes associated with the goat, the traditional symbol of lechery, and indirectly the devil, a master of lechery seducer. The goat image recurs later in the narrative when Jones recalls the words of a young former lover: "You old goat! You think I'm goin' to stay in this stinkin' apartment with you slobberin' over me day after day?" (87). Through the goat image, Petry renders Jones a repulsive figure.

While Petry employs the goat image to reveal Jones' lust, she uses dog/wolf comparison to signal its progress from a passion to a threatening, irresistible compulsion. In Lutie's imagination, the gaunt, hungry-looking, Jones appears dog-like, "snuffing on [Lutie's] trail, slathering, slobbering after [her] like some dark hound of hell" (25). Lutie later dreams that Jones metamorphoses from a dog to a wolf; it is a revolting scene: Jones "and the dog had become one . . . . The same man, but with the dog's wolfish mouth and dog's teeth---white, sharp, pointed, in the redness of his mouth. . . . the long fangs closed on her hand. Her hand and part of her arm were swallowed up inside the wolfish mouth" (192). This nightmare serves three purposes: first, to foreshadow Jones's attempt to rape Lutie; next, to indicate the extent to which lust has overtaken Jones; and finally, to emphasize the threat he has become to Lutie. The narrator describes the surreal rape attempt: " . . . the man was trembling with his desire for her as he dragged her toward the cellar, and the dark hall was filled with the stench of the dog and the weight of his great body landing on her back" (236). The image of Jones as a dog/wolf underscores his lustful, dangerous, and predatory nature.

Petry next compares Jones to a snake, the universal symbol of evil. Min, whom Jones has come to loathe, imagines him breathing "with a sharp, hissing sound . . . the same sound that she had heard snakes make" (358). As Jones becomes increasingly hostile to Min, she protects herself by hanging a cross above their bed. It works, for Jones with "his hands itching to do violence," desists when he notices the cross. It stops him in his tracks: "When he saw the great gold cross. . . he stood still. It was like an accusing finger pointing at him. Almost immediately, he started backing away from the slight of it" (140). With this depiction of Jones, Petry appeals to a tradition dating from the Middle Ages, a time when "the sign of the Cross was considered the surest defense against the snares and stratagems of malignant spirits. The very mention of the Lord often sufficed to put to flight the fiends of hell" (Rudwin 135). Associated with a snake, Jones becomes an even more repulsive and dangerous figure.

Depicted then as both snake and fiend, Jones then becomes associated with envy and wrath, two of the Seven Deadly Sins closely associated with Satan. Both Jones and the fallen angel of the Bible and of *Paradise Lost* are motivated by envy. Like Satan, who will never be permitted to enjoy the sensuous pleasures of Paradise, Jones will never be able to enjoy the sensual delights he thinks Lutie offers. In *Paradise Lost*, as Satan pines . ". . . the more I see/ Pleasures about me, so much more I feel/ Torment within me" (9.120-121), he reflects on his own diminished state and then plots revenge "on him who next/ Provokes my envy, this new favorite/ Of Heaven, this man of clay" (175-176). Similarly, imagining the delights Lutie's husband has enjoyed with her, Jones cannot shed his envy. Regarding Bub as a young Adonis, Jones torments himself, thinking , ". . . the child was an exact replica of his father---that unknown man who had held Lutie in his arms, caressed her breasts, felt her body tremble against him" (88). Comparing himself to Lutie's husband, Jones endures pangs of inadequacy similar to the impotence Satan feels before God. Elucidating this point, Ernest Becker explains "envy is a signal of danger that the organism sends itself when a shadow is being cast over it, when it is threatened with being diminished" (12). Both Jones and Satan regard themselves as inadequate, and they are beset by gnawing envy that continually reminds them of their diminished state.

Jones's ego is further damaged once he learns that Junto, the white landlord, desires Lutie. He erroneously assumes that Lutie has rejected him because she prefers white men. He thinks, "Black men weren't good enough for her . . . . He had seen that kind before. No use for men of their own color." For that reason, he vows, "He'd fix her good" (283). At this point, Jones, like Satan, devises a vengeful, secret scheme because as Leonard E. Doob explains, "Evildoers may find it rewarding to have the frustrator subjected to a painful experience" (91). To hurt Lutie, whom he cannot engage directly, a deeply frustrated Jones determines to ruin her son. As a result of his Iagoesque villainy, the action quickly rushes to Bub's arrest, Boots Smith's murder, and Lutie's flight. "The simplest definitions of evil," says a recent essayist, "begins with whatever makes a child suffer" ("The Evil at the Dragon's Feet" 66). In depriving Bub of his mother as well as his childhood innocence, Jones commits a nearly unforgivable evil: the dooming of a child to the whirlwind of misfortune.

Just as envy motivates Jones, it also perversely animates Mrs. Hedges, who is trying to procure Lutie for Junto, and he intends her irreparable harm. Mrs. Hedges does not want Lutie to become Junto's mistress, which as degrading as it is, would at least have carried status, however dubious. Rather, she intends to transform Lutie into an expensive whore. Studying Lutie's good looks, she muses: "With that thick, soft hair, Lutie offered great possibilities for making money. Mr. Junto would be willing to pay very high for her. Very, very high, because when he got tired of her himself he could put her in one of those places on Sugar Hill" (256). To that end, she constantly tempts Lutie with the idea that "a nice white gentleman" is interested in her. Envy motivates Mrs. Hedges, an envy engendered by the knowledge that she never will possess Lutie's womanly appeal. Attractive, decent, and desirable, Lutie epitomizes what Mrs. Hedges has always lacked and wanted: beauty and desirability. "Seeing the way [Lutie's] hair went softly up from her forehead, looking at her smooth, unscarred skin, and then watching her walk out through the door with the long skirt gently flowing in back of her" (241), Mrs. Hedges recalls the fire that left her own mountainous body scarred, her limbs disfigured, and her bandanna-covered head forever bald. Motivated, then, by envy---and greed---Mrs. Hedges tries to destroy Lutie.

That Mrs. Hedges seeks Lutie's moral destruction can be deduced from Petry's use of snake imagery to depict her piercing eyes. To Lutie, they are "as malignant as the eyes of a snake" (6); they are "eyes like stones that had been polished. There was no emotion, no feeling in them, nothing visible but shiny, smooth surface" (239). To the narrator, Mrs. Hedges' eyes are "hard black eyes full of malice" (75). Even Jones notices "her eyes cold and unfriendly like the eyes of a snake. No expression in them, but you knew you weren't safe" (106). Through the snake image, Petry alludes to Mrs. Hedges's envy as well as to her dissembling---at first, she lies to Lutie about knowing Junto. Moreover, this image evokes the Evil Eye tradition of folklore, which holds that an individual with the evil eyes can harm an object of envy by merely looking at it. Mrs. Hedges envies Lutie and, for that reason, has no qualms about encouraging her to enter into an arrangement that would be degrading to Lutie and embarrassing to her son. For their evil intentions and acts, Virgil places procurers in the eighth circle of hell, where horned demons lash them incessantly. Mrs. Hedges would be deserving of that punishment.

Lust reappears in the figure of Boots Smith, the bandleader, whom Lutie eventually murders. In order to seduce Lutie, Boots offers her a singing contract that never materializes. He reveals his attitude toward Lutie as he contemplates Junto's request that Boots procure Lutie for him: "Was he in love with her? . . . . No. He just wanted her. There was a challenge in the way she walked with her head up, in the deft way she had avoided his attempts to make love to her. It was more a matter of itching to lay his hands on her than anything else" (263). Petry chooses an appropriate name for this character. The OED identifies "Old Boots" as a name for the devil, the arch deceiver, which Boots proves himself to be by setting Lutie up with Junto under the pretext of having her come to his apartment for the money he has promised for Bub's defense. At their first meeting, Lutie studies Boots: "There was no expression in his eyes, so softness, nothing to indicate that he would ever bother to lift a finger to help anyone but himself" (152). Versfeld writes that "evil is present in a nature not as something but as a lack of something which that nature should have" (41). Boots Smith lacks compassion because of the betrayal and pain he himself has experienced. Therefore, when Lutie approaches him for money to help her son, he rushes to exploit her and to betray Junto. His thoughts are a telling indictment: "He hadn't intended to in the beginning, but he was going to trick [Junto] and [he] would never know the difference. Sure, Lutie would sleep with Junto, but he was going to have her first . . . . After all, he's white and this time a white man can have a black man's leavings" (423). With hardly a thought, Boots is willing to defile and prostitute Lutie to satisfy his lust and desire for revenge. That Boots is bad luck---even for himself---becomes clear through the cat imagery Petry employs. At least three times in the novel, cat imagery signals Boots's predatory nature. He reminds Lutie, for example, of "a cat, lean, stretched out full length, drawing itself along on its belly, intent on its prey. . . . His body was lean, . . .and as he lounged there, his arm on the bar, his muscles relaxed, she thought again of a cat slinking quietly after its prey" (152). At another point, Boots walks out of a bar "cat-footed, his face as expressionless as when he came in" (27). Boots, however, does not walk away from the evil he intends for Lutie. Trapped by his own lust and treachery, he is destroyed by the evil he unleashes.

Representing omnipresent evil and the deadly sin of pride, Junto is the ringmaster in the nightmarish domain he controls. With Mrs. Hedges's counsel, he has built an empire of tenements and profits from the helplessness of its inhabitants. Junto has money, power, and influence; he can manipulate events that enable Mrs. Hedges to operate a profitable brothel in her neighborhood undisturbed by the police, that help Boots Smith dodge military service even though he has been drafted. As Junto sits in one of his clubs---silent, detached, master and lord of all, Lutie observe him:

> Somehow even at this distance his squat
> figure managed to dominate the whole room
> . . . . Whenever she had been in here, he had
> been sitting at the same table, his hand
> cupped behind his ear as though he were
> listening to the sound of the cash register;
> sitting there along watching everything---the
> customers, the bartenders, the waiters."
> (146)

By virtue of his power and position, Junto feels entitled to an exceptional – looking woman like Lutie. Confident that she will accept him, Junto dismisses Boots's suggestion that Lutie may refuse to sleep with a white man. "Money cures most things like that," he replies (275). A throughgoing materialist, Junto typifies the kind of pride manifested in egocentric love, an exploitative perversion, which, according to Versfeld, "degrades all reality to the category of the usable, with oneself as the end" (29). Junto wishes to use Lutie to satisfy his lust and his ego, and, if Mrs. Hedges can be believed, to swell his already overflowing coffers. Lutie eventually begins to understand the evil that Junto represents. Unaware that he will also be at Boots's home when she goes there for the money Boots has promised to lend her, Lutie nonetheless feels a sense of dread, no doubt the result of "smelling out evil," as her grandmother would have identified the sense of foreboding. En route, Lutie feels a palpable evil with every step. At Boots's apartment, this evil finally bodies forth as Junto, who confidently rises when Lutie enters, stands, and then leans "his elbow on the mantel," expectantly awaiting the assignation. The evil that Junto exudes resides in a lust and a marauding egocentrism that assaults decency and disrespects human dignity. It is born of a pride that causes men like Junto to feel entitled to a black woman's body, to regard their own rise from poverty to privilege, as Junto has done, as a position they have earned, and not to consider the misery of others. In spite of his tender feelings for Mrs. Hedges, Junto really cares about no one but himself and his own pursuits. What Gregory the Great writes of Pride aptly applies to Junto: ". . . and when he thinks he surpasses others in all things, he walks with himself along the broad spaces of his thoughts and silently utters his own praises (qtd. in Payne 73).

Junto, Boots Smith, Mrs. Hedges, and William Jones are sources of intended and actual evil in Lutie's life. Motivated by the deadly sins of lust, envy, wrath, or pride, they have a devastating impact upon Lutie's life. Yet, ultimately, Lutie must be held responsible for the devastation and defeat she suffers from individual acts of evil. Her own willfulness, a type of pride, manifested in unwise reliance on her own limited understanding and strength as well as an intense hatred for whites dooms Lutie and her son.

Lutie's willfulness compels her to act unwisely. Her unilateral decision to leave her family for an eventual two-years stay provides a telling example. When her husband, Jim, is unable to find work, Lutie secretly secures a housekeeping job in Connecticut in spite of an oblique warning from an Italian storekeeper that she is making a mistake. During that period, Lutie also decides without consulting anyone that she will visit her family less frequently in order to save money. After the marriage, predictably, crumbles, she arrogantly (or defensively) asserts she would not have left Jim had he asked her to stay. The reality is that Jim had not wanted Lutie to leave, and she knew it. Wounded pride prevents Lutie from trying to save her marriage. Consequently, she denies herself a husband who loves her and robs her son of a father whom he loves and needs. In effect, Lutie sacrifices a marriage and a family to save a house, which she loses anyway. By not consulting her husband, Lutie oversteps the boundaries inherent in a marital partnership and severs the familial bond.

A different type of pride, bordering on self-righteousness, convinces Lutie that she should leave her father's home to seek her own place. Openly disdainful of her father's lifestyle, Lutie fears that Bub will be corrupted, especially by her father's girlfriend, Lil. Respectable, decent, and moral, Lutie considers Lil a tramp. As she ponders renting the apartment on 116th Street, Lutie weighs her alternatives: "You can sit down and twiddle- your thumbs while your kid gets' a' free education from your father's blowsy girlfriend [Lil]. Or you can take this apartment" (19). This type of shallow either-or thinking fails to consider all of the advantages of remaining with her father or the disadvantages of leaving. When Lutie moves, Bub loses a home where he is cared for and, equally important, supervised. Never once does Lutie suggest that he has been neglected or mistreated by Lil, her father, or the roomers. In their new environment, however, Lutie worries constantly about Bub's lack of supervision after school and the potential dangers of the street. Considering the outcome, Lutie's short-sighted self-righteousness and, again, her willfulness place her son in the clutches of the devious super who causes his arrest and destroys his family. In this context, Lutie's optimism about moving into her own apartment is especially ironic: "With the apartment, Bub would be standing a better chance, for he'd be away from Lil" (25).

Lutie's pride causes her self-delusion. Although she witnesses the pernicious effects of her new environment upon others, Lutie thinks she will not become one of its casualties. To her mind, "She wasn't afraid of its influence, for she would fight againt it . . . she would fight back and never stop fighting back" (56, 57). Later, she declares, "I'm young and strong, there isn't anything I can't do" (63). In addition to these feelings of power and control, Lutie congratulates herself for having found a way out of the street. Thinking that she will be singing with Smith's band and imagining a better life for herself and Bub, Lutie exults:

> And the thought that she had been able to
> accomplish this alone, without help from
> anyone, made her open the street door of the
> apartment house with a vigorous push. . .
> .and as she stood there smiling, her face and
> body glowing with triumph, she looked as
> though she were dancing (230).

It is indeed ironic that Lutie has accomplished nothing: The singing contract does not materialize, and she learns too late that the evil embodied in Boots Smith, Junto, and Mrs. Hedges have vanquished her. By deluding herself into thinking that her solitary strength is sufficient to accomplish her goal, Lutie underestimates the evil she faces and leaves herself vulnerable to the evil machinations of others. One of her biggest mistakes is not taking Jones seriously when she senses the danger he poses. Once Mrs. Hedges has prevented his attack, Lutie does nothing to protect herself or Bub from him. Although she worries, with good reason, that he may takeout his hostility towards her on Bub, she decides not to report Jones to the police or to take any precautions. Incredibly, she never informs Bub of the attack, nor does she monitor his subsequent contacts with Jones. Instead, Lutie becomes so preoccupied with acquiring the funds to leave the street, she turns her son over to her enemy. Furthermore, in the case of Boots Smith, although Lutie understands his larcenous attitude, she still seeks money from him. It is only after his murder that she thinks about contacting her father, someone who surely would have helped her. The coup de grace, however, is the evil that infects Lutie herself. Having come to value money as the greatest good, she becomes obsessed with earning and saving. For the sake of money, she leaves her young son alone at home, afraid of the dark, to pursue a pipe dream dangled by a slick con man. She emphasizes the necessity of saving and decries the lack of money with such desperation that Bub, alarmed at her frustrated cry of "Damn being poor! . . . God damn it!" decides, in spite of his initial misgivings, to help Jones, his fiercest enemy, catch a fictitious mail thief.

Not only does Lutie 's preoccupation with money hurt Bub; it also harms her. As Lutie becomes increasingly desperate, she relaxes her moral rectitude and becomes an exploiter. At her first meeting with Boots, for example, she muses, "He had probably tossed out this sudden offer with the hope that she'd nibble at it. Only she wasn't going to nibble. She was going to swallow it whole and come back for more until she ended up as a vocalist with his band. She turned to look at him, to estimate him, to add up her chances . . . . It wouldn't be easy to use him" (115-152). This attitude signals Lutie's degenerating moral sense. Isolated from a network of support and separated from her spiritual self, Lutie becomes ever more vulnerable to others and to her own frailties.

Equally destructive is Lutie's wrath, a deadly sin, manifested in her hatred of whites. Bitter about the limited opportunities for gainful employment available to men of color, Lutie also experiences the hostility engendered by racial stereotypes. Although she avows, at one point, that hatred leads nowhere, Lutie allows her frustration to feed her hatred. Even when she acknowledges that it is partly responsible for Bub's plight---"Lately, she had been so filled with anger and resentment and hate that she had pushed [Bub] farther away" (406)---Lutie cannot control it. Her hatred intensifies as she faces Boots, whom she resent for trying to procure her for Junto. Failing to recognize her own complicity in the evil she faces, Lutie lashes out at Boots: "This quick surface anger helped to swell and became a part of the deepening stream of rage that had fed on the hate, the frustration, the resentment she had toward the pattern of her life" (428). Thus, when Boots strikes her, she defends herself by clobbering him repeatedly with a candlestick. Boots becomes an anvil on which to vent her pent-up rage. If it is true that hate destroys, then perhaps Freud's view is true: not to destroy ourselves, he says, it may be necessary to destroy someone else. In a desperate act of murder, Lutie may have been trying to save herself, perhaps from the painful recognition of her own responsibility in the nightmare her world has become.

Indeed, this nightmare is the revelation of the evil encamped around Lutie, where predators tread upon the ground of her physical and moral being. In her enervated moral condition, owing to her own frailties, Lutie is powerless to protect herself or her son from their onslaught. To prevent such devastation, the novel suggests, one must confront evil not on its own terms but in one's own inner territory where it also abides.

Note
1.Ann Petry, *The Street*, 1946. New York: Houghton Mifflin, 1974. This reference and subsequent ones are taken from this edition.

Works Cited

Becker, Ernest. *Escape from Evil*. New York: The Free Press, 1975.
Bloomfield, Martin. *The Seven Deadly Sins*.   Michigan: Michigan State University Press, 1967.
Doob, Leonard E. *Panorama of Evil: Insights from the Behavioral Sciences*. Westport: Greenwood, 1978.
"The Evil at the Dragon's Feet." *Time* 19 June 1995, 66.
Lyman, Stanford M. *The Seven Deadly Sins*. New York: General Hall, 1989.
Payne, Robert. *Hubris: A Study of Pride*. New York: Harper & Bros., 1970.
Petry, Ann. *The Street*. 1946. Boston: Houghton Mifflin, 1974.
Rudwin, Maximilian. *The Devil in Legend and Literature*. New York, 1970.
Versfeld, Marthinus. *A Guide to the City of God*. New York: Sheed and Ward, 1958.
Wilson, Angus, et al. *The Seven Deadly Sins*. London: Sunday Times, 1962

'Beating Unavailing Palms Against the Stone': Spatiality, Sexuality,
Stereotyping, and the Myth of the American Dream in Ann Petry's *The Street*
(2004)
Ama S. Wattley

Sexual stereotyping of the black woman is an issue that Ann Petry addresses in
her 1946 novel *The Street*. Petry's protagonist Lutie Johnson, is defeated by the
hostile environment in which she lives, and by the harsh social realities, racism
and sexism, as she attempts to succeed.

In his essay, "Ann Petry's Demythologizing of American Culture and Afro-
American Character," Bernard Bell argues that one of Petry's concerns in *The
Street* is to show how myths about America get debunked when they are applied
to African Americans, particularly African American women, because of the
racist beliefs and discriminatory forces at work against them.   To show that
American myths of success are often one-sided, Bell points to the difference
between Lutie's environment and that of the family for whom she works for two
years, the Chandlers, noting that "Petry's use of symbols of confinement and
contrasting images of the white world [. . .] give structural and thematic
coherence of the novel. The wide, quiet tree-lined sunny main street of Lyme,
Connecticut, where the Chandlers live in gracious luxury is contrasted with the
drab, violent, [and] over-crowded streets where Lutie's economic, racial, and
sexual circumstances trap her" (109).

In this essay, I return to Bell's argument and examine how in the *The Street*
sexual stereotyping of the black woman is an issue that Ann Petry addresses in
her 1946 novel and how Petry uses physical spaces that are narrow, small, and
confining as well as harsh social realities such as racism and sexism to relate to
the way in which Lutie is trapped and constricted within her urban environment
as she attempts to realize the American Dream.

W. E. B. DuBois's concept of the veil in *The Souls of Black Folk* is important
in understanding confinement and discrimination in Petry's novel.   Writing
about his first experience with discrimination, DuBois says: ". . . [I]t dawned
upon me with a certain suddenness that I was different from the others; or like,
mayhap, in heart and life and longing but shut out from their world by a vast
veil" (44). In *The Street*, Petry writes about Lutie's sense of exclusion while on
the subway, in the Chandler's home, and in Junto's Bar and Grille (i.e., while in
the white world):

> It was, she discovered slowly, a very strange
> world that she had entered. With an entirely
> different set of values. It made her feel that
> she was looking through *a hole in a wall* at
> some enchanted garden. She could see, she

> could hear, she spoke the language of the
> people in the garden, but she couldn't get
> past the *wall*. The figures on the other side
> of it loomed up life-size and they could see
> her, but there was this *wall in between which
> prevented them from mingling on an equal
> footing. The people on the other side of the
> wall knew less about her than she knew
> about them* (41; emphasis mine).

Like DuBois's veil, Petry's wall symbolizes an awareness of the forces of racism that shut black people off from the economic, political, and social opportunities to which whites have access. Early on in her experiences with the Chandler's, Junto, and other whites, Lutie believes the wall is a naturally occurring structure that does not allow whites and blacks to associate with one another. Later, however, Lutie concludes that the wall is a man-made barrier intentionally "built up brick by brick by eager white hands" (324) to keep blacks "hemmed into an ever-narrowing space, until [. . .] [they are] very nearly walled in" (324). Lutie learns, then, that it is not that whites are prevented from mingling with black people on an equal footing, but that they [whites] have no desire to do so. Whites like the Chandlers and their friends, Junto, and others could see black people beyond the figurative wall. Instead, the wall is deliberately constructed by whites and it creates distance between whites and blacks so that no real understanding takes place. Rather than see blacks as individuals, white people like the Chandlers and their friends, the people on the subway, and even Junto are more comfortable remaining ignorant about black people or negatively categorizing them.

In *The Souls of Black Folk*, Du Bois writes that "[I]t is a peculiar sensation, this double-consciousness, the sense of always looking at one's self through the eyes of others, of measuring one's soul by the tape of a world that looks on in amused contempt and pity" (45). In the *Street*, Lutie is constantly seeing herself through the eyes of other white characters in the novel. What she sees through their eyes is herself as sexual object or as a woman of easy virtue. Petry's utilization of Du Bois's concept is most apparent in an early scene on the subway when Lutie is returning home after work:

> She got off the train, thinking that she never
> felt really human until she reached Harlem
> and thus got away from the hostility in the
> eyes of the white women who stared at her
> on the downtown streets and in the subway.
> Escaped from the openly appraising looks of
> white men whose eyes seemed to go through
> her clothing to her long brown legs. On the
> trains their eyes came at her furtively from

behind newspapers, or half-concluded under
hatbrims or partly shielded by their hands.
And there was a warm moist look about
their eyes that made her want to run (57).

Lutie is reminded via the hostile eyes of the white female passengers that she is
perceived as a wanton woman who will entice the white women's husbands.
She is aware, from the lustful stares of the white men that they view her merely
as an exotic Other with whom they wish to have sex. In such settings, Lutie's
ego diminishes because she realizes that white people are looking at her in
stereotypical ways, and not as an individual. Such settings are what Lutie will
face throughout the novel. To communicate a sense of double-consciousness,
Petry ties to Lutie's realizations descriptions of space and size, which are small
and under the gaze of whites. For instance, after "hostile or lustful eyes of the
white passengers on the subway, "[Lutie] noticed that once the crowd [of
blacks] walked the length of the platform and started up the stairs toward the
street, it [her self-worth] expanded in size. The same people who had made
themselves small on the train, even on the platform, suddenly grew so large
they could hardly get up the stairs to the street together" (57-58). In other
words, the expansion in numbers of black people once they were out from under
the gaze of the white passengers relates to the increase in blacks' sense of self-
worth. The platform expands in size only when the black passengers are away
from the white commuters; their egos grow to normal sizes. Petry returns to
descriptions of space and size in the novel in order to communicate the way in
which other people's perceptions of Lutie stifle her ability to grow and to
become the best person she can be.

II

On the street, Lutie finds herself being viewed not only by whites but also by
blacks in ways that contrast with the image she has of herslf. In the novel, 116th
Street is the territory of Mrs. Hedges, a neighbor in Lutie's apartment building.
Mrs. Hedges is always present at the first floor window of this building, looking
out into the street and watching the people as they go past. When Lutie first
sees Mrs. Hedges, she takes an immediate dislike to her: "It was the woman's
eyes. They were as still and as malignant as the eyes of a snake. She could see
them quite plainly---flat eyes that stared at her---wandering over her body,
inspecting and appraising her from head to foot" (56). A good judge of
character, Lutie will learn later that Mrs. Hedges operates a small prostitution
ring from her apartment, and Mrs. Hedge's appraisal of her on their first meeting
is toward that purpose: Mrs. Hedges will try to *tempt* Lutie into working for her,
for as she concludes, money is the bottom line; the means by which one obtains
it is of little importance (417). But, Lutie will not be enticed by Mrs. Hedges's
money. When Lutie refuses Mrs. Hedges's offer , the madame "scowl[s] after
her. After all, if you needed money, you needed money and why anyone would
act like that when it was offered to them she couldn't imagine" (417). Mrs.

Hedges never thinks that perhaps Lutie has morals or that for Lutie mere survival does not take precedence over concerns about morality.

Mrs. Hedges's offers (to set Lutie up with a white man) angers Lutie who is reminded of the sexual legacy between black women and white men dating back to slavery, and of the sexual harassment by white men that black women continued to face. "At first, she merely fumed at the top of her mind about a white gentleman wanting to sleep with a colored girl. A nice white gentleman who's a little cold around the edges wants to sleep with a nice warm colored girl. All of it nice---nice gentleman, nice girl, one's colored and the other's white, so it's a colored girl and a white gentleman" (417). The reality for Lutie is that slavery allowed rape and sexual exploitation of black women, and its abolition had not done much to curb the sexual harassment and assault that black women faced at the hands of white men.

In Lutie's view, Mrs. Hedges is not much different from Mrs. Chandler and her friends or the white people she faced daily on the train and elsewhere who believed that "if a girl [is] colored and fairly young, why it stood to reason she had to be a prostitute. If not that---at least sleeping with her would be just a simple matter, for all one had to do was make the request" (45). Just as Mrs. Chandler's friends believed all young, attractive black women were ready and willing to sleep with their husbands, Mrs. Hedges's actions suggest she believes that all poor, young, and attractive black women should be ready and willing to earn extra money by sleeping around. The questions raised here is are the two perceptions of black women---that of the Chandlers and their friends (i.e. of whites) and that of Mrs. Hedges---based on racist beliefs? Generally, critics have suggested Mrs. Hedges operates not from racial stereotyping but from an attitude of economic pragmatism. She seems motivated by the realization that, other than prostitution, few avenues are open to black women to make strides economically. Nevertheless, for Lutie, the image of the black woman as sexually permissive is the same for whites and for blacks like Mrs. Hedges. Devastatingly, the space of Mrs. Hedge's street is confining. Confining also is Mrs. Hedges's perception of Lutie as a potential prostitute. Thus, the street and the image go hand in hand in Lutie's mind, and she feels trapped and unable to escape both.[1]

Petry also describes confinement via architectural space and the black males's perception of the black female. Upon first meeting Jones, the superintendent of her apartment building, Lutie senses a desire emanating from him that makes her feel uneasy. As with Mrs. Hedges, Lutie correctly gauges Jones's perception of her. He views her as a sexual object that he wishes to possess. Moreover, Jones believes that Lutie will be rather easy prey. In his mind, all it will take are a few cheap presents---a pair of stockings or some earrings---and she will make herself available sexually (99). Upon his introduction to Lutie, Jones refers to Lutie as "young little thing." Even while showing her her prospective apartment, he fantasizes sexual intercourse: "She went into the kitchen and the bathroom and he made himself stand still. For he knew if he followed her in there, he would force her down on the floor, down against the worn floor boards" (99). Later, in the story, Jones does attempt, unsuccessfully though, to rape Lutie.

Again, Petry uses descriptions of space to show that Jones's view of Lutie is limiting to her. As Lutie walks up the stairs ahead of Jones to view the apartment, she notices that "[t]he halls were so narrow that she could reach out and touch them on either side without having to stretch her arms any distance. When Lutie and Jones reach the fourth floor, Lutie thinks that instead of reaching out for the walls, the walls were reaching out for her---bending and swaying toward her in an effort to envelop her" (12). Two pages later, Petry transfers this action from the walls to Jones." While in the apartment, Lutie "force[s] herself to start walking toward the kitchen. As she went past him, it seemed to her that he actually did reach one arm out toward her, his body swaying so that its exaggerated length almost brushed against her" (15). Petry ties together the way in which both the space of the hallway and Jones's perception of and deviant behavior toward Lutie serve to stifle and restrict her. Petry uses the same verbs, "reaching" and "swaying," to describe both the movement of the walls and the movements of Jones, suggesting that Jones is as restrictive of Lutie as are the walls. By objectifying Lutie, Jones diminishes and devalues her identity in the same way that the "reaching" walls seem to obscure and contain her.

Petry contrasts the space of the apartment and the street with Junto's bar and grill and with the Chandler's house. While Petry describes the apartment and the street in terms of their small, narrow, and engulfing dimensions, she describes the bar and grill and the Chandler's house in terms of their vastness. The bar and grill is the place where the neighborhood residents go to unwind after dealing with the daytime pressures of survival in a world that is hostile to their very presence. Lutie, too, considers Junto's bar and grill to be a haven, a place where she can go to escape from the cramped quarters of her apartment, and "for a moment capture the illusion of having some of the things that she lacked" (144). Because of its spaciousness, Junto's establishment gives Lutie a sense of freedom: "The big mirror in front of her made the Junto an enormous room. It pushed the walls back and back into space; [. . .] it pushed the world of other people's kitchen sinks back where it belonged and destroyed the existence of dirty streets and small shadowed rooms" (146). The first sentence of Petry's description, however, suggests that the big mirror only creates the appearance of spacious size. In fact, because of its apparent immensity, Lutie is deceived into believing that it is a space where she can feel liberated from the restrictions and perceptions faced in the subway, in the street, and in the apartment. The Junto is a place where black and white people co-exist harmoniously. The white employees greet the black patrons graciously, not with the grudging respect or lack of respect that blacks were accustomed to receiving from whites at large. Petry states that the white bartenders' "courteous friendliness was a heartwarming thing that helped re-build egos battered and bruised during the course of the day's work" (143).

What lies underneath this harmonious interracial environment, however, is the same kind of economic oppression faced by blacks in the larger society. Petry has already informed us of the many black men, including Lutie's estranged husband Jim, who cannot find jobs. Despite this fact, the Junto, which is situated in a black neighborhood, employs only white bartenders. Blacks patronize the Junto but they do not work there. So, while the Junto seems to be a space that is more liberal and integrated, in actuality, it is a microcosm of the economic oppression that blacks faced in the larger society.

Like the illusory spatial enormity of the Junto, the white man who owns it, Mr. Junto creates the illusion that he does not hold racist or stereotypical notions about black people. Mrs. Hedges considers him a friend because he helped her start her prostitution business when she was a homeless woman living on the street. Boots Smith, the young musician who works for Junto, thinks he is color-blind because "[t]here was never anything in Junto's manner, no intonation in his voice, no expression that crept into his eyes [. . .], nothing that he had ever said or done that indicated he was aware that Boots was a black man" (163). This, however, is Boots's perception of Junto before he learns of his desire to sleep with Lutie. When Boots learns this, he finally sees Junto as the manipulator that he really is:

> He looked down at Junto seated at the table
> and swallowed an impulse to laugh. For
> Junto's squat-bodied figure was all gray---
> gray suit, gray hair, gray skin, so that he
> melted into the room. He could sit forever
> at that table and nobody would look at him
> twice [. . .]. Yet he had them coming and
> going. If they wanted to sleep, they paid
> him; if they wanted to drink, they paid him;
> if they wanted to dance, they paid him, and
> never even knew it. (225)

Junto is an invisible power in the community, owner of a majority of the apartments, whorehouses, and nightclubs in Harlem. He exploits the black people, sucking the economic life out of their communities for his own economic gain, while not attempting to give back anything, more or less, that is legitimate for the black patrons who support him.

As stated earlier, Lutie falls prey to the illusion of the Junto, never realizing that at the same time that she is feeling the space to be free, Junto is observing her from the back of the bar in the same lustful and sexualized manner as does Mr. Jones. At this point in the novel, Lutie sits in the bar and grill, unaware of the instrumental role Junto will play in her failure to leave the confinements of the street. Because Junto wants Lutie for himself, he cuts off her avenues of opportunity for escaping the street and realizing the American dream. He anticipates that she will eventually come under his control. Lutie is also not aware, throughout most of the novel as a matter of fact, that the "nice white gentleman" with whom Mrs. Hedges wants to set her up is Junto. By the end of the novel, Lutie will come to realize that Junto is another man who gazes at her with lasciviousness and who objectifies her.

The Junto is also the place where Lutie makes the acquaintance of Boots Smith, who entices her with the prospect of a singing job. However, this job is not without conditions, for Boots euphemistically hints that sexual involvement is a requirement for the job. Like Jones, Boots possesses an aggressiveness when it comes to the pursuit of sex, and his aim is to dominate women.[2] With Lutie, his desire is to somehow conquer and subdue her proud spirit: "There was a challenge in the way she walked with her head up, in the deft way she had avoided his attempts to make love to her. It was more a matter of itching to lay his hands on her than anything else" (263). Not surprisingly, however, when Boots finds out that Junto wants Lutie for himself, the female character quickly becomes expendable. Boots weighs his present lifestyle of money and other material possessions against his former position as a porter in a train, and he decides that Luite [or the value of the black female image?] is not worth giving up the comfortable existence he will lose if he does not follow Junto's orders. Boots agrees to go along with Junto's scheme of not paying Lutie for singing at the Casino, and he acts as a pander for Junto----e.g., purchasing for Lutie a pair of rhinestone earrings as a present from Junto. Like Mrs. Hedges, Boots views things in terms of economic pragmatism. Like Mrs. Hedges, he also seems unable to comprehend why Lutie is unwilling to sleep with Junto, after all, "Junto's rich as hell . . . What you got to be so particular about? There ain't a dame in town who wouldn't give everything they got for a chance at him" (428). Boots and Junto possess predatory desires for Lutie. Like society at large, they shatter her opportunity to escape the street and realize the American dream. Because of their machinations, Lutie must choose between her desire to succeed and her desire to preserve her independence and moral and ethical principles.

The Chandler house is another architectural space that Petry uses to contrast enormity of discrimination and confinement. In Lutie's eyes, it is the most beautiful place she has ever seen, "like something in the movies, what with the size of the rooms and the big windows" (38), and it is in contrast to all the camped and crowded quarters where she has lived. Petry's comparison of the Chandler house to a movie set is more than a way of contrasting Lutie's physical environment to that of the Chandlers; it is also a clue to their opposing existences and experiences. Near the end of the novel, Lutie will go to a movie and find that what happens on the screen is in no way similar to the kind of life she lives nor to the physical environment in which she lives (412). This is also true of the Chandlers' existence. Their lifestyle might as well be portrayed in a movie because what they have obtained in terms of success cannot hide their failure as husband and wife or as mother and father.

When Lutie first goes to work for the Chandlers, she not only views their home as a model of what she wishes to aspire to obtain, but their principles for achieving success that Lutie internalizes and adopts:

> After a year of listening to their talk, she absorbed some of the same spirit. The belief that anybody could be rich if he wanted to and worked hard enough and figured it out carefully enough [. . .]. She and Jim could do the same thing, and she thought she saw what had been wrong with them before— they hadn't tried hard enough, worked long enough, saved enough. There hadn't been any one thing they wanted above and beyond everything else. These people had wanted only one thing—more and more money—and so they got it. (43)

Lutie naively adopts the methods of the Chandlers without stopping to think about the differences between her reality as a black woman and their reality as whites, or how these different realities may hinder her chances of success. Hence, taking as a role model a family so different from her own shows that Luite is unaware that the obstacles to her advancement as black female or as black mother will be much greater than they are for the Chandlers. Moreover, in adopting the Chandler's values, Lutie has already begun to blame any failure to advance on personal faults rather than on institutional and societal racism and sexism.

Lutie's internalization of the Chandlers' philosophy is also apparent in her identification with Benjamin Franklin:

> She shifted the package into a more comfortable position and feeling the hard roundness of the rolls through the paper bag, she thought immediately of Ben Franklin and his loaf of bread. And grinned thinking. You and Ben Franklin. You ought to take one out and start eating it [. . .]. Only you ought to remember while you eat that you're in Harlem and he was in Philadelphia a pretty long number of years ago. Yet she couldn't get rid of the feeling of self-confidence and she went on thinking that if

> Ben Franklin could live on a little bit of
> money and could prosper, then so could she.
> (63-64)

While Lutie does recognize somewhat that living in a different time and place affects prosperity, what she does not seem to realize is that so too does one's race and sex.[3] Because she is a black woman, Lutie is bound to face many more impediments in her attempts to prosper, more than did Ben Franklin. Racial and sexual discriminations restrict the types of jobs black women of the 1940s are allowed to have, as well as their ability to advance in them. In short, they are limited in the amount of money they can earn in order to prosper. As Farah Jasmine Griffin notes:

> Lutie fails to read the silences and the
> absences which undergird [Ben Franklin's]
> manual for success. While he provides her
> with an ethic of hard work and thrift, she
> fails to see how Franklin's notion of success,
> grounded on a system of chattel slavery and
> on a discourse whose subtext constructs her
> as inferior, acts to her detriment. Even
> though she continues to suffer from and be
> defined by definitions of black women that
> first emerged in Franklin's day, she does not
> make the correction. (115)

Lutie does not realize, at this point in the novel, what she comes to realize at the end—that as whites, the Chandlers and Ben Franklin do not face the kinds of oppression and discrimination that she does as a black woman.

Lutie is not, however, unaware of the destructive part that racism plays in the lives of black people. She recognizes the discriminatory forces at work on her street . She observes the lack of job opportunities available for black men, including her estranged husband Jim, and she is aware of the inequality present in the type of jobs that black people are allowed to have. Hence, Lutie is not wholly blind to how racism manifests itself or to the debilitating effects it has on black people as a group. Rather, it is as an individual that Lutie discounts the stigma of racism and sexism. She believes that, as an individual, she can overcome whatever obstacles of racism and sexism she encounters. Describing herself as "young and strong," Lutie believes "there isn't anything [she] can't do" (163). Throughout the first half of the novel, Lutie displays this determination and optimism with statements such as "They'd never catch her in their dirty trap. She'd fight her way out" (74). Furthermore, "she was going to stake out a piece of life for herself. She had come this far poor and black and shut out as though a door had been slammed in her face. Well, she would shove it open; she would beat and bang on it and push against it and use a chisel in order to get it open" (186). So while Lutie is aware of the oppression of blacks by whites, she is determined to beat the odds. Believing that she had found the secret to success in the philosophy of the Chandlers and Franklin, Lutie attempts to adhere to it and expects to advance. However, Lutie soon comes to realize that she is not exempt from the oppressive forces of racism and sexism, that hard work and careful planning are often not enough when one is constantly being discriminated against, oppressed, and exploited.[4] Rather, she learns the hard way that with each advancement that one makes through hard work and sacrifice, acts of racism and sexism can cause one to retrogress.

III

In his book *The Black Woman in America*, Robert Staples writes that "Regardless of how often [the black woman] has attempted to provide her own definitions of herself, she has never been able to force the dominant society to accept [her] validity" (xi). Staples's words certainly prove true in Lutie's case. Throughout *The Street*, Lutie refuses to act in ways that contribute to the perpetuation of the stereotypes of the black woman as promiscuous and as sexual object. While Lutie could have taken Mrs. Hedges's suggestion or acquiesced to Junto's desires, and thereby obtained enough money to escape the street, she does not do any of these things because her values and sense of self contrasts with the way society perceives her. Lutie renounces the avenues she is given to succeed because all involve a devaluation of her selfhood and do not allow her to maintain her dignity. Eventually, her experiences with racist and sexist stereotypes and with economic opportunities that reduce her to a sexual object lead to frustration. She comes to compare herself to animals at the zoo:

> There was a moment, before the great hunks
> of red meat were thrust into the cages, when
> the big cats prowled back and forth,
> desperate, raging, ravening. They walked in
> a space even smaller than the confines of the
> cages made necessary, moving in an area
> just barely the length of their bodies [. . .].
> They were weaving back and forth,
> growling, roaring, raging at the bars that
> kept them from the meat, until the entire
> building was filled with the sound, until the
> people watching drew back from the cages,
> feeling insecure, frightened at the sight and
> the sound of such uncontrolled savagery.
> She was becoming something like that.
> (325)

Again, spatiality is used to explain Lutie's situation. Again, Petry brings the reader back to the realization that like the caged animals, Lutie, too, is confined to a small space---the street---from which she is unable to escape. In addition, she is trapped by the racial, sexist stereotypes through which she is defined. The animals' meat is like Lutie's dream of success ---within sight, but nevertheless unreachable. The bars keep the animals from the meat just as the invisible but impenetrable wall keeps Lutie and other black people from attaining their goals. As a result, Lutie goes around in a circle, just as the animals move in the cage, never quite advancing from the place where she began.[5]

---

[1] Interestingly, unlike Lutie, who is objectified because of her attractiveness, Petry describes Mrs. Hedges as lacking in attractiveness and femininity due to scars and burns she sustained in a fire. Mrs. Hedges, then, is spared the predatory gaze that Lutie's appearance continually elicits from men. In fact, her homeliness proves advantageous and serves, in part, to give her power. As Carol Henderson points out, Mrs. Hedges's "lack of femininity allows [her] a greater amount of freedom to "command spaces and places that [Lutie and Min] cannot" because their "subject and object positions cause them to operate within certain socially inscribed spaces" (861). Similarly, Keith Clark observes how Mrs. Hedges's "defeminization" allows her to maintain a "hard-fought place in the white male power structure" (499). He also mentions, however, that Mrs. Hedges recognizes that such a position of power involves an "unwillingness to exploit her own body in the sex-money nexus" (499). Nevertheless, Mrs. Hedges is not adverse to exploiting the bodies of the other black women on the street. Her appreciative appraisal of Lutie's body is in keeping with her role as part of the white male power structure that seeks to objectify black female bodies. Therefore, her gaze is just as unwanted.
[2] Petry does not restrict her commentary on the sexual harassment and exploitation of black women to the white man. By including Boots and Jones as victimizers of Lutie, Petry emphasizes the following: "while racism caused white men to make black women targets, it was and is sexism that causes all men to think they can verbally and physically assault women sexually with impunity. In the final analysis [. . . ,] it is the sexism motivating these assaults that is important not just the racial background of the men who initiate them" (hooks, *Ain't I A Woman* 68).
[3] Several scholars have noted the gullibility and naivete of Lutie's identification with Ben Franklin. Marjorie Pryse, for example, observes that although Lutie heeds her grandmother's warning to be distrustful of white men because of their lasciviousness toward black women, she still "chooses as her model a white man, Ben Franklin" (124). Several scholars have pointed to Lutie's grandmother, among others, as a better model for Lutie. However, as Farah Jasmine Griffin notes, "Lutie's memory of her grandmother engages in a tug of war with her retention of Ben Franklin's autobiography. While her grandmother's spoken voice tries to guide her through the psychic maze of the street, the written text of Ben Franklin [. . .] influences her more" (115). It seems, then, that where the issue of material success is concerned, Lutie believes

she must follow the strategies and examples of whites who have achieved the level of success to which she aspires. Doing so, of course, blinds her to alternative models, as well as to rational critique.

[4] Several scholars have pointed to Lutie's internalization of the myth of the American dream as her biggest flaw. You-me Park and Gayle Wald, for example, write that Lutie is "responsible for her investment in the ideology of an American dream that professes to be gender-and race-neutral" (618), while Keith Clark argues that whereas Mrs. Hedges and Min are able to "undermine the myth [of the American Dream], altering it to ensure both economic survival and varying degrees of emotional stability" (496), Lutie is defeated.

[5] As You-me Park and Gayle Wald state, Petry offers Lutie "movement without the promise of mobility, choice without the promise of agency" (619), with the likelihood of imprisonment looming large even as Lutie flees the city.

A Neglected Study in "Whiteness"---Ann Petry's *Country Place* (2004)
Martin Japtok

Of the 398 entries in Hazel Arnett Ervin's *Ann Petry: A Bio-Bibliography* (1993), a mere 39 as much as mention Ann Petry's *Country Place*, and only a handful of these entries are articles, books, or dissertations that devote significant critical energy to the novel. *Country Place* appeared in 1947 but, unlike *The Street* (1946), the novel did not find a readership, presumably because it is set in a small New England town and has a cast of white characters. Bernard W. Bell's mentioning of the novel in *The Afro-American Novel and Its Tradition* (1987) suggests as much. After a brief description of *Country Place*, he concludes that "[b]ecause the major characters are white, and because time and place are more important thematically than color and class [the novel] is not as relevant . . . to our theory of a distinctive Afro-American narrative tradition as [found in] *The Street* and *The Narrows*" [1953] (180). Of Petry's three novels, *Country Place* clearly remains the least appreciated and the most understudied. In an article on "white life novels" by African American authors, Robert Fikes, Jr. has suggested that "the controversy over [the white life novels'] authenticity" and the charges of "betrayal of one's proud heritage" (105) may have contributed to the critical neglect of works such as *Country Place*. For whatever the reason, it appears critics have not found it easy to read *Country Place*, or to place it in the African American canon.

Critics who have provided critical discussions of *Country Place*, such as Sandra Alexander in an entry in the *Dictionary of Literary Biography* (1988) and Thelma J. Shinn in "Women in the Novels of Ann Petry" (1974) describe *Country Place* either as "essentially raceless" (Alexander (143)---presumably meaning that it is not concerned with matters of "race"---or as a novel that proves "[Petry's] novels are not limited ethnically" (Shinn 110). Implied by critics such as Alexander and Shinn is that black writers writing about whites are to be praised for indicating a wider horizon---i.e., they "transcend geographical and racial boundaries" (Alexander 140). In this essay, I wish to extend critical discussions of *Country Place*. I suggest that rather than being merely a "raceless" novel, Petry's *Country Place* actually focuses on "race," albeit "whiteness."

II

David Roediger's anthology *Black on White: Black Writers on What It Means to Be White* has collected African American writers' responses to the phenomenon of "whiteness," from the 1830s to the present. Roediger's anthology reminds us that the study of "whiteness" has a long tradition in African American literature. In his introduction, Roediger traces several themes acknowledged by black writers in their responses. The two most pervasive are feelings of fear and notions of ownership---themes associated with whites starting as early as slavery or "The deep associations of whiteness with terror and with property . . . ." (3). In *I Heard It Through the Grapevine*, Patricia Turner testifies to the ongoing and fear-inspiring potential "whiteness" has had in African American literary culture. Also rumored by Turner's sources are suspicions of white businesses, white corporations, and white governmental institutions that might not act in the best interest of the black community. In such works, the "overall theme" is that organized anti-black conspiracies threaten the communal well-being and . . . the individual bodies of blacks" (3).

The point suggested by Roediger, Turner, and others is that much of the scholarship on "whiteness" has focused on material underpinnings---i.e., what specific economic gains "whiteness" brings and how it serves to secure and to perpetuate those gains. Given the history of relations between Americans of African and of European descent, one would expect "whiteness" to be linked to terror and property. While there is evidence to support these conclusions, the "wages of whiteness" are also metaphysical. W.E.B. DuBois may have said it best: "All through the world this gospel [of white supremacy] is preached[ed] . It [whiteness or white supremacy] has its literature, it has its priests, it has its secret propaganda and above all---it pays!" *(Darkwater* 44). DuBois' rhetoric also links the realms of finance and of the spirit, but the very focus on getting paid---i.e., materialism---which is the short-hand term one may use for the state of "whiteness," is already a kind of spiritual condition, or the lack thereof, though it also feeds on very real and material exploitations. The point is African American literary works dealing with the issue of "whiteness" explore both material and spiritual dimensions.

What interests me here is the "liturgical" aspect of "whiteness"--- its "spiritual" manifestations as revealed by African American writers. In works such as *Country Place*, whiteness is exposed as a pervasive desire for ownership. Ownership becomes the focus of life; it absorbs and colors all other activities. As DuBois indirectly proposes, "religion" provides a useful way to approach an understanding of whiteness (*Darkwater* 30) Commonly defined as "a set of beliefs concerning the cause, nature, and purpose of the universe . . . , usually involving devotional and ritual observances and often containing a moral code governing the conduct of human affairs," or, more simply, religion is "something one believes in and follows devotedly" (*Webster's* 1628), the term "religion" outlines parameters within which the phenomenon of "whiteness" can be comprehended not merely as an ideology based on racism but as comprising an entire world view. Such as delineation of "whiteness" is not merely interesting for the study of the invention of whiteness. As recent studies have shown---foremost among them Toni Morrison's *Playing in the Dark*--- conceptualizations of "whiteness" and "blackness" are complimentary, and this is certainly the case in a significant body of African American literature. In her essay on *Seraph on the Suwanee*, Zora Neale Hurston's "white life" novel, Laura Dubek notes that "Hurston shows whites living racially structured lives built by people of color while at the same time striving to maintain boundaries between themselves and these laborers" (347). Just as material conditions---white wealth built on black labor---complement one another, so do literary portrayals, and the roots of that complementarity must ultimately be looked for in socio-historical conditions and their ideological context.

Country Place depicts the conversion of all values into material values and links this greed-driven "materialization" to "whiteness." Such a depiction, one might argue, carries with it the danger of essentialism. However, given the vengeance with which some "white" people have exploited people of color worldwide, and given an intellectual climate, provided by, for instance, (European and American) nineteenth- and twentieth-century nationalism, which tends to look for the essential traits of a people, one should not be surprised that authors have turned to "whiteness" when attempting to understand what drives (some) white people. As William Pfaff has said, "Nationalism is an emphasis on . . . distinctness at the expense of the similarities of mankind as a whole, and for that reason, nationalism easily becomes an aggressive attempt to impose the difference [however imagined] as a superiority" (54). The conceptualization of "whiteness" by African Americans in late nineteenth- and twentieth-century African American literature can usefully be seen as a response to and an analysis of "white" notions of superiority often employed in nationalist ideology.

For instance, in Charles Chestnutt's *The House Behind the Cedars* (1900), a novel which generally questions and undermines the notion of "race," the narrator John Walden desires to pass as a means to gain prestige and wealth, and as a direst result of his lineage: "The blood of his white fathers, the heirs of the ages, cried out for its own, and after the manner of that blood set about getting the object of its desire" (163). Chestnutt combines an imperial acquisitiveness with the idea of inheritance to conceptualize what it is that makes "whiteness." (A similar conceptualization of whiteness is found embodied in Petry's Glory and, to some extent, in Mrs. Gramby in *Country Place*). Ownership and "whiteness" are part of the same discursive field in *The House Behind the Cedars* and "blackness" plays a complementary role. What emerges in much African American literature of the late nineteenth century and of the first half of the twentieth century is a dichotomy memorably phrased by W.E.B. DuBois in *The Souls of Black Folk*: "all in all, we black men see the sole oasis of simple faith and reverence in a dusty desert of dollars and smartness" (8). In other words, one side of the dichotomy is spiritual or moral superiority, characterized by altruistic behavior and "racial" solidarity, a bastion of strength where one is without legal rights; the other side is its complement, the tragic flaw or lack of spirituality and resulting rampant materialism. This dichotomy, which sees African Americans as establishing "a kind of spiritual counterculture to white materialism," as Cynthia Schrager notes (554), surfaces very prominently in African American novels concerned with "passing." In many passing novels, the stark juxtaposition of characteristics associated with "blackness" and "whiteness" forestalls the potential disintegration of a culture if part of its membership decides to leave. In other words, passing literature advocate preserving the strengths of African American culture, but they may be also the strongest expressions of the black-and-white dichotomy. Pasing literature often presents "blackness" in terms of altruism, spirituality, and artistry---one might think here of James Weldon Johnson's *Autobiography of an Ex-Coloured Man* (1912) or of Jessie Fauset's novel *Plum Bun* (1928)---and "whiteness" in terms of the proverbial "mess of pottage" which the ex-coloured man tells us he has gained for trading his blackness.

But more than being a response to white supremacy, the association of "whiteness" with materialism strikes at the philosophical core of the concept. To understand the philosophical basis of "whiteness," it is useful to look back to John Locke's pronouncement that "every Man has a *Property* in his own *Person*" (qtd. in Pateman 13). While the form "whiteness" taken in the United States is specific, analog forms have developed in other colonized areas, especially in those under British control, and in Europe. One can understand how "whiteness" developed in the American colonies as a ruthlessly pragmatic ideological concept, a unifying element against people who had what settlers were interested in and against people who were systematically exploited. But the philosophical basis of "whiteness" as African American literary works suggest, was already in place. And an integral part of that philosophical basis is located in Locke's concept of freedom: Locke conceived of the individual as proprietor of his or her own person and of his or her capacities and attributes. Freedom, therefore, is expressed as the independence from the wills of others and is a function of the possession of oneself. Individuals relate to each other as proprietors and thus society consists of relations of exchange between proprietors (MacPherson 3 & 262ff). This concept of freedom migrated to the U.S. with the European settlers, who were thus already primed to understand metaphysical concepts in terms of ownership.

In *Freedom in the Making of Western Culture*, Orlando Patterson provides insights that help to explain how a philsosophy of the nature of freedom grounded in ownership became color-coded in the context of colonialism. Patterson defines personal freedom as the state that "gives a person the sense that one, on the one hand, is not being coerced or restrained by another person in doing something desired and, on the other hand, the conviction that one can do as one pleases within the limits of other person's desire to do the same" (3). "Sovereignal freedom," however, "is simply the power to act as one pleases, regardless of the wishes of others" (3/4). In essence, one can recognize "whiteness" as a desire not for personal but for sovereignal freedom, a freedom with inbuilt connotations of ownership, as described by Locke. "Whiteness" imagines not merely the ownership of oneself and one's own capacities, but the untrammeled freedom to infringe on the liberties of those who are not "white," specifically in terms of their property, whether it be their persons, their capacities, or their assets. In U.S. history, "whiteness" has come to mean not merely liberty of persecution from others, but the ownership of other people's property or, indeed, of other people.

Early capitalism in the United States conceived of freedom as a function of property, and it was freedom that the early settlers initially sought---be it economic or religious freedom. Economic success was the call most European immigrants sought in the years to come, and many found it , but whatever the initial motives for emigration from Europe might have been, that success came to be based on notions of sovereignal freedom, which made "whites" value their own liberty but not that of others. Such an attitude later translated into first a cultural and than a "racial" supremacy which allowed some whites to be at ease with exploitation. The concept of "whiteness" absorbs all of these notions: it is a "racialized" entitlement to freedom imagined as a function of possession, inextricably linked to the idea of ownership, or of owning as the highest value--- in other words, materialism, but a materialism with religious overtones. The later is what DuBois recognizes when answering his own question, " 'But what on earth is whiteness that one should so desire it ?'" . . . [T]hat whiteness is the ownership of the early forever and ever, Amen!" (*Darkwater* 30). (In *Country Place*, Petry has Mrs. Gramby, an aristrocrat, to come to a very similar conclusion).   Ann Petry's novel *Country Place* is permeated with this conceptualization of what it means to be "white," a conceptualization that has at its heart the idea of ownership and possession as the building principles of life. Displacing and subsuming emotional and spiritual considerations, it may be said to this extent that whiteness functions also as a religion.

III

Current neglect of African American works exploring the notion of "whiteness" is undeserved. As bell hooks has said, African Americans have a " special" knowledge of whiteness gleaned from close scrutiny of white people," a knowledge meant "to help black folks cope and survive in a white supremacist society" (165). Or, as Trudier Harris states "the necessity within the black folk community for understanding more about the oppressor than the oppressor understands about Blacks" (qtd. in Roediger 302). The neglect of "white life novels" has its odd side: they have often been read as not being relevant to a discussion of "race" though as in Petry's *Country Place* they seek to pierce the protective cloak around the category of "whiteness" and to expose "whiteness" as a specific identity rather than let it be understood as a kind of normative "Americanness."   The lack of black readership for "white life novels" thus appears to illustrate what analysts of "whiteness" have claimed: that whiteness is invisible, and that this invisibility shrouds power relations. As Charles Mills cautions in *The Racial Contract*, "part of what it [whiteness] requires to achieve Whiteness . . . is a cognitive model that precludes self-transparency and genuine understanding of social realities" (18). The end result "whiteness" will be simply assumed as the norm. George Lipsitz cautions "[a]s the unmarked category against which difference is constructed, whiteness never has to speak its name, never has to acknowledge its role as an organizing principle in social and cultural relations" (369).   Cheryl Harris, George Lipsitz, and others have successfully described "Whiteness as Property," showing that there has been a historically traceable "Possessive Investment in Whiteness."   African American writers on whiteness such as Ann Petry have attempted to make "whiteness" visible, to show it as a state of being. How ironic, then, that these works themselves have become invisible. I submit as preliminary evidence as analysis of some aspects of Ann Petry's novel *Country Place*.

Ann Petry is a particularly well-qualified observer of "whiteness," given that she spent much of her life living in very predominantly white surroundings. Her family was "one of only two black families in the small town of Old Saybrook" (Mobley 347), and , after schooling in its public school and at the University of Connecticut, she "worked as a pharmacist in the family-owned drugstores in Old Saybrook and Old Lyme" (Ervin 571). After ten years in Harlem (1938-48), Petry returned to Old Saybrook to live. Arthur P. Davis has remarked that, in *Country Place*, Petry wrote about a lifestyle and an environment which "in all probability she knew better than the life she wrote about in *The Street* (qtd in Mobley 354).

In his discussion of *Country Place*, Robert Bone sees its characters functioning as symbols of certain character traits. For instance, Lil, the mother of one of the main characters, is said to "[suggests] vulgar materialism and acquisitiveness" (182). But the problem of materialism runs much deeper in the novel and is not merely confined to Lil. When the narrative turns to relationships, it often adopts a vocabulary of ownership. When Johnnie Roane, a young soldier just returned from World War II and one of the main characters, arrives at his hometown, he is ecstatically happy to see his wife, Glory, but she receives him without enthusiasm. Johnnie experiences a moment of happiness when, for a short while, Glory seems to want him again; on that occasion, he ponders, "Nothing could touch him now because he *had* Glory. Just before [Johnnie] went back to sleep, he decided that he had never *lost* her . . . ." (131- my emphasis). But no characters embodies the longing for ownership better than Glory herself, whose name, as Roger Rosenblatt has noted, "[contains] all the promise of small town America, indeed the flag itself" (139). Glory thus functions as a representative character. The reader sees Gloria through the eyes of the narrator, who is also the town's drugstore owner---a perspective Petry was familiar with, having grown up in a pharmacist drugstore. The narrator describes his impressions of Glory upon first meeting her as a customer in his drugstore:

> . . .she had the most amazing eyes I had ever
> seen. They seemed to blaze in her face; due
> partly to the color . . . but due mostly to the
> way she looked at things. It was as though
> she tried to see all of a thing at once,
> devouring it, because she was impelled to
> decide then and there, in that first hungry

> glance, whether it was something she would
> want and had to have; or whether it was
> undesirable, completely worthless, and
> therefore to be discarded, quickly. (99/100)

The passage emphasizes the pronounced binarism of Glory's world view: all things are related to her either as potential possessions or as waste. Being animated solely by the desire to own, she appears as the embodied principle of commodification, of the notion that "the marketplace is . . . ubiquitous and invisible," as Wai-Chee Dimock explains in a discussion of Edith Wharton's *House of Mirth*, and that "the realm of human relations is fully contained within an all-encompassing business ethic" (783). *Country Place* illustrates the ubiquitousness of the marketplace in Glory's relations to all those surrounding her.

In an internal monologue occurring shortly after Johnnie's return from the war, Glory assesses her own situation: "All of them get what they want but me. He gets New York and painting and she [Johnnie's mother] gets her son back from the war---that's what she wanted. I'm the one that everything goes wrong for. She's happy' he's happy. I won't have it. It isn't fair" (52). Glory shows herself as jealous, as covetous of the feelings of others, regarding feelings as a kind of possession, something one can "get." That happiness is configured as a function of possession becomes even clearer when Glory engages in similar covetous musings a little later. Again she complains that "the whole town is happy, everybody but me. They have the things they want---all of them " (62). Happiness, a state of *one's spirit*, thus is assumed to result from owning things, and the more things the better, as the nicely ambiguous phrase "all of them" implies. The pursuit of happiness becomes the ownership of happiness, or the happiness of ownership, a materialist conceptualization of a mental state that is consistent with the belief that ownership is the central purpose of life, *"something one believes in and follows devotedly."*

Family relationships, too, can be seen in terms of possessions, as is illustrated when Glory loses herself in daydreams about owning the town's largest house, Mrs. Gramby's house. Mrs. Gramby is Glory's mother's mother-in-law, and also quite old, so that Glory's hopes of someday owning the Gramby house are not entirely unrealistic: "Well, one of these days this place would belong to Momma. Momma [can't] live forever and then [the house] would be [mine]" (56). There is not much love lost in this mother-daughter relationship throughout the novel; nonetheless, Glory's statement has a chilling quality in that it reduces the parent to a conduit of property, the means by which ownership of possessions is passed on. Ironically, not much later in the novel, it is Glory who complains about her mother's lack of empathy and emotion: "She's always been like this, talking about herself; everything for her is food and clothing and shelter" (69). Glory's comments on her mother's materialism provides a moment for readers to reflect: Glory is capable enough recognizing the transformation of all emotions of/for her mother into the wish for possessions, a voracious longing excluding full recognition of the needs of others, but she is unable to diagnose the same character trait in herself, much less free herself of it.

Even the affair between Glory and Ed, as gas station owner specializing in affairs with married women, can be understood in terms of materialism. Glory expresses her desire for him repeatedly in a language of ownership. Disturbed by her husband's return from the war, thinking his presence might spoil the incipient affair, and worried about the prospect of aging, Glory has taken to meeting him regularly, but the affair has not yet been consummated. On occasion, before one of those meetings, she shares "I've never had anything I really wanted, and if I don't hurry up and get it it'll be too late" (75). Unbeknownst to her, her husband's arrival will facilitate the affair. While Ed, known for his affairs with women already "owned" by other men, has been merely eyeing Glory, never initiating a sexual relationship. Upon Johnnie's return from the war, Glory becomes more interesting to Ed; he could "steal" her. Ed's action is informed not merely by the desire to possess, but also by the desire to possess what is not his. He wants to own what is already valued and "owned," but without the responsibilities of ownership. Ed exercises "sovereignal freedom."

But not merely the lower or lower, middle class characters in Petry's *Country Place* are infected by the obsession of ownership. One year earlier in *The Street*, Petry depicted whites, or more, specifically, white Anglo-Saxon Protestants, as embodying "strange values." The novel's protagonist Lutie Johnson works for a wealthy Connecticut businessman and his family and closely observes them. Although her employer Mr. Chandler and his associates are graduates from Yale, Harvard, and/or Princeton, Lutie notes that "once these men went into business they didn't read anything but trade magazines and newspapers" (42). Anything other than business loses their interest, because "[w]hat they wanted was to be rich---'filthy' rich, as Mr. Chandler called it" (43). As with Glory and as with the Chandlers and their friends, the world revolves entirely around the acquisition of things.

Lutie reflects on the mental habits of her employer in a passage that nicely illustrates the absorption of metaphysical concepts such as "spirit" and "emotion" by the world of money:

> It was a strange world of strange values
> where the price of something called Tell and
> Tell and American Nickel and United States
> Steel had a direct effect on emotions. When
> the price went up everybody's spirit soared;
> if it went down they were plunged in gloom.
> (43)

Lutie Johnson sees the "spirit" of her employer effected by stock prices, and the passage reveals the degree to which the Chandlers converted all values to market values.

In *Country Place*, Lennox's last aristocrat, Mrs. Gramby, shows herself as being similarly vulnerable to this conversion of values. Upon learning that her son Mearns has been betrayed by his wife, Mrs. Gramby, who becomes profoundly sad, turns to her jewels and pearls for comfort:

> I must touch something else, look at something else, she thought. To sit on a night like this, a dark night full of wind, and think of ugliness, of faithlessness, of the mean in spirit---I cannot do it. She put a string of pearls from a worn velvet case, put them around her neck . . . . There was something else she wanted. She reached inside the safe again, took out a diamond ring . . . Mr. Gramby had given her the diamond when Mearns was born. (155)

While connecting an object with the memory of a person appears unremarkable enough in and of itself, the context makes clear that Mrs. Gramby expects solace from putting on her jewelry---no other strategy for seeking relief or sympathy occurs to her, indicating that objects connected to wealth and power substitute here for spiritual solutions.

When reading a passage in which Mrs. Gramby thinks of her family line, of transmitting name and property to descendants, one realizes that, for Mrs. Gramby, the function of property and inheritance is, ultimately to provide an illusionary safety, as well. Mrs. Gramby contemplates her son Mearns' marriage to Glory's mother Lil, a marriage she disapproves of because she (rightly) suspects Lil of mercenary motives and because Mearns and Lil (who is too old) will not have any children: "Nothing worse could have happened to him. The name would die out. Lillian [her daughter-in-law] was too old to have children . . . . The name would disappear, lost down the reaches of time. No heirs, no issue, the line ended." (83). Inheritance and heirs here are stays against mortality, are the ends in a battle against time. In the religion of ownership, time and mortality are the ultimate enemies, since they put an end to ownership---are barriers that can be overcome, in an illusory fashion, through the passing on of ownership, titles, and "names." Though Mrs. Gramby realizes the futility of the battle against time, a later passage makes clear that ownership has indeed been the issue at stake in her musing over her family "name," but through Mrs. Gramby (Petry?), there is a higher level of consciousness. Looking back over her life and realizing that all power ultimately comes to nothing, she wishes she could "show the town how impossible it is to control the earth, to arbitrarily decide who is *to own it"* (89; my emphasis). In many ways, Mrs. Gramby's internal monologue is philosophical contemplation related also to the question of race. In her will, Mrs. Gramby leaves much of her possessions to the very inhabitants of the town who have suffered from white Anglo-Saxon exclusion: She wills her house to her African American housekeeper Neola and her gardener, a Portuguese immigrant, and she hires a Jewish lawyer as the executor of her will, a person who has been much discriminated against in Lennox. Connected to her earlier statement of the futility of arbitrarily deciding who is to own "the earth," a phrase ringing with imperialist pretensions, and with Biblical overtones, Mrs. Gramby's will may be seen as an act of restitution of stolen goods , of returning possessions to those who have been wronged or exploited. Revoking her will to possess and declaring a "post-humus" solidarity with those wronged by "white" aggressive and exclusive materialism thus can be understood as Mrs. Gramby's attempt to revoke "whiteness."

However, here it is useful to remember Ruth Frankenberg's caveat that "Whiteness changes over time and space and is in no way a transhistorical essence. Rather, . . . it is a complexly constructed product of local, regional, national, and global relations, past and present" (Frankenberg 236). For instance, Catholics, while benefiting from "whiteness," are also excluded from the exclusively Anglo-Saxon Protestant "whiteness" as Petry's New England town conceptualizes it, and they have not been allowed to have a church on the main street, unlike all other denominations in Lennox. Accordingly, Mrs. Gramby's will includes Catholics, donating "land on the main street, formerly known as the Gramby Pasture . . . to Saint Peter's Roman Catholic Church, to be used in any way the church desires" (262). Gramby's action is in an obvious subversion of the town's religious snobbery. By the same token, Johnnie Roane, who decides to leave New England to go to New York and pursue his art---a decidedly unmaterialistic decision---also gets rewarded in Mrs. Gramby's will. Her will thus appears as an instrument to correct past wrongs and to steer people in the right direction.

Mrs. Gramby's attempt to direct (or redirect?) Lennox's fate is not without feudalist overtones, coming, as it does, from the last grand dame of a wealthy New England family, who still is determined, however benevolently, to guide people's fates through money. The apparent societal exclusion of Neola , the Portuguese and the Jewish lawyer, none of whom are seen as having any meaningful interaction with any "white" townspeople save Mrs. Gramby, makes it unlikely that the mere transmission of money, however, a well-meaning gesture, will fundamentally change the social structures of this New England town. But, the reader is left to decide.

Once read as a novel concerned with the question of what constitutes "whiteness," Petry's *Country Place* may be seen not as an oddity, but as part and parcel of Petry's oeuvre, as foreshadowing the materialistic heiress Camilo

Treadway Sheffield of *The Narrows*, or as harkening back to Lutie's Connecticut employers in *The Street*. More importantly, maybe, *Country Place* and a number of other neglected "white life novels" expose the extent to which notions of "race" in general, and of "whiteness" in particular, are both a function and a result of a crass and ruthless materialism religiously adhered to by its proponents. Writers such as Edith Wharton, Henry James, and Mark Twain have also explored the impact of capitalism and materialism on human relations, but African American writers such as Petry, DuBois, Baldwin and others have explored the "spiritual" dimension of that impact and its connection to "whiteness." Their explorations indict "whiteness" as the religion of ownership for (some) white people, a religion warping the character of its devotees. In a time of corporate mergers, almost universally greeted with amazement and awe, of enthusiastically embraced ever-increasing computerization, of so-called "re-engineering," of dwindling support for Affirmative Action, and of the privatization of healthcare and welfare, such as indictment merits serious attention.

Works Cited

Alexander, Sandra Carlton. "Ann Petry." *Dictionary of Literary Biography, Vol 76: Afro-AmericanWriters 1940-1955*. Ed. Trudier Harris, Detroit: Gale Research , 1988. 140-147.

Bell, Bernard W. *The Afro-American Novel and Its Tradition*. Amberst: University of Massachusetts Press, 1987.

Bone, Robert. *The Negro Novel in America*. New Haven , Ct: Yale UP, 1965.

Chesnutt, Charles. *The House Behind the Cedars*. 1900. Athens, GA: University of Georgia Press, 1988.

Dimock, Wai-Chee. "Debasing Exchange: Edith Wharton's *The House of Mirth*." *PMLA* 100 (1985): 783-92.

Dubek, Laura. "The Social Geography of Race in Hurston's *Seraph on the Suwanee*." *African American Review* 30.3 (1996): 341-351.

Du Bois, W.E.B. *Darkwater: Voices from within the Veil*. New York: Harcourt, Brace and Howe, 1920.

_____. *The Souls of Black Folk*. 1903. New York: Bantam, 1989.

Ervin, Hazel Arnett. "Ann Petry." *The Oxford Companion to African American Literature*. Eds. William L. Andrews, Frances Smith Foster, and Trudier Harris. New York: Oxford University Press, 1997. 570-72.

_____. *Ann Petry: A Bio*-Bibliography. New York: G. K. Hall, 1993.

Fauset, Jessie Redmon. *Plum Bun, A Novel Without a Moral*. 1928. Boston: Beacon Press, 1990.

Fikes, Robert, Jr. "Escaping the Literary Ghetto: African American Authors of White Life Novels, 1946-1994." *Western Journal of Black Studies* 19.2 (1995): 105-112.

Frankenberg, Ruth. *White Women, Race Matters: The Social Construction of Whiteness*. Minneapolis: University of Minnesota Prees, 1993.

Harris, Cheryl. "Whiteness as Property." *Black on White: Black Writers on*

What It Means to be White. Ed. David Roediger. New York: Schocken Books, 1998. 102-118.

hooks, bell. *Black Looks: Race and Representation.* Boston: South End Press, 1992.

Lipsitz, George. "The Possessive Investment in Whiteness: Racialized Social Democracy and the 'White' Problem in American Studies." *American Quarterly 47.3 (1995): 369-387.*

MacPherson, C. B. *The Political Theory of Possession Individualism: Hobbes to Locke.* Oxford: Clarenden Press, 1962.

Mills, Charles. *The Racial Contract.* Ithaca, NY: Cornell University Press, 1997.

Mobley, Marilyn Sanders. "Ann Petry." *African American Writers.* Ed. Valerie Smith. New York: Scribner's, 1991. 347-359.

Morrison, Toni. *Playing in the Dark: Whiteness and the Literary Imagination.* Cambridge, MA; Harvard University Press, 1992

Pateman, Carol. *The Sexual Contract.* Stanford: Stanford University Press, 1988.

Patterson, Orlando. *Freedom, Vol 1: Freedom in the Making of Western Culture.* New York: Basic Books, 1991.

Petry, Ann. *Country Place.* 1947. Chatham, NJ: Chatham Bookseller, 1971.
_____. *The Street.* Boston: Houghton Mifflin, 1946.

Pfaff, William. *The Wrath of Nations: Civilization and the Furies of Nationalism.* New York: Simon & Schuster, 1993.

"Religion." *Webster's New Universal Unabridged Dictionary.* 1996.

Roediger, David R., ed. *Black on White: Black Writers on What It Means to Be White.* New York: Schocken Books, 1998.

Shinn, Thelma J. "Women in the Novels of Ann Petry." *Critique, Studies in Modern Fiction* 16.1 (1974):
110-120. [See elsewhere in this text]

Webster's New Universal Unabridged Dictionary. New York: Barnes and Noble Books, 1996. 1628.

Race Trumps All Other Identity Markers: Reading Ann Petry's *The Narrows* as
an Anti-Lynching Text
Deirdre Raynor

The Narrows, published in 1953, is an anti-lyching text. It examines the ritual
associated with American lynching. debunks the myth of the black male rapist,
demonstrates the complicity of white woman in the ritual of lynching, and
exposes the role of the media in the perpetuation of racial violence in American
society. Lynching, an execution without due process of the law, has been
traditionally in the United States a ritual executed by a mob against an
individual who commits an alleged crime or is perceived to transgress against
social codes (Dray viii).

Trudier Harris, writing in *Exorcising Blackness* (1984) argues that given the
ritualistic nature of lynching in the United States the act was designed,
especially following Reconstruction to instill fear in African Americans who
stepped out of the socially, politically, and economically prescribed space, and
to reinforce notions of white superiority (18-19). In *The Rope and the Faggot*
(1926), which is based on personal investigations of lynching in the 1920s,
Walter White's main argument is that the unique form of racial violence
practiced in the United States comes out of the desire of white Americans to
control the black labor force and to secure places in the top runs of the economic
hierarchy that exists in the United States (105) Such research by White dispels
what he refers to as the "big lie"---i.e., that black men were being lynched due to
the threat they posed white women through rape. The works of Trudier Harris
and Walter White are useful in providing an analytical frame for discussing
Petry's *The Narrows* as an anti-lynching text. Petry's novel, as mentioned
earlier, reveals the intersections of racial and sexual oppression by calling into
question the "big lie" associated with the myth of the black rapist, and she
illustrates the connection between sexuality and lynching. In addition, Petry
uses her novel as a vehicle to challenge the dominant racial and sexual ideology
of the 1950s in which the novel is set. As part of the anti-lynching tradition in
African American literature, Petry's text increases social and political awareness
of the fact that black bodies were under siege in the mid-twentieth century.

Anti-lynching literature like Petry's *The Narrows* illustrates the conflict
between American culture's supposed reverence for women and the degradation
of African American women. In *Southern Horrors*, Ida B. Wells Barnett
describes the conflict by stating:

> To justify their own barbarism they (here
> she is referring to white males) assume a
> chivalry which they do not possess. True
> chivalry respects all womanhood, and no
> one who reads the record, as it is written on
> the faces of the million mulattoes in the

> south, will for a minute conceive that the
> southern white man had a very chivalrous
> regard for the honor due women of his own
> race or respect for the womanhood which
> circumstances placed in his power. (30)

Trudier Harris has suggested that lynching reinforced white superiority. Petry expands this notion and suggests that not only do white males have the power to illicit fear in African Americans, but that white women also provoked fear. In traditional anti-lynching narratives usually the lynch mob is comprised of white males. In *The Narrows*, Petry shows the complicity of white women in the ritual of lynching by having Camilo, a white woman, make the claim that Link, a black man, raped her. Petry takes things a step further. She centers Camilo's mother, Mrs. Treadway, within the white mob. As the story unfolds, Widow Treadway, Captain Sheffield, Camilo's husband, and two other white men, kidnap Link. Shortly before his death, Link reveals that it is Mrs. Treadway whom he fears the most:

> He dismissed the three men as unimportant,
> all of them cut from the same tree, perhaps
> Elm, a soft wood no good for burning. But
> the woman. The woman is dangerous. It's
> in the face, the eyes, the mouth---
> determination, intractability. Danger in the
> shaking. There's a tremor running through
> her that she can't conrol, running all through
> her body. Not fear but hate. (399)

By placing emphasis on the hatred of Widow Treadway, Petry debunks the mythical image of the pure asexual white woman. But Petry reinforces what Harris has cited as a true cause of lynchings---to reinforce superiority. Mrs. Treadway and the Captain fear that Link will somehow infringe upon the social and political privileges associated with their whiteness if his relationship with Camilo is perceived as a consensual relationship. So, supposedly Mrs. Treadway and the Captain proceed to protect the honor of Camilo. Understood, however, the Captain is motivated to kill Link as a result of his jealousy. Rather than leave anything open for interpretation, Petry makes it very clear that Link has not raped Camilo. In fact, Petry lets it be known that Link resisted using violence against Camilo when the thought crossed his mind. The point is that it was much easier for the lynch mob to justify their actions based on an alleged rape than on the jealously centered around the social impropriety of the white woman (here, Camilo) who voluntarily becomes involved in sexual relationships with a black man (here Link), and of the black man (here Link who acquiesces).

In *The Narrows*, Petry suggests also that to a certain degree, white women are used as scapegoats by lynch mobs. As Calvin Hernton notes in *Sex and Racism in America*, historically speaking,

> While she did not actually lynch and castrate
> blacks herself, she permitted [involuntarily]
> her men to do so in her name. The black
> man became the object of mutilation in and
> through which . . . white men [not white
> women?] could drain themselves of guilt,
> fear, and inadequacy. (17-18)

Although Hernton focuses on lynching in the southern United States, this quotation is applicable to what happens to Link and Camilo in the north. Both Link and Camilo are controlled by the white patriarchal powers that Camilo's husband and the matriarchal Mrs. Treadway represent. Both Link and Camilo become pawns in the race war. Given race relations of the 1950s, Link and, to a certain degree, Camilo are trapped in the social milieu.

In addition to exploring the ritual of lynching in *The Narrows*, Petry explores also the impact of racist stereotype—e.g., the black brute---on the psyche of the African American. As a historian, Link has a clear understanding of the historical roots of the oppression of African Americans in America and of the role of stereotypes. There are three key scenes in *The Narrows* that emphasize the power of the stereotypes and the potential they have for undermining the self-image of the African American. The first scene takes place in Link's elementary classroom. Link is ten years old and he knows intuitively what are the perceptions of his peers and of his teachers about what it means for him to be African American.

The teacher and children in Link's class single him out for abuse due to his blackness. For instance, his teacher, Miss Dwight, decides that the class should put on a minstrel show as a fundraiser for the Parent Teacher's Association. She gives Link a typical minstrel part. And she notes that in addition to exaggerated speech patterns, she expects him to "act sleepy and be late for everything" (134). To add further injury to insult, Miss Dwight claims that Link is a natural Sambo, for, as she points out to the class, in the tradition of Al Jolson who put burnt cork on his face to blacken the skin, Link would not have to use any burnt cork because of his natural blackness. The narrator goes on to point out that this was the first time Link "was ashamed of the color of his skin" (135). Implied by the narrator is how segregated the races are despite the illusion of integration in the northern schools. But stated by the narrator is that the white children are an "invulnerable group, welded together by their whiteness, and [Link], the outcast, the separate one, [is]. . . ostracized by a gesture, a look, a word" (33). The school scene will foreshadow what happens to Link once Camilo rejects him and falls back on her whiteness and class privilege.

The next time Link seems ashamed of the color of his skin is following his first confrontation with Camilo (the second key scene used by Petry to emphasize the power of stereotypes). Link's mother, Abbie Crunch, discovers him and Camilo in Link's bedroom. There is tension and anxiety associated with interracial relationships in the 1950s. In fact, interracial relations are prohibited socially and legally in much of the United States at this time. Petry illustrates the intense climate surrounding interracial relations via the angry exchange between Link and Camilo and through their descriptions of each other following their dismissal by Abbie. Camilo calls Link a "black bastard" (257). The derogatory phrase Camilo uses to describe Link draws attention to Link's blackness. Although Link refers to Camilo as a "bitch" prior to her calling him a "black bastard," Link does not mark his insult by bringing race into the conflict. Camilo does.

When spoken by Camilo, the phrase "black bastard" takes on great significance in this text. The phrase has negative connotations given the history of American slavery and the history of interracial sexual liaisons in which children were produced. During the slave period, a rule was set in place: The child followed the conditions of the mother. In short, if one's mother was a slave, and the father was the mother's white master, the child was designated as black, as slave, and as illegitimate. Camilo's use of such a derogatory phrase to describe Link conjures up the precarious position of African Americans in relation to whites. Camilo's use of such a derogatory phrase brings also to the forefront another stereotype of the African American male---the black buck. At this point in the novel, Link comes to view his relationship with Camilo in terms of the master-slave relationship---with Camilo in the role of master (of mistress), and he in the role of slave. Link goes so far as to imagine himself on the auction block, Camilo examining him as a physical specimen suited to be a "plantation buck" (280). Link even recognizes the gifts from Camilo ---markers of her ownership of him to further underscore the relationship. Petry underscores the master-slave relationship between Camilo and Link when she writes, "Bought and sold, he thought. Bought at an auction, sold again at the death of the owner, part of an estate to be disposed of at the death of the owner, along with his [her] horses and cows . . . ." (280). Imagined or real to Link, Camilo was always giving him presents and for him this was an example of a "Kept man. Stud" (280).

Link begins to see that he has become one of Camilo's many possessions, and the differences in their socio-economic class status only heightens his feeling of objectification. Petry explores Link as object and stereotype—black buck/black stud and black brute/black rapist. She suggests the stereotypes are rooted in a repressed and perverted sexuality on the part of those whites (Captain Sheffield and others) that espouse the rhetoric or myth of the black male to their ends, including the heinous crime of lynching. The last way Petry explores the controlling stereotypes is to expose the role of the media for its perpetuation of racist stereotypes. For example, the local newspaper, the *Monmouth Chronicle*, covers the story of an escaped convict who happens to be African American. In a racist and biased way, the picture of the escapee appears next to a picture of the white woman, Camilo, who is being presented as a rape victim. As Petry writes, the picture "that took up the center half of the paper" also

> showed the convict not as a man but as a
> black animal, teeth bared in a snarl, eyes
> crazy, long razor scar like a mouth, an open
> mouth, reaching from beneath the mouth to
> the chin . . . . [E]veryone who saw the
> picture would remember and wake up in the
> middle of the night covered with sweat,
> because this terror, this black terror had a
> shape, a face; and they would remember the
> headline NEGRO CONVICT SHOT . . .
> (377)

The newspaper's caricature of the black convict reinforces the unwritten law governing race relations in the 1950s. Unstated is that the best way to deal with a suspected African American menace to society (e.g., the black brute or the convict) is to kill him.

The functions of the headline in the *Monmouth Chronicle* are twofold. First, it garners the "appropriate" racist response. The story focuses on the traditional claim of black terror posing a threat to white womanhood. The journalist responsible for the racist propaganda "wrote down simply, and untruthfully, that the black convict, the brute, the escaped murderer, had attached the frail housewife, when he found her along in the big farmhouse" (377). Although the white "frail housewife" described here tells the reporter that the escapee does not rape her (he startled her and consequently she screamed), both the reporter and the woman's husband silence her and collaborate to create a story that reinforces a stereotype, and, in the minds of some, justifies the killing (the lynching) of the convict.

This particular story in the *Monmouth* runs parallel to the story of Camilo's claim that Link raped her. The two stories are connected to a certain degree in that the perceived female victim of the so-called black brute is silenced and displaced by more powerful forces. These forces gain power due to, in the case of the housewife's husband, the reporter, and Camilo's husband, a whiteness and maleness; in the case of Camilo's husband, he gains (or maintains) economic privilege, as well.

Here lies Petry's indictment of the media. Petry depicts both visual images and journalistic writings as powerful tools used by whites in the media to perpetuate certain stereotypes and to justify violence directed against African Americans. Petry also indicts the media for its role in perpetuating racism and crimes against African Americans. Jubine, the photographer mentioned at key points in the novel, photographs Camilo, following her auto accident that involves a DUI, the mangling of a black child, and her attempt to run over Link. Bullock the publisher of the *Monmouth* refuses to use these pictures in the periodical. Bullock's excuse is that Jubine's photographs pose a threat to the sanctity of white womanhood. Understood by the reader is that Jubine's photographs would undermine the confidence of white hegemony and any beliefs by those who believe themselves to be superior to African Americans.

Bullock acknowledges the power of the media to influence societal perceptions. When Jubine publishes the pictures of Camilo in a New York newspaper, Bullock accuses Jubine of "hav[ing] tried the case, handed in a verdict . . . .[In fact] . . .[h]e'd made the Treadway girl look like a whore and made the nigger look like Apollo" (365). Through her critique of the media, Petry reveals what Earl Hutchinson describes in *The Assassination of the Black Male Image*: a plot rooted in America's sinister racial past to destroy literally the image of the black male and the black man (17).

While *The Narrows* is clearly an anti-lynching narrative, it ends in an ambiguous way. In the introduction to the text Nellie McKay asserts that Petry

> gives the reader an unfamiliar twist to the traditional tale. Like a mighty Samson pulling down the pillars of the Philistine' temple with him, Link's death is symbolically avenged in the collapse of the Sheffield empire: Camilo's mother and husband are exposed as Link's murderers as they attempt to dispose of the body as old clothes for the Salvation Army (xii).

It is true that the ending of *The Narrows* differs from the ending of most anti-lynching narratives in that police officers surround the perpetrators of the murder. Usually anti-lynching narratives end with legal officials claiming that the victim died "at the hands of persons unknown" despite physical evidence to the contrary, including, for instance, pictures of the lynch mob killing its victim.

In the ambiguous ending of *The Narrows*, the narrator fails to describe what happens to Mrs. Treadway and Captain Treadway after they are caught in the act of disposing of Link's body. Despite Mckay's reading that the Sheffield's empire collapses, there is no textual evidence to support this claim. The presence of the police officers at the site where the murderers had planned to discard of Link's body has no real significance. In other words, the police officers do not serve as markers of the collapse noted by McKay.

The actual lynching of Emmett Till, a youth who transgresses against social codes in Mississippi occurred two years after the publication of *The Narrows*. The murderers of Till were poor white folks; the murderers of Petry's Link Williams were rich white folks. Yet the criminals in both cases were protected by their whiteness and privileges. The accused in the Emmett Till trail are freed. Mrs. Treadway and Captain Sheffield are not brought to trial by the end of the novel, suggesting as in the Till case, exoneration.

What happens to Mrs. Treadway and Captain Sheffield is somewhat irrelevant. What is important about this text is what it reveals about the economics of lynching (execution without due process) as exemplified by the class conflict between Link, Mrs. Treadway, Camilo and Captain Sheffield; by myths used by racist whites to justify lynching Link; and by the role of the media in its perpetuation of stereotypes and racial violence. Furthermore, as an anti-lynching text, *The Narrows* underscores the pervasiveness of American racism and inequality. While intersections exist between race, class, and gender, Petry is clear in stating, race trumps other identity markers within a racist society. By exposing some of the effects of racism in both African America and in White America in the world of fiction, Petry moves beyond simply writing what has been perceived by some as an interracial love story.

Works Cited

Dray, Phillip. *At the Hands of Persons Unknown.* New York: Random House, 2002.
Giddings, Paula. *When and Where I Enter: The Impact of Black Women on Race*
    and Sex in America. New York: Morrow, 1988.
Gunning, Sandra. *Race, Rape, and Lynching: The Red Record of American Literature, 1890-1912.* New York: Oxford University Press, 1996.
Harris, Trudier. *Exorcising Blackness.* Bloomington: Indiana University Press, 1984.
Hernton, Calvin. *Sex and Racism in America.* New York: Doubleday, 1988.
Hutchinson, Earl Ofari. *The Assassination of the Black Male Image.* New York: Simon and Schuster, 1994.
Petry, Ann. *The Narrows.* New York: Mariner Books, 1999.
Wells, Ida B. *Southern Horrors.* Amherst, NY: Humanity Books, 2002.
White, Walter. *Rope and Faggot: A Biography of Judge Lynch.* Indiana: University of Notre Dame Press, 2001.

Unmasking the Black Female Cultural Hero: A Jungian Analysis of Min's
Journey from Invisibility to Identity in Ann Petry's *The Street* (2004)
Iris M. Lancaster

In order to move from invisibility to identity, one must willingly commit to an
individuation process that permits the birth of a new self. Unlike the quest
journey, which gives birth to healing and self-preservation, the individuation
process allows for an unveiling of the authentic self. The path to individuation
is difficult because one must take slow, yet heroic steps, while on the road to
shedding the burdens of invisibility. These steps become heroic because a
person who is able to face his or her invisibility, and the reasons for its
conception, is one who is not afraid to look back at past images and stereotypes
in an effort to move forward and toward self-restoration. Following this strain
of thought, Joseph Campbell, writing in his text, *A Hero With A Thousand Faces*
(1949), defines a hero as a "man or woman who has been able to battle past his
personal and local historical limitations to generally valid, normally human
forms" (19). In Ann Petry's *The Street*, Min is such a woman who heroically
battles past the negative images faced by black women prior to 1946 and the
harmful stereotypes of the silent and abused (mentally and physically) black
woman.

Utilizing Campbell's idea of the hero helps put into perspective the reasons
that many African American novelists construct female characters who act as
disablers of past stereotypes and negative images of African American females.
Characters such as Iola in Francis Harper's *Iola Leroy* (1892), Angela Murray in
Jessie Fauset's *Plum Bun: A Novel Without a Moral* (1929), and Janie Crawford
in Zora Neale Hurstron's *Their Eyes Were Watching God* (1937), heroically
battle past and present personal limitations to become powerful characters who
help reinvent and rewrite the African American female character.

Believing that African American writers constructed characters to heroically
battle past negative images, Mary Helen Washington, in her introduction to
Midnight Birds (1980), asserts, "With the written word we . . . sculpt the heroic
molds for our own ceremonies" (xiv). Perhaps in an effort not only to sculpt a
positive cultural hero for black women, but as a way to continue to heroically
battle past historical limitations for the black female character before 1946, Ann
Petry published *The Street*. In this essay, *The Street* is regarded as an historical
production that depicts the struggles of three black females as each attempts to
shed the burdens of invisibility. In this revolutionary novel, Petry picks up the
journey of reinventing the black female character---a journey that began with
writers such as Harper, Hurston, and Fauset---by writing Min as a woman who
willingly commits to the journey from invisibility to identity.

Min's heroic journey from invisibility to identity can be traced using
archetypal images presented in Carl Jung's individuation process. Jung's
process helps "[to] construct a path to self knowledge" (Singer 134), one that a

person who is determined to find his or her own identity must travel. The individuation process involves the realization of three archetypes: persona, shadow, and anima/animus. This developmental journey is not an easy accomplishment because it involves a complex movement from darkness to light and from shapelessness to form. When this process is complete, an individual is equipped to organize his or her life in a way that points toward restoration of the inner self. Without an examination of the three major archetypes---persona, shadow, and anima/animus---Min, the abused female, cannot be seen as a character who moves from a masked persona to an unmasked identifiable cultural hero. Reading the journey via these three archetypes helps Min realize 1) her past limitations as an abused woman, 2) the darkness she lives in because of her fragmented and abused psyche, 3) her struggle to be released from this psychological prison, and 4) the self as it is reborn and individualized.

The first archetype in Jung's individuation process is the persona. The persona "mediates between the person and society" (Singer 134) because it is the social mask a person wears to adapt to the perceived expectations of others (Russell-Chapin and Rybak 171). Because the persona/mask is that which a person hides behind to satisfy societal needs, he/she is often in danger of adopting an identity that is not his or her own. Subsequently, individuals who feel forced to exist in accordance with societal expectations become repressed, unable to function not only in the outer world, but in their inner world as well.

Min's persona is one that permits her to live in a battered, isolated, and silent state. In the cocoon created by this persona/mask, Min is oftentimes read as insignificant. However, it is important to note that the realization of the persona is the first heroic step in Min's journey to find her new identity. Min's journey is complicated because she seems, at first, unwilling to submit to the truth that hides behind the darkness of the mask she has chosen to live behind. Consequently, critics' initial response to Min---the shapless, invisible woman who lives with Jones---is that she is insignificant to the restorative power of this novel. Thus, Min is recognized sometimes by critics as a woman who is irrelevant to Petry's efforts to portray women as cultural heroes. However, this negative view of Min destroys what Petry attempts to do with this novel---to create a positive female character who looks at how her life connects to others in an effort to construct a plan to move from behind the mask society has created for her.

In his text *Blackness and Value: Seeing Double* (1999), Lindon Barrett believes:

> Petry constructs narratives that convene and interweaves the actions and lives of a broad array of characters not necessarily by bringing an array of characters into the direct contact or conversation with one

> another but by pursuing the way their lives
> affect or speak to each other through the
> relaying wakes of their actions in a populous
> narrative world. (4)

Because Min is able to see how her life is effected by Lutie Johnson (the female "fair-skinned" protagonist) and Jones (the male antagonist/Min's live-in companion), Min is able to feel the dehabilitating shackles of invisibility, which govern her increasing need to reinvent her self.

The first time the reader comes in contact with Min is when Lutie hears whispering as she waits in the hallway outside of Jones's (the Super's) apartment. When she (Lutie) enters the apartment, she sees a shapeless, invisible form that has melted into brown:

> Next to the sofa was an overstuffed chair
> and she [Lutie] drew her breath in sharply as
> she looked at it, for there was a woman
> sitting in it, and she had thought that she and
> the dog and the Super were the only
> occupants in the room. How could anyone
> sit in a chair and melt into it like that? As
> she looked, the shapeless small dark woman
> in the chair got up and bowed to her without
> speaking . . . That must be the woman I
> heard whispering. (Petry 23)

It is important to note that Min bows to Lutie who is the epitome of black beauty because she sees herself as insignificant (a background to Lutie's foreground, a melted brown standing next to a vibrant yellow woman). By melting into the sofa, Min becomes repressed, silent, and powerless to step from behind the mask. The powerlessness that Min feels, thus, explains why the dark brown upholstery of the sofa swallowed her up until she was not only "scarcely distinguishable from the chair itself" (Petry 24), but also explains the persona of the silent and obedient woman. Min's desire to be accepted by Jones (a representation of a patriarchal society) permits her to read from the familiar script of the voiceless, abused black woman.

As Min accepts the role of the abused black woman, she, as Keith Clark phrases it in his article "A Distaff Dream Deferred? Ann Petry and the Art of Subversion," fits "the classic 'abused woman' paradigm: conditioned by a patriarchal society to see herself as worthless" (499). Clark goes on to recognize that "[Min] tolerates and rationalizes a life of violence---physical, sexual, and economic" (499) because she feels she must hide behind a *persona* that does not reflect her true inner self. When Jones, Min's abusive common-law husband, brutally slaps and kicks her just like she was the dog, Min again runs for cover behind the persona, a mask that accepts silence and submission:

> Only last night when she leaned over to take
> some beans out of the oven, he kicked her
> just like she was a dog. She had managed to
> hold on to the pan of beans, not saying
> anything, swallowing the hurt cry that rose
> in her throat . . . . (Petry 117)

Min has found so much comfort behind this persona. When she decides to visit the Prophet David---a conjure man---she does so not as an escape from psychological and physical abuse, but as a way to further into it. She is sure the conjure man will assist her in finding a remedy that will force Jones to acknowledge her existence, rather than tear it down. As she waits for the conjure man to see her, she begins to have a conversation with herself. This conversation is the first step by Min to realize, yet still ignore, that she is living behind a persona created by society:

> [H]ere she was sitting waiting to see the
> Prophet David---committing an open act of
> defiance for the first time in her life. And
> thinking about it that way, she was
> frightened by her own audacity. For in
> coming here like this, in trying to prevent
> Jones from putting her out, she was actually
> making an effort to change a situation.
> (Petry 126-27)

Because she accepts the conjure man's list of things to do to keep Jones from putting her out of the apartment, Min is making also a conscious choice *to live*, frightened, behind the persona. She agrees to "burn candles every night at ten o'clock for five minutes," "clean the apartment everyday," "hang a cross above the bed," and use a special medicinal powder if "he [Jones] gets violent" (Petry 135). These directives further support the idea that Min is living her life according to prescribed gender roles within a patriarchal society. To even think cleaning a house everyday will help solidify her place in Jones's life *is* preposterous, yet Min is determined to live according to society's expectations (or behind the persona). For a long while after she visits the conjure man, Min sinks deeper into the comfort of living behind the persona; yet, once she discovers there is truth hidden in the shadow/darkness behind the persona, she begins to see a way out of this psychological prison.

The second archetype in the individuation process is the shadow, which exists in the darkness behind the persona/mask. "The shadow is inferior to our personality, that part of ourselves which we will not allow ourselves to express"

(Singer 134). Jung suggests, "To become conscious of the shadow involves recognizing the dark aspects of the personality as present and real. This act is the essential condition for any kind of self-knowledge and it, therefore, as a rule, meets with considerable resistance" (*Aspects of the Feminine* 165). When the reader first comes in contact with Min, she is, without a doubt, resistant to going against the rules set forth by the collective unconscious. However, because this is a restorative text, Min does not remain afraid of facing the truth that lies in darkness created by the shadow. In the shadow, Min sees light in the darkness; a light that lets her discover psychological strengths and abilities that help her find a way to reinvent the self.

Min sinks into the darkness the shadow creates, but this move is positive because inside the darkness that the shadow provides, she begins the process of restoring not only her identity, but also the identity of the black female cultural hero. Min's progression out of the shadow is gradual, yet in her slow ascent out of this suffocating, psychological prison, she constantly bumps into an image that resembles a woman who is becoming conscious of a new, stronger identity.

A myriad of occurrences begin to take place in the house after Min visits the Prophet, yet the changes do not bring Jones close to Min, but they do bring Min closer to her new identity. Min has lived so comfortably behind the persona of the voiceless and obedient woman that she has forgotten she actually has a voice, an identity hidden somewhere in the darkness. "Funny how she got to believe that not having to pay rent was so important, and it really wasn't. Having room to breathe in meant much more. Lately she couldn't get any air here" (Petry 362). Inside the darkness the shadow provides, Min is able to see strengths, weaknesses, and abilities she did not know she possessed. Giving herself time to contemplate her life situation, Min realizes that Jones, "had swallowed the room up until she could see nothing but him....[H]e had become a giant that blotted out everything" (363) in her life. Gradually, as Min confronts the shadow, she disconnects herself from the identity society has assigned her, and begins to restore her psyche. As the restoration process starts, Min begins to draw visible lines around her invisible body.

Critic bell hooks claims in her text, *Remembered Rapture: The Writer at Work* (1999) that "confronting that shadow-self can humiliate and humble. Humiliation in the face of aspects of the self we think are unsound, inappropriate, ugly, or downright nasty blocks of one's ability to see the possibility for transformation that such a facing of one's reality promises" (8). When Min acknowledges the shadow, she has to recognize that she has lived a life hidden behind a mask, honoring an identity that is not her own. Recognizing this psychological fragmentation is the second heroic step by Min toward becoming a cultural hero for the black woman. When Min begins to consent to the idea that there is truth in the shadow, something phenomenal happens: she begins to breathe in.

The third archetype in the individuation process is the anima/animus. The anima/animus "are those unconscious parts of ourselves that carry the mystery of the sex which is not ours" (Singer 134). The anima is the feminine psychological tendencies within a man, and the animus is the male psychological tendencies within a woman. The woman possessed by the positive animus is always in danger of losing her femininity, her adapted feminine persona. Min, despite this danger, recognizes that even in the face of losing her femininity, realizing her positive animus will help her construct, with a strong, distinct voice, her own initiative, judgments, and opinions (just like a man).

Unearthing her eternal masculine characteristics help her discover herself set apart from society's expectations for the voiceless female character. Min's positive animus (or her female soul image of man) unleashes "masculine traits," such as strength, courage, and aggression (traits once associated with Jones). Min laments, "It was because of the evilness of Jones. She could feel the weight of it like some monstrous growth crowding against her. He had made the whole apartment grow smaller and darker; living room, bedroom, kitchen---all of them shrinking, their walls tightening about her" (Petry 362). As the walls begin to close around her, Min realizes that her inner self has been denied a right to freedom because of her fear of facing her own identity. Min acknowledges, with the help of her new masculine psyche, that she can be a woman, and still exercise her right to have a commanding voice:

> She ought to be going . . .The trouble was she didn't know why she was going. There was something that she hadn't satisfactorily figured out, some final conclusion that she hadn't reached. Ah, yes . . . It was because if she stayed here she would die---not necessarily that Jones would kill her, not because it was no longer safe, but because being shut up with the fury of him in this small place would eventually kill her. 'And a body's got a right to live,' she said softly.
> (Petry 368)

As Min discovers the positive animus she becomes assertive and immediately begins to take hold of her life. Without delay, she decides it is time for her to move away from Jones, the apartment, and the street. As she begins to feel comforted by her newfound "right to live" inside her new identity, Min, still unsure of her future, finds the courage to turn her back on her fears and leave the street.

Heroically, Min stands up and proceeds to rewrite the ending for the black female character (who, prior to 1946, was abused physically, emotionally, and mentally by both white and black society).   Joseph Campbell insinuates that only "birth can conquer death---the birth, not of the old thing, but of something new.   Within the soul, within the body social, there must be---if we are to experience long survival---a continuous "recurrence of birth" to nullify the unremitting recurrences of death" (16).   In other words,   Min's contribution must be perceived as an heroic rebirth, in a long line of rebirths (i.e., Hurston's Janie Crawford and Fauset's Angela Murray) and as one that continues the journey of unmasking the black female cultural hero.   When Min's identity is reborn, she not only gives birth to the self, but she rewrites the life of the black female character.

Realizing she can be a woman and have a strong voice, Min steps across the accepted borders and begins to reposition positively herself and the black female character; she metamorphoses into the body of a female character who is unashamed of her new voice and identity.   Thus, Min's choice to leave "the street," with the pushcart man, should be seen as a conscious choice to live free from masked darkness.   According to Carol Henderson, Min's "narrative illustrates the contradictory impulse of the street as both a delimiting and immeasurable space.   It becomes evident that in order to be recognized as an individual, one must create a space where one can develop a self---vocalized and uniquely identified---within the context of one's immediate milieu" (859).   The space Min has created forces her to disconnect from the street because it [the street] limits her progress into womanhood.   Even though many readers may see Min's choice to leave the street with the pushcart man as a conscious choice to revert back to an abused, submissive mentality, this scene effectively ends Min's individuation process and allows her to become her authentic self:

> . . . a woman living alone really didn't stand
> much chance.   Landlords took advantage
> and wouldn't fix things and landladies
> became demanding about the rent, waxing
> sarcastic if it was even so much as a day
> behind.   With a man around, there was a big
> change in their attitude.   If he was a strong
> man . . . they were afraid to talk roughly.
> (371)

Min, who has realized her positive animus, has begun to respect her new, powerful, capable voice.   She begins to understand that she is now in control of her own life and her own identity.   When she makes up her mind to befriend the pushcart man, she is making a decision to fight for survival in a world that sometimes closed the door on the progress of womanhood.   Min survives because "she has learned that a woman didn't stand much chance alone" (Shinn 5).   When Min says, "Say, you know anywhere a single lady could get a room?" and then pauses to add, "But not on this street," she is creating a new space, one that welcomes her role as a cultural hero thriving in the light of a new identity.

Individuation means that one becomes a person, an individual, a totally integrated personality. "The challenge of individuation, of discovering and affirming the unique human being each of us is potentially, is the challenge of being open to the experience, of being able and willing to be touched by life and affected by others" (Wagenseller 270). The energizing, restorative quality of Min is her ability to challenge her life in relation to societal expectations. Min chose not to sit idly by and let her life lead her; eventually she heroically leads her life out of the darkness. According to Thelma Shinn in her article "Women in Ann Petry's Novels" (1988), "Petry's first concern is for acceptance and realization of individual possibilities---black and white, male and female. Her novels protest against the entire society which would contrive to make an individual less than human, or even less than he can be" (120). Neither Petry nor Min were afraid to travel into the darkness in order to find ways to rejuvenate the spirit of the black female character.

Min began as a shapeless form, but when she chooses life over death, she becomes an image for black female characters who would eventually follow her (e.g., Celie in *The Color Purple*). By acknowledging the persona, then the illuminating darkness the shadow provides, Min begins to understand that she has been unhappily living invisibly. Min unveils her positive animus which allows her to gain a voice and the strength to find a new identity, one that permits her to breathe. Critics' initial response to Min—the shapeless, invisible, abused woman---has been that she is irrelevant to the story. Hence, Min is recognized sometimes by critics as a woman who is extraneous to Petry's efforts to portray women as the kind of cultural hero who would be equal to characters like Janie Crawford and Angela Murray. Yet how can critics claim Min is insignificant when it is obvious as Barbara Christian argues in *Black Women Novelists* (1980) that "Petry understood the stereotypes that were inflicted on black women, for her female characters are decidedly intended to counteract them" (65). Christian goes on to state, "She [Petry] sets up characters with particular characteristics that match specific stereotypes and then proceeds to show how they are not quite what they seem. In doing so she both adheres to and deviates from the standard images" (65). Petry creates the character of Min as an emotionally and physically abused woman, as a submissive female, but only as a unique way to present Min as a woman---battered and emotionally broken---who moves from invisibility to identity. "Ann Petry's fiction reveals an author who can see through the illusions of the American way of life that distort[s] and destroy[s] individuals. As a rebel, she seeks to tear down the walls that trap people, white and black, into meaningless existence" (Lattin 72). At the end of Min's individuation process, both Ann Petry and Min become rebels as each heroically fights to unmask the black female cultural hero.

Works Cited

Barrett, Lindon. *Blackness and Value: Seeing Double*. Cambridge: Cambridge
        University Press, 1999.

Campbell, Joseph. *The Hero With A Thousand Faces*. New York: MJF Books, 1949.

Christian, Barbara. *Black Women Novelists: The Development of a Tradition, 1892-1976*. Westport, Conn: Greenwood, 1980.

Clark, Keith. "A Distaff Dream Deferred? Ann Petry and the Art of Subversion." *African American Review* 26.,3 (1992): 495-505.

Henderson, Carol E. "The 'Walking Wounded': Rethinking Black Women's Identity in Ann Petry's *The Street*." *Modern Fiction Studies* 46.4 (2000): 849-867.

hooks, bell. *Remembered Rapture: The Writer at Work*. New York: Henry Holt, 1999.

Jung, Carl. *Aspects of the Feminine*. Trans. R. F. C. Hull. NJ: Princeton University Press, 1982.

Petry, Ann. *The Street*. 1946. Boston: Houghton-Mifflin, 1991.

Russell-Chapin, Lori and Christopher Rybak. "The Art of Teaching Jungian Analysis." *Journal of Humanistic Education and Development* 34.4 (1996): 171-81.

Shinn, Thelma. "Women in the Novels of Ann Petry." *American Literature* 60.4 (1988): 110-120.

Singer, June. *Boundaries of the Soul: The Practice of Jung's Psychology*. Rev. ed. New York: Anchor Book, 1994.

Wagenseller, Joseph. "Spiritual Renewal at Midlife." *Journal of Religion and Heath* 37.3 (1998): 265-272.

Washington, Mary. *Midnight Birds: Stories by Contemporary Black Women Writers*. New York: Anchor, 1980.

Select Bibliography

Articles, Book Reviews, and Books

"An Interview with Ann Petry." *Artspectrum* (Windham: Regional Arts Council, Willimantic, CT) September 1988. 2-4. Reprinted. Hazel Arnett Ervin. *Ann Petry: A Bio-Bibliography.* New York: G. K. Hall, 1993. 98-100.

Andrews, Larry. "The Sensory Assault of the City in Ann Petry's The Street." Hakutani, Yoshinobu, ed. *The City in African-American Literature.* Madison, NJ: Fairleigh Dickinson University Press, 1995. 196-211. [Reprinted in this text].

"Ann Petry." Voices from the Gap, 2003. http://voices.cla.umn.edu

Anzaldua, Gloria. *Making Face, Making Soul, Haciendo Caras: Creative and Critical Perspectives by Women of Color.* San Francisco: Aunt Lute, 1990.

Bande, Usha. "Murder as Social Revenge in The Street and The Women of Brewster Place." *Notes on Contemporary Literature* 23.1 (January 1993): 4-5.

Barrett, Lindon. *Blackness and Value: Seeing Double.* Cambridge: Cambridge University Press, 1999.

_____. "(Further) Figures of Violence: Tne Street in the American Landscape." *Cultural Critique* 25.3 (1993): 205-37.

Barry, Michael. 'Same Train Be Back Tomorrer': Ann Petry's The Narrows and the Repetition of History." MELUS 24.1 (Spring 1999): 141-59. [Reprinted in this text].

Bell, Bernard W. "Ann Petry's Demythologizing of American Culture and Afro-

American Character." Pryse, Marjorie and Hortense Spillers, eds. *Conjuring: Black Women, Fiction, and Literary Tradition.* Bloomington: Indiana University Press, 1985. 105-115. [Reprinted in this text].
_____. *The Afro-American Novel and Its Tradition.* Amherst: University of Massachusetts, 1987.
Bell, Roseann P., Betty J. Parker and Beverly Guy-Sheftall, eds. *Sturdy Black Bridges: Visions of Black Women in Literature.* Garden City, NY: Anchor/Doubleday, 1979.
Bone, Robert. "Richard Wright and the Chicago Renaissance." *Callaloo* 9.3 (Summer 1986): 446-68.
_____. *The Negro Novel in America.* New Haven: Yale University Press, 1965.
Bontemps, Arna. "The Line." *Saturday Review of Literature* (22 Auguat 1953): 11.[Reprinted in this text].
_____. "Tough Carnal Harlem." *New York Herald Tribune WeeklyBook Review* (10 February 1946): 4. [Reprinted in this text].
Bryant, Jackqueline. "Postures of Resistance in Ann Petry's The Street." *CLA Journal* 45.4 (June 2002): 444-59.
Burns, Ben. "Off the Book Shelf." *Chicago Defender* (9 February 1946) [Special Collections, BostonUniversity]. [Reprinted in this text].
Busby, Margaret. *Daughters of Africa: An International Anthology of Words and Writings by Women of African Descent from the Ancient Egyptian to the Present.* New York: Ballantine Books, 1994.
Carby, Hazel. *Reconstructing Womanhood: The Emergence of the Afro-American Woman Novelist.* New York: Oxford University Press, 1987.
_____. " 'It Jus Be's Dat Way Sometime': The Sexual Politics of Women's Blues." DuBois, Ellen C. and Vicki Ruiz, eds. *Unequal Sisters.* New York: Routledge, 1990
Cayton, Horace R. "Ideological Forces in the Work of Negro Writers." Herbert Hill, ed. *Anger and Beyond: The Negro Writer in the United States.* New York: Harper, 1968, 37-50.
Childress, Paulette. "A Womanist Social Protest Tradition in Twentieth Century African-American Literature: Fiction by Marita Bonner, Ann Petry, Dorothy West, and Gwendolyn Brooks." DAI, 1999.
Christian, Barbara. "A Checkered Career –The Street by Ann Petry." *The Women's Review of Books.* 9.10-11 (July 1992): 18 [Reprinted in this text].
_____. *Black Feminist Criticism: Perspectives on Black Women Writers.* New York: Pergamon Press, 1985.
_____. *Black Women Novelists: The Development of a Tradition, 1892-1976.* Westport, CT: Greenwood Press, 1980.
_____. "Ordinary Women: The Tone of the Commonplace." *Black Women Novelists: The Development of a Tradition, 1892-1976.* Westport, CT: Greenwood, 1980.
Clark, Edward. "From 'The Street' to the Garden: Recollections of Ann Petry." *The Boston Sunday Globe.* 27 July 1997. N16.
Clark, Keith. "A Distaff Dream Deferred? Ann Petry and the Art of

Subversion." *African American Review* 26.3 (1992): 495-505. [Reprinted in this text]

Collins, Patricia Hill. *Black Feminist Thought: Knowledge, Consciousness, and the Politics of Empowerment.* New York: Routledge, 1990.

Condon, Garrett. "Ann Petry." *Northeast Magazine* (8 November 1992): 1-7.

Conrad, Earl. "A Woman's Place in Harlem." *Chicago Defender* (2 February 1946): 13.

Dandridge, Rita B. *Black Women's Blues: A Literary Anthology 1934-1988.* New York: G. K. Hall, 1992.

Davis, Arthur P. "Current Literature." *Journal of Negro Education* 25.4 (Fall 1946): 649-50. [Reprinted in this text].

_____. *From the Dark Tower: Afro-American Writers 1900 to 1960.* Washington, DC: Howard University Press, 1974.

_____, Sterling A. Brown and Ullysses Lee, eds. *The Negro Caravan.* New York: Arno, 1941.

Davis, Thulani. "Family Plot." *Village Voice*, 10 March 1987: 14-17.

Delano, Page Dougherty. "Loose Lips Sink Ships": Women and Citizenship in Wartime Culture (World War II, Ann Petry, Chester Himes, Kay Boyle, William G. Smith, Gertrude Stein), DAI, 1996.

Doyle, Sisten Mary Ellen. "The Heroines in Black Novels." Johnson, Willa D. and Thomas L. Green, eds. *Perspectives on Afro-American Women.* Washington, DC: ECCA (Division of Educational-Community Counselor Association, Inc.), 1975.

Drake, Kimberly. "Women on the Go: Blues, Conjure and Other Alternatives to Domesticity in Ann Petry's The Street and The Narrows." *Arizona Quarterly* 54.1 (Spring 1998): 65-94. [Reprinted in this text].

Dubey, Madhu. "Narration and Migration: Jazz and Vernacular Theories of Black Women's Fiction." *American Literary History 10.2 (Summer 1998): 291-316.*

DuCille, Ann. *The Coupling Convention: Sex, Text, and Tradition in Black Women's Fiction.* New York: Oxford University Press, 1993.

Eisenger, Chester E. *Fiction of the Forties.* Chicago: University of Chicago Press, 1963.

Emanuel, James A. and Theodore L. Gross. *Dark Symphony Negro in Literature in America.* New York: Free Press, 1968.

Ervin, Hazel Arnett. "Adieu Harlem's Adopted Daughter: Ann Petry (12 October 1908 – 28 April 1997). *Langston Hughes Review* 15.1 (Spring 1997): 71-73.

_____. "Ann Petry." Andrews, William, Frances Smith Foster, and Trudier Harris,eds. *The Oxford Companion to African American Literature.* New York: Oxford University Press, 1997. 570-572.

_____. *Ann Petry: A Bio-Bibliography.* New York: G. K. Hall, 1993.

_____. "The Subversion of Cultural Ideology in Ann Petry's The Street and Country Place." DAI, 1993 [Revised version in this text].

_____. "Just a Few Questions More, Mrs. Petry." *Ann Petry: A Bio-*

Bibliography. New York: G. K. Hall, 1993. 101-103.

Feld, Rose. "Tragedy on Two Levels." *New York Herald Tribune Weekly Book Review* (5 October 1947): [Reprinted in this text].

Fein, Esther B. "An Author's Look at 1940s Harlem Is Being Reissued." *New York Times* (8 January 1992): C13.

Fikes, Robert Jr. "Escaping the Literary Ghetto: African American Authors of White Life Novels, 1946-1994." *Western Journal of Black Studies* 19.2 (1995): 105-112.

Fitzsimmons, Lorna. "The Socially 'Forsaken Race': Dantean Turns in Ann Petry's The Street." *Notes on Contemporary Literature* 30.2 (March 2000): 6-8. [Reprinted in this text].

Ford, Nick Aaron. "From Test Tube to Typewriter." *Afro-American* (Baltimore) (11 December 1948): 3.

"From Pestle to Pen." *Headlines and Pictures* (March 1946): 42-43.

Fuller, James E. "Harlem Portrait." *Pittsburgh Courier* (9 February 1946): [Special Collections, Boston University]

Garvey, Johanna X. K. "That Old Black Magic? Gender and Music in Ann Petry's Fiction." Saadi, Simawe, ed. *Black Orpheus: Music in African American Fiction from the Harlem Renaissance to Toni Morrison*. New York: Garland, 2000. 119-151. [Reprinted in this text].

Gates, Henry Louis, ed. *Black Literature and Literary Theory*. New York: Methuen, 1984.

_____ and Nellie Y. McKay, eds. *The Norton Anthology of African American Literature*. New York: W. W. Norton, 2004.

Gayle, Addison, Jr. *The Way of the New World: The Black Novel in America*. Garden City, NY: Anchor/Doubleday, 1975.

Giddings, Paula. *When and Where I Enter: The Impact of Black Women on Race and Sex in America*. New York: William Morrow and Company, 1984

Gloster, Hugh. "Race and the Negro Writer." Addison Gayle, Jr., ed. *Black Expression: Essays by and About Black Americans in the Creative Arts*. New York: Weybright and Talley, 1969, 255-259.

Green, Marjorie. "Ann Petry Planned to Write." *Opportunity: Journal of Negro Life* 24.2 (April-June 1946): 78-79.

Greene, Lee. *Blacks in Eden: The African American Novel's First Century*. Charlottesville: University Press of Virginia, 1996.

Griffin, Farah Jasmine. *'Who Set You Flowin'? The African-American Migration Narrative*. New York: Oxford University Press, 1995.

Gross, Theodore L. "Ann Petry: The Novelist as Social Critic." Lee, Robert A., ed. *Black Fiction: New Studies in the Afro-American Novel since 1945*. New York: Barnes and Noble, 1980. 41-53.

"Harlem Made Ann Petry Write." *PM* (3 March 1946): M4.

Harris, Trudier. "On Southern and Northern Maids: Geography, Mammies, and Militants." *From Mammies to Militants: Domestics in Black American Literature*. Philadelphia: Temple University Press, 1982.

Henderson, Carol E. "The Body of Evidence---Reading the Scar as Text: Williams, Morrison, Baldwin, and Petry (Sherley Anne Williams, Toni

Morrison, James Baldwin, Ann Petry), DAI, 1995.

_____. "The 'Walking Wounded': Rethinking Black Women's
Identity in Ann Petry's The Street. *Modern Fiction Studies.* 46.4 (2000):
849-67. [Reprinted in this text].

Hernton, Calvin C.. "The Significance of Ann Petry." *The Sexual Mountain and
Black Women Writers, Adventures in Sex, Literature, and Real Life.* Garden
City, New York: Anchor/Doubleday, 1987. 59-88. [Reprinted in this text].

Hicks, Heather J. "Rethinking Realism in Ann Petry's The Street." *MELUS* 27.4
(Winter 2002): 89-97.

_____. " 'This Strange Communion': Surveillance and Spectatorship
in Ann Petry's The Street." *African American Review* 37.1 (Spring 2003):21-
38. [Reprinted in this text].

Hill, James L. "Parellels in Black and White: The Two Worlds of Fiction of Ann
Lane Petry." *Journal of Arts and Sciences* (Albany State University) 1.3 (Fall
1996): 15-26.

Hill, Patricia Liggin, Bernard W. Bell, Trudier Harris, R. Baxter Miller, Sondra
A. O'Neale, and William J. Harris, eds. With Horace C. Porter. *Call and
Response: The Riverside Anthology of the African
American Literary Tradition.* Boston: Houghton Mifflin, 1998.

Hill-Lubin, Mildred A. "African Religion: That Invisible Institution in African
and African-American Literature." Anyidoho, Kofi, Abioseh M. Porter,
Daniel Racine, and Janice Spleth, eds. *Interdisciplinary Dimensions of
African Literature.* Washington, DC: Three Continents, 1985.

Holladay, Hilary. *Ann Petry.* New York: Twayne, 1996.

_____. "Holding Together, Breaking Apart: Communities and
Relationships in Ann Petry's Fiction," DAI, 1993.

_____. "Narrative Space in Ann Petry's Country Place." *Xavier
Review* 16.1 (1996): 21-35. [Reprinted in this text].

hooks, bell. *Remembered Rapture: The Writer at Work.* New York: Owl Books.
1999.

_____. *Yearning: Race, Gender, and Cultural Politics.* Boston: South End
Press, 1990.

Hogue, Lawrence W. *Discourse and the Other: The Production of the Afro-
American Text.* Durham, NC: Duke University Press, 1986.

Hughes, Carl Milton. "Common Denominator: Man." *The Negro Novelist:
1940-1950, A Discussion of the Writings of American Negro Novelists 1940-
1950.* New York: Citidel, 1953. 147-193.

_____. "Portrayals of Bitterness." *The Negro Novelist: 1940-1950,
A Discussion of the Writings of American Negro Novelists 1940-1950.* New
York: Citidel, 1953. 41-113.

Hull, Gloria T., Patricia Bell Scott, and Barbara Smith. *All the Women Are
White, All the Blacks Are Men, But Some of Us Are Brave.* New York: The
Feminist Press, 1982.

Isaacs, Diane. "Ann Petry's Life and Art: Piercing Stereotypes." DAI, 1982.

Ivey, James. "Ann Petry Talks about First Novel." *Crisis* 53.2 (February 1946):
48-49. Reprinted. Ervin, Hazel Arnett. *Ann Petry: A Bio-Bibliography.* New

York: G. K. Hall, 1993. 69-71.

_____. "Mrs. Petry's Harlem." *Crisis* 53.5 (May 1946): 154-155.

Jackson, Blyden. "Of Irony in Negro Fiction: A Critical Study," Ph.D. Diss., 1952.

Jaskoski, Helen. "Power Unequal to Man: The Significance of Conjure in Works by Five Afro-American Authors." *Southern Folklore Quarterly* 38.2 (June 1974): 81-108.

Jones, Amy Robin. " 'There is no Place': Geographical Imagination and Revision in Novels by Ann Petry and Jo Sinclair," DAI, 1996.

Joyce, Joyce Ann. "Ann Petry." *Nethula Journal* 2 (1982): 16-20. [Reprinted in this text].

_____. *Warriors, Conjurers and Priests: Defining African-Centered Literary Criticism.* Chicago: Third World Press, 1994.

Lattin, Vernon E. "Ann Petry and the American Dream." *Black American Literature Forum* 12 (1978): 69-72. [Reprinted in this text].

Lauter, Paul and Richard Yarborough, eds. *Heath Anthology of American Literature*, vol 2. Boston: Houghton Mifflin, 2000.

Littlejohn, David. *Black on White.* New York: Viking Press, 1966.

Locke, Alain. "A Critical Retrospect of the Literature of the Negro for 1947." *Phylon* 9.1 (First Quarter 1948): 7.

Lorde, Audre. *Sister Outsider.* Freedom, CA: The Crossing Press, 1984.

Lucy, Robin Jane. " 'Now is the Time! Here is the Place!': World War II and the Black Folk in the Writings of Ralph Ellison, Chester Himes, and Ann Petry." DAI, 2002.

McDowell, Margaret B. "The Narrows: A Fuller View of Ann Petry." *Black American Literature Forum* 14 (1980): 135-41. [Reprinted in this text].

McKay, Nellie Y. "Introduction." *The Narrows* by Ann Petry. Boston: Beacon, 1988. vii-xx.

_____. "Ann Petry's The Street and The Narrows: A Study of the Influence of Class, Race, and Gender on Afro-American Women's Lives." Maria Diedrich and Dorothea Fischer-Hornung, eds. *The Changing Status of American Women from the 1930s to the 1950s.* 112-140. New York: Berg, 1990. [Reprinted in this text].

Mobley, Marilyn Sanders. "Ann Petry." Valeria Lee, ed. *African American Writers.* New York: Scribner's, 1991. 347-59.

Morris, Wright. "The Complexity of Evil." *New York Times Book Review* Section 7 (16 August 1953): 4. [Reprinted in this text].

Nance, Merle. "Four-Star Novel." *People's Voice* (16 February 1946): S-6. [Reprinted in this text].

O'Brien, John. "Ann Petry." *Interviews with Black Writers.* New York: Liverright, 1973. Reprinted. Ervin, Hazel Arnett. *Ann Petry: A Bio-Bibliography.* New York: G. K. Hall, 1993. 72-77.

Olsen, Tillie. "One Out of Twelve: Writers Who Are Women in Our Century." *Silences.* New York: Delacorte/Seymour Lawrence, 1965.

Park, You-Me and Gayle Wald. "Native Daughters in the Promised Land: Gender, Race, and the Question of Separate Spheres." Davidson, Cathy N.,

ed. *No More Separate Spheres! A Next Wave American*
Studies Reader. Durham: Duke University Press, 2002. 607-34.
Petry, Ann. "Ann Petry." *Contemporary Authors: Autobiography Series*. Vol 6.
Detroit: Gale Research, 1988.
_____. "The Novel as Social Criticism." Hull, Helen, ed. *The Writer's*
Book. New York: Harper and Brothers, 1950. Reprinted. Ervin, Hazel Arnett,
ed. *African American Literary Criticism, 1773 to 2000*. New York: Twayne,
1999. 94-98.
_____. *Country Place*. Boston: Houghton Mifflin, 1947. Reprint. London:
Michael Joseph, Ltd., 1948. Reprint. Chatham, NJ: Chatham Bookseller,
1971. Foreign Reprint *Tempeste*. Translated by V. E. Bravetta Roma: Jandi
Sapi, 1949.
_____. *The Street*. Boston: Houghton Mifflin, 1946. Reprint. New York:
Pyramid, 1946, 1961. Reprint. London: Michael Joseph, Ltd., 1947. Reprint.
New York: Signet, 1947. Reprint. Boston: Beacon, 1985. Reissue. Boston:
Houghton Mifflin, 1992. Foreign Reprints: *A Rua*. Translated by Ligia
Junqueira Smith. Sao Paulo, Brazil: Companhia Editoru Nacional, 1947. *De*
Straat. Translated by Vertaald Door and H. W. J. Schaap. Amsterdam: N. Y.
De Arbeiderspers, 1948. *De Stratte*. Berlin: Druck and Veratbeitung, n.d.
Die Strasse. Translated by von Marinette Chenaud. Bern. Switzerland:
Verlag Hallwag Bern, n.d. *En Kvinne I Harlem*. Translated by Oversatt Av
Erik Farland. Oslo: Tiden, 1947. *Gaden*. Copenhagen: Aschenog Dansk
Forlag Kobenhaun, 1946. *Gatan*. Translated by Olof Hogstadius. Stockholm:
Ljus, 1947. *La Calle*. Translated by Julio Vacarezza. Argentina: Ediciones
Penser, n.d. *La Rehob*. Translated by Aaron Amir. Tel-Aviv: N. Tversky
Publishing House, Ltd., 1947. *La Rue*. Translated by Martine Monod, Nicole
Soupault, and Philippe Soupault. Paris: Charlot, 1948. *The Street*. Translated
by Ryo Namikawa, Tokyo: Kaizo Sha, 1950.
_____. *The Narrows*. Boston: Houghton Mifflin, 1943. Reprint. London:
Gallancz, 1954. Reprint. New York: Signet, 1955. Reprint. London: Ace
Books Limited, 1961. Reprint. New York: Pyramid, 1971. Reprint. Boston:
Beacon, 1988. Foreign Reprint. *Link and Camilo*. Berlin: Propylaen-Verlag,
1955.
Pettis, Joyce. "Reading Ann Petry's Tne Narrows into Black Literary Tradition."
Hubbard, Dolan, ed. *Recovered Writers, Recovered Texts*. Knoxville:
University of Tennessee Press, 1977. 100-120.
Poirier, Suzanne. "From Pharmacist to Novelist." *Pharmacy in History, 27-33*.
Madison, WI: American Institute of the History of Pharmacy, 1986.
Pryse, Marjorie. " 'Patterns Against the Sky': Deism and Motherhood in Ann
Petry's The Street." Pryse, Marjorie, and Hortense Spillers, eds. *Conjuring:*
Black Women, Fiction, and Literary Tradition. Bloomington: Indiana
University Press, 1985. 161-31. [Reprinted in this text].
Rabinowitz, Paula. "Domestic Labor: Film Noir, Proletarian Literature, and
Black Women's Fiction." *Modern Fiction Studies* 47.1 (Spring 2001): 229-
255.
Redding, J. Saunders. Review of The Narrows. *Afro-American* (Baltimore) (12

September 1953): 2. [Reprinted in this text].

Reynolds, Clarence V. "Ann Lane Petry" (A Tribute). *Black Issues Book Review* 4.4 (July/August 2002): 79-81.

Review of Country Place. *The New Yorker*. (11 October 1947): 122. [Reprinted in this text].

Rickman, Ray. "Ann Petry Revisited." *American Visions* (Washington) 5.1 (February 1990):56.

Royster, Beatrice Horn. "The Ironic Vision of Four Black Women Novelists: A Study of the Novels of Jessie Fauset, Nella Larsen, Zora Neale Hurston, and Ann Petry." DAI, 1975.

Schraufnagel, Noel. "The Protest Tradition in the Forties." In *From Apology to Protest: The Black American Novel*. Deland, Fl: Everett/Edwards, 1972. 10-20.

Shinn, Thelma J. "Women in the Novels of Ann Petry." *Critique, Studies in Modern Fiction* 16.1 (1974): [Reprinted in this text].

Smith, Barbara. "A Familiar Street." *Belles Lettres* (January/February 1987): 4. [Reprinted in this text].

_____. "Toward a Black Feminist Criticism." *Conditions: Two* 1.2 (October 1977): 25-42. Reprinted. Ervin, Hazel Arnett, ed. *African American Literary Criticism, 1773 to 2000*. New York: Twayne, 1999. 162-171.

Smith, John Caswell, Jr. A Review of Country Place. *Atlantic Monthly* 180 (November 1947): 178, 182. [Reprinted in this text].

_____. A Review of The Street. *Atlantic Monthly* 117 (April 1946): 172. [Reprinted in this text].

Smith, Valerie. "Split Affinities: The Case of Interracial Rape." Hirsch, Marianne and Evelyn Fox Keller, eds. *Conflicts in Feminism*. New York: Routledge, 1990, 271-87.

Solomon, Irvin D. and Marty Ambrose. "Race and Gender Conflict in Ann Petry's The Street: Lessons in Symbolic Interaction from the 'Middle Period' of Black Literature." *McNeese Review* 37 (1999): 1-13.

Streitfield, David. "Petry's Brew: Laughter and Fury." *Washington Post*. 25 February 1992, E1-2.

Sullivan Richard. "Injustice, Out of Focus." *New York Times Book Review* (28 September 1947): 12. [Reprinted in this text].

Taylor, Ivan. "Current Literature on Negro Education." *Current Literature* 23.1 (Winter 1954): 60-61. [Reprinted in this text].

Tetsuo, Yamaguchi, Midori. *Feminine Fiction from Across America*. Tokyo: Bunri Company, 1978.

Thomson, Rosemarie. "Ann Petry's Mrs. Hedges and the Evil, One-Eyed Girl: A Feminist Exploration of the Physically Disabled Female Subject." *Women Studies: An Interdisciplinary Journal* 24.6 (September 1995): 599-614.

"The Street 'Still Unchanged.' " *Hartford Courant*. 7 March 1969: 32.

Troupe, Quincy. "A Conversation with Terry McMillan." *Emerge* (October 1992): 51-56.

Wade-Gayles, Gloria. "Journeying from Can't to Can and Sometimes Back to Can't." *No Crystal Stair:Visions of Race and Sex in Black Women's Fiction*.

New York: The Pilgrim Press, 1984. 148-156. [Reprinted in this text].

Wall, Cheryl . *Changing Our Own Words: Essays on Criticism, Theory, and Writing by Black Women.* New Brunswick, NJ: Rutgers University Press, 1989.

_____. "On Freedom and the Will to Adorn: Debating Aesthetics and/as Ideology in African American Literature." George Levine, ed. *Aesthetics and Ideology.*

Washington, Gladys. "The Narrows." McGill, Frank, ed. *Masterpieces of African American Literature.* New York: Harper Collins Publishing Group, 1992. 869-874.

Washington, Mary Helen. "Black Women Image Makers." *Black World* 23.10 (August 1974): 11.

_____. " 'Infidelity Becomes Her': The Ambivalent Woman in the Fiction of Ann Petry and Dorothy West." *Invented Lives: Narratives of Black Women 1860-1960.* New York: Doubleday, 1987. 297-306.

Weir, Sybil. The Narrows: A Black New England Novel. *Studies in American Fiction* 15.1 (Spring 1987): 81-93. [Reprinted in this text].

Willis, Susan. "Eruptions of Funk: Historicizing Toni Morrison." Ed. Henry Louis Gates, Jr. *Black Literature and Literary Theory.* New York: Methuen, 1984, 263-83.

Williams, Barbara. "Prodigal Daughters: Female Heroes, Fugitivity and "Wild" Women in the Works of Toni Morrison (Women Characters), Zora Neale Hurston, Ann Petry, (African American Women Writers). DAI, 1996.

Williams, John A. and Charles F. Harris. *Amistad 2.* New York: Randon House, 1971.

Williams, Sherley Anne. Review of *The Street. MS* (September 1986): 23. [Reprinted in this text].

Wilson, Mark K. "A MELUS Interview: Ann Petry – The New England Connection." MELUS 15.2 (1988): 71-84. Reprinted. Ervin, Hazel Arnett. *Ann Petry: A Bio-Bibliography.* New York: G. K. Hall, 1993. 88-98.

Winters, Kari J. "Narrative Desire in Ann Petry's The Street." *Journal X: A Journal in Culture and Criticism* 4.2 (Spring 2000): 101-12.

Wurst, Gayle. "Ben Franklin in Harlem: The Drama of Deferral in Ann Petry's The Street." Buelens, Gert and Ernst Rudlin, eds. *Deferring a Dream: Literary SubVersion of the American Columbiad.* Basil: Berkhauser, 1994. 1-23.

Ya Salaam Kalamu. "It Didn't Jes Grew: The Social and Aesthetic Significance of African American Music." *African American Review* 29.2 (Summer 1995): 351-75.

Yarborough, Richard. "The Quest for the American Dream in Three Afro-American Novels: If He Hollers, Let Him Go, The Street, and Invisible Man." MELUS 8.4 (Winter 1981): 33-59. [Reprinted in this Volume].

Yglesias, Jose. "A Classy-Type People." *New Masses* (9 December 1947): [Special Collections, Boston University]

Index

About the Editor and Contributors

MERLE NANCE authored "Four-Star Novel," a review of *The Street* in 1946 for *People's Voice*.

JOHN CASWELL SMITH, JR. authored a review of *The Street* in 1946 for *The Atlantic Monthly* and a review of *Country Place* in 1947 for *The Atlantic Monthly*.

ARTHUR P. DAVIS (1904-1996) was an educator, editor and literary critic.

BEN BURNS authored "Off the Book Shelf," a review of *The Street* in 1946 for the *Chicago Defender*.

ARNA BONTEMPS (1902-1973) was novelist, poet, librarian and literary critic.

SHERLEY ANNE WILLIAMS (1944-1999) was a novelist, poet, educator, essayist, and literary critic. A major novel by Williams is *Dessa Rose*.

BARBARA SMITH is co-founder of Kitchen Table: Women of Color Press. An educator, editor, and literary critic. Her edited works include *Conditions: Five, the Black Women's Issue* (co-edited with Lorraine Bethel), *All the Women Are White, All the Blacks Are Men, But Some of Us Are Brave: Black Women's Studies* (co-edited with Gloria T. Hull and Patricia Bell Scott). *Home Girls: A Black Feminist Anthology* and *The Reader's Companion to U. S. Women's History*. This collection, *The Critical Response to Ann Petry*, is dedicated to several pioneering women critics of African American literature, including Barbara Smith.

BARBARA CHRISTIAN (1943-2000) was an educator and literary critic. She authored countless articles on African American literature, especially on black women writers. Her authored books include *Black Women's Novelists: The Development of a Tradition, Teaching Guide to Black Foremothers, and Black Feminist Criticism: Perspectives on Black Women Writers. The Critical Response to Ann Petry* is dedicated to several pioneering women critics of African American literature, including Barbara Christian.

RICHARD SULLIVAN authored "Injustice, Out of Focus," a review of *Country Place* in 1947 for *The New York Times Book Review.*

ROSE FELD authored "Tragedy on Two Levels," a review of *Country Place* in 1947 for the *New York Herald Tribune Weekly Book Review.*

J. SAUNDERS REDDING (1906-1989) was editor, educator, and literary critic.

WRIGHT MORRIS authored "The Complexity of Evil," a review of *The Narrows* in 1953 for *The New York Times Book Review.*

IVAN TAYLOR was an administrator, educator, and literary critic. A scholarship fund exists in his name in the English Department at Howard University.

VERNON E. LATTIN 's article "Ann Petry and the American Dream' first appeared in 1978 in *Black American Literature Forum*, now called *African American Review.*

JOYCE ANN JOYCE is Director of the Women's Studies Program at Temple University.

RICHARD YARBOROUGH is currently associate professor of English and Faculty Research Associate with the Center for African American Studies at UCLA in Los Angeles. He has lectured and published on African American literature and U. S. popular culture, with essays on writers such as Frederick Douglass, Pauline Hopkins, Harriet Beecher Stowe, Charles Chesnutt, and Richard Wright. The associate general editor of the *Heath Anthology of American Literature,* he is also the general editor of Northeastern University's *Library of Black Literature* reprint series.

BERNARD W. BELL is the author of numerous articles on African American literature. His authored books include *The Afro-American Novel and Its Tradition* and *The Folk Roots of Contemporary Afro-American Poetry.* He is editor of *Modern and Contemporary Afro-American Poetry;* co-editor of *Call and Response: The Riverside Anthology of the African American Literary Tradition.*

THELMA J. SHINN's article "Women in the Novels of Ann Petry" first appeared in *Critique: Studies in Modern Fiction* in 1974.

GLORIA WADE GAYLES is Director and Faculty Mentor to the Spelman's Independent Scholars (The SIS Oral History Project) at Spelman College in Atlanta, Georgia.

CALVIN C. HERNTON (1933-2001) was poet, novelist, essayist, educator, and literary critic.

MARJORIE PRYSE is professor of English and Women's Studies at the University of Albany, State University of New York. Her most recent book (co-authored with Judith Fetterley) is *Writing Out of Place: Women Regionalism, and American Literary Culture*. Forthcoming works include a book on race and psychoanalytic objective relations in American literature.

MARGARET B. McDOWELL's article "The Narrows: A Fuller View of Ann Petry" first appeared in 1980 in *Black American Literature Forum*, now called *African American Review*.

SYBIL WEIR's article "The Narrows: A Black New England Novel" first appeared in *Studies in American Fiction* in 1987.

NELLIE Y. McKAY teaches in the Afro-American Studies and English Departments at the University of Wisconsin, Madison. Since publishing *Jean Toomer, Artist, a Study of his Literary Life and Work* in 1978, her scholarly work includes co-editing *The Norton Anthology of African American Literature*, Harriet Jacob's *Incidents in the Life of a Slave Girl* and Toni Morrison's *Beloved*. Her interest in Ann Petry dates back to the 1970s. *The Critical Response to Ann Petry* is dedicated to several pioneering women critics of African American literature, including Nellie McKay.

KEITH CLARK teaches in the Department of English at George Mason University. He is the author of *Black Manhood in Ernest J. Gaines, James Baldwin, and August Wilson*. His edited works include *Contemporary Black Men's Fiction and Drama*. Other essays on Petry have appeared in *Ann Petry's Short Fiction: Critical Essays* and the forthcoming *An Ann Petry Encyclopedia*.

HAZEL ARNETT ERVIN is an associate professor of English at Morehouse College where she teaches senior-level African American literature courses. A Fulbright Scholar and UNCF/Mellon Fellow, Ervin is the author of *Ann Petry: A Bio-Bibliography* and articles on Petry which appear in *The Langston Hughes Review, MAWA,* and *The Oxford Companion to African American Literature*.

With Hilary Holladay, she has edited *Ann Petry's Short Fiction: Critical Essays*. Her edited work includes *African American Literary Criticism, 1773 to 2000*. Her most recent work is *The Handbook of African American Literature*. A forthcoming work is an encyclopedia on Ann Petry.

LARRY A. ANDREWS is Dean of the Honors College and associate professor of English at Kent State University. He specializes in nineteenth-century relations among Russian, French, and German literatures. An exchanged teacher once in Poland and Russia, Andrews has published articles and book chapters on literature by the Russian, French, and African American.

LORNA FITZSIMMONS is an associate professor and Coordinator of Humanities at California State University, Dominguez Hills, in Los Angeles. She specializes in comparative literary studies, film studies, performance, and aesthetics.

JOHANNA X. K. GARVEY teaches at Fairfield University, where she is also Chair of the English Department. Founding co-director of both the Women's Studies Program and the Program in Black Studies: Africa and the Diaspora, Garvey has published numerous articles on twentieth-century literature, including a recent essay on Dionne Brand in *Callaloo*. Forthcoming works include a book on contemporary Caribbean women writers.

KIMBERLY DRAKE teaches American literature, women's studies, and writing at Wesleyan College. She is completing a book-length study of twentieth-century American protest novels.

CAROL E. HENDERSON is an associate professor of African American literature and American literature at the University of Delaware (the Newark campus). Her recent publications include *Scarring the Black Body: Race and Representation in African American Literature*. Her articles have appeared in referred journals, the *Dictionary of Literary Biography* and *Alizes, Journal of the Universite de La Reunion* in France.

HILARY HOLLADAY is a professor of English at the University of Massachusetts Lowell. She is the author of *Ann Petry* and co-editor of *Ann Petry's Short Fiction: Critical Essays*. Her most recent work is *Wild Blessings: The Poetry of Lucille Clifton*.

MICHAEL BARRY is an associate professor of literature at the University of Detroit Mercy, where he has taught since 1994. In addition to teaching courses in American literature after 1865 and literary theory, Barry is completing several articles on postcolonial literature and cultural relativism.

HEATHER J. HICKS is associate professor of English at Villanova University. She has published articles on T. Coraghessan Boyle, William Gibson, Marge Pierce, and Joanna Russ, exploring how these writers redefine categories of race and gender in a contemporary context. Hicks is currently writing a book on how American authors have depicted transformations in the meaning of work since World War II.

ANNIE S. PERKINS is Chair of the Department of English and Foreign Languages at Norfolk State University. Her areas of specialization are British and African-American literature, especially the poetry of Gwendolyn Brooks. A forthcoming work includes a collection of essays on Brook's sonnets.

AMA S. WATTLEY is an associate professor of English at Pace University in Pleasantville, New York. Her area of specialization is African American literature. Other published articles are on playwrights Aishah Rahman and Amira Baraka.

MARTIN JAPTOK is the author of the forthcoming work *Growing Up Ethnic: Nationalism and the Bildungsroman in African American and Jewish American Fiction.* Editor of *Postcolonial Perspectives on Women Writers from Africa, the Caribbean, and the U.S.,* Japtok also has published essays, mostly on African American fiction and issues of ethnicity and identity. He teaches at Palomar College.

DEIRDRE RAYNOR is an assistant professor at the University of Washington, Tacoma where she teaches American Ethnic literature. Her primary scholarly interests include African American literature, Native American literature, multicultural pedagogy, and diversity in higher education.

IRIS M. LANCASTER is a doctoral candidate in the Department of English at Texas A&M University-Commerce. A version of this paper was first read at the College Language Association Conference in Nashville, Tennessee, in 2004.